THE FAMILY MAN

Solutions To Permanently Eradicate Domestic Violence, Child Abuse, and Bullying

Photo By CharMarie Photography www.charmariephotography.com

Solutions To Permanently Eradicate Domestic Violence, Child Abuse, and Bullying

THE FAMILY MAN

Solutions To Permanently Eradicate Domestic Violence, Child Abuse, and Bullying

Solutions To Permanently Eradicate Domestic Violence, Child Abuse, and Bullying

THE FAMILY MAN

SOLUTIONS TO PERMANENTLY ERADICATE DOMESTIC VIOLENCE, CHILD ABUSE, and BULLYING
A.W. BURGESS

THE A.W. BURGESS GROUP
A.W.ooo BALTIMORE

Solutions To Permanently Eradicate Domestic Violence, Child Abuse, and Bullying

COPYRIGHT

Solutions To Permanently Eradicate Domestic Violence, Child Abuse, and Bullying

ACKNOWLEDGMENTS

This book is dedicated to all the victims and victimizers of domestic violence, child abuse, and bullying. I thank God, Jesus Christ, and the Holy Spirit for sparing my life when it was evident that my life was worth nothing to anyone, and I had zero reasons to live on this earth. I thank God for carrying me on His shoulders during those days when I could not see the next day on the horizon. I rise today with incomparable energy, drive, and resolve because the Holy Spirit lives in me; thus, my little light shines for the entire world to see! To Jesus Christ my best friend, comforter, and the source of my purposeful existence. I thank You for dying for me when I was so unworthy of such a sacrificial display of love. I thank You Three for never giving up on me!

To my wife Trena, I thank you for loving me despite my previous history as a violent domestic violence offender, abuser, and bully. In all my dreams, I would have never believed God would have given me the prettiest genius, and most fiercely competitive woman on the planet to run next to me as my partner in this marathon called life. I thought I was incapable of loving another woman again after being tortured by women and family as a child and after torturing friends and family. You are a phenomenal mother, and a superior example of a Godly woman. I thank God for your life and unconditional love. You made me believe I could love a woman again when I had resolved in my spirit that I should date until death. You are a beacon of love who inspired me to believe it was possible for a monster to transform into a man and then a Family Man™.

To my girls, Antoneya, Ava, Andira, Anisa; and my loving grandchildren Justin, Jaxon, and the ones still in heaven, I thank God for entrusting me with you; His most precious possessions. To believe I could be trusted to healthily love a baby without a proper example in my life was unfathomable that God made a reality. Once I saw you enter the earth, I knew then that I had to do everything to love, pray, provide and protect you. I will always keep you safe and never abandon you as your Father because I know that feeling and would never have you experience a pain that can only be filled by Jesus. Your presence makes me realize every day how much I love Jesus, your mom, and myself, but also how much they love and trust me. I rise each day purposefully because of you. I hope you always know how much I love you for just how God made you!

I pray I left you with a proud legacy! Always know Daddy loved you!

CONTENTS

Solutions To Permanently Eradicate Domestic Violence, Child Abuse, and Bullying

TACKLING THE PROBLEM AT THE SOURCE! WHAT HAPPENED?
WHO DID THIS TO YOU? ACCOUNTABILITY BEGINS WITH ME!

To God, all victims of violence, the abusers, bullies and violent offenders, I owe you the sincerest apology from my heart and soul! Please trust and forgive me when I say that I wish many years ago I could have gotten this book in the hands of the individuals who could have possibly been inspired or used the solutions I am offering to have prevented bringing any harm to another person and themselves. I know firsthand what it feels like to **NOT** be appropriately loved and shown how to love another properly, and as a result, I became a domestic violence offender, bully, and abuser of someone else's child. I am completely accountable for my horrific actions in hurting others and offer no excuses to make light of those I have harmed, bullied, and abused. I contributed majorly in attempting to destroy God's property and my victim's physical, mental, and emotional well-being! I had no right or authority to commit such vile and heinous acts towards another human being! My purpose on this planet is to inspire humanity by providing solutions to permanently eradicate violence against all children, women, men, and LGBTQ! I will protect these innocent victims by taking the violence away from the predator. Domestic violence directly or indirectly leads to child abuse and bullying! This will be my legacy!

To the individuals I have victimized, tortured, traumatized, and abused physically, verbally, psychologically, emotionally, and mentally, I apologize sincerely from the genuine parts of my heart and soul. I am sincerely apologetic and fully accountable for the pain that I have caused that negatively impacted your life! I live with the guilt of knowing that I intentionally harmed you when you never did anything wrong to deserve my malicious treatment! You were totally innocent and did nothing to deserve my abuse. I am doing everything within the limits of my capacity to ensure the millions of dysfunctional people just like me get the mental health and wellness they require to permanently eradicate harming another individual, animal, community and themselves as a result of being a domestic violence offender, child abuser, or bully. I am ending the cycle of violence and abuse right now for the future generations who will perpetuate love instead of hate. Other innocent families, individuals, and communities should never be paying the penalty for these offender's crimes.

Abusers like me must understand that their mental health is as equally important, if not more significant, as their physical health and they must get help now not tomorrow. It is not a request to get help now, but rather, it is a requirement to get help now because someone's life & legacy depends on it.

This book is for the sole purpose of saving the lives and legacies of children, women, men, and any individuals or animals harmed or impacted by domestic violence, child abuse, and bullying, while ridding bloodlines and generations of cyclical, perpetual violence, and abuse from the victimizers of these crimes. I pray this book reaches the souls, hearts, and minds of abusers, violent offenders, bullies, their families, friends, bosses, activists, victims of violence, abuse, bullying, rape, molestation, sexual assault, and harassment.

This how-to guide is for any individuals who wish to be a change agent to bring about a permanent and prosperous change to prevent violence, bullying, and abuse against any human being or animal regardless of their gender, identity, lifestyle, demographics or religious affiliation. *I am not calling out victimizers, batterers, abusers, bullies or violent offenders, but rather, I am calling them in to get the required mental health help, so they can permanently stop harming others and themselves.* I will partner and stand with the victims of domestic violence, child abuse, bullying, rape, sexual assault, and sexual harassment. I will do the same for offenders too! No more public shame or character assassination to either the victim or the victimizer for the ones who have made the courageous decision to come forward voluntarily, and without political pressure, so they can be healed. I want victims and victimizers to come forward out of the dark to get help before they are harmed or harm others. I want volunteers to come forward to be "MenTours™" and "WomenTours™" in partnering with me in serving those in need! I need everyone's loving help!

My decision to confess publicly to being a domestic violence offender, abuser & bully is I do not want to see another victim or victimizer harmed along with the destruction of their family and legacy. I paid the ultimate cost for someone else's crime and as a result of my own self-destructive, manipulative, and controlling behavior, along with my ignorant decisions to not get the appropriate mental health solutions as a result of being abused, assaulted, neglected and a tortured soul as a child, I went on to brutally assault personal relationships, corporate family, friends, and a dog named Toby*. These were individuals who loved me unconditionally and put up with my craziness, despite the extreme reciprocated physical, verbal, psychological, emotional, and mental torture I put each of them through. I systematically destroyed my legacy, and many once in a lifetime experiences and opportunities as a result. I do not want anyone to experience what I have done to others, what others have done to me, and the things I have put myself through that can never be made right.

I am calling in, not out, myself first and all the bullies, abusers and violent offenders like me, making a non-judgmental, heartfelt, genuine plea to them to get help! Our victims, fellow humanity, the animal kingdom, and family bloodline are screaming for us to stop harming them and ourselves! I sincerely apologize to "All" the victims of any abuse and violence that I have directly or indirectly caused during my only life on this planet. To my wife, kids, the generations of Burgess grandchildren who will be innately impacted in my bloodline, my mother, grandmother, cousins, aunts, uncles, my former friend and victim Michelle, her husband and children, the Thompson family, her dog Roscoe* and my dog Toby* the boxers, Dr. William Harvey and Hampton University, the McDonogh School, Oklahoma State University, the late Elrod Hendricks and his family, the Baltimore Orioles, Grade School and College friends and professors, the many coaches and teammates along with their parents that supported me as a youth to be the best student, athlete, friend and human being, but due to my horrific decisions to commit vile acts of violence, bullying and abuse against the individuals who loved, cared, provided, and protected me, I let you and my legacy down! If possible, in your heart and soul, please forgive me. I certainly respect if anyone does not forgive me.

I want to ensure that I do my best in my one lifetime to safeguard any person I can reach in person or with this book, so they do not systematically destroy and impact the lives and legacies of others, and their own, by not choosing the appropriate solutions to prevent violence against any human being or animal! I apologize to those individuals I could not reach in time to prevent them from harming others and themselves and especially those that needed the encouragement to come forward to get themselves or a loved one help. I do not want anyone to end up in a jail or prison cell or worst on a psychiatric ward, or suicide watch, because of ignorance and careless disregard for another human being's feelings! I do not want you, anyone you may know and love, or your legacy to die! I want those who have struggled with violence and abuse to be proactive and not reactive towards their mental health and choosing self-love over hate by changing their evil, violent behavior and get the necessary help required to learn how to cope forever in life with violence and abuse! I want those individuals who have never been violent or abusive to help me help those who are by being mentours™, womentours™, partners, and shining examples of how to cope and live a purposeful, balanced, energetic, abundant, happy life!

The greatest regret I have in life was taking too long to get help for my violent behavior, as well as howling and letting someone know family members were harming me as a child. Those secrets and silence led to my violence towards others and me. I paid the price for a crime I never committed as a child and ultimately ended up reciprocating that violence to innocent family members and friends. I will spend the rest of my life trying to save lives and legacies of victims and victimizers, so they do not end up perpetuating and experiencing the incredible pains and losses I have had in my life!

Victims should not be the first person to reach out to their victimizer for their healing. The victimizer should be more accountable and aware that the healing process begins when they, the victimizers, proactively apologize to their victims, when their victims are ready to receive their apology. The strongest and most in control person are the individuals who realize they have a severe personal deficiency and they proactively become accountable to a permanent solution! Do you know how mentally strong and courageous you must be to overcome and survive abuse publicly? Victims are suffering in silence! We can never blame the victims! If we blame them, the cycle of violence continues!

Victimizers must stop running from being an offender and come forward to admit they are a violent offender, abuser or bully publicly? Many victimizers are heroes publicly and zeros privately. You are embarrassed and ashamed to admit that you are a victim, as well as admitting to the world you are or have been a predator against someone who is innocent and defenseless. If the strength is in the admission then surrender to your deficiencies and admit your pains clinically by getting help & stay committed to being mentally healthy. The most dangerous person is the person who is not accountable and aware of their mental health and behavior and how their violence and abuse impacts others. As a society, we should never publicly shame or assassinate the character of a victim or any individual who is abused and or seeking healing! What I know now is what you do not know and do about yourself can truly hurt you and others!

The bottom-line: ***Evil Should Never Define Your Life or Legacy!***

Abusive monsters are not born…. they are created. We are all born to love and manufactured to hate! The truth is, someone is pushing their pain, abuse, and illness by way of force or choice, onto an innocent person who is undoubtedly unaware and incapable of stopping that predator's agenda. How can you properly love anyone or anything if you have never been properly loved? When you hurt someone or damage something, you are hurting & damaging yourself! If you abuse her or your child, you are abusing yourself! You bully them, you are bullying yourself! You hate them. You hate yourself! Who would do that to their self? Your physical well-being must match your mental well-being! Abusing someone physically and then also torturing them mentally is the ultimate sign you urgently need an intervention! Bruises may heal, but the psychological effects may linger for a lifetime for an individual.

I ignorantly refused to take the sincere, genuine advice immediately from individuals who honestly had a concerned love for me and my welfare! I chose to not get help for my violent temper and high propensity to violence towards humanity and my dog Toby*, and it cost me a path in life that I wish upon no one. I plead to all violent offenders, child abusers, and bullies to please stand up, step forward, speak out and GET HELP NOW! This mission is about ridding every home of domestic violence and child abuse and every school of bullying with the result being we helped to save lives and legacies! *I want to provide sincere, nonjudgmental hope to any abuser that it is possible to permanently eradicate domestic violence, child abuse, and bullying!*

We can all choose to scowl publicly and growl at the abuser and violent offenders who opt not to get help to heal themselves from what ails their mind, body, and soul! However, I warn against shunning or overly judging the abusers or victimizers, if we do not offer a realistic, tangible approach and permanent solution to get them healed, and not treated. We owe this to the victims.

I want my mother, aunt, and uncle to know that this book was never written to embarrass them publicly or diminish their respect level and legacy with others. My intent is to show others that they, like you and me, can survive trauma with the right solutions to live a productive and happy life, despite the challenges or obstacles that violence and abuse may put in your life. My family should know that whenever the first person goes forward to tackle an unpopular social issue, they often times pay the price with their sacrifice, but ultimately time will show the world that their intent was to make humanity better and more peaceful.

Violence of any kind impacts an entire community! We can never blame or judge the victims of domestic violence, child abuse, and bullying and must always take a victim at their word until it is proven otherwise! The truth will always come to light and we as a society should never put a mute button or muzzle on the victim to silence them from getting justice and freedom from the devastating pain caused by a victimizer. I pray I help to take off the muzzles of the victims as well as convincing their abusers to stop putting muzzles on individuals who actually care for them and their mental health wellness.

We only get one lifetime on earth. What will your legacy be to those who know you? How will your obituary read or what will be inscribed on your tombstone? Will you be in a cemetery in a lonely grave destined for hell or with other abusers and violent offenders, with a headstone engraved with an epitaph and obituary that reads "Here alone lies a prolific abuser, destroyer of self-esteem and happy spirits, a quitter, doubter, coward, bully, an intimate partner abuser, a wife-beater, a domestic torturer and terrorist, humanitarian hater, a profound perpetrator of hate, violence and abuse and as a result promotes generational curses in bloodlines and one who murders legacies? This person did not care about the welfare of those who loved them, and the spouses and children relying on them to provide, protect and pray for them!" If you do not want this to read on your tombstone or obituary, be a loving person and get the required help now to become the loving person you and others want you to be! Your Heavenly Brother... A.W. Burgess

Please follow and like me and FAMILY MANKIND™ on Facebook, Instagram, Twitter, YouTube, Google+, Pinterest, Snapchat! Please go to our corporate website **www.familymankind.org** for more information about us and how you can get involved as a volunteer, Womentour™, Mentour™, Corporate Partner, Sustainable Sponsor or Donor. I want to support you and your initiatives and pray we can effectively collaborate. I can not do it alone! I really need you!

I sincerely thank you now and forevermore for however you wish to help partner and affiliate with me and FAMILY MANKIND™! You are a blessing! You truly are saving lives and legacies! For more information on partnerships, training, bookings, speaking engagements, conferences, corporate and personal appearances, you can also connect with me at **www.awburgess.com** or by email at **awburgess@awburgess.com** or text at **704-287-0086** or Toll-Free at **1-833-3HOWLER (1.833.346.9537). THANK YOU AND MUCH LOVE TO YOU!**

Solutions To Permanently Eradicate Domestic Violence, Child Abuse, and Bullying

ME and MY UNCLE CHIP. HE WAS ONE OF THE CLOSEST EXAMPLES OF A MAN'S MAN. HE WAS MY UNCLE...NOT MY DAD! HE DID NOT GROW UP IN MY HOME! NO ONE SHOULD FILL ANOTHER MAN'S ROLE TO RAISE HIS CHILD, UNLESS HE IS NOT MAN ENOUGH OR FIT ENOUGH TO TAKE ON THE RESPONSIBILITY! IF YOU ARE BLESSED TO BE A FATHER, IT IS YOUR ROLE ONLY & NO ONE ELSES!

Solutions To Permanently Eradicate Domestic Violence, Child Abuse, and Bullying

MY BIRTH CERTIFICATE!
ANSWER THIS: WHAT IS MISSING ON MY BIRTH CERTIFICATE?
IT WILL BE MISSING FOR MY ENTIRE LIFE! (*Answer Is At The Bottom*)

THERE IS NO FATHER'S NAME LISTED ON MY BIRTH CERTIFICATE!
THIS WAS A SIGN THAT HE WOULD BE MISSING IN MY LIFE FOREVER!
A FATHER IS A MAN OF GOD! AMEN TO THE MAN WHO CLAIMS HIS
CHILDREN AND WHO IS A FAMILY MAN! _NO MAN EVER CLAIMED ME!_
I HAVE SPENT FOREVER IN THE LOST AND NEVER FOUND BOX!

Solutions To Permanently Eradicate Domestic Violence, Child Abuse, and Bullying

D.A.D- DIDN'T ACCEPT OR ABANDON DUTIES!

What Should I Call You? What's Your Title? Dad, Father, Pop, Sperm Donator, Captain, Emperor, Ghost, Magician, Abandoner, Wanderer, Rolling Stone, Drifter? Why Did You Leave Me? What Did I Do For You To Discard Me? You Did Not Accept Your Duties!

Were you ever here or there for and with me? Was that your voice I heard when I was swimming inside of mommy saying you were going to take care of me? Did you watch me get delivered into this world the first day of my life? Were you the first thing I ever saw when I first opened my eyes? Did you give me my first bath? Did you get me home safely from the hospital? Will you die for me? Should I trust your advice? Can I depend on you forever? Did you ever care about me? Did you protect me? Did you feed, house, educate and clothe me? Did you provide health coverage for me? Do you have life insurance? Did you provide reliable transportation for me? Did you walk me to or from the bus stop? What sound, lifelong advice did you give me? Did you advocate for me? Did you video my first footsteps? Do you want me to follow in your footsteps and do to my kids exactly what you did to me? Will you teach me my ABC's, 123's, and how to tie a tie or my shoes and brush my teeth and go to the potty? Will you show me how to ride a bike? Will you read to me and tuck me in at night? Will you scare off the Boogie Man and check under the bed and in my closet to ensure I am safe before you turn off the lights? Will you teach me how to pray or play and live well with others? Will you show me how to celebrate someone else's great fortune? Will you show me how to be accountable to others and for my actions? Will you be there for my first day of school? Will you be at my graduations? Will you take me to visit colleges and then send me off to one? Will you co-sign for me? Will you teach me about the birds and the bees? Will you pre-qualify my dates? Will you teach me how to have excellent credit and a clean driving and criminal record? Will you be in my wedding? Will you be there for me when my babies come into the world? How will you respond when you first hear that I died? Will you attend? Will you show me how to cope in life and relationships? Will you show me how to love? Will you love me? Forever?

Thank you for placing me in the lost and found treasure chest never to be claimed as a son by any other man! My prayer in life is to become a man's man, a good guy, and a FAMILY MAN™ as a result of you permanently abandoning me! You placed me there knowing no one would come for me and step up to claim me or vouch for me like a shipwrecked vessel stripped of its identifying name and numbers forever lost at sea! You see, I am a trillion miles away floating around lost in a black hole in space just plummeting to earth. Oh yeah, you choose not to see and are not conscious of my existence on land, at sea, or in space! Will you at least send an AMBER Alert or Code Adam out for me? You never came for me! You never sent for me! They are charging you a dollar a minute at the daycare for not picking me up on time. They are wandering around the store looking for you and calling you on the intercom and your cell phone describing me and making you aware that I am in this treasure chest and making me aware that no one treasures me. I am worthy to be loved. You will treasure my love. Come for me! Send for me! When you see me, you will know that I am yours and belong to you. I stand out from the rest even though they are treasured gifts too. I look like you, or at least I resemble you in ways! I beg of you to do everything humanly possible to make your way over to me like a strategic alligator looking for a meal or defending its children and territory with a purpose. Some say I act, sound, and dress like you! Get me before I hurt myself, or potentially harm someone else, or something comes to destroy me!

Daddy, that is "church" which equals "love." There are no "churches" in the wilderness or concrete jungle! I believe it, even though I do not want to believe it. It is the Wild West out here in this lost desert, and I am not John Wayne with a gun, I am Lil' Wayne with a gun and mommy is at work. What will come of this? I am an oddity because the odds of me winning in life without you are stacked against me. I will prove the statistical gatherers and analytical authorities that I will not perpetuate what you did to me! I will never do unto others what you dealt unto me. I will be everything opposite of your dysfunction! I wish you would have come for me or called and just told me you loved me and was proud of me and so appreciative and grateful that God had personally chosen you with the privilege to be my dad and me as your son. Words and actions do matter because my life matters. I am lost without you and am not whole, but rather I am stuck in this spinning spiritual black hole in space and blue hole vortex like the Bermuda Triangle. I am riddled with holes in my head, and there's nothing funny about it because I don't want to be holey and filled with holes, I want to be made whole and holy spiritually, filled with love!

I have visited and seen better fathers in prison than on the streets! I've seen parents send their entire monthly check of $25 to their kids from prison! I've seen men send sweet and genuine homemade gifts and birthday cards home from prison to their children! I am done with you! No more wasted time on you! You are a zero! This coming from the one you never claimed! Sincerely Not Yours, A.W. Burgess!!!

Solutions To Permanently Eradicate Domestic Violence, Child Abuse, and Bullying

My wife's daddy never bought her a tampon, deodorant or basic living necessities in her lifetime! He never contributed to her education in any fashion even though he came from wealthy parents and he has a college degree and education from a Divinity College, but she could not complete her education…No Dough! My wife believes he may have a master's degree but does not know in what. She believes he even worked for NASA. Sounds crazy does it not, but this is not unusual to me or many others who were abandoned by their fathers! I never really gave too much thought about my dad growing up in Baltimore because there were no dads around in my household and barely around in my family and the ones we thought were solid turned out to be sausage head hypocrites or weren't the actual paternal dads anyway! In fact, my limited exposure to great dads and men, in general, came by coaches in my little league recreational teams, a few teachers and church administrators, Sunday school teachers, and several neighbors who let me cut their lawns like Mr. Tex, Mr. Ryan, Mr. Rich, Chester Washington, Joe Butler, Mr. Bus Owens, Mr. Dorsey, Mr. Leonard, my uncle's Pete, Joe, Carl, David, Chip, Thomas, Bill, Bev! When I think of the word father, I think of the poem "Footprints!" Daddy don't leave me! Don't abandon me! Will you carry me on your back when times are tough. Don't abandon your responsibilities as a parent! Don't desert your post or go AWOL (Absent Without Official Leave) as a leader! What made you leave your baby, Dad?

I hear a baby crying! What would any sane human being do if they were in an arm's reach of a crying baby? Who could ever leave or harm a crying baby? The baby is already in pain because that is why it is crying. Is the baby hungry, thirsty, needing their diaper changed, or are they too cold or hot and need proper sheltering or are they crying or dying for attention which is communicating to their parent and screaming to the world that they are in desperate need of love! Be an Emperor penguin daddy and raise me by the example of the King of the cold! No matter how cold it gets, the Emperor penguin never leaves his babies! He hovers over them and takes the blast of the arctic wind head-on, face to face! He defends his babies to the death of a foe trying to harm his babies! He feeds them and does not leave them until they are of a mature age to do so for themselves! If for any reason they get away from his covering he can recognize their cries despite the thousands of other babies crying out!

Can you hear me or my cry daddy! Do you recognize my voice or do my screams fall on deaf ears? Are you abandoning me? Daddy, do you know who Captain Francesco Schettino is? He was *the Captain of the wrecked cruise ship*

Costa Concordia that ran aground off the Italian coast in 2012, killing 32 people, and as a result, he was charged with manslaughter and abandoning ship! He denied these charges even though there was video footage of him abandoning his post and leaving the ship well before his 4200 passengers and crew left. He was sentenced to 16 years in prison. [1] **I WAS GIVEN A DEATH SENTENCE FROM YOU DAD!**

I am not judging Captain Schettino because until we are put in that exact situation, we genuinely do not know how we would respond in that same scenario. The difference though is that before you take on the daunting task and responsibility of captaining a ship, airplane, bus or rideshare vehicle where you are responsible for getting live passengers and human and animal cargo to their destination safely, you must know if you are properly trained to complete the mission! You know the appropriate protocols and processes to execute the delivery, and you definitely should be accountable for your responsibilities and know how to provide solutions to any issues that arise during your shift! Worst case, make a "May Day" or 911 call to get help and always know that you can pray and ask God for help or a miracle! As fathers, we have to always right the ship as Captain and be the last person off the ship! We have to ensure the ship is safe for the next voyage and secure against the dock, so it does not float away. You should be like the captain of the Titanic and commit to the captain's oath where you ensure the safety of your human cargo first, preserving life, and if necessary, then your final requirement is to save yourself last by going down with the ship. You never abandon the ship! You cannot go back to make up lost time, but you can make it right, now! Schettino was a coward's coward!

Am I too naive or too old school to want to believe that men can stay and raise their children and will never consider leaving their children regardless of their relationship with their children's mother? I am baffled, disappointed, and disgusted at the thought that another man would not be there to take care of his kid and would abandon them or throw them away like garbage or harm them physically, mentally and emotionally! Abandoning fatherly duties is a crime as it pertains to fathers abandoning their children and responsibilities as a parent! Cowards come in many forms, but there's a special sense of shame reserved for dads who abandon their kids!

Let us put fatherhood or abandoning your children in this same perspective! How and why do you leave your baby alone? How do you impregnate a caring, loving woman, or worst, an equally irresponsible woman, and judge her for choosing to abort the baby or put the baby up for adoption or forced foster care and you were not there or involved or actively engaged in the baby's welfare or future? How could you do that to them or God? Why would you do it to yourself? I am not judging you or her. I am loving and hugging you! You never leave! You do not kill your baby!

When a woman, regardless of being responsible or irresponsible, has chosen to carry and have your baby, again, your baby, and has not decided to give it up for adoption or foster care or the choice to abort, has she boldly told the world that she really loves her baby and wants to have a baby with you! She believes you can and will provide, protect and pray for her and your baby! As a man and father, I would dread knowing that I was the reason for a woman wanting an abortion or to put a baby up for adoption because she loved her baby enough not to want me around it or she didn't believe I would be the best responsible option & that I would not be there for her and the child! I do not resent not having a father ever in my life. I have learned to live without one. I only wish I could have known the other side of my family who is supposed to make me a complete individual. Maybe God did not think I would be safe around them, assuming that my father was the product of violence and abuse and just maybe that was why I never had an opportunity to be a part of that side of my family, but rather, God saw it best that I be apart from my family and that He would be my Father and stand in the gaps whenever I needed that filled!

When a baby comes into this world it is naturally born to love and hate is a learned behavior that is generally impressed upon or influenced by someone else. Kids learn what they live, see, and hear and then they consciously or unconsciously apply it. I must break generational curses of abusers. Abusers are not born, they are created. We are born to love and manufactured to hate! Somebody is pushing their pain, abuse, and their illnesses, by way of force or choice, onto another innocent person who is undoubtedly unaware and incapable of stopping that individual's agenda. Whether it is seeing or hearing, one is learning the behavior from some individual(s), television, movies, books, magazines, radio or any other forms of mass communication such as the internet and social media outlets. *Charles Manson* was born "No Name" by his mom who traded him for a pitcher of beer. His only "happy moment' was when his mom came home from a 3-year prison stay and she hugged him. He did not get anything for Christmas, and she sent him away to never take him back. He was illiterate, molested in 'boy's school' and literally begged to stay in jail.* [2] By no means do I shed a tear for him and his crimes against others, but is there any wonder why he turned out the way he did? What an incredible image! What first goes on that birth certificate speaks volumes! Where are you, Daddy? Thank God we can always depend on our heavenly Father who will never leave us!

It is not natural to be born a hater, violent physical or mental abuser, pediphiler, rapist, arsonist, or murderer! It is like a baby or child that has never laughed or smiled! What caused that baby or child to stop laughing, smiling, or loving? If you are laughing or smiling uncontrollably and then suddenly someone comes up to you and suddenly severely pinches you or punches you in the face or gut your smile suddenly retreats to a frown or a look of bewilderment, and your body sends out negative signals because now you are focused on pain! Imagine this behavior happens consistently enough to become the norm or enough to impact you for the rest of your life, all you ever know or remember is the pain. It could also lie dormant and not resurface until triggered! Because of the exposure to hate or violence, now this individual knows how to inflict pain on others and is immune to love, hate or violence! If all you have ever known is hate and have never been loved or shown how to love another human being properly, how is it possible to normally love another human being, animal, plant, or valuables? How can one never be adopted and be in foster care until they age out of the system? If it were me, I would think, "No one wants to love me or has ever loved me? What is wrong with me? Where do I go from here? How is it that I am an unlovable person? I am a baby too!"

How do we function in a dysfunctional world? Violence and destructive behavior will surface if there is never any coping skills learned to diminish or forever suppress this learned behavior! Whatever happens to you is eventually what you learn to do to others! Whatever you are exposed to is what you possibly will expose to others! If your parent(s), guardian(s), never love you or love you inadequately, how do you learn to love others adequately or sufficiently if no adequate or sufficient love is in you? If you are exposed to pornography or alcoholism or pyrotechnics or violence or horror movies, why is it a surprise when children and adults become what they have been exposed to at impressionable times in their lives! I hated the weekends because of the way my mom tortured my spirit with the drunken spirits in her, but I loved going to my aunt's home because she showed me love, as well as, X-Rated cable shows and the tempting attractions at her house and in the city? And why? Lack of parenting! I have seen better fathering from those in the penitentiary!

As a father, your children should always wake up in your residence until they go to college, into the military, or leave to start their own life as an adult. Who should care more about your children than you? Who is taking your children to the doctor or dentist for their regular checkups? Unless you're working in some capacity or are in the hospital due to illness or an emergency, are you with your children on their birthday, a monumental special occasion, and all family holidays? You never, ever, ever leave or abandon your children and responsibilities as a father. How can you live across the street from your mother or father and your mother or father has an entirely new family and sees you as just another neighbor... a million miles away? Do you not know predators are looking at your kids as prey because they know there is no alpha male or female there to protect their offspring! Who's praying/preying?

Take your kids, no matter what their age is, 2 minutes old or 102 years old and place them in a remote area of woods while they are asleep and just walk away leaving them alone with no food, clothes, or sheltered protection from the elements and predators. What do you think is going to happen to them? How would you feel if something happened to them? Do you even care what happens to them? How would you feel if something or someone attacked them or even killed them? Would you actually do this as a father? Do you see any male animal attack or abuse the mother of their very own offspring? Do they kill their own offspring? And to think, God gave man dominion over the animals! Only the mothers are defending their babies like grizzly bears and Nile crocodiles? I now understand why the black widows kill the male donors of their offspring? *#DON'TLEAVEME&MOMDAD!*

As a man and father, I was chosen by God, the creator of all mankind on the earth, to parent, provide, protect and pray for His precious and priceless creation, a live human being, and the thought of bringing pain in any shape or form to a baby is simply repulsive and never acceptable. If we were born in God's image, then that means I was born to create and not hate. The even greater thought of harming God's property is boldly audacious and foolish! I am a simple thinker in that I do not understand how a father cannot understand that his obligations as a parent are a requirement and not a request that is not securely fulfilled until his baby can provide, protect, and pray for themselves and even then the father still needs to leave life insurance and a legacy of love and best life skilled practices and wisdom!

As a father, I never have an option to lose because I am working with no safety net or network of partners that will stand in the gap on my behalf when I die! I have a family and a disabled daughter who cannot survive on her own amongst the predators in our society. Who will ensure her safety and welfare? You have to be a definitive man and mature adult. You provide, protect, and pray for your family. No man should ever call a woman fat or body shame her and play mental games with her psyche. I have no right to hurt someone else's baby or the baby God entrusted me to care for on His behalf. I have no right to ever harm God's beautiful property!

Fathers give you swag in that anything you do or touch, you have the confidence to succeed and the courage to keep your head up and keep moving forward when you are short of success! God blesses motion...no atrophy, doubt or rigor mortis will set in your body, mind, or spirit when you have your father's endorsement and full support! Dad, Father, Sponsor, Sperm Donator do you hear me now? Did you abuse my mother to the point that your abuse eventually taught my mother to abuse me and consequently me to hate and abuse myself and those closest to me? I did not abuse her Dad, you did, not me, and now I understand why she did not get help sooner. I wish you had gotten help sooner before it spilled over onto my head, nose, and mouth? I hate that I have those violent antibodies in my body, but I love that I got help with the abuse you and others infected me with and was cured enough to not tragically abuse my wife and kids. I paid for your crime Dad! ***If I am sitting down today, it is because I will not stand for domestic violence!***

Dad, I forgive you and understand why and it is all love and forgiven at this point. I get "it" and "it is" all good now for me! I have found the meaning in the suffering. I am no longer lost because I have found my way and I know where I am going. I am seeing my kids doing productive things with their lives and we support them and their dreams. This baby who was not supposed to live has succeeded without any of your help. My heart and mind are not cold or bitter. They are healthy. I carry no chips on my shoulder! I know I was forced to be a man without your helping hand. It was not my fault! I stumbled! I tripped! I fell down! But I got up to stay up and stand up for me, my children and their children. I got up for the children in my bloodline to stop the violence and pain! Why didn't you? You left me behind!

I wish my dad realized the strength of a woman...a woman like my mom! I imagine he was like some men who underestimate the power of a woman or who does know the strength of a woman but simply does not respect them just because they are a woman. How can a woman be weak in any form when God made them strong enough to carry and deliver a baby. The strength it takes to endure the pains of carrying and delivering a baby. The "Her"culean strength it takes to feed, protect, house, educate, and raise a child! Women almost never abandon their babies as compared to the number of men who make babies only to abandon their parental duties and fatherly obligations. ***#MOMISTIREDANDNEEDSYOURHELPDAD!***

Why are some dads so ***doggone insecure***? The answer is they are twisted and backward in their thinking and are not "secure in" their manhood and as a result, that "dog is gone on to another innocent victim to abandon the mom & litter!"

Solutions To Permanently Eradicate Domestic Violence, Child Abuse, and Bullying

Nonetheless, I had to be the man since mine was not! The only positive thing I can say about my dad is that I am 1000% positive that God sometimes uses even the most negative situations and people to bring something positive to the earth. The only father I ever had and knew was my Father in heaven. He never abandoned me or harmed me and only treated me in a loving way. I am not the only one who was abandoned intentionally. The amazing beauty though is I am not the only one He loves. Because of Him being my Father, I was able to fearlessly emerge from the valley of the shadows of death unscathed! Thanks for carrying me on Your back and shoulders Father in the sand when my biological dad did not bother to care and stay! I will never forget that You never abandoned me. I will never abandon my children!

JAMES ERNEST THOMPSON

THIS IS THE ONLY PICTURE I HAVE OF THE PERSON THEY SAID WAS MY DAD! CAN YOU IMAGINE HAVING ONLY ONE PHOTO OF YOUR PARENT? I AM LUCKY TO HAVE IT! HOW CAN ANYONE HAVE A RELATIONSHIP WITH SOMEONE FOR A SIGNIFICANT PERIOD OF TIME TO ONLY POSESS ONE IMAGE? THIS HAS NEVER MADE SENSE TO ME, BUT IN LIFE I GUESS MANY THINGS ARE ONLY ANSWERED BY GOD, AND THAT IS WHAT I HAVE TO TRUST WAS BEST FOR ME!

A righteous man and father in the home is a blessing from God who puts the "Man" in Amen. Where are the men? There is a major difference between a male and a MAN and a dad and a FATHER. Men and Fathers never abandon their wives, children, and duties/responsibilities as a Family Man™. Adam, look what you caused!

James Thompson*- How can I ever know all of me if I never knew a fraction of you? Thank You so much for _not_ teaching me how to be a Family Man™! I AM better off!

I AM

I

AM

FULLY ACCOUNTABLE,

WITH NO EXCUSES, FOR MY

BEHAVIOR, HAPPINESS,

AND MENTAL WELLNESS!

AS A CONSEQUENCE FOR

BEING AWARE OF THIS,

I AM

THE SOLUTION

TO MY DOMESTIC VIOLENCE,

ABUSING SOMEONE'S CHILD,

AND

BULLYING INNOCENT PEOPLE

The Progress-Index   Monday, January 6, 1992   B

Children learn discipline from their first teachers

"The will is made of steel. You can hold it. You can bend it . . . on the other hand the most common mistake that parents and teachers make in handling discipline has to do with using anger to motivate children instead of using action to motivate children."

— Dr. James Dobson

Discipline of our children is needed. Society could not exist if people acted without regard for others. Why then is there so much disagreement about the subject?

One reason is that many people misunderstand what discipline means. The word "discipline" comes from "disciple," meaning someone who follows the teachings of another. Discipline therefore means a learning experience — not punishment or tears, but a chance to learn how to live in a social world.

The long-term goal of teaching discipline is putting the child in charge or the ability to achieve self-discipline. Children have to learn to rely on themselves rather than on you or other adults to tell them what to do. Discipline should help children take over the responsibility for their own behavior. Of course, when your child is about to hit a friend on the head with a baseball bat, you can't wait for the long-term effects of discipline to take place. While children are still learning self-control, they need to be protected from hurting themselves and other people. They have to be shown how to behave in appropriate ways. The short-term goal of discipline is to control the children's behaviors on a daily basis.

In working toward these long and short-term goals, it helps to question what message your child is trying to tell you by the misbehavior. Many times when a child misbehaves he or she is trying to accomplish things that you yourself want him to achieve, such as being independent, expression of feelings, learning new skills.

Children don't always know the best ways to do these things as they are in the process of learning self-expression.

The next time your child misbehaves, ask yourself these questions:
• Am I expecting my child to do more than is capable of at this time?

Deborah Higginbotham

• Are my child's possessions or feelings of self-worth being threatened?
• Is my child trying to learn something or practice a new skill?

You don't have to like all your child's behaviors. But by trying to understand the message of each misbehavior, you can find a technique that is more likely to be effective in changing the behavior.

There is no one right way to discipline. Rather, there are a variety of techniques that can stop misbehaviors and, at the same time, encourage self-discipline. Some examples of choices include:
• Letting your child make some decisions and choices.

• Giving reasons for your rules.
• Taking the child away from trouble.
• Utilizing taking away privileges, time out or spanking.

Punishment, if used too often, can lose its effectiveness and may even have negative side effects. It can arouse anger or cause the child to forget why he was punished in the first place. Discipline takes time and self-discipline for the parent. Children will repeat misbehaviors. It is vital that whatever method of discipline chosen be consistently applied. Keep in mind your long and short-term goals, your child and the particular situation. In general, younger children need more direct control. As they get older, you can make more use of reasons, choices and natural outcomes. The parent is the child's first teacher and counselor. Parents help the child to develop at an early age with the physical, emotional, social and intellectual capabilities the child will employ for a lifetime.

• *Deborah W. Higgenbotham is license clinical social worker and he her practice at Hopewell Family Guidance Center.*

3

I LEARNED VIOLENCE BASED ON HOW I LIVED AS A CHILD

Solutions To Permanently Eradicate Domestic Violence, Child Abuse, and Bullying

M.O.M- MURDERER of ME? MAKING of a MONSTER or MAN?

You Are One Half: Setting The Tone Of How I Will Love And Treat Other Women!

I want the world to know that I love my mother and all of my family! My mother and aunt were victims of heartless, insecure, and cowardly violent domestic violence offenders. I am not offering excuses to justify how I became their victim, but I understand how without the appropriate mental health and wellness solutions, the victim eventually becomes a victimizer. No one should ever be mad at my mom or aunt because they were victims too, struggling to cope, and was only playing the crooked hand that was dealt to them. Here is my love letter to my mom to free me.

Mom, I want to believe you loved me after God created me and let you borrow me. I just am not overwhelmingly convinced that you wanted me because of dad! I know for sure God loved me first but am not sure if you were second. I believe you tried to love me the only way you knew. I do not think you ever knew how to love me properly because of the way you were abused! I was not clueless in that I could feel you did not love me as you should have! You could not have because it was not possible, and I understand now. I know why now! It was my birth dad's fault. He traumatized you! I felt the trauma at conception, in the womb, and beyond.

I apologize for bringing you a pain that caused you to drink your way into oblivion, but the alcohol did not mask how much you hated me because you told me and the entire world how much you did despise my existence in those very drunken moments and other demeaning ways of hatred. Is it that I resonate something in your psyche that causes you to want to hurt, harm and embarrass me, rather than a desire to want to love and embrace me? Did I remind you so much of your abusive domestic violence offender boyfriend, that it was the reason why you tried to kill me? Was it because I was too light-skinned and not dark enough for your liking? Was it my curly black "good hair?" If I had looked or acted like you, would that have prevented you from trying to harm me? I hate weekend nights and Miller beer!

If you could turn time back, would you have protected me better, rather than abandon me, leaving me to fight off the predators by myself? Would you have been prouder and less embarrassed by me to make you want to come to my games? Would you have come to my games sober? Would you have come to my games at all? I do not blame you for the neglect or purposely not coming to my defense to protect me from other abusers, because you were doing to me what someone had done to you! I do not blame you, mom. I know you were only playing the game with

Solutions To Permanently Eradicate Domestic Violence, Child Abuse, and Bullying

a half a deck of cards expecting to win. Maybe you abandoned me purposely at times to prevent yourself from harming me. I hate you got caught driving drunk with me in the back seat! I caused you to make that decision too? I paid a price for that too?

I do not know why I was blamed and punished for a crime I did not commit. I do know now why I was ashamed to be born. James Thompson caused it all! I blame him to a point! God chose you for me, but you never chose me for you…why?

How could you treat your school kids better than me? How could you be a better person at work, a hero, and a zero at home to me? I was confused as to why you wanted to kill me, my will and my spirit? You did not want me to smile or be happy? I became a violent reason and a cause for people not to smile! A frown? :(

I protected you and kept silent so that you and others would not get in trouble, and that is because I believed you and your siblings could and would change and would get the necessary help that would have prevented all of you from harming me again! I no longer sit in silence worried about violence and my safety or anyone else's for that matter. I broke the silence of violence and generational abuse curse in my bloodline and DNA! That cycle has ended and will never appear again.

I hug my kids and wife and tell them I love them! I attend their school events and social activities. I listen to them and their stories. I ask them how they feel and how was their day? I loved and cared enough about them and their welfare, before I ever met them, to get the required treatment so I would never think or even try to kill them or their spirits or their dreams. I want them to have and live a healthy, phenomenal and productive life free of parental child abuse, bullying, and domestic violence. Today, I am the reason for people to smile and laugh. I AM A MAN Ma!

Until I die, I will live to ensure my children and the children of many others, regardless of their age, will be properly loved and protected from violent offenders, bullies and abusers and never neglected, abused or bullied by their parents, partners, spouses, and classmates for just being a child or the closest victim. I always try to find the silver lining and positive meaning in everything negative that finds its way on my plate in life. God chose me to represent the violent offenders, bullies and abusers and partner with those who they have abused to stop the violence and abuse, so others will not be victims of violence and abuse like you and me.

I would not have been able to do such, had you not did what you did to me and the ultra-negative consequences it caused that turned me from a violent and hostile troubled and depressed youth, abused child, successful athlete, abusive high school boyfriend, to a budding college student and corporate intern, to an evil hypocritical monster of a college boyfriend, to a prisoner, to psychiatric patient, to a street pharmacist and community degenerate thug, to a productive, healthy man, husband, father, business person, benevolent humanitarian, altruist, philanthropist, and a selected citizen in heaven. I owe that honor to you and thank you for the opportunity to serve others as a result of the pain I endured from you and your siblings. Thank you, Ma, and I pray I see you and your siblings in heaven with the many people who say they love me and those that I love! It is best for me now that I love you from a distance with no communication, so my heart stays healthy! A.W.

I want people to know I do not want to ever harm my mom! I do not want any harm to anyone in my life. It is tough for people to truly understand my life because what they see today is a certified, genuine, authentic, secure man and a bonafide FAMILY MAN™! Many do not understand the journey because all they see is the final destination of a lost soul that has been found. Living with pain is a daily suffering. However, what I now know is surviving means you have the opportunity to discover the meaning in the suffering. You have to kill what is killing you to live. Silence and secrets are friends of all forms of violence trying to kill you!

Every chapter in this book has significance and purpose to me. Because we cannot choose our parents and this one is titled "MOM" and you only get one birth MOM in life, I wanted to end it in a unique, yet significant and respectful, fashion!

My family is probably like 95% of most families who struggle with some dysfunction or another. As I became more mature and accountable for my mental wellness and an individual discovering what were the exact roots of my dysfunctional behavior, I eventually began to realize that my family was exactly like most families who opt not to proactively deal with their family dysfunctions, believing that the problems will either go away or eventually correct on their own which is what continues the deadly cycle of quiet violence and abuse. ___Silence kills!___

I resolved in my mind with no excuses, passes, or justifications that the abuse, trauma, and neglect that I experienced was simply as a direct result that my mother was dealing with a deep cutting pain so hurtful and traumatic for any one person to deal with single-handedly, let alone a 21-year-old single parent who was lonely & facing head-on the thought of trying to raise a boy in Baltimore, all in her senior year of college. To conquer the world without a co-parent and the after-effects of the domestic violence and abuse from my biological sperm donor who most people refer to as dad, and the devastating untimely death of him, for certain short and long-term postpartum depression, and not to forget that during those days, the family shame and embarrassment brought on by being pregnant while in college and having a baby as an unwed mother, had to be an incredible mountain to climb alone. It had to be a daunting task to be pregnant and still being abused! I feel for you Ma!

I know my mother wanted to do right by me at times in my life, and probably had decent intentions for me. She either was in such a hunt to be loved by a man or accomplishing something in her career or other aspirations, that she didn't always manage her priorities in loving me the right way and settled for ways to appease her insecurities, self-esteem, or good name for survival purposes and that ultimately pushed me away from her and my family. When she chose men and her career endeavors over me that was one thing. To not stand up for me against other family members who were fighting and bullying me; torturing me with their weak scare tactics or harassing and demeaning me; her hateful epithets and rants during her drunken weekend stupors; and embarrassing me at my sporting events made it painfully clear to me that I had to be my own man--a FAMILY MAN™! I love you still Ma! I may have been born under crazy and death, but I still survived to love! I will always call you Ma! I have to live my life away from your form of painful love!

In a crazy way, I have to thank God for allowing my life to play out as He intended it to be, because I would never have met my wife, we would have never married, I would not have had my four beautiful and incredibly special daughters, my grandchildren would never have called me Pa-Po, I would have never written this book for people like you and me, and I would never have been the human rights activist, domestic violence expert, victimizer and victims advocate, and an impactful change agent for domestic violence offenders, child abusers, and bullies that I am to this very day! Thank you for helping me help others. God chose us to get love here!

I thank you Ma for just being yourself and allowing God to intervene at the most needed times when I needed His mighty righteous right hand to shield me from death, self-destruction, and the deadly consequences from growing up and raised as a fatherless, poor, product of a single-parent, black male in Baltimore, Maryland! I forgive my family and you for all of your deficiencies and dysfunctions that were taken out on me for a crime I never committed against any of you because I know you were perpetuating what was in your and Jimmy's DNA and bloodline! I know you were only responding to the abuse Jimmy inflicted upon you! Jimmy skewed your judgment when he hit you in the head! How were you supposed to love me after the love was taken from you? How were you to love me properly when I reminded you so much of him! I will always love you Ma and my entire family too!

The forgiveness I gave you healed me. I pray it heals you permanently too! My kids and their kids and their children's, children's, children will be better parents as a result of this healing. I truly am sorry that I created such animosity that made me an aversion to you to the point that you disliked me so much that I was a disgusting, repugnant, repulsive and revulsion of a human who caused you and others to be hostile to me because I was an abomination you hated and loathed. I apologize for causing you that pain. When you said, "I wish I never had you!" and "I should have flushed you down the toilet when I had a chance to abort you!" how do you ever take that statement back and erase it from my memory? Drunk or not, you said what was in your heart and your conscious spoke. That's okay because God had to get me here. God had me! He flushed me out of you to get me to this earth to begin and complete a phenomenal mission! I flushed the violence, "it," all away!

I have gone from being a Baltimore bastard baby, to boy, to bully, to the monster, to the prisoner, to the psychiatric patient, to healed, to a friend, to husband, to father, to Family Man!™ Now I am someone's Pa-Po and I am headed to HEAVEN! The lessons I learned doing my time in our house and around other negative influences in Baltimore were priceless. I thank you for making it easy for me to attend McDonogh. I have no regrets about how things have gone in my life because destiny had to happen for me to be where I am today as a MAN. I just want you to know that I believe I would have really made you proud had you been more involved in my life. I wanted to excel in everything I did for your approval and satisfaction. I wish you could have seen me perform personally because you would have known then and only then, that I was playing to make a better life for you. I wanted you to be my number one fan and cheerleader. I wanted you to treat me the way you served your career! Why did you **NOT** understand that the most important work you did was within the walls of your home as a secure and mature **PARENT**?

I want the world to know that it is just about impossible for a child to ever stop loving their mom, regardless of how the mother treats her baby. I am certain because through all of the roller coaster of emotions I have had with and for my mother, I never ever wanted to have her totally out of my life. I always felt that I would never get into heaven if I did not obey or love my mother and so that respect I had for God and His commandments is what always drew me back into loving my mother. I love her, but I am certain that it is probably best for me and my mental wellness to simply love her from a distance. Sincerely Your Son, A.W. Burgess :)

Solutions To Permanently Eradicate Domestic Violence, Child Abuse, and Bullying

If the world can understand the power of love then most will understand why I say I know my mom is a victim of domestic violence and should be considered a heroic survivor of a torturous individual. She truly did not deserve the treatment that James Thompson gave her. Anyone who knows her today will tell you that she is one of the most giving and caring individuals to her family, friends, and all of humanity. She will give her everything to those in need of any help. She has been a faithful servant to her church, community, and the many citizens of Baltimore. She is the type of person you can call a friend to those who admire and respect her.

I have forgiven her, and the world should too! None of us sets out to be a bad parent who harms their child but based on how we were raised or the set of circumstances that impact our relationships with our children, and without proper coping skills and parenting techniques, along with outside resources to get help, any of us can be subjected to circumstances beyond our control and dreams.

Although it was never said to me, and actions speak louder than any words, I know you loved me as best as you could, and I thank you for doing the best you could with the cards that were dealt to you. I know you loved me because you always came home regardless of how long you were gone. I know you tried with your best intentions and that will be sufficient for me. A woman alone can't make a man a MAN Ma! I know that you tried, and I can live with that now! I forgave you a long time ago for not protecting me better from harm! I know you did not set out to harm me in any form or fashion. I know it was never your fault or intentions to hurt me.

I will always continue to end all of my personal and corporate conversations with my family, friends, customers, clients, and you, with I Love You! (Pictured Below Are Two Of My 4 Children & Their Phenomenal Mom Trena Burgess)

Solutions To Permanently Eradicate Domestic Violence, Child Abuse, and Bullying

P.S. Ma —WHY IS NO FATHER'S NAME LISTED ON MY BIRTH CERTIFICATE? WAS I THE PRODUCT OF A RAPE? IF HE WAS NOT THE FATHER, THEN WHO IS OR WAS MY FATHER? I WISH MAURY WAS AROUND IN THE '70s FOR DNA TESTING TO TELL ME THE TRUTH! IS THIS WHY THE STATE DENIED ME HIS DEATH BENEFITS? WHO IS/WAS THE DONOR Ma? WHY WOULD THERE BE NO MAN'S NAME ON THE BIRTH CERTIFICATE Ma? *MAN DAMN!* *#NO MORE SECRETS MOMMY!*

Solutions To Permanently Eradicate Domestic Violence, Child Abuse, and Bullying

USA Today, 07.12.18, Cops Pulled Back; Violent Crime Rose[4] WHY?

$2.00 ■ THE NATION'S NEWS

USA TODAY
07.12.18

NEWSLINE

IN SPORTS

WITTERS SPORT VIA USA TODAY SPORTS

Croatia stops England in extra time 2-1

Team secures a spot in World Cup finals on Sunday against France

Federer: Retirement not on the table

wiss sensation not giving up after uarterfinal upset at Wimbledon

' NEWS

urricane Chris urns in Atlantic

n could clip Newfoundland, da, late Thursday, cause floods

ONEY

np threatens -ranging tariffs

th Chinese could increase prices, including for oxygen

The Rock's s ranked

y's never-ending charisma list a hit not to be missed

A TODAY PODCASTS STEN UP!

Mornings are chaotic, and so is the news cycle. USA TODAY's 5 Things podcast covers the day's top tories in less than five olitics and sports to d tech.

free at Apple Home or wherever favorite podcasts.

The surge of shooting and killings has left Baltimore as easily the **deadliest large city** in the USA. Its murder rate reached an all-time high last year at 342 deaths.

"We have a community that is afraid," says the Rev. Rodney Hudson of Ames United Methodist Church in west Baltimore. DOUG KAPUSTIN FOR USA TODAY

Cops pulled back; violent crime rose

After Freddie Gray's death, Baltimore police appeared to look the other way on the beat

Brad Heath
USA TODAY

BALTIMORE – Just before a wave of violence turned Baltimore into the nation's deadliest big city, a curious thing happened to its police force: Officers suddenly seemed to stop noticing crime.

Police officers reported seeing fewer drug dealers on street corners. They encountered fewer people who had open arrest warrants.

Police questioned fewer people on the street. They stopped fewer cars.

In the space of just a few days in spring 2015 – as Baltimore faced a wave of rioting after Freddie Gray, a black man, died from injuries he suffered in the back of a police van – officers in nearly every part of the city appeared to turn a blind eye to everyday violations.

They still answered calls for help. But the number of potential violations they reported seeing themselves dropped by nearly half. It has largely stayed that way ever since.

"What officers are doing is they're just driving looking forward. They've got horse blinders on," says Kevin Forrester, a retired Baltimore detective.

The surge of shootings and killings that followed has left Baltimore easily the deadliest large city in the USA. Its murder rate reached an all-time high last year; 342 people were killed. The number of shootings in some neighborhoods has more than tripled. One man was shot to death steps from a police station. Another was killed driving in a funeral procession.

What's happening in Baltimore offers a view of the possible costs of a re-

See BALTIMORE, Page 6A

BALTIMORE*

You Can Take A Boy Out Of The Concrete Jungle. Can You Take The Concrete Jungle Out Of The Boy? Where You Are From Impacts Where You Are In Life!

I am and will always be beyond proud to say I am from Baltimore, Maryland. But candidly speaking, once I left Baltimore there was a period in my life when I had "Anal Glaucoma" to returning to Baltimore.... my "a** could not see" me ever returning to Baltimore! Again, I am a die-hard Baltimorean proud to wear my Baltimore colors well as an Orioles and Ravens fan. However, though, my feelings are always conflicted about Baltimore like a never-ending tug of war match wearing no gloves. It is a diabolical city that built me and broke me at the same time. It is a magical place in that perception is not always the reality in that there are a lot of smoke and mirrors when it comes to hidden agendas and relationships. A place where you are alive and dead at the same time! A place that for your punishment, if you get served a life or death sentence, whether you are incarcerated or not, it still equals the death of a life! Either way, you die physically or psychologically from an imprisoned soul — a place where you have to run to achieve a successful life, or you will ultimately be running for your life. It is where your pain is equal to your weight standing on top of your head and heart. We swipe cards because there are no cards to swipe. Like a tiger taking a swipe at your head, Baltimore's citizens are always swiped at in life by some entity's paws trying to get their greedy grips on your money or your talents which will feed their needs and filthy desires.

The majority of the city is filled with blue-collar workers singing the blues for working long hours and eating the bottom of the bay blue crabs because we have little access to wealth. 33% try to make it, 33% try to fake it, and 33% try to take it! We don't swipe debit or credit cards, we swipe and pinch other people's cards and anything else we can get our claws formidably clenched like a vice with no unlock pin. There is no one depositing or crediting anything to our lives. When you are viewed as an insignificant pawn where people only use you for their benefit and advantage, and you aren't even in control of your future, tell me how do you view your life today, let alone believe you will see or want to see tomorrow? 1% make it!

Being broke financially is nothing compared to being broken mentally! Being broke mentally causes your mind to enter a world where you become hopeless and helpless, or it turns you into a passionate person who proactively decides to take life into their own hands versus being strangled by the hands of life who has no conscience because you are just an insignificant pawn easily pawned for pennies.

When we were young, we were told by the world that you had to go to college to get a degree because a high school diploma was not enough to get a solid career or a job with incredible benefits. Boom, you go earn the B.S.(Bachelor of Science) college degree. You get on the job in your career, and you see that you are not being promoted faster or making the maximum amount at your position because you do not have a master's degree and so you spend the money and sacrifice time from your family and go get the master's degree. In the meantime, you find out the very people you trained, who you now call or called boss never had the credentials you were told to go get and they knew someone who knew someone, and they were hooked up by an -ISM (Favoritism or Nepotism) or grandfathered into their career and pay grade. How would you feel? Either way, you were victimized by economic hypnotism and the magic that moves the mirrors and places you in a box that you can never escape from unless you are Houdini because the rules of the game have changed now that you have APPEARED. Or worse, you spend all the money and time to get a Ph.D. and then corporate America tells you that you are overqualified for the position & they cannot afford to pay you what your Ph.D. should bring. B.S.

Bull S***! Wait! First, I was not qualified enough and underpaid. Now I'm overqualified, and they can not afford to pay me what I'm worth and what I went to school for so I can earn at the top pay grade in my field, and now somebody changes the rules to the game or changes the height of the goal and landscape of the golf course. Baltimore taught me to know the value of my life and that I am worth what I believe I am…Priceless! If you don't value your life, no one else will, and they will pimp and prostitute you and your soul until you are left to become a zombie or just someone waiting to die a slow death. Should you make it, fake it, or take it? People are fronting until they are stunting! But what happens when you are confronted????

One of the things we did not fake is when we played football and baseball on concrete and asphalt. As great of an actor or actress native Baltimoreans may be, how do you fake domestic violence, no money, hungry, homeless, no clothes, child abuse, bad hygiene, bullied, and molestation? Baltimore is affectionately known as the "Charm" City by its citizens. Do not get fooled by the deception because I know firsthand that Baltimore should be renamed and "coined" the "Harm" City because everyone is chasing coins and paper and they will harm you to get theirs and keep theirs! It's a place where you don't want the "Money on your head!" "Money on your head" signifies a price on your life for someone to kill you. Yes, Baltimore puts the "harm" in "charm" city all over the evil economic forces of money! "Ball-Til-I-Get-More!" "Ball-Til-I-Get-2-The-Morgue!" Crime does not payout the same for some!

Baltimore is a place that depending upon your home environment you either have life or death spoken into your life, legacy, and dreams! I have a love-hate relationship with Baltimore like Cain and Abel because it is a hypocritical environment where there are no concerns for consequences and where impulsiveness, irrational thinking, and nefarious behavior thrives. You battle between these diabolical dichotomies. One of the few places on earth where you have the heartless and heartbroken built in the same individual. Where there are equally significant hero cops and zero excessive force and discriminatory police officers. The taxpaying citizens hired and paid law enforcement to be "peace" officers for the community to uphold the law, but a few didn't understand or hear the swearing-in correctly and heard they should enforce the laws by being "piece" officers taking a "piece" out of you're a** as they hold you up taking the law into their own hands. These are the "piece" officers who put the uncivil in civil servants and civil rights. Know justice know peace! No justice, no peace or piece for some!

Baltimore is the set-up city! You are set up to have a tremendous failure, then tremendous success, then failure, then ultimately redemptive success. You are set up by the devil, then God, then the devil, then God! Hate appears then love comes about, then hate reappears, then, at last, love appears! And just when you think you have made it, here comes death, then life, then death, then life! Your fall from grace is swift but the come-up is Mt. Muthaf*****! It is a complex, smooth & bumpy ride on the up & down seesaw of Baltimore life. S*** or get off the pot!

In Baltimore, you did not shake certain people's hands because you may not get your fingers back! A place where predators and "pray-dators" reside in the same church, school, home, gang, and team. Their only interest is what they can get out of you or into you such as your labor and money or their certain body part or influence. A sinister clan of financial and sexual molesters lives in these spaces.

It is a city where only your immediate family, friends or classmates know your real "government name" because you go by an affectionate nickname or street alias name or what ails or stands out about you after about fourth grade like Poochy, Bubba-Chuck, Black, Man, Boogie, Suede, Swendell, Teenyman, Ed from Ireland Street or Dukeee Breath Steve! The funny thing is no one knows anyone's last name or first name when the police come around! Selective amnesia, wise counsel or love?

Baltimore is a violent "Hotspot" that *"THROWS"* out chilling, mind-blowing crimes to its taxpaying citizens from its most vile, heinous, untrustworthy and reprehensible basement impoverished city dwellers. This is a place where we love *THROWING* things! We *THROW* acid in people's faces or *THROW* homeless people into the harbor! We love to *THROW* the Holy book of the Bible at innocent people and it's where an overworked, underpaid, uncaring, compromised, misrepresented, non-negotiating public defender of the ignorant and poor gets people *THROWN* into the penitentiary system and cycle of recidivism and poverty or *THROWN* into the back of a steel cushioned paddy wagon thus *THROWING* them into a coma, & consequently *THROWING* someone's baby into the grave or into the streets to fetch the government's taxed beer, pharmaceutical drugs, lottery tickets or worst where we *THROW* the baby out with the bathwater and into a scalding hot bathtub or *THROW* a pillow over their faces or *THROW* them off the 12 story project balconies into the pavements! Again, this is the "Harm" City!

This is the place where we put the "K" in Krazy! Has the "Baltimore Plan" worked for the government and its poorest citizens? Our land gets devalued as we do as citizens so that someone can buy our land and our labor for peanuts with no peanuts in the shells. How do you make a peanut butter sandwich with no peanut butter? We are only good enough to be the slaves who do 99% of the work for 1% of the income with no health or death benefits or retirement plans with just barely enough to live because our shelves are bare, and a bear is on our back so we are required to fill out paperwork and stand in lines for hours to get subsidized housing, supplemental-income, subsidized food stamps and subsidized healthcare that is not accepted by the best doctors or pharmacists. Then someone else comes along to buy our rat, bed bug and roach-infested "home" because the land and it's human labor can be bought for a dollar or cents on the dollar. Then they renovate the building, not the people in the building, or better yet demolish the building and the residents so that they become super wealthy off of this equitable land deal and off the wholesale labor the people will provide with their sweat equity. We get a lifetime contract of supplemental housing, food stamps, and health benefits as part of the deal. It sounds like the rats, roaches and bed bugs got a better deal than the citizens. The citizens didn't have landlords; they had con artist slumlords, devious politicians, paid for inspectors and environmentalist.

I always see Baltimore as a wall that has a picture of Jesus hanging on the wall next to a hole in the wall from a violent punch! It is a daily fight for justice versus injustice in a corrupt city and strategic systems designed to entrap people into a cycle of poverty and criminal activity to fund government budgets. Why and how else did guns, crack, pills, and heroine get into our communities to give us temporary relief from poverty with marked bills, scraped off serial numbers on guns, attractive drug packages and vials? It is the blessing and curse at the same time because what you think is a gift from God is a setup from Satan. You see the prettiest human being ever in life, but you do not know that they have an STD or worst, a highly contagious disease like Ebola that can kill you in a very short period and thus you are now a carrier, passing it on to spread to others. It is true Darwinism where you either choose to fight or flee to survive. Most have no choice but to stay and try to survive!

People keep it real, yet they will rob you to survive! Only the strong survive here or is it the weak and foolish stay because they have limited options? They opt to stay and die from unfulfilled dreams, broken promises, or a broken heart due to the fool's gold of being a "Hustler" by pimping, selling bootleg DVDs, clothes, perfumes or worst, dealing drugs like weed, meth, opioid pills, pharmaceutical prescription pain pills, crack, crank, dummies, liquid codeine, powdered cocaine, black tar "smack" heroin, being a stick up kid, or neighborhood booster, robbing drug dealers, being a hit or con man or high tech fraudster while committing other serious crimes like burglaries, home invasions, bank, liquor store, 7-11s, business robberies, and carjackings for the car, parts, or rims or just for fun and the hell of it, just to make a fast dollar. All of these examples of criminal activities occur because these individuals truly believe they will never get caught, or worst, they do not care if they get caught because they do not fear anyone! They fear no one in their family, or lives for that matter, the police, jail, penitentiary, God, Satan, or any other form of consequences, because they need the money to survive! Death is a come up!

Death by natural causes in Baltimore is a rarity and not normal because you have to live long enough to die naturally. Some look at jail, prison or any form of incarceration as a vacation or a way to get three solid daily meals, hot showers, clean sheets, their own bed and bathroom, toothpaste and toothbrushes, medicine, healthcare, heat or air conditioning, visitors, mail, a job, income, and entertainment! Quietly, there are some there to get peace of mind, peace and quiet, education, and bible studies. Sadly though, there are many there looking for this simple thing called love and encouragement from others and for anyone to acknowledge their existence as a human being while some are seeking protection from family and friend molesters!

Solutions To Permanently Eradicate Domestic Violence, Child Abuse, and Bullying

Nonetheless, Baltimore is a town where you keep an edge on your attitude and your eyes remain wide open because someone is always trying to screw you figuratively and literally 24/7 regardless of if it's your family, friends, neighbors, employer, or a horribly raised pit bull that is going to pay the price with their life or someone else's. Baltimore breeds you to gamble because they have legal gambling like the lottery, race track, and casinos so you can win a few dollars to get you addicted and use to "playing!" The game is they are "playing(conning)" you by saying it is for entertainment purposes only and to add injury to insult, they put the disclaimer in the fine print that says "please call the gambling hotline if you are no longer having fun and have become addicted!" What can they say to comfort you now that your house is in foreclosure or already occupied by the new residents? The entire insides of your home are at the pawnshop or recycling center, and your kid's college fund is gone and ghost-like your spouse and family, and you have street goons and goblins looking for you for their money and now both eyes are black from the constant punches from a guy named Susan and your nose is packed with horse shizzle from the results of the Preakness!

The bottom line is the more you spend gambling, the more you lose and the more the goons and government make! We are conditioned in Baltimore from birth to gamble with our lives because we are only playing the hand of cards we have been dealt! Baltimore is who put the black eye on the black-eyed Susan? Baltimore is where the laws are in a two-faced race whereas when you get caught by the police for selling or using, regardless, possession of crack, which is a mixture of cocaine and baking soda heated up in water until it bonds into a solid piece of rock and then you "crack" it up into pieces that you sell based on the weight and or size, you get many years in prison, even more on parole, and a lifetime of exclusion because you are a convicted felon with a permanent drug conviction record. Get caught with pure cocaine and you get a substantially less sentence, probation, or sentenced to a drug treatment facility, a program or halfway house and upon satisfying the conditions of the program, the charges are often dropped, dismissed, or expunged or it never reached court because of a high price, well connected and influential attorney who has greased an official's palm at a luxurious resort, 5 star restaurant, on the golf course, at the 19th hole, at the exclusive tennis club or has simply paid and satisfied the demands of the ransom. If you do not have the money to pay for your private lobbyists, stay out of criminal enterprises or get used to long vacations behind the concrete and steel embedded walls.

As crack dealers, we often sold on the *corner* streets of Baltimore or in the dark *corners* of the projects. Where do you normally see retail pharmacy stores? Typically, they are on high trafficked *corners* throughout America. What's the difference between the crack dealer and the *corner* pharmacy? The *corner* pharmacies, along with drug manufacturing companies, pay to have lobbyists go to Washington "DC", "Drug Conspirators," to solicit Congress(con-men) and the Senate(sin-ate-whores) to pass their drugs so they can legally sell their drugs on the *corners* just like the drug dealers sell on the *corners*, but the difference is one has the legal authority to do so, and the other is operating illegally! Legal versus illegal for the same purpose of giving an individual a chemical substance to take away the pain! Juvenile detention versus charged as an adult? Street CEO pharmacist versus Corporate CEO pharmacist? Ask "Big Meech" Flannery, Rayful Edmond, "Fat Cat" Nichols, Pappy Mason, Bumpy Johnson, Frank Lucas, "Alpo" Martinez, AZ Faison, Richie Porter, Freeway Ricky Ross, Larry Hoover, Kenneth "Supreme" McGriff, Guy Fisher, Pablo Escobar, and Avon "Bodie" Barksdale how fair the system was and is to the "Kingpin" drug dealers compared to the people who supp"lied" them. Where are you Oliver North? He's with the contras. Never trust anyone or anybody with "con" in their descriptive name like "contras" and "Congress!" If progress means to move forward, what does "Congress" mean? The laws work for whom?

Did they want to stop the drugs from hitting the streets by arresting the drug users and their dealers or did they purposely not want to arrest the original manufacturer of the drug? The system will never stop the money from the original supplier but will pawn off the street dealers to a lifetime behind bars to further the careers of prosecutors and judges and where they upgrade their careers and bank accounts with other backdoor relationships as well. The now convicted felons who had to pay incredible amounts of ungodly money for the best attorneys who had the best chance at getting them off or a reduced sentence and "voila" they still lost their money and freedom which was split by their attorneys and the judges and some prosecutors, and the state and federal government criminal system now collects from the taxpayers to be the ward of these long-term convicts. Baltimore is now implementing this system with our children in their schools by charging our grade school juveniles with crimes and keeping them in the system because they are worth more to the penal system as a housed criminal than they are in the public-school system as a regularly attending law-abiding student. It will always be about money, greed, politics, corruption, deception, death, control, systems, power, and respect.

Solutions To Permanently Eradicate Domestic Violence, Child Abuse, and Bullying

Where some devious people take in foster children for the sole purpose of getting an income and not because they are in love with the children or the idea of serving and saving another human being's life! They are saving their own lives and serving themselves! They do not show these kids the love they deserve and the love they have never received! These are throwaway kids whose senses and instincts tell them they are with people who are more interested in the check than checking on their welfare and care. These kids feel unloved! And we wonder why some of these same children run away or turn to drugs and alcohol addiction or a life of crime and abuse and violence towards others. We wonder why they turn into evil, sociopathic monsters who commit the most unthinkable heinous crimes against humanity! Did they turn into such or did we assist in creating the diabolical monster? All I know is we are born to love and receive love but when anything opposite of that is shown or learned, only terror can justifiably appear and show you the idea of love!

In Baltimore, our kids grow up fast out of force, not a choice, because they are forced to do, see, and hear things they should never have had to do, see, or hear as children! Like raising your siblings as if you were the parent because your parents or grandmother or aunties or caregivers are incarcerated or working a minimum wage job and they are in the social services donut hole and trap regarding how much in food stamps they can receive because they have some income thus forcing you to bow down to the streets to start selling drugs or your body to eat, pay bills, buy clothes and pay rent. Or you witness your parent or caregiver do drugs and then become an entirely different person with characteristics that embraces aggression, violence and annoyingly aggravating by your existence. Or you participate in their cons and crimes. Or you become a teenage parent, or you are self-allowed to watch porno because no one is home or they are home, and no one is watching or monitoring you or your activities. Or you walk in on your mom's boyfriend having sex with another woman. Or you watch your mother and aunts get beat up by their unsuitors or watch them cheat on their spouses and insignificant others. Or your 14-year-old cousin has a baby, 5 abortions before 21, or your girl cousin is raped at vacation bible school after the graveyard visit by a freckled face family friend who was one of the teachers. The bottom line is kids should not be raising kids and conducting parental responsibilities like preparing meals, babysitting, doing and helping with homework as if they are paid tutors, doing laundry, providing entertainment, changing diapers, bathing, grooming, and dressing their siblings for school and bed. Or how about you go to the Baltimore "Block" as a rite of passage, to see your uncles talk to the prostitutes. Or you are witnessing people sniff cocaine or smoke "love boat" which is laced weed at weekend house parties or on Sunday's at the softball games. Or you look forward to the trip to the liquor store to get your Goetz Caramels, Utz Chips, Slim Jims or pickled sausage or eggs, so your family member or friend can pick up their "package" in an inconspicuous brown paper bag without forgetting to play the lottery and then hurrying off to meet the weed man or woman which was often a relative or longtime family friend. Or you go to the Preakness or Atlantic City, so your family can gamble with your college funds.

Or you go to your aunt and uncle's house for the weekend to see them play wage and risk cards and dice games, gambling for money while also drinking, doing lines of coke, and you look forward to it because your aunt and uncle, who are in an open relationship, have Super TV where you can watch porno and where your cool aunt allows you to have a Miller High Life Pony beer as long as you never touch your uncle's poisonous cannabis ivy plants, located on the front porch in vanity planters, that will make your hands fall off. Or in your residence, you see, and smell weed being smoked and sold by your uncle, his girlfriend, and his friends! The same girlfriend who had sex with his best friend's brother, who too was considered my uncle's friend. I guess the buzz around town was that my uncle's friend was just following the Baltimore "G-Code!" The Baltimore "G-Code" stands for "Greed, Gank, Goon, Gobblin, Got, Gangster, Gigolo Code" when it used to stand for "Gentlemen's or Guy Code" which was an unwritten agreement between men was that we would never have anything to do with disrespecting one another by crossing the line of a friend's girlfriend or wife!

Is this why Baltimore is home of "You are not the father!" Where good men thought they were the dad, but they were the only one on the planet not to know that they were not the biological father? Now that's some Houdini, gangster magic! I wonder if these men will die from a punch in the gut like Houdini when they find out the children they have been raising since birth and paying child support for is not their own, even though they have paid for them. I have read online and seen on television many horror stories where if you ever want to know if your kid is yours for certain, tell your lady you want to get life insurance on your kids and the insurance company is requiring a DNA test to ensure you are the father before they put insurance on the kids and so you have to submit a DNA test, and you just have to pick up an Identigene kit from the pharmacy or the insurance company! If she does not question it, no problem. If she questions it, possible problem. If you think she might buck or get pissed at you for not trusting her or questioning her fidelity and commitment to you, you have got a decision to make. Some children look identically like their father and after taking a paternity test it turned out they were not the father. She was smart enough to find someone who looked just like you! I am 1000% sure that people get really good at deception & secrets! Trust is the key!

For most, your family costs you most of your pains and personal issues! For example, as a youth, your mother loads you in her car one Friday evening, and the car is not the only thing gassed up, and she catches a DUI/DWI with you under the floor mats, and she gets a trip to jail to dry out with no charges. You do not even remember who picked you up or how you got a ride home, but somehow the charges she never received stuck with you for a lifetime. Then she gets home sober, only to pick up where she left off, as, on a many weekend night, she paces back & forth in the hall, shouting, "I hate you! I wish I never had you! I wish I had flushed you down the toilet when I had the opportunity to do so!" Where this child says to the parent, "I wish I were never born!" & the parent replies, "Me too! I agree with you because you being born destroyed my life!" To no amazement, on one Saturday evening in Baltimore, it's no wonder why she tried to kill him by smothering him in his sleep! Maybe he would have been better off aborted or smothered to death? **Not to God!**

Where your mother says she loves you, but then she gets drunk, comes to your baseball game in a drunken stupor, trips walking, stumbles and rolls down a 50-foot hill with another drunken parent right on her heels with hay in her 30"-inch Afro bush and him in a 48" inch Mexican sombrero looking absolutely ridiculous, and your teammates and their parents shout in concern, "whose mother is that?" and your cousin laughingly screams, "That's my cousin's mother!" That was not the last time she would appear to a game in that fashion, dressed to embarrass her son purposely! This child tried to beat a system that was beating on him every day!

Where you become homeless after your junior year of college because you beat your uncle's a** because he stole thousands of dollars from you that you earned as a legitimate intern for a thriving multi-million dollar privately held company, along with clothes and shoes that ended up outside on the ground being thrown from your mom and grandma because they said "you think you are better than us because you are a college student who talks and acts white!" Thank God for the night shift, so he only had to sleep in his car until his friend Jay's Mom welcomed him into her home until she moved and sold her home! The entire idea to go to a predominantly white, privileged, college preparatory school, on an athletic sports scholarship that was earned, was their idea to get this young man away from the violence and temptations of the streets of Baltimore such as drug dealing, being a hitman, stealing cars, robbing others or becoming a teen dad, which was consuming young black males at the time, and he gets criticized for being in college and speaking proper when 7 years previous, he did not know proper grammar or what a thesis statement or preposition was and was headed to a life of street economics and science. Ironically, his mother had a master's degree in Elementary Education!

Baltimore's the same place where his grandmother believed that he only got a vasectomy "so no mistakes would pop up outside of his marriage!" Or when he told his mom he was getting married, she immediately said, "Is she pregnant? She is not? Then why are you marrying her? Are you telling me the truth? Why marry her and why now? You do not owe her anything do you?" These statements are coming directly from a person who has never been married or even remotely in a successful, respectful, vested interest relationship! Her judgment in men was incredibly ridiculous seeing how she was abused and violently disrespected by the sperm donor or donator we will call his dad. The second man who was married and produced his first brother who was stillborn. The third man produced his second brother who was born when he was 15 and who is the last seed from a shady, noncommittal, irresponsible, non-paying child support, character, who donored 14 kids, (who really knows the actual numbers because he was in the military), by 10 or so different baby mommas, (who really knows the exact numbers because he was in the military), of which he was married who knows how many times, (but again, who really knows the actual numbers because he was in the military)! ***Man Damn!***

Again, it is Cain versus Abel and love versus hate, where you have brothers killing, raping, robbing, molesting yours and their very own brothers, sisters, parents, children, babies, the elderly, the disabled, teachers, cops, Freddie Gray*, Phylicia Barnes*, Tahjir Smith*, Zahra Baker*, Shaniya Davis* or anyone! Where we have torture houses for victims of crimes and crimes against family members, legal and illegal gambling spots, pool halls, cash, stash, and late-night "shot" and 24-hour trap houses for the dirty birds to fly high for the drug-addicted fiends, sex offering chicken & crack heads! No one is safe, & no one gets a pass! You cannot run, & you cannot hide. If you scream, no one will hear you & for sure no one will dial 911 or come to rescue you. You rescue you because no one is looking to save!

Baltimore is as deceptive as a tick or mosquito bite in that you get bit and are not aware of the bite and before you know it, you are deathly ill, and no one can figure out why you have to have blood transfusions. Do you have meningitis? Are you septic because you have the West Nile disease or Ehrlichiosis? You must be aggressive, aware, and constantly vigilant because if you are not, you will eventually be a victim of a vigilante or savage or witness a heinous act of silence violence!

They say the early Baltimore Oriole bird gets the early morning worm (money or opportunities that lead to getting money), but I am telling you that the city is filled with ravenous Baltimore Ravens that never sleep and come out at all hours of the day and night looking for fresh or decaying meat(money or opportunities that lead to getting money), so they can eat, buy clothes, jewelry, other non-assets or feed their addictions! Consumed with acquiring expensive things of no value such as athletic apparel like Jordans, custom clothes, jewelry, Highline luxurious cars, rims, & women, along with territorial turf respect yet we do not own any assets such as stocks, bonds, IRAs, homes, and rental properties, but the only thing we do own are depreciating items and debt! We do not have a 401k or portfolio of investments, but instead, we invest in military and law enforcement grade bullets and assault rifles typically used in wars such as AK 47s, Tech-nines, and AR 15's to protect our drug proceeds and the cash stash trap houses that we do not even own.

The Baltimore culture is "Magic." The teachers tell us that with a great education "You can have anything that your heart desires!" as if it magically appears with a degree. My takeaway from them as a kid was if you can dream it you can possess and be it. As I got older, I realized a magician was a master of deception, manipulation, and expert at timing and wordplay to convince the brain to believe something it didn't see...a liar! There is no magic when it comes to the hard work needed to possess what you want to be or possess materialistically. The very people who are helping you to commit crimes will be the same ones who will be helping to plan your robbery and murder! They will be helping the police, DEA, FBI, ATF, IRS, CIA, or any other "Alphabet Boys" in law enforcement to plan your arrest so they can either replace you or save themselves from an incredibly long-life changing incarceration in the state or federal penitentiary or witness protection program. Your friends become your foes! Your closest friends are the ones who actually kill you!

Baltimore is a place where you can be killed if you do not have permission to come into and walk through the projects even though no one who resides there owns an inch of the property! Thinking like this makes as much sense as the Maryland Institute For Boys which was an institution built to help correct wayward boys from horrific family situations when it turned out to be everything opposite of what it was designed to be for boys. The intent was probably to "help" turn boys into men, but it turns out there were a lot of health officials, who were never shown how to be men, allegedly "helping" themselves as predators by "harming" and further damaging the boys and perpetuating violence and abuse on the very individuals needing love and instruction on a different way to cope through life. The very ones sworn to serve & protect these kids harmed them just like their parents & caretakers, & these will be the horrific experiences they will have their entire lives. These experiences harden children's hearts, souls, and spirits as minimal human beings. You become a real menace to society, a careless recidivist criminal offender, where the laws do not apply because statutes, law enforcement, lawyers, clinical health officials, administrators, and anyone else like their abandoning families could care less about protecting them or their rights! Now, does that make any sense?

Baltimore is complicated in the sense that your family, friends, classmates, fellow church members, fraternity brothers, and sorority sisters tell you they want you to win in life, but the truth is they hope and pray that you lose because they do not want you to do better than them unless they can benefit from your success. You have no one in your family attend your games as a youth and in high school with any frequency or consistency, but when you appear in the U.S.A Today paper as one of America's top athletes and the rumors start circling about being drafted by a professional franchise, everyone wants to make sure you did not forget them when you made it and got the million-dollar payday. Where were they when you had strangers and no one cheering for you other than caring coaches like Ron and Jack Kowitz, family friend Andrew Locust, and a great friend's dad, Wilbert White? You will forever love them for loving you and making you feel relevant & significant!

As you get older, life takes its proper course and other coaches came and went with their children no longer on my team and there was nothing of a vested interest in it for them. But then a strange occurrence appears when you are about to seemingly make it big financially as an athlete, rapper, entertainer, celebrity, Wall Street trader or hedge fund manager, or just an average Joe or Joan who lands a great job or wins the lottery. You begin to see who now shows up, or magically appears in your life when the money comes rolling in and then watch who rolls out or disappears like a magic trick, when the money and opportunities are gone, and they can no longer benefit from your life. Like the lottery, they want you to win in life even though the odds are stacked against you and strangely, you have those same people praying against you and praying that you lose! I love Ron and Jack Kowitz and their wives and children, Andrew Locust, and Wilbert and Rose White because that was never the case because they showed up when I had no money! They imparted priceless love and healthy doses of wisdom that served me well at the time. I wish they could have been my parents just because of their level of care for me and their very own children. They were there for me with heavenly intentions!

Why is Baltimore a complex dichotomy of a city? Baltimore is a city where I can honestly say I love it and hate it at the same time! The same city that built me nearly killed me! It is a place where your parents, caretakers, or guardians are heroes at work but zeros at home! It is a place where the "First 48" television show would never solve the majority, if any, of the murders within the first 48 hours because the streets do not talk, an army of detectives would never sleep, and the police would never want to be on camera because we just might see them committing and covering up their crimes against citizens.

Recidivism thrives here with glee and no conscious or care because you are only as good as your financial options and so the risk of going to jail or prison is sometimes a better option! A place where kids have to choose to either be educated by schoolteachers, street pharmacists, or prophets. A place where kids look forward to school, so they can get two meals to eat and hate when school is out because they do not get two meals to eat. A place that murders it's Robin Hood heroes like Anton Carter*(R.I.P) who was at least trying to sow a seed of positivity into the community to anyone who was willing to listen humbly! We are the official home of single muvas(mothers) and favas(fathers), baby muvas and baby favas, grandparent parents, and guardians, vacant, abandoned, or excuse-filled, promise-making, heartbreaking, never can count on, unreliable, non-child support paying, will deny you, paternity test only has proven, locked up, see you at visitor's day, maybe or maybe not you will be at my birthday or holidays, and definitely not a PTA meeting, fathers!

The streets of Philadelphia created T-Shirts in 2002 with "Stop Snitching," and then in 2004 Baltimore street certified the "Stop Snitching" campaign with its official video "snitches get stitches." [5] These snitches get stitches because they are b*****s who end up in ditches is how I took the saying! We even printed T-shirts with the slogan and wore them with a badge of honor with bullet holes in them. But what happens when someone kills or commits a heinous crime against our loved ones, friends, or homies? Now we want both forms of justice, which are street and in the courts! Now we want the police to do their jobs and find out who is responsible for this crime and bring them to justice. The streets think you are a b**** if you snitch, but as soon as their momma, child or homie is killed, then it is a b**** when no one snitches to solve their loved one's murder. The problem is there is such mistrust for police, and the system or people are too afraid to come forward because of the intimidation factor of retributed violence. Witnesses cannot come to court to testify if they are dead or nearly dead or fearing death! That is the trap or is that entrapment or street politics that are just complicated?

The funny thing about snitching is the very gangsters who do not believe in snitching will often turn to snitch when they are facing serious prison time or the death sentence. Sammy "The Bull" Gravano, Frank Lucas, Nicky Barnes, Alpo Martinez, and Whitey Bulger* are just a few of America's most heinous and respected gangsters who turned to snitching to save their own lives, and you cannot blame them! They are playing the game of life to save their life. Many are living in witness protection programs. Snitching is yelling and telling to saves lives and legacies! If you saw your loved one's house on fire, would you call 911 or would you make them aware by screaming "fire!" while running into their house or would you loudly shout outside for them to get out or would you call them? Would you have a problem doing that for your family, neighbor, classmate or co-worker?

The truth is snitching is a set up to cover our eyes, ears, and mouths to convince us that…reciprocated violence, revenge, & street justice is good; covering up crimes is the right thing; it's okay to kill each other, along with innocent (Not guilty until proven innocent by a judge or jury right?) poor white and brown people like Freddie Grey*; the cops who allegedly killed him are not guilty/convicted and set free; deceptive, crooked cops, false street prophets, drug dealers, home invaders, stick up kids, carjackers, hitmen, family and non-family pedophiles, along with money-loving, sexually deviant preachers, priests, educators, caretakers and lying hidden agenda empty promise-making politicians who rape us literally & with their policies of greed that supersedes their constituent's need and stealing money and benefits from the average citizen are innocent? Not snitching is an atrocious disgust!

The brother or sister serving their form of street justice and retribution backfires because now they end up in jail for life or on death row for premeditated first-degree murder and now the family of the individual they killed for murdering their "fam" is now looking to serve the same street justice on them. This becomes a never-ending perpetuating cycle of death where the end result is a sentence to the cemetery in a grave or the "Cement-ary" in a penitentiary cell. As a result, children do not look forward to going home or school because of the abuse, violence, and bullying and look more forward to running away or using drugs and alcohol as a way to forget the abuse! What is the sense of a child fearing going home or school? Something is seriously fundamentally wrong with a child fearing their home! The reality is most folks who hate snitches and who are making the hardest street code claim that "snitches get stitches because they are b****** who end up in ditches" are the very ones who end up as snitches in the system to save themselves from getting killed by others or the state injustice, profit, exclusion, and execution system that is trying to give them hundreds of years behind bars or a trip to death row for political numbers, career advancement and financial purposes to sell canteen products and services. My point is crime does not pay. If you do the crime then take what comes with it. If someone who is doing dirt and then decides to now become righteous because they have been caught, well they know how the street responds…witness intimidation becomes their reality because they are cowards!

Even more ironic and moronic is that these same street soldiers who hate snitches want someone to snitch when their loved ones become a victim of a crime! Is it snitching or coming forward to serve a righteous plate of justice by simply telling the truth to help a life? There are tons of cowardly bullies on the streets, in jail, along with a trillion dead souls in prison or in the grave, because of bull shizzle street codes & because no one stood up to the cowardly bullies and crooked cops!

My city is a place where most little boys want to be tough as nails to prove their manhood, and so they act hard or are recruited by thugs to be gangsters. What no one in the game of life or on the streets will ever tell them is the criminal "games" you play always ends where the gangsters get the grave. Whether it is the actual gravesite or the concrete cemetery that I respectfully call the "Cementary" where a life sentence is a death sentence, and a death sentence means you die in prison! You sell drugs to survive to stay alive, but the reality is you're just surviving in a criminal jungle where there are too many negative elements in the environment conspiring to kill you or hold you captive that it is virtually impossible to survive alive! You lose!

How many have retired successfully from their criminal enterprises and nefarious activities? Did Pablo Escobar*, John Gotti*, Al Capone*, Bonnie* and Clyde*, the Unabomber Ted Kaczynski, Osama Bin Laden*, the original Golden State Killer and rapist who was a cop, Joseph James DeAngelo Jr or Gary Ridgway who is also known as the Green River Killer, convicted of 49 separate murders making him the most prolific serial killer in United States history or murderous nurse Charles Cullen, Charles Manson*, American Gangster Frank Lucas, William Bonin who was the Freeway Killer in California, who dumped the boys and young men he raped and murdered by freeways, as did Randy Kraft or the Grim Sleeper Lonnie Franklin Jr, or Anthony Sowell who murdered prostitutes, or Charles Ng who tortured people in his "dungeon" at a cabin in the Sierra foothills and the Night Stalker, Richard Ramirez, get away with their crimes? Did El Chapo or BTK make it? You will get caught! Your life is over and done! You will be locked up for life!

What the streets never tell you about being a drug dealer, gangster, rapist, murderer or hoodlum is that it is your gangster family who ends up murdering you to cover up your and their crimes or snitching on you to save their butts! Again, go ask Sammy "The Bull" Gravano, Nicky Barnes or James "Whitey" Bulger* about what the game of criminal enterprises gives back to you! Better yet, ask these snitches, oh, my bad, criminal confidential informants, how living as a government informant in the witness protection program is just another way to die while living because you are always worried when someone is going to find you and kill you for what you have done to them or someone they care about or work for! Do not be deceived by a one-way friend. Crime does not pay! Your death will be the payment!

Baltimore is a city where your mother is actually your grandmother, and your auntie or sister is your actual birth mother and the man who for the past 18 plus years you have been calling your dad has just been informed by a court-ordered or home DNA paternity test, or maybe Maury told him that *"he is not the father!"* A place where before you are born you are already an uncle or aunt. ***MAN DAMN!***

Hear me loud when I say Baltimore is a two-meaning city where everyone says they "Keep it REAL," when in fact some are FAKE as a \$3-dollar bill. The word real, R.E.A.L stands for "Really Effective At Loving or Really Effective At Lying!™" Love is true, and of course, lying is hate! Love is the light and lying is the dark. Love is life and lying is death! This is how I view Baltimore and the world. It's a city where life is painfully clear yet complicated and confusing — a dynamic city where parents birth you out of love or lust or both, but then one or both abandons or abuses you or both. Now, that is real! I will repeat the meaning of R.E.A.L!!!

Here, fathers turn out to be heavenly sperm donors or affectionately known as baby daddy donators, and yet they choose the penitentiary and grave over their responsibilities. Here, kids visit correctional facilities as visitors or guests, and not the library, to the point they believe their parent or loved one is "stuck in the mirror" because their parent is on the other side of the glass and they cannot touch them!

Where 25% will see their self "stuck" in the mirror one day. Where mothers choose men, or is it lust or a financial opportunity, over their children and the prospect for responsible caring and protecting their babies! Where the females are lions in the jungle because they are required to do all the hunting to feed the male lion, her cubs, and the entire pride. There is no pride in having a male Lyin'(liar) or a male Lying (laying down) on the couch! Be a LION Brother! Get out there and work with pride!

Women are to be treated like the Lion Queen except for doing all the work to feed the family! A man should take pride in providing and protecting their family and especially serving their mate! Women were taken and made from man's rib! The ribs are in our sides. They were put here by God to be by our side, next to us, not behind or in front of the male, but to compliment us as equals! We're here to help one another! Together! To Get Her! Two Get Her! Together! Together! Twogether!

Women are rightfully called females (FEE-Males), not FREE-Males because as a male you have to pay a generous and privileged fee for the right to serve them and have them stand next to you. Money comforts females because it assures them they will be cared for properly, as they and your children should be comforted. Money assures them of your commitment to take care of them. They shouldn't have to worry about starving, unsafe or no shelter, no transportation, and utilities being cut off. Money provides comfort like food, weapons, clothes, shelter, etc. in the wilderness! You do not value money until you are starving, homeless or in need of a weapon when someone or something or the weather is trying to kill you!

There is a FEE to pay because as always, cheap things are not good, and good things are not cheap, and you generally get what you pay for! Yes, FEE is providing financially, but it also means showing respect like opening doors, sending sweet nothings like edible arrangements or her favorite flowers or chocolates to her job, complimenting her on her great looks, outfits, hairstyle, cooking! Letting her know how much you appreciate her as a parent, your friend, spouse, lover, and support system! As a man, an alpha male wolf that is, if you want to find love, pride, and comfort in your relationship with your queen or alpha female, to keep her comfortably at your side, always keep her comfortable by providing and protecting knowing she was put here to save us from being alone by loving us with reciprocal love and respect! If you want always to see the F.E.M.A.L.E, always pay the FEE, so she never wants to FLEE! Don't turn her into a FLEE-MALE™ because you did not fulfill the commitment you promised her and God! If you want her always to be next to Y O U, you better DO what you got to DO to keep her next to you, especially if you like sleeping with both eyes closed at night! Always stay in hunt mode like a male lion in the jungle or an alpha wolf in the wilderness! She fell in love with the hunter who was doing things at the beginning of the relationship to capture and win her heart and soul! FEMALE = FEE-MALE™, FREE-MALE™, FLEE-MALE™!

In Baltimore, we want to eat steak and lobster but end up on welfare and food stamps eating crabs, peanut butter and jelly, ramen noodles, "wish" sandwiches and spam, while we watch others eating the steaks, lobster and ham that we paid for with our freedom and lives! We were pushed to the city when the wealthy individuals ran to the county then they helped us kill each other to build the system to the point the land's value became nothing, so they can repurchase it for a dollar, so they could move back to the city and run us back to the new low land called Baltimore county! The houses that were once known for profound poverty-stricken areas are now profound profitable properties filled with equity and full pot bellies laughing to the bank. A cycle of GENTRIFICATION that will repeat!

Baltimore is a town where the kids grow up fast because the money is coming in slow. Consequently, children raise children either as a result of their teenage pregnancies or by force because daddy or mommy is dead, in prison, in and out of jail, or mommy or daddy is addicted to something, preventing them from coming home to parent and are in the streets rolling with their demons. Now, it may also be that their mother is working the late shift and does not get back in time to get them off to school! I have seen elementary school boys and girls know how to professionally style and braid hair like they were licensed cosmetologists! This is the city of half-brother and sister siblings because poppa or momma was either a rolling stone deadbeat parent or a person who got caught up in illegal activities or addictive drugs and neither could not, would not or should not have waited for the other to change their ways, get out of rehab, prison, a mental hospital or resurrect!

A city where the East side is the beast side and it indeed is the Wild West side of Baltimore where the West was never won and where Murphy Homes and Lexington Terrace housed its best bankers and pharmacists, despite being in the hole or pit, on top of its reinforced concrete where someone's babies planted their faces! Where these same R.E.A.L people keeping it on a 1000 know the hit HBO show "The Wire" was b.s. because many of the actual people whose lives were depicted did not get paid! I guess HBO kept it REEL HOLLYWOOD and R.E.A.L HOLLYHOOD too, like the government, by exploiting poor people of all colors, like all the government agencies have done and are continuing to do to this day and until Jesus comes back! That is why in Baltimore we have no fear because F.E.A.R means False Evidence Appearing Real! In this case Really Effective At Lying!™

Our professional basketball team was called the Baltimore Bullets and the soccer team was named the Baltimore Blast! Where the private white high schools and colleges proudly cherry-pick and recruit the best eligible and poorest black and white athletes in the hood, docks, or trailer parks so their teams can receive a boost in their win columns in exchange for a proud boost in their donations from their boosters, investors, and alumni. The school and their businesses thrive, but unless that athlete makes it big, they will probably return to that same pit or hole where no one is coming to boost them up out of there! The wealthy like to win at ALL cost!

This is where black men make less money annually and have less of an opportunity to be hired than a man living in a third world underdeveloped country, but yet he can get a gun or drugs faster than a job or library card. When you are always taught as a male youth that to be a man, you must provide for & protect your family, regardless of your educational level, & when you are not able to do that, what does your life become and where do you go in life from that point? Do you become a creator or a waiter? A creator is proactive & makes it happen or are you a waiter meaning you are reactive and waiting for things to happen! Do you swim out to the ship or do you wait for your ship to come into the port? Are you accountable or do you play the blame game and are a scrub, bum, or excuse filled sloth?

Baltimore systemically emasculates boys and men, defeminizes girls and women, and turns them into soft savages always trying to prove their manhood and womanhood. That's like a great white shark trying to prove it's a shark with no teeth. The men act like women, and women are often forced to act like men. The women are forced into the role of provider and protector because the men are either on the "D.L.," the "Down Low" with their sexuality and are gay or bisexual or claim to be neither because they are too afraid or embarrassed to come out of the closet to the world or are simply weak and irresponsible and choose to abandon their role as a father, husband, boyfriend, provider, protector, comforter, and man! Let me be definitively clear in that there is absolutely nothing wrong with someone choosing a certain sexual orientation and or lifestyle because only God judges, not me!

I have got a love for all humanity and especially since my uncle was gay and my aunt was a lesbian, I would be the last person to hate someone for their choice of sexual identity! The problem for me with the "DL" dude is I do not care about how you sexually identify yourself as gay or lesbian. I am cool with all that because I am not a judge of men or women, that is strictly reserved for God! My problem is with the lying and deception of hiding behind the curtain of a man who ends up spreading a potentially fatal disease like aids or another STD to an innocent, unknowing, undeserving woman and often the mother of this lying male figure. The lack of accountability, transparency, and just flat-out lying is what eats at me. Stop your lying and own it! Stop breaking up families because you are not definitive man!

In Baltimore, mean and evil men turn men into women and women into men! These demonic men demean and emasculate boys to be the polar opposite of what they see respectfully as a man and the only person who is sweet to them and becomes their idol and what they grow up to emulate is their mother! These mean and evil men turn their sweet daughters to dudes and bitter babes! Therefore, these sweet babies hate the next man in front of them, and once these men show signs of what their daddy represented, they are "out" of the relationship; "out" of the house; "out" of the closet and "out" of their mind. Why? It is very simple! Dad was "out!" He showed them it was okay to be "out" in the dark! He did not show them LOVE!

The other issue is these men are not taking care of teaching the right values to their children, and thus these children are taught to believe this is the normalcy of a father, and so the sons perpetuate this deadly cycle of lying as a way of normalcy in all of their relationships and become deceptive manipulators who scurry from their fatherly responsibilities and the daughters learn to accept this behavior from their babies' daddy or daddy's, and continue this devastating cycle of broken relationships and commitments where the single parent mom, who grows into the single parent dad and grandmother, becomes the only head of household, solely responsible for the burden of providing financially, protecting, praying for, educating, entertaining, and being everything for their children. How dare these men dare to assault and abuse women, and they are abusing their right to be a father!

The only man worse than them is the man who violently abuses pregnant women and children! If men could only know the unsettling feelings of anxiety, vulnerability, and fear that women and children are confronted with every single day! I look to the day when these cowardly hypocrites have other men aggressively approach them without, although coming very close to, (I cannot advocate violence or abuse of any kind against any human being or animal unless it is legally justified) violently assaulting them so they can know and feel what women have to confront daily continuously! This is why such men are looking for women to treat them like their mothers did and why daughters are conditioned to taking care of their grown-up little maternal boys acting as boyfriends, husbands, and baby daddies.

These gladiator women end up being their enabling surrogate mommas who keep them on the nipple, never severing the umbilical cord, pacifying them, while also keeping them cuddled and unaccountable. They pay his child support to his other baby's mothers and buy them a PlayStation or Xbox gaming system with all the hot games with a 75" 4k, Ultra HD television; Jordans and other athletic apparel; buying, financing or leasing them a car or motorcycle; paying all their bills, including keeping money on their jail and prison account books so they can purchase canteen items like they are at an all-inclusive 5 star rated vacation resort; visiting and writing them while they are on this criminal retreat consistently like they are in the hospital in critical care, when they are in jail or prison, even though when they are free on the streets they do not pay their child support to all their baby's mothers and never support their children by going to church, any PTA meetings, musicals, plays, recreational sporting events, a date night, a trip to the park, museum or movies. To add insult to injury, when this Baltimore jailbird gets released from its cage, the woman actually throws him a prison release welcome home party like he's a military hero coming home from a long deployment at war, while also moving in his other children only to discover she is not his only woman! ***MAN DAMN!***

The final icing on the virtual wedding cake, with the bride and groom on top, is when the final chips are put on the table. The free-spirited Oriole abandons her and the kids for the other woman, man, jail, prison, addiction or death. He sprints from his responsibilities, leaving her with all the debt, bad credit, no assets, no help, no hope, no dreams, no trust, no esteem, a broken heart and spirit, an STD, all the pain, and more than anything, no love! However, she still rises from the ashes of devastation because her will was not broke and her love for her children with God's help, wills her to first place as she crosses the finish line baring her scars and crosses!

When it comes to "public" versus "private" anything in Baltimore, you have to choose either by choice or force! If you do not believe me, then answer these questions! Would you rather live in public housing managed by the housing authority, aka the projects, or live in a private gated community? Would you rather attend a public school or private institution for educational purposes? How about a public defender or private attorney to represent you, your rights, and your freedom should you ever have to face a judge or jury for any case brought against you? A public clinic or hospital or a private healthcare facility? A public bathroom/shower, your private home or clubhouse bathroom/shower? A public water fountain or your own home water filtration systems such as your refrigerator or water cooler? Public equals free! Free means death, increased risk of an unlikely outcome on your behalf, a loss of your freedom and civil rights, which is living as though you are dead, or you wish you were, potentially your health diminishes which leads to a certain disease and again death to consequently follow, and your education, which determines how you choose to live your life! It is the difference between being set free to go home or being locked up in a house of bondage and horrors! It literally is life versus death when it comes to choosing "public" versus "private" in Baltimore!

This city is being raised by praying, tired and broken-hearted grandmothers and aunties! A city where we are known for blue crabs! The crabs in the barrel define Baltimore to me where brothers and sisters do not help or encourage other brothers or sisters and hate supersedes love due to money, power, respect, ignorance, jealousy, envy, and just plain out sinful reasons! Where we "pinch" one another, like the pincers on crabs, for money until you scream "Uncle!" "Dad" was not there!

A city that has and always will have a drug and murder crisis even though the White House is less than an hour's drive away with politicians who want to emphasize a drug abuse epidemic in red states and cities and help his constituents who are white when just like the color of the Maryland crabs it's brown and poor white citizens sing the "blues!" Focusing on Chicago who has fewer murders per capita than Baltimore when your backyard is scorched in Baltimore and DC! A city or should I say jungle, filled with deviant predators where it all looks excellent during the day, but at nightfall, the helicopters, sirens, and street predators hit the streets and come out of the closets in your home too! I wish there were surveillance cameras in our homes as much as they are throughout Baltimore city! Would the cameras prevent violence and abuse in our homes because they certainly have not kept the crime rates down in Baltimore? Cameras mean nothing if you cannot talk!

NBA great Carmelo Anthony, a man I pray I meet one day and who has represented Baltimore well, nearly got caught up in the Baltimore trap soon after making it to the NBA when *he appeared in a video supporting a cause that he and many others like myself believed was a great cause against snitches and crooked cops! His belief in the cause almost derailed his opportunities! He says, "It was a joke"* [6] and I believe him! The Baltimore trap is where you go off and make a successful life for yourself and family, but keeping it real almost always claims you as a victim because it pulls you back to Baltimore like a holy vortex, only to find

Solutions To Permanently Eradicate Domestic Violence, Child Abuse, and Bullying

out it is a quicksand filled black hole trying to pull you down like the Maryland crabs in a barrel. A place that builds your character to be successful in the world, but you never can return to give back some of the intellectual equity you have acquired as an ode to my Baltimore! Baltimore is a paranoid schizophrenic city with multiple personalities that try to build you up foundationally, but then tries to kill you at the same time! Baltimore hugs you and then mugs you!

In the first days of 7th grade, we were told by the school principal and administrators that 1 out of 4 of us black boys will die, be in jail or prison, be strung out on drugs, will be seriously injured or will experience a traumatic experience where you will end up permanently disfigured or hospitalized, all before the age of 25! This was when administrators didn't have to have a parent's permission to talk about their personal feelings or social opinions as they do today! That won't be me! I will beat those statistics! I will prove him wrong. Has this man just given me purpose, or did he speak death into my life? As fate would be, he was right. Many of my childhood great friends like Darell Dixon were dead before 25, assassinated in his teens as a result of the violence associated with dealing drugs. As much as I fought never to be captured or imprisoned by a spoken death sentence, the traumatic experience eventually caught up to me in September and October of 1991 in the state of Virginia just a month after my 21st birthday! ***MAN DAMN!*** He and others spoke death into our lives... not life! What if he had told us that 3 out of 4 of us will be highly successful? I wonder what would have become of me and many of my classmates had he spoken life into our spirits and souls, inspiring us to rise above death? Biggie, Tupac, & Nipsey Hussle rhymed about their deaths & it came to be!

In Baltimore, sticks and stones definitely will hurt your bones, but words definitely will hurt you too! Words have life and death in them. I wish Ann Iverson, NBA Hall of Famer Allen Iverson's mom, was everyone's mother because she always spoke life into her son "Bubba Chuck!" I can still recall hearing her vehemently stating, "My baby is going to be something special! All of you trust me when I say he is something special! My baby is going to the NBA or NFL! Y'all trust me!" She never spoke death into Chuck's life, and he truly believed his mother when she told him he would be successful, prosperous and touch people all over the world! She supported him despite her economic circumstances to the point where she made stupendous sacrifices just so her little boy Bubba Chuck could have Air Jordans to play in a significant basketball tournament where her baby's talents could be on full display! What an incredible motherly sacrifice and deliverance of support!

Ann Iverson is perhaps one of the mightiest human beings I have ever seen in my lifetime, regardless of gender or financial stature! She is undoubtedly one of the purest examples of possessing an authentic and genuine love for her children, despite the painful situations she had to endure! I wish I would have had a mother cheering and screaming for me at my games the way she and Mike Tomlin's mother did because I always wanted to play for my first cheerleader and the one person on the earth responsible for caring for me.......my mom! She missed out on greatness!

In Baltimore, no R.E.A.L woman wants a man with esteem and trust issues or a weak-minded man. What always bothered me was two people make a baby but only one parent, if that, raises the baby. What village are some people talking about? Where you don't even get told about the circumstances surrounding the death of your father until you are 17 and approach your mom and grandma, and the truth becomes clear that no one ever had any intentions of loving you and your life was a mistake in their eyes, and this is why you do not even know where your birth dad is buried.

Sure you experience love here, then heartbreak, then tragedy, then triumph where you are in love, but then your mate, lover, or spouse cheats on you and has a baby outside of your relationship. You are tired of the disrespect and abuse and decide to break it off, and then in an unbelievable display of audacious hatred, they throw acid in your face, disfiguring your face but strengthening your will and resolve! One of the most shocking days of my life during my summer break in high school, was when a classmate who I believed at the time was like a genuine big brother, tragically lost his cousin to a drug overdose. 48 hours prior to this very moment, his entire family was on cloud zillion because his family's fortune was about to permanently change forever because his cousin had just hit the jackpot by being the overall second pick in the NBA draft lottery and in 48 hours his cousin, the lottery pick, was dead from cardiac arrhythmia induced by a cocaine overdose. What? How or why does that happen? Then several years later, his deceased cousin's younger brother was murdered at a Maryland mall over a perceived minor insult and died in the same hospital his brother had died in years prior. Only in Maryland can the lightning death strike the same family twice? I do not need any more inspiration!

Then Freddie Gray*(R.I.P) dies as a result of the injuries allegedly suffered while in the custody of the Baltimore Police. The Baltimore citizens nearly burn down the city along with cop cars, looting, violence, and protests break out. The Mayor and D.A. then provides hope, words of wisdom, and peace to calm the citizens, and then the cops get arrested, the cops go to court, Freddie's family allegedly gets the check, none of the alleged cops go to prison, and the Mayor, D.A., protesters, and the citizens go silent as if they have now joined Freddie! Voila! Smoking mirrors and magic tricks appear! "No justice! No peace!" It's more like "Know just-ice(money)! Know peace!" I know I just want to take a piece out of....

Then there were *eight corrupt Baltimore cops, where all but one was indicted on robbery, extortion, and overtime fraud in March 2017 after a lengthy FBI investigation. They were members of an elite squad of highly trained officers tasked with seizing illegal guns, but they used their power and authority to steal money, drugs, guns, and resold the very guns and drugs they were tasked to remove off the streets of Baltimore!* [7] As a result of cops like these in Baltimore, the suspect charged with the alleged murder of 16-year-old Phylicia Barnes' killer was acquitted three times. [8] The North Carolina teen was just in Baltimore visiting relatives when she went missing until her body was found and identified in the Susquehanna River a few months later. [9]*

I know there are solid law enforcement representatives in Baltimore, and I am not talking about them and their commitment to the oath. However, this has been a city where there are a few good men and a few crooked cops! A city that let Phylicia Barnes' and Freddie Gray's alleged murderers go free because of a few wayward cops! A city of injustice and no peace! If you want justice, you have to give the system a sizeable piece of the money pie because it's not free! Follow me!

What sense does that make when as a parent you innocently send your 16-year-old to visit family in Baltimore and you never see her alive again and have to now wait to see her in heaven? Again, Baltimore rears its beautiful, ugly dual heads of justice and injustice like the former mayor Sheila Dixon, an African American, who was the first female Mayor in January of 2007. *January 2009 she was indicted on twelve felony and misdemeanor counts, including perjury, theft, and misconduct. She allegedly misappropriated gift cards intended for the poor. She was subsequently found guilty on one misdemeanor count of fraudulent misappropriation, and she received probation provided she resign as mayor as part of a plea agreement, effective February 4, 2010!* [10] She proves that Baltimore and all of its temptations and temptresses will quickly turn a hero into a zero. Did the poor citizens ever see those gift cards? How much money was on those gift cards?

A place where a native hero like Reggie Lewis*(R.I.P) goes from a star NBA player with the Boston Celtics, collapses on the court, goes respectfully to the grave, and then returns to the court of public opinion as a "drug user, who died as a result of his addiction" even though he was cleared to play by the very best cardiologist, putting a disgraceful, unnecessary asterisk next to his legacy when it was clearly unproven of his demise, all because one of his childhood friends said *"he had seen Reggie do drugs in the past."* [11] *Naturally, he has recanted his story* [12] probably in fear of the loving Baltimore justice that may be served to him. If I were Reggie Lewis*(R.I.P), I would probably say from heaven, "That's Baltimore love! With friends like these, who needs friends?"

The people outside of Baltimore say, "BMore stands for "You have got to "be more" careful when you are in Baltimore!" because at any time anyone is subject to be raped, robbed, or murdered regardless of where you are in Baltimore. What is even more remarkable about Baltimore is the belief where most individuals growing up in poverty do not even realize they are poor because their single mothers and grandparents are making chicken salad out of chicken shizzle every single day!

This, along with the propensity of violence and crime is why these same individuals want to be the "first" to make it out of their impoverished environment and show off their mansion in their exclusive and private neighborhoods, luxurious jewelry, custom-made clothes, expensive and limited edition automobiles, boats, jets, and even their bank account statements and credit cards, yet, they are the "last" to help another brother or sister with a hand up to help them get up off their backs and the very "last" to offer you a job, meal, letter of recommendation or endorsement, a word of encouragement, and definitely not a dollar or loan even though someone obviously had to help them to become successful by extending their helpful hand. This is why Baltimore is a place where trust is eroded to extinction and where strangers in foreign places are friendlier than family or friends, and that's not always a safe or good thing!

In Baltimore, you live every day like it is your last because it just may be because all you have ever heard was "tomorrow is not promised to anyone!" Consequently, this is why I have no attraction to visit Baltimore because as much as I would love to visit, I cannot stay because something bad is bound to happen. It's not a matter of if, but when something bad is going to happen to you.

Baltimore has street pharmacists and their supporters checking the calendar aggressively throughout the month for their ***RELEASED*** government subsidies. Dates that signify ***making*** money or waiting for the mastermind or general to return to get money and power. We want our homeboy ***RELEASED*** to get back to work. Here we specialize in ***RELEASING*** balloons. Balloons for the monthly ***RELEASE*** of food stamps and disability checks! These are the same balloons for the **RELEASE** party...recently **RELEASED** from jail, the penitentiary, probation, parole, the hospital, or worse, in the air to celebrate and remember the life of a dead loved one!

It is like Druid Hill Park which was built with a zoo for family enjoyment and other entertainment purposes such as a picnic destination or lovers' lane or enjoying the pool and other sports recreational activities and music events, but over time it turned into a drug and money exchange point, murder factory and dead body drop off and destination! Was the zoo built for the animals or the citizens of Baltimore? The purpose of the park? A place where some of the people refer to themselves and others as dangerous, detestable, lost cause zombies, gorillas, goons, and goblins! A place where, as a child, you wonder are children on the side of the milk carton really missing and are in danger or did they run away to be safe or did a family member, friend or stranger kill them and bury them at the park? A place where some of us love to SHOP. The difference though is we love to SHOPLIFT!

This is the type of place where your boyfriend, girlfriend, or spouse will set you up to be robbed or murdered over pennies! Where there is only one way in and one way out of your hood! Where you understand why they committed suicide because all they ever knew was poverty, filth, roaches, rats, hunger, waiting for the first & a check or in long government lines, truancy, left-back (failed school grade), welfare E.B.T. cards, WIC, handouts, borrowing, embarrassment, you are ugly, tight and non-name brand clothes and shoes, never well-groomed, always praying for a miracle under the Christmas tree and every day but especially on their birthday, holidays and Christmas because they have been abandoned, no one loves them, 20 plus families passed on adopting them to where they timed out of the system because the foster care parents do not really care about them but care more about the money, and your constant thoughts and pressing burdens are "Why did I not get adopted? No one wants me? No one individual loves me? Will someone adopt a highway or animal before me? God does not even hear my prayers? Why should I or you live to see another day? To hell with living! If I die, no one will attend my funeral!"

People in Baltimore can be so deep and conscious, while also shallow and unconscionable at the same time. The average Baltimorean has trust issues. Oh yeah, we trust you, but we verify because we are sinister skeptics! We are always thinking the worst and therefore you never see the positive in the negative because all you ever experience and expect is the worst-case scenario! As a form of protest, some of Baltimore's finest citizens nearly burned down, looted, and vandalized their own communities after Freddie Grey's* death at the hands of alleged corrupt Baltimore law enforcement, but did absolutely nothing once those same alleged offenders were found not guilty, thus freeing those same alleged corrupt individuals and sending a message of precedence from the local Baltimore government to its tax-paying citizens that we will kill you and get off scot-free by using your tax dollars to pay for our freedom and reputation management. *If the alleged officers were innocent, why did the city settle for $6.4 million dollars, with Freddie Grey's family?* [13] Why would I pay my neighbors a dime to replace their windows if they had no proof that it was one of my children who threw a rock or ball and shattered their window? I guess this is why we say to our spouses and significant others with such fervor that, "I love you to death," because we just may literally be the individual who "loves them to death" because if you can not have them, then no one else will ever have them as well. In my case, I think people "hated me to life!" They loved Freddie's family to his death. Why can't we say, "I Love You To Life!" in any relationship?

A place where you are a Prisoner of War. A P.O.W. who acquires the *"Stockholm Syndrome" which is a condition that causes hostages to develop a psychological alliance with their captors as a survival strategy during captivity. These alliances, resulting from a bond formed between captor and captives during intimate time spent together, are generally considered irrational in light of the danger or risk endured by the victims.* [14] You have feelings of trust or affection felt in certain cases of kidnapping or hostage-taking by a victim towards a captor that as much as you hate Baltimore is as much as you love it because you can never divorce Baltimore or your family because it is eternally holding you hostage in your heart and mind, despite the despicable acts of pain inflicted upon you, like those by my mom and aunt, and just growing up in Baltimore! To add to this syndrome, *because you have been exposed to such traumatic events firsthand,* [15] upon your release from your captors, you do not even realize that you are now suffering from *urban Post Traumatic Stress Disorder (PTSD)* [16] and you have never served in the military or in any law enforcement capacity. Your brain has been exposed to nonnormal things!

Maybe it is caused by the years of sleep deprivation from hearing the obnoxious police, ambulance, and fire engine sirens or "ghetto birds" (helicopters) flying loudly all night and day with their bright spotlights looking for a criminal or being out on the corner or in the pit hustling 24/7 or where there is no independence due to the constant gunfire that sounds like it is 4th of July! Maybe it is the sight of dead bodies and babies in it's alleys or teenage pregnant mothers and fathers where

5-year olds have the street instincts of a 50-year-old veteran corrupt police detective who quickly graduates to 11-year olds being forced to become business strategists, schemers, and criminal financial providers by becoming pharmaceutical distributors or a seasoned non-licensed automotive recovery service expert or a home goods and electronics purveyor! These babies are forced to be adults when they are children!

Baltimore is a place where you do not know where your dad is buried or any of his family! You have zero positive life stories about him. For all you know he could be buried in Baltimore, Maryland or Richmond, Virginia, or a memorial cemetery for veterans, or in an urn on someone's mantle, buried at sea or on another planet, because no one knows, or refuses to tell you. I am in the same place as him!

We have the historic row houses in Baltimore, but there is nothing historical about our youth and high levels of recidivism where they are habitually always finding themselves in a row of lineups where they end up in the penile system housing or a return to the government's public housing! A city where the ghetto birds, commonly referred as helicopters, fly over the future purposely gentrified boarded-up row homes with 1000 feet of various colored extension cords sticking from the windows and being powered by an unconscious or strong-armed neighbor where the drug dealers and highly addicted users reside until it gets hot or when dead babies and bodies are found there or in the alley and reappear in black body bags. This worthless residence that has housed dead souls and demons will be bought legally for only a dollar, gutted, remodeled, and then sold for hundreds of thousands of dollars, if not millions, for mixed family usage purposes!

The new mixed usage owners, like the drug dealers and government tax revenue experts, saw the abandoned building as an investment property opportunity for flipping profits and tax purposes. Once the place is all fixed up and newly renovated, the new home equity seeking residents do not understand the crying sounds and hurried footsteps in the dark of lost souls coming from the basement, walls, and attic that only come out at night and the wee hours of the morning! Is it the cries from toddlers because they awakened to gunshots, racing dirt bikes, police, fire trucks, and ambulance sirens or is it because they awakened neglected to an empty house or is it because they know that before the age of five their credit score is in the tens because their mom or dad or family member used their name and social security number to secure a residence, utilities, cable, and credit for loans and never repaid a dime thus destroying their credit history before the age of ten. With family and friends like these, who needs family and friends!

I should have known my senior year was not going to be fulfilled because the last day in Baltimore was simply a tragic prelude! Was it my girlfriend's aunt or family friend who saw me at the harbor being hugged by a pregnant woman and assumed I was the father when in fact I was not and that I was being hugged for helping the pregnant woman's boyfriend. This assumption set off an irreversible set of horrific circumstances. Was it the homeless man being pushed in the harbor by a friend who nearly drowned? Or was it being pulled over to a stop in my car by a helicopter in front of my car! I do not even remember opening the door to get out of my car or my feet touching the ground. With my body perpendicular to the ground, I think I levitated out of the car with my arms extended in the do not shoot pose and almost instantaneously my face was buried so deep into the black asphalt I could smell the tar with a knee on my neck and a foot on my back. Then I hear on the policeman's Walkie-talkie, "It's not them!" As fast as they pulled me to a halt was as fast as they vanished when they learned we were not the culprits who just robbed and murdered the owner of a nearby liquor store---talking about mistaken identity and your life flashing in front of you. It did not matter anyway because I have never been scared of death. I always felt there was no value or purpose to my life because I was already dead. Therefore, I do not fear consequences, the law, law enforcement and of course death! What does my life mean if my parents never wanted/loved me?

We know domestic violence almost always occurs mostly at home, but look at the extensions of violence, abuse, and bullying that randomly shows up to glorify itself, and never at an opportune time, at the mass shootings in our schools, churches, hospitals, malls, movie theaters, concerts, video game tournaments, and work! Where is a true sanctuary if you cannot have peace at church, home, or work or you are relaxing and enjoying yourself via entertainment by going to the mall, a concert, movie or gaming tournament and instead of the peace and joy you were hoping to achieve, you now have to carry a "piece" to give you peace of mind just so in the randomness appearance of violence you are proactively prepared for an active shooter!

But then again, Baltimore is the home of the Baltimore Academy and Emmy Awards for the best actors and actresses who deceptively stumbles, limps, or wheels themselves into court drunkenly sober and with casts and braces on along with crutches so they and their attorneys can nefariously get their monthly disability and social security checks! Google *2016 Baltimore Justice Department report* to know how I feel about the stellar Baltimore Police Department.

Baltimore is the place that produces a global winner of mass appeal in Michael Phelps, the greatest winningest Olympian ever and conversely produces a mass murderer in David Katz, just because he was a loser eliminated in a video gaming tournament! Think about traveling to Jacksonville, Florida to have fun at a competitive "gaming tournament" and before you know it "Baltimore" shows up like this:

3 dead, 11 injured in a mass shooting at Jacksonville NFL Madden '19 video game tournament. Jacksonville, Florida law enforcement have identified David Katz of Baltimore, Maryland. Katz is believed to have opened fire with at least one handgun shortly after 1:30 p.m. during a "Madden NFL 19" tournament, authorities said. Among the dead was 24-year-old David Katz of Baltimore, Maryland a defeated contestant in the tournament. Police say he killed himself after opening fire on other competitors.[17] That was some R.E.A.L bull shizzle! Mental health 101! Michael Phelps is the epitome of a winner & David Katz is a sore loser!

Baltimore is symbolic of a dual mindset that lies in many cities throughout the United States of America and the citizens who reside in them. The mindset is a spirit that is either love or death that resides in an individual's heart and soul. You have the power to choose what you put in your heart or soul as it pertains to how you choose to love or harm others. I thank God for being a Baltimorean, but my goal is to be a kingdom citizen! It is a city where a few of its citizens and Baltimore itself, permanently has an asterisk next to its name! A city where its citizens do conquer their deficiencies and force their fears to submit while they make the seemingly impossible, possible! A place where you do not wait for your ship to come in you swim out to the ship and storm the helm, and if no ship appears, you build your own ship like Noah and create your own charted voyage.

Baltimore is me, and I am Baltimore! It is definitely a R.E.A.L place. Really Effective At Loving and Really Effective At Lying.™ I am 1000% Really Effective At Loving others and forgiving others for the pain and past experiences. I will never allow myself to be defined as a throw-away or deplorable and detestable human being who never contributed anything positive into the souls and minds of humanity. But instead, I will live and die as a benevolent, altruistic, philanthropic, humanitarian who has run and endured a turbulent and prosperous marathon with no finish line. Baltimore motivated me to go get it because I have no excuses or reasons but to absolutely make it! The Baltimore drive is what motivated me in corporate America and what drives me to stay self-employed. Being self-employed means, I carve out my own path, so I own and operate on the terms that are important to me. I am from Baltimore! An employer once asked me "Do you think outside of the box?" I replied, "No! I have never been in a box!" How far have you come from where you are from is what I asked him in reply to his question? I love you to life Baltimore! I will always love Baltimore because it truly defines who I am which is a person who has lost in life, but with no excuses, who will end up a winning champion in life helping others, despite the hands they were dealt. A.W. Burgess*

Here are just a few individuals who were either born, raised, or made their career in Baltimore and who have made a significant contribution to the world. I pray that one day I impact the world to be placed on this list.

David T. Abercrombie, Spiro T. Agnew, Grant Aleksander, Yari Allnutt, Tori Amos, Carmelo Anthony, Bess Armstrong, Howard Ashman, John Astin, Tavon Austin, David Bachrach, Penn Badgley, Virginia S. Baker, Florence E. Bamberger, Gary Bartz, Bernadette Bascom Robbie Basho, Sylvia Beach, Jacob Beser, Eubie Blake, Nili Block, Tyrone "Muggsy" Bogues, John R. Bolton, Keith Booth, Julie Bowen, Tony Bunn, Elise Burgin, Beverly Lynn Burns, Cab Calloway, John Carroll, Ben Carson, Sam Cassell, Dennis Chambers, Norman "Chubby" Chaney, Josh Charles, Samuel Chase, John Christ, Tom Clancy, Martha Clarke, Kevin Clash, Ta-Nehisi Coates, Hans Conried, Kenny Cooper, Miriam Cooper, Thomas Cromwell Corner, Elijah E. Cummings, Ida R. Cummings, Harvey Cushing, Thomas D'Alesandro, Jr., Clay Davenport, Henrietta Vinton Davis, Angela Dawson, Dan Deacon, Buddy Deane, Olive Dennis, Divine Harris Glenn Milstead, Juan Dixon, Sheila Dixon, Mary Dobkin, Fitzhugh Dodson, Henry Grattan Donnelly, Art Donovan, Joey Dorsey, Dru Hill, The National Association for the Advancement of Colored People (NAACP), Mary White Ovington and Moorfield Storey, Mildred Dunnock, Ferdinand Durang, Adam Duritz, Charles S. Dutton, Joni Eareckson Tada, Louis E. Eliasberg, Cass Elliot, James Ellsworth, Donald Elliott, Joan Erbe, Ellery Eskelin, Damon Evans, Diane Fanning, Anna Faris, Steven Fischer, George Fisher, F. Scott Fitzgerald, Paul Ford, Jane Frank, Antonio Freeman, Mona Freeman, William H. French, John Friedberg, Paul Friedberg, Bill Frisell, Joe Gans, John Work, Mary Garrett, Lee Gatch, Rudy Gay, Herb Gerwig, Garretson W. Gibson, Adam Gidwitz, Duane Gill, Anita Gillette, Dondre Gilliam, Ira Glass, Philip Glass, Jacob Glushakow, Duff Goldman, Tamir Goodman, Jaimy Gordon, Brian Gottfried, Edith Hamilton, Elaine Hamilton, Louis Hamman, Mary Hamman, Dashiell Hammett, Steve Handelsman, Frances Harper, Elaine D.

Harmon, Ken Harris, David Hasselhoff, Emily Spencer Hayden, Raymond V. Haysbert, Maya Hayuk, Mo'Nique Hicks, Alger Hiss, Katie Hoff, Billie Holiday, Eleanora Fagan Gough, Sidney Hollander, Johns Hopkins, John Eager Howard, William Henry Howell, Christopher Hughes, Sarah T. Hughes, Lillie Mae Carroll Jackson, Harry Jeffra, Bryant Johnson, Delano Johnson, Natalie Joy Johnson, LaKisha Jones, Thomas David Jones, Brian Jordan, David Kairys, Al Kaline, John Kassir, Chris Keating, William Henry Keeler, Stacy Keibler, Thomas Kelso, John Pendleton Kennedy, James Lawrence Kernan, Stu Kerr, Greg Kihn, J. William Kime, Mel Kiper, Jr., Benjamin Klasmer, Jim Knipple, Jeff Koons, K-Swift, born Khia Edgerton, Ruth Krauss, Steve Krulevitz, Henrietta Lacks, Bucky Lasek, Maysa Leak, Jerry Leiber, Noah Lennox, Barry Levinson, Kevin Levrone, Hank Levy, Reggie Lewis, Reginald F. Lewis, Kevin Liles, Eli Lilly, Walter Lord, Los, Morris Louis, G. E. Lowman, Katharine Lucke, Edmund C. Lynch, Marvin Mandel, William C. March, Mario, Todd Marks, Thurgood Marshall, Nancy Mowll Mathews, Aaron Maybin, Angel McCoughtry, Jim McKay, Theodore R. McKeldin, H.L. Mencken, Ottmar Mergenthaler, Kweisi Mfume, Barbara Mikulski, Jamie Miller, Steve Miller, Clarence M. Mitchell, Jr., Keiffer J. Mitchell, Jr., Parren Mitchell, Thomas Hoyer Monstery, Garry Moore, Lenny Moore, Bessie Moses, Robert Murray, Clarence Muse, Anita Nall, Ogden Nash, Gary Neal, John Needles, Jeff Nelson, Edward Norton, Brandon Novak, Ric Ocasek, Madalyn Murray O'Hair, Martin O'Malley, Elaine O'Neal, Ken Ono, Dorothea Orem, William Paca, Tim Page, Jim Palmer, James A. Parker, Nicole Ari Parker, Bob Parsons, Travis Pastrana, Nancy Pelosi, Clarence M. Pendleton, Jr., Vincent Pettway, Michael Phelps, Tom Phoebus, Jada Pinkett Smith, Mathew Pitsch, Greg Plitt, Art Poe, Edgar Allan Poe, Jack Pollack, Gordon Porterfield, David Portner, Parker Posey, Emily Post, Enoch Pratt, Thomas Rowe Price, Jr., Helen Dodson Prince, Robin Quivers, Hasim Rahman, Jane Randall, John Rawls, Lance Reddick, Chris Renaud, Hilary Rhoda, Adrienne Rich, Cal Ripken, Jr., Brooks Robinson, Frank Robinson, Martin Rodbell, Josh Roenicke, Adeke Rose, Carroll Rosenbloom, Francis Peyton Rous, Christopher Rouse, James Rouse, Mike Rowe, Ruff Endz, David "Davinch" Chance and Dante "Chi" Jordan, Mike Ruocco, Dutch Ruppersberger, Babe Ruth, Rye Rye, Pat Sajak, Al Sanders, Paul Sarbanes, William Donald Schaefer, Jason Schappert, Kurt L. Schmoke, Gina Schock, Dwight Schultz, Elizabeth Ann Seton, Tupac Shakur, lived on Greenmount Ave in East Baltimore for two years, Richard Sher, Pam Shriver, Sargent Shriver, Eli Siegel, Jeff Siegel, David Simon, Bessie

Wallis Warfield Simpson, Upton Sinclair, Christian Siriano, Sisqó, Cameron Snyder, Maelcum Soul, Melissa Stark, John Steadman, Michael S. Steele, Gertrude Stein, Andrew Sterett, Richard D. Steuart, Donald Symington, Stuart Symington, Tate Kobang, Evan Taubenfeld, Michael Tearson, Mark Texiera, Jon Theodore, Martha Carey Thomas, Tracie Thoms, F. Morris Touchstone, Michael Tucker, Joseph Tumpach, Jack Turnbull, Charles Yardley Turner, Jerry Turner, Kathleen Turner, Anne Tyler, Ultra Naté, Johnny Unitas, Matthew VanDyke, Evan Sewell Wallace, Henry Walters, Dante Washington, John Waters, John K. Waters, Earl Weaver, Chick Webb, Wendy Weinberg, Matthew Weiner, George Hoyt Whipple, Reggie White, Bernard Williams, LaQuan Williams, Montel Williams, Reggie Williams, Oprah Winfrey, David Wingate, Danny Wiseman, Edward Witten, James Wolcott, Bernie Wrightson, Natalie Wynn, John H. Yardley, Steve Yeager, Frank Zappa, Joanna Zeiger, Lillian Zuckerman, Tammy Rivera, & A.W. Burgess. Hello!

Just for your reading pleasure, I leave you with some headline news! Please know that this is the same old song and dance for me. Enjoy! **BODYMORE, MD!**

Baltimore Homicide Rate Is On A Record High, Deadlier than Detroit and Chicago [18]

Associated Press Published 6:47 p.m. ET Sept. 25, 2018, | Updated 6:49 p.m. ET Sept. 25, 2018

New crime statistics released by the FBI place Baltimore's homicide rate last year well above that of any other large American metropolis, making it an anomaly in the national crime landscape for U.S. cities with populations over 500,000 people.

The 342 homicides notched last year in Maryland's biggest city yielded a punishing homicide rate of 56 per 100,000 people, according to the FBI's annual Crime in the United States report released Monday. Earlier this year, Baltimore had announced 343 slayings for the year, but three deaths were reclassified, eventually bringing the total to 342 in the city of roughly 615,000 inhabitants. The per capita rate was a record high for the city.

Among major U.S. cities, Baltimore was followed in the FBI's annual tally by Detroit, which last year recorded a homicide rate of 40 per 100,000 people; Memphis, Tennessee, with a rate of 28 per 100,000; and Chicago, with a rate of 24 per 100,000. But some smaller cities reported a higher homicide rate than Baltimore's. St. Louis, with a population slightly over 300,000, had a rate of 66 murders per 100,000 people.

Overall, the FBI says the national violent crime rate decreased by 0.2 percent from 2016 to last year, making Baltimore's record tally stand out even more for large urban centers. In comparison, Houston, with over 2 million residents, had a rate of 12 homicides per 100,000 people. Boston, with less than 700,000 residents, had eight slayings per 100,000.

Violent crime rates in Baltimore have been notoriously high for years. In recent decades, the city's gritty realities helped make it the setting for hard-boiled crime shows such as "The Wire," "The Corner," and "Homicide." But there's been a worrying march of killings since the 2015 death of Freddie Gray, who suffered a fatal injury in police custody, that eventually set a new per-capita high in 2017.

Baltimore's leaders are hopeful this year could mark somewhat of a turnaround. So far in 2018, crime is declining, with homicides down about 16 percent compared to the same stretch of time last year. Killings are down by over 30 percent in some troubled neighborhoods where authorities are focusing attention, according to City Hall.

"One murder in Baltimore is one murder too many. But I am convinced that by addressing the root causes that give rise to hopelessness and eventually to criminal activity, we will make Baltimore safer for all residents," said Mayor Catherine Pugh in an email Tuesday. She took office in December 2016.

But crime experts note that Baltimore's leaders have been failing to get their act together for a long time.

David Kennedy, a professor at John Jay College of Criminal Justice in New York City, said that what's distinctive about Baltimore is that it's been "unable to muster any kind of strategic and lasting response" through the course of its violence epidemic. He contrasted it with Chicago, one of the deadliest cities in the country but a place where he believes leaders have a clear focus and a plan.

The main reasons for Baltimore's violent crime problems are the subject of endless interpretation. Some attribute the increase to the fallout of the opioid epidemic and Baltimore's longstanding status as a heroin market, or to systemic failures like segregated neighborhoods, unequal justice and a scarcity of decent opportunities for many citizens. Others have pointed the finger at police, accusing them of taking a hands-off approach to fighting crime since six officers were charged in connection with the 2015 death of Gray, a black man whose mysterious fatal spinal cord injury in police custody triggered the city's worst riots in decades.

In addition, there's been serious instability at the top of the police force and scandals and missteps have worsened a trust deficit in city neighborhoods. Baltimore is also struggling to implement a consent decree mandating reforms after federal investigators detailed longstanding patterns of unconstitutional policing and excessive force in the eighth largest municipal police department in the United States. The underlying conditions that produce violence always matter. But on the other side, what matters is whether a city is able to frame up and implement a response to the violence. And one of the fundamental facts about Baltimore is that it's really never been able to do that," Kennedy said in a Tuesday phone interview. "There's been persistent political and law enforcement dysfunction in Baltimore going back pretty much as far as anybody can look."

Daphne Alston, a co-founder of Mothers of Murdered Sons and Daughters United, sits in St. John's Alpha and Omega Pentecostal Church on Dec. 9, in Baltimore. Alston's 22-year-old son, Tariq Alston, was murdered in 2008. (Salwan Georges/The Washington Post)

As police struggle to solve homicides, Baltimore residents see an 'open season for killing' [19]

By Wesley Lowery, Steven Rich and Salwan Georges December 27, 2018

BALTIMORE — *Daphne Alston used to go to every funeral.*

A co-founder of Mothers of Murdered Sons and Daughters United, Alston has worked with hundreds of families here, helping them navigate the pain, paperwork, and logistics that come with each killing. But recent years have brought such a spike in violence that there are now too many funerals for Alston to attend. She has enlisted other members of her group to help her with outreach to the families of the slain, sometimes going to three or four funerals each day of the weekend.

A key component of that outreach was once helping families endure the legal proceedings that followed — and sitting next to them during the trials. But this year the court cases are scant. Alston knows of just a few killings for which anyone has been arrested.

As Baltimore has seen a stunning surge of violence, with nearly a killing each day for the past three years in a city of 600,000, homicide arrests have plummeted. City police made an arrest in 41 percent of homicides in 2014; last year, the rate was just 27 percent, a 14-percentage point drop.

Of 50 of the nation's largest cities, Baltimore is one of 34 where police now make homicide arrests less often than in 2014, according to a Washington Post analysis. In Chicago, the homicide arrest rate has dropped 21 percentage points, in Boston it has dropped 12 points and in St. Louis it is down 9.

Baltimore is also one of 30 cities that have seen an increase in homicides in recent years, with the greatest raw number increase in killings of any city other than Chicago, which has four times the population. While homicide rates remain near historical lows in most American cities, Baltimore and Chicago are now both seeing murder tallies that rival the early 2000s.

The wave of violence here began not long after the April 2015 death of Freddie Gray, a 25-year-old black man arrested in West Baltimore and placed — hands cuffed, and legs shackled — in the back of a police van. There, he suffered a severe neck injury and lost consciousness. He died in the hospital about a week later.

Gray's death prompted massive protests that at times turned to riots. The years since have come with a documented officer slowdown — patrol officers say they are hesitant to leave their vehicles and have made fewer subjective stops of people on Baltimore's streets. That, coupled with a crisis of police legitimacy as residents express distrust and frustration with the force, has fueled a public safety emergency in parts of the city, community leaders say.

"It's an open market, open season for killing," said Alston, whose son Tariq was murdered in 2008. "After Freddie Gray, things just went berserk."

A mural depicting Freddie Gray is seen along Mount Street near Gilmor Homes in the Sandtown-Winchester neighborhood. His death in police custody continues to reverberate across the city. (Salwan Georges/The Washington Post) A dramatic shift in 2015

While there is evidence for and against a nationwide Ferguson effect — the theory that crime increased after 2014 as police faced more scrutiny following the shooting of Michael Brown in Ferguson, Mo. — in Baltimore, there is an indisputable Freddie Gray effect. As violence in the city has risen since 2015, the likelihood of a killer being arrested has dropped precipitously.

For most of the decade before 2015, Baltimore's annual homicide arrest rate hovered at about 40 percent. Since 2015, the arrest rate hasn't topped 30 percent in any year. And while most cities saw their arrest rates drop gradually, Baltimore's decline was sudden — plummeting 15 percentage points in 2015, after Gray's death, the largest single-year drop for any city already solving less than half its homicides.

"Our clearance rate isn't what I think it should be," Baltimore Police Commissioner Gary Tuggle, who has been running the department on an interim basis since May, said in an interview. "We've got a really, really talented homicide unit, but we're understaffed."

Tuggle, who noted that violent crime is down from its peak levels last year, said that the depressed arrest rate is due to a combination of factors. In many cases, detectives struggle to find cooperative witnesses. Police grapple with community relationships still deeply singed by the unrest that followed Gray's death. And, perhaps most crucial, the department's homicide detectives are overwhelmed.

Solutions To Permanently Eradicate Domestic Violence, Child Abuse, and Bullying

Each Baltimore detective, on average, now is responsible for nine homicide cases and, with other suspicious deaths factored in, about 31 total active cases, Tuggle said.

A Post analysis of homicides nationwide found that major police departments that have success in making arrests generally assign detectives than five cases a year.

"Our average caseload per detective is far higher than it should be," Tuggle said. "Generally, if we can't clear a case and get it off of the board within the first 25 days, chances are it's going to be a lot longer. If we can ever get it off of the board at all."

Community leaders and residents say that leaves hundreds of families who have been robbed of a loved one without a chance at seeing justice done. Of the 1,002 homicides between 2015 and the beginning of this year, just 252 — one out of every four — resulted in an arrest.

[Murder with Impunity: Where killings go unsolved]

"It's a cold case," said Cynthia Bruce, whose son Marcus Tafari Samuel Downer, 23, was shot and killed in Baltimore in July 2015. "They have a suspect and the detective is confident that someone witnessed my son's murder, but people are scared to come forward because of retaliation."

Downer died in Northwest Baltimore, near his grandmother's home. Bruce said that the word on the street is that her son had jokingly messed with — either kicking or sitting in — a neighborhood child's stroller, prompting someone to summon the child's father. When the father arrived, he brought a gun, Bruce said she has heard from neighbors.

Downer was shot 19 times in broad daylight. It has been three years; no one has been arrested.

Cynthia Bruce, a member of Mothers of Murdered Sons and Daughters United, at St. John's Alpha and Omega Pentecostal Church. Bruce's 23-year-old son, Marcus Tafari Samuel Downer, was killed in 2015, and no one has been held accountable. (Salwan Georges/The Washington Post)

Rubin Avenue in Baltimore, where Downer was shot and killed in 2015. (Salwan Georges/The Washington Post)

Bruce holds a necklace with photos of her son. Bruce said police have a suspect in her son's slaying, but witnesses have been reluctant to talk. (Salwan Georges/The Washington Post)

"My son was killed senselessly, and the person is just walking freely as if nothing happened," Bruce said.

The killings, both solved and unsolved, are clustered in a small number of the city's neighborhoods — even as the citywide homicide rate has soared, there are neighborhoods that are safer today than they were before Gray's death in 2015.

The 'butterfly' effect

Solutions To Permanently Eradicate Domestic Violence, Child Abuse, and Bullying

The neighborhoods that have seen the most violence are familiar to social scientists and experts in Baltimore: They fall within what is known as the city's black "butterfly," a set of neighborhoods that spread out to the east and west of the city's center.

Homicides have soared in several neighborhoods since Gray's death. Sandtown-Winchester, where Gray died, has seen 22 more homicides in the three-year period since Gray's death than it did in the three years before he died. Southwest Baltimore saw its homicides rise by 35, and Greater Rosemont has seen 26 more since 2015.

In each of those neighborhoods, police make an arrest in fewer than 25 percent of cases, including 16 percent in Sandtown-Winchester.

These areas long have been among the city's most economically depressed and, because of years of residential segregation, populated almost exclusively by low-income black residents.

"This structural violence contributes to the street violence that we see," said Lawrence Brown, a Morgan State University professor who coined the term Baltimore butterfly in 2015. "What hypersegregation does is that it distorts social dynamics. You don't have resources in these communities, and people have to fight for every little crumb. And then comes the violence that ends up on the evening news."

A pedestrian walks along North Fulton Avenue in Baltimore's Sandtown-Winchester neighborhood on Dec. 10. (Salwan Georges/The Washington Post)

Local criminologists and activists say that the surge in violence and the police department's low success rate in solving homicides is directly linked to the deep distrust both highlighted and stoked by Gray's death.

"This boils down to the relationship between communities and police," said Tara Huffman, director of criminal and juvenile justice programs at Open Society Institute-Baltimore. "They need people to come forward, they need people to answer the door when they knock, and they need people to talk to them on the scene."

"You cannot coerce that," she said. "You can beg and plead all you want to. If the relationship is screwed up, you're simply not going to get the help that you need to solve these crimes."

And those relationships, never great, have been further damaged within a few tumultuous years.

[In many homicides, police believe they know the killer's identity but can't get a witness to cooperate]

First came Gray's death. Then state's attorney Marilyn J. Mosby announced that she would charge six of the officers involved, enraging the local police union and, some local leaders say, further encouraging officers to police less actively. Many Baltimore community leaders fear that shift helped drive the uptick in violence.

Prosecutors failed to secure a single conviction in the case — abandoning the prosecutions after a mistrial and two acquittals — prompting a new round of anger from residents who wanted to see officers held accountable.

In the meantime, city and police department leaders were locked in tense negotiations with the U.S. Justice Department, which launched an investigation after Gray's death and ultimately concluded that Baltimore police regularly violated residents' civil rights.

"This is a city where law enforcement has felt massively under siege, and where there was one of the worst police killings ever for which there was no accountability," said Phil Goff, president of the Center for Policing Equity, which works with police departments across the country.

Officers block a CVS that caught fire near West North Avenue and Pennsylvania Avenue during a protest for Freddie Gray in Baltimore on April 27, 2015. Gray died from spinal injuries after he was arrested and transported in a police van. (Jabin Botsford/The Washington Post)

People attend a rally outside Baltimore City Hall after it was announced in May 2015 that criminal charges would be brought against all six officers involved in the Gray case. None of the officers were convicted at trial. (Jabin Botsford/The Washington Post)

Then another policing scandal arose: Eight members of an elite "Gun Trace Task Force" pleaded guilty or were convicted in federal court of widespread abuses across Baltimore. An investigation found that officers set people up for baseless searches, stole property and money from residents, and carried toy guns to plant on people.

"All of the things that could happen to a police department to create a culture of murder with impunity are all happening in Baltimore," Goff said.

The department also was grappling with near-constant leadership upheaval, including three police commissioners just this year.

As the murder rate soared, Mayor Catherine Pugh (D) fired Police Commissioner Kevin Davis in January and replaced him with Darryl De Sousa, who in turn resigned just four months later after facing federal charges of failing to file tax returns. De Sousa later pleaded guilty to the charges.

Tuggle has run the show since May as an interim commissioner. The mayor's choice to replace him, current Fort Worth Police Chief Joel Fitzgerald, is awaiting city council confirmation but the secretive process by which he was selected has raised skepticism that was further stoked when he refused to provide the Baltimore Sun with a copy of his résumé.

"We have an unstable department," said Ray Kelly, chief executive of the No Boundaries Coalition of Central West Baltimore, an activist group that has been involved in police reform efforts. "It's just a whole lot of chaos that we have to get beyond before we can start seeing any change."

Tuggle acknowledged that the leadership shake-ups have had some impact on the department's ability to prevent and solve crime.

"The department really needs a level of continuity, and I'm really hopeful that going forward they'll get that," he said.

Tuggle also emphasized strides he believes the beleaguered department has made in the months since he took over. He said homicides are down about 10 percent from last year, and that in recent months violence has begun to decline even in some of the city's most difficult zones.

For that, Tuggle credits the city's violence reduction initiative, in which city agencies work to focus social services and resources on the city's most violent neighborhoods, meeting at 8 a.m. daily to strategize.

"I certainly see the relationship between the community and the police improving. I've seen substantial improvement since I've been here," Tuggle said. "There is a sense of urgency on the police department's part to get justice for each and every victim that is out there."

But as cases go unsolved, a growing roster of family members of the slain are frustrated with what often feels to them like an inadequate effort to bring them closure.

"When people have been traumatized and they don't get the justice that they need, it makes them distrustful," said the Rev. Andre H. Humphrey, commander of the Baltimore Trauma Response Team, a group of chaplains that helps police respond to violent crime scenes. "Not just of law enforcement, but of everyone."

On the second Sunday afternoon of every month, a dozen or so mothers and fathers of homicide victims gather around folding tables spread across the crimson carpet of a meeting room at St. John's Alpha and Omega Pentecostal Church in West Baltimore.

The church sits a short walk from where Freddie Gray was taken into police custody and just a few blocks up North Avenue from the CVS that was torched during the riots and has since been rebuilt. The rest of this area looks, more or less, unchanged from 2015: a desolate maze of boarded-up rowhouses, crowded liquor stores, and underattended churches.

James Dixon, a victim-witness advocate with the Baltimore Police Department, speaks during the Mothers of Murdered Sons and Daughters United monthly meeting in Baltimore on Dec. 9. He assured the group that the department is doing everything it can to bring killers to justice. He was met with skepticism and frustration. (Salwan Georges/The Washington Post)

December's gathering started a bit behind schedule, though, because Alston had trouble getting to the church. There had been a shooting just a few blocks away, so she had to detour around the crime scene.

Each meeting begins with an open floor, in which families of victims can give updates on their cases. Then guests have the opportunity to talk about community programs or upcoming events.

In 2016, the Baltimore Police Department hired two victim-witness advocates, who work with the homicide unit and aim to help families affected by slayings. At the recent meeting, the gathered mothers heard from James Dixon, one of those advocates. He quickly sensed skepticism and frustration.

Dixon assured the group that the department is doing everything in its power to bring their loved ones' killers to justice. He said his very job was a sign of those efforts — since Baltimore is one of just a few major cities with full-time victims' services staff.

But it's a challenge, he said. Often, the leads that the mothers hear on the street don't pan out. In other cases, witnesses who share details with the family of the slain clam up when police approach.

"It's easy to beat up on the police and say that they're not doing their job," said Dixon, clad in a tan suit and yellow bow tie, as he paced the front of the room. "At the end of the day, if there's not a witness ..." And then the debate began. The gathered women peppered Dixon with questions, prompting round after round of disagreement. The mothers said they feel like some victims are treated differently than others, but Dixon insisted that's not true. Dixon suggested that the community needs to be more cooperative with police and with prosecutors. The mothers seemed unconvinced.

After about 2½ hours, the meeting adjourned, with Alston even more dissatisfied than she was when it began. "People are losing their children every single day, and everybody profits off of our pain, but nobody wants to hear our cry," Alston said, downtrodden as she put on her coat and headed out the sanctuary's side door. "I guess we have to just keep going to funerals." Daphne Alston closes her eyes as she listens to James Dixon speak about police efforts to solve homicides. (Salwan Georges/The Washington Post) Rich reported from Washington. Kimbriell Kelly and Ted Mellnik in Washington contributed to this report.

To: The Elected Politicians in D.C., From: A.W. Burgess

You really do not care about poor people! If you want to sit back and judge Baltimore for where it is as a city, understand you are either part of the problem to why it is in its current state or please be a part of the solution instead of offering a negative opinion that does nothing to better Baltimore. You are only as good as your choices and options in life. Give the citizens of Baltimore better options for education, economics, employment, and housing! Come over here and see how the citizens live and decide whether it is even fit for an animal other than rats and roaches.

Solutions To Permanently Eradicate Domestic Violence, Child Abuse, and Bullying

Cynthia Bruce, a member of Mothers of Murdered Sons and Daughters United, at St. John's Alpha and Omega Pentecostal Church. Bruce's 23-year-old son, Marcus Tafari Samuel Downer, was killed in 2015, and no one has been held accountable. (Salwan Georges/The Washington Post) **_NO ONE HAS BEEN HELD ACCOUNTABLE FOR THESE MURDERS?_**

<u>America does not want a solution to violence or recidivism,</u> *no more than a solution to energy such as a car that can go 1000 miles on a full tank of gas! America would rather build a billion dollar sports stadium to a billionaire team owner of a professional sports franchise or no corporate taxes for 20 years to billion dollar companies rather than build broken citizens into productive individuals while building a fair and balanced justice, health, and educational system that keeps EVERY citizen safe and healthy. America's citizens want to feel safe and secure first before they are entertained by a sports game! Citizens deserve to win in the game of life first!*

Baltimore Named Nation's Most Dangerous City By USA Today [20]

February 19, 2018, at 7:25 pm Filed Under: Baltimore Homicide, Baltimore Killings 2017, Homicide, Killings

BALTIMORE (WJZ) — *USA Today has named Baltimore the most dangerous city in the country.*

The paper analyzed police crime data in the nation's 50 biggest cities, which revealed Baltimore had the highest per capita murder rate in the nation with nearly 56 murders per 100,000 people — a record for the city. The rate outpaced New Orleans and Detroit, with a rate of 40 and 39 killings per 100,000 people, respectively.

Baltimore's 342 murders in 2017 was an increase from 318 in 2016.

Baltimore — the most populated city in Maryland with more than 615,000 residents — had more homicides last year than Philadelphia, Los Angeles, and New York City. Philadelphia, with 1.5 million people, tallied 317 killings; New York, a city of 8.5 million, had 290 murders; and Los Angeles, with 4 million residents, recorded 286 homicides, according to USA Today

Baltimore has seen a decline in homicides so far this year. Through Monday, 32 people had been killed, compared to 47 killed at the same time last year. The latest murder came Monday night when two masked men walked into a barbershop near Patterson Park and shot two people, one of them fatally.

The incident occurred in the 3200 block of Eastern Avenue, where police found a 35-year-old man suffering from a gunshot wound. He was taken to an area hospital where he later died.

"Two suspects on the street right now that we are trying to get a hold of that are responsible for this," said Baltimore Police spokesperson T.J. Smith. Councilman Kristefer Burnett says the city's image could affect tourism, and residents could pack up and leave.

"It was definitely heartbreaking," he said. "We have a lot to offer, but when the narrative is so much violence and that is the reality, there is so much violence, it becomes very difficult to control that."

But some residents say Baltimore's new title doesn't fit.

"I've been in Baltimore my whole life and I don't feel like I am in danger every day," said Tameka Cottman.

Baltimoreans want the world to look beyond a headline and see its charm.

"It's a shame when people who don't come in the city and don't experience the city, don't have relationships here want to make comments about it," said Rachel Cybor.

I DO NOT GIVE A RATS BEHIND ABOUT BEING SENTIMENTAL ABOUT EXPERIENCING BALTIMORE! BALTIMORE IS THE "HARM" CITY AND NOT THE "CHARM" CITY BASED SOLELY ON MY EXPERIENCES, THE CULTURE, AND A SYSTEM THAT IS IN PLACE IN BALTIMORE TO EXTERMINATE POOR PEOPLE WHO LOOK LIKE ME OR SHARE THE SAME DEMOGRAPHICS STEMMING FROM POVERTY.

LIKE MANY OTHER CITIES IN AMERICA, BALTIMORE IS A TRAP CITY BUILT TO EXCLUDE AND RECIDIVATE A PORTION OF IT'S CITIZENS FOR MONEY & POLITICAL REASONS TO BUILD JAILS AND PRISONS, TO GET OTHERS ELECTED & KEEP OTHERS EMPLOYED! A RECIDIVISM SYSTEM THAT WOULD MUCH RATHER INCARCERATE YOU THAN HEAL & EDUCATE YOU! THE POLICE, ATTORNEYS, SHERIFFS, JUDGES, WARDENS, CORRECTION, PROBATION, PAROLE OFFICERS, CANTEEN VENDORS, BAIL BONDSMEN, CONSTRUCTION COMPANIES, CORONERS, BANKS, ADVERTISERS, EMTS, HOSPITALS, GUN & BULLET COMPANIES, FUNERAL HOMES, REALTORS! WE LOSE!

BALTIMORE IS A TISSUE CITY BECAUSE YOU ARE JUST ABOUT CRYING AT THE INJUSTICES THAT OCCUR THERE EVERY DAY! I WOULD LOVE TO RETURN THERE TO BE A SIGNIFICANT PART OF THE SOLUTION, BUT I AM NOT TOO CERTAIN I WOULD BE WELCOMED WITH OPEN ARMS TO A SYSTEM THAT DOES NOT ALWAYS EMBRACE LOVING SOLUTIONS THAT ACTUALLY WORK. I WOULD CERTAINLY WELCOME THE OPPORTUNITY TO HELP THOUGH IF I CAN TRUST THE RELATIONSHIP OF THE PARTNERSHIP! I WILL NEVER GIVE UP ON BALTIMORE BECAUSE I BELIEVE ALL THINGS ARE POSSIBLE IF PEOPLE ARE OPEN TO REAL CHANGE AND NOT CHANGE$$$$! I WILL ALWAYS LOVE YOU MY CITY AND COUNTY FOR MAKING ME A MAN...
I WILL ALWAYS HAVE LOVE FOR YOU IN MY HEART

BALTIMORE

WHERE ARE THE FATHERS OF THESE MURDERED YOUNG MEN?

THE MOTHERS HAVE TO ENDURE ALL THIS INCREDIBLE INSURMOUNTABLE AMOUNT OF PAIN ALONE?

WHERE ARE THE FATHERS TO SUPPORT THEIR EX-WIVE'S AND BABY'S MOTHERS

DURING A PHENOMENAL MOMENT OF LOSS? ARE THEY IN JAIL, PRISON,

DEAD, SERVING OUR COUNTRY ABROAD, AT WAR, ON DRUGS, OR ON THE MOON?

WHY WOULD THEY SHOW UP NOW IF THEY HAVE NEVER BEEN THERE?

THEY WERE NOT THERE FOR THE BIRTH OF THE BABY, SO WHY SHOW UP

NOW? OR DO THESE SO-CALLED MEN ONLY SHOW UP WHEN IT BENEFITS

THEM? THEY WERE NOT THERE FOR BIRTHDAYS, HOLIDAYS, OR GRADUATION!

THEY WERE NOT THERE FOR THESE YOUNG MEN WHEN THESE YOUNG MEN

NEEDED FATHERS TO BE THERE FOR THEM AT CRITICAL TIMES IN THEIR

LIVES? I KNOW THERE ARE SOME GOOD MEN WHO HAVE BEEN THERE FOR

THEIR SONS AND THEIR SONS STILL ENDED UP DEAD...THEY ARE THE EXCEPTIONAL FAMILY MEN!

WHERE THE HELL ARE YOU MAN FOR YOUR YOUNG SON AND DAUGHTER?

WHERE THE HELL ARE YOU CO-PARENT FOR YOUR CHILDREN'S MOM?

I DON'T CARE WHAT HAPPENED TO YOU TWO! BE THERE FOR "THEM" UNTIL YOU TAKE YOUR LAST BREATH BROTHER!

Solutions To Permanently Eradicate Domestic Violence, Child Abuse, and Bullying

21

Football Top 20

FINAL TOP 20

No	School	Rec.
1.	McDonogh	9-1
2.	City	11-0
3.	Severna Park	10-2
4.	Meade	8-3
5.	Annapolis	8-3
6.	Milford Mill	13-0
7.	Linganore	11-2
8.	Havre de Grace	11-2
9.	Overlea	10-2
10.	Gilman	7-2
11.	Aberdeen	8-2
12.	Loyola	8-3
13.	Frederick	7-4
14.	Broadneck	7-3
15.	Franklin	8-3
16.	Randallstown	7-3
17.	Paliotti	10-0
18.	Damascus	7-4
19.	Oakland Mills	7-3
20.	Mt. St. Joe	5-5

22

Solutions To Permanently Eradicate Domestic Violence, Child Abuse, and Bullying

McDONOGH

A Lifetime of Priceless Education...A Lifetime of Priceless Friendships!

McDonogh is a private school funded by the estate of John McDonogh for orphan boys! The interesting part about that is I came home from the hospital a partial orphan. I say partial orphan because from looking at my birth certificate there is no father listed. The name in the "Father of Child" section is blank and so would be the permanent void and emptiness in my life that was never filled by any man for the record. I was born without a legal father on record? Why and how was that possible to not know who was my father? Did my mom have me via the immaculate conception? Did an alien randomly attack her? I am in a rare class of children whose parent died before they were born and so I will never have a chance to know what the feeling is to call someone dad or hear some man proudly say, "That's my child! That's my boy! That's my little man! That's my son!" It truly is a bizarre place to be in because there was never a substitute or substantial man who wanted to be my father. I would have made a great son to some man seeing how the women in my life never saw any interest in supporting me and my sports career. In hindsight, my father was worse than the women and men in my life because he did not want to be a parent so bad that he got killed because of his violent nature and behavior.

What was fascinating to learn later in life is that I came home to a house owned by McDonogh! My Grandpa was a bus driver for McDonogh who made an honest living for his family. In the eyes of most, if he was judged solely on his credentials and demographics, he was a poorly educated, low wage earner, insignificant "colored" bus driver. But to anyone who crossed his path, regardless of age, color, education level or economics, he was a significant soul who embraced the spirit of being a protective and altruistic surrogate father to the children who rode on his bus. He carried the precious human cargo to and from school as if they were his own or he was the sole secret service agent guarding the children of the President of the United States of America. All he ever had in his heart was love and an angel's concern for the welfare of others. Before he died, he saved my cousin Teeny and me from drowning in a stream of water. As toddlers, we had somehow drifted away from the house and ended up in an area of the stream that wouldn't allow us to get back to the dry embankment. Barely walking, he pulled us out of the water to safety using his cane. I will never forget that he and Grandma also saved enough money for the family to build a modest home. I will always be grateful for the incredible sacrifices that my Grandmother and Grandpa made for my entire family. Both are the best examples of pure loving intentions to become a loving family and who put the essence in me to become a FAMILY MAN™!

My two uncles attended McDonogh too, but only my late uncle, Morris "Chip" Burgess*(R.I.P), graduated in 1974 making him one of the first minorities to graduate from McDonogh. He attended there from first grade until he graduated from its upper school as a senior. It wasn't long after that that my grandpa died, and we soon moved to Baltimore. My only remembrance of McDonogh following my Grandpa's death is when we would take a Sunday ride to the country to pick apples from the McDonogh orchards, feed the horses in the horse stables, and visit the men who worked with my Grandpa. These men admired and revered my Grandpa with such high respect and regard equally to the love and affection they displayed to their dogs in the kennels that I enjoyed petting and watching them get fed or do disciplinary tricks. As time set in and I got older and more involved in sports and mischievous outside activities, I visited McDonogh and the men rarely.

It was not until the fall of 1983 that McDonogh became relevant to my life again! I had just finished a football game where I had an exceptional game with my Randallstown homeboy Tommy Davis and was waiting for a friend's dad to take me home when a friendly, stealthy, quite portly, conservatively looking white man approached me and stated, "My name is Mike McMillan, and I am the varsity football and baseball coach at the McDonogh School. May I speak with your mom or dad?" I quickly told him that "I did not have a dad and my mom does not come to my games." He looked bewildered but continued to prod in a nosey fashion about why I did not have family at the game? What does this guy want from them? He asked, "Can I have your home phone number so that I may speak with your mom about an opportunity!" I gave him the home number, and he kindly said he "would call my mother soon to talk about the opportunity to attend McDonogh." There was absolutely no way I was going to "that kind" of a school where you were required daily to wear a collared shirt, tie, blue or black blazer, khaki pants, wingtip shoes, and a suit to school. The only time I had to dress like that was to go to church, court, a wedding or funeral. That school represented the epitome of privy, highly intelligent and wealthy white students because that is how my family respectfully spoke of McDonogh around me my entire life. My uncle Chip was a legendary smart man in my family! When anyone spoke of him, they always said he got his brilliant wits from being a graduate of McDonogh! On the other hand, my other uncle Chub who also attended McDonogh had flunked out because he was not smart enough to handle the McDonogh curriculum. Chub was the lazy uncle who always gave me hell. He stole money from me, wore and ruined my brand-new clothes and sneakers, sold and did drugs, was the insecure one who bullied me, always offered horrendous advice and fought me like I was his age when he was eight years older than me. He always tried to intimidate my cousins and me, but because I was the only one who would stand up to him and confront him about his behavior towards my things, I was the one always caught up in a violent encounter and engagement with him! It's because of him and the violence and abuse I suffered from him and my aunt Annie that I even entertained McDonogh. The other reason to go McDonogh was just to get away from my negligent mom who always put men and her career before me!

At that point, I just wanted my own room and bed, peace and quiet to study, and a bathroom I didn't have to wait in line to use. I despised hearing depressing old school love songs stuck on repeat and a drunken mother pacing the halls at the wee hours of the weekend mornings shouting, "I should have aborted you! I should have flushed you down the toilet! I hate you! You were a mistake!" I was tired of this routine and hearing other demeaning, drunken gibberish, and most importantly to me would be no arguing, fighting, torturous games, violence or abuse towards me!

My mom was totally for me attending McDonogh because it afforded her the opportunity to spend even more time with her weak a** degenerate boyfriend and even less time with me. At thirteen, I was headed towards either chartering a gang or being a violent drug kingpin with my closest friends who were classmates since we were in elementary & junior high. She knew I was too dangerous for her!

It was 8th grade and I was walking around with my grandmother's .22 caliber handgun in my pants or book bag. I did not really need the gun but just in case, it was on me. In my mind, I always knew that if I were put in a pinch I would shoot any brave one who threatened me! At that age, a gun commands respect!

All my friends and my cousin had the name brand clothing and athletic shoe apparel, along with the jewelry that attracted the girls and gave you respect with your peers! Not having the latest clothes, shoes, fashion or even haircut meant you were not fresh or relevant, but more than anything it shouted to the world that you were poor, and your parents weren't worth a diggity damn, so you weren't worth a diggity damn! What I never understood was when I would ask my mother to buy me Jordans or other name brand apparel, she would tell me she did not have the money or because she was a teacher she did not make enough to afford them for me or her bills were high, or she did not make as much as my cousin's mom or that she was building my character and that I should be proud to wear a few clothes from cheaper non-name-brand discount department stores! I can still hear my cousin and friends chanting on the very first day of junior high school, "Here comes Wrangler, he's one tough customer, and he's got the stuff when the going gets rough, yeah!"

Izod, Polo shirts and Members Only jackets were at their peaks and my mom would go out of her way to buy a shirt that had a logo of a fire-breathing dragon or a skipping pregnant kangaroo, or a regular old man standing next to a donkey drinking water alongside a river rather than the alligator or a jockey on a horse playing polo. My version of the "Members Only" jacket was an "All Permitted" jacket! Why were my cousins and friends rewarded for being average students in grades, sports and attitude and I was the opposite who never got rewarded with the things I thought were significant? How could they afford those things if their parents made less money and were less educated than my mother? I was always planted on frustration and confusion with my mother because she would reward others with gifts of money and other meaningful things like her time or supporting other people's dreams which should have meant less to her than me. It was confusing!

What was on my brain about attending McDonogh was will I be smart enough to stay and how would I fit in with my "white" McDonogh family when I never really fit in with my actual family? Will people care about me? Who will leave me or want to hurt me as I get closer to loving them? Will they even know that I exist? Will they care if I exist? Will they miss me when I'm gone? How can I escape this pain? How do I cope? Alcohol, drugs or both? Should I take a dope trip on the LSD/Acid space shuttle where my serotonin and dopamine receptors will interfere with my moods, and I can hallucinate in a place better than the one I am currently experiencing? Or should I get the PCP angels to dust me off, so I can somehow see shapes, patterns, and colors that are not there in reality? I just wanted to feel euphoric and not be panicked or tortured with paranoia, anxiety, and loneliness. I felt safer, more comfortable and in control if I just stayed to myself. Childhood trauma and drama sucks to no end. Depression and suicide sucks more as a child! That is it! I am going to McDonogh to escape the pain and violence and get my own room! I was tired of fighting my aunt and uncle and having my mom not do a damn thing.

And then voila, I appear in an English class with the incomparable Desmond Corcoran.*(R.I.P) What a beautiful human being. I recall during one of my first days of school, as he would randomly call on students to read a passage out of a classic novel, Please Lord! Don't let him call on me to read. As fate would have it, eventually my name was called. Mr. Corcoran, with his signature Irish accent and his sincere and genuine articulation, exclaimed my worst nightmare, "Mr. Burgess, would you be so bold, but yet so kind, to please read the thesis statement beginning on page one!" I wondered, "What the hell is a thesis statement? And where is it located on page one?" I paused awkwardly, and to my amazement, the young female student sitting directly to my right instinctively knew I was clueless and put her finger on the first word of the thesis statement. I began reading to the best of my ability, and though I do not remember the exact words of the thesis statement, I do remember one word that caught me completely off guard.

The word was "melancholy" and I pronounced it "Ma-Lank-Oh-Lee"! Mr. Corcoran quickly responded after I finished speaking and replied, "Mr. Burgess, thank you so very much for reading. You mispronounced the word "Melancholy" though. The correct way to pronounce and annunciate the word is "Melon-Caulie!" Mr. Burgess do you know the meaning of the word "Melancholy?" Uh oh! I'm being put on the dime in front of all these smart students, so I have to say something smart to show everybody I belong at McDonogh! I pondered for a second, with the room silently waiting for me to speak as if I was E.F. Hutton about to give investment advice, and then these following brilliant and defining words came out of my mouth to define "Melancholy!" "Yes, sir Mr. Corcoran. I know what the meaning is of the word "Melancholy!" Melancholy is when a watermelon and cauliflower have sex to produce a "Melon-Caulie!" And then the unstoppable, deafening roar of laughter bellowed out of my classmates and Mr. Corcoran. Mr. Corcoran laughed so hard that he turned burnt orange-red. He had to excuse the class twice to get air to catch his and my classmates' breaths. He said that he "always enjoyed a great laugh to stimulate the soul!" He thanked me for giving the class "a moment to remember that from time to time you have to take time out to just laugh!" Our moment was so endearing for me. If I could've crawled under the carpet, tiles, or dirt I would have!

The beautiful thing about that entire "Melon-Colley" experience is that not one of my classmates then or my entire four years at McDonogh ever called me stupid or made me feel that I did not belong in a class with them. Their gracious response then and during my tenure, set the tone that there would never be any derogatory judging or belittling of me. Mr. Corcoran was such an inspirational teacher who truly took a concerned interest in each student's appreciation with reading and writing. His love for his family and his priceless expressions with his articulate Irish accent that eloquently put me at ease and shares a love and appreciation for reading and writing! "Put your mind out to pasture" rings loudly in my head like the McDonogh church bell clock that never seemed to stop chiming! He would have class outside on the most beautiful days for us to embody the spirit of nature, so we could always be inspired to write passionately about a subject matter rather than write for a grade! His passion and patience should be training for all teachers in all grades and subjects. This "Melon-Colley" experience got me closer to Mr. Corcoran such that it moved him to pair me up with a student tutor and lead me to one of the most brilliant minds and souls of a human being ever to grace the earth. He introduced me to the incomparable Ceres Horn.

And then "Voila!" Ceres Horn walks into my life! My street instincts have always protected me, and I know that was God's way of rewarding me because I didn't have parents in my life around me to protect me and so whenever you lack something in your senses God provides you stronger senses to accommodate for the ones you lack. My initial instincts told me immediately that Ceres Horn was the smartest and sweetest human being I had ever known. She was beyond genius and had a level of sincerity that only God gives to certain individuals for a specific mission from heaven. She was so approachable even though everyone on campus was simply in awe, respectfully, of her intelligence. Mr. Corcoran emphatically stated, "She will help you immensely beyond the classroom if you just understand her methods to educational success!" I trusted him and looked forward to the tutoring seeing how some other student could help me when they were my age. What I didn't know at the time was Ceres was already on her way to being a published writer and was on track to graduating from McDonogh at the age of 15.

She had goals of attending one of the best Ivy League schools to become an astronaut. I had never been around anyone who had such seemingly impossible goals, but after spending many tutoring sessions with her, and seeing how she approached studying and writing papers, it was crystal clear that she would be whatever she sought to be. She asked me, "Did I enjoy reading and writing?" I told her no and that I hated it because I didn't see the purpose of it and that it was just so boring and a waste of time! Then, she sprinkled some of her magic and wisdom on me. She said, "If you had to pick anything to read that wasn't boring, what would it be?" I told her, "I'd read anything about sports, girls in bathing suits, cars, deejaying, hip hop music, comedy, clothes or jewelry." That is when she said, "Hey! The reason you do not like writing is that you do not like the subjects you have to write about!

Would you like to read a magazine or book if it had any of those subjects in them?" I told her "yes." She then said, "I would bet you only read the sports section of the newspaper! Am I right?" How did you know, I replied? She went on to say that, "Regardless of the subject matter, if you can't choose the subject, you have to own the subject better than anyone as if it is one of your favorites! You must challenge yourself to find what is interesting about the subject matter so that it feels like a hunt to find gold or discover the pieces to the puzzle! The fun is in the hunt. Do you like challenges? Do you like winning? Do you like being second or last? Do you want an A or F?" Woe Nelly! WOW! Undoubtedly, she was the absolute BEST EVER!

I was stunned that this girl had this kind of confidence, not arrogance, for being what I thought was going to be a docile nerd hiding behind books in the library. She was definitively a wolf who stayed hungry and in a relentless search for the prize! She won me over by challenging me to be better than what I was yesterday. When she showed up with about fifteen finished copies of the same paper she had just turned in for a class, I thought she was tutoring fourteen other students, when in fact, she was telling me these were her rough drafts of the paper she had just turned in for a grade. For that week's tutoring, my homework was to read the first five papers to find the reasons or subtle differences in the papers. When I say I thought this would be a fruitless task and a waste of my time, I was thinking how boring of a week and weekend I would have, reading this boring paper times in a row!

To my surprise, each paper sent off different messages because of the way she had written them from a tonality aspect or even a change of a completely different perspective. This girl was a genius in that I would have never thought you can have these many different perspectives on a given topic. I now can see why Mr. Corcoran would tell us to "Free your mind! Let it out to pasture!" He was describing everything she embodied in writing to the umpteenth degree! After many months of her tutoring, my appreciation for reading and writing lead to an incredible difference in my English grades and overall academic appreciation because not only did she show me how to properly write a paper and read a book of any sorts, she taught me how to study and have a sincere relationship with professors. To this day, I owe much of my academic awareness and expression to her and the many levels of inspiration seeds that she instilled in my psyche. She went on to graduate from McDonogh at age 15 and enrolled and was accepted at Princeton University at age 16 where she majored in astrophysics. She was so sweet! I was with a scientist!!!

I was and was not really looking forward to the fall of 1986, my junior year at McDonogh, because the girl of my dreams had just left for a two year stay in Barbados with her family because her dad's company had him there for a two-year assignment and so the one cheerleader and full-time supporter who was coming to my baseball games when she could, would be gone away. Her absence meant I had no one to go to the proms with nor anyone in the stands. That was okay because I was used to it. Nonetheless, this would have been my first year without having Ceres there to help me educationally, and I wanted to prove to everyone that I would make it on my own without her tutelage! I was focused to make Ceres proud of me!

Life was not going great personally by way of family relationships, but I was part of a band of brothers called "The Union!" I didn't allow hazing, so I formed big brother relationships with Poochy Davenport, Kofi Carpenter, Kevin Wilson, Bobby Newton, Jermaine Walker, Stan Dorsey, Tony Lawson, Cortland Wylie, Julian Wright, and many others, as was for me by Derek McEwen, David Bostic, Alan Robinson, John Rallo, John Gast, Cheis Garrus, Jerry Bias, Trini House, Mark Vincent, Geoff Trussell, Mark McCrea, Carlo Gilotte, Boyd Byrd, Dusky Holman, Devon Dodson, Greg Bell, Peter Pittroff, Vince Angotti, Gian Aleece, Rob Young, and Mark Koski. We had a brotherly bond that was unbreakable, regardless of race, religion, economics! Genuine respect & love for each one! I will always love them!

But then there was this one kid who gravitated to me as if he was on a mission to be the best high school lineman on the team in McDonogh history since my great coach Biff Poggi or possess the relentless heart of Richard and Joe Bosley III or the tenacity of Steve Inge and Alan Robinson. He reminded me of a young John Rallo who was always looking to get stronger in every aspect of his life. His name was Brandon Wilson, and he looked up to me because of my athletic achievement and the respect I had on and off the football field by fellow students, faculty, players, and coaches.

I enjoyed answering the millions of questions he had for me regarding girls, working out and being a captain on the football team. He, like Poochy and the others, was the little brothers I never had even though I had a one-year-old baby brother named Tony. Due to my actual brother Tony's age of barely one, my hectic sports schedule and workout regimen, having a weekend job with Brandon at a local pizzeria at Owings Mills Mall, along with my McDonogh academic and athletic commitments, & writing Michelle as often as possible, I never formed a relationship with Tony because I despised his father and just thought my 35-year-old mother was an idiot who always chose bad men and other things as a greater priority than me and to have a baby at 35 with an irresponsible 50+ year-old gigolo who never took care of his previous fifteen+ kids scattered all over Baltimore and the U.S. was just dumb and one of the many reasons that kept me from going home on the weekends. This was the same guy we both saw cheating on her. Why would I want to form a bond with a baby from them when no one ever bonded with me? Who needs them?

I welcomed having Brandon as a little brother who I worked with on the weekends at the mall and who I worked out with or studied in the library with my other dorm brothers. McDonogh was great now with my grades getting better, solid friendships, my athletic skillsets getting better and better, and now having legal cash in my pocket, God Bless you Darell Dixon*, all I was focusing on was getting to a division one college athletic program or being drafted by a Major League Baseball team, preferably the Baltimore Orioles. I was beyond focused and driven to be the very best athlete in the country. And then boom, like a ton of bricks falling on your head, in the biggest game of the year for our football team, I was the lone reason why my high school football team lost the game to our rival Gilman Greyhounds. I did not just let my teammates and coaches down, I let the entire school and alumni down. I carried this lost in my soul because I knew how much it meant to beat Gilman. The seniors will never forgive me, I thought! Al Robinson & John Gast did!

Going into the Thanksgiving, Christmas, and New Year's holiday season, all I could think about was getting stronger and faster, so I would have an incredible finish to my junior year athletically and educationally. That's what the goal was until January 4, 1987, hit the calendar. And then, "Voila!"

According to the Baltimore Sun[23], *on January 4, 1987, Ceres was killed in an Amtrak rail crash near Chase, Maryland. She was returning to Princeton to take a special course in relativity when her train was struck by a Conrail freight train. The engineer of the Conrail train had been smoking marijuana and failed to stop at a signal. He served four years in prison. Ten years after the collision, the McDonogh School of Owings Mills, Maryland decided to build a 448-seat theater in her memory.* **___MAN DAMN!___** Why God? Why? Why her? Did you need her back too?

After that happened to Ceres, all I truly cared about was getting to college, so I could get to the dream of playing a professional sport. I cared less about people or studying for tests or writing papers for grades because all I could see was the worst in people and not the best! I saw how people were positioning themselves around me especially when the word got out that I was being asked to try out for the

U.S.A. Junior Olympic team for baseball and that all the division one schools were going to offer me a scholarship and that the Orioles were scouting me for the future.

No family. No Michelle. No Ceres*! I just despised coach Paul Smith* and Coach "Mac"*! My brothers Jay Woods, Alan Robinson, York Eggleston, Bobby Williams, John Gast, Larry Chang, Mark Howie, Don Evans, Damon Young, Mike Liberatore, Terri Dowla, Eric Aldrich, and Poochy, along with my dorm parents the Sanborns, Seals, Holts, Jeff Sandler, and Mr. McManus got me focused on finishing the school year. I did not care about pleasing anyone but myself. I hid behind a fake smile to cover what was killing me inside. I was depressed and confused!

I was elected by the student body to serve during my senior year as the Vice President of the Student Government, but my candidacy did not last long because before my senior year even started, as a junior, I was caught plagiarizing and was put on probation for a year from the school administration. Consequently, this amounted to my entire senior year in obscurity because it cost me the opportunity to serve as the senior class Vice President of the Student Government. I was self-destructing and couldn't get out of my way. I didn't give two damns about anything or anyone at that point because no one gave a damn about me! *F***'Em!*

Fast forward to the fall of 1987! I went to football camp with a chip on my shoulder. I could still be the Captain of the football team, but I couldn't be the Vice President of the student body? Guess what coaches, I will not play by your rules. I will not play defense ever again. Here I was the hardest hitting player on the field and who played varsity defense since I was a freshman and here I was putting the middle finger up to the coaches during my senior year. I could care less about the end of the year political awards that did not go to the deserving players, so I could care less about the coaches and teachers and anyone else that did not know the real deal. I had coaches who knew I was the best player and never called or called back any prospective colleges on my behalf. How could I be the best player on the state's number one team, and I never got any respectable football college offers. Blackballed!! These coaches are full of shizzle! Middle finger up to all of them! Bring on the Gilman Greyhounds! I'm ready to fight Leon Newsome! Where are you, Gilman? Where are you Trey Maldrone, Donald Bentley* & Charles Shufford?

I was literally in the biggest and last high school football game of my life against our archrival Gilman, whereas, if we won, we would more than likely be ranked first in the state of Maryland by the Baltimore Sun newspaper, when an overwhelming epiphany came upon me. I turned my head towards the sidelines, and

I saw one of my teammates receiving a tremendous bear hug from their father. Their dad had such a proud and rejoicing look on his face to where he became so overwhelmed that he began to tear up. I saw other fathers and grandfathers too, react similarly, and some were boldly standing there holding their son or grandson's hand and helmet as if their son was just elected president of the United States of America. Returning to the sideline, you could feel the love and excitement from these men and my teammates.

After the game, much later, back in my dorm room, I kept replaying those images in my head because I was enamored with why their dad and grandfathers reacted the way they did. Were they hugging their sons because they were so proud that they were on the varsity team that had just become the number one ranked football team in all of Maryland? Was it that their sons had just accomplished something they had never accomplished in their lifetime such as playing football or making the varsity team or just being a champion or did they know their sons would never play college football and this was the end of the road for football for them? Their dads and grandpas were there enjoying the experience via family time showing respect, adoration, support, and appreciation, and were simply proud because they were witnessing greatness in a moment of time in the life of their precious baby boy who had grown to be a respectful, hard-working kid, in and out of the classroom and on the football field. These young men never were a disciplinary issue or gave them grief and frustration as a youth, but rather, my teammates gave them something to be tremendously proud of and gracious enough to embrace with love and joy. Because of this love, they simply took the air out of my teammate's bodies with an impressive bear hug and a firm handshake. I began to tear up and cry uncontrollably quiet! Why did I not have any parents on the sidelines or in the stands for the biggest and final game of my high school career? These were the same feelings I had always felt in my entire youth playing recreational league football, basketball, and baseball. I was always arguably the best athlete on the field at any point in my playing days but there was never anyone there to see and support me consistently like my friend Wilbert's dad, Mr. White, or Kevin and Brian's dads Ron and Jack Kowitz, or Stan's dad, Mr. Dorsey, or Roger's adopted dad, Belford Davis, or Johnny and Anthony's mom and dad, Joyce* and Chester Washington*, or Mark Howie, Bobby Williams, Don Evans', York Eggleston, Rob and Damon Young, Casey Clark, Andy Linden and George Persky's parents, Derek McEwen, Cheis Garrus and Al Robinson's single-parent dads, Jay Woods, Jerry Bias, Kofi Carpenter, Eric Aldrich, Tony

Lawson, and Alonzo "Poochy" Davenport's angelic single-parent moms, and John Rallo, Billy Bryant, Antonio Hunter, John Pride, Terrence White, Warren Polsten, and John Gast's passionate, always at every game parents! Cortland Wylie's dad epitomized fatherhood! Ryan Hendricks' father Elrod was a professional Major League baseball player and coach for the Baltimore Orioles, and his dad or mom, or both attended his games and ran a summer youth baseball camp that employed many of us for our first paying jobs. These were phenomenal Family Men and Women!

All of these parents still made it to the games as often and consistently as possible, despite their hectic schedules or fatigue and who were rightfully busy in their own lives juggling their parental and professional responsibilities and duties, and they still managed to get to their children's games along with sometimes being a coach, or assistant, or transportation for their children and children like me who did not have a ride to or from practice or the game! I wonder if my family would have come to my games had I made it to the professional ranks of baseball or football? I was so hard on the outside, but on the inside I somberly wailed because I figured maybe no one came to the games because I was an embarrassment to them or because I had horrible grades at McDonogh and was probably the lowest ranked student in my class, or because I had been put on probation from the school administration for plagiarism in my junior year which cost me the opportunity to serve as senior class Vice President of the Student Government!

But then I thought, was it because they thought I did not want them to come to my games because of all the violence and fighting in my youthful years where my mother never protected me or defended me between my aunt and uncle or that they thought I was better than them and acted or sounded white. I then just chalked it up to my mother, as she had always done previously, just made something else other than me, more of a priority such as her career, her beer, her weekend or newest boyfriend, her pregnancy, her stillborn baby, her depression, her retreat, then getting her Master's Degree, or going into the military, or helping her boyfriend start a business, then managing his tour bus transportation business, then managing him because he was a serial cheater who was not her husband, and once my brother Tony came along, he became her number one priority, and I was just shelved, as always, and left to survive and cheerlead on my own! What did I do to make her hate me and not want to see me play or support me as I witnessed these other parents?

When my tears dried from within and I collected myself after several minutes and several deep gasps of air, I realized I had never indeed known what happened to or where my father was buried. I did not even know he was dead until around the third or fourth grade when I was tasked, like most grade school students, with making a Father's Day card and a new substitute or temporary teacher, who apparently did not know my parental situation, asked me "Why are you making a Father's Day card for your Mom and Grandmother and not your Father?" Now understand something clearly! This was the seventies when we did not have all the rights of privacy & disclosure as we do today, with I.E.Ps (Individualized Education Programs), where the school administrators ensure an awareness to the facts of individual students personal and health situations to all faculty and staff who come into contact with these children with "special needs circumstances" like me, for exposure to litigation purposes, so no one would be sued. She would have never known my situation unless of course, she had spoken to my grandmother who was the school's custodian and she would have only seen or heard from my mother if I had gotten in trouble, not at a PTA meeting. My reply to her was, "I don't have a father who lives with me!" She asked, "Why not?" I replied, "I don't know, but my cousins Teeny, Rachel, Nicky, Jason*, and Stephanie's dads don't live with them like me!" She went silent and walked off quickly yet bewildered. Back then, I don't believe there were as many white single-parents as it is almost commonplace today or acceptance and normalcy of single-mothers, and fathers too today, regardless of ethnicity. No teacher or anyone ever said anything to me again regarding how, why, or where my father was around Father's Day! I assumed he was probably where my cousins' dads were, with the exception of Ruth because I remembered my hilarious and great-uncle Pete's death. I bet that teacher went back and got the scoop on me from another faculty member or staff or quite possibly my grandmother.

     Nonetheless, I sincerely do not know how or when it got in my mind, but I began to tell other kids and adults, when asked innocently in conversation about my father, I would proudly and emphatically say he was a green beret, ranger, and seal who died in the Vietnam War flying or jumping out helicopters or airplanes in combat. I told the story countless times in the school sandbox during recess and other play periods during my youthful days at Winands Elementary School. My friends, especially the boys, use to be in awe and wowed that my dad was like G.I. Joe. One asked me, "Did I have his medals and flag?" because he wanted to see them. Of course, I embellished and ignorantly lied and replied, "Yes! But I cannot show them to you because they are buried with him!" I had never seen a flag or medals in my house, other than the flag at school that we stood and pledged to every morning in class and the one that Ruth showed me of uncle Pete's that my aunt Mary* had received at his burial for his time served in the military. After I dried my eyes and took those gasps of air on my dorm room bed, that night it became painfully clear to me that I wanted to know what happened to my dad. How did he die? Hmm!

That following weekend I asked my mom to come and get me from school so that I could spend the weekend at home. She came that Friday evening and I wanted to ask her about my father with my grandma present because my mother had a way that depending on the topic, she could be very evasive or conversely furious and upset, and thus I would not get the answers at all, or some of them, or half-truths mixed with vagueness. My mother's passive-aggressive spirit is why I wanted my grandmother there to get the unadulterated and unfiltered truth about my father's death and what actually happened to him and my mother's relationship in detail!

My grandma worked until midnight, so the moment came that late Saturday morning, almost afternoon, when I sat in one of my grandmother's chairs that she had near the foot of her bed, with my mom to my left in the other chair, and my grandmother lying casually on her made bed, I proceeded to ask them about my dad. "Uh! Um! Whatever happened to my father? How did he die?" As if all the air, at that very moment, rapidly escaped the room, my grandmother's jaw dropped, mouth wide open in shock, a piercing melancholy scream bellowed from my mom's soul and a crying scream and chant of "No! No! Noooooo! I knew this day would come!"

She rocketed out of her seat as if she was blasting off like the space shuttle! She ran down the hall as if she were completing an Olympic 100-meter race like an Olympic sprinter on their way to a world record, repeatedly screaming, "I knew this day would come!" She then ejected herself out of the house, into her car and then subsequently squealed all of her tires as she peeled out of the driveway. Then my grandmother gathered herself and began to tell me the truth, the whole truth, and nothing but the truth, in great detail, about how my dad had actually died!

It all began on a Sunday afternoon when my dad uninvitingly and abruptly visited my grandparents' rented home located on a McDonogh school property about 150 feet west of an active railroad track and about 250 feet east of an active river, creek, brook, or basin that sat down from an overpass bridge. McDonogh was where my dad met my mom and where they became friends and eventually a couple. His name was James Ernest Thompson, and he was twenty years older than my mother. After a few dates and more time spent with my dad, my mother soon realized that my dad was incredibly abusive, controlling, violent and flat out MEAN. My aunts and uncles verified to me that my dad was the "prettiest, most handsome man they had ever seen, along with being a great dresser, always polished and well-groomed, very health and body-conscious, and always a man who smelled good." However, they went on to say that "as great as he appeared on the outside was the polar opposite of how he treated your mother and us! He would beat her up in public, in front of us, or spit on her and we really couldn't do anything because he would threaten or intimidate her and us and he would display a gun to us, and we were scared to do anything, let alone tell anyone, especially our parents!" They told me my mom was "trapped by him like she was under his spell like a voodoo doll! He controlled her mind and body, and we all feared him! Whenever your mom tried to break it off and leave him, he would manage to convince her to stay and give him one more chance with him promising her and us he would never hurt her again. We believed him every time! He accused her of cheating! He was the one cheating!"

What is amazing to me is during my four years at McDonogh, not one person who was employed there when my family and father worked there, ever said anything to me about him. I have only seen one picture of him in my entire life and little did I know that for all the times I visited the school library, I could have tried to look up his picture because McDonogh put every employee and student into the annual yearbook. Nonetheless, to my amazement, I also learned he had the Napoleon's "short man's" complex because he was a petite man who barely stood 5' foot 2" inches and my mother is 5' foot 4" inches and all of my uncles stand north of 6' feet tall and they feared him! I guess that gun and my dad being at least twenty years their senior and his diabolical propensity for violence would have the average person fearing for their life. They could not do anything physically with him because of his willingness to use a gun. I have always said, "size does not matter when it comes to harming or killing anyone because regardless of your size, or theirs too, a bullet is not but so big, but it will kill you because of speed and force!"

When my dad arrived in my grandparent's residence, uninvited, of course, my mother and grandmother made it crystal clear that my mother was done with him and that she was no longer his girlfriend or friend for that matter. He got incredibly belligerent after they asked him several times to leave and before they knew it he pulled out his gun and pointed it directly at my mother and grandmother and shouted he was not going anywhere until she took him back. After hearing all of the commotions and witnessing my father pull out his gun to hold my mom and grandmother at gunpoint, my grandpa quickly retreated to get his shotgun, and before anyone knew it, my dad and grandpa were at a standoff. My grandpa says, "Jimmy! This is the very reason why she and we cannot have you around her or the baby that will eventually be here! Put the gun down while you still can so we can talk this thing out! Cooler heads will prevail Jimmy!" After the more reasonable talk from my grandpa, Jimmy put the gun away. They convinced him time apart from one another would be a good thing, to work on themselves before the baby arrived. He left the home physically, but mentally, he was as crazy as a rabid runover dog!

My family had two family friends over at the house this day, who were innocently visiting my uncles, and who too were friends with my mom and aunts. As the two men exited the house, they came under a hail of gunfire. My father shot at them. He was extremely jealous and had always suspected my mother was sleeping with one of them and that she dropped him because she was really in love with one of them and that one of them was the baby's father and not him and that my mother was trying to pin the baby on him. Everyone heard the gunfire and called the police. They explained to the police what took place and that my dad had taken off behind the family friends in his car, shooting at them.

In less than an hour, my dad was justifiably shot and killed by the Baltimore police because when the police got behind him, he shot at them and they consequently shot back killing him. The most remarkable thing to me is I will always have fond memories of these old men who would give me money and candy and always call me "Curly" and was always edifying me! The one who showered me the most was the coolest to me because he had this pimp walk because he walked with this stylish cane. Little did I know that these kind and generous men were the two young men my dad had shot at that fateful Sunday and that the reason the gentleman walked with the cane was that my dad shot him. They were beyond forgiving and understanding men! They could have easily been mad at me. Wow! ***MAN DAMN***!

Here I was again, going through the holiday season without my girl, the revelation that my father was a piece of crap, and the anniversary of a great friend's death approaching. At least I was working, getting stronger for my final high school baseball season and a possible chance of making it on the U.S. Olympic Baseball team. I could see myself drafted and was biting at the day I graduated high school because I knew my girlfriend would be back in the U.S. to be with me. Then boom! "Voila!" Almost a year to the day at the anniversary of Ceres Horn's death, on January 3, 1988, my little McDonogh brother, friend and co-worker at the pizzeria, Brandon Wilson was killed on the New Jersey Turnpike in an auto accident. What?

Again? **_MAN DAMN_**! Why? Again God? Really? And just when I thought death was over, my mentor and advisor to the Black Awareness club died too!

It was during this time that I had my first thoughts of suicide. I was living like a hermit banished to my room because I could not participate in any significant school activities that meant anything outside of sports. I could never enjoy my success as an athlete. The school wanted to surprisingly acknowledge me in front of the entire school for being one of the top 51 baseball players in the entire United States according to the newspaper USA Today and as they were making the announcement at lunch in front of the entire school, I laid on my bed back in my dorm room unaware of the presentation. Why did they purposely not tell me?

As a child playing youth sports, I was used to winning and accepting awards by myself with no fanfare that it was a downer for me to receive attention for a singled-out accomplishment and not a team accomplishment. It is eerily quiet and lonely at the top and the bottom of success! It is like it is your birthday and no one acknowledges you all day. There are no birthday gifts, balloons or cards, cake, special dinner or party planned in your honor. You and your life are dishonorable to them! When you are dishonorable, you get discharged and legally evicted. There is no celebration of your life. This means that when you die there will be no one at your funeral or a memorial to honor you. Who will write your obituary or eulogize you when there is no funeral? There will be no balloons released to heaven in remembrance of your life. You will die alone with no one paying any respects!

I was an athlete-student at McDonogh, not a student-athlete, bought or brought in for entertainment purposes by the adults. I was approached by the head football coach after a game in which I simply dominated my peers. Would Coach Mac have approached me if I had of put up a horrendous game and did not stand out from the other players? It was not about the academics because he did not come to my junior high school to talk about coming to McDonogh because of my grades. The truth is I was approached only because of my skill sets and talents on the football field and not because of the best intentions of getting me a quality education for my benefit. I was an athlete-student, not a student-athlete. That is what I thought then.

The truth though is I understand now that it was a blessing that Mike McMillan approached me. I am so grateful that he thought enough of me to ask me to come to McDonogh. I thank God for McDonogh showing me the significance of lunch and dinner "Family Style" and talking with family during a meal. I appreciate being a horse mucker, getting up at 6 a.m. to clean out horse stalls. The horses were like babies and were purely instinctual. Something was relying on me to eat and live in a clean and healthy environment. Someone was entrusting me to take care of the horses. Me? Why me? I do not know anything about horses. Horses are so beautiful!

There was a day in my life that I will share with you in great detail later in the book where it hit me like a ton of crack pipes, that I had just killed my McDonogh legacy, reputation, and overall good name! I destroyed what my grandfather James Burgess* and Uncle Chip* had built for other Burgesses following their heritage! I got a notification in the '90s that many people had nominated me for the McDonogh Athletic Hall of Fame (HOF)! As years passed, many people would nominate me and question me why I was not in the HOF before so many others! I couldn't understand why I wasn't elected since I was recognized by U.S. Today in 1988 as one of the top 51 baseball players in the entire United States of America! Was it because I did not attend the special recognition ceremony for that achievement or because in my junior year I was caught plagiarizing and lost all my executive privileges as a student for a year surrendering my Vice-President of the Student Government position or was it because McDonogh did not want me in their Hall of Fame because I morally do not represent the values of John McDonogh or the other highly esteemed associates included in the McDonogh family or is it that I just bring shame, embarrassment, and dishonor to the McDonogh brand that no one wants to associate themselves? I know now why I was not elected into the Hall of Fame and you will soon see why as well! Regardless of whether I am never accepted literally or figuratively speaking, by any McDonogh alumni or the Hall of Fame, a substantial positive piece of my life and legacy at McDonogh will always be ingrained in my heart, mind, and spirit! On my hands and knees, I bow before God and ask for everyone in my McDonogh family's forgiveness, and I most respectfully and sincerely apologize to my Granddad*, Grandmom and Uncle Chip* for bringing shame and embarrassment to your legacy! Coach Mac* & Paul Smith* I love you!

Looking back at my athletic career at McDonogh, I was playing a high stakes game of poker with a loaded deck. My attitude stymied my destiny with people who probably would have given a damn about me had I not shut down and took accountability for my actions and stopped pointing the middle finger at everyone except myself. I put myself in that position when I chose to get emotionally lazy and not look for the positive in the negativity and drama that I created. I should have used the negativity to fuel me to greatness instead of using it to set others and my legacy on fire at McDonogh with my coaches and the school administrators.

Some say McDonogh is debatably one, if not the very best, college preparatory schools in the nation but I will take anyone to the mat like my friends Derrick Asbell, Greg D'Alesandro, Damon Royster, Dave Farace, Rob Young, John Rallo, Mark Koski or Greg Bell use to fiercely do during their wrestling days and fight to the death to argue that McDonogh is a life preparation school! McDonogh's preparation of its students is what made college easy because I was beyond prepared compared to the average incoming freshman. I was probably ready for graduate studies! I can humbly say thank you to my McDonogh classmates who I now call friends, faculty, administrators, alumnus, and the parents of my classmates, for making me a believer that diversity and love for all humanity regardless of race sincerely does exist in the often, divisive times in America. Thanks, Ceres Horn*!

To Casey Clark & his entire family, you are my saints in the sense that when I needed a friend to show up in the final hour when I was at the lowest point as a Family Man, you singlehandedly inspired many of my McDonogh family members to help! I will never forget your generous act of benevolence and love. You literally helped me feed my family and keep on my lights and water! You are forever in a special place in my heart! Thank You!

MY GRANDPA WAS A FAMILY MAN WHO LEFT A LOVING LEGACY! THANK YOU MARK and ARI BLUM and McDONOGH FOR NAMING A HOME IN MY GRANDPA'S HONOR! HIS LEGACY LIVES FOREVER!

On November 11, 2018, one of the greatest moments in my life occurred when my Grandpa Burgess was commemorated by having a home named in his honor, by the McDonogh School for his 39 years of dedicated service and the incredible impact he made to the students and faculty of the McDonogh School as a bus driver. What a statement of character and a legacy that will live on throughout time. I was so proud that Mark Blum thought so much of him as a person and his commitment to an exceptional work ethic. I wept because I can not imagine how difficult it was just to be recognized as a man during those days let alone how he and others paved the way for people like me to attend such a prestigious school to receive an incredible education in and out of the classroom, and I repaid his sacrifices with a trip to the penitentiary.

I felt I had destroyed and tainted my Grandpa's legacy and let him and our family legacy down and brought shame to our family name. I thank God that my Grandpa's legacy wasn't compromised because of me.

I get that McDonogh may never honor me in the Sports Hall of Fame, but I am utterly thankful that my Grandpa's work ethic and level of care for kids is what made him respected and honorable! He and my uncle Chip were definitive Family Men to me! Amen to them and all the honorable individuals at McDonogh who judge individuals on the content of love in their heart and spirit. Amen to the Blums and McDonogh for giving me a reason to visit with my grandchildren so that they can see how a great, stand up guy, and Family Man gets rewarded for his life's works because of a phenomenal spirit, attitude, work ethic, and love for all of humanity!

This is exactly why I so desperately wanted to be in the McDonogh Hall of Fame! I wanted my legacy to be seen by any of the generations of Burgess's that hard work will be recognized by someone in authority and you can never take that away! My reward will come from God! I am so beyond ecstatic that my grandpa is represented at McDonogh for life!

McDonogh

Solutions To Permanently Eradicate Domestic Violence, Child Abuse, and Bullying

MᶜDONOGH SCHOOL
Marc Village Directory

1
HUNT HOUSE
In honor of German H. Hunt

3
HARRIS HOUSE
In honor of George W. "Pee Wee" Harris

5
SMINK HOUSE
In honor of Douglas I. Smink
Honorary Alumnus '73

7
WHITE HOUSE
In honor of Robert C. White

9
SEIGMAN HOUSE
In honor of Robert E. Seigman '64

11
McKIBBIN HOUSE
In honor of Martin H. McKibbin, Jr.
Honorary Alumnus '96

21
GUSTAFSON HOUSE
In honor of Carl O. Gustafson '39

23
DIEHL HOUSE
In honor of Lee A. "Pop" Diehl

24
WORKING HOUSE
In honor of C. Richard Working

25
MAISEL HOUSE
In honor of Frederick C. "Fritz" Maisel, Jr. '37

26
PETERS HOUSE
In honor of Herbert "Herb" Peters

27
LYNCH HOUSE
In honor of Willis K. Lynch '28

28
WENDER HOUSE
In honor of Mina R. Wender

29
DIXON HOUSE
In honor of Ann H. Dixon
Honorary Alumna '06

30
BRITTON HOUSE
In honor of Jennifer R. Britton

31
CORCORAN HOUSE
In honor of Kathleen M. Corcoran and
J. Desmond "Des" Corcoran
Honorary Alumnus '01

32
SCOCOS HOUSE
In honor of Theodore E. Scocos

33
STEPHENS HOUSE
In honor of Lewis W. Stephens '45

35
RAMSAY HOUSE
In honor of Alfred Ogden Ramsay

37
SMOOT HOUSE
In honor of Robert C. Smoot III '51

41
THOMAS HOUSE
In honor of Agnes M. Thomas
Honorary Alumna '90

43
WANN HOUSE
In honor of Mel Wann

45
JASPER HOUSE
In honor of Arthur Jasper

46
BURGESS HOUSE
In honor of Anne Burgess
and Hugh F. Burgess

47
HORNER HOUSE
In honor of Kenneth C. Horner
and Family

48
HARLEY HOUSE
In honor of David E. Harley

49
EYTH HOUSE
In honor of Howard C. "Dutch" Eyth
Honorary Alumnus '74

50
DAWSON HOUSE
In honor of Leah Watts Dawson

51
COX/ABBOT HOUSE
In honor of Cynthia A. Cox
and W. Wright Abbot

52
MARTIN HOUSE
In honor of Louis F. Martin, Jr.
Honorary Alumnus '02

53
HARRISON HOUSE
In honor of Barton Harrison

54
GREGA HOUSE
In honor of John T. Grega

55
JAMES BURGESS HOUSE
In honor of James W. Burgess

56
MacHAMER HOUSE
In honor of Harry A. "Mose" MacHamer
Honorary Alumnus '73

57
BIRD HOUSE
In honor of J. Edward Bird

58
SEAL HOUSE
In honor of Cheryl Working Seal
and William A. Seal III

65
MacMULLAN HOUSE
In honor of John F. "Jack" MacMullan

67
McMILLAN HOUSE
In honor of Victoria E. McMillan
and Michael S. McMillan

HOUSE #55- THE JAMES BURGESS HOUSE

Solutions To Permanently Eradicate Domestic Violence, Child Abuse, and Bullying

McDONOGH AND InROADS: *BUSINESS RELATIONSHIPS DO HAVE MEANING*

Marvin Wilson(Left) Is An Incredible Man, Father, Son, and Friend Who Helped Me When Very Few Would! I Will Always Be Grateful That He Did Not Judge Me Because Of My Past!

Solutions To Permanently Eradicate Domestic Violence, Child Abuse, and Bullying

TUESDAY, JANUARY 6, 1987   THE SUN

CRASH OF THE COLONIAL

Victim Ceres Horn, Princeton student at 16, was 'something special'

By Katie Gunther Kodat

A high school graduate at 15, an Ivy League freshman at 16, an athlete, an actress, — by any standard, Ceres Millicent Horn was an exceptional young woman.

"So much promise," said Martin McKibbin, Ceres' history teacher and basketball coach at McDonogh School in Reisterstown. "She was something special."

Sunday, after spending the holidays with her family in Cockeysville, Ceres boarded the 1:11 p.m. Amtrak Colonial at Penn Station — bound for Princeton University, where she was an astrophysics major.

Sixteen hours later, her lifeless body was pulled from the wreckage of the worst train accident in Amtrak history.

"What a waste," Mr. McKibbin said yesterday. "To me, to the nation, to the society. . . . She wanted to be an astronaut, and I'm sure she would have made it."

"She was just a special, special person," Ceres' aunt, Mrs. Robert Sharkey, said tearfully yesterday.

A student at McDonogh since 1978, Ceres (pronounced sir-EES) was the oldest child of two Johns Hopkins University professors, Dr. Roger A. Horn, a professor of mathematics at the Homewood campus, and Dr. Susan D. Horn, a professor

in health policy and management at the School of Public Health. The Horns and their two younger children — Corinne, 14, and Howard, 9, both students at McDonogh — live on Falls Road in Cockeysville.

Dr. William C. Mules, the headmaster at McDonogh, described Ceres yesterday as a "very talented, very talented youngster who did a lot of things very well.

"She's taken academic honors from McDonogh by the truckload over the years," he said. "She was one of the top students in her class. I'm looking at her records right here, and she got nothing but A's through her entire career."

Dr. Mules said Ceres — a National Merit Scholar — finished her high school studies in three years by "accelerating and taking courses way beyond what her classmates would take."

In addition, he said, Ceres distinguished herself as a member of the varsity softball team and as an actress in school productions — playing Miss Marple in Agatha Christie's "Murder at the Vicarage" and taking a major role in last spring's production of "Anything Goes."

Ceres continued to pursue her interest in drama at Princeton, where his advanced placement course in her advanced placement course in U.S. history. "In the advanced placement test [administered by a nation-

CERES MILLICENT HORN

"Anything she got into, she did full bore," Dr. Mules said.

Mr. McKibbin — whom Dr. Mules described as one of Ceres's favorite teachers — taught Ceres in

al testing service], she got the highest mark they give," Mr. McKibbin recalled.

In addition to academic pursuits, Ceres was a forward on the junior varsity basketball team at McDonogh under Mr. McKibbin's coaching.

"She was very quick; we kind of built the press around her," he recalled.

Mr. McKibbin noted that Ceres joined the novice women's crew team at Princeton, "the sport where her determination, energy, strength and everything would pay off."

"She stopped by the classroom to see me [when she was home for the holidays] and it took me a second to recognize her," he recalled. "Her shoulders were much broader. She was a slight girl before . . . and she had just had her hair done and she looked very attractive. She had a beautiful smile.

"She was so enthusiastic about everything," he continued. "About life, about learning . . . so enthusiastic that it was contagious. It influenced everyone: teachers, students, friends. She had so much energy. She enjoyed life. She had a great sense of humor. She was always making up jokes, playing with words . . . oh, gosh, she would often come up after class with some pun on something I had said during the class."

News of Ceres' death was broken

to McDonogh's students during a morning assembly, Dr. Mules said.

"All the students were brought together. We had a prayer and a moment of silence," he said. "There was absolute, dead silence in a meeting of several hundred students. . . . Some of them went out with me to visit the family later in the day."

In addition to her parents and siblings, Ceres is survived by her maternal grandmother, Mrs. Demeter Dadakis Nelsen, and her paternal grandparents, Mr. and Mrs. Woodrow A. Horn.

She is also survived by an uncle, Sophocles Dadakis of Westport, Conn.; an aunt and uncle, Mr. and Mrs. Robert Sharkey of Baltimore and six cousins.

Funeral services have been scheduled for 11 a.m. Friday at Second Presbyterian Church, Stratford Road and St. Paul Street. The family requests that memorial contributions be made to the Ceres Millicent Horn Scholarship Fund at McDonogh School.

Dr. Mules said he planned to schedule a memorial service for Ceres at McDonogh sometime this week.

"When faculty remember her, they'll remember her because she had every reason in the world to be intellectually aloof and never, ever was," Dr. Mules said.

23

Ceres Horn Was A Genius Gem Of A Person In and Out Of The Classroom!

She Was So Caring and Genuine To Take The Time To Teach Me How To

Read and Write! But More Than Anything, She Showed Me How To Care About

My Education and To Never Settle For The First Draft In Anything! <u>*BRILLIANT*</u>

Solutions To Permanently Eradicate Domestic Violence, Child Abuse, and Bullying

Ceres Millicent Horn
1970-1987

24

AN EXCEPTIONAL INTELLECT WITH AN ALTRUISTIC SPIRIT

Solutions To Permanently Eradicate Domestic Violence, Child Abuse, and Bullying

Princeton Student, Two Sisters, Among the Dead

January 6, 1987

BALTIMORE (AP) _ Ceres Millicent Horn was "intellectually a superstar,"
A freshman at Princeton University at age 16. Sisters Kirsten and Corrine
Luce were "two top-notch kids."

They and 12 other people, including a woman and her 7-year-old grandson,
Died Sunday in an Amtrak crash near Baltimore.

Miss Horn, a daughter of two Johns Hopkins University professors, had
been returning to the Princeton Campus in New Jersey when the train
crashed.

"This was a beautiful child, a marvelous child," said her mother, Susan
Horn. "She was very bright, very mature and a loving child. She was so
thoughtful And considerate."

Miss Horn, who graduated last year from the private McDonogh School in
Owings Mills was in the top five of her class. She hoped to be an astronaut.

"She was an exceptional kid, intellectually a superstar," said William C.
Mules, headmaster at the school where she won awards in oratory,
Chemistry, Mathematics, and German.

She was vivacious, brilliant and talented." Said Martin McKibbon, a
teacher in the advanced placement program at McDonogh. "She was very
quick intellectually and physically. I'm sure everyone here is going to
come up with the same thought: what a waste to the nation, what a waste
to society." [25]

McDonogh recalls Brandon Wilson as one always there to help out

By Mike Farabaugh
Evening Sun Staff

Brandon Christopher Wilson has left his mark at McDonogh.

The 16-year-old student-athlete was to be buried today following morning memorial services at the school. His life ended tragically Sunday morning in an automobile accident in Camden County, N.J.

"Brandon had driven his brother to Connecticut and was returning here when, apparently, he fell asleep at the wheel," said Wilson's father, Joseph.

Football coach Mike McMillan described Wilson as a hard worker, one who had earned a competitive academic scholarship to McDonogh for the ninth grade.

"I can't remember ever seeing Brandon when he wasn't smiling," said McMillan. "He was a super kid, a scholar, very responsible, and he would give you the shirt off his back to help out."

A junior, Wilson earned a spot on the varsity football team in 10th grade, then took over the starting left offensive tackle position this past season. He was 6-feet-2, 250 pounds. His improved play and strong blocking was instrumental in the Eagles' going 9-1 and ending the season No. 1 in *The Evening Sun* Top 20 rank-

McMillan. "We were a senior-dominated team, but he showed so much promise. I was very pleased when he was elected to be a team captain for next season. He was always helping out, carrying the water, whatever, to make things easier for someone else."

Running back Antoine Burgess called Wilson more than a teammate.

"Brandon and I have lived together -- we both boarded at the school -- and we worked at the same pizzeria in Owings Mills.

"He was always coming to my room looking for something to eat. We could always talk about anything, girls, how Coach Mac was treating him or me at practice, you know, the things guys talk about.

"He was always talking about paying off his car, helping out his family. One night he even took a pizza to Coach Mac's house around 10 o'clock."

Brandon Wilson made a habit of helping out. When he realized the varsity wrestling team had no heavyweight this season, he volunteered to fill the void. He never had wrestled before, but his record thus far was 8-1, including an exciting overtime victory over his opponent from Gilman at the McDonogh Christmas Tournament.

Why did he decide to wrestle?

"... needed him," said his father.

26

THERE WAS A TIME WHEN DEATH JUST SEEMED CONSTANT!

Solutions To Permanently Eradicate Domestic Violence, Child Abuse, and Bullying

Brandon Wilson: Th... Eagles had made him their captain for the 1988 football season.

27   **MY FRIEND BRANDON! I MISS YOU, MY BROTHER!**
Solutions To Permanently Eradicate Domestic Violence, Child Abuse, and Bullying

28

USA TODAY TOP 51 HIGH SCHOOL BASEBALL PLAYERS

TOP 8 OUTFIELDERS

Hugh Walker, Jacksonville H.S. (Ark.)
Sean Brown, Granada Hills H.S. (Calif.)
Wendell Ansley, Plainview H.S. (Tex.)
Damon Mashore, Clayton Valley H.S. (Concord, Calif.)
Mike Robertson, Servite H.S. (Anaheim, Calif.)
Antoine Burgess, McDonough H.S. (Md.)
Chris Hart, Harrisonburg H.S. (Va.)
Jon Zuber, Campolindo H.S. (Moraga, Calif.)

29

photo by Bill Gates

Liberty Road's Antoine Burgess takes a lead off of first base during Liberty Road's 10-2 beating of Reisterstown Monday night at Hannah Moore. Burgess, who played for McDonogh, had two hits in the game and threw out a runner at the plate from center field. He'll attend Oklahoma State on a full baseball scholarship in the fall.

30

FROM McDONOGH TO OKLAHOMA STATE UNIVERSITY

McDonogh I Love You! You Are My Family! Thanks For The Incredible Education and Experiences With Even Better Genuine and Lifelong Friendships! You Have Always Been There For Me! I Will Always Love You For Preparing Me Well Educationally! I Know I Represent The Very Reason Why John McDonogh Established McDonogh in 1873...Orphan Boys-The Unwanted! The Throwaways! If Possible---I Pray You Will Forgive Me One Day --Your Brother And Your Friend For Life! Antoine W. Burgess, Class of '88

Solutions To Permanently Eradicate Domestic Violence, Child Abuse, and Bullying

Me, Teeny Turner, and Ruth Dorsey September 1976
First Day of 1st Grade
Cousins Who I Call My Brother and Sister

My Other Cousin Rachel Griggs(Right) and Cousin Ruth Dorsey(Left)

Solutions To Permanently Eradicate Domestic Violence, Child Abuse, and Bullying

MANHOOD vs. BROTHERHOOD

You Serve Me The Man vs. I will Serve You, My Brother

When I was a kid, I starved for a father! I have always believed that had I had myself as my dad, I would have been in the NFL or played Major League Baseball. To have a dad show you how to be a man and treat a woman, girlfriend, or wife at those monumental times in your life is critical! Playing sports or a musical instrument or theater arts or being a Boy or Girl Scout and even just attending the PTA meetings, there is nothing like having your own personal cheerleader who is absolutely proud of you regardless of how successful you are. Indeed, they may wish you are the next megastar professional at whatever you are participating in, but the sheer fact that you are competing with your best effort and attitude and are beyond trying to be the very best you, lets them know you are not comfortable or lazy.

When I looked at the success of some of history's most prominent and impactful people, what I saw was the successful end product of support and encouragement from an active father, mother, or dual parental presence. But seeing how I was a boy, what stood out to me and what intrigued me most was how much they talked about and emulated their dad and mom's work ethic. I saw it in many successful students and athlete's parents during my school and playing days, and I still see that same formula for success today in married couples who are fully engaged in their children's lives with phenomenally strong and resilient parents. I know all of their journeys were not easy ones because being a spiritual person, I know that ***"To much is given, much is required and expected!"***[31]

As a street soldier, I know there is a trail of blood, sweat, and tears, along with tons of incredible sacrifices and losses made by all parties for their loved one to become that successful in sports, business, and in their personal experiences. Even if some of their journeys did not end in a fairytale, they did not end in tragedy and that is the testimony to their phenomenal feats of love and conquering spirits to never have given up or surrender to evil or death. To this day and forevermore, many people are and will continue to be benefactors of their successes and most painful and personal losses.

When I was pledging a fraternity back in the fall of 1989 at Hampton University, which at that time was the Hampton Institute, I was completely sold out to the opportunity of becoming a fraternity brother for the Omega Psi Phi Fraternity before I had even stepped on a college campus.

When I was a young boy, I had no say in attending church regularly because it was "mandated" by my Grandmother every Sunday. I hated church because of the hypocrisy of my family, but as I have always said, "Some things are a request and some things are a requirement!" This was a requirement without exception. I took on some spectacular and memorable a** whoopings behind the old church which was just a few feet from the graveyard as a result of my inability to stay in one place for long time spans, commonly known today as ADHD-Attention Deficit Hyperactivity Disorder, and a profane disdain for church and my glutton for parental punishment because "I was embarrassing them and could not sit still and act right and good as the other kids" and so consequently I got my behind cut and bruised at church by my mom. I hate rose and sticker braw bushes with their thorns on their ends, to this day. I attributed church with humor, harm, hate, and HYPOCRISY.

Church for me was toxic and boring after Sunday school was over because there were no more cookies, juice, and fun kids' activities. I became embittered with the church because it was also very judgmental and political. I wondered why my gay uncle and lesbian aunt always attended different churches and never visited our church! I assumed it was because they lived too far from our church and so that's why they never attended. Because I am a spiritual believer and not a religious person, with a believer's discernment, instinct, and intuition, my belief is that my favorite uncle and most endearing aunt were either made to feel uncomfortable and unwelcomed, or they themselves did not want to be embarrassed, awkwardly confronted or bring unsolicited shame and unwarranted attention to my grandmother who was their mother!

It was torturous to me. For a child like me to have to sit through hours upon hours of whooping and hollering, listening to goopity goo gospel that made absolutely no sense to me, or at best applicable, and was just unbearably inhumane to me, my intellect and my attention span. And lo and behold, God forbid if it was a visiting long-winded holy roller pastor who was truly trying to kiss up to our pastor and the congregation so that his "special offering plate" was stacked with cash! Worst yet was sitting through a quarterly revival because we may have gone in there on Sunday morning and left out on Saturday evening! I would have paid a trillion dollars for them to sit down, stop talking and just let us go!

Do not get me wrong about going to church to get the word. I get that, and I do not judge anyone who goes or does not attend. It is just that at that time in my youth, I could not relate to what the pastor was preaching because what he was preaching was not what was going on in my residence. The only cheek that got turned for me was the other side of my tail. My abusers were in church not listening!

How do you honor your mother and father if one was dead and the other tried to kill you in your sleep? My aunt and uncle were always fighting me as if I were an adult! My uncle would steal my money and clothes even though he sold and used weed. My mom, aunts, uncles, and cousins were adulterers. My family was consumed with alcoholics and drug addicts! I could not get a decent night's rest whenever my mother would violently and drunkenly pace the halls knocking on my locked door shouting demoralizing comments aimed directly at piercing my self-esteem. Everybody was coveting the neighbor's everything and bear false witnessing to me! I do not want to do to others what was and continued to be done to me! I just wanted to be a good and positive kid and friend to those people around me! I just wanted to be loved and appreciated by the individuals who should have been loving and appreciating my life. I just wanted to matter and be relevant and respected.

How I learned to cope at church and in school classes was I just started to look for the positive in the negative of attending marathon church dissertations and services. I enjoyed it and excitingly looked forward to and loved it when a church member or someone caught the Holy Ghost and ran around the church babbling gibberish like they had just lost their mind and were running to freedom or were dancing so hard, jumping back and forth in the same spot, while beating up their neighbors sitting next to them or the grandest of them all was when someone just fell out and I mean blacked out to the point of unconsciousness and could not be reverse tranquilized or revived by smelling salts or ammonia or even awakened by a thrown bucket of scalding or ice water, the music stopping or the pastor dropped the mic! Only Jesus could have touched them to be awakened!

However, before they went completely out, you can see them, and their eyes scope out who and what was next to them to ensure that they would be caught before they hit the ground or that their fall would be softened by the plush carpeting and their wannabe mink or shearling coat and purse already laying on top of the carpet.

As I matured and grew bored with the same old predictable antics from the pastor and other artists, speechwriters, musicians, praise and worship dancers, clothiers, caterers, directors, actors, actresses, and entertainers in the church, I started to pay attention to the real men of the church who just silently moved and executed their duties with grace. Some of the genuine men at the church I attended were members of the college black fraternity that I was so eager to join was Omega Psi Phi or more commonly known as the Q's, Omegas, or Q-Dogs! I saw the way they always excitingly engaged with each other, as well as the other men of the church who were nonmembers of any organization or members of other fraternities or men's organizations such as the Alphas, Kappas, Sigmas, Iotas, or Masons.

What stood out to me was how incredibly involved in the business and operations of the church all these men were participating. I really enjoyed the cookouts at the church and watching the men fundraise, set up the events, purchasing the supplies and products, helping and cooking the food on the grill, serving the people, eating last, and then cleaning up the food and packing up the venue.

I was not used to seeing men in this capacity because there were no men in my residence doing anything remotely to helping set up or pay for anything, let alone preparing or serving a family meal or cleaning up after everyone. I never saw any man do that until church. I thought they were brave warriors because of the raised keloid "horseshoes" they had branded on various body parts, as well as the phenomenal display of tattoos that represented the fraternity in poignant body places. Also, half of them were sculpted strongman figures as if they were bodybuilders or ex-football players and the others were superpowers who came in the shape as supernatural educated men who were brilliant in their respective careers. I would safely bet that most were longtime married men to even stronger, brighter, and more successful career-oriented women who were sweethearts with angelic souls!

At 16, I learned that my girlfriend's dad was an Omega Man and that many more famous individuals had pledged Omega Psi Phi! Man, it was a wrap on what fraternity I was going to pledge in college after I learned that all those highly successful men were Qs. The truth though was that I enjoyed the opportunity to bond with certain individuals who would have been in my eyes, loving brothers for life!

The foundation of the fraternity was built on the principles of manhood, scholarship, perseverance, and uplift. The motto was "Friendship is essential to the soul!" [32] *This was all set up in 1911 by 4 educated men at Howard University, in Washington D.C., just under an hour drive away from Baltimore. The founders were undergraduates Oscar James Cooper, Frank Coleman, and Edgar Amos Love, along with their faculty advisor Ernest Everett Just.* [32] To remember their names I use to think, "Cooper and Coleman are Just about Love!"

When I initially met my future big brothers during the informal interview process, they asked me "If I could only choose one, which of the four Cardinal Principles of Manhood, Scholarship, Perseverance, and Uplift did I best represent?" I told them I put my life on Manhood because I was a "Man" from the "Hood" of Baltimore. I went on to disclose my real reason for choosing Manhood was that I wanted to be a phenomenal leader in the professional corporate environment at Ingram Industries and at home as a husband and father where I would be a provider, protector, and spiritual beacon to my wife and children someday. I continued to say I never had or knew what a father was or a fully attentive, engaged and protective mother, and that I wanted my own family to love without harm and judgment, and who would reciprocate love back to me without a cost or hidden agenda. These big brothers loved me unconditionally.

I can honestly say I never was hazed or witnessed any hazing to anyone. Why would I want to join an organization that believed to make a man of me and a healthy, productive, functioning member of society, my brothers had to violently assault and abuse me physically, mentally, verbally, or emotionally? That is not manhood or brotherhood, nor was that what the founding brothers intended for the fraternity or wanted as their legacy given that they weren't too far removed from slavery and the incredible violence they faced from living in such a racist society during the close of the late 1800s and early to mid-1900s. There is no way distinguishable, higher learning, educated black men would have believed in advancing the black man and his causes by intentionally physically and psychologically torturing and brutally hazing their future brothers if they truly believed "Friendship is essential to the soul!" It was never an option. Never!

Hazing would have been monumental hypocrisy, if not sacrilegious, for them to promote bullying, violence, and abuse given that one founder wanted to be a minister (Edgar A. Love) and who ended up with the title "Bishop" and another a practicing physician for 50 years (Oscar J. Cooper) who earned the title of a licensed "Doctor!" Hazing, bullying, violence, and abuse against their own brothers or to even know of Omega Men and fellow brothers committing violence and abuse against others and especially women and children would have broken the oaths of all the founder's souls that all would have been eventually sworn to uphold as genuine and authentic men and friends. Besides, do you think the slaves, other blacks and the supporters of slaves and freed blacks who lost their lives would ever think while hanging from a tree that they would ever be killed or tortured at or by the hands of another slave, a black person or a sympathizing supporter?

Given my stance on manhood and brotherhood, I was enthused to follow big brother Q, Floyd Pettaway from Pompano Beach Florida who was Mr. Q in my eyes and who represented the spirit and significance of being an Omega Man. My other pledging big brothers Nathaniel Pierre Armstrong lll, William "Bill" Parrish Jr, and Robb Patterson from East Orange, New Jersey exemplified ManHood and hustling. I had a great Q big brother and advisor from Baltimore in Dwayne Cooper, who had the sweetest mom ever, who always encouraged me and gave the best brotherly advice as an awesome mentour. My fellow pledge brothers Fruqan Mouzon, Paul Chin, Vernard McBeth, Walter Neighbors, Howard Harvey, Eric Abrams, Mark Duncan, Samuel Tre Riddle, Carlton Weddington, Byron Rainey, Ashanti Shackleford, Carlos Walton, Brian Foster, Brian Williams, Vladimir Jean Charles, Elijah Woods, and a few others who I sincerely apologize to for forgetting their names, were simply my brothers from another mother who I know I will see in heaven one day because they were exceptional friends and blood brothers to the end. Friendship truly is essential to the soul!

As we were pledging, and I was living the dream, I truly realized the power of mind over matter in that one night I literally did pushups for 2 straight hours. I became a believer in that if you focus on something long enough, your mind will make your body accomplish things you didn't think were possible. I couldn't even open the door to my car the next day. I also realized that being an Omega Man meant you were the strongest man physically and mentally on the earth and that nothing could kill you...not even you if you just put your mind to the task.

And then voila, it all came to a grinding halt when the president of Hampton University, and a fellow Omega Man and brother, Dr. William Harvey, said that there was a "new intake" process for pledging Q. The bottom line was that in order to qualify for membership into the fraternity, every student's tuition had to be paid in full with a zero balance at that very moment. I was paying month to month and living month to month. To come up with that kind of cash meant I had to rob a bank or take out student loans. Both options were never up for consideration because that would have been a death sentence for everything I was trying to avoid doing in life and the sole reason I was out of Baltimore and into college. What was I going to do to become a Q? I certainly was not going to borrow money from anyone because respectfully, I did not have anyone to go to on short notice for legal cash.

Solutions To Permanently Eradicate Domestic Violence, Child Abuse, and Bullying

The death sentence came in the form that I could not pledge the Omega Psi Phi Fraternity Incorporated! I felt like I had just been mule kicked in the head, face, teeth, gut, and below the belt! I sat there in absolute shock and disbelief. What the flip? This was Armageddon! That loss of not being permitted to join the brotherhood was sobering and enlightening in that it has stuck with me to this day such that figuratively the Omega Man, and all pledgees of frats and sororities, is always going to be the strongest and last person standing on the earth regardless of Armageddon.

Ultimately though, what pains me further is that because I am a convicted felon and a non-college graduate, I can never be a Q, an Omega or brother. I will always tell anyone to stand on what they believe because if you do not believe in it enough to die for what you believe, then you just may get killed during the process and that would just be foolish vanity. Many people just wanted to join the fraternity for vanity purposes because of walking and strutting around campus like a peacock with their fraternity paraphernalia or the line stepping and barking chants that drew crowds and caught the attention from women. This attention usually meant you were able to get sex, clothes, gifts, food, or money from such women or groupies who probably would have never given you their time or the fact that being a brother opened up career opportunities for you from the network of other successful brothers who were already established in corporate America in various career capacities and for some it meant that you were obligated and required to volunteer your time to charitable efforts! It was none of that for me. I just wanted to be a brother; a *__friend__*!

They, like many other Q's, or Omega Men as I prefer to call them, such as Jay Woods, Marvin Chambers, Victor Williams, Mark Duncan, Adell Pickens, Marvin Williams, and Randy Harris will always have a definitive place in my soul and heart as *__friends__* but more so as brothers who happened to be phenomenal men just like the men at my church in Baltimore. They were then and to this day, brothers who I will always have a love for because I know their hearts were always true to me like the loyalty that only man's best *__friend__* can provide! I owe my man Kevin Brown, a Q's Q, Omega man, who was a *__friend__* to me when I only had Jesus!

I know the reason why God did not allow me to pledge Omega was that at that time, I was a hypocrite who was certainly not worthy of being a fraternity brother because I did not represent manhood. I would have shamed and embarrassed the fraternity! How could I embody the principles of manhood and uplift if I was abusing my girlfriend physically, emotionally, verbally, and many other ways of degrading a *__friend__*? How could I be a Q & I was not an essential *__friend__* to her soul?

Also, God knew then that the journey I am on today included all men and women including the other fraternities and non-fraternity associations and more importantly the sororities, so I can be a sincere partner and brother, and prayerfully, an honorary member in any of them because of the love I have for their missions and mankind.

God's mission for me is to be a brother to any individual requiring love and protection! What I did learn about pledging was that you must test the limits of your mind and you will see that there are no limits! When you put your mind to something you can accomplish anything, and you will be pleasantly surprised with the end results! I also learned that you must be prepared because poor preparation promotes pain. The greatest lesson of all by the great men of Omega Psi Phi showed me that ***"Friendship is essential to the soul especially if you follow the principles of manhood, scholarship, perseverance, and uplift" and that you will be the last and only MAN left on the planet even after the earth has been destroyed by Armageddon because of the resilience & will that is within you! I cannot be killed!***

Because my grandpa died when I was 4, I never appreciated him or the many other men who stayed married for 20 plus years to the same woman. I did not see these types of individuals as "the man" but rather just as an ordinary Joe who boringly worked all day and night and came home to the same old woman and routine. I admired in awe, and more than anything, RESPECTED, the players and hustlers who were drug dealers, gangsters, pimps, boosters, and athletes getting big bands, stacks and racks of cash with the baddest (prettiest) women, exotic whips(cars), gear (clothes), blinged-out ice (jewelry), and luxurious cribs (homes). You could tell if they had money based on how much other guys feared or respected them. These were the guys we'd say to others as "You know G-Money is "The *Man*" now slinging (selling drugs)!" Back then, and to this very day, when I approach a friend I respect, I greet them with "My *Man*! What's Poppin'? What's Crackin'?"

When I would see someone in the media, who I considered a hero or respected them from the mountaintop like Adrian Branch, Brian Jordan, Michael Jordan, Len Bias, Deion Sanders, Andrew Locust, Antoine Harris, Bo Jackson, Rodney Monroe, Reggie White, Spike Lee, Reggie Williams, Vaughn Hebron, Lamar Smith, Michael Jackson, James Brown, or Muggsy Bogues, I would be like, "That's my *man* throwing down!" "That's my *man* getting his money!" "Nobody can stop him unless they beat the *man* to be the *man*!" "He's the *man*!" "I'm the *man*!" We even referred to the police as "the *man*!" Sure, we knew them as five-o, but we also would say, "Don't go down there right now because it's hot and the *man* is out there!" When someone said you were the **man**, it was because they respected you on the highest level and wished they could attach to you as a child does to their parents. The truth of the matter is that we were starving for a father and because there was not a single significant *man* and fatherly "presence" in our lives, we had to settle for "presents" and substitutes to complement our egos and ultimately fill the void of an absentee father. Think about it this way. To have a pair of fresh, spanking brand-new Air Force Ones, Suede Pumas, or Shell head Adidas gave you instant credibly by your peers! But to have a blazing new pair of Air Jordans was an entirely different perspective to the point where people would say and make you feel like, "You the *man*!" That was an incredible boost to your ego to hear someone compliment you on your shoes. You would poke your chest out and walk around like you were the King of the world! That is why I call them "Heir" Jordans!

Why do you think Michael Jordan's logo and brand are *titled "Jump Man?"* *The "Jumpman" logo is owned by Nike to promote the Air Jordan brand of basketball sneakers and other sportswear. The logo is a silhouette of Michael Jordan, "The Man!" performing a slam dunk.*[33] Michael Jordan is and probably will always be the king of the court and shoes with my man LeBron being the heir to his throne until the one and only King returns.

Jordans symbolized a person with money. As soon as you got off the scene, people would say "How does "money" get his paper and peanuts? Does he come from money or is he hustling?" When I was the star athlete, I was referred to by most as "the big man on campus who will eventually be a million-dollar athlete!" We saw people wearing Jordans as hood millionaires. Jordans are utopian limousines for your feet! They are therapeutic and refreshing! They are euphoric and are as addictive as the worst drug or bad habit you could ever have. They are such a must-have that people get up in the wee hours of the morning to stand in lines for them to ultimately wait to pay several hundred or thousands for them? I have heard of individuals who have hundreds of pairs of Jordans in their homes literally under lock and key, with guard dogs and with surveillance cameras recording as if the Jordans are in a bank's vault. I know of people who have had their utilities cut off, so their children could play in certain basketball tournaments whereas their kid would not be the only one without a pair of the new Jordans dawning their feet. Both tell me they were investing in their children's basketball career and the shoes because they can resell the Jordans in the future for more than they originally paid for them.

But are they worth taking another man's life for so they can make you feel like a man or be the man for having them? How many people have been robbed, assaulted or even killed over having them? Are Jordans just like violence in that it is so much about the respect factor that if you do not have them, you may be willing to resort to and are capable of violence, bullying, and criminal activity to acquire a pair? What sense does it make that you are willing to take another man's life or permanently lose your life as you know it in exchange for a lifetime behind bars for a temporary feeling of manhood exuberance, a boost of self-esteem and respect?

Why? It is all because Michael Jordan will always be **_the man_** to those who love and respect him and his game! His swagger on the court with his tongue out because he is the world's best trash talker who could back it up! His majestic dunks and dunks over seven-footers! The game-winning buzzer-beating shots! A winner of six championships! The Greatest of All Time and one of the greatest scorers and defenders. A Hall of Famer! His notorious winning prowess and swag because he always bet on himself confidently, in business, on private jets, or anywhere playing in the game of life or games such basketball, cards, dice and on the golf course! And all with the greatest shout out to his father with a mimicking tongue and cheek swag that said, "I am just like my father, and I respect my dad so much that I am just like him as a man & winner by having my tongue out when I am balling, just like my dad who is the man!" Michael Jordan will always be "**_the man_**!"

Why do you think Muhammad Ali always shouted, "I'm a bad man!" James Brown, the "Godfather of Soul" said he was "Super Bad" and "This is a Man's World!" Denzel, now you know you are the man or woman when you are known by just your first name, once shouted to the entire "hood" implying that he was the man by emphatically saying, "I'm the man up in this piece!" Ali said he was faster and stronger than Superman because he was faster than a speeding bullet, more powerful than a locomotive, and able to lift tall buildings! Alexander O'Neal was an "All True Man!" Ralph Tresvant said we need "A Man with *SENSITIVITY*!"

If you need to make yourself feel that good about yourself, get an adrenaline or B12 shot or buy a fresh pair of Js! For the record, I have never purchased a pair of Jordans in my entire life because growing up in Baltimore, although my mom could afford to buy me a pair, she never wanted me to shine but instead tried to embarrass me by purchasing a pair of Bobo the clown shoes, which never made sense to me. This embarrassment motivated me to hustle to sell whatever I could such as soon to be expiring Frito-Lay products that I *borrowed for an indefinite period* from my great friend, and eventual McDonogh classmate, Cortland Wylie's dad. Mr. Wylie, who worked for Frito Lay, would set Frito-Lay boxes filled with nearly expired chips out near his trash cans and eventually, with his permission, on route to school I would get them just before school to sell to my classmates.

As much as I always wanted to buy Jordans for the respect that came with having them, I never bought them because of the negative attention they brought to young dudes in Baltimore. You were likely to get robbed, assaulted, or possibly killed over a pair of Jordans. If I did not have something of value like Jordans, a fancy watch or clothes and accessories, then I was less likely to be a victim, but also less likely for me, who always stayed strapped after 6th grade, to not have to reciprocate violence and abuse towards those individuals trying to harm me or my friends as we walked to and from school and during times at the basketball court. Another reason I never bought them was I always believed my uncle would steal them or sell them for money and my mother would never have believed me if I told her he did either to me. I probably would have killed him or someone else who would have tried to take them from me during that time in my life. Jordans meant you were to be respected as a man! Jordans meant you were "*the man*" with money!

By the time I could buy them I was attending McDonogh with a uniform and conservative dress code and a negative stigma tied to Jordans that black youth who were poor, yet owners of Jordans were considered ignorant and ghetto because they would rather look good but sacrifice paying for books or school supplies. I did not want to bring that kind of attention to myself either. Maybe one day I will sign a lifetime contract with Air Jordan and receive unlimited pairs of signed Jordans and LeBrons after we work together to eradicate domestic violence, child abuse, and bullying. Jordans represent unparalleled respect and being the man you are supposed to be in life by achieving success through incredibly hard work and sacrifice!

Love conquers all like LeBron's friends advocating for him because at times as a child he was in some situations that his father should have been there to handle head-on...not his mom. Reciprocating the love back to his friends and forging a bond that will never be broken, LeBron is the type of brother who truly is "My brother's keeper!" I say this because when you look at his life, he is a shining example of brotherly love and serving others. He makes people's dreams a reality!

There is only one King, and He (God) is the King of All Kings! Do not ever let anyone put the title of "King" on your career. Look what happened when the world claimed Mike Tyson was the "King" of Boxing. Elvis Presley was crowned by society as the "King" of Rock and ironically, his future son in law, Michael Jackson, was formally christened as the "King" of Pop. James Brown was hailed the "King" of Soul, Richard Pryor was first touted as the "King" of Comedy, Tupac and Biggie had society divisively wedging a fight between them for the title "King" of Hip-Hop and Rap! They crowned Biggie as the "King" of New York! Ronnie Coleman was crowned the "King" of bodybuilding. T.I. has been known as the "King" of the South. Meek Mill, the "King" of Philly! Eminem the "King" of Detroit! Bun B, the "King" of Houston! Kanye, the "King" of Chicago! R. Kelly is known as the "King" of R&B and is the self-proclaimed & promoted "Pied Piper." *The Pied Piper was a rat-catcher hired by the town to lure rats away with his magic pipe? When the citizens refused to pay for this service, he'd retaliate by using his musical instrument's magical power on their children, leading them away as he had the rats?* [34] Poor Prince! His name means the son of a king! Look at what happened!

What happened to these individuals is the deception that society plays on some of the most successful human beings to ever live on earth. These individuals were given rare talents by God that were exclusively only meant for them. But somehow "man" purposely designed a strategic plan of destruction, deception, violence, and abuse. Man craftily raised them to levels of immortality and financial security to give them any worldly possession and access to the most critical and influential humans on earth. Then "Voila!" Here comes a life of pain, loss, no peace, paparazzi, divisiveness, people trying to torch them and their loved ones in the media or with death threats, no personal fulfillment, low to no self-esteem, depression, and paranoia. Then only to fall from the highest graces of mankind and the death of their lives, legacies, good name, and careers. The irony is when they die; their estate becomes more valuable dead than alive!

Like King Kong, the world wants to capture you to make money off of your talents that they are captivated by, but the minute you do not comply say goodbye because you are about to die figuratively or literally! Before you know it, you are on stage in front of a sold-out crowd and then before you know it you are at the top of the Empire State Building only to get shot down from on high to plummet to earth to die in the streets. Look how the world & media are there for your rise and demise! Never let anyone give you the title of King for anything! Even King Kong, Godzilla, and The Godfather died in the end! The Kings of Comedy are not spared! How many world leaders have been assassinated as Kings and dictators! Most Kings once declared are killed like Jesus and Dr. Martin Luther King Jr. There is only one King!

LeBron is called "King" James because of his last name *in association with the Bible version and reference that came from King James of England who was prompted to produce an English Bible because of the poor and prejudicial copies being circulated in England. King James feared these could be used by inflammatory religious and political sects.* [35] LeBron has never been crowned the "King" of Basketball because there is and never will be a definitive "King" of the NBA. Bill Russell has more championships, 11 in total, than anyone in the history of the sport and no one has ever thought of putting the "King" in front of his name because he is a "man" who never got snared by society's deception and rather he bullishly and uncompromisingly defeated the injustices head-on as a "man!" Not to say the others were not men, but when society defines you as a "King" of something and promotes you to where people treat you like you are "a" or "the" "God" of anything, there is a price that can never be fully paid for a title that has already been claimed and paid for at the cross. What happened to Jesus when He claimed to be the Son of God? Most had a love for Bill Cosby as America's dad and king of NBC!

What will the world and society do to you if you let someone crown you as "King" and you think you are "God" because of your position in life and how you treat others? Okay, you are a highly successful individual who earns a significant amount of money and has influence and power over people! Does that give you the authority or permission to treat people violently or abusively? What do you think will happen when you are so arrogant and a bully and think you will never have to pay for how you have abused others? What happened to all the political world and domestic leaders and "Hollywood" movie executives, entertainers, actors, music and fashion moguls who were crowned "King" and were found or accused of being tyrants, rapists, murderers, and dictators who intimidatingly ruled as bullies without conscious and with senseless malice? They lost their positions of power, money, corporations, public respect, and more than anything their families, livelihoods, and legacies. Some have even lost their lives.

When you do not stand up for your mental health and to the eradication of domestic violence and child abuse against women and children, the only outcome will be the loss of lives and legacies! LeBron will never fall into the snares of trouble the way so many others have because what separates him from those who fell from grace and wealth is that LeBron willfully, respectfully and humbly serves others. He meets their needs humbly and respectfully as King Jesus did when He would perform miracles such as feeding the starving thousands or making a blind person see or even as simple as washing the feet of other servants.

Man wants you to serve them as the worst tyrants, dictators, and Kings in history have done! They only want you to serve them and wash their feet, laundry, and car while continually giving them money and gifts and if you do not, they will exile you or kill you literally or figuratively! They will tear you down whereas LeBron wants to build you up and never tear you down literally or figuratively. He started a school to build better lives and outcomes for deserving children. He built the Cleveland Cavaliers and delivered more than a championship to the cities of Cleveland and Miami and state of Ohio and Florida and plans to do the same in L.A. for the Lakers, just like MJ did for Chicago and Illinois and for UNC Chapel Hill, the Charlotte Hornets, and North Carolina. Both delivered hope and mental wellness by winning throughout the regular season and playoffs. There is no greater feeling than when your personal and favorite team wins a championship. Both made others and their lives and legacies around them on and off the court better, and as a result, they achieved better results, opportunities, and contracts too. This is why I love the relationship Jay Z has with Ta-Ta Smith. Brothers for life! Beyond the grave!

LeBron is a real brother's keeper in that when you look at the relationships he has with his friends from childhood, he has kept his promise to them, as they have to him, that they will always be friends and in love with one another no matter the fame or money or politics or anything. Their love is truly unconditional and filled with mutually reciprocated respect. I do not think most people understand what the phrase "My Brother's Keeper" really means.

People do dumb stuff all day every day because they stop caring about their life and do not give a damn about the consequences and who it impacts, so they get up on some bull shizzle where they do not give a flip about the relationship and succumb to impulsivity and become disillusioned! To most, a brother's keeper only applies if both people are benefiting and getting something out of the relationship, but the minute one party thinks they are not receiving an equal amount of value back or nothing at all in return, the relationship terminates, and the honeymoon is over. That is a one-sided relationship that is simply selfish and greedy. I will keep you as my brother as long as you keep on giving me things, but the minute you stop giving me things I will stop giving you things and more than anything, I will stop being your loving brother. The love I have seen with Lebron is unconditional and impenetrable. He truly is a man's man. You can't have a one-way street relationship!

I have respect for such people, their family, journeys, as well as the many other individuals running charitable nonprofits to serve others in need for their many contributions to humanity that are done in the dark with little to no fan awareness for public sympathy or corporate campaigning. They are "Stars" for a reason because they let their "Little Lights Shine!" They are special because their lives serve as a testimony to incredible sacrifices, unmatched hard work, and a willingness to serve others despite their tragedies. They do not participate in excuses, but rather they find solutions to make their lives and the lives of others better! They can all be viewed as "THE MAN" by society's standards of success, but I will always love and respect them first as men and women who loved others enough to call you their brother or sister by their benevolent, altruistic, and philanthropic actions. Those actions and the spirit of love is how I will always know them until I die and join them in heaven one day. Like them, "*I AM A MAN! I AM A BROTHER's KEEPER!*"

I know now that the good Lord knew at that time I was not supposed to solely be a member of the Omega Psi Phi fraternity because I would have been an absolute shame as an abuser to the organization and the many men and women who proudly represent and are affiliated with the Qs. I did not represent manhood, scholarship, perseverance, or uplift at that moment. Friendship definitely could not have been essential to my soul based on how I served and treated others. God knew this moment would come where I could be a brother to ALL fraternities, sororities, or any professional groups gender-specific or not for the charitable efforts I will partner with and serve them without any prejudices or biases. I will be able to stand with corporate, church, community, political, educational, health, LGBTQ and private leaders of incredible organizations and will be able to represent the best attributes of ALL organizations and support ALL their agendas as a loving brother would with no judgment, hidden agendas or for selfish reasons. I want All of my brothers and sisters to always know that **"I LOVE YOU FOREVER!"**

ARE YOU REALLY LIVING AS A BROTHER'S KEEPER OF LOVE? DO NOT EVER LET THE WORLD CROWN YOU OR CALL YOU KING OR GOD OF ANYTHING BECAUSE YOU WILL HAVE HELL TO PAY FOR SUCH A TITLE! THERE WAS A MOVIE OF A FAMOUS SHIP THAT SANK AS A RESULT OF HITTING AN ICEBERG. A MAN WAS AT THE HELM OF THE SHIP SHOUTING HE WAS THE KING OF THE WORLD. THAT SHIP SANK AND HE DIED IN THE FREEZING OCEAN!

SOMEBODY'S BABIES!
WHO IN THEIR RIGHT MIND WOULD INTENTIONALLY HARM A
BABY? REGARDLESS OF AGE, WE ARE ALL SOMEBODY'S BABY!

(TEENY TURNER AND ME)

NO ONE SHOULD HAVE HARMED ME!
I HAD NO RIGHT TO HARM GOD'S PROPERTY!
I HARMED SOMEBODY'S BABY!
I AM SORRY FOR HARMING MY FORMER
GIRLFRIEND, WIFE, FAMILY, FRIENDS, and FUTURE!
I SHOULD NOT HAVE HARMED MYSELF!
I PAID A PRICE FOR A CRIME I NEVER COMMITTED!
AS A RESULT
I LEARNED TO HARM OTHERS AND MYSELF TOO!
TO KNOW WHAT I KNOW TODAY,
I WOULD HAVE TOLD SOMEONE
I WAS BEING HURT
BY PEOPLE WHO SHOULD HAVE LOVED ME!

Solutions To Permanently Eradicate Domestic Violence, Child Abuse, and Bullying

MY VICTIM and GODSENT ANGEL

How Do You Hurt The One Who Loves You More Than You Love Yourself?

And then "Voila!" A miracle appeared in my life one Friday evening when I decided to attend my cousin Teeny's basketball game. Wilbert White, my great childhood friend, and someone I will always consider a true diehard of a man and father to his children, along with my cousin Teeny, both said I needed to meet this girl who they considered a homegirl named Michelle Thompson! They said she was perfect for me and I was perfect for her. Naturally, I was suspicious because if she was perfect for me, why had they not or any of the other sexually aggressive guys in their school want her? They felt she was a good girl with a great head on her shoulders and was someone from great stock! They said her parents were both professionals who lived in a nice community in this particular section of Baltimore! Those were code words for she was not fast, meaning, she was not sexually active and has a two-parent home where they could not or did not want to work that hard getting past the gatekeeper parents to have a girlfriend! Michelle was too conservative and clean-cut for them despite being cool! Was I a conservative now?

Seeing how at age 14, I was living away from home, in the dorms at ultra-conservative, liberal arts, private college prep school McDonogh, where everyone and everything was the polar opposite of anything black such as speaking proper English or displaying royal etiquette, wearing Jordans or name brand designer clothes and jewelry, or just resembling any of the remnants of the hood or projects, they thought she would be good for me and me for her! Before I knew it, she was standing in front of me. She was everything I had hoped for in a blind set up being that she was incredibly pretty and possessed an even more beautiful warm and angelic disposition. I was smitten with her because from the onset she was different from the typical Baltimore girls with whom you had to always dress to impress or flash the cash to give the appearance of a successful baller, or you had to be some incredibly popular athlete or "Billy Badass" who everybody feared and respected! These were all the characteristics I possessed that got me shipped off to McDonogh because the belief was I was not going to see 18 at the rate I was going when it came to my associations and activities in the Baltimore public school system.

Michelle saw me exactly for who I was, and that was simply a guy looking for someone to share quality time and conversations with consistently. She complimented and supported my focus towards getting to healthier dreams for my life such as going to college and becoming a corporate attorney, versus just focusing on sports and getting to the pros with no strategies to fall back on if those dreams did not pan out. She had me thinking about being a FAMILY MAN™ like her dad who came home every night to his beautiful, equally educated, strong, and highly successful wife and mother of his children! She gave me insight into what a healthy relationship looks like between a husband and wife and how to communicate and raise children appropriately and together! She even showed me how to properly care for a dog, through her pet dog, who was a boxer breed, named Roscoe. She taught me what a friend looks, sounds, and acts like in a vested relationship! She was love!

Until that point in my youthful life, I had never seen any man in my household properly love a woman nor a woman appropriately love a man! I've witnessed & heard violence of all sorts at all levels in all kinds of places such as my female teenage cousin being raped by a Sunday and Vacation Bible School teacher who was a family friend; My aunt, who despite the number of times she went toe to toe as a young child with me, smacking, scratching, punching or hitting me with the rotary dial telephone in the face or head; When she ran over her husband with her car breaking his foot and the time she came home with a black eye from her married boyfriend; The time when someone she inadvertently cut off in another car pulled up next to us and called us a "bunch of black baboons" and we followed her to her house, pulled up in her driveway, and before the woman could get out her car or even pull the window up, my aunt smacked the living shizzle out of her face just as my mother smacked the crap out of Steve the postman for calling us the N-Word!

Or was it the time my uncle-in-law hit my aunt, and my mom loaded us in the car so fast that before we knew it we were at their home and before my uncle knew it he was bleeding profusely from his head because my mom and aunt had cracked him in the head with a beer bottle! I know he was not feeling so high once he got his wig peeled back with the 32 oz bottle of Miller High Life beer. This act of violence probably came about as a fight from one or the other getting caught cheating as both always cheated on one another! Or maybe it was watching the porn on my aunt and uncle's cable television channel called "Super TV" or at friend's houses watching the porn on cable or tapes! I was **_exposed_** to too many things XXX!

Or how about my uncle's... my gay one and my two straight ones, who had the gay and straight editions of porn and slutty magazines out in plain view or stashed accordingly, but to latchkey kids who are used to knowing when people are coming or going that's like telling a prisoner there's a key to unlock the cell door in their cell...all they have is time and energy to find the reward so it is not a matter of if they will find it, but when they will find it! Or maybe it was when I watched a family friend take an empty bottle and hurl it over to the other team's bench that landed on the face of a young lady forcing her to go to the hospital in the ambulance. Or watching my friends, during the summer following my senior year when at a neighborhood pool a full-scale race riot broke out and I watched white boys and girls get their asses handed to them because they were unfairly outnumbered and before I knew it here come the ghetto birds (police helicopters) and sirens as Billy Bryant and I were ducking chairs, fists, bullets, and the cops as we got away in Billy's car only for a similar incident to occur several weeks later on the "block" at Pollock Johnnies!

Or maybe it was witnessing firsthand a homeless man being pushed into the Baltimore Harbor for just being homeless because another man was tired, annoyed, and fed up with this homeless man begging him for money. Or how about the weekend gambling card tournaments and coke parties at my aunt's or uncle's homes. Or family members breaking into other family members homes to steal jewelry and other valuables to pawn to feed an addiction or pay bills to cover gambling debts and losses! Or maybe it was watching my mother and aunts date married men, and consequently, I got a stillborn brother out of the deal!

Maybe it was because my uncle and family friend took us to the famous Baltimore "Block" to see them talk shizzle to the sexy hookers and prostitutes they referred to as "working b*****s" and when they did not get what they wanted from these "b*****s" because these "b*****s" would not accept their negotiated price offerings for a sex act! My uncle David* and Timothy should have known that these were Baltimore "b*****s" and even they knew the value of their lives and services! What is crazy for me is that how can anyone purposely call someone a "b****" just by their profession and you don't even know the person well enough to determine if they are a "b****" or not. What I do know is there are plenty of male "b*****s" too that I refer to as "Mitch's," who are not streetwalkers, prostitutes, or escorts, but are the true "b*****s" for abandoning their financial responsibilities and other fatherly and spousal duties by bullying and battering their wives, women, and children. The code on the street always was you never involved women and children whenever you engaged in any violence or abuse. Little boys are always taught you never hit girls. My aunt taught me that "you never hit a girl or woman, but it is okay to smack a "b****!" How confusing of a message is that to send to any child of any age?

Solutions To Permanently Eradicate Domestic Violence, Child Abuse, and Bullying

Can you imagine how I felt when Michelle asked me over to her house to meet her parents? When a girl tells you she wants you to meet her parents what is she communicating to you? I was unbelievably happy and excited about the opportunity! She cared or trusted me enough to invite me into her home because where I am from very few strangers were permitted to come by the house, especially an individual from the opposite sex. It truly was not until I saw Michelle's parents lovingly engage one another, that I had first properly viewed a healthy marriage. I was blown away when I saw her grandparents, both maternally and paternally, with equally exceptional loving and respectful relationships! I was in awe and disbelief at the notion that people could have a long-term truly monogamous relationship free of violence and abuse! This was an absolute miracle for me even to be close to such a person as Michelle. Yes! I finally have someone in my corner and can see healthy love up close and not just an episode on the Cosby show. And just when I was receiving a healthy dose of love, "Voila," she moved to Barbados because her dad's job relocated him. Michelle's going to Barbados? Why? Why now God? Why? Why? Every time I would get close to receiving or giving love, the person leaves me because it is my fault. This time it is not my fault Lord! To heck with love! I thought. I hate love because it seems to always hurt and retreat to somewhere else.

The only love that never left me alone and what I could always rely on was sports. It never hurt me in any capacity. It never tried to kill me physically, mentally, verbally or emotionally! I did not believe in love because it always hurt me or abandoned me. I would much rather hurt it or abandon it before it hurt or abandoned me again! Love did not become tangible to me until I met Michelle! After she left for Barbados, I fought bouts of depression for the next twenty-four months. I finally had someone in my life who truly loved me and was not going to stop loving me, abandon me, neglect me, embarrass me, choose another man, beer or a career over me, while choosing not to attend my games, and then to add insult to injury, turn around & harm me by not protecting me from others. She would never hurt or harm me. She was now gone, and the only thing that kept me going was her love letters from Barbados that we both sent to one another quite frequently! I even once visited her and her family for nearly a month in Barbados during the Christmas holidays.

My last two years of high school was an absolute disaster personally. I withdrew from people and focused solely on getting to the professional ranks of baseball and football by getting into a division one program that would allow me to play both sports like my heroes Bo Jackson, Deion Sanders, and Brian Jordan.

My focus on sports became optimal, and I did not give a damn about grades or making new friends. What do you do when you do not have your best friend around?

Once I realized that my high school SAT and ACT scores were just enough to qualify for college and that all I needed to maintain was a 2.0 grade point average, my high school focus on education was to the point where I did not give two craps about the coaches because I could see that they did not really have my best interest in mind and that their interests were in helping other people and perpetuating their hidden agendas. I felt the sabotage and knew what was going on politically.

After I got caught for plagiarism in the latter part of my junior year, it only got worse for me and my relationships with the coaches, school administrators, faculty and staff. I welcomed the hate because I knew the truth that the school looked at me as an embarrassment and lazy talent who had never received their full blessings because I was a hoodlum who had respect from the majority of the school, and they could not understand why the mass population would put their arms around such a bad boy who defied all of their rules for living on campus and in their classrooms. Getting caught naked with Michelle in my room or coming in late after curfew or having contraband in my room just set people against me even though I knew they were committing greater criminal offenses in their homes. My offenses were at best immoral but not illegal. You are mad at me because I would not support and perpetuate legacy and traditions that I believed would harm me or others like spending the weekend at Maj's or going over other faculty member's homes for inappropriate activities. I was tired of the hypocrisy of my family and my McDonogh family too. I could not serve my student government position as the Vice-President of the Student Body and other significant student club positions but, I could still be captain of the football and baseball teams and President of the Black Awareness Club. Lead the sports and social clubs?

With Michelle in Barbados I went to my senior prom, the only prom I went to at McDonogh, with an awesome friend Terri Dowla. She was gracious, to say the least. I gave her my jerseys as a gift for just being my friend at McDonogh. Why did I want to celebrate a school that I assumed did not want to celebrate me? I went to another prom and it was a complete disaster because the girl I went with could not understand why I was so loyal to Michelle. Would you be loyal to someone who was loyal to you? **No McDonogh coach ever helped me receive a scholarship!**

At that time, graduation could not come fast enough. I watched the politics play out by way of how the awards got handed out to the undeserving people who had not put in all the work and all the crap I had endured at McDonogh. I never celebrated the graduation nor was any party thrown in my honor. To this day, I have very few keepsakes of McDonogh. I worked out all-year-round for four years!

Off I go to Oklahoma State University to fulfill my lifelong dream of playing Major League Baseball and in the NFL. But then the depression from high school reappeared with a vengeance. I could not focus on my dreams because I was so occupied with wondering what my girlfriend was doing in Virginia at Hampton University. What an idiot I was to worry about who she was with versus trusting her and caring for her wellbeing just as a loving friend. I could not see my future destiny!

These are the moments in life where children and young adults truly need sound advice and counseling from a trusted source such as a parent, friend, mentor, teacher or coach. This is the line in the sand or fork in the road moments when you need the voice and ears of reason! I did not reach out to anyone because, in my entire life, I never had anyone I could sincerely trust to reach out to for fear of retribution or for the appearance of being weak or crazy. I did what I always did by trusting the only person I had always relied on and trusted...me! I shut down in full depressed mode. In my mind, I was going crazy. Reaching out to Michelle then was not as easy as it is today via cell phone, text, email or by Facebook, Instagram, Twitter or Snapchat. I was beginning to lose my will to fight, live, or survive. Death's talking!

My passion and drive left me because I became fixated on bull shizzle. I left Oklahoma State on a full scholarship due to lack of focus and injuries! Lack of focus leads to horrible decisions, poor choices and bad judgment. I left a full scholarship, a free education, while also playing a college sport and the opportunity to play a pro sport possibly! Who does that with no plan b strategy? As a result, I cost myself the possibility of living a supernatural life! Your talents and body of work should never cause another person to lose their life! But rather, your talents should benefit and enhance the lives of others. I allowed my ego and a fixation on misplaced love to screw me! I needed a man and a father at that time in my life!

Michelle was such an awesome, caring and amazing person who had the special spirit of an angel. Her parents, sister, family, friends, dog, and neighbors were equally as genuine and loving to me as she always was to me. I can honestly tell the world that I never recalled one incident where she picked, provoked or prodded me into an argument. It was all about me, and I was the one with the controlling and jealous disposition. I was the insecure person with low self-esteem who was immature and violent and abusive physically, emotionally verbally, and mentally. I was the one with all the violence and abuse against her while playing all the mind games and stressing her to the point where if we were to have had children, I know I would have caused her to miscarry our babies. God would have kept those angels with Him in heaven because He knew she and those babies did not deserve a life with me. Like a wild and untamed apex predator, it was not possible for me to love her the way her grandpas and dad had loved their wives! I thought she wanted to wife me, but instead, God wanted to knife me out of her life rightfully! I was wrong for her on so many levels. I was so mentally unhealthy, and God and she knew it! She was the innocent victim living under the constant threat of death.

August 28, 1991, four days before returning to my senior year of college! Just before heading back to school I had dinner with Michelle's parents. Michelle had already headed back to Hampton a day or so before me. I was sharing with them how I had received an incredible sendoff message from the C.E.O, E. Bronson Ingram of Ingram Industries and how excited he was for me to complete my senior year at Hampton and join him in Nashville following my graduation to attend Law School at Vanderbilt, so I could eventually be a corporate attorney for his company.

We talked about me marrying Michelle in the near future and babies. It was an exciting forecast, to say the least, when her dad spoke about helping me to pick out a wedding ring with their neighbors' help. But little did I know, and rightfully so, that would be the last time we would talk about pleasantries together at the same table. I did not know that the weapons of my violent past were forming against me!

I will not tell you what happened next because you will soon find out in the very next chapter but know my days of being a sustainable aggressive domestic violence offender had come to a head with Michelle. She rightfully decided to end the 6-year relationship as high school sweethearts. She loved me but was not in love with me, nor the abuse, violence, or disrespect. I was oblivious to why I had the gumption and audacity to question and be confused and baffled about why she broke up with me! Here I was again alone at the hands of my own destruction! All I ever wanted to be was relevant, not alone, and loved! I will come back!

Many people to this day wonder in disbelief how could I, of all people, end up in the worst places on earth for abusing the girlfriend I loved so very much? The answer is simple in that I refused to get help and the necessary professional treatment. I was a certified fool. I was a crazy boyfriend who was psychotic. My behavior threatened her life to the point she eventually realized she would never be my wife! I assaulted her in private and in public. I was the ultimate loser because no one with a sound mind would love a woman like her and then abuse her! I was an ignorant, arrogant, fool! I was a dysfunctional and psychotic fool trying to function in a relationship with a non-dysfunctional individual! How was that going to work?

My behavior and overall treatment of her was despicable and deplorable at best. Sure I had moments where I was loving and gave the appearance and best intentions of a future husband and best friend, but how relevant do those things mean over time to a future wife when you commit incredible acts of violence and abuse that are simply acts of treason in your relationship. I was a positive negative!

After so many times of forgiving me, I am definitely certain now that she realized, just like my mother probably did with my dad, that there was absolutely no end to the violence, abuse, and maltreatment, and so from just a self-preservation position and a general love for self, she had to take a justifiable stand for her life. What I realize now is that every time I verbally, physically, emotionally or psychologically abused her, in reality, I should have pulled out a mirror because I was really verbally, physically, emotionally or psychologically abusing myself.

If I called her a b****, I was really calling myself a b****. If I smacked or assaulted her, I was really smacking and assaulting myself. If I choked her, I was really choking myself. If I told her she wouldn't be shizzle without me, I was really telling myself that I wouldn't be shizzle without her. With abuse when you are harming someone else, you really are harming yourself. You are harming her family, your future family together, and the chances of reconciliation and redemption. The relationship is over forever and the only person to blame is the coward in the mirror, not a future family man! ***MAN DAMN!***

When someone tells you that they are no longer in love with you and you are not the one for them, realize that they are telling you they no longer want to be with you or associated with you because you have obviously shown them enough for them to feel that way about you! I had damaged our future with my propensity for violence and abuse towards her. She was innocent and I could not see that I was murdering her self-esteem! I fired myself from our relationship. She didn't quit us!

I remember being angry for her wanting to break up with me as if she had no choice or freedom to get out of such a toxic relationship that I created and sustained. I was narcissistic in that I thought, "How could she break up with me when I made her relevant?" I would have not wanted me based on how I treated her!

Oh, what shameless ignorance on my behalf! I did not own her. I was not the God who made her. I was not the mother who suffered through the insurmountable pains of childbirth. She was not my property and I did not own her. I had to right to harm her in any form or fashion. She was God's property and I had harmed someone's baby that God had trusted to raise. How dare me!

My question to abusers today and to all people in any type of personal or corporate relationship is, "Why in the hell do you want to be with anyone or anything that does not want to be with you or no longer is in love with you?" Man, oh man, I wish that statement was plugged into my psyche when my former girlfriend said that she no longer wanted to be with me in the capacity of a boyfriend/girlfriend relationship. I should have respected her enough and her wishes to be single or with someone else. If I had really loved her as I once believed, and if I had really loved her as a friend, I would have respected her wishes and allowed her to freely move on to the destination God had for her life that did not include me. If I had really loved her, I would have never harmed her or anything she loved, in any capacity! I was a selfish, narcissistic, psychopath who did not deserve to be in love with anyone or anything at that time because the bottom line was I was not in love with me!

Due to my reckless actions, unprecedented levels of disrespect, and obvious displays of violence and abuse of all sorts, she was right to feel that way, and she certainly had the right to move forward with her life. Hear me clearly when I say that this type of rhetoric from a loved one is indeed the beginning of the end of whatever relationship you thought you might have had with your loved one! Let them go on with the freedom to live their life without you or without being in a monogamous relationship. If you were working for a company and they told you they were parting ways with you and that they were no longer happy with your performance as an employee and that they were severing the relationship, could you continue to work there, or would you leave willingly and eventually look for another job? Most of us would look for another job or field of work versus coming back to harm your boss or others you think harmed you! Get a new career and a new relationship with yourself first before you go jumping around to the next relationship! How would it look to keep coming into a job you are no longer an employee? How would the next job look at you if your work history was spotty?

The answer is apparent that you would move on without incident and you would be removed by security or the police if you did not leave the premises. I'm telling you because I love you, and I wish someone had taught me better for these types of scenarios, to get the hell away from them as fast as possible because you are not the one who makes them happy! Leave immediately if possible and if you have children then work out the details as far as a scheduled arrangement to co-parent healthily, but regardless of how much you love them it is time for you to get yourself corrected and either get to the person meant for you only or as was the situation in my case, get professional psychological help to prevent these same heart-breaking scenarios from resurfacing again in your life!

Just as they have a right and deserve to be happy, so do you! I never again in my life will ever be in any relationship where I know I am doing all the right things to please people for their acceptance, but rather the only person I need to please and win their acceptance is myself and God Almighty! No person is that significant to lose your life and freedom over unless it is your children or you are a sworn civil servant, or your hero senses kick in to save someone's life. Michelle taught me that based on her strength to leave me!

What I will always share with everyone is that if you really care about the individual who is abusing you or you are an abuser who truly cares about the devastation you are inflicting upon a loved one, and you definitively cannot control your violent and abusive behavior, then you must tell, pardon me, YELL, to anyone who is in a position to help you! Had I not gone to hell on earth, I would have ended my life a long time ago or ended someone else's life a long time ago or best-case scenario, I would have quite naturally and consequently moved on to abuse and traumatically terrorize other women, people, children and pet animals. I would have continued a cycle of horrible violence!

The truth of the matter, and sad reality is, had my former girlfriend not thought enough about preserving her own life once she realized it was not possible for me to change after all of the passes she had given me and that it was heartbreakingly and blatantly obvious that I was not remotely choosing to move forward to change, the best possible thing she could do and did was to tell her parents and the authorities. She stopped enabling me. I should not have expected her to because I put her in that predicament. I was wrong to put her in a position to enable me. She enabled me because she loved me as a friend and only hoped, cared and believed I would change for the better. Even still, and she had all the reasons not to do so, she still showed me mercy when she stressed to the judge and all authorities that all she wanted then and all she ever wanted for me during our entire relationship, was for me to get the necessary help so I would not continue to hurt her, anyone or anything, and especially myself. Of all the people on the earth, how could I hurt her? I ruined a friendship with the one who actually cared for & loved me! ***MAN DAMN***

I live each day wondering how I could have ever been smart enough to get to my senior year of college and yet be so utterly stupid and deaf to her sincere recommendations to get help, blind to the facts of my violence towards her and others, and naively unaware of my own mental health capacity. How could I have been so ignorant? Why would any sane and rational person behave in such a vile and reprehensible manner that would push away the very individual, might I add, the only individual at the time, who was desperately trying to help me, and this was the same person that I had violently abused in so many demeaning ways?

I am incredibly contrite and ashamed to know that I hurt her and so many others. She did everything right, and I managed to punish her for a crime she never committed against me. My eyes tear like a broken water faucet, my heart shutters, and my belly wants to throw up its contents, repulsed at the very notion that I was the sole reason, the root cause, the eye of the storm who could not see the bands of despicable destruction that I was purposely inflicting upon the only light in my dark world, the only defender of my existence and the only person who trusted me enough to want to love me and I simply did not know how to reciprocate the same love back to her properly!

Her love was filtered, and refreshingly pure and organic while mine was unfiltered, toxic, and shockingly filthy with the impurities of dysfunctional soot, pain, and self-hate! My violent actions towards her made it seem obvious that I did not want her, but I did not want her to leave me or worse, be with anyone except me. How selfish and hypocritical! That is like violently and purposely breaking your most hated and unfavorite toy into a million pieces and then throwing the pieces into the garbage can, and you have a friend who says they will take those broken million pieces and you will not let them get the broken million pieces of the hated broken toy out of the trash. What was worthless to me would definitely have been priceless to someone in their right mind. I did not want my girlfriend or friend to be happy because I was not happy internally.

If I ever had the opportunity, and maybe this is my one and only opportunity to do so, I would say humbly and respectfully that I want to apologize to you sincerely, your Mom, Dad, Sister, Grandparents, Aunt, Cousins, Roscoe, your Husband, Children, Sorority Sisters and friends for the pain and abuse I caused you and them during yours and their life! I was infinitely wrong for the way I treated you physically, verbally, mentally, and emotionally! I possessed a weak heart and mind and single-handedly destroyed the friendship that I comfortably took for granted. I was an egotistical, unaccountable, liar, impulsive, traitor, disloyal, unthoughtful, always right, hypocrite who if I had been in my right mind, possessed a peaceful resolution in my heart, and a spiritual sound soul, I would have recognized your love for my life! I thought I had made you relevant when in fact it was you who truly made me relevant. I was not a leader. I was a cowardly bully. You were the mature one. I was the hero in public but a zero in private with you when you deserved nothing short of a man's man just like your father, grandfathers, and husband! I emphatically emphasize being a hypocrite because of the people who loved and knew us. I was a woman beating, control freak, mind game player, cheater, heart and soul breaker!

I was incredibly deceptive because anyone knowing me would never have believed I was a monster to her based on how I presented myself to them. At that time, I was honestly who they thought I was, a Dr. Jekyll. It is just that I had never displayed Mr. Hyde to anyone publicly other than my Mother, Grandma, her, my Aunt Annie and Uncle Chub, my closest cousin Teeny, too many close male friends that I bullied in grade school, and even my dogs Smoky* and Toby*! I guess that's why they call him Mr. Hyde because he truly "Hides" who he really is inside and only the individuals closest to him can actually see and feel who he is as a total person! Everyone thought I treated her like a queen and princess, but the truth was I treated her like an enemy and prisoner of the palace, rather than see her as a genuine friend and ally! Even worst is knowing that I was the cause and centerpiece of inflicting pain upon her when I should have been the complimentary center peace of love and happiness to her life! I disrespected her and controlled her!

Truthfully, I am not worthy to ask for her and anyone else's forgiveness for how I treated her and all the pain I caused! She was everything I should have been when I think of how she, her family and friends treated me! I am responding to her apologetically and with full accountability to let her know that I am forever apologetic for the oftentimes insane, ridiculous, sinister, and unwarranted pain, trauma, abuse, and violence against her that also impacted her family, friends and the future I may have harmed her or them. I should have accepted her help!

I was beyond wrong when I hit her physically or with my tongue verbally or played mental and emotional games with her! She was strong and I was the ignorant coward who was actually hitting myself and playing mental and emotional games with myself! She was somebody's baby and I abused her. How could I have abused anyone's baby? ***MAN DAMN!***

Solutions To Permanently Eradicate Domestic Violence, Child Abuse, and Bullying

When I think about that statement, my state of mental health was clearly and definitively not well! Who beats their self-up or calls themselves a b**** or stupid and piece of shizzle? Who purposely kills their self-esteem and their dreams of happiness? I was a self-esteem killer and a bully!

I was so young and dumb, I never let her know enough how much I truly loved, appreciated, and respected her as a friend and human being! I should have let her know at the beginning and end of each day, and as a matter of fact, as often as I could, how much I loved her and appreciated her kindness and friendship! I should have greeted her with a hug and a kind word and an "I Love You" before bed, and as we awakened in the morning and every time we parted one another. Why didn't I treat her as if I knew this was her last day on the earth and this would be the only and last time I would ever see her? I was sick in the damn head!

I know she will be in heaven one day and I just pray I will be there to see her and her family and introduce them to mine, to thank her for trying to get me the help I so desperately needed at the sacrifice of me abusing her, my friend, but yet I still ignorantly denied grabbing her extended hand of help! ***MAN DAMN!***

I feel like Tom Hanks in the movie "Castaway" when he is finally reunited with his fiancé after four years on a deserted island, and he learns she has moved forward and is married with a child and his fiancé told him not to get on the plane due to the inclement weather! She could see the storm before it arrived. He opted to go to work, thus right into the storm and a plane crash. Look at the price it cost both of them. I should have listened to her and got help! I still cannot believe I hurt her the way I did. She was somebody's baby and I had no right to harm God's property. I am so sorry! As a father of daughters, I cannot imagine anyone harming them! But yet I did that to her parents! I apologize with the sincerest gesture to her parents because they raised a quality human being fit for the very best man on the earth.

The truth though is it was not what was in God's plans! The Lord's Will had to be done! This means as much as I may have wanted and dreamed to be married to my teenage love Michelle, it wasn't in God's plans, or it simply wasn't meant to be! It was meant for both of us to meet our spouses, marry them, have children with them, raise these children, set them upright in life, have grandchildren, then retire together until we get to heaven together! It was God's plan for us to be exactly where we are supposed to be today! It was the only way for me to get healed!

I was so pissed at myself because I knew how great of a person, woman, friend and eventual wife and mother Michelle would be! I lost an incredible friend and future wife who never did anything wrong to me to deserve how I violently abused her mentally, physically, verbally, emotionally, and psychologically. She paid the price for a crime that she never committed...a price that belonged to me. I was not good enough to deserve her and the opportunity to parent our babies! I was not a mature enough and secure enough man for her at the time!

I had to surrender to the truth that she was meant for an individual who was as equally strong, mature, and authentic as her. God had to release her to her destiny without me. Why did I have to put her through such a horrid ordeal to know how to properly love myself and the next woman and women in my life? It was just a part of His great plan! Why did I wait so long? I should have kept her safe and protected!

This entire experience of domestic violence and abuse was only preparing me for the next chapter in my life to pay for what I had done to Michelle, our families, friends and to my future! The entire experience was to show me how to properly love myself and others, so I can show millions of others how to cope in life and how to love themselves and others properly, so they do not harm themselves, others and their legacies. This entire experience showed me how to be a secure man!

Michelle will always be a Godsent angel to me and the world! I pray that Michelle and her family one day forgives me because I will always be beyond sorry for harming her, her family and friends! I pray that she will forgive me for being such an evil and malicious person! I have already accepted that she does not owe me forgiveness for what I have done to her and her family and friends. I emphatically am sorry for harming her in every way that I did! I apologize! I was wrong to harm!

I thank Michelle for being my friend who truly showed me how to love appropriately! I only wish I knew then how to love her properly without violence and abuse because she certainly did not do anything to me to justify how I treated her! God, please forgive me!

She was truly a Godsent angel to a psychopathic narcissist who had given up on love and God! I am tremendously blessed to have met her, learned from her and her family and friends. I am beyond disappointed that I could treat someone so innocent and nice who always had my best interest. We will be judged by God one day based on how we loved and treated one another during our time here on earth! I pray he forgives me for how I treated His angels like Michelle and the many others!

I CAUSED- LOOK AT WHAT DOMESTIC VIOLENCE LEADS TO and CAUSES BECAUSE OF DOMESTIC VIOLENCE.........CHILD ABUSE and BULLYING...

I CAUSED SOMEONE TO LOOK OVER THEIR SHOULDER?

I CAUSED SOMEONE TO BE AFRAID & SCARED OF ME... TO HIDE FROM ME?

I CAUSED SOMEONE TO FLINCH WHEN I JUST WAIVED GOODBYE?

I CAUSED SOMEONE TO CALL THE AUTHORITIES ON ME?

I CAUSED SOMEONE TO CHANGE THEIR NAME?

I CAUSED SOMEONE TO CHANGE THEIR PHONE NUMBER and ADDRESS?

I CAUSED SOMEONE TO CHANGE THEIR JOB?

I CAUSED SOMEONE TO CHANGE THEIR RELIGION and HATE THEIR GOD?

I CAUSED SOMEONE TO BE MANIPULATED and CONTROLLED BY ME?

I CAUSED SOMEONE TO PURCHASE A GUN OR OTHER WEAPON?

I CAUSED SOMEONE TO LOVE SOMEONE ELSE?

I CAUSED SOMEONE TO VOTE FOR A STRANGER?

I CAUSED SOMEONE TO BE A LIAR TO LOVED ONES and FRIENDS?

I CAUSED SOMEONE TO TAKE ON A NEW PERSONALITY?

I CAUSED SOMEONE TO TAKE KARATE OR YOGA OR GUN CLASSES?

I CAUSED SOMEONE TO TAKE DRUGS OR ABUSE ALCOHOL?

I CAUSED SOMEONE TO PRAY AND TO NOT PRAY?

I CAUSED SOMEONE TO LOWER THEIR SELF ESTEEM?

I CAUSED SOMEONE TO COMMIT SUICIDE?

I CAUSED SOMEONE TO HATE THEMSELVES AND OTHERS?

I CAUSED SOMEONE TO BE SILENT and PUT ON PERMANENT MUTE?

I CAUSED SOMEONE TO HARM SOMEONE ELSE OR A PET ANIMAL?

I CAUSED SOMEONE TO TURN THEIR SMILE INTO A FROWN?

I CAUSED SOMEONE TO DRESS DIFFERENTLY?

I CAUSED SOMEONE TO WEAR A DIFFERENT HAIRSTYLE & MAKE-UP TOO?

I CAUSED SOMEONE TO HAVE SEX BY FORCE...NOT BY CHOICE?

I CAUSED SOMEONE TO RUN FOR THEIR LIFE?

I CAUSED SOMEONE TO CHANGE LAWS?

I CAUSED SOMEONE TO BE A VICTIM OF HOMICIDE OR FEMICIDE?

I CAUSED SOMEONE TO DRIVE HOME IMMEDIATELY?

I CAUSED SOMEONE TO CREATE A CYCLE OF VIOLENCE?

I CAUSED SOMEONE TO NOT MAKE EYE CONTACT?

I CAUSED SOMEONE TO COWER OR BE A COWARD?

I CAUSED SOMEONE TO LOSE AT LIFE?

I CAUSED SOMEONE TO GIVE UP ON DREAMING?

I CAUSED SOMEONE TO FEEL A CONSTANT THREAT OF DEATH?

I CAUSED SOMEONE TO WITHDRAW FROM SCHOOL and SOCIETY?

I CAUSED ALL THAT PAIN? NO WAY! NOT ME! NOT POSSIBLE! *YES, YOU!*

INGRAM INDUSTRIES INC.

E. BRONSON INGRAM
PRESIDENT

ONE BELLE MEADE PLACE, SUITE 1400
NASHVILLE, TENNESSEE 37202
TEL 615 474 2100   FAX 615 730 1001

August 31, 1989

Mr. Antoine Burgess
Ingram Distribution Group Inc.
8201-B Stayton Drive
Baltimore-Washington Industrial Park
Jessup, MD 20794

Dear Antoine:

I very much appreciate your nice letter and tee shirt. I enjoyed meeting you and the opportunity to have a visit at lunch and am delighted you were able to get a look at our Nashville operations and a little better understanding of what the rest of the company is about.

INROADS is giving you an opportunity to see what business is and how it works. If you really apply yourself, both during your internship as well as getting the very best education you can possibly absorb, there is unlimited opportunity for you to grow and advance at Ingram after you graduate. I hope and expect that we will do a good job in monitoring and supporting your internship but, in the last analysis, it is really up to you and how you apply the talent that you have. I hope you have a very successful upcoming school year and look forward hopefully to getting by Jessup next summer for another visit.

Sincerely,

Bronson Ingram

E. Bronson Ingram

/msd

MR. INGRAM WAS SIMPLY THE BEST! HE WAS A DREAM MAKER FOR MANY PEOPLE! HE BELIEVED IN ME WHEN I HAD VERY LITTLE REASON TO BELIEVE IN ANY HUMAN!

Solutions To Permanently Eradicate Domestic Violence, Child Abuse, and Bullying

IMPULSIVE MOMENTS THAT CHANGED MY LIFE

Think Twice! Don't Roll The Dice! You Choose! Prison Or Paradise?

On August 28th, 1991, four days prior to returning to Hampton University for my senior year of college, I had dinner with my girlfriend Michelle Thompson's parents. We were discussing me and Michelle's marital plans, Michelle's desire to be a schoolteacher, me going to law school in a JD-MBA program in the spring, grandchildren, and my future as a corporate attorney with Ingram Industries. I recall reminiscing with them about how I appreciated them so much for being as involved in my life to the point where I truly felt they were my actual parents. They were very helpful to me when my Mother and Grandmother threw me out of my home, thus making me homeless because my Mom and Grandma believed I "acted too white for them!" I was so excited to have them as my future in-laws and the thought of Michelle and my future as parents were even more elating.

I arrived in Hampton the very next evening, I was asked by Michelle that night to come over to her apartment because she desperately wanted to speak with me. Because I had such a long day of travel and unpacking, I insisted on the following morning. I arrived at her apartment the next morning eager to see my girlfriend. However, when I arrived at her place, she had an entirely different agenda. As I stepped in the doorway, I immediately saw all of my possessions and those I had given her over our 6-year relationship. As I sat down, she said, "So do you think you can have your cake and eat it too?" I exclaimed, "What are you talking about?" She repeated the same and so did I. Finally, she stated, "Well it does not matter at this point because you and I are over!" I commented several times, "Are you serious? You have got to be joking!" It wasn't until she told me to get out of her house or else she was going to call the police that I actually believed her. When I told her that "I was not going to leave until she gave me a real reason for ending our relationship" she decided to call her dad. Shortly after he spoke with her, he got on the phone with me and asked me to "leave the apartment until he could learn more about the situation." I told him "I would!" Before I left the apartment, I asked Michelle one last time to tell me, and she simply refused stating again that "I thought I could have my cake and eat it too!" In the act of utter frustration, I smacked her. Thinking she would tell me if I physically intimidated her I continued to smack her around. I only stopped when she curled up in the fetal position after I pushed her down a flight of steps. By the time I got to the bottom of the steps, I was filled with

Solutions To Permanently Eradicate Domestic Violence, Child Abuse, and Bullying

remorse and my eyes full of tears. She angelically said, "Please leave because I know my neighbors are calling the police and I do not want you to go to jail." After I got her to her feet, I hurried to my car. I got in my car and said to myself, "What the hell just happened? It is over for sure!" I drove home blind from the tears in my eyes.

As I sat in my condo, I now realized that I had just sensationally pushed away the last person on the earth that loved me and cared for me. She was there for me when I became homeless and had to ask to stay at a friend's home months later. She was there for me when I returned from Oklahoma State walking away from a once in a lifetime full scholarship and possible Major League Baseball contract. She was there when my Mother stated she "wished I was dead and that she hated me." And still, despite this violent assault, she did not call the police. Sadly, neither did the neighbors. The tragedy for me was that despite the attack, my mind was still selfishly fixated on why she left me. Huh? My mind was warped. I was sick as hell!

After a few weeks of harassing Michelle by phone, with little to no communication and eventually stalking her at her residence to no avail, I became a recluse. I constantly meditated on the fact that all my life I believed I had given the best to man and that all I ever got in return was the worst of man. All I ever experienced on an intimate level was loss and pain. In my life every time I opened up and confided in someone they either died or left me. I began to believe that the reason they left was that I had pushed them away. I dwelled in the bowels of self-pity to the point that I was incorrigible. I truly believed I was better off dead than alive. At least then I would not hurt and moreover hurt someone else at the expense of my actions. It was during these days that I believed suicide was my only way out.

I recall sitting in my apartment alone for weeks. The day I decided to take my life was dreary. I looked to the sky for a sign or answer. Damn, this must have been fate because all I saw were black clouds! I was drunk! Later that evening, as I prepared for my date with death, I had a gas can in one hand and a cigarette lighter in the other. As I began dousing myself with diesel duel, I knew this was the right thing to do. Unaware of the fact, I doused the lighter with so much gas that it would not ignite. I was so overwhelmed by the consumption of fumes that it knocked me out rendering me unconscious. Had it not been for the unbearable cries of my 6-month boxer pup Toby*, who was out on the balcony and was crying because it was so late in the early morning, dark, cold, and raining, forcing my neighbors to bang on the door, that eventually awakened me from my diesel and alcohol-induced sleep.

It was following that incident that I realized I would not be around long. However, I knew that before I left this earth, I had to let Michelle know that I was wrong for the way I mistreated her throughout our relationship. I was a spoiled, self-centered, immature young adult who believed the world and its inhabitants only appreciated you if they were the benefactors and could get something out of you—namely money. I always reacted impulsively without using any rationale thinking when I believed this to be true. I did not think about Michelle's feelings. Instead, I fed my impulsiveness to find out the truth as to why she left me and why she did not come to see me in the hospital.

I decided to go to her class and speak to her. When I saw her, she was amazed that I had lost so much weight. When you go days without eating those things happen because your mind is preoccupied on seemingly more important things than food. I demanded she speak to me and when she said "No! We'll talk later!" I took it as another brush off of hers and that because I was truly going to kill myself soon, I did not have that kind of time. I told her to "come with me in a serious intimidating tone." I grabbed her by her arm and insisted she come with me. She cowardly obliged and we proceeded to my car. I insisted all I wanted to do was talk to her. I know now that she believed I was going to hurt her because she kept asking me "Did I have a gun?" I kept assuring her that "I did not," but given the circumstances, I certainly see why she believed I did even when I did not.

I drove 3 hours from Hampton, Virginia to someplace in Maryland where we stayed at a hotel. The entire time in the car and the hotel room we talked. When we settled in the room, we continued to talk. She asked me could she use the phone because she "Did not want her roommate to worry!" I said, "of course." She proceeded with the call. She asked me "Could we leave early in the morning so that she could get to her early morning classes." I said "yes." Upon checkout around 6 am, we were greeted warmly by the checkout clerk and soon after by 2 FBI agents. They informed me that I "was being charged with abduction, use of a firearm in the commission of a felony, and assault with a deadly weapon." I insisted "I never had a gun," but they said, "because she believed I had one it was as good as having one."

As I sat in jail, mentally intoxicated from the thought of how my life had drastically changed in less than 30 days from that original meeting with Mr. and Mrs. Thompson, I could not get my mind off the fact that Michelle still had not told me why she had called it quits other than me having my cake and eating it too. I was desperate now to kill myself. After posting bond, my attorney sent me to Easton

State, a local psychiatric hospital to be evaluated. All they did was medicate me and let me sleep all day and night. Because I was committed voluntarily, I could leave at my discretion. After about two weeks of just lying around, I decided to leave.

My attorney believed that if I just stayed away from Michelle and focused on my future, she could get this situation resolved without me ever having to do any time and that she could get this situation expunged so that it would not affect my future as a corporate attorney. Upon her advice, I decided to withdraw from Hampton and enrolled at the University of Baltimore. I went back to Baltimore because of my Mother's and attorney's recommendation to the court, and so I began staying with the man I hated, Milton Dorsey, my Mother's estranged boyfriend and father of my younger brother Tony. I do not think I ever said more than 25 words the entire time I knew Mr. Dorsey, so going to his house was quite strange. I sat in his apartment for two weeks all alone because he was a commercial bus driver and stayed gone for weeks. The only thing different about me being alone this time was that two days upon my arrival to Mr. Dorsey's I stopped somewhere in Maryland near D.C. and bought my first legal gun. I had to wait for my registration to go through, and it did, because I had not been convicted of a crime at this point and so it never showed up. I felt like a one-year-old trying to take care of myself as I sat there with that gun. I should never have been left alone in that environment.

I was not in his apartment for 2 weeks when I received a page from a college friend from Hampton. He informed me that "the reason Michelle left you was that she was secretly having an affair with someone else and that it was she who was having her cake and eating it. She had no better way of telling me other than to make me feel it was my fault so that she did not look like a whore in front of her sorority sisters and parents." Yo! What? I blanked! I do not even remember hanging the phone up! I became nauseous to where I vomited on the door of my car trying to get it through the window. How could she do this to me is what I thought? I immediately headed south to Hampton! This was it! I knew then that I was going to see her one last time and then I was going to kill myself in front of her.

I knew I could not roll up on her so after enlisting the help of my friend Joe Parron we proceeded to Michelle's apartment. As it would be, as Joe pulled up, Michelle was getting out of her car. I do not even remember Joe stopping the car or me opening the door, and before I knew it I was out in front of Michelle crying like a baby with the gun to my head asking her "How did we get here?" I told her to "Get in the car with Joe so that we could go talk." She exclaimed, "I have to go to counseling therapy and that if I did not show up, they would think the worst!" I told her "Joe will drive you!" She got in but immediately said, "I am scared because of the gun!" I said, "The gun is for me and me only!" I emptied the bullets out and put the gun in my waistband. We proceeded to her destination where before she exited she said, "If you wait for my counseling to end I will return and talk to you!"

The rest is history. Joe and I waited in the car! The police soon arrived as if they had found an America's Most Wanted fugitive. I was placed into custody without bond this time. Other than the few times in court I never saw Michelle again. I was charged again with the same crimes of felony abduction and possession of a firearm in the commission of a crime. This time I was looking at a combined 36 years. My attorney threw her hands up with me as she took my money. The judge ordered/recommended an intense psycho evaluation after my sentencing to be conducted while in custody since he had sentenced me to only six years.

So I get to the penitentiary and not long thereafter I was sent to the *Central State Hospital in Petersburg, Virginia, a psychiatric hospital once named the Central Lunatic Asylum, that housed the criminally and mentally insane. It was the first institution in the country for "colored persons of unsound mind." Central State Hospital serves the Greater Richmond Region of Virginia, providing forensic psychiatry and civil admissions ranging from short-term treatment to long-term intensive treatment for the most seriously mentally ill.* [36]

After I was placed on a ward with the "Not Guilty By Reason of Insanity," I came to realize through sessions with my doctor that I was lucky to have gotten this far in life without killing myself or someone else. He brought out of me 21 plus years of trauma that just reached its epicenter. He discovered in me what I had been searching for all of my rational years of life. Remember when I told you earlier when I was 17 years old, during the McDonogh-Gilman game, when it dawned on me "What happened to my Father? Who was he? What did he do for a living?" I knew from my grandmother's account how he had died before I was born and that he had a bad temper because everyone said that is where I had got mine. I just did not know how his death had anything to do with me ending up in prison and the ward of a psychiatric hospital with the criminally insane. Why did she hate me? Not want me?

When I asked my Mom, remember, she immediately became overwhelmed with sadness and let out a cry from the inner sanctums of her soul. My grandmother went on to tell me that my father was shot and killed by the Baltimore police because he was trying to kill my Mom. The truth was, my Mom was pregnant with me and decided to break up with my father because he was beating her, spitting on her, and controlling her. She did not want to bring a child into this world only for it to see its father abuse its mother. She called it quits and told him that if he could ever change she may consider getting back with him. Beyond that, she was content on raising me with the help of her parents. My dad could not accept this and continuously threatened my Mother. He insisted on being in her life despite her continuous letters of rejection. So when It finally came to a head many months before I was to be born when my father appeared unannounced at my mom's house with a gun and then the eventual gunfire from my dad at the two young men leaving their home, it was my Mom who called the police. A chase and shootout ensued, and my father was shot and killed justifiably by the Baltimore police. I believed God took him from my life because God knew that only He, God Himself, was the only suitable Father for me and not my biological. Okay, so she called the police and feels she caused his death. How did I end up here? What did I do to pay for his crimes of abuse?

My mother always blamed herself for my dad's death because she made the call. She knew her son would grow up with no dad. She became a loner and eventually grew to be a drinker. She had a stillborn baby with a married man I never spoke ten words to in my life. It was shortly after that that my Mom tried to kill me by smothering me in my sleep. Had it not been for my aunt Annie keeping an eye on me and hearing my hand knocking against the wall and the curtain rod falling in my Mom's room awakening my aunt, and the blood of Jesus on my and my Mom's life, I would not be here today. I still do not for sure, but I believe my Mom went away for a small-time. Where I do not know! We have never discussed the matter.

But to add injury to insult, the very aunt who came to my rescue ended up carrying the violence and abuse torch by being the very person to begin using me as a source to abuse and torture since she was or had been tortured from the men in her life and the hands she was being dealt in life such as being unemployed and on food stamps. She took out everything violently on me. Both were in past and current traumatic relationships where they were horrifically abused or abandoned. What she and my mother also taught me were the protocols on what to do after violence occurs when you are the victim of abuse in these violent encounters in that "What goes on in this house stays in this house!" and how to stay on mute and self-silence to violence and internalize these events and go on to conduct business as usual as if these events never occurred and that there would be further consequences if I said what happened to me to anyone like my Grandmother who worked the second shift, 3:30 p.m. to midnight, Monday to Friday. This was intimidation and bullying!

What they gave me was the blueprint on how to justifiably and violently abuse women and how to cover it up by using bullying and empathy to convince your victim that you will not do this to them again. According to my Aunt, "It was never okay to hit a girl, but it was okay to smack a b****!" Man, that was confusing advice to me, but it became a justifiable position to take when I conveniently wanted to pull it out. My uncles, older cousins, and other family friends told me that "A man never cries, and a man never kisses or holds a chick's hand in public, because if he does, he is a punk a** b**** who was a soft muthaf****** gay N-word, faggot a** b****!" It now made sense when I called Michelle a b**** for thinking I was a soft, faggot a** b**** or gay N-word for wanting to hold my hand at the mall because all that rang in my head was my aunt, uncle, and other family friend's advice about dealing with women and other people. But again, I wondered why am I sitting in a penitentiary psychiatric hospital talking with a mental doctor? Children do learn what they live. Not all kids take such experiences and become abusive! I did!

The problem was, no one got me help! I was left to my own resolve as a child to come up with my own solutions to my abusive behavior. Until the phenomenal doctor pulled these stories out of me, I never realized these traumatic incidents in my life, along with no parental discretion and the endless first-hand accounts and exposure to domestic violence, demeaning words and mind games, torturous situations, unaccountable weak men, violence against dogs, racist hate crimes, exposure to adultery, cheating, pornography, gay and lesbian lifestyles, drug selling, drug usage, horror movies, gambling, alcoholism, adultery, suicide, family court drama, child rape, a stillborn baby brother, my 7th grade classmate, Ceres, Brandon, Boonie and Darell's death, would become so suppressed in me that they would affect my life later down the road with all my relationships personally and corporately, especially the individuals who were closest to me like my Mom, Aunt, Uncle, Teeny, Michelle, classmates, school-age friends, and my dog Toby*.

The violence only worsened for me when my aunt thought it was funny to try and scare me and my cousins by punishing us by having us retreat to the basement in the complete dark to have us sit there in the dark on the steps as if we were in concentration camps or walk completely in the dark to the back of the basement to touch the far-off distant wall. When her scare tactics only worked on my cousins by making them cry, the game no longer became funny when I never cried or displayed any fear. The game became totally focused on me and how do I break this little boy's will since he is not scared of anything? This was when the punches and slaps and spitting in the face started showing up and getting hit in the head or face with rotary house phones or anything else meant to knock a child's block off. I imagine she was trying to beat me into submission as a bully does. In my mind, all I could ever think was, "As soon as I get big enough and strong enough, I am going to beat these b*****s into the dirt! My mom for trying to kill me, embarrass me, and not protect me! My aunt for trying to torture and emasculate me! And my uncle just because he is a straight-up punk a** b**** who thinks he can get away with intimidating my cousins and me, along with stealing my money and clothes! I swear to God I am going to try and kill them as soon as it is humanly possible for me to do so!" This was when I began to work out and get stronger as an athlete. The reason why I was never scared of or feared anything was mentally I was already dead and had nothing to live for any way or no one who would care if I was alive or dead. When your mother tries to kill you and then does not believe you when you tell her of the torturous things her siblings are doing to you, you stop giving a flying flip about life. Then to make matters more confusing, your aunt, the person who saved you from the hands of death from your mom, goes on to torture and fight you. The rage just continued to grow! This rage served me well as the school and neighborhood bully and an even greater threat on the football and baseball field.

All my mother and family ever spoke to me about my father was the tongue of death and not life. Little boys often emulate their dads regardless of if their dads are heroes or zeroes. When my family and their friends always told me, "You are mean just like your father. You are as evil as your dad. You think you are all that just like your dad? You are a high yellow piece of crap!" I should have flushed you down the toilet!" I began taking on the very things they hated because I knew it would hurt them because that was my way of harming people who harmed me. The problem was I did not even realize that I was acting like them when I was dealing with others close to me. It turns out in my case that I was emulating a whole bunch of people for all the wrong reasons. I became what I was living! Continue the cycle!

Therapy sessions pulled this garbage out of my life and more importantly out of my mind. I got on the road to recovery and never looked back. I credit the Lord for my deliverance into the spirit of truth. Through the mercy and grace of Jesus, the judge suspended 30 years on sentencing day and sentenced me to 6 years in prison. In retrospect, I did not think of the consequences and how my actions would not only affect Michelle's feelings, her liberty, and her wellbeing but her parent's feelings as well. My gun was legal because it was a registered Maryland firearm, but because I had communicated a threat with it in Virginia, I was absolutely guilty. I was more concerned about my feelings than her feelings. The bottom line was that I was out of line, out of control, and truly in the wrong.

I was wrong for forcing my will on her. All of my young life I had been accustomed to people catering to me and doing whatever I pleased. I was an All-American High School athlete who had his choice in going to just about any college in America. I had been a great athlete since I was seven years old. It was through sports that I began to see how people showed favoritism to the best players. It was through sports that I saw how people "help" star athletes. It was this "help" that changed the rules for me and got me special consideration when I needed "help."

It was this "help" that was a deadly formula for me as a young athlete because I became conditioned to believe that this was how the ball bounced in life. What happened was I believed that I did not have to have a respect for authority, rules, or protocol because when it came to me, none of those things applied. I truly lacked respect for my family and friends because I viewed them as piranhas that were looking at me as a payday and for what I could do for them. I know now that those people at that time who were close to me—such as my mother, my cousin Teeny, and Michelle really did care about me—I did not respect myself and had fallen out of love with me. I had become my Father and all my young life I believed I would never be that man. As hard as I fought not to be him, I became him and did not realize it until it was almost too late to save my soul and moreover, my life!

I battled the spirits of trying to understand how can you love and respect anyone if no one who is supposed to love you ever shows you how to properly love and respect another person and also if you first do not love and respect yourself? How could I have ever expected them to draw near to me and love me accordingly? I had no humility and lacked self-control. They did not deserve my psychotic tantrums and maltreatment. As extremely phenomenal as I was as an athlete, I was as extremely bad to the ones who were close to me and loved me. The confusing part was I could not figure out why I treated them so bad. What was the issue?

During the early days of my incarceration, I would be in total disbelief like how in the hell did I end up here when I should be in college right now finishing my senior year of classes and enjoying all the festivities with my classmates and my girlfriend? I literally remember being dazed and confused until the concrete and steel or the electronic prison doors or the profane words of a jail or prison philosopher quickly reminds you where you are! I initially thought, "How could Michelle put me in here? All the years together and the sacrifices I made for her, and this is how I am repaid? I thought about how for the last two years of high school I remained loyal to her when she and her family moved to Barbados for her dad's job. I thought about all the opportunities of sex and other experiences with other girls I passed on out of my commitment and loyalty to her! I thought about how I missed her so much that I foolishly left a full scholarship at Oklahoma State and moreover, the chance to play for the Baltimore Orioles, to join her at Hampton University! How I remained loyal to her, and she did not reciprocate loyalty back to me! As I write these statements today, I write these words in disgust, shame, and in tears! It should have never been a notion of "How could she put me in here?" I put myself there! She is not the blame nor the excuse! I did this on my own accord and forced my controlling and impulsive will upon her, and consequently, I ended up in the penitentiary! How or why did I do this to myself, my future, my legacy and most importantly, my friend Michelle? Love for myself should have been my first and only thoughts? I was beyond arrogant and ignorant, but in hindsight, I was more blasphemous, selfish, unaccountable, & not concerned about the welfare of Michelle or anyone else for that matter. I put myself in jail, prison, and the mental hospital!

I foolishly left Oklahoma State due to being injured and bored with sports, a tad lovesick, no parental guidance and support, and although I knew I had the focused discipline and structure to play college sports on the highest stage to be drafted by the Orioles, my focus was off center and set on being with her! She made sacrifices too during the last two years of high school, and with certainty she was loyal too and truthfully, knowing what I know and believe now, she never owed me anything as significant as a reciprocation of loyalty and sacrifices as one has as a married individual! She did not make vows to God or me, pledging her loyalty and sacrifices. Had I been more mature and even more equipped with better coping skills and asking for help by way of counseling, I would have known that her word and character alone should have been sufficient enough for me to accept as her friend! I should have been focusing on my God-given talents of hitting home runs out of the park as a player for the Oklahoma State Cowboys or the Baltimore Orioles instead of violently hitting and putting my hands-on Michelle! I caused my own destruction, not her. She told me the relationship was over and that should have been enough! But no! I needed a justifiable reason for the split, and I could not see that the violence, abuse, mind games, disrespect, & humiliation were not good enough. She had every right to leave a lying, abusive & violent person, not a man, like me! Why did I not listen to her? Also, when a woman says, "She loves you, but she is not in love with you!" that is the statement of death! Today, the only and best advice I can offer anyone is ***"Why would you want to be with someone who does not want to be with you? You cannot make someone love you who does not want to love you!"***

I thought the worst of my girlfriend and women in general when I should have been thinking the best of her, trusting and believing her versus being jealous and having distasteful images in my head of her and someone else! She was not the one who gave her friend a reason to doubt the sanctity of the relationship. It was me! I was the one who was cheating and lying and manipulative. I was the insecure one. I was the one not playing by the rules! I was not worthy to have a gem of a human being with such an angelic spirit. I was a lame bully and coward who did not keep the unwritten promise of a genuine friend to love and be true always and forever. She was sweet, and I was bitter! I was having my cake and eating it too.

The entire time she was in Barbados my mind wondered what she was doing and who she was doing versus thinking the best of her as a loyal friend. What is sad is to know now that being in control is not worrying about what you cannot control and really only giving attention to what matters need controlling. I did not own her and was not married to her, and even if I were married to her, it still would not have given me the right to try and control her. She was God's property, and I had no right to disrespect or damage His priceless possession! She had the right not to tell me or explain in great detail or justify to me why she was ending the relationship. It is like firing an employee in an "At-Will" state in that she could legally fire me without cause. She had free will to let me go. My will should have let her go freely!

I was so damn diabolical, egotistical and blind to the simple fact that I was a horrible boyfriend and friend who was a domestic violence offender and abuser of multiple types such as physical, verbal, psychological(mental), and emotional. I was a habitual offender who made it more difficult for her after each offense to want me in any capacity. I kept chipping away at her esteem and the foundation of our friendship until there was nothing worth standing in the remote resemblance of love. How was she to ease the pain after each horrendous moment of abuse? How ridiculous and remarkable that I expected her to smile and be jovial or better yet, lovey dubby or huggie after my offensive behavior. I guess after someone smacks you in the face and tells you are a piece of crap that you should smile and act like you are saying your vows to one another. My expectations were warped!

Man, that is just so damn cruel, unusual, inhumane, evil and beyond ridiculous on my behalf to treat a friend, as well-intentioned as she was, for my welfare. How could I do that to her of all the people on the planet? She was the soldier in the relationship who knew the value of her life. She was the warrior who saved my life with her formidable behavior to say ***ENOUGH IS ENOUGH!*** She knew this would probably be the only way I would receive the necessary help for my life. How could I do this to her and her family and friends? How could I do this?

God's Will is powerful! He always puts me where I am supposed to be and with the people who I am supposed to be around. It was not His destiny for us to be together as husband and wife! I told her and many others my entire young life that I was going to have only girls as children and a set of twins in that mix. I always assumed they would be with her, but God had a higher and different place and plan for both of our lives. His plan was more significant so we could serve others and make an even more positive impact in the lives of people God chose for us. I regret not listening to Michelle, my friend, a best friend, who suggested I get counseling throughout our relationship! By not listening to her and not trusting that she had my best interest, it did not just cost me a trip to the penitentiary and psychiatric hospital, it cost me an incredible legacy and friendship with a person who ultimately had my best interest in mind and was 1000% right about me getting help to get mentally healthy! She was right, and I was wrong for harming her and the people who loved her. I pray one day she and everyone she's connected to will be able to forgive me.

She was either breaking up with me, or at the victim's impact statement to the judge before he formally sentenced me, when she stated that "Antoine was going to be a great "FAMILY MAN™ and provider," it's just that "He was not the one for me," and that "she had moved on successfully with her life and that I had to do the same with mine and with counseling!" These were words that I did not want to hear at the moment, but words that were intended for the right reasons and without maliciousness. She was right in the sense that I would be a great FAMILY MAN™, but little did I know I would end my life as "The FAMILY MAN™" making an impact to save the lives and legacies of women, children, animals, and their abusers!

I struggled with trying to figure out why I abused my girlfriend and those closest to me. Trying to unlock that puzzle in my head was like trying to figure out the Pythagorean Theory or Rubik's Cube the very first time you are introduced to it.

Of course, for me, that solution was not discovered until after I was in the penitentiary and psychiatric hospital when everything that was good and profitable for me and my future, personally and professionally, had already disappeared never to return like Michelle and law school. Can you imagine a magician calling to the stage volunteers from the audience for his disappearing trick and after he swings his magic wand over the box they are contained in and chants out the expression, "Voila! Poof! Be Gone!" As he pulls back the curtain, the crowd bellows, "Oohs and Ahhs!" His performance wows them. But how will they respond and what will they say if his willing participants and volunteers from the audience never reappear or are never seen alive again? That is how I feel about what I did to Michelle and my future with her and Ingram Industries both personally and professionally. I did that at my own free will to loving and willing participants and volunteers in my life and future? My controlling behavior, or better yet, my out of control behavior now has the key to unlock the mystery to my nefarious history and the people who paid the ultimate price and sacrifice cannot benefit because of me! I will live with that for the rest of my life. My apologies will never be enough, so my actions have to speak for me even well after I am no longer on the earth. Quite frankly, Michelle's parents raised two angels, and I am just fortunate enough to say that I thank God for sending Michelle and her family, to show me how to love another properly.

I had to go to prison and be on a psych ward to find out that I did not have any coping skills. I did not know how to lose properly. I never found grace in being second at anything. I could criticize any, and all individuals but could never take an ounce of criticism about myself. I always hurt the ones who loved me. I cared about a few people in life because only a few people ever cared about me. My dad, who was shot and killed by the police, died before I was born. My mother tried to kill me by smothering me when I was a toddler. I witnessed my aunts get physically abused. I still hurt over my mom losing my little stillborn brother Anthony! I literally fought my aunts and uncles as a child as though I were a grown man. I punished my cousins physically and mentally. I truly despised my Mother for her alcoholic binges and her weekend gambling sprees. Her DWI with me in the back of the car was painful to witness firsthand. I hated that she never came to my games but hated her more when she showed up in a drunken stupor beyond embarrassing. I suppressed these incidents without knowing how to deal with them. I never dealt with any of those issues until I arrived in prison and the State Hospital in Petersburg. Thank God for the excellent treatment I received from the prison counselors and Dr. Miller Ryans*, my psychiatrist. I was able to effectively deal with those issues and move on with my life. I wish I had spoken to a school counselor or therapist earlier in my life!

I am sincerely sorry that I put Michelle through such chaos because I did not know how to function in any relationship properly. To date, and forevermore, I will never use my early childhood experiences as an excuse for maltreatment and misbehavior towards any individual. *"Excuses are tools of the incompetent, which builds monuments of nothingness, and those who specialize in using them seldom accomplish anything."—Anonymous!* Thanks to the Qs for introducing this poem!

I should have been more mature about the situation. I am truly sorry for my actions against her and live each day regretting the horrible choices I made. I should have gotten clinical help, of which she recommended to me time and time again prior to the incident, to deal with the issues I possessed at the time. I was a mental and physical manipulator. If I did not get my way I would play mind games and if put to a pinch I would fight the ones (man or woman) who were close to me. I would push away the most important people in my life and did not understand why.

After proper counseling sessions, prison and medical officials exclaimed: "I was a fish out of water in prison because of my positive attitude, future outlook, and resolve of the situation regarding Michelle and my Mom." They were "surprised that I had made it this far with much success given the disturbing ordeals I had experienced as a child." With their recommendations and support, I was early paroled on January 7, 1993, after serving only 14 months of my 6-year sentence. I was on parole for approximately two years and have had zero contact with Michelle. I have never been arrested for anything since being paroled and will never associate with anyone who is negative. I reunited with some of my family before my release, and they have been an instrumental part of my life ever since.

I immediately found work selling cars for incredible companies such as Walden and Hall Automotive, Bowditch Ford, Casey Automotive Group, and Hendrick Automotive Group. I enrolled at Old Dominion University and became a volunteer at the Friends of the Homeless shelter in Newport News, Virginia. I have been married for nearly three decades to the finest and most ferocious woman on the planet, am a father to 4 amazingly beautiful, witty, and exceptionally brilliant daughters, and 2 grandsons who are shining examples of God's love. I love my family dearly and do everything to provide a safe, secure, mentally healthy, balanced and loving environment. I will never take my mental health for granted because in doing so I will compromise everything of significance to my life that is not for sale!

I cringe at the thought of abusing my wife or anyone abusing my daughters the way I treated my former friend Michelle. She never deserved to be treated in the manner I treated her. Some days I sit and ponder that had I never did what I did to her, I would have at least had a chance to still be her friend. I even blew the chance to tell her how truly sorry I was for negatively impacting and inconveniencing her life. She was a kind and sincere person who deserved a better life mate than me. I wish I were a fraction of the person than who I am now. I will never satisfy my debt to society until no innocent individual, child, or animal suffers or dies from domestic violence, child abuse or bullying. For that reason alone I will always be encouraged and enthused to be an active and productive part of my community, family, state, and government and be an advocate to ensure violence, abuse, and bullying are permanently eradicated. My life and legacy will prove how much I loved mankind!

HUMANITY, I NEED YOUR HELP! WILL YOU PLEASE FORGIVE ME FOR MY VIOLENT PAST? I WILL SHOW THE WORLD MY COMMITMENT TO PERMANENTLY ERADICATE DOMESTIC VIOLENCE, CHILD ABUSE, and BULLYING, SO WE CAN TOGETHER HELP SAVE THE LIVES AND LEGACIES OF INNOCENT PEOPLE LIVING IN FEAR AND THOSE INDIVIDUALS SUFFERING FROM MENTAL ILLNESS! PLEASE HELP!

Solutions To Permanently Eradicate Domestic Violence, Child Abuse, and Bullying

I WAS EXCEEDINGLY GREAT AT GETTING SOMEONE TO FALL IN LOVE WITH ME, BUT I WAS HORRIFIC AT GETTING SOMEONE TO STAY IN LOVE WITH ME. IT WAS NOT A MATTER OF IF I WAS GOING TO PUSH THEM AWAY, IT WAS A MATTER OF HOW SOON THEY WOULD LEAVE. EVERY PERSON CLOSE TO ME ALWAYS LEFT ME, SO I WAS TO ASSUME THAT I WAS ALWAYS THE REASON FOR THEM LEAVING AND THAT THEY WOULD EVENTUALLY LEAVE BY THEIR CHOICE OR BY MY FORCE OF ABUSE!

DOMESTIC VIOLENCE COST ME SOME INCREDIBLE RELATIONSHIPS WITH PHENOMENAL PEOPLE! IT WAS NOT MEANT FOR ME TO BE IN THEIR LIVES, NOR THEY IN MINE! I TRUST...

FROM THE CHAIRMAN OF THE BOARD- PHILIP M. PFEFFER

INGRAM

INGRAM DISTRIBUTION GROUP INC.
347 Reedwood Drive · Nashville, TN 37217
(615) 361-5001

Philip M. Pfeffer
Chairman of the Board

August 23, 1989

Mr. Antoine Burgess
Ingram Distribution Group Inc.
8201-B Stayton Drive
Jessup, MD 20794

Dear Antoine:

Thank you very much for your note of August 21 and the enclosed t-shirt. I enjoy sailing very much and a t-shirt with a sailboat is just right.

I enjoyed meeting you in Nashville and I am delighted that you had a opportunity to visit our operations here. I hope that you learned a lot about our company during your visit.

I am delighted to have you on board and I look forward to working with you in the years ahead.

With best regards.

Sincerely,

Philip M. Pfeffer

jfh

John M. Donnelly, Jr. Closes 34 Year Career With Ingram Industries Inc.

John M. Donnelly, Jr. closed a 34-year career with Ingram on July 1. His career began in 1955 with the Ingram Oil and Refining Company. In 1963, he became active in the barge business and was subsequently named Executive Vice President, President and then Vice Chairman of the Board of Ingram Barge Company.

At the time of his retirement, he served as a Director and Executive Vice President of Ingram Industries Inc.

"John Donnelly and I started at Ingram together in 1955 and we have been close friends and, in effect, business partners ever since," said Bronson Ingram, President of Ingram Industries Inc. "I will truly miss his ready support and wise counsel while continuing to enjoy our friendship."

Donnelly was a founding board member and later Chairman of the Board of The National River Academy in Helena, Arkansas. In 1980, he served as Chairman of the Board of the American Waterways Operators, the national trade organization for the barge and towing industry, and, since then has continued to serve on the board of that organization. More recently, he has held the office of vice chairman of the Board of Directors of Goodwill Industries in Nashville and currently is a vice chairman of the President's Committee for the Nashville Chamber of Commerce.

A native Nashvillian, Donnelly was a 1951 graduate from Vanderbilt University and also attended Naval Officer Candidate School in Newport, Rhode Island.

Bigach Joins Ingram Video

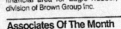

Jeff Bigach has joined Ingram Video Inc. as Vice President of Finance and Administration. Making the announcement was John Taylor, President.

Bigach comes to Ingram from Aladdin Industries, the Nashville-based manufacturer of housewares, where he was controller for the consumer products division. He has also worked in the financial area for Eagle Rubber, a division of Brown Group Inc.

Associates Of The Month

April: Martha Lee, Senior Telephone Sales Representative, Ingram Book Company

May: Clint Grandstaff, Facility Services, Ingram Distribution Group Inc.

Recent Retirements

Alfonso P. Custodio, Ingram Distribution Group Inc.

Joy Lindsley, Ingram Distribution Group Inc.

Albert J. Pavolini, Ingram Barge Co.

Carl H. Seale, Ingram Barge Company

William Simpkins, Ingram Barge Co.

Ingram Materials Joins In At Kirkpatrick's Field Day

Kirkpatrick Elementary School in Nashville is Ingram Materials Company's adopted school through the Project Pencil program. On May 11 and 12, Ingram took part in the school's Field Day activities by furnishing ribbons and candy to the kindergarten through 4th grade students.

The prizes and goodies were distributed by "Dofuss the Clown," Mike McCluskey, Equipment Inspector Trainee at Ingram Materials. McCluskey and other Ingram associates were present both days of the event.

Ingram Materials' Project Pencil Coordinator Ronnie Pritchard coordinated the annual event. According to Pritchard, plans are underway for the next school year, and they include a continuation of the tutoring program.

Three Students Added To INROADS Program

Three students have been added to Ingram's INROADS internship program — Brent Taylor, Jonathan Chihorek and Antoine Burgess.

Taylor is interning with Ingram Barge Company in Nashville. He will be working in the Claims area under the guidance of Larry Hays, Manager of Claims and Safety. A graduate of McGavock High School, Taylor begins his freshman year at Tennessee State University this fall.

Chihorek is a first-time intern with Ingram Micro D – West. He is working as an Associate Sales Representative in telemarketing. A graduate of Mission Viejo High School, Chihorek will be attending the University of California at Berkley this fall, majoring in Marketing.

Burgess is the first INROADS intern in the Jessup distribution center of Ingram Book Company. His summer will be spent working in various positions throughout the faciltiy. A native of Randallstown, Maryland, he graduated from McDonogh School and is a freshman majoring in Finance at Hampton University in Hampton, Virginia.

INROADS is a national career development organization for minority youth. Ingram has been supporting INROADS for over 10 years.

Bettle Knight Retires

On June 23, Bettie Knight closed a career spanning over 20 years.

She first joined Ingram in 1965 and has worked continuously in Employee Benefits and with Tennessee Insurance Company since 1970.

For over 10 years, Knight handled Payroll in Employee Benefits. Transferring to Tennessee Insurance Company following the purchase of that company, she remained there until her retirement, holding the position of Executive Administrative Assistant.

Bettie Knight (seated) with long-time friends and coworkers from Ingram Industries and Tennessee Insurance.

Solutions To Permanently Eradicate Domestic Violence, Child Abuse, and Bullying

37

E. BRONSON INGRAM 1931 – 1995~Artist:Ann Street~ Date Created:1996 Owner/Location:Vanderbilt

Attending Vanderbilt one year, Bronson Ingram received a B.A. degree from Princeton University in 1953. Having become a trustee on Vanderbilt's Board of Trust in 1967, he served as Vice President from 1988 to 1991 and President from 1991 until his death in 1995. Mr. Ingram formed one of the nation's largest and most successful privately held companies, Ingram Industries, Inc. He and his family endowed four faculty chairs in three Vanderbilt schools; endowed scholarships in women's and men's golf; endowed the Orrin Henry Ingram Scholarship in Engineering Management; made gift for various research projects in the School of Medicine; and endowed the Ingram Scholars Program in 1994, one of Vanderbilt's largest gifts. Named in his memory are the Vanderbilt-Ingram Cancer Center and the Ingram Studio Arts Center.

Solutions To Permanently Eradicate Domestic Violence, Child Abuse, and Bullying

38

BURGESS, ANTOINE WILLIAM

Baltimore, Maryland; Student, Vice-President Trainee; b: Aug 4, 1970; p: James Thompson and Delores Burgess; ed; Hampton Inst, BS in Bus Fin 1988-92; career: Ingram Indus, Inroads Intern, Operations VP Trainee 1989-; Vector Mktg Corp, Sales Rep 1987–89; civic: Inroads-Baltimore Intern Org 1989-; Fin Mgr. of Am Assn, VP 1988-; Tutorial Service for Dysfunctional Blk Youths 1986-90; Maryland Sp Olympics Vol 1984-; Rosewood State Mental Hosp, Vol 1985-; Meals on Wheels 1987-; Maryland Salvation Army Soup Shelter Home 1986-89; Students Against Drunk Driving 1987-91, Pres 1989-90;FCA 1984-88, Pres 1985-87; honors: City of Baltimore Comm Serv, Vol of the Yr. Award 1989; Rosewood State Mental Hospital, C. Markland and Kelly Award 1988; Inroads Inc, Intern Training Award 1991; Ingram Indus, Distinguished Intern Award 1990.

➢ I received this award while in the Southampton Correctional Center!

➢ I was incredibly upset at myself that day for letting so many people down!

I ALWAYS WANTED TO BE A WANTED PERSON…NOT WANTED* BY POLICE

WANTED

ANTOINE W. BURGESS

Description: Ht.- 5'11", Weight - 195 lbs , skin- Light Brown
Eyes- Brown, Hair- Black/curly, Scars- None
Aliases - Toine, B∘More, Sèchue, Cadrè , DOB-8/4/70

Burgess is wanted on felony charges for the abduction of Michelle M. Thompson and misuse of a firearm. These crimes occurred on October 28,1991 and November 13,1991. For any information leading to his arrest, please contact the Hampton Crime Line at 722-3844. A $10,000 cash reward is being offered.

SKETCH BY MY CELL MATE DARNELL ROGERS

Solutions To Permanently Eradicate Domestic Violence, Child Abuse, and Bullying

39

Commonwealth of Virginia

WARRANT OF ARREST

FELONY

☐ EXECUTED by arresting the Accused
☒ named above on this day:

....11/14/91.... 9:51pm....
.... DATE AND TIME

....
.... ARRESTING OFFICER

....
BADGE NO., AGENCY, AND JURISDICTION

DEBORAH S. ROE
Attorney at Law

Patrick B. McDermott, P.C.
532 Settlers Landing Road
Hampton, Virginia 23669

(804) 722-0611
FAX (804) 722-1312

WARRANT OF ARREST — FELONY

← Hampton ....
CITY OR COUNTY

Co. Traam .... VA. CODE ANN. §19.2-71, -72

General District Court   ☒ Criminal   ☐ Traffic
☐ Juvenile and Domestic Relations District Court

TO ANY AUTHORIZED OFFICER:
You are hereby commanded in the name of the Commonwealth of Virginia forthwith to arrest and bring the Accused before this Court to answer the charge that the Accused, within this city or county, on

or about.... 11-14-91 ....
DATE

....did unlawfully and feloniously in violation of Section

18.2-47 .... Code of Virginia: Abduct Michelle

M. Thompson By Force Threat or

Intimidation, deception And without

Legal justification access, with the

Intent to deprive such persona of

her liberty

WARRANT OF ARREST — FELONY

← Hampton ....
CITY OR COUNTY

VA. CODE ANN. §19.2-71, -72

General District Court   ☒ Criminal   ☐ Traffic
☐ Juvenile and Domestic Relations District Court

TO ANY AUTHORIZED OFFICER:
You are hereby commanded in the name of the Commonwealth of Virginia forthwith to arrest and bring the Accused before this Court to answer the charge that the Accused, within this city or county, on

or about.... 11-14-91 ....
DATE

....did unlawfully and feloniously in violation of Section

18.2-53.1 .... Code of Virginia: Use A Firearm

in the commiss of a felony while

Abduct

1 OF 4 FELONY WARRANTS FOR MY ARREST

Solutions To Permanently Eradicate Domestic Violence, Child Abuse, and Bullying

```
                              DEPARTMENT OF CORRECTIONS               13:51.3
                              DIVISION OF ADULT SERVICES
                              UNIFORM COMMITMENT REPORT

                         ** L E G A L    U P D A T E **
    PAGE  1
                                                CURRENT DATE: 11/18/92
    STATUS: ACTIVE                              CLERK ID: JAK
                                                VERIFICATION CLERK ID: CAC

    INMATE NUMBER:  196546    NAME:  BURGESS         ANTOINE     WILLIAM

    CURRENT LOCATION:  SOUTHAMPTON RECEIVING UNIT     DATE RECEIVED:  10JUL1992

    JAIL CREDIT DAYS: 00240    JAIL GOOD TIME: 00120    SEN START DATE:  13NOV1991

    GCA LEVEL:  2  20/30  TOTAL SENTENCE:   006 YEARS  00  MONTHS  000 DAYS

    ANTICIPATED DISCRETIONARY PAROLE ELIGIBILITY DATE:                05JAN1993
    ANTICIPATED MANDATORY PAROLE RELEASE DATE WITH 00 ADJ-DISCHG DAYS:  19MAR1995



    THE ABOVE ANTICIPATED DATES ARE BASED ON THE ASSUMPTION THAT YOU WILL CON-
    TINUE TO EARN GOOD TIME AT YOUR PRESENT EARNING LEVEL AND THAT YOU WILL NOT
    HAVE EARNED GOOD TIME TAKEN FROM YOU BY AN ADJUSTMENT COMMITTEE ACTION AS A
    RESULT OF MISBEHAVIOR.  LOSS OF EARNED GOOD TIME OR A CHANGE IN YOUR GOOD
    TIME EARNING LEVEL MAY CAUSE YOUR ANTICIPATED DATES TO CHANGE.

    EVENTS LISTED BELOW IN DATE ORDER REFLECT TRANSACTIONS AFFECTING ANTICIPATED
    DATES OF ELIGIBILITY AND RELEASE SINCETHE LAST UPDATE ON
    SEPTEMBER 03, 1992.

    14OCT1992    ADJUSTMENT COMMITTEE ACTION:  POSSESSION OF CONTRABAND
                 THIS REPORT ORDERS THE LOSS OF 00000 GOOD TIME DAYS.
                 PENALIZED 0000 DAYS; 00000 TOTAL DAYS LOST FOR PAROLE TO DATE .
                 PENALIZED 0000 DAYS; 00000 TOTAL DAYS LOST FOR RELEASE TO DATE .
                 UNEARNED-PAROLE: 0000 TOTAL: 0000;  -RELEASE: 0000 TOTAL: 0000
                 00 DAYS IN ISOLATION         00 DAYS IN PREDETENTION
                 OTHER PENALTY:REPRIMAND
```

6 YEAR SENTENCE FOR A PREVENTABLE CAUSE...*MAN DAMN!*

Solutions To Permanently Eradicate Domestic Violence, Child Abuse, and Bullying

XII. YOU MUST _NOT_ HAVE BEEN CONVICTED OF A FELONY.

connected with the production, administration, judging, or distribution of the Program such that his or her participation in the Program could create the appearance of impropriety.

IX. If you are selected as a participant, you must be willing to travel to and reside at one (1) or more undisclosed locations in the United States for up to six (6) weeks in August/September/October, 2010 (or as otherwise scheduled by Producer). Economy travel to be paid by Producer.

X. You must not currently be a party to any pre-existing contractual obligations with any third party that would prevent you from participating in the Program, prevent Producer and OWN from exploiting any and all rights granted by you (if chosen) in connection with the exploitation of the Program and/or prevent you from entering into a talent hold agreement with OWN.

XI. You must not currently be signed to a hosting or talent holding deal with a television network/channel, production company or other television related entity.

XII. You must **not** have been convicted of a felony.

XIII. Producer reserves the right in its sole discretion to change or amend any or all of the eligibility requirements set forth above at any time.

Have you at any time been convicted of a felony, sanctioned by any professional ethics body, licensing board or other regulatory body or by any professional or scientific organization?

☐   No

☐   Yes

Please explain in the space below. Your application will be reviewed by the Ethics Committee, which will contact you for further information within four weeks of receipt. As a result, the review of your application may be delayed. For more information about the review process, see Review of Applications for Membership or Affiliation in *** by the Ethics Committee.

I NEVER WANT YOU TO EVER HAVE TO CHECK YES OR BE REJECTED!

(HERE IS AN ACTUAL SIGN POSTED IN A HAIR SCHOOL WHERE I WENT TO GET MY HAIR CUT BECAUSE THEY WERE SOLICITING VOLUNTEERS TO HELP THE STUDENTS GET CREDIT HOURS AND VALUABLE HAIR LESSONS)

Currently the Hairstyling Institute of Charlotte, Inc. & Metropolitan Hair Academy are NOT excepting any convicted felons. If you are a convicted felon and wish to be placed on our waiting list, please inform us and we will be glad to contact you when an available spot opens. We do apologize for any inconvenience to you.

CONVICTED FELON. THE COST? A LIFE SENTENCE!
Will You Be An Activist or Recidivist? What Cost Are You Willing to Pay?

If You Were To Ask Any Child...

What Do You Want To Be When You Grow Up?

What Do You Dream Of Being One Day?

No Child Would Ever Say,

"A Permanently Disenfranchised Convicted Felon!"

If any person had told me that in just 2 months of entering my senior year of college that I would be in the newspaper twice for committing a crime against another person, I would have told them they had the wrong person pegged because I was destined to a life of love and money. I would have told them that they were out of their mind because I was headed for marriage and law school and there was nothing that was going to derail my dreams, and me going to jail was an absurdity. Wrong Bro! Permanently Excluded and Forever Judged! Plans can change! Some say, "*Never say what you would never do!*" *Never do what you should never do!*

HU STUDENT ABDUCTED BY FORMER BOYFRIEND [40]
November 1, 1991, CHERYL L. REED Daily Press

HAMPTON- A 21-year-old Hampton University student was abducted by her former boyfriend Tuesday afternoon outside Phenix Hall and taken to Maryland, where he held her against her will that night, police said.

Antoine Burgess, 21, of the 2000 block of Nettles Drive and a former HU student, is charged with abduction, use of a firearm in commission of a felony and assault and battery. He was released from jail on $7,500 bond, said Hampton Sgt. Craig Michael.

Burgess approached his former girlfriend, Michelle Thompson, 21, about 3:30 p.m. Tuesday and tried to talk to her about their relationship, Michael said. He got her to walk with him to his car.

At the car, he pushed her inside and slapped her when she tried to leave, Michael said. He also told her he had a gun, but never showed her a weapon.

Solutions To Permanently Eradicate Domestic Violence, Child Abuse, and Bullying

Burgess then drove to Jessup, Md., outside Baltimore, and checked them into the Red Roof Inn. "He made her spend the night with him, and they talked most of the night about their former relationship," Michael said Thursday.

During the night, Thompson was able to call a friend and through code tell her friend where she was. Thompson's friend alerted the victim's father, who met his daughter as Burgess was checking them out of the motel.

Thompson and her father immediately went to the Maryland State Police and reported the incident and then called Hampton police.

Burgess had turned himself into Hampton police by the time they were notified, Michael said.

BALTIMORE MAN JAILED IN SECOND ABDUCTION [41]
November 16, 1991, DAVID CHERNICKY Daily Press

HAMPTON- A 21-year-old Baltimore man is in Hampton's jail after he abducted his former girlfriend for the second time in two weeks, police say.

This time, Antoine Burgess, who was released after his arrest earlier, used a pistol and is being held without bond.

Burgess is accused of abducting Michelle Thompson, 21, a student at Hampton University. Thompson was leaving her apartment when Burgess confronted her in the parking lot at Hampton Club condominium on Pacific Avenue shortly after 7 p.m. Thursday, police spokesman Sgt. Craig Michael said.

Records indicate that Burgess may also be a HU student, a jail official said. He said a man unaware of Burgess's intentions, Joseph Parran, 22, drove Burgess to the lot. "Burgess stepped from the car, drew a handgun and ordered the woman into the car," Michael said Friday. Thompson and Parran persuaded Burgess to unload the weapon, a .38-caliber Ruger pistol, and Parran drove them to an office on Enterprise Drive where Thompson was to keep an appointment, Michael said. Thompson entered the office and called police.

When officers arrived, they found Burgess with the revolver in his waistband still waiting for his former girlfriend, Michael said. Burgess surrendered without incident.

Burgess was arrested in Hampton Oct. 30 after he forced Thompson into a car on the HU campus. He drove to a Maryland suburb, where he forced her to spend the night in a motel with him, police said.

During the night, Thompson managed to call a friend and was able to surreptitiously convey her location. Thompson's friend alerted the victim's father, who met his daughter as Burgess was checking out of the motel.

MAN DAMN!

Solutions To Permanently Eradicate Domestic Violence, Child Abuse, and Bullying

What is the cost of going to jail, prison, psychiatric hospital, and permanently being labeled a felon? Going to prison is like having two funerals! One individual going in the ground literally or figuratively and one going on the prison grounds literally or figuratively! Your credibility is compromised, jeopardized, and seemingly gone forever! You are viewed as a convicted criminal for your entire life! Have you ever done or said something in your life that you wish you could take back? Something you wish never happened and you have regretted saying or doing it ever since? Something you have had to pay for the rest of your life. Imagine those individuals who had lapses in judgment and chose to drive drunk or while under the influence and eventually ended the night by killing a passenger in a stranger's car or even a friend in their car? How do you get that person's life back now that you have killed them? What apology can you offer their family and friends to comfort them? How can you repair their broken hearts and erase their tragic memories of this fatal event? Can you say, "Case never closed or a ship that will never find a dock?"

Being a felon is a lifetime sentence like a tattoo or burned in brand! It is the past that stays as your presence and future forever. It is the past that keeps coming back to haunt you as a recurring non-redemptive nightmare that repeats itself every night. What is the very first thing that comes to your mind when you hear that someone is a convicted felon? How do you ever get a great paying career in corporate America with "smart" analytical unemotional robotic computers with artificial intelligence data and algorithms that automatically disqualify you based on your criminal background, social media presence, zip code, demographics and level of potential corporate legal exposure? How do you explain your criminal past to an unempathetic robot? Robots and their programmers do not care? You are excluded!

Up until my vote was truly needed in the National 2016 Presidential election race, I was a permanently disenfranchised felon by the good ole southern sweet exclusion Lose Dixie laws of the state of Virginia. I had forfeited my basic constitutional rights as an American citizen, for being convicted of a felony crime, such as the right to vote in any election anywhere in the America! I could not run for any office, nor serve on a jury, nor purchase or be in possession of a firearm, nor be a notary public, nor acquire or hold certain professional licenses, nor serve in the military. Hell, I was surprised to be granted a driver's or marriage license. Virginia probably had a law against me voting who had the best chili or dessert dish in a church baking competition. I cannot even drive for Uber or Lyft. I lost my 2nd amendment rights to bear arms. I cannot stand my ground, protect myself or my family and defend my family at home because I do not have the legal right to purchase, own, or possess a firearm! The only right I have is to just bare arms, and I do mean nothing in my arms, hands, or pockets because I do not have a right to bear arms to protect myself as the 2nd amendment rights granted me. I cannot own or even be a General Manager for specific franchises such as automotive manufacturers, restaurants and most publicly traded companies. Permanently disenfranchised means you are often permanently frustrated. Despite your talents, you are permanently excluded from participating in the ownership and political process. This means you typically can no longer make real money! *MAN DAMN!*

I know the feeling of being forever disqualified and a justified rejection. I am one of the best athletes in the history of McDonogh's athletics, but being a felon means I am never allowed or eligible to be admitted as a member of the Hall of Fame because of its moral turpitude clauses that exclude me. Plus, it sends a horrific message to the McDonogh family, alumni, faculty past and present, contributors, and supporters that you can be a felon and still get a pass into an enshrinement of exceptional athletic individuals on and off of the field. That hurts because I worked to be one of the most exceptional individuals on and off the field. I am a lifetime member of the McDonogh Hall of Shame, ALL because of domestic violence and abuse! I forced my own McDonogh family to sentence me to an eternal ban which is a Hall of Famer's death sentence. I paid for my crime by finishing the sentence from a judge but am banned forever from my McDonogh family? *MAN DAMN!*

Certain colleges and universities would not take a chance and open the opportunity for legal exposure or establishing a precedent for all felons to apply there if they accepted me! They accepted my application, but most acceptance letters I got was mostly anybody "except" you! I could not go into the military or work as a civilian on any military base, school, post office, bank, airport or hospital. I could not even volunteer in certain places. Would you want any felon around you or your children or loved ones? When I would disclose I was a convicted felon who had served time in the penitentiary and a psychiatric hospital, some girls would never return or accept my calls. I have had my bosses in certain jobs tell the other managers and me that "We do not hire felons and anyone with an arrest record because we have enough candidates trying to work here so we never even have to consider them or their crimes! As long as I am here and am the boss making the hiring decisions, we will never hire anyone with a felony background or arrest record period!" The amazing part about his declaration was that our millionaire owner was, at the time, currently under Federal house arrest serving a one-year sentence for a felony conviction until he received a full Presidential Pardon which permanently cleared his felony conviction and criminal background. I've had another say, "Now that we have gotten rid of all the felons, we can move forward as a company!" He must have forgotten all about me and my history. I even was turned down from a reality show before I could even submit my application to them because they vehemently stated, "No felons' applications will be accepted! All applications will be denied! Don't fill the application out if you are a felon because you will never have an opportunity?"

I served my prison sentence and was released in January of 1993 and was shocked and incredibly thankful and blessed when the Governor restored certain rights to felons like me so that we could vote in the 2016 election. I had not voted in more than 25 years! I was excluded from all of those rights even though over the majority of many years I probably paid more taxes and tithes than the average citizen because my income was in the highest earnings bracket. I am a permanent citizen of the distressed and dysfunctional community you speak of that is always left behind. I served my time, and yet I am a permanently disenfranchised felon for the rest of my life! ***THAT IS OKAY BECAUSE THE TAIL WON'T ALWAYS BE LAST!***

Since January of 1993, when I was 22, I have had to hustle and earn my way into excellent paying jobs and eventually becoming self-employed, to support my wife of many decades, four daughters, and now grandchildren. Since I could never purchase or possess a firearm as a felon, I had to go beyond working hard enough to earn a substantial income to put my family in the very best zip codes, so they could live in the safest neighborhoods and attend the best possible schools both privately and publicly. Conversely, I have experienced the financial hardships families of chronic and critically ill individuals have. I have had a home foreclosed, a car repossessed, a 300-beacon credit score, and many slammed doors closed as a result of not being hireable or desirable by companies. ***GOD WILL RESTORE!***

I know the feeling of getting released from prison with no secured jobs or educational opportunities, wondering the entire time, who was going to hire a felon or welcome a felon to their campus since my felony abduction began on the campus of Hampton University where my former girlfriend and I were students. I know firsthand the countless personal and professional rejections where your manly dignity and esteem are emasculated when you try to get a real wage paycheck and the stripped pride of knowing you are not in an honest career that affords you the opportunity to provide income and benefits for your family. I know the feeling of losing the opportunity to be a BMW or American Honda-Acura franchise dealer! I know what it is like to not be licensed or receive professional certifications as a result of being a felon! I have seen the signs in hair schools that stated, "Felons Do Not Apply!" What is even crazier than seeing this attitude towards felons was when someone from my wife's family called the dealership where I was earning 6 figures annually with no degree, a wife and 4 daughters, demanding to speak to the head manager to disclose to him that I was a felon and they wanted to ensure that they were aware that they had hired a violent offender out of Virginia and Baltimore. The blessing was that the head manager pulled me to the side to tell me that he was once a "Hell's Angel" type person and knows what it is like to have made mistakes in judgment as a youngster and once he matured he realized the error of his ways and was thankful for the many people who helped him out following that young lifestyle. He was an angel to me after that day and showed me that there are some redemptive individuals like him and Rick Hendrick on the planet, regardless of my race or past.

When I got out of the penitentiary I constantly thought about who would want to be with me after having such a troubled soul? My first few dates were tear-jerkers and real because I promised myself I would never withhold my criminal and domestic violence background from the next woman. I had many girls on different occasions tell me they could never be my girlfriend because I was a felon who was violent towards women. Man, oh man. The truth hurts and helps at the same time. For someone like me who was always use to being welcomed with a smile by most people, hearing such negative sentiments and doses of reality always hurt to the soul because I had earned the right for people to feel that way towards me! There are very few things in life you can settle when a simple apology does not ever make things right with people you did not even personally hurt. Their reaction was justified and who was I to try and convince an individual who was rightfully scared. How would I respond to one of my daughters if they told me their brand-new boyfriend had just been released from prison for crimes stemming from violence and abuse against their previous girlfriend? I do not want anyone to experience what I experienced with women, new friends, and potential employers and school administrators. How would you respond? Would you have dated or hired me?

The overwhelming regret and remorse that comes upon you once the dust clears and settles are like the death of the closest and only friend you have ever had in your life. I would commit a despicable act of domestic violence or abuse, or both, and after some time had passed after the incident, I quickly realized that I was so wrong for harming an individual who honestly did not deserve my cowardly and deplorable behavior. The saddest truth of all is that initially, Michelle would tell me that I would get better and that she believed me and trusted me when I said, "I would never do "IT" again to her!" That was a contract and commitment I would renege on and never keep and thus the justifiable reason why she could not see me as her husband, baby's father, friend or anything significant to do with her future. I know she had come to the reality and finality that ***"If the people around you will not change, change the people around you!"*** **I WAS THE CHANGE!** In all fairness and transparency to her, she must have told me over and over and over to get professional help and that she would be willing to come with me and we could do it together to save our relationship, friendship, and future together. I was extremely ignorant, full of pride and embarrassment and clueless to the level of love she was extending to me and even more naive to needing professional mental therapy.

In hindsight, she was the superwoman with X-ray vision who could see my fragile mental capacity and the desperate medical attention I so needed. She was the only one who could ever see the generous heart, beauty, and kind spirit in me. The truth is, in these types of contentious equations, only the individual in need of care or God Himself is the only being who can save you from yourself. I could not save myself because I thought and truly believed I could beat the violence and abuse syndrome on my own. I came up with every lame and bull crap excuse to avoid seeing a professional healthcare individual or institution! I will tell anyone willing to listen that my foolish decision to avoid getting help and my former girlfriend's loving advice was not just the death of my relationship with her and her family, but this was the death of my life and existence as a free citizen of the United States of America and even more so, the possession of a free mind and spirit.

Within 2 weeks I was sitting on two different occasions as an inmate in the Hampton city jail for felony abduction, possession of a firearm, and felony assault. That is correct! Twice! Within months after that, I was headed to the penitentiary and a trip to the psychiatric hospital for a criminal evaluation and an intense involuntary court-ordered treatment regimen on the ward for Virginia's worst psychotic criminal individuals who were often convicted and sentenced there for "Reasons of insanity purposes!" Excuse the pun, but the crazy part of being there was I felt that I would get the help I always needed. I was there by force of a judge's court order and so it was time to get right and realize I had no choice but to surrender to the toxic truth that I was an abuser and violent offender who was only going to eventually take my own life or someone else's if I did not get healed. I submitted and surrendered "IT" all to my doctor! He creatively pulled out all of the toxins, diseases, and cancers that were riddling my body of all of its nutrients and functions. I was being overwhelmed and consumed from within by my own dysfunctional crap. Imagine if you never went to the bathroom to urinate or excrete all the waste that continues to build up in your system. Eventually, you become septic, and your biological systems begin to fail and shut down until you go into shock and die.

I pray this book and my contributions as a humanitarian shocks you into getting professional help now before you go into shock from a significant other or family member giving you the shocking news that they no longer want to be your spouse, friend or they want you out of their house and life forever. I do not want anyone to feel the shock of being arrested and sentenced to serve a lengthy prison sentence such as life without parole or worse yet sentenced to death. I will never forget the shock of waking up on the cold slab of a jail floor and steel bed. I will always remember the shock of jail and prison steel bars and the opening and closing of cell doors. The shock of the horrendous amount of time spent behind those bars doing nothing productive. The shock of hearing the horror stories of other people's crimes and the sentences these inmates are now serving. The shock of how bad your life must be for you to be in the penitentiary or psychiatric hospital. The shock of no visitors or communication from anyone who you once considered a friend. The shock of the few visits I received was from the very individual who never protected me and who hated me to the point she tried to kill me with her own hands. The shock of being paroled to the drug infested hood you told your mother not to parole you.

For some, prison is the ultimate time out and "go to your room!" It is often too late for some to get the solutions to domestic violence, child abuse and bullying especially if they receive a life sentence. The sad truth is had they got the necessary coping and life skills they were more likely to not end up in prison. What is more diabolical is many will receive the same rehabilitation in prison that they could have received before coming to prison. Domestic violence, child abuse, and bullying is a preventable issue! The difference is the abuser's mentality to choose to receive help!

What many individuals, like myself at one time in my life, who commit violent acts and bullying against women and children never quite understand is that as a result of their abuse they are serving life sentences of trauma to their victims. When in contrast and reality, all they have to do as abusers is serve out their criminal sentence or walk away and abandon the relationship or surrender their rights and responsibilities as a parent. What a devastating trail of trauma and tears and the destructive aftermath bestowed upon the innocent victims who have to cry daily through such pain until they gain the strength, if they ever do, from the pain to cut the trauma baggage off their backs, out of their minds, and out of their lives forever. That is not a fair exchange of love. A vested interest in any deal is where both parties win and get something positive out of the deal. **Abusing a girlfriend is child abuse!**

This was a hijacking of someone's heart, a severing of their soul, and a mugging of their mind. Every time you hit and abuse her or your child violently, you put a nail in the tire of your relationship which holds up the vehicle and keeps it in motion. Every time you do something good, take the nail out and replace it with a plug? How long and far do you think you will get before a major blow out occurs? Moreover, how safe do you think your victims feel and how much confidence do you now have in that multi-plugged tire(relationship)? Was it built by the manufacturer to perform optimally with all those plugs in it? Then why do you continue to put nails and plugs in it? How long can a run-flat tire, which is a pneumatic vehicle tire, meaning the tire's engineered to make use of gas or pressurized air, travel when it was designed to be able to resist the effects of deflation when punctured, and able to continue driving after loss of air pressure for a limited speed and distance? Most allow one to travel a limited distance usually no more than 50 miles and at a slower speed generally under 50 miles per hour, before needing to be replaced. Also, oftentimes vehicles equipped with run-flat tires do not have a spare back up and if they are not installed and mounted properly to ensure the best operation with a functioning Tire Pressure Mounting System (TPMS), drivers can potentially drive on an underinflated tire without realizing it, putting them at a high risk of tire failure. The point is, it is not a matter of if you will fail at committing another domestic violence or child abuse offense, it is a matter of when you will offend again if you do not have the proper coping and life skills system installed and mounted properly! It is all about a healthy "BALANCE" to your life!

When you have a history of violence and abuse and have done time for it, you walk daily on a slippery slope with the public and especially those who proclaim to have a relationship with you. If you are easily provoked and go from zero to a hundred in no time, you best stay away from any individual or entity who will call the police on you even if you have not threatened any harm to them. So often is the case where spouses, loving mates, friends, and employers know they control your fate with the police. Now, to keep it on a 1000%, you should not be putting them or yourself in that predicament for them to have to make the decision to get law enforcement involved. Never stay with anyone who holds you hostage to your past!

Any person who feels like the law can solve your domestic violence issues instantly is sadly mistaken! But do understand that if law enforcement is dispatched to your location, know that they are approaching with extreme caution because domestic violence calls are some of the most dangerous calls for law enforcement to respond to! Comply when they arrive and know that one false move or hostile words can often evoke lethal and often fatal and justified force! Provocative people are dangerous to be around if they are not on the same harmonious path with your change towards being a nonviolent, tempered and civil individual! One of the most regrettable things about being a domestic violence offender and convicted felon is no one believes you when you say to the authorities that "They hit me or threatened me first!" Provocative people know this truth very well and hold it over your head for life. I beg of people to never put themselves in my shoes because you shake your head every day knowing you are set up to lose and that whenever 911 is called, get ready to pay a lifetime of consequences for a few seconds of misguided judgment. As a felon, I stay on a slippery slope that at any given moment, it is easy for me to return to prison if I put myself in a position to be arrested and return to jail.

Success only comes by trying. Do not fall into the path and laziness of recidivism. Recidivism is a mindset. A culture! Prison is like a dead body going into the cemetery, in that, once you go in, you or your spirit never comes out if you do not have the right mindset to get healed from what caused you to end up there initially. If you do not get a permanent solution to your mental issues, I can say with absolute certainty that you will continue to stay connected to the criminal system or you will be mentally imprisoned for the rest of your life. You have to get the coping and life skills that you can apply in your daily living and engagement with others to permanently and successfully prevent you from ever returning to a life of physical and mental incarceration. Recidivism is the systemic hateful spirit that wants to keep a consistent revolving door of going back and forth to jail and prison. The systemic forces of violence and abuse against women and children will continue to prevail if your mind and environment do not change permanently for the better. You cannot expect people to change for the better if you do not first change and show them the permanent solutions to your personal issues. People will naturally fear you or flee from you if they cannot trust and believe you are truly transitioning to a quality human being they can feel safe around. You are never going back to jail or prison.

Never look back. Do not look back because if you do you just may be looking at your future. If you look forward and focus on what is in front of you, then you will see the future and the limitless dreams and opportunities. Have you ever tried to walk forward while looking backward? Have you ever tried to drive a car forward while looking back or better yet, drive the car in reverse while looking forward? Both are wrecks waiting to happen. Which direction are you eyeing when you are walking and driving forward? What happened to Lot's wife who looked back? Salty!

There are forces who only care about making money off the crime and not reforming the criminal. Not providing adequate access and educational awareness to mental health and recidivism is great for business. Where are the appropriate solutions for ending domestic violence, child abuse, and bullying? I am not speaking of attending anger management or proper parenting class to get a certificate for a month or two or going to detention as a permanent solution to eradicating domestic violence, bullying, and child abuse. Not getting the proper solution guarantees that violence and abuse will surely return in the near future as sure as you can predict that there will be a tornado, hurricane, or cyclone during their annual seasons when it is not a matter of if one catastrophic event will happen but when the horrific event will occur and who it will impact. America wants you to stay a recidivist.

Candidly speaking, what does one mistake cost you? It indeed is a mistake you cannot afford. If a neurosurgeon, anesthesiologist or pharmacist makes an error, what does that mistake cost that patient, client or them? Both run the risks of losing their lives personally and professionally! Have you ever had a mortgage, car, or student loan payment? Even if you have not, it is like living in an apartment where you make a lifetime of payments, and you never have a chance to own the property you have been paying for the last 80 years! That is right, you are still making payments on a home or car or student loan, and the bank will never give you the deed, title, or Degree until you finish paying them but that is the catch, there is no date of maturity, and you will pay until you die, and your heirs will still have to pay your lifetime debt to society! Can you imagine paying for the same car that has been in the junkyard for 80 years? Own your mental health and build equity in it.

Let me digress further before I delve into the initial question of what does one mistake cost that has sent me on my purpose for my one life! People ask me all the time what was the experience like in the penitentiary? For some like me, I imagine my entire life to that point was preparing me for a place that many say is the closest place to hell on earth, even though there is no record of anyone ever coming back with pictures or videos of people's vacation in hell! If you are like me and are not afraid of death or are not easily intimidated or scared of any human being or animal on the earth, then maybe you may make it in the luxuriously nefarious hotel penitentiary! But if you are not built for hell, stay the hell away from crime.

After paying your dues to society, a person is to never earn a living thereafter? I get malpractice, but they cannot have another opportunity to make a living? As a kid like me, when you survive death from the hands of your mother and the abusive physical and mental tactics from a malicious aunt and coward uncle, you feel like you have already survived being on a deserted cursed island and so prison is almost a reprieve from your near-death experiences because you have already been face to face, eye to eye, and cheek to cheek with death and been in the clutching palms of King Kong in the Baltimore jungle. If you have stood there firmly with your boot heels dug into the clay-like tar as the frontline soldiers, even though you hear the beast coming aggressively through the jungle tearing trees down and clearing a path directly towards your destination, there is no fear in your heart because your mind, body, and soul have already become weapons, and so you fear no evil, are unbreakable, cannot be tortured any longer, and could give a damn about death because the reality is "You cannot kill what is already dead and willing to die again!" The scariest or bravest person will always be the individual who has resolved that death is just a destination because we all are going to die eventually, and it is not a matter of if but when you will! I do not give nare damn about death.

The truth about going to the penitentiary is once you do time for a felonious offense or you are a habitual offender with an extensive criminal past, you will always pay for the crime! With the level of competition towards a job paying a competitive salary, society and corporate America are excluding individuals with arrest records through computer analytics and artificial intelligence to limit their legal exposure for hiring an individual with a criminal background even though they may receive a tax credit for hiring an individual with a criminal background. Why would they have a desire or critical need to hire anyone with a criminal background when there are other qualified individuals without a criminal history?

Once you do time, you will always pay for the crime? I thought it was you get convicted and sentenced by a judge or jury, then do the time you owe society as a consequence for your crime, then you get set free now that you have paid your debt in full to society! What no one informs you of is that you just flew from one birdcage with reinforced steel bars to another cage with reinforced, electrified invisible bars! Now, I truly understand that all crimes are not equal and that some individuals will always be officially certified as a dangerous or permanently deviant and evil individual. I truly get that wholeheartedly! But if that be the case, why are such heinous offenders allowed to return to the streets anyway? The answer is $$$!

The political process and justice system is not always just and has its share of loopholes and prejudices, especially if you have exceptional money to get exceptional results from exceptional lawyers, political relationships, and affiliations of influence such as when you can get your criminal or arrest records expunged or granted a full pardon from a Governor or President. The old saying in business is, "Time is money!" Unless you have the money to pay in exchange for your time, do not do the crime because with no money you are going to pay with your time until the end of time! If you commit a crime, get used to and prepare yourself for the permanent and long-term societal judgment, exclusion, rejection, legal discrimination, and electrified invisible bars! Get used to the negative consequences that come with being labeled as a felon or a person with an arrest record or a person with an asterisk next to their name or in their employment file or warned by law enforcement to approach with caution because they have a criminal history. You have got to mentally resolve that this is just how some people in society, not all people in society, think. No Redemption! No Forgiveness! I cannot stress that you must always, always, always think about the consequences and what will my actions cost me immediately and in my future!

When you are going through something, you may think at that very moment that you do not give a damn about who or what or how this will impact your life. Once you get caught and have time to retrospectively reflect on the criminal severity of your crime and now realize the error of your crimes and sound judgment, you begin to constantly think about the possible real-time you must serve in front of you. You begin thinking about an exit strategy out of this life-changing situation because you are in full awareness of the penitentiary vacation you are about to face head-on with foreign "tourists" who are greater torturers than you! You are now spending unrecoverable years of your life with other dysfunctional individuals, and prayerfully you receive the "rehabilitation" and "treatment" you need to permanently heal you from what caused you to commit a crime that landed you in prison.

The irony is you could have received this rehabilitation and treatment without coming to prison. Now you get paroled or receive probation when you are discharged from prison or jail and are quickly smacked in the face with reality when you are filling out an online application that there is a box to check next to a question that says, "Have you ever been arrested?" Followed by other boxes to check with even better questions such as "Was it a misdemeanor or felony?" "What was the nature of the crime?" "What was your sentence?" "Are you currently on probation or parole?" "May we contact your probation or parole officer for verification?" "When was your last offense?" "Was a gun involved?" Then they clean up their questions by stating that "Your criminal history and background will not exclude you from the hiring process or prohibit or prejudice any hiring managers from discriminating against you." Let me ask you this question, "Would you hire you if you had other qualified individuals with no criminal history, arrest record or arrest record?" Oh, by the way, if you have the gift of gab and can sell sand at the beach or ice to Eskimos, God Be With You and God Bless You because the days are evaporating for companies that actually let you fill an application out in person to be turned in to an on-site manager. You may think you are a smooth talker but it is not possible to talk your way into a job if you NEVER get a call to interview!

What makes anyone want to harm anyone or anything? What makes someone want to commit a heinous crime on a spouse, friend, child or animal? Why or what makes you snap? Why do you want to take your pain out on someone who is not trying to harm you? What would your bosses, colleagues, or employees think of you if they knew you were an abuser of women, children, LGBTQ, your boyfriend or even animals, at any time of your life? What would your family or friends speak of you if they knew you went home every night or perhaps once a year to violently abuse your spouse or child? Just think before you end up in the clink because you will be judged for a lifetime by family, friends, schools, colleges, universities, Hollywood, businesses, franchisers, banks, fraternities, potential spouses, clergy, employees, customers, halls of fame...etc. etc.

What the penitentiary and psychiatric hospital taught me was that you have to be accountable for your life! Outside of being known as "The FAMILY MAN™" and "A Wolf," I am often called "Mr. Accountability" in my role as a business consultant specializing in business development because I teach and preach that "Accountability equals Awareness," in that you have to be aware of yourself at all times and take responsibility for your actions while taking initiatives to ensure you will better your life and those who you engage within society! What do you do exceptionally well and where are your deficiencies and inefficiencies that keep you less than or at best average, so you can be working towards a solution to what is ailing you? If you never know where you are deficient you will never find a solution.

My job and purpose in life are to make people better performers, not bitter performers at work and in life! The irony for me was that I was always the hero in corporate America and around outsiders but a zero at home and with those who were closest to me. I could not figure out why I was such an abusive individual to the people closest to me and why I did not care about the consequences to my malicious behavior. The solution to my violent and abuse deficiencies in my life was not solved until I was sitting in the ward of a criminal psychiatric hospital in Petersburg, Virginia in early 1992.

Here I was on the ward with some of Virginia's historically worst criminally insane offenders. Most were paranoid schizophrenics who had committed heinous acts against family members! This place made the penitentiary look like a peace corps mission outing with Mother Teresa. I saw on several occasions various longtime male residents having sex in the showers like they were married couples holding hands and conversing and doing their daily walk around the neighborhood. It was so habitual and routine that it was a horrific ritual that I never got used to and simply had to find the humor in the craziness of schizophrenia. It was disturbing!

Seeing any individual snap and go off was not unusual for me because I witnessed individuals lose it in my neighborhood in Baltimore and on many occasions I was the one who lost it and became that crazy dude. I just never took my clothes off or walked around holding my shoes in my hands telling people "I have already put my shoes on so let's go!" I watched my family friend Tub perch on an average American mailbox in the complete nude. Was he experiencing the remnants of P.T.S.D, LSD, crack, heroin, ecstasy, or opioids? I do not know from what it stemmed from or caused the crazy reaction. I do know it was just someone dealing with a pain they had no solution or cure for at the moment except for calling the cops because people were scared. For me, it was just Baltimore humor at its best moments and preparation for my time in the psychiatric hospital! I witnessed a solidly built, 6-foot 5-inch, 300 lb., silverback of a man, sprint to top speed and throw himself into an enclosed television fixture. It looked unrealistic when it was happening because we all thought he would stop running, and when he did not, you could not help to think "What in the hell is wrong with him?" Then you see him stunningly rise from the unimpacted, impenetrable television stand and think, "that was one of the most impressive and spectacular daredevil stunts and feats of strength that I have ever witnessed live without it being Evel Knievel or someone getting killed." It was just pure craziness mixed with sadness, laughter, and empathy.

And like magic, "Voila!" it was my time to meet with the doctor. This tall, bald, African American man who had no eyebrows or facial hair. He was cordial yet dry and all about his business. This was the beginning of the breakthrough and peeling off of the layers of pain that were causing the chaos in my life. He kept asking me "What was my trauma? When did it begin? Where did it all derive from?" I kept telling him initially that I did not know why I repeatedly abused my mother and girlfriend physically, verbally, emotionally, psychologically, mentally and any other forms of abuse and violence! I was a witty college student making excellent grades, a former champion athlete, a rising and budding corporate leader and intern at a phenomenal company. If anyone could stop abusing his mother and girlfriend along with beating up his aunt and uncle, it was me. He told me to tell him of every violent episode I could remember and to not withhold any details for him to help!

I shared everything in my childhood that I have already mentioned! When I started with my first abusive encounter with Michelle he told me to talk slowly! I told him everything I could remember from the incidents in high school, college, to the incidents that landed me in prison! He said, "Now go back to the incident at the mall! We were at the mall one Friday night in the mid-eighties. Friday night at the mall then was huge. She wanted to walk around the mall holding hands. As I came around to open her door as a gentleman would do, I was happy to be at the mall with my girl. I opened the door and she went to extend her hand as if to gesture to hold her hand. I said to her, "Do you think I am a f*****g faggot or soft ass N****?" In my mind, I am screaming! "Are you implying I am gay, or I have female tendencies or ways?"

In my head, all I could hear was my uncle's and older cousins shouting, "Boys are hard like soldiers who never cry and never hold hands in public with girls unless they are gay!" Dr. Ryans said, "Stop right there!"

He went on to ask about all the males who gave me that advice. He asked me, "Did any of the males who gave me that advice have successful relationships or marriages?" Of course, the answer was no. He went on to say that, "All of the examples I had of male and female figures living inside of my home or who my mom exposed me to or put me around or in front of were deadbeats and cowards who set me up to fail in relationships with any and all women if not any relationship. He said ***"The way your mom, uncles, aunts, and other family and friends lived,*** *with their wild, reckless, and unaccountable lifestyles and all that you witnessed and all the violence you were subject to and the way you were treated and tortured, it is surprising that you did not kill yourself or others by now!* <u>*Son It Was Not Your Fault The Way You Turned Out!*</u>*"* I had just paid a price for a crime I never committed as a child! I should never have had to go to prison to be freed of what was causing me to be violent to Michelle and so many other people! I was healed!

And then "Voila!" it all made sense to me why Michelle wanted to hold my hand at the mall! I did not know what the significance was of public displays of affection or as people refer to it today as PDA. She obviously came from a loving, married, two-parent home. She was only doing what she saw her parents do at the mall which was show love towards each other publicly by holding hands. PDAs are healthy for mentally healthy and functional people and individuals who truly love one another and themselves. I wish I could have done then with Michelle what I do now without hesitation, reluctance or regret with my wife because she truly deserved to have a person show her respectful love that is reciprocated equally.

Little did I know she was showing me how to love appropriately and receive love. I wish that my uncles and cousins had taught me that another meaning for gay is happy and not to judge gay or lesbian people! I recall the violent gay and lesbian outbursts during heated card games. I ultimately learned to embrace gay and lesbians from my gay uncle Boonie and lesbian aunt Dusty who I have always loved unconditionally and wholeheartedly and who were the rare and exceptional family members who always showed me love on the rare times I saw them growing up.

As I would say to my former girlfriend Michelle after the many of my crazy episodes, "I promise "IT" will never happen again and I will never talk to you so harshly and disrespectfully! I am better now. I know I can beat this! I am not like those other guys!" I would beg for forgiveness or let time pass until I guilted them or blamed them or simply waited for them to come back around to me or I would apologize with gifts and money to buy clothes or pay off her credit cards.

How I know Michelle truly and sincerely loved me more than I loved myself and certainly more than I could have ever loved her back at the time was she always forgave me, always believed I could change, always allowed me to be intimate with her shortly after an abusive or violent incident which I now know was her way of truly showing her commitment to our relationship and giving her love, heart, and support. She would always tell me in a sincere, loving, gentle and angelic manner that "I needed to seek help by way of professional counseling, a church pastor, a school official, or a psychologist. She never told anyone to protect my reputation while I was slowly chipping away at her esteem, mental and emotional dignity, and her purpose! She was foregoing her ego to keep mine intact when my ego was not worthy of anything respectful. She was royalty, a beautiful Queen that never deserved my bullying, disrespect, mind games, physical and verbal assaults along with my tortuous behavior and mannerisms. She was the true friend and ride or die woman all men want next to them to the grave. She was the spirit with a loving soul and genuine disposition. She was pure gold! I was a shiny piece of pyrite!

Acknowledge me for who I am today and where I want to be tomorrow is what you scream as a released felon or an individual with a criminal background! You did the crime so now you must do the time in and out of jail and prison? Time is money! When you are required to sit down so does the opportunity to earn money! Prison is not a place you go to for your dreams to come true, but rather a place that totally kills your dreams or abolishes the individual's pursuit of happiness, fulfillment, and purpose! I awakened every morning in a cell at the same nightmarish confusion of how my life ended up here. There is no way I am living a nightmare! Let me find the positive in this negative is what I had to convince myself. I had to find out why I hurt people in of all places, a penitentiary psychiatric hospital!

I have to be one of the rarest examples of where the crime actually pays. I am the exception where I had to come to prison to get my healing! But do understand me clearly when I say that unless you receive a Presidential Pardon, having a felony arrest record along with a prison and psychiatric hospital stint in your background is like having an STD that has no cure or treatment and stays with you forever, with the only difference being that the disease dies when you do but the legacy of being a felon who served time in the penitentiary and received treatment in a psychiatric ward is permanently affixed like a bad tattoo to you and your legacy!

The second someone learns that you are a felon they immediately have an opinion that typically is not a favorable perspective. Truthfully, you cannot blame them because before any of us were felons, what did we think when we first learned about someone having a felonious background, let alone an arrest record. If you met someone for the first time and the first thing out of their mouth was "I am a convicted felon," what would be the first thing you would think of them? Would you judge them, hug them or wonder what their crime was? My mind used to immediately think murderer, rapist, bank robber, thief or drug dealer. Why else would they stress the point that this person was a felon? Being arrested is one thing, but the word felon is an entirely different level of severity! It is like the difference between being sentenced to serve your time at a jail, except for places like Riker's Island in New York, versus the penitentiary. The seriousness and intensity of the penitentiary means the propensity of violence and crime and the likelihood of an inmate becoming a victim of a violent crime is greater in the penitentiary. The mere hearing of the word penitentiary sounds like electrocution to my ears. There are very few people who want to be affiliated with a convicted felon who has served time in the penitentiary and a psychiatric hospital. To them, I imagine they feel it is like purchasing a King Cobra or Black Mamba and you have never handled a snake before in your life without the vials of antivenom, and one thing you believe for sure is that it is uncertain when this highly venomous snake will strike and possibly kill you. Now do not get me wrong about jail. There were many tough guys who left jail different than they arrived and those secrets will go to the grave with them. Countless dudes wearing M and M make-up and skirts by force and not by choice because they ran into a ravenous lone wolf who did not give a flying flip how big or strong you thought you were on the streets! Everybody has to go to sleep, eat, shower, and use the toilet! How tough are you? Can you sleep with both eyes open?

What is lifelike in the penitentiary? "Enter to learn, depart to serve!" If that is the motto hanging on banners at many colleges and universities that we give to our aspiring young, educated professionals, what should be the motto at the entrance for the penitentiary doors? "Enter to get your healing! Depart to heal and serve others!" should be a beginner's goal! But what if you are never going home? I encourage any man or woman to be involved in community service like FAMILY MANKIND™ for the rest of your life so much that you fill voids in your life with love by serving others and impacting their lives as much as they are impacting yours.

There was very little difference between the penitentiary versus the psychiatric hospital except for the psychiatrist who saved my life. He was the difference in my life. I was on the ward for the individuals who were already convicted of heinous crimes or those like me who were court-ordered and being evaluated psychologically. These individuals had committed some of Virginia's most heinous crimes! I was on the ward for the criminally insane. Most had committed murders, and nearly everyone had schizophrenia. Everyone else was either asleep or depressing zombies walking in circles all day having their own conversions with their own imaginary friends and family. I remember thinking that I have been to three of the closest places that could be considered hell on earth or at least one step closer to the grave... Baltimore, the penitentiary and now the psychiatric ward! What the hell was God trying to show me! What is the message?

Eight months previous, I was at a summer leadership conference as an INROADS intern for Ingram Industries, whereas the C.E.O, Mr. E. Bronson Ingram tells me, "If you just work hard and smart A.W., you and your family will live an awesome and phenomenal life!" How was it possible to be there not so long ago and now I am here with some of Virginia's most violent and heinous offenders? In the penitentiary, you are dealing with society's worst of the very worst. Most have truly troubled souls if they have souls at all. Murderers, rapists, arsonists, child molesters and baby killers, assassins, terrorists, cannibals, psychopaths, diabolical geniuses always scheming to perfect their next crime, and other highly venomous and toxic nefarious packs of hyenas and vampires disguised as humans. I saw some of the so-called hardest dudes, regardless of size, muscles, race, influence, demographics, or gang affiliation, get turned into prey and turned out by a group of sex-starved predator butt savages and before you know it the prey was wearing colored M and M lipstick or make-up and getting violently gang-raped until it became submissive consensual love! Now they know exactly how their victims must have felt before, during, and after they violated the innocent. Isn't Karma a pain in the butt? Justice has a way of being served by the most unofficial officials of law enforcement! Bodybuilders were getting their wigs peeled back, and they no longer speak with bass in their voice and are scared of gnats after they got scalped.

Prison is not the place to use as a revolving door unless you are an apex predator and that is the only place you should ever be housed unless you take pleasure in being a gang's or someone's pawn or princess. I do not care if you are a ten-foot, thousand pound muscle man who is a black belt trained killer, you can get got and you will be hunted down like Goliath because in the penitentiary it is a dark and cold jungle, wilderness, forest, Everglades, or whatever you decide to refer it as, it is the closest place to hell on earth, and regardless of your physical stature or strength, a family of hellish fire ants will kill you and carry you back on a gurney platter to their Queen, and if you are so lucky, you may only be tagged once by a single black mamba that will run you down and continuously keep tagging you! Remember too that an Anaconda is non-venomous, and it can consume you whole after it squeezes the life out of you! You will not survive because everyone is in boot camp trying to rise through the ranks by earning their prison credibility stripes off the backs and butts of the weakest and strongest! If that can happen to a seemingly invincible strong-arm Superman, what does the average citizen have to protect themselves from such predators who are going nowhere soon?

Size and speed do not matter to predators. I survived because I was a wolf, MAN and R.E.A.L G whose presence and aura came before people and what they saw and more importantly what they felt was the spirit of an individual who was already dead and committed to taking others to meet the maker. *I had dominion over the animals on earth* [42] because I was God's greatest creation. It says in the Bible that, *"No weapons formed against you shall prosper!"* [43] Weapons are going to form against you, and bad things are going to come at you and cross your path, but they will not win or conquer you if you have a rod and staff, Jesus, to comfort you because Jesus is with you in the valley of the shadow of death! In prison, it is whoever is the hungriest and most strategic. It is who has the greatest will who will get what they want or what someone else is willing to do by choice or force! The inmates are one thing, but the guards, if not under accountable and forthright leadership, can be just as predatory in some institutions. They are locked up and doing time too.

God Bless Kalief Browder* and his family. He was the innocent individual sent by God to show how injustice operates in the criminal injustice system. He should never have lost his life, but some of us are martyred to bring about a better existence for those individuals coming after us. The criminal injustice system and man cost him and his mother their life! I will always say though that there are some great people in the law enforcement arena who are trying to enforce justice the right way and are doing everything in their given position to be right by their fellow mankind, and they are laying their life on the line each day as they enforce the laws and do time with these inmates. The citizens of New York will forever owe Kalief!

And then there is ratchet old recidivism. *By definition, recidivism means repeated or habitual relapse, as into crime.* [44] I have had friends who stayed in and out of jail as if they were high wage-earning road warriors working a job that kept them on the road for significant stints or a military person on a long-term deployment or a wealthy individual who spends part of the year out of the country in some remote wealthier country like beautiful Monaco or a retiree bluebird who flies to Florida for the frigid winter months of their home state and returning in the livelier spring months! When jail or prison becomes a better option and place to live than your actual home with your family, America has a serious problem! If the only place you could go to receive proper nutrition or medical treatment would you go there? How about a safe environment free from child molesters, muggers, stick up kids, drug dealers, and addicts, or violent home invasion burglars? How about a place where you can get your own bed and get a quality education? How about a place where you are relevant and not invisible? How about a place where you can receive love? A place where you can be yourself and be a part of a family you call your gang! A place where you can work out and get healthy? A place where you can make money and have worldly possessions? A place where you can get all of your reading and television programming and other forms of entertainment such as gambling or sports or even taking the time to write rap lyrics or even a book? A place where you are the man or woman. A place where you find peace of mind?

I remember trying to figure out why one of my friends was always in and out of jail. As fate would have it, I went to his house one night and then it became crystal clear why he was a habitual offender. Imagine an eight hundred square foot home with two bedrooms, one bathroom, a kitchen and living room that housed at least thirty to fifty people on any given night. Everyone was packed in there like maggots inside of a dead caucus. Now I see why he was in and out of jail and why he was pleading for me to let him sell drugs for me. He wanted a better life for himself and family. The problem was he was not built for the drug game, and all the hidden forces snared in crevices that eventually sniff out every seller and user. He was not built physically or mentally to sell crack let alone anything out on the corners. No way I was going to put his life in harm's way because someone would have been robbing him on a daily basis as if they were practicing how to properly rob a drug dealer at gunpoint! This would have become my problem to bust back!

What was crazier than anything was I met him through his mother who was incredibly addicted to crack and was one of my best customers and referral generators. She had the audacity to ask me if she could sell drugs for me since I would not let him sell for me. I told her that she and he could sell all day for me if she paid the cash retail price upfront for at least two ounces of crack, which for them would have been nearly impossible for them to have that kind of cash on hand. For me to give them the two ounces on consignment or front her the drugs upfront until they could pay me back was completely out of the question because in those days a person could lose their life if they didn't pay for their consigned drug tab! I watched them both deteriorate to the point of desperation, and for me, that was one of those tipping point signs that it was nearing the time to get out of the drug game! The ultimate point came when a drug dealer guy I once knew from jail and his family was responsible for killing a local police officer who was one of the good cops in the community. Everyone loses when law enforcement is unjustifiably killed from violence just like when one of our innocent black, brown, yellow, red or white children and women are murdered!

At this point in my life, I was back in college, selling cars, working at Red Lobster and trying to begin a relationship with a woman named Trena Walden. Because of my hectic schedule, about the only time of day I had to sell drugs was after 11 pm. I could not get out to the block as often as I wanted because Trena was occupying my remaining time and asking a million questions like she was an interrogator instructor for the FBI or CIA at Quantico as well as a CSI expert collector. Where are you going this late? With whom are you going? What are you going to be doing? When are you coming back? Are other girlfriends and wives going to be there? I remember my soldiers selling for me wearing my pager and answering machine out, telling me to get to the block, so they could buy more drugs and make more money! I no longer could deposit poison and ravage the community with people who were robbing others to get money to support their drug habit. My conscious and level of mature accountability had finally appeared in my life! I never sold a crumb or bump of crack ever again in my life. As for my friend who I desperately tried to keep out of the losing man's game, he ended up in Federal prison for exchanging food stamps for crack! I even heard he had become so hardened that he would even sell crack to pregnant women. He got a prison stint that would have beached a sperm whale!

Felon Cost? I have paid the ultimate price by compromising my good name and reputation! Punishing someone over and over for the same crime after they have paid with their time and restitution is a death sentence. I truly am empathetic towards restricting individuals for certain crimes against certain individuals in that I would never expect a child abuser, child murderer, or child molester ever to be granted a job or housing near children! I absolutely understand that, but they cannot vote? I get taking away their right to bear arms, but they cannot get food stamps to eat since no one has or will employ them? Not being permitted to vote, serve in the military or government positions or hold certain jobs or be a notary public or own a weapon legally to defend themselves or their family or go on certain television shows or travel to certain countries should be viewed on the individual and their crimes. I get it 1000%!

Here is a list of a few things you give up when you chose to become a felon versus getting help to prevent you from ever becoming a criminal. All I will ever say is "Think Twice Before You Roll The Dice For Your Life!" Here is a sample of what happens when you choose not to get mentally healthy. Things are far worse for permanently disenfranchised convicted felons like me in Commonwealth states like Virginia and Kentucky whereas unless you are pardoned or given a reprieve from a Governor more than likely, you lose most of your basic rights as a citizen for the rest of your life. Just know it is never worth losing your rights as a citizen.

CONSEQUENCES OF A FELONY CONVICTION [45]

By: Christopher Reinhart, Associate Attorney

Here is a list of the consequences (other than a fine and imprisonment) of a felony conviction.

SUMMARY

A convicted felon:

- *1. loses the right to become an elector and cannot vote, hold public office, or run for office, although he can have these rights restored; 2. is disqualified from jury service for seven years, or while he is a defendant in a pending felony case (CGS § 51-217); 3. loses the ability to have firearms; and 4. could lose a professional license or permit, although licensing agencies are restricted in their ability to revoke licenses because a person cannot be disqualified from engaging in any occupation, profession, or business for which a state license or permit is required solely because of a prior conviction of a crime except under certain conditions.*

Employers can ask job applicants whether they have been convicted of a crime although federal anti-discrimination laws place some restrictions on the use of criminal histories. State law also prohibits employers, including the state and its political subdivisions, from taking certain actions against people who have their conviction records erased by an absolute pardon.

In addition, a number of statutes apply to people convicted of certain felonies or types of crimes.

- *1. The State Board of Education (SBE) cannot issue or renew, and must revoke, a certificate, authorization, or permit to someone convicted of certain crimes. The SBE can also take one of these actions if the person is convicted of a crime of moral turpitude or of such a nature that the board feels that allowing the holder to have the credential would impair the credential's standing. 2. The Department of Children and Families must deny a license or approval for a foster family or prospective adoptive family if any member of the family's household was convicted of a crime that falls within certain categories, which can include felonies. 3. Landlords can evict a tenant who was convicted of a violation of federal, state, or local law that is detrimental to the health, safety, and welfare of other residents. Federal and state law for public housing allows eviction based on conviction of certain felonies. Different rules apply to older adults. 4. "Megan's Law" requires a person* to register on a sex offender's list for certain periods for committing certain sexual offenses (CGS § 54-250 et seq.). The offenses include felonies such as first, second, and third-degree sexual assault. Also, anyone convicted of a sex offense requiring registration must provide a DNA sample (CGS § 54-102g). sep.5. Someone convicted under federal or state law of a crime involving possession or sale of a controlled substance is not eligible for federal assistance for higher education expenses for certain periods. sep.6. State law bars anyone convicted of a drug possession or use felony under federal or state law from receiving benefits under the temporary assistance for needy families or food stamp programs unless the person (1) has completed his court-imposed sentence, (2) is satisfactorily serving probation, or (3) completed or will complete a court-imposed mandatory substance abuse treatment or testing program (CGS § 17b-112d).

In addition, private organizations may also consider a person's criminal background. For example, Little League recently adopted regulations to check volunteers and employees for convictions of crimes against or involving minors.

VOTING RIGHTS

A person forfeits his right to become an elector (a voter) upon conviction of a felony and commitment to prison and cannot vote, hold public office, or be a candidate for office (CGS § 9-46). But the law allows the right to vote to be restored after he has paid all fines and completed any time served in prison and parole (CGS § 9-46a).

In addition, every elected municipal officer or justice of the peace must be an elector in his town, and anyone who ceases to be an elector of the town must immediately cease to hold office (CGS § 9-186).

A felon regains the right to vote by (1) contacting any voter registration official and (2) providing written or other satisfactory proof that he has been discharged from confinement or parole and has paid all conviction-related fines (CGS § 9-46a).

GUNS

It is a criminal offense for a felon to possess a firearm or electronic defense weapon (CGS § 53a-217). The law defines a "firearm" as a "sawed-off shotgun, machine gun, rifle, shotgun, pistol, revolver, or other weapons, whether loaded or unloaded from which a shot may be discharged" (CGS § 53a-3(19)). A person convicted of a felony is not eligible for an eligibility certificate, or a permit to carry a pistol or revolver, and the certificate or permit is automatically revoked for a conviction of a felony (CGS §§ 29-28, 29-36i). In addition, the person must transfer any pistols or revolvers to someone eligible to possess them or the Public Safety commissioner (CGS § 29-36k).

EMPLOYMENT

Many statutes authorize government agencies to revoke or suspend licenses or permits for conviction of a felony. But the law also restricts the ability of agencies to do so. A person is not "disqualified to practice, pursue or engage in any occupation, trade, vocation, profession or business for which a license, permit, certificate, or registration is required to be issued by the state of Connecticut or any of its agencies solely because of a prior conviction of a crime" (CGS § 46a-80(a)).

Connecticut law declares a public policy of encouraging employers to hire qualified ex-offenders (CGS § 46a-79). A person is not disqualified from state employment solely because of a prior conviction of a crime. The state can deny employment or a license, permit, certificate, or registration if the person is found unsuitable after considering (1) the nature of the crime, (2) information pertaining to the degree of rehabilitation of the person, and (3) the time elapsed since the conviction or release (CGS § 46a-80). These statutes (CGS § 46a-79 et seq.) prevail over agencies' authority to deny licenses based on the lack of good moral character and to suspend or revoke licenses based on conviction of a crime. But they do not apply to law enforcement agencies, although an agency can adopt such a policy (CGS § 46a-81).

Licenses, Permits, And Conviction Of A Felony

Many licensing and permit statutes authorize an agency to suspend or revoke a license or permit based on conviction of a felony, including the following.

1. Architects (CGS § 20-294).

2. Private detectives, watchmen, guards, and patrol services (CGS § 29-158).

3. Professions under the jurisdiction of the Department of Public Health specifically including healing arts, medicine and surgery, osteopathy, chiropractic, naturopathy, podiatry, physical therapists, nursing, nurse's aides, dentistry, optometry, opticians, psychologists, marital and family therapists, clinical social workers, professional counselors, veterinary medicine, massage therapists, dietician-nutritionists, acupuncturists, paramedics, embalmers and funeral directors, barbers, hairdressers and cosmeticians, and hyper trichologists (CGS § 19-17 and various other statutes).

4. Attorneys (CGS § 51-91a).

5. Judges, family support magistrates, workers' compensation commissioners (CGS § 51-51i).

6. Radiographers and radiologic technologists (CGS § 20-74cc).

7. Midwives (CGS § 20-86h).

8. Licensees for (a) electrical work; (b) plumbing and piping work; (c) solar, heating, piping, and cooling work; (d) elevator installation, repair, and maintenance work; (e) fire protection sprinkler systems work; (f) irrigation work; and (g) sheet metal work (CGS § 20-334).

9. Major contractors (CGS § 20-341gg).

10. Lead abatement consultants, contractors, and workers (CGS § 20-481).

11. Public Service Gas Technicians (CGS § 20-540).

12. Public Accountants (CGS § 20-281a).

Solutions To Permanently Eradicate Domestic Violence, Child Abuse, and Bullying

13. *Psychologists (CGS § 20-192).*

14. *Individuals and businesses selling insurance (CGS § 38a-702k)*

In addition, statutes prohibit licensing a convicted felon as a pawnbroker (CGS § 21-40) or a professional bondsman (CGS § 29-145). A person convicted of a felony cannot be employed as an agent, operator, assistant, guard, watchman, or patrolman, subject to the general state policy (CGS § 29-156a). The Department of Consumer Protection can suspend, revoke, or refuse to grant or renew a permit for the sale of alcoholic liquor if convicted of a felony (CGS § 30-47).

CGS § 19a-80 allows the Public Health commissioner to suspend or revoke a daycare provider's license if any employee having direct contact with children has been convicted of any felony in which the victim is under age 18.

Licenses, Permits And Certain Crimes

Other licensing and permit statutes include provisions on suspension or revocation on conviction of certain crimes (such as those related to the profession, fraud, or extortion) or lack of good moral character. These could involve felony convictions. These statutes include the following.

1. *Consumer collection agencies (for actions of a partner, officer, director, or employee) (CGS § 36a-803).*

2. *Real estate appraisers (CGS §20-521).*

3. *Occupational therapists (CGS §20-74g).*

4. *Real Estate Brokers and Salespersons (CGS §§ 20-316, 20-320).*

5. *Service dealers, electronics technicians, apprentice electronics technicians, antenna technicians, radio electronics technicians (CGS § 20-354).*

6. *Sanitarians (CGS § 20-363).*

7. *Landscape architects (CGS § 20-373).*

8. *Interior Designers (CGS § 20-377r).*

9. *Hearing aid dealers (CGS § 20-404).*

10. *Community Association Managers (CGS § 20-456).*

11. *Pharmacy licensees (CGS § 20-579).*

12. *Practitioners distributing, administering, or dispensing controlled substances (CGS § 21a-322).*

13. *New home construction contractors (CGS § 20-417c).*

14. *Physical therapy assistants (CGS § 20-73a)*

The consumer protection commissioner can refuse to issue or renew a home improvement contractor or salesman registration of anyone required to register as a sexual offender. The Home Inspection Licensing Board can refuse to issue or renew a home inspector license or a home inspector intern permit to anyone required to register as a sexual offender (CGS §§ 20-426, 20-494).

State Employees

The state Personnel Act permits state agencies to discharge classified employees for incompetence or "other reasons relating to the effective performance of [their] duties" (CGS § 5-240(c)). Its regulations allow the state to dismiss employees who are convicted of a (1) felony, (2) misdemeanor committed while on duty; or (3) misdemeanor committed while off-duty that could affect their job performance (Regs. State Agencies § 5-240-1a). In most cases, it must give employees notice and a hearing prior to dismissal. And a union member may grieve and get an arbitrator's ruling on whether the conviction was just cause for discharge under the specific terms of the union contract.

Pam Libbey of the Department of Administrative Services (DAS) reports that the department does not have a policy specifying when background checks, including criminal history checks, must be done for state job applicants, and each agency sets its own rules.

Private Employment

Asking job applicants to indicate whether they have been convicted of a crime is permissible, but Title VII of the Civil Rights Act of 1964 appears to restrict an employer's ability to use criminal background information in the hiring process (42 USC. § 2000e, et seq.). The Equal Employment Opportunities Commission (EEOC), the federal agency that enforces Title VII, has decided that disqualifying people who have criminal records from jobs is discriminatory because the practice disproportionately affects African American and Hispanic men. (Those two groups have much higher criminal conviction rates than do Caucasian men.)

The EEOC has ruled repeatedly that covered employers cannot simply bar felons from consideration but must show that a conviction-based disqualification is justified by "business necessity." The legal test requires employers to examine the (1) nature and gravity of the offense or offenses, (2) length of time since the conviction or completion of sentence, and (3) nature of the job held or sought. Under this test, employers must consider the job-relatedness of a conviction, the circumstances of the offense, and the number of offenses (EEOC Compliance Manual, § 604 Appendices).

Pardons

State law prohibits employers, including the state and its political subdivisions, from taking certain actions against people who have their conviction records erased by an absolute pardon. An employer cannot require an employee or prospective employee to disclose such records or deny employment or discharge an employee solely because of records. An employment application form asking for criminal history information must contain a clear notice that the applicant need not disclose erased information and that he is considered never to have been arrested and can swear it under oath (CGS § 31-51i).

EDUCATION

The State Board of Education (SBE) can revoke a teacher or school administrator certificate or an authorization or permit (such as those held by athletic coaches, substitute teachers, and teachers teaching outside their endorsement area) of a person convicted of a *crime of moral turpitude or of such a nature that the board feels that allowing the holder to keep the credential would impair the credential's standing (CGS § 10-145b(m)(1)).*

The SBE must revoke a certificate, permit, or authorization when the holder is convicted of certain crimes. This includes convictions for (1) a capital felony; (2) arson murder; (3) any class A felony; (4) a class B felony, except first-degree larceny, computer crime, or vendor fraud; (5) risk of injury to a minor; (6) deprivation of a person's civil rights by a person wearing a mask or hood; (7) second-degree assault of an elderly, blind, disabled, pregnant, or mentally retarded person; (8) second-, third-, or fourth-degree sexual assault; (9) third-degree promoting prostitution; (10) substitution of children; (11) third-degree burglary with a firearm; (12) crimes involving child neglect; (13) first-degree stalking; (14) incest; (15) obscenity as to minors; (16) importing child pornography; (17) criminal use of a firearm or electronic defense weapon; (18) possession of a weapon on school grounds; (19) manufacture or sale of illegal drugs; and (20) crimes involving child abuse (CGS § 10-145b(m)(2)).

The SBE can deny certificate, authorization, or permit application if the applicant has been convicted of a crime of moral turpitude or of such a nature that the board feels that granting the credential would impair its standing (CGS § 10-145b(m)(3)). The SBE cannot issue or reissue a certificate for a person convicted of one of the crimes listed above until at least five years after the person finishes serving his sentence (including probation or parole) for the conviction (CGS § 10-145i).

FOSTER FAMILIES AND ADOPTION

The Department of Children and Families (DCF) must deny a license or approval for a foster family or prospective adoptive family if any member of the family's household was convicted of a crime that falls within certain categories of crimes, such as (1) injury or risk of injury to a minor; (2) impairing the morals of a minor or similar offenses; (3) violent crimes against a person; (4) possession, use, or sale of controlled substances within five years; and (5) illegal use of a firearm or similar offenses (Conn. Reg. § 17a-145-152). These crimes include felonies. DCF can also refuse to renew a license for the same reasons.

HOUSING

The general summary process procedures and those that apply to renters of mobile manufactured homes allow a landlord to bring eviction proceedings against a tenant who was convicted of a violation of federal, state, or local law that is detrimental to the health, safety, and welfare of other residents (CGS §§ 21-80, 47a-23).

Public Housing

Causes for eviction from public housing are slightly different for elderly people and others, but both are subject to eviction for certain felonies. Federal regulations for a federally subsidized project allow a landlord to evict a tenant only by judicial action pursuant to state or local law unless preempted by federal law or action of the United States (24 CFR § 247. 6).

Solutions To Permanently Eradicate Domestic Violence, Child Abuse, and Bullying

Under federal and state laws, an elderly person may only be evicted for good cause. The elderly (over 62), blind, and physically disabled cannot be evicted except for good cause. Good cause, relevant to a senior housing complex, includes voiding of the rental agreement because the tenant was convicted of using the premises for prostitution or illegal gambling, or material noncompliance with the rental agreement (CGS § 47a 23c). (See OLR report 2002-R-0734 for more information).

There is also cause for eviction from public housing when someone is associated with someone arrested for a drug-related offense. Federal law appears to authorize HUD to evict tenants who associate with people arrested or convicted of drug-related offenses. In fact, the law prohibits a tenant's eviction except for cause.

One ground for eviction under federal law is serious or repeated violations of the material lease terms, such as failure to pay rent, fulfill tenant obligations, or other good cause (24 CFR § 966.4 (l)(2)(i)). One of the provisions that the law requires in leases by federally assisted housing agencies is an assurance that a tenant, members of his household, guests, and other people under the tenant's control will refrain from engaging in drug-related criminal activity on or near the premises. "Drug-related criminal activity" means the illegal manufacture, sale, distribution, or use of a controlled substance or possession with intent to engage in these activities (24 CFR § 966.4 (f) (12)). (See OLR report 2000 -R-0256 for more information.)

The law gives public housing authorities certain discretion when evicting tenants for drug-related criminal activity. Specifically, the authority may consider all the circumstances of the case, including the seriousness of the offense, the extent of participation by family members, and the effects that the eviction would have on family members not involved in the proscribed activity. In appropriate cases, the authority may permit continued occupancy by uninvolved family members. The housing authority may also require a family member who engaged in illegal drug use to present evidence of his successful completion of a treatment program as a condition of continued occupancy (24 CFR § 966.4(l)(5)(i)).

STUDENT LOANS AND AID

A higher education student is not eligible for federal assistance if he is convicted under federal or state law of a crime involving possession or sale of a controlled substance. This includes grants, loans, or work assistance. For a conviction of possession, a person is ineligible for one year for a first offense, two years for a second offense, and indefinitely for a third offense. For a sale conviction, a person is ineligible for two years for a first offense and indefinitely after a second offense. A student can regain eligibility before the end of the specified period if (1) he satisfactorily completes a drug rehabilitation program with certain criteria or (2) the conviction is reversed and otherwise removed (20 USC § 1091(r)).

PRIVATE ORGANIZATIONS

Other organizations may consider a person's criminal background. For example, Little League regulations for the 2003 season require volunteers and employees to undergo annual background checks and prohibit anyone convicted of a crime against or involving a minor from participating as a volunteer or employee. At a minimum, the regulations require local leagues to check the sex offender registry in the state where the applicant resides or, if unavailable, a state criminal background check if allowed by law. Leagues can elect to conduct a national criminal background check (see OLR Report 2003-R-0048).

I am still trying to find my rightful place in society since I have been permanently disenfranchised by Virginia law. I have completed the judge's sentence, paid fines, and have made full restitution to Michelle and the State of Virginia. I have never had any contact with Michelle or any members of her family. The person I am today is trillions of miles away from the person I was when I committed those offenses. I am married with a beautiful family structure, a businessman, and a devout man of God. However, most regrettably, I am a permanently disenfranchised felon. My greatest disappointment in life and my only regret is that with respect to this situation I have allowed my kid's future to be jeopardized due to my actions. I have always felt that even though I was set free in January 1993, the chokehold of being a convicted felon has always haunted me and bound my goals and dreams. Most kids idolize and respect their parents until they can form their own opinions. I wonder how my kids will react when it is finally disclosed that I am a convicted felon. The thought hurts because I have no excuse and am not about to begin to play the blame game because the only person at fault was me. When will I be set free?

Jerome A. Gray, an official with the Alabama Democratic Conference once said, "At what point does the state's hold on inmates cease?" [46] As a felon, I am always told what I cannot do instead of what I can do. As a felon I cannot vote, hold a public officials seat, adopt children, serve on a jury, serve in the military, mentor inner-city youth, qualify for state and federal occupational licenses and loans, act as a notary, volunteer in certain business sectors, hold certain positions within a church, be awarded certain government contracts due to certain security levels of clearance, and cannot work at certain jobs because almost all job and loan applications rightfully ask the question have you ever been convicted of a felony? As a felon, you must distance yourself from various public and private officials because your affiliation can hurt that person's credibility. As a felon, I cannot go into certain jails and prisons to give spiritual counseling and general uplift to inmates due to security. I cannot get into certain schools, universities, and programs due to their strict codes of moral conduct and ethics. I cannot participate in certain social groups and organizations such as the masons and fraternities. I certainly cannot purchase a firearm in order to protect my family. I cannot get certain business franchises, become a person of influence, and impact my community since as a felon you are prejudged, stereotyped, least likely to be hired in a respectable, high paying job, and constantly reminded of your past. I am not really a U.S. citizen because I am not permitted on certain premises, always discounted, not taken seriously, seen as a threat, never trusted, publicly ostracized, not credible in legal proceedings, and are seen as a liar. I cannot retain professional licenses such as an attorney, doctor, c.p.a, dentist, mortgage banker, real estate, or an insurance broker. I cannot participate with local civic groups that work with government agencies such as the FBI community outreach programs. I cannot even become a coach to my daughter's recreational sports teams. I can do ten thousand deeds of good, but once someone learns that I am a felon the deeds are overshadowed by my past.

I am sincerely sorry for what I did. How is it that this wrong can never be made right? This is a slate that can never be wiped clean? I have a bounty that is always on my head! How can I feed my family, tithe appropriately to my church, and pay my taxes if I cannot earn a certain living because of the restrictions set forth due to my felonious background? I am a mute in my community because my vote literally does not count, and I really cannot have an opinion about an election because my opinion has no influence and will not make a difference. People of all races died fighting for the right to vote. I cannot defend my family in the event of a home invasion due to not having the right to bear arms. I cannot defend my country because I cannot serve in the military. I have to watch foreign citizens come into our country, become a legal citizen, and gain the right to vote. All I can do is observe them. I will be forced to watch my daughters grow up and have the opportunity to vote more times than me and who are rightfully more of a citizen as toddlers than I ever will be. The Iraqi's can scream freedom. Far worst criminals can vote and hold government jobs because the state they committed the crimes in allows them to do so under the law. I cannot volunteer for the Big Brothers and Sisters programs, nor can I adopt a deserving child.

I was in the wrong, and if it is the will of God that I should be permanently disenfranchised for the remainder of my life because of my actions, then I must accept this and find resolution in the fact that I apologized, and it is what it is until I die. Even if that becomes the reality of my position as a U.S. citizen and my rights, I will never be held captive in my mind regarding the matter. My mind will always be justifiably free because I paid my debt to society and God has been forgiven me!

Solutions To Permanently Eradicate Domestic Violence, Child Abuse, and Bullying

I do want you to know that I am not a cannot, could not, can never be, undriven, unenthused, lazy person. I am in hot pursuit of leaving a positive legacy to my wife and children. I am the core of our family financially and truly control the financial, educational, spiritual, and future destinies of my wife and kids. I do not want to be in a large number of people who are unable to participate in our democracy because of Virginia's permanent disenfranchisement laws. Disenfranchisement laws conflict with the basic notions of justice and discourage what society ought to be promoting: those criminals who have completed their sentences be allowed to return to society as productive citizens. *"The process of voting is one of the most sacred processes in our democracy,"* said Hilary Shelton, *director of the NAACP's Washington Bureau. "Our hope is that former inmates will participate fully in our democracy, take ownership of their communities, and become law-abiding citizens. The right to vote is fundamental to that."* [47] I want to feel like my vote and voice really does count and has an impact on someone. I do not want to spend my days and nights wondering why in some parts of the U.S. released convicted felons can vote because their rights were restored once they served their sentence as well as those inmates who can still vote even though they are incarcerated.

"Every United States citizen has the right to vote once they reach eighteen and register. However, once someone breaks the law and is convicted that person is extracted from society and imprisoned until he has paid his debt to society. Once released, the ex-convict must show that they want to be a participating and viable citizen again. They must show that they have learned from their mistakes and that they no longer participate in criminal activities that are harmful to society and its citizens. Voting is a right until you have been convicted of a crime, then it becomes a privilege that one must earn the right to have back." [48] Unless convicted of Treason, why should a felon who has served his sentence be further punished by the loss of his fundamental civil rights? It has been nearly 3 decades since this crime occurred. I am a great asset to my family, friends, employees, church, and community. What do you think happens when a man cannot feed his family or just be a man? That is a dangerous proposition for any human being trying to survive!

Each day I realize as a felon that I will never again be allowed to take part in some of the fundamental rights of this country, simply because of my past transgressions, of which I am sincerely apologetic. I also wonder daily if this policy is obviously contradictory to the principles behind not only the right to vote but to the principles behind the entire United States Constitution. Each day I wonder how my friends, colleagues, business associates, neighbors, pastor, and church members will respond when they learn of my personal criminal background. I know too well that most people respond unfavorably when they learn of an individual's background. I once had a boss reply, "As long as I am in charge, a convict will never work here!" Had he read my file to know of my background prior to my employment I would never have been allowed to work there for eight years as a manager. I know my actions made me a felon, but no one can ever be truly ashamed and embarrassed as me. I embarrassed my family, friends, Michelle, her family, friends, and my good name. Moreover, I felt I shamed myself to God. I harmed His property! Forgive me!

Once released, I never fell back to the violent ways of life that landed me in prison. I have made a great career in business. It was my agenda in 1993 to not only transfer myself into a beacon of integrity but to change the negative stereotype of a felon. I accomplished this by realizing early in my young career that the foundation of any relationship is trust and credibility. I built my reputation on being trustworthy, altruistic, and enthusiastic. After what I had been through prior to, during, and after prison, I realized that given the second chance I had been given in life by God that I would spend the rest of my life as a quality human being who appreciates life each day, and all that it has to offer. I am trying to realize my dreams as a husband, father, entrepreneur, humanitarian, and philanthropist. I know that the Lord put me in prison for a reason greater than my understanding. I know now that in order for me to have great things occur in my life I had to first endure great things!

I am approaching many years of being self-employed and am enjoying the impact that I am having on other folk's lives. I want to impact every family and community in the world, in the future, by being financially sound to support and create programs that will preserve lives. I would love to create a program for men, women, and children who abuse their significant others, family members, and classmates so that they do not face the road I had to travel. People are only as good as their options. I want to give people choices and options in life. I pray that I will be judged for who and what I am doing today and where I wish to be tomorrow.

I despise everything that a felon represents. I do not represent the principles of a felon. I represent the spirits of love, faith, and integrity. I have a commitment to fulfilling my responsibilities and role as a husband, father, provider, employer, neighbor, activist, and friend. Sometimes in life, all you have is your good name and your word, and that is how people judge you. Without you truly knowing who I am today and forevermore I give you my word that I am truly a phenomenal, trustworthy, quality human being, trying to help God save lives and legacies.

I recall wondering why God allowed my life to happen this way. But if I am trusting in Christ, I never need to ask, "How could He let that happen to me?" God may never reveal all His reasons to me, but He has revealed His character to me. His character assured me that He never makes mistakes, is never uncaring, and that He never separates Himself from our need. The need I face for making the FAMILY MAN™ a successful company is great because I and many millions of others have a positive legacy waiting! I have individuals relying solely on me to exist, and I owe them my labor of love! The bottom line is God did not influence me and the devil did not make me do it. I was impulsively wrong, accountable, and responsible for my own actions. I will not minimize it, make light of it, or justify it with excuses! I am sincerely sorry for what I did to my victims because I negatively compromised the future destinations of many individuals!

If prison and jail is more attractive and sexier, compared to what you deal with at home, how many convincing arguments do you have to make to an individual that is choosing how to survive and self-preserve with the basic choices of being a human being such as food, water, shelter clothing, sanitation, education, and healthcare. The solution is rooted in what is causing the pain and suffering and getting the appropriate coping skills and techniques to permanently extinguish the problems and pain! Then comes economic and education solutions to provide purpose and fulfillment and reasons for someone to live!

Serving others in need opportunities and activities to keep them focused on others and not just on their pain! Sometimes you can be healed by healing others needing a bigger bandage and carrying heavier baggage than you! Activities breeds activities! These individuals need new environments because the definition of insanity is doing the same things over and over again expecting different results! I saw a better life when I got out of the dungeon! It is hard to dream in those dark places when the light is off in your head. Your mind is on the pain and not the pleasure! My mission is to eradicate violence and abuse against women and children and prevent recidivism!

What does one mistake cost or questions by the recidivists? What do you need to succeed? It costs you meaningful things like your good name, reputation, brand, legacy, once in a lifetime opportunities such as meeting and doing business with people like Oprah, Mark Burnett, Tyra Banks, Tyler Perry or Rick Hendrick,

Automotive Manufacturers like BMW, Toyota, Ford, General Motors, VW, Mercedes Benz, American Honda, Hyundai, KIA, Subaru, Mazda, or Nissan that would permanently allow you to take care of generations of Burgess's and their employees' families!

The thousands of people who lost their lives for basic rights to vote are crying in heaven because you broke the law and lost the right to vote! You can do a million charitable deeds of good for humanity, and one mistake or error in judgment will also cost your children's, children's children. People make mistakes and errors in judgment daily, and naturally, depending upon the severity and degree of their crime, most deserve a second chance and should not have to pay for their mistake or lapse in judgment for the rest of their entire life. I am not naive enough to believe that there are individuals and situations where these individuals do disqualify themselves from an eternal, infinite redemption pass due to the heinousness of the offense and for those individuals God bless them. So you pay the price over & over?

My goal will always be to serve those individuals who want to be healed of what is triggering their violent and abusive behavior, so that no one else's life and legacy, including theirs, is harmed or killed! My mission is to be the ultimate positive example of what your life can and will be after you have been arrested or incarcerated and served your debt to society and the coping skills and techniques needed to follow up to resolving your mental health issues and dealing with other individuals in society.

My non-profit company FAMILY MANKIND™ will be to domestic violence offenders, child abusers, and bullies what Alcoholics Anonymous is to individuals struggling with alcohol and chemical addiction and what Susan G. Komen and St. Jude's Hospital is to those impacted with cancer and other very serious life-threatening illnesses. We will be the catalyst that breaks the toxic bloodline legacy and perpetuation of domestic violence, bullying, and child abuse while "howling" away the silence of domestic violence, bullying, and abuse towards students, women, and children, and in the process, ending recidivism. FAMILY MANKIND™ will create "HOWLERS" who will never stand for violence and pain!

Police and law enforcement say the most dangerous call is a domestic violence call and the most disturbing and heartbreaking call that sticks with them their entire life is the crime against and involving children. If I can impact any person to save a life or prevent harm against another human being, then my life will have served a significant purpose and defined meaning that my family for generations will most certainly be proud! There is nothing more honorable than serving and improving the lives of others! There is nothing more valuable than preserving and helping to save the life and legacy of an innocent individual!

When I was in the penitentiary, I asked the Lord to permanently heal me and deliver me from the domestic violence and abuse sickness! HE did! Now I fight this cause! I am talking directly to the domestic violence offender, bully and child abuser to get the required help to permanently stop the violence and abuse against women and children because what I do know for certain is that bullying, violence, and abuse progresses from bad to worse to a tragedy. It all can be prevented if the abuser decides to make the change, so they can change their destiny and those who they are impacting with their behavior. Get all the help you can get on the outside by choice, rather than, getting the same health by force on the inside of a penitentiary cell or psychiatric hospital. With Your God, the impossible can and will be possible! It is not a matter of if but when those impossibilities become POSSIBLE realities!

The only stripes I want to earn are the stripes from those who served in the military, law enforcement, or community servants and activists. Street stripes are earned by acts of violence and are often followed by tattooed, tear dropped eyes and released balloons headed to heaven. The penitentiary and street credibility stripes come at a high price and often times with losses tied to them such as your freedom or your life. I do not want anyone to experience what I went through by way of losing great friendships, career opportunities, legacies, my freedom, my pet, and nearly my life. I do not want anyone to be responsible for violently harming any woman, man, child, member of the LGBTQ community or animal! I want anyone who is a domestic violence offender, bully, or child abuser to get help now before they end up where I did or worse. Want to go to prison now? Do not wait or even hesitate to get help for your violent or abusive behavior. You are better than being a bully! Your reputation, legacy, and bloodline are screaming for you to be the one that stops the generational curses of domestic violence, bullying, and abuse!

The bottom line is there are consequences for the rest of your life when you are labeled a domestic violence offender, child abuser or bully! When will your exile end you may wonder? Quite possibly never! The victims of your crime live and serve a life and death sentence impacted by your violence and abuse. What about the consequences for the rest of your victim's life? When will their exile end? Quite possibly never I surmise! Do not put yourself in that box ever my friend!

Solutions To Permanently Eradicate Domestic Violence, Child Abuse, and Bullying

Being a domestic violence offender is like a baby walking across a busy highway just after learning to walk, not aware or conscious of the dangerous vehicles approaching at 70+ miles per hour! It is a Rubik's Cube! I have love and faith that if I could get help and permanently eradicate violence and abuse so can you! Never forget that my greatest mistake was taking too long to get help? Get help why you still can! Get help now before something happens that you didn't plan! Love you!

WHAT HAVE YOUR MISTAKES COST YOU?

WHAT HAVE YOUR MISTAKES COST OTHERS?

TEENY TURNER, RUTH DORSEY, & ME
I SHOULD HAVE NEVER LEFT THEM!

Solutions To Permanently Eradicate Domestic Violence, Child Abuse, and Bullying

FYI About PRISON: It is better to fight and lose than to never fight at all! It is about respect, relationships, and loyalty in prison! Violence is always present in prison! Your mental toughness has to be stronger than your physical toughness. Sure you can be eight feet tall and 8 hundred pounds of pure muscle, but you still have to go to sleep, take a shower, get groomed and eat! This requirement makes anyone vulnerable regardless of size. The question then becomes are you ready for the fight for your life and manhood when it comes, because it is not a matter of if "it" will come, but when "it" will come! You will get tried but will you get got? You have to fight to survive! Do you want to fight for your life in or out of prison? How many of us are in prison in our minds and not behind bars? How many innocent people are in prison in their relationships, homes, school, church or work? *A bullet is small & it will kill you!* <u>**YOU DON'T HAVE TO GO TO PRISON TO BE FREED! YOU CAN GET HEALED NOW!**</u>

Solutions To Permanently Eradicate Domestic Violence, Child Abuse, and Bullying

SOUTHAMPTON CORRECTIONAL CENTER! THIS IS NOT A PLACE YOU WANT TO TAKE A PHOTO! I DO NOT WANT ANYONE TO GO TO PRISON BEHIND A PREVENTABLE ISSUE. THERE ARE TONS OF HOSTILE VIOLENT OFFENDERS WHO ARE LOOKING FOR A GOOD FIGHT IF VIOLENCE IS WHAT YOU ARE LOOKING TO PERPETUATE! THE DIFFERENCE THERE IS ARE YOU THE PREDATOR OR PREY?

Solutions To Permanently Eradicate Domestic Violence, Child Abuse, and Bullying

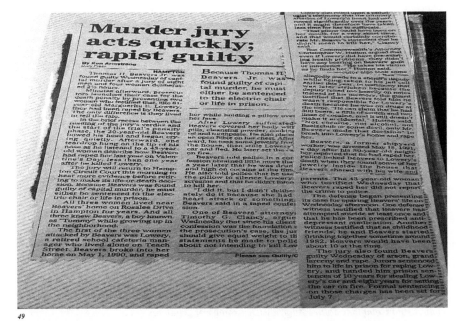

49

My Cell Mate Thomas Beavers. He Died By Lethal Injection In 1997

50

Solutions To Permanently Eradicate Domestic Violence, Child Abuse, and Bullying

TERRIFIED YOUNG MAN' IS TO DIE [51]
KEN ARMSTRONG Daily Press
July 8, 1992, Hampton

When Thomas Beavers Jr. was a baby, his mother tried to kill him.

When Beavers was 5, he started sniffing gasoline. In elementary school, he twice had to repeat a grade because of learning disabilities. In ninth grade, he dropped out. His abuse of drugs and alcohol got worse. Twice, he tried to kill himself.

Then, when Beavers was 18, he killed a neighbor while raping her. After that, he raped two other neighbors. He told authorities recently that if set free, he'd probably rape again.

Those were just a few of the facts presented Tuesday to Hampton Circuit Court Judge John D. Gray, who had to study the timeline of Beavers' life and decide whether it should end in the electric chair.

Defense attorneys argued that Beavers' life should be spared, that he grew up in a troubled family and had never been able to break the chains of drug addiction. Prosecutors argued that Beavers should be sentenced to death, that his life's spiral of violence showed he would remain a threat to society.

"What has been going on with Mr. Beavers the last 10 years is a road map to the electric chair," said Commonwealth's Attorney Christopher W. Hutton.

On Tuesday, four days shy of Beavers' 21st birthday, Gray upheld a jury's recommendation and sentenced Beavers to death. The execution date was set for Nov. 23, 1994.

It was the fourth time in the past 10 years that a defendant received the death penalty in Hampton.

On the evening of May 1, 1990, Beavers broke into the Teach Street home of Marguerite E. Lowery, 61, a retired school cafeteria manager who lived alone in Beavers' neighborhood. Beavers raped Lowery and suffocated her by holding a pillow over her face. He later told authorities he used the pillow only to stifle Lowery's screams, not to kill her.

Nine months later, Beavers broke into his next-door neighbor's home and raped her. Three months after that, he raped yet another woman who lived in his family's neighborhood.

Upholding a separate jury's recommendation, Gray also sentenced Beavers on Tuesday to life in prison for raping the third woman, along with another 20 years for breaking into her home. Beavers also received a life sentence for raping Lowery, another 10 years for burglarizing her home and eight years for setting her car afire.

Before being sentenced Tuesday, Beavers asked the judge to spare his life.

"I stand before this court as a terrified young man," he said. "I feel great pain and anger for what I have done to others. ... I'd just like to state that I am sorry for what I have done."

Members of Beavers' family said afterward that instead of being sentenced to death, he should have been given a chance to turn his life around.

Solutions To Permanently Eradicate Domestic Violence, Child Abuse, and Bullying

"He's sick, but they don't want to help him. They just want to kill him," said Elsie Kostyal, the defendant's aunt.

Thomas Beavers Sr. said he's convinced his son didn't mean to kill Lowery. "He wasn't in his right mind. Why kill a man over drugs and everything when it's not his fault?" he said.

The father also accused prosecutors of using the case to make a name for themselves. "They're using other human beings to make their way in life," he said.

Hutton declined to comment on those statements, other than to say that the case received little publicity and that the father was probably "emotionally distraught."

The defendant's wife and 2-year-old son attended Tuesday's hearing, but Beavers' mother did not. Defense attorney Timothy G. Clancy told the judge she was "conspicuous by her absence."

"He has a mother who to this day can say nothing good about him, a mother who when he was an infant tried to kill him," Clancy said during sentencing arguments.

Thomas Beavers Sr. said afterward that his wife suffered severe depression after giving birth to her son. When the baby was only a few months old, she took him into the bathroom and locked the door. Thomas Beavers Sr. said he had to break the bathroom door down, then take the infant - his skin blue from his being held in cold water -to the hospital.

LETTER FROM THOMAS BEAVERS AUGUST 8, 1992
HE WROTE THE LETTER ON MY BIRTHDAY!

WHO GROWS UP BELIEVING THEY WILL LIVE WITH A FUTURE DEATH ROW INMATE? WHO DO YOU KNOW LIVING ON DEATH ROW! I WOULD HAVE NEVER DREAMED THAT NIGHTMARE EVER!

I Still Can't Believe I Had A Friend Who Died By Lethal Injection!

2:30 Am 8-4-93

Dear, Burgess

Hey What's up, Nice to hear from you.
i hope your fine & well?
B-mow i tell you things are fuched up here,
We only come out to eat that's it.
Two hours a day an after dinner we stay
out 3 hours. We go out side 3 times a week,
for 2½ hours the law library same time as well.
They call a cell block here a POD it's 5 building
here in in building 1 we have A-pod B-pod & C-pod
im in C-pod 24 cells to a pod B&C are
death row A is the pod fuck you, this
not death row. The rooms here are 1 man cells
with a window an a writing table the food
is not good some times. i go to the library
alot too fine some thing to help me on my case
Well about your letter to me you ask how
my falings are its like this i did some thing
wrong by law an by God all i can do is
pray for Gods help an go on to fight for my
life. B-mow i may only have 5 to 8 years
left on this earth, so i will make it
the best as i can. Hey about "y" that had 30 years
well men will be men. why he did that is
some thing he as to live with. You know it just
gos to show you how some one can be at times

Solutions To Permanently Eradicate Domestic Violence, Child Abuse, and Bullying

I CAN RELATE TO WHAT LIFE IS LIKE ON DEATH ROW

B-more you said you want to help me any way you can. Well i thank You very much for feeling that way. to me i would feel wrong to ask you for anything i hope you understand its up to you to do what's in your heart B-more i respect your words as man an good friend. The people who give me money is my Mom & Dad it's not much an i don't ask them for money or any thing.

You know i turned 21 on death row 7-11-93 B-more the things you said in your letter to me is what im doing you know about the inner self. That's all i have us a person so i do pray to help with my problems an to be successful spiritually.

Your friend Miss Davis i would like to here from her!

May God be with you all ways

Your friend, Bear

Take Care

I WAS IN A SUICIDE PREVENTION PROGRAM

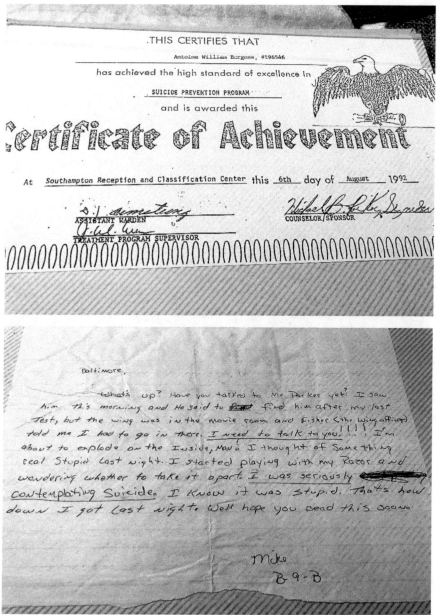

I ENCOURAGED OTHER INMATES TO GET THE REQUIRED HELP

Others Encouraged Me: Gwendolyn Jackson and Carlos Walton

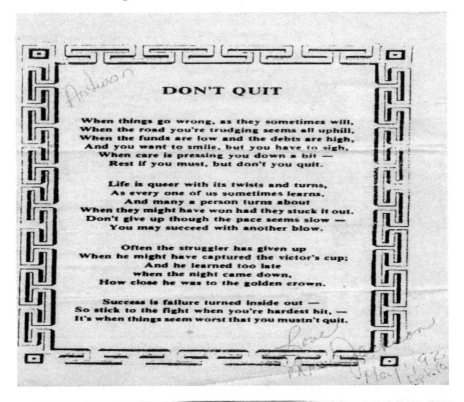

DO NOT BENCH YOUR SELF IN LIFE DUE TO YOUR MENTAL HEALTH

Impulsiveness, stubbornness, ignorance, ego, and not being accountable or aware of my mental health challenges cost me dearly. I benched myself in the game of life as a result of my horrific decisions. I blew the opportunity to become a licensed attorney, automotive dealer, insurance agent, hospital contractor, and even the opportunity to own certain franchises that no one in their right mind would ever turn down. I could never become a General Manager at any automotive manufacturer dealership as a result of being a convicted felon, even though I was brilliant enough to own one! The best day and worst day was when two automotive manufacturers wanted me to become a franchised dealer only to find out shortly thereafter that it was not possible for me! To know that I cost my children, grandchildren, great-grandchildren and so forth, the opportunity to live an abundant, privileged life is unequivocally the worst feeling for a father, husband, and grandpa. I let them down. I wanted to give them the very best life that any man could offer them, even when I am no longer on this earth. _**MAN DAMN!**_

SPEAK LIFE INTO THE ATMOSPHERE

It was not so long ago that I, Antoine Burgess, a junior finance major, from Baltimore, Maryland, took time to analyze myself. During this process, my objective was to come up with adjectives that would give a conclusive description of my character. Based on my personality, achievements, and goals, the adjectives that best describe me are serious and compassionate.

Why am I serious? I am a career oriented person who believes that one must go to any extreme to get what he wants out of life, just, as long as in attaining this success one sets their goals high, but in perspective with reality and the law.

Also, because I am black, I can not be content with the nine to five, eight hour work day. I have got to be concerned about working ten, twelve, or fourteen hour days, so that my work is so sharp, I am judged on it, rather than the color of my skin. As a result, when I graduate from Hampton, I plan to go directly to law school in hopes and prayers of becoming a practicing corporate attorney with a Ph.D. in Law.

Why am I compassionate? My heart almost fails when I think about marriage and setting up a family. I love to think about things such as my wedding day, my wedding night, my honeymoon, being loyal and respectful to my wife, having kids, being an emotional and financial provider for my wife and children, family, and community. But more than anything in this world, and this involves both being serious and compassionate, I am going to be the father who will always be there for his wife and children. I do not want to be amongst the statistics of those black fathers who abandoned their family, kids, and life.

By only the blessings of God, I pray I attain these goals.

YOUR SPIRIT IS LISTENING TO BRING IT INTO EXISTENCE

Solutions To Permanently Eradicate Domestic Violence, Child Abuse, and Bullying

THE WOLF and THE WOLVERINE

Solutions To Permanently Eradicate Domestic Violence, Child Abuse, and Bullying

THE WOLVERINE
Another Person's Trash and Nightmare is Another Person's Treasure and Dream!
Loving Me in Spite of Me! Bless Your Life Trena!

I was probably a good 90 days out of the penitentiary at the ripe old age of 22 when I got a call from a college friend, from Hampton University, who stated, "Mannnnn! We've got to get down to Club Paradise," a strip club located in Newport News, Virginia, because there was supposed to be "a Jet Beauty of the Week centerfold model coming there to dance, and she is a must-see in person!" To young black brothers like me, page 43 of Jet magazine was like a prestigious men's centerfold magazine with the significant difference being the Jet Beauty of the Week was fully clothed in a bathing suit. In fact, in Virginia that was the case with their so-called strippers too because they were dancing with bikinis on and they never shed the bikinis! "I'm there!" I said.

Growing up in Baltimore and traveling to Washington D.C., I was exposed to seeing strippers in the nude on the Baltimore block and the Foxy Playground bar and nightclub on Georgia Ave in D.C. Setting the record straight about strippers, I respect them above all! Why? Do you know how strong, purposeful, and confident you have to be to shed your clothes in front of strangers? How many people could do that for money? Is it by choice or force to work such a job? Most times it is because you are only as good as your options to feed yourself or your children! Better options equal better choices. Better choices equal better money & lifestyle!

I truly and respectfully appreciate their communication and closing skills, hustle game and commitment to get legal money without having to sell their souls or bodies to the devil to make an honest dollar. I have always loved them with a passion not just because of their beautiful bodies and faces, but it is because of their hustler's ambition, purpose, mentality and resolve that I respect and share with them!

How or why would I judge them if I viewed and judged myself just like them, as a closer, hustler and boss and not a whore or b****? Like them, you are only as good as your options at the time and being a freshly released and paroled permanently disenfranchised convicted felon, I resorted to what I knew to make money to take care of myself and that meant being a dope boy selling crack and cars while going back to college. I had to do what I had to do to survive with the dramatic difference between me and the strippers being that what I was doing was illegal, immoral and just downright killing and devaluing the quality of life in the very community I lived. I was an impulsive convicted felon with limited options trying to begin a life as a man with no help from abusers! Cardi B, Amber Rose, & Jessica Dime proves *"**Never Judge Me Where I Was! I Just May Be Your Boss One Day!**"*

Going to see pretty women to have a beer or two or to fraternize with the fellas kept me sane, but the reality was it was keeping me from being depressed and lonely. These women and men were therapy to me that I desperately needed and wanted. Besides, the activities reduced my chances of being incarcerated or being killed or robbed, even though I never feared or worried about either because I was already incarcerated and dead in my mind, body, and soul. Me selling drugs, like them dancing, was a direct reflection of the lack of parental support I had which trained my choices to not care about the consequences or care about who the f*** knew what I was doing to feed myself. Would I've sold drugs if I was serving them to a loved one? Would they be dancing if they were dancing in front of their dad?

No one was offering me jobs or money as a freshly minted Virginia permanently disenfranchised convicted felon, yet the Virginia Commonwealth did not mind offering their unsolicited opinion of me being a convicted felon and that no respectful individual or company would ever hire me! When I saw young or older ladies stripping, I wish I could have saved them and given them a better opportunity to upgrade from dancing with no hidden agendas or "G" strings attached.

I wished that I could have stripped the bull shizzle and pain out of their lives and minds forever and filled it up with love and money, so they could be doing what they wanted to be doing versus what they had to be doing! Many of these women were students trying to go to or stay in school or were single ladies and moms trying to feed themselves and their babies because no one else was filling in the financial gaps and voids. I could never even judge the ones who were doing it to feed their habits because what I know is there is a pain in them they are trying to forget, treat or remedy, and that says to me that at least they are not robbing or stealing from others to support their habit. They are just trying to cope with the pain!

I have always viewed strippers as the remnants of insecure, weak, lying, lazy men in relationships who promised to take care of their mothers and them, or abandoned fathers like mine who deserted their responsibilities and chose not to be accountable or engaged to their daughter's well-being! These cowards called Dad should be called **_Dead_**! Show me a weak man & I'll show you a broken weak family!

That is why when I first saw Trena, whose stage name was "Mercedes," as beautiful as she was externally, I was melancholic and could not see her for her heart, but rather the product of a failed father! I gave her an empathetic $50-dollar bill for a one-song dance, and she did not have to do anything...No Lap Dance, No Private V.I.P intimacy, No Flashing of her flesh, No Motor Boarding, Nooooothinnng as we say in the streets! I just wanted her to know she was valuable and that her life had a purpose! I was saddened by the fact that how could someone so beautiful have to resort to dancing in a bikini in a hole in the wall bar in her hometown! Do you know how embarrassing that had to have been for her? Her daddy is now called ***DEADDY*** because he gets a failing E for effort! ***MAN DAMN!***

I proceeded to play pool when one of the assistant club managers named Rob said, "Let me holler at you!" He "wanted me to talk with the dancer named Mercedes, because he knew I could help her out with no strings attached as far as either getting her enrolled in school somewhere locally or a solid job." He told me "She was working part-time at Food Lion as a cashier and bagger to help her blind mother out with the bills because ends were not meeting and that she wanted to help her family and get back into college in New York at the Fashion Institute of Technology or return to Hollywood to regain her position as a model and actress."

Rob said he "Did not want her to get comfortable dancing or the money because he saw many good girls come in with ambitions and goals. They never leave the club to pursue their dreams because men or life hits them and throws irrevocable curveballs, causing many to strike out in life or they just settle for the money!"

And then "Voila!" Before I knew it, I was eye to eye sitting across the table from the most beautiful and prettiest woman ever made by God! I remember her scent and her eyes just melted me. She was the prettiest girl I had ever seen in my life! **This woman's goal should never have been dancing on a pole in a hole!**

She was very direct with me, and I do not recall her even looking at me in the face. If she was a "G" string diva, then the "G" should have stood for "Gangster" and string should be replaced with strong! She was "Gangster Strong" to me by the way she carried herself! She was not f****** around or going for any bull shizzle because she was focused on doing what she had to do legally and morally until she could do what she wanted to do outside of dancing in a club in a bathing suit in front of horny and corny men. ***This grind is why strippers go from the pole to the palace***!

The conversation we had was brief, and to this day she cannot recall remembering my face or conversation, but she remembers I had on a nice silk shirt and that I had given her $50. What I did not know then was I was literally there for her very first individual dance set and was one of her very first customers and confirmed in her mind that she did not have to sell her body or do acrobatic tricks for a dollar. She said that I had given her that justification that made her realize she was worth more than the typical $1 given by cheap men. It reaffirmed to her from her very first day of dancing of what she already had decided which was that she never was going to do anything against her set of ethics, values or morals like No In or Out of the Club Relationships, No Lap Dances, No Private V.I.P Intimacy, No Flashing of Her Body Parts, No Motor Boarding, No Nothing! She knew her worth!

I gave her my business card which had a symbolic ying-yang logo and all of my contact information on it and told her to contact me should she ever need my assistance for anything. Over the next few weeks, I never heard from her. I recall sitting in my bed one morning before school thinking, "I wonder how that girl Mercedes is doing! I hope she has made enough to take care of her blind mother!"

And then, "Voila!" I had just bought a sports car and was traveling down Warwick Blvd in Newport News, Virginia with the sunroof open, windows down, and music **bumping** out of the speakers. To my amazement, as I looked to my right, there she was walking. It was Mercedes, the most beautiful girl I had ever seen, from the club. I passed her, but just as I was about to enter the intersection, a revelation or some may say a spirit overwhelmed me and I looked up at the sky out of my sunroof and GOD spoke to me...*SHE COULD BE THE ONE! TURN AROUND*!

With nearly any hesitation, I bussed a U-turn. Before I knew it, I was slowly strolling in my car at 2 miles per hour with the hazard lights on praying that no one would hit me from the rear, next to my dream girl. "Give me the words God!"

"Don't I know you? Don't you go to the university?" To my amazement and excitement, waiting anxiously for her first reply, she stated, "NO!" And as if I had never stopped, she continued walking forward. I remember thinking again, "God give me the **right** words to say to this Goddess so she can give me a chance!"

After about 25 minutes curbside and at least 20 cars roaring by honking their horns, God found the words for me and I was able to convince Mercedes that I had met her at the club via Rob's introduction. Considering the 100+ degree of heat, she allowed me to take her home which was only a few miles down the road. She later confessed to me that she "had a hidden shank in her right hand and that had I made any aggressive moves she would have sliced my faces to shreds!" Lord Have Mercy!

Nonetheless, I walked her to her door and gave her another business card and emphatically replied again, "Should you need a ride anywhere, at any time, for any reason, just give me a call because I am 2 minutes from you." She kindly said, "Should I need a ride, I will call you!" Then she entered her townhome and the moment was over for Mercedes and me. Oh well. Man, I was praying for weeks for her to call. She never did. The crazy thing is I thought about her for months to no avail. I prayed she was okay and that we would somehow meet again.

One day before I had to go to work at Red Lobster as a bartender, I decided to drop by to check in on her. I was dressed in a formal black tuxedo which was the standard uniform at that time for bartenders at Red Lobster. I went to the door and rang the doorbell hoping she would be the one to answer. Instead of her answering the door it was her mom. I smiled kindly as her mom opened the door and said, "May I help you?" "Yes, mam, I replied. Is Mercedes available to come to the door?" She said, "I don't have anyone here by that name. What does she look like?" I said, "She's short and very pretty!" She smiled and said, "You must be talking about my daughter Trena. Wait a second! Let me get her for you. Who shall I say you are?" I said, "Tell her it's Q!" (I was called Q, which is short for "Seque" because when I was in prison, a close partner of mine named Dwayne Cephas said we should have aliases in prison for female visitors and pen-pals, so it sounded more attractive to the ladies. When I asked Cephas why I should be called Seque, he said, "The Muslims told him I should be called Seque because I had spoken constantly about the fraternity of Q's and Baltimore so much that I should be called Say Q, spelled Seque formally." I asked him what Seque meant, and he said "He didn't know. Make some s**t up Baltimore!" I told him that "Seque stood for the beautiful one!" He was like, "Hell yeah Baltimore. I've gotta come up with some bulls**t like that for myself to impress the honeys!" My boy Cephas was a true brother's keeper in prison.

Here I was on parole, telling Mercedes' mom that my name was Q. She called Trena's name aloud for her to come to the door. As she was calling for Trena, I could see someone appearing at the top of the second-floor steps, looking down to see who was at the door. At that very moment, I could see Trena stomp her feet in disgust with her mother as if to say, "Why in the hell are you calling me to the damn door momma? I don't want to see that Mutha******!" After several louder, "Trena you have a guest!" calls by Trena's mom, Trena came balling down the stairs with an agitated look of disgust with her mom, and before I knew it, she was standing at the door alone with me. I was still on the outside of the door when Trena replied in a short and stern tone, "Yes! What do you want?" I replied, "I was in the neighborhood and decided to stop by to see if you needed a ride anywhere." She quickly spurted out, "What did I tell you I would do if I needed a ride?" I said, "You told me you would call me." She said, "Did I call?" I said, "No!" She said, "Then what does that mean?" I chuckled, and before I knew it, the door was being respectfully slammed in my face. I remember thinking, "Damn that chick is raw as a muthaf*****! Oh, well, I tried. I will never see her ever again in life! C'est La Vie!" I had just blown my chances to ever be with the prettiest woman on earth!

Several weeks later, I am at Red Lobster, and I am called to the phone for a personal call. The only calls I had ever received at Red Lobster was from my parole officer doing a job verification call. That is who I thought it was and so when it was not I was baffled. But to my surprise, the most magnificent sounding voice was on the other end of the line. "Hello, is this Q?" "Yes, it is. Who is this?" "This is Trena Walden. You know me as Mercedes!" I could not believe I was talking to my dream girl. I was talking to the prettiest woman on the planet. I could not believe it. She went on to say that she "wanted to take me to the Sade concert in Richmond and that she had backstage passes." Sade was my girl. I would be there with Trena Walden?

If I were not on parole I would have said yes, but because the concert was in Richmond and out of my allowed travel zone I could not possibly go. Also, I was scheduled to work and always believed I had to work the schedule that I had agreed to. I was committed to Red Lobster because they first gave me, a permanently disenfranchised felon a job when no one else at the time would! I told her with the sincerest apology that, "It breaks my heart Trena to tell you I cannot go to the Sade concert with you because I have to work, and I literally cannot afford to take any time off because I may lose my job! I will take you anywhere you want to go, with all the expenses paid by me on my day off!" I could not risk going back to prison!!!!

I was rolling the dice with any future opportunities with my dream girl, but there was no way I was ever going back to prison behind a bad or impulsive decision. I loved myself more than the thought of a dream date with my dream girl. I could not risk it for her sake or mine. If I violated my parole, there would never be another chance to impress such a woman. She replied, "I'm sorry to hear that you cannot go with me, but I promise I will give you a call the day before your day off so that you can take me out!" She kept her word, and we eventually began going to different places enjoying each other's time and conversation. I really enjoyed talking with her.

The day was Halloween, October 31, 1993. Trena, who was a trustworthy friend to me was damn near hanging out with me on a daily basis. I enjoyed her company and her conversation. I enjoyed looking at her face because it was absolutely the prettiest face I had ever laid my eyes on in my entire life. She received a message from her mom to come home immediately. The time was around 5 pm, and I was on my way to Red Lobster, so I told her I would drop her off.

When we got to her home, she was emphatic that I came into the house. So I followed her in, and she told me to wait on the couch. Within seconds I could hear her mom's voice yelling and screaming. As I looked around the home, it became painfully evident that the house was in complete disarray as if a tornado had blown through and knocked over everything, spilling clothes out of draws and onto the floor.

When I looked up, my friend Trena was standing in front of me teary-eyed and cowering in front of me. Her mother was kicking her and her oldest sister out, and she had nowhere to go. I asked her was she ok and she said. "She had nowhere to go!" What Trena did not know about me was that several years prior I was thrown out of my home by my family for something I did not do to my uncle and I was made homeless. God had me here for this very moment as a test for the testimony!

Had it not been for my great friend Jay Woods and his sweet and beautiful mother Linda, I would have been homeless two times in my life versus the one time where I was homeless and living out of my car, bird bathing at Walmart, showering in truckstop hubs, and staying in a warehouse at Ingram Book Company in Jessup, Maryland. I knew what it was to be rescued because of Jay and his mom and I knew what it was like to be out of options and had nowhere to stay on the planet.

I told her she could stay with me until she could get on her feet or until this moment clears up with her mom. She was adamant about not living with a man she was not married to or a person she barely knew all of 90 days. She said that she "would not stay with any man because there are always strings attached and she didn't want to play that game because she had seen what that situation looks like firsthand with her mother and dad, and that was not an option!"

I have always been a quick thinker when it comes to coming up with solutions, so I said to her almost immediately that "What if it were possible for you to get an apartment and you don't have to worry about paying rent for two years?" Of course, she was like, "How is that possible?" I told her, "Since you will not stay with me because you do not trust the terms of the arrangement, why don't you let me take my apartment out of my name and put it into your name and that way I stay with you, and if you do not want me to stay, you can kick me out at any time? I have already pre-paid the lease for two years, and you do not have to worry about paying rent for two years. I will even have them change the locks and issue you a new key and that way the only way I can get into the apartment is if you let me in at your will." She said, "You would do that? You would really do that?" I said, "Let's do it before they close. Before we go let me call Red Lobster to let them know I will be late." My friends at the leasing office made it happen and before I knew it, "Voila!" Trena could not believe it until she saw her name on the lease and she got the keys. I know in my heart she would have done the same for me, if not more.

Fast forward to Monday, February 28, 1994, when I get a call to the dealership from Trena. She stated she, "I have some critical things to share with you when you get home!" This was the last day of the month in the car business, and so I knew I would be getting home late. What could it be other than she was going back home to her mom's townhome or she needed money? When I got home, she greeted me immediately at the door and told me to join her in the kitchen. I took my blue blazer and tie off and grabbed a beer from the fridge and chugged it down. I grabbed another beer, and before I knew it, Trena was standing across from me with anxious eyes and folded arms. I said, "What's up? What's so important?" She said, "Well. I have been talking to my mom here lately, and we have been having some great conversations about a few things that are quite important to me and I need to ask you an important question!" I am thinking, "Here comes the money question!" To my amazement, the question she asked me completely knocked me slam off my foundation. Trena replied, **<u>WILL YOU MARRY ME</u>?"**

I immediately thought she was joking but quickly realized she was not. In that instant, I thought, "Somebody loves me enough to want to be with me for the rest of their life? Somebody thinks enough of this permanently disenfranchised convicted felon to want to be with me? Somebody wants to have children with me? Somebody wants to have my last name? I am a piece of shizzle unworthy of a woman's love. I do not want to hurt Trena!"

I quickly responded to Trena by saying, "Yeah I will marry you. When do you want to get married? Friday?" She said, "Yes!" I was married that Friday at 3 pm. I am approaching 30 years of marriage, and every day I still cannot believe I am married to my dream girl and the most beautiful and smartest person I have ever seen on the planet. I wake every morning with the person God sent directly for me!

If I had to describe Trena, and I am quite confident that my children would agree wholeheartedly *she is me with a wig on her head*! She is nothing to play around with when it comes to respect. As I share with all men, one of the secrets to being married for multiple decades is always keep respect as a priority in your relationship with your spouse or mate so that you can always keep your commitment to one another sacred. Sure you are going to have your fair share of arguments that can come off as unsettling, but just never cross the lines of no return because when you create reasons for uncertainty and cause your significant other to feel insignificant or anxious and doubtful about continuing the relationship with you, an entirely different set of problems will take over your relationship and overwhelm both parties to the point where people feel they cannot breathe and be themselves in a relationship that they cannot recognize! My wife has always had the freedom to speak her mind with no threats. Her not being able to speak her mind is insane!

To put it simply, if you want the person you fell in love with to keep staying in love with you, continue to build on your relationship by building them up and not tearing them down. Do the things you did to acquire their love and respect at the beginning of the relationship! Never settle and get comfortable with them or take them for granted because when you do, you welcome a ton of bull shizzle into the relationship like outside influences such as family, friends, and others with their various solutions to your personal relationship issues. Let them be who God made!

Their best intentions and opinions probably do come from a loving place because they care, but does their suggestion benefit both sides if their ideas are just as dysfunctional as the both of you and worst? If I had listened to the one-sided dysfunctional opinions of people from broken relationships, I would have been divorced shortly after being married. The advice they're giving they don't even use.

Get help and always seek counseling from qualified individuals who have been in relationships where they found robust solutions to overcome the deficiencies in their relationships. Seeking informative and beneficial solutions from individuals who were in tumultuous relationships will only tell you what not to do or tolerate in a relationship based on their specific situation, when what you truly also need is the solutions that will tell you what is required to make the relationship move forward, or in some cases if you step too far over the lines of disrespect or the intent is clear one does not want to do the things to better the relationship, what now makes sense to do for solid and sound reasons is to move on and part ways with someone who indeed is not healthy for you or them to stay in a committed relationship.

The bottom line is I sincerely try with the best intentions to do everything I can to keep my wife and friend Trena as happy as humanly possible with no limitations. The older generations of successful individuals in successful relationships will tell you that *"A happy wife makes a happy life!"* I agree, but also say, *"If you want to sleep with both eyes closed at night to keep your life, do everything you can that is humanly possible for your wife!"* I do not want to wake up with 1000 plastic spoons in my chest! Keep her satisfied! Keep her interested in the guy she fell in love with many moons ago by listening to her and having meaningful time and conversations together. Stay hungry after her like you first did!

Trena is the wolverine because I once saw on separate occasions, a starving pack of wolves and a hungry bear, get run off by a single wolverine who was so ferocious and impenetrable that the wolves realized this was a battle for a meal not worth the potential of losing their lives over, or risking serious injury and moved on to see another day, while the bear quickly scurried up a tree to avoid any injury. What truly separates us is I can candidly say that I give an edge to my wife in the category of strength and respect is that I can go to my grave knowing that there is no way I or any man on the earth could ever endure the painful process and birth of a baby. Men could not endure a single Braxton Hicks contraction! **Tolerance level!**

My wife and many mothers have the ferocity of a female crocodile that protects the nest and a female grizzly bear that protects her cubs from anything trying to harm their unborn or born babies. One of the most dangerous places a human being could be is near a crocodile's nest or when a mother grizzly bear is traveling with her cubs! You can be consumed alive or be mauled to death in either scenario! Mothers do not naturally walk away from their children, whereas, men can casually stroll or run for their lives away from their unborn or born offspring. I need these men to be kings and emperors to their children as the emperor penguins who never abandon their paternal responsibilities. Male emperor penguins never abandon their newborns! *"After a courtship of several weeks, a female emperor penguin lays one single egg then leaves! Each penguin egg's father balances it on his feet and covers it with his brood pouch, a very warm layer of feathered skin designed to keep the egg cozy. There the males stand for about 65 days through icy temperatures, cruel winds, and blinding storms."* [52]

If a penguin can stay with their newborns and help raise their babies, why would an adult man abandon his children at their most vulnerable time in life? We as men must realize we must complement our women in raising our children! Whether it is as a husband, boyfriend, or co-parent. In my heart and mind, this is why the women of the world are the strongest human beings on the planet! They do not ever leave or abandon their parental responsibilities! Do you know how strong a mother has to be to put her baby up for adoption? Do you understand the incredible level of love a mother has to have to surrender her baby to strangers? Who would go through the nine months of pregnancy and the pain of birth not to enjoy the pleasures of parenting the offspring that you love? To walk away or not walk away?

To sign your parental rights over must be one of the most challenging things to do as a human yet most loving gesture to provide a better life for your baby. Trena possesses this strength for our children despite having a father who went into a Chinese restaurant to eat while his daughters who had not eaten and were hungry waited in the car for him only for him to come out of the restaurant empty-handed and with rice in the corner of his mouth. The irony is not only is he the son of millionaires, but he has also won lawsuits where he never gave Trena a penny of money or provided as much as a box of tampons or a tube of toothpaste. F*** him!

My wife and I were two spirits in the dark trying to find the light in one another! My instincts and intuition tell me that I am only here by the grace of God and that the bond we have is because my mom tried to maliciously and intentionally kill me while I was in the dark waters of her womb. I thought the knocks were nudging me around from drums beating or perhaps my mother's heart was pounding. Because of the torture my dad put my mom through, the trauma had an impact. Was my mother beating on her belly to try and purposefully get rid of me? I was incredibly traumatized as a baby to the point where I came out so small that they thought I was premature because I was only 4 pounds. My wife was premature too! Trauma by dad? You can call yourself dad after you torture your pregnant woman?

Our mothers went home from the hospital before we did. We spent weeks in pediatric intensive care in the incubators oftentimes alone. Our mothers were violently abused before and as pregnant women. My mother tried unsuccessfully not so many years after that to smother me, but I think the third time was a successful "harm" because my baby brother was stillborn from an affair with a married man who had no interest in my mother or me. If at first or second you do not succeed, try, try, or die, die again. God Bless my mother who was tortured and rightfully did not want to have a baby from a horrifically violent and abusive man. I get it now as an adult and parent, and I guess my mom needed to be loved and suffered from bad judgment in the men's department. I thank god for Trena asking me to marry her because I doubt that if she did not ask me to marry her, I am not too confident I would have ever thought I was worthy of being any woman's husband and life mate, let alone believe I should be some child's father. God had a different destiny for us!

When a man finds a wife, he finds a good thing. And he finds favor with the Lord! [53] *He shall leave his parents and cleave to his wife. They should be equally yoked. A man should cleave to his wife!* [54] I honestly cannot see myself ever being without my wife because she chose me to be in her life at a time that I had completely given up on love and the entire concept of marriage and family. She became an inspiration to me because I wanted to make everything that was ever wrong in her life right or anything she had ever lacked I wanted her to have. She had given me hope and love and those four priceless gems called Antoneya, Ava, Andira, and Anisa. My daughters and wife are the very reason I exist, outside of the love for the Lord. I am forever thankful to God and Trena for giving me my daughters! I see the very best of my wife in each of my girls! They are all incredibly beautiful, witty, emotional, intelligent, and are resourceful and relentless fighters. They are us! Wow!

I had an entirely different appreciation for my wife after an incredibly painful defeat against kidney stones. I acted like a damn fool when the pain from the kidney stones kicked in and knocked me off of my feet. The doctor told me *"Your pain is about a million times less than the pain a woman experiences during childbirth!"* What the hell! No man could possibly endure that pain and God knew it. How could I ever harm Trena physically, mentally, verbally, or emotionally after she endured that pain for us? How could I ever abandon her or them? #Neverleaving!

The other time I can distinctly remember feeling an incredible loss and appreciation for my wife was when I was returning a rental car, and although she was directly following behind me, she got lost and ended up at the wrong return center. No one could reach her because she had left her cell phone home and it was dead, so all of my calls went straight to voicemail. Because my life is fixated on domestic violence and child abuse and I see and hear the worst-case scenarios more than the positive ones, for some strange reason a weird feeling of loss just all of a sudden overwhelmed me. I immediately began to think the worst! I was so shelled!

Man, who would love me unconditionally for me and all of my drama and dysfunctional baggage the way she has for these past decades? Who will want a rehabilitated domestic violence offender and an abusive convicted felon as she did so many moons ago? Who will ask me to marry them? Who will love my kids and care for them as much as she did? Who will be there for my daughter if her debilitating seizures return, and she has to spend weeks or months in the hospital or at home watching our sick child as I continue to earn a living for us, so we do not lose everything again? I must have left a million voicemails with different responses and various emotions. I called my kids and others to no avail. I stopped, and I prayed. Then after a total of nearly two hours, she called me. I was of course joyfully invigorated, and after telling her how much I loved her and could not see my life ever without her, I thought Man, I have got to stop reading about and watching so many crime and violence shows. I am losing my damn mind! ***MAN DAMN!***

It took me no time to figure out why my wife became what she is as far as relationships with men, me, and children in general. Her mother tried to be an honest corporate person who worked 9 to 5 Monday to Friday with full benefits early in Trena's baby years. However, her mom was unable to earn a living for an extended period consistently. Her mother was declared legally blind when she was a youth, and her father has just about always been on his mommy's bosom and monthly payroll, waiting for his inheritance or drumming up a scheme. He was literally the baby of the bunch among his siblings. He was and is used to getting his way like a spoiled brat! He has never grown up to take responsibility for his parental duties!

Her dad had the government or some individual sponsoring him when her mother did everything to feed her baby girls. He was a beater (BEAT HER) and cheater (CHEAT HER). He beat his wife, and he was a habitual cheater who cheated on his wife with other women and cheated his children out of living a healthy and prosperous life. He has never bought my wife a tampon, pencil, paper, deodorant, a bra or pair of panties. I have had to pay for his inadequacies in my entire marriage to always prove to my wife that I would never do to her what he did to her mom, her and her sister. I can understand Trena's mother's dilemma and am empathetic towards her mother because her dad broke the marriage vows with his domestic violence and adulterous ways and never lived up to be a provider or protector, but instead, he was an immature degenerate who has never taken proper, consistent care of his children and wives. My wife's heart will never be right until he apologizes!

The other man or fatherly example in Trena's life had domestic violence issues with her mom, and Trena too, with the difference being he was honorable in that he never abandoned his duties as a father, surrogate, friend, and for many years was the glue that helped my wife's mom feed the kids. He has been a phenomenal dad to his child and surrogate to Trena and her sister and never abandoned being a father. He will always be an example of how to learn from past relationship mishaps; how to be an accountable man, father, and lover of your baby's mother's other children. I applaud and salute him. I have incredible love and respect for Trena's mother and him working as responsible, mature adults, to secure the best possible future for their children despite not being in a formal marital relationship. They made it work! I am still praying and holding on that Trena's dad can change to become a FAMILY MAN™ so he can impact his former wives, baby mothers, children, grandchildren, and great-grandchildren before he leaves this earth. If I can change, along with Trena's "step in dad," so can her dad! Come on Brother! Co-parenting works when you stay focused on the needs of the children! Apologize to your children, former wives, & baby mother's so both of you can heal! Serve them!

Naturally, domestic violence, abandonment, & contract breaking men was Trena's example of a man. She always wanted to be independent and never wanted to rely on a man or the handouts from the government. She got conditioned by her father honestly, but she was going to be contrary in that she was going to fight for her children to have the best healthcare, education, and life, seeing how she was never rightfully afforded the opportunity given how she was raised in such a horrific and abusive environment by her father. The other man who fathered her youngest sister was a decent man, but at the end of the day, she was not his child and he never married her mom, which naturally had an effect on Trena and ultimately me.

Her mom, grandmom, aunt, and sisters are sheroes in my book because they not only survived the physical and mental violence and abuse from the men who should have been loving them the right way, they taught their daughters and sons to be fighters and not to settle for weak, cowardly, bull**** people who are only interested in what they can get out of the relationship versus what the men will be contributing positively to a healthy relationship. I love my mom, aunt, mother-in-law, sisters-in-law, aunt-in-law, grandmothers, & grandmas-in-law because they are like black mambas in that they are incredibly beautiful, but nothing to play with because they are physically and mentally lethal. They are so strong they can break bricks with toothpicks! ***MAN DAMN!*** They conquered all forms of domestic abuse!

I wish I could have prevented them from being victims. These women have overcome incredible pains and losses! My daughters are growing to understand those positive attributes, and like their mom, they will soon be legally permitted owners of handguns and assault rifles. I love Rosetta, Margaret, Barbara, & Lita for their resilience. They fought for their children despite being harmed by insecure men. These women did not give up on life or their responsibilities to their babies, as many men did. I salute men like Alfred Graham Mens, George Hicks Jr., James *Man* Smith, Samuel Joseph, Andre Battiste, & Keith Gaines. These are true Family Men who try to do everything for their family & kids as possible! ***Women run the world!***

My greatest accomplishment outside the births of my children is that my wife Trena asked me to marry her! Me? Someone loved me enough to ask me to marry them. Someone loves me enough for the truest commitment and epitome of love? To this day I still cannot believe someone thought enough of me as a human being to want to be married to me! I had to oblige her. She is the beauty, and at one time I am sure I and society would have considered myself the beast!

There were times when that beast was unleashed on Trena verbally and physically early in our marriage where I was just downright demeaning and wrong. I never threw a punch or fought her like a man, but candidly, violence is violence and I should have never treated her in any negative manner. My faith, all the lessons I learned in prison from Dr. Miller Ryans*, my will, wisdom, and my children keep me loving her respectfully until Jesus taps me on the shoulder to go home. What message would I send to my kids and Trena if I was an abusive dad and husband? I would definitely have to sleep with both eyes opened for fear of the WOLVERINE!

My wife is my bride, and it is not meant for me to ever beat on her physically, verbally, mentally, emotionally, or sexually as if she was my property! The thought of harming her in any fashion is despicable to me because I cannot imagine hurting the one person who loved me enough to want to be with me forever and the one who endured all of the pain carrying and birthing my four children on three occasions! There is absolutely no way I could ever see myself inflicting pain on her. She loved me in spite of my history of domestic violence, abuse and criminal background as a permanently disenfranchised convicted felon. Who would select me with those types of credentials preceding me? She selected me when I can honestly say I never intended to ever be in love with another human being or animal following my release from prison. A night not under the same roof with my wife is a nightmare! My wife was the missing link that put me back in sync as a man!

To sum up who and what Trena is to me is simple! She too was absent a father in her life at critical times where the guidance of a father could have changed the outcome of her life in a positive manner. She too comes from a pedigree of traumatized women who were tortured by domestic violence. She too comes from a stable of strong, single mother homes where she learned the power of prayer and a requirement to love the Almighty God, Jesus Christ, and the Holy Spirit! She too is still waiting for her father to say, "I am sorry for abandoning you, your entire life!" We both probably will not hear "sorry" from either one, even though I believe her dad still has time to say so! Her dad is a confessed believer in Jesus Christ, and I believe he will eventually do right by all his kids and their mothers before he has to give an account to God about how he treated them. God used him to get them here!

Again, she is me with a wig on! She is the "Wolf Whisperer!" She single-handedly tamed me when, as a wild and abandoned wolf with no pack to call my own, she got with me at my most unwanted and undesirable time in life. What woman in her right mind would want as their boyfriend a recently released from prison, paroled, convicted felon, and certified psychotic domestic violence offender, bully, and abuser? She was as crazy or crazier than I was, to be around me, let alone want to be my friend. She is the truth who has always kept it gangster from Monday to Sunday with me. What I know now was she was free but imprisoned by the dysfunction and trauma she had experienced as a child and young adult. I was healing her as she was helping to heal me. Lastly, if I am the crazy wolf and she tamed me, what does that make her? It makes her a fine and ferocious wolverine. Trena is An Alpha Female! A Warrior! A Wife! A Wonderful Life Partner! I LOVE HER! She loved me in spite of me being me! I will always pay any FEE for her!

THIS IS WHAT CELEBRATING 25 YEARS OF MARRIAGE LOOKS LIKE!

HOW CAN I SHOW MY WIFE ANYTHING LESS THAN LOVE? SHE TRULY LOVES ME!

The female wolf appears to hide under the male. She's actually covering his throat from their assailant, whilst pretending to be scared.

55

IF I AM AN ALPHA MALE WOLF AND SHE TAMED ME, WHAT DOES THAT SAY ABOUT HER? SHE IS TRULY ONE OF THE MOST PHENOMENAL PEOPLE ON THE PLANET AND I AM BEYOND GRATEFUL TO CALL HER MY FRIEND? HOW COULD OR WHY WOULD I EVER HARM THIS INDIVIDUAL WHO ENDURED THE PAIN OF HAVING MY 4 CHILDREN? SHE LOVED ME WHEN I NEVER BELIEVED I COULD OR WOULD EVER BE LOVED AGAIN! GOD KNEW I NEEDED HER WHEN SHE CAME INTO MY LIFE! I TRULY HAD GIVEN UP ON LOVE! SHE ABSOLUTELY PLAYED A SIGNIFICANT ROLE IN SAVING MY LIFE!

56

BMW MASTERS ACADEMY PHOTO (October 1998)

Solutions To Permanently Eradicate Domestic Violence, Child Abuse, and Bullying

A subsidiary
of BMW AG **BMW of North America, Inc.**

October 19, 1998

Antoine William Burgess
Henrick Imports
6950 East Independence
Charlotte, NC 28227

Dear Antoine William:

Congratulations on your acceptance to the BMW Masters Academy!

You are one of the select few that have been nominated by a BMW of North America manager to the BMW vision of the future.

Completion of this industry leading program will ensure that when you return to your retail center you will have increased confidence and knowledge to continue to represent the BMW product. One of the key aspects of this program is based on BMW Best Practices, which will further prepare you to meet the professional expectations of our customers in this highly competitive marketplace.

Your schedule for the three days at the Masters Academy is aggressive and packed with information. Be prepared for very active days; the facilitators involve you in a myriad of activities that fully immerse you into BMW culture and product. This will include BMW Manufacturing tours and presentations, interactive discussions with BMW management and workshops on the most current, relevant topics to continue your Masters status.

Included in the tuition is airline transportation, transfers to and from Greenville airport, hotel accommodations, breakfasts, lunches and dinners. You will be responsible for miscellaneous charges such as telephone calls, laundry, etc.

Enclosed is a general outline of the program; more details will be waiting for you at check-in at the Marriott. The weather in Greenville/Spartanburg in November will be cool, please be prepared.

To make your airline arrangements, please call the BMW Travel Department at 1-800-446-TRIP and identify yourself as a participant in the BMW Masters Academy.

When you arrive in Greenville, please go to the baggage claim area and the Marriott Hotel will provide your transfer. Use the hotel information phone to notify them that you are there.

Marriott Hotel   Phone   864-297-0300
One Parkway East   Fax   864-281-0801
Greenville, SC 29615

Headquarters
300 Chestnut Ridge Road If you have any questions, please call Kathy Fay at (201) 307-3963.
Woodcliff Lake, NJ 07675

Mailing Address We look forward to seeing you in Greenville at the welcome reception on November 17th at 6:30 p.m.
PO Box 1227
Westwood, NJ 07675-1227 Sincerely,

Telephone
(201) 307-3840

Facsimile T. W. Strahs
(201) 930-1178 Professional Development

Enclosure

Printed on Recycled Paper   98.3W Masters Academy (1-17-98)

Solutions To Permanently Eradicate Domestic Violence, Child Abuse, and Bullying

57

BMW DIVERSITY and MARKETING CONFERENCE...
(NOVEMBER 1997)

Solutions To Permanently Eradicate Domestic Violence, Child Abuse, and Bullying

10/23/97   09:31   FAX 770 5523850   BMW NA SO.REG.   +++ HENDRICK CLT   001/002

Vice President &
General Manager
Southern Region
BMW of North America, Inc.
A subsidiary of
BMW AG

Axel H. Mees
October 22, 1997

Mr. John Fornshell
Hendrick Imports
6950 E. Independence Blvd.
Charlotte, NC 28227

Dear John,

Throughout my tenure in the Southern Region, I have said that it is our responsibility at BMW of North America to devote 50% of our efforts on today's issues and the remaining 50% on setting the stage for the future.

When we compare our business and the market place from September 1993 until today, we see why this strategy is so critical. Our mutual success is truly founded in creativity and proper strategic planning.

Today, I write you to ask for your continued support to promote our business interest. The Southern Region has taken the initiative of sponsoring a conference which will address the critical issues of diversity and marketing. Our future business depends on us not only understanding the importance of this topic but the challenge to act.

I am pleased to announce: *Diversity and Marketing to African-Americans.* This conference will represent a first step toward future dialogue across other diverse groups. It is my sincere hope this conference will provide participants and BMW a greater understanding of emerging trends and opportunities and provide an information base that will help shape future actions by BMW in addressing diverse markets.

Among the invited speakers will be Mr. Vic Doolan, President of BMW NA, Mr. Len Posey of Drake-Beam-Morin, Mr. Keith Elliott of Southeast Research and Mr. Carol Stewart, BMW NA, Manager Retail 2000.

In considering participants I felt it important to invite African American individuals who have experience with this topic and have shown a successful understanding of BMW through their performance. After speaking with your market team, I am pleased to inform you that Alfred Glover and A. W. Burgess of your BMW Retail Center were nominated to attend this conference. Your Market Manager will be in touch with you to confirm Alfred and A. W.'s attendance and will extend a personal invitation to Alfred and A. W. to attend the conference.

Southern Region
1290 Hightower Trail
Atlanta, GA 30350

Telephone
(770) 552-3810

Facsimile
(770) 552-3850

The conference is scheduled for November 11th and 12th in Greenville, South Carolina. Attached is a tentative agenda and fact sheet for this special event. I look forward to seeing you at the MAC Meeting next week.

Regards,

Axel Mees

Axel Mees
cc: Market Manager

57

Solutions To Permanently Eradicate Domestic Violence, Child Abuse, and Bullying

NAACP NATIONAL CONFERENCE REPRESENTING BMW and HENDRICK

58

BMW of North America, Inc.

A subsidiary
of BMW AG

To: Mr. John Fornshell
Executive General Manager
Hendrick BMW

From: John Haley
Sales & Marketing Manager
BMW of North America, Inc.

Date: July 7, 1998

Re: 89th Annual NAACP Convention (Atlanta, GA.)

Dear John:

Thank you very much for your approval to send A.W. Burgess to this year's NAACP Convention in Atlanta, GA.

As you are aware, the Hendrick Automotive Group has been very supportive the past three years by having a BMW Sales Specialist attend the convention. We are pleased that A.W. Burgess will represent Hendrick BMW and we also recognize the outstanding job he has done since graduating from the BMW Sales Academy.

Mr. Burgess will be assisting me with the BMW vehicle exhibit at the Georgia World Congress Center on July 11-14, 1998. His airfare and hotel lodging will be covered by BMW NA. I will contact him to make arrangements for delivery of his airline tickets and also provide further instructions for this important event. Again, thank you for your support.

Regards,

John Haley

cc: Mr. Victor Doolan, President of BMW of North America, Inc.

naacpexhibit.doc

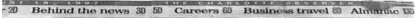

THE BOTTOM LINE: I HAD TO PROVIDE FOR MY WIFE and CHILD RELYING ON ME TO LIVE THEIR BEST LIFE! IT MOTIVATED ME TO BE THE VERY BEST BMW SALESPERSON IN THE WORLD and BEST EMPLOYEE FOR THE HENDRICK AUTOMOTIVE GROUP! NO ONE COULD OUTWORK ME IN MY MIND BECAUSE I OWED IT TO MY FAMILY and MR. HENDRICK! WHEN YOU GO TO WORK......WORK!

59

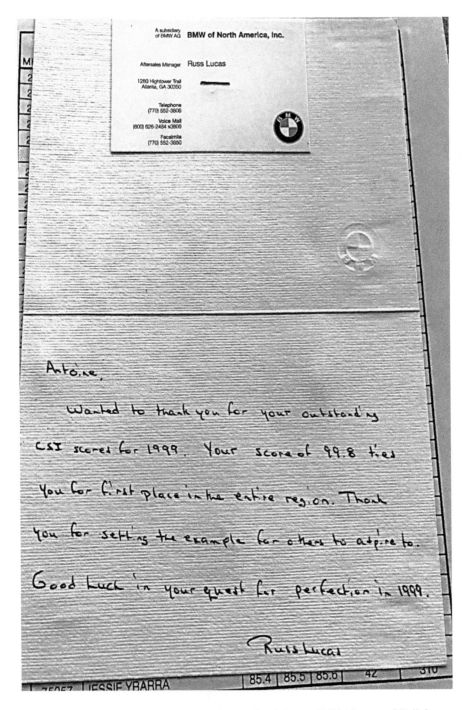

Antoine,

Wanted to thank you for your outstanding CSI scores for 1999. Your score of 99.8 ties you for first place in the entire region. Thank you for setting the example for others to aspire to.

Good Luck in your quest for perfection in 1999.

Russ Lucas

Solutions To Permanently Eradicate Domestic Violence, Child Abuse, and Bullying

Dan Crowe, Acura Remarketing Manager,
Dave Porter, Hendrick Acura General Manager
and Ray Mikiciuk, Acura Zone Manager

A.W. Burgess, Hendrick Acura CPO manager

Hendrick Acura

(continued from page 1)

keep existing clients happy instead of having to earn a new one," notes General Manager David Porter. "Great customer service is 10 times more cost-effective than trying to draw in new customers." The payoff is measurable annual increases in repeat and referral business. Yet Porter is not content to rest on the laurels of 60 to 70 percent return clients.

"An exit survey helps us carefully target who is buying CPO products," he continues. "We ask where they live, what they do for a living, what they watch on TV and where they went to research their purchase." As a result, Hendrick can laser-target its advertising at the most likely buyers, and sales consultants can be trained to recognize and easily break the ice with walk-in clientele.

Porter's long-term philosophy stretches back 13 years, when he began working for one of the organization's used-car departments as a sales consultant. "Today, I've been GM for two and one-half years, and we continue to hire and promote from within." The approach provides a continuity that upscale buyers in the Charlotte community value.

What qualities does Hendrick look for in its sales staff?

"Integrity. Integrity. Integrity," chants A.W. Burgess. He believes that skill is important but secondary to attitude,

especially since his clientele consists of owners who will call back and report the slightest misstep.

This is not likely, considering the outstanding success of a dealership that refuses to accept recession as more than a mindset.

Recession-Beating Tips from the Front Line:

- **A job loss is not a deal-breaker.** "Because of the Internet, career-minded individuals bounce back fast," points out Burgess. "People will still need a mode of transportation for their next job."
- **Faltering fleets work for you.** Perks like a company car may vanish in tight times, while sales territories of traveling reps have widened. (The actual increase was 10 to 12 percent in 2002, according to CitiCapital.) Both are good reasons for customers to consider CPO, an afford-able option to purchasing a new vehicle that is backed by a comprehensive limited warranty honored at any participating Acura dealership.
- **Knowledge provides selling power.** Since customers are holding on to their money, sales consultants need to be empowered with both product knowledge and comparison literature. Hendrick Acura stresses product strengths,

Continued on page 4

5

#1 Certified Pre-Owned Dealership In America In 2001 and 2002

Solutions To Permanently Eradicate Domestic Violence, Child Abuse, and Bullying

<u>OR</u>

ANY MAN WHO CALLS A WOMAN A FAT WHORE

OR

BODY SHAMES HER

OR

CONTROLS HOW SHE WEARS HER MAKE UP,

OR

CONTROLS WHAT CLOTHES SHE CAN WEAR

OR

WHO SHE CAN BE FRIENDS WITH

OR

CONTROLS HOW MUCH MONEY SHE CAN HAVE

OR

WHERE SHE CAN GO

OR

ELECTRONICALLY TRACKS HER EVERY MOVEMENT

OR

CONTROLS WHAT SHE CAN SAY OR DO

OR

CONTROLS HER SEXUALLY

NEEDS HELP NOW OR THE OUTLOOK WILL BE H<u>OR</u>RIFIC!

Solutions To Permanently Eradicate Domestic Violence, Child Abuse, and Bullying

NEVER TAKE YOUR SPOUSE, CHILDREN, FAMILY, OR FRIENDS FOR GRANTED, BECAUSE WHEN THEY ARE NO LONGER HERE ON EARTH WITH YOU, YOU NEVER WANT TO HAVE ANY REGRETS FOR WHAT YOU SHOULD HAVE TOLD THEM OR WHAT YOU SHOULD HAVE EXPERIENCED WITH THEM WHEN THEY WERE HERE! LET THEM KNOW HOW YOU FEEL ABOUT THEM NOW SO YOU WILL NOT HAVE REGRETS!

I THANK GOD FOR THE BEAUTIFUL FRIENDS MY FAMILY HAS BEEN BLESSED TO HAVE MET THROUGH THE YEARS. OUR RELATIONSHIPS HAVE BEEN INCREDIBLY MEANINGFUL AND REFRESHING GIVEN THE OBSTACLES WE HAVE FACED AS A FAMILY. GOD HANDPICKED OUR FRIENDS AND FAMILY TO BE THERE FOR US WHEN ALL WE HAD WAS A PRAYER TO GIVE THEM BACK. I THANK YOU AND ASK GOD TO BLESS YOUR LIFE!

MANY OF MY FRIENDS I NO LONGER CALL FRIENDS BECAUSE THEY TRULY ARE FAMILY! THANK YOU FROM THE SINCEREST DEPTHS OF MY HEART! I THANK AND LOVE YOU!

Solutions To Permanently Eradicate Domestic Violence, Child Abuse, and Bullying

I WROTE THIS FOR MYSELF WHEN I TURNED 40 & NO ONE WOULD HIRE ME

Who is A.W. Burgess?

A.W. BURGESS: Antoine William Burgess

AGE: 40, Born August 4, 1970

WIFE: Trena; Married 17 years

KIDS: Antoneya (Big Sissy,15), Ava and Andira (twins 11),& Anisa (The Baby, 9)

BIRTHPLACE: Baltimore, Maryland   **CURRENT CITY:** Charlotte, North Carolina

STRENGTHS: Never comfortable with being comfortable. Fear of failure drives me! Benevolent, altruistic, philanthropic. Rapport, Respect, Relationships, Results! Employee & Customer Satisfaction! Consistently winning. Always finds the positive in the negative. Thick skin...Short Memory! I think outside the box because I have never been in the box! Transparent! Professionally aggressive! Revitalization/turnaround, strategic, loyal, structured, confident, listener, ultimate team player, kind, generous, discerning, strength under control, operates within order, consistently exceeds expectations, committed, runs on high octane jet/NASCAR fuel, passionate, relentless, purposeful, radical with a cause, pursues excellence, humble, driven, dethrones negativity, knows when to cut bait. I do not judge and opt to give second chances.

WEAKNESSES: Losing keeps me up at night searching for ways to win; a workaholic who is married to his job, worrying about how to impact and serve others. difficulty understanding why some individuals do not think, care, or are as compassionate as me about certain things, and why some individual's work ethic, transparency, and drive isn't like mine! Sensitive to other's pains inflicted by ruthless predators...ie, Zahra Baker and Shanyia Davis, and foster kids.

GREATEST ACHIEVEMENTS: (1)A relationship with Christ! (2)My wife asked me to marry her!

GREATEST DISAPPOINTMENTS: Convincing myself I had no significant purpose in life, such that I did not deserve to live & allowing my kid's future to be jeopardized due to my actions.

ONE-WORD SELF DESCRIPTION: Altruistic-Generally concerned about the welfare of others!

FAVORITE MOTTOS: See it through, 12P's, Excuses, and Invictus. Friendship is essential to the soul. It is you're love for God that will be the source of your love for others. Love in the spirit for our fellow brethren and for all the needy people of the world, or someone that you loved very dearly suffering some terrible tragedy. For in the way you judge, you will be judged!

HOW OTHERS WOULD DESCRIBE ME: The Unitarian Humanitarian. Always concerned about the welfare of others; lovingly brings the best performance out of everyone; a humbled man's man; purposeful warrior, lives to serve others, an extraordinary human; a phenomenal energy with a relentless pursuit to win; an advocate for those who can't speak for themselves; the calm in the eye of the storm. Redemption, Humility, and Contrition at it's ultimate best! Magnetic!

TOMBSTONE INSCRIPTION: "I pray my work speaks for itself. I pray my life experiences convinces many individuals and entities to always put the needs of others first before self. I pray that all who were connected to me are still benefiting from my life services—my legacy!

WHAT DOES A.W. STAND FOR?: Amazing Will, Always Working, Always Winning, At Work, A Workaholic, All Women(a wife & 4 daughters), A Warrior, An American Winner Wonder!

FAVORITE BIBLE CHAPTERS: Romans 12, Titus 2, 1 Corinthians 13

FAVORITE PRINCIPLES: Benevolence, Altruism, Philanthropy, Redemption, Contrition

Solutions To Permanently Eradicate Domestic Violence, Child Abuse, and Bullying

**MY FRIEND & BROTHER LITTLE RICKY*(R.I.P) A BROTHER NEVER FORGETS!
LITTLE RICKY HENDRICK ALWAYS KNEW THE VALUE OF HIS LIFE!**

IT WAS GREAT WATCHING HIM LIVE OUT HIS DREAMS AS A YOUNG MAN!

Ricky Hendrick

Biography

Ricky Hendrick is proving that the apple never falls far from the tree. Following the successful lead of his father Rick Hendrick, Ricky got started in racing at an early age and wasted no time in putting his talents on display. Success came to both father and son very early in their respective racing careers.

The parallels are striking when you consider that the elder Hendrick built a 1931 Chevrolet that set drag strip records at the tender age of 14. Ricky, at 15 years of age, dashed to five victories in the 1995 Legends Series Summer Shootout during his first year of organized racing.

While competing in the 1996 Legends Summer Shootout Series' Semi-Pro Division, Ricky posted one win and three other top-five finishes. He then graduated to late model stock cars in 1997, competing at tracks in South Boston (VA), Myrtle Beach (SC) and Concord (NC).

After watching his father Rick reach racing's pinnacle for a third straight season, Ricky Hendrick knows the bloodlines are working in his favor.

Quick Facts

Born: April 2, 1980
Residence: Charlotte, NC

- Son of legendary NASCAR team owner and auto magnate Rick Hendrick
- Posted five victories in his first formal season of racing in the 1995 Legends Summer Shootout Series (Chargers Division).
- Won the 1996 "Next Generation" special event competing against the children of NASCAR drivers Dale Earnhardt, Morgan Shepherd and Barry Bodine.
- Advanced to the Legends Series' Semi-Pro division in 1996 and claimed one victory along with three other top-five finishes.
- Started racing late model stock cars in 1997 at tracks in South Boston (VA), Myrtle Beach (SC) and Concord (NC).

Solutions To Permanently Eradicate Domestic Violence, Child Abuse, and Bullying

REDEMPTION
Refuse to Lose because You Possess the Will to Win!

Many folks in 2004, and still to this day, wonder why I chose to leave a stellar corporate automotive management career that had financially secured me in the six-figure income bracket. Anytime there are issues concerning your family's well-being, you realize it is a requirement to take a break, not a request to do so. My youngest daughter, who was three at the time, was battling refractory epileptic seizures. Because epilepsy was so new to my wife and me, the ordeal became so overwhelming that for the first time in my adult life, I was genuinely trying to handle a situation that I could not resolve with money, relationships, or my intellect. I knew I had to physically be there for my family without the concern of getting back to work for fear of losing my job. All I knew was that my daughter had fallen into a medical condition known as "status epilepticus." This is a condition where one continues to have repetitive seizures, and unless you get the appropriate medication or neurosurgery, you will eventually damage the brain. She was so critical that they wanted to helicopter her to the nearest hospital who could accommodate her condition, but due to the weather, she had to be transported via ambulance from Charlotte to the University of North Carolina, Chapel Hill's intensive care unit.

As I sat in the ICU, I realized then that life causes interruptions. The question then becomes how do you respond to that specific interruption? Do you listen to that interruption and be genuinely concerned about your family's needs for that period? Business and the process of earning a living for my family was always going to be there, but my loved ones will not. I needed to take the necessary time to deal with those pressing issues right then and there, to make certain things were back in place or close to being in place when it came to my daughter and family's health. Once they were content, I could consider other options for my professional career.

These sentiments were inspired by Rick Hendrick, a man who I affectionately and respectfully refer to as Mr. H. I had the blessing to work for a man who had incredible successes and failures. When you experience supernatural losses where you are living but are actually dead on the inside, and there is nothing or no one who can comfort you or settle your spirit, regardless of your money, power, political connections or influence, your sanity, integrity, love level and will are tested to the very core. He battled a fatal disease, got tried in the media for alleged crimes, lost family members and friends due to natural causes and a fatal plane crash, but despite all the drama, heartbreak, losses, and negativity, he pushed through the pain and was the linchpin that kept his family and company together until he received a clean bill of health both personally and corporately. God restores!

You have to go through some seemingly unconquerable and incurable tests to give a supernatural *test*imony to the world. His inspiration resolved in me a belief that ***a setback is only there to elevate the comeback***. I looked at trials and tribulations as a sign that I was about to get upgraded to a better position in life. If you pull an arrow back on a bow, it definitely gets harder as you pull it further back, but that tension just means that when you release it, it is only going to come out of the bow with more speed to get to its intended target faster and straighter. When my daughter got critically ill, I thought of him. He would say **"A.W. when it gets thick and seemingly impossible to most people, you must, *Refuse to Lose!*"** I added on to it that the reason you must **"*Refuse to Lose!*"** is that God chose you, so you must **"*Possess the Will to Win!*"** He is one of the most competitive yet caring and giving people on the entire earth! If I had to describe Mr. H, he is **"*Pure Benevolence!*"**

Mr. H is a spiritual man with supernatural resilience who has come face to face with tremendous tragedy but managed miraculously to triumph over these incredible tragedies! How does one ever heal from the unexpected loss of their child, parent, or other significantly close family members and friends? Where does the strength and resolve originate or come from every day following the loss? Who provides the light to your dark days? What settles your spirit to make it through the seconds of each day? How do you win after such an overwhelming loss where it seems as though time and your heart stops? It is this same strength and amazing grace that I see in the resolved spirit of Sandra and Chancellor Lee Adams, along with the many individuals who are lifetime members of the organization "Mothers of Murdered Offspring" and Gold Star family members! God carries us in the pain!

I owe Dr. Miller M. Ryans*(RIP), for providing the solutions to my healing while I was in prison and at Central State Hospital, the biggest thank you for solving the puzzles in my head as it pertained to violence and abuse. I thank God for Margaret "Maggi" L. Curry Williams, the compassionate *female* Dean of Students who trusted and allowed me the opportunity to try and finish my college education at Old Dominion University when no one would accept me as a convicted felon. Thank you, Maggi Curry Williams, Carlos Walton, Gwendolyn Jackson, Pam Smith of Inroads Baltimore & the University of Baltimore, along with E. Bronson Ingram*, for never giving up on me despite the situation I put myself in after being arrested.

This supernatural, miraculous strength and merciful grace are stronger and more magnificent than any of the forces of nature such as a hurricane, tornado, tsunami, or earthquake that will knock you off your feet, blow you into oblivion, or sweep you away never to be seen again! Yet in spite of it all, these phenomenal human beings still rise each day to slay the many dragons of life. I see this same spirit in the victims of domestic violence, child abuse, and bullying! They no longer stand for or stand down to violence, abuse, and bullying, but instead, they stand up to these cowardly evil forces and slay them on a daily basis. These individuals are my sheroes and heroes and are supernatural phenomena and inspirational blessings!

What Mr. H never knew or understood about me and my feelings for him was that he could never know how much he truly changed my life when eight years prior, he gave a permanently disenfranchised convicted felon life and confidence when his company hired me. Who would give a convicted felon with no college degree, the opportunity to earn a six-figure income, with benefits, and the chance to advance in the management ranks of the company other than an individual who understands the essence of love and forgiveness? He restored me as a MAN!!

He did and his management team such as John Fornshell, Phil Humbert, John and Mike Desmond, David Porter, Jim Sabo, Greg Hayes, Wayne Simpson, Doug Winchester*, Chris Little, Jack Green, Doug Weaver, Mike Bostic, Harold Hamilton, Linwood Bolles, Dick Rife, Gary Davis, Kirk Heppler, John Lampkin, Randy Watkins, Mike Smith, Sandi Poole, Libby McElduff, Roger Mesiemore, Sherry Underwood, Reggie Suble, Phil Wood, Chris Maroules, Cynthia Hamm, Tony Esposito, Peter Barc, Paul Wantz, David Foster, Dale Knorzer, Mike Mihoch, Keith Black, Randy Threatt, Tom Fulp, Wes Watkins and Patrice Wood who embraced me as a brother and friend! I was destined to win because of the help I had from my fellow brothers and sisters like Alfred Glover, Kris Beacham, Stacy, and Monica Walker, Larry & Joy Foster, Shirley Europa, Cristina Love, Ed Keady, Brian Porta, Richard McGough, Laurie Sabo, Isaac Powell, Dentist Shaw, Henry Williams, Brandon Lawyer, Karen Fairley, Cindy Williams, David Livingston, Terri Wilson, Bill Guggenbiller, Mitzi Cribbs, Robert Lee, Tony Clawson, Mike Johnson, Chris Das, John Weisenberger, Fred Dagenhart, Henry Jonas, Sharon Lipa, Padej Yakamna, Scott Marks, David Rosenbaum, Dick Hoppe, Whitney Brackett, Delano Santos, Kevin Leitch, David Melton, Donnie Lind, Tony Debastani & Ali Talebi.

He never knew how much I cared for him, Todd Rose, Alice May-May Liggons, and his entire family including Papa Joe and his dog. I treated his business as if it were mine. I treated his family as if they were mine. Why? I loved him for the sole reason of redemption! *Jack Gross of the 1 Jeans Group summed it up best when he said, "There's a responsibility of all of us to try to help people that may be made a mistake in their life! Just because you make bad decisions doesn't make you a bad person!"* [61] Mr. H validated me as a human being and made me realize that my life was significant and purposeful and that I was relevant to his company and others close to him. The company did not see me as a convicted felon who was a permanently disenfranchised felon according to the state of Virginia, but rather they saw me as an equal opportunity employee given the opportunity to make a name and an honest living for his self and family. Alfred Glover, Patrick Kelly, and Damian Mills, my fellow brothers, gave me a second chance when they hired me as a business development consultant. Reggie Hubbard believed in me enough to run his dealership. Each one of them are true men of God who will definitely be in heaven.

Alfred solidified his love for me when he would invite me to his family functions during holidays, and I never got invitations from my own family. When Alfred invited me to his wedding and his parents' funerals, it was the ultimate gesture of saying to me I was his friend. Reggie Hubbard took me solely for my expertise and the man he viewed me as that day and not when I was a young and dumb kid. Damian Mills trusted me purely as a brother's keeper. Patrick Kelly and John Fornshell believed in me and saw the potential to execute regardless of my past that was in my rearview. Brian and Jason Hackney gave me validation when my fellow brother Ed Keady asked them what they thought of me and the services my company provided and they both, along with Kenny Gullette, stated, "A.W. is absolutely worth every dime and more of a family member and not just another business vendor servicing the dealership! He is a difference & profit-maker who cares about people!"

Allison Walden*, Ron Ward & Piper of Red Lobster took me as is. Thomas and Joyce Moorehead, Peter Boesen, Jeremy Guenther, Carroll Wayne Stewart, Mark Samples, Bill and Steve Talbott, Dimaggio "Nick" Nichols, Brad Johnson, Emir Abinion and his family, and Shon Jennings believed in me enough to hire me when no one else would when I first became self-employed! These men and women are indeed my brothers and sisters who do not know how much I thank them for allowing me to be a FAMILY MAN™ to provide for and protect my wife, 4 daughters, and grandchildren. Marvin Wilson vouched for me when I needed a certified corporate reference to prove that I was actually looking for employment. He was the 1st to help me! They restored me as a man and human with real feelings.

With Mr. Hendrick, all the bad of my criminal background was pardoned? Giving extraordinary opportunities to many people who would never have been hired, qualified or certified by a resume, or interview and especially a background check at an even more ridiculous salary. The charitable gifts no one will ever know about because they were mostly all done anonymously because he wanted God to get the glory and credit and for people to keep their dignity and privacy and not broadcast via the media to gain positive public relations and marketing for himself or his company. These are the actions of a humanitarian that I admire respectfully. Thanks for not judging me forever. I have few regrets in life, but I wish I would have listened to John Desmond when he said, *"Be patient A.W.! Do not do anything stupid because I have something good for you coming up soon! Just be patient Bro!"*

My plans for the rest of my life are to become one of the greatest benevolent, altruistic, and philanthropic humanitarians of all time. I want to be used in that capacity for the business world and public to advance the vision of FAMILY MANKIND™, and use my ministry of business to impact, protect, and improve the lives of people. I wish I could do this for free because ***whatever you would do for free is indeed what you should be.*** God will provide for my family and me because He knows the mission in my heart! I believe that God will forever use me, and my abilities to benefit the lives of others. In everything I do, I will always seek to create opportunities, not so much for me, but others. Serving the public is not something to be taken lightly. You are dealing with people's lives, futures, and legacies. I am not pursuing my dreams to be in the spotlight. I am aspiring only to serve people to change the condition of their lives and our communities---this is my passion.

I am genuinely concerned about the welfare of others. Whether or not you are somehow connected to me, you should never want. You should never know hunger, be without clothes, shelter, education, proper medication, and moreover, be without a connection to mental health. If you are lacking and are connected to me, I have failed you. I am the person who creates plans of actions that address real issues facing our communities. The difference though is that I enthusiastically see the projects through to their completion as a solution. I will execute until resolute!

However, these plans must be strategically mapped out to be achieved in a timely fashion. Unless there is leadership in corporate America to recruit other minds that are greater than what we have already seen in our communities today and get the required feedback or ideas to prevent the current issues, we have not done our service to the community. We must become radical, tireless, warriors like Mr.

H so that we stop being passive and reactive waiting on someone else to solve our problems or give us a handout. People in the community are crying out but because there is a lack of leadership, resources, and willing participants--- their cries go unheard! I hear their cries and am taking on challenges that are unfavorable to most—if I do not, who will? Will you help me help others? You already have living proof of what the payoff is which is an accountable, productive member of society.

It is incredibly difficult to first tell anyone that you are a convicted felon who has served time in prison and a psychiatric ward, especially when you first meet them in any capacity. Even after nearly 30 years of being a released parolee, not everyone has an understanding care or heart to my situation and that is okay because I caused those sentiments and accept the consequences. I apologize for putting anyone in that space. I am a trillion miles away from that 21-year-old dysfunctional, lost, impulsive, violent & unconscious kid. I'm the example of a reformed offender!

Mr. H, Mr. Walden, Ron, Piper, Alfred, Miller, Patrick, Reggie, Damian, Tom & Joyce, Peter, Carroll, Jeremy, Mark, Bill, Steve, Mr. Nick, Brad, Emir, Pat, Gabby, Dani, Marvin, Maggi, & Shon, I sincerely thank you for giving me a hand up. My family and I thank you for giving me a second chance at life. Thank you for redeeming me and restoring my faith as a human being and a believer. As a father and husband, when you have a dependable, well-paying job along with a career with benefits, you can provide, protect, and pray for your family, it validates you as a FAMILY MAN™! You gave me back my dignity and manhood! I truly Love You! Because of people like you, I AM A.W. Burgess, A MAN & THE FAMILY MAN™!

THE MOST IMPORTANT CAREER I WILL EVER HAVE IS AS A FATHER!!

AND NOW AS A GRANDPA TOO…CALL ME PA-PO!

JUSTIN and JAXON I LOVE YOU FOR BEING GOOD LITTLE GUYS!
YOU WILL BE A FAMILY MAN ONE DAY TOO!

Solutions To Permanently Eradicate Domestic Violence, Child Abuse, and Bullying

WHAT DRIVES YOU TO BE THE VERY BEST EACH DAY? *LOVE?*

Solutions To Permanently Eradicate Domestic Violence, Child Abuse, and Bullying

MY WIFE AND KIDS! I WOULD HAVE NEVER IMAGINED BEING MARRIED WITH 1 KID! GOD TRUSTED ME OF ALL PEOPLE WITH AN INCREDIBLE WIFE AND 4 KIDS! MY KIDS ARE A BLESSING TO ME BECAUSE THEY ARE PROOF THAT GOD ANSWERS PRAYERS! I AM THANKFUL GOD TRUSTED ME WITH HIS BABIES!

Solutions To Permanently Eradicate Domestic Violence, Child Abuse, and Bullying

MY KIDS! OUR KIDS

THE MOST IMPORTANT CAREER I WILL EVER HAVE WILL BE AS A FATHER

They Are 24/7 Recording Sponge Devices! Many Become Carbon Copies Of You!

I was exposed to way too much violence as a child! As a parent, if you do not change your nefarious destination, your children will likely end up there too! Do not be to your child what you hated about your parents. Do the exact opposite of what you hated. When children see and hear too much, they are destined to repeat and live what they see and hear from you. If we were created in God's image, then that means we were created to be like God. When we say, *"Lord, Let Your Will Be Done!"* [62] We must believe that we are saying, *"Lord! I Will Let My Will Be Done!"* Our children must know they are created to be like God and not created to hurt themselves or others but are created to be creators of love! God is love!

I stand heartedly transparent in this chapter concretely believing we must trust and allow the will of God to dominate and drive our lives and our children's lives to the destinations He has preserved for them and us! I must chant internally and repeatedly, **"Lord! Let My Will Be Done! Lord Let My Will Be Done! If It Is Meant To Be, Then Lord Let It Be! If It Is Meant To Be, Then Lord Let Me Be It!"** I can no longer worry or stress about the negative things going on in my life when I am ultimately in control of my life and even the outcome of my dreams. Me controlling my ultimate destiny is like me telling you the exact winning numbers to tonight's Powerball Jackpot or tomorrow night's Mega Millions lottery! If I could determine those types of things, I would be the wealthiest person, and the lottery would cease to exist because people would never lose. What I realized is that in life I must be in control of what I can control. Anything else I do not worry or lose any sleep over because worrying will kill me and my will. Raising children is trying to predict the exact winning numbers of the lottery. Do you before you are done in by your kids or others!

As a parent, our goal is to try and set our children up for a successful life! We are teaching them how to survive in the jungle of life! We teach them their ABC's and 1, 2, 3s and how to say their grace before they eat, and how to pray before they go to bed just after we have read them a book or a significant Bible passage. We feed and clothe them and drive them to purposeful events as though we are their chauffeurs for their entire young lives even past college days sometimes! We bought all the required school supplies for everyday class needs and special projects for that all-important presentation and grade. We make sure there are always gifts for their birthdays and their friends' birthdays and under the Christmas tree! And please don't forget the cupcakes for their class or going to the Monday Milk with mom and donuts with dad and the daddy-daughter dances and dates! Let us not forget the school and church plays, recitals, sports events, and musicals you proudly attended. Not to mention getting the time off to see them graduate from pre-k, kindergarten, 5th grade, middle school, high school, and college. And before you blink, life hits!

Being there literally for them bedside as they give birth to your grandkids and you are pleasantly surprised with not just seeing your grandchildren for the first time, but you get the bill for your daughter's delivery! They must have served this to the wrong dad. Oh, that is right, your daughter is a baby and her baby's daddy is an unemployed, nondriver's license, no car or transportation, no high school diploma, dropout, pill-popping, drug user, drug selling, thief, unkempt, twisty hair, woman beater! Who in their right mind would say, "Now that is my future husband and baby's daddy!" Also, he was living rent-free, with no house key, in a two-bedroom home with his unmarried grandparents of 40 years, because his father was in the penitentiary and his mother had never cared for him the way he thought she should have been. My daughter sure knows how to pick a winner. Not only did she get abused by this buster and herb he was sticking her up for paycheck and food stamps to buy their drugs instead of buying food and diapers. He was in jail when the second baby boy was born, and they came home from the hospital to stay at my house. These two boys are going to be winners and make a difference in the world, or they will be worse than their parents and grandparents after seeing and hearing what they have seen and heard as babies, toddlers, and little boys.

As a dad and father, you pray that one day your daughters grow up to marry someone just like you or better. There was a time in high school and college when I would have never wanted any of my future daughters to marry someone like me. Someone who would have never been able to love them the right way and the way young girls in healthy relationship homes see their dad treat their mom in a healthy loving fashion with no violence or abuse whatsoever. My point to all of this rhetoric is parenting is tough! But who wants to be responsible for planting bad seeds that ultimately ruin your child's one lifetime, and even worst, creates the DNA of a failed bloodline doomed to pass these bad genes and traits to the next generations? No one is perfect, but sometimes the cost of failure comes at an even higher price for innocent children and society to pay!

Never abandon your responsibilities as a parent because when you do, you have just boldly told your child that something or someone is more important than your love for them. When you do this, you can rest assured that your child will never forget what you have done to them. You have to be there for them literally! I get my strategy and negotiation skills from not having a ride to and from games, so I had to know when and how to properly ask a teammate, parent or coach for a ride. I had to have a sincere rapport with my teammates, their parents, and coaches so I could justify asking for a ride to and from home. I realize today that me asking a parent or coach for a ride was incredibly dangerous because some of these coaches and parents could have possibly been child molesters or abusers.

People should not be allowed to teach, coach, counsel or mentor kids if they have not received the necessary training to ensure they will not perpetuate pain to children or if they have not raised their own properly or if it can be proven that they are from an incredibly dysfunctional home full of violence, abuse, and bullying. They should be thoroughly vetted like they are going into the FBI, CIA, or Secret Service as if they are providing security detail for the President. Often times, teachers, coaches, mentors or counselors stand in for parents where a parent is absent in the life of a child, student, or athlete and so many kids are looking at these influential figures of authority as respectable surrogates. Our kids are vulnerable!

What healthy advice can these influencers possibly give our kids who are the most impressionable? They can give phenomenal and influential advice if there is no engaged parent to balance their advice and perspectives on various life situations. This is why both parents should be actively involved and engaged in all of their children's activities interactions with adult authorities who can influence your kids' perspectives on life. These individuals should be working in concert with the parents as a compliment to the parent's belief systems and core life values.

Parents show you how to prepare for life's obstacles, so you know how to conquer them. A great parent teaches you how to use the defroster when it is raining or cold outside and cannot see out the windshield! They show you the little details such as how to look both ways before you cross the street or why you check each door and window at night before you go to sleep at night! They show how to groom yourself and use proper etiquette to act in public respectfully. They teach you how to pray or meditate depending on your beliefs and care about treating others with love and respect. They tell you and show you how and why you should never break the law. This is the making of a solid citizen and humanitarian. This is why as parents you can never neglect, abandon or abuse your children, spouse, intimate partner or pet! You can never, never, never, never cut off communication with them.

Time races and before you know it your children are graduating! You do not want to be that deadbeat parent who did not help your children by contributing positively to their educational and life success. You want to now show up when they are graduating when the blood, sweat, and tears have dried! Mothers need to stop coddling their kids when it comes to giving so much doggone respect to their piece of crap deadbeat baby's dads or donors. Tell them at a respectable age who that mother or father f***** really is and what he did to you and your babies. He was the irresponsible one who blew up the family by being a coward who chose not to get help. This is when your children will say, "I do not need you to be my father, mother or friend now! That window of opportunity has permanently closed. I need you to be a friend and a grandparent to my children and your grandchildren."

When it comes to parenting troubled children, you must understand that if children are not in motion regarding being involved in positive activities then they often will create their own negative experiences! *The Bible says,* ***"Idle hands are the devil's workshop,"*** [63] and if that is the case, then you have got to put them on the treadmill! You must occupy their minds and bodies to tire them out and release the negative energy and lactic acid, which builds up in your body by getting them up and out of the house and into positive activities that will enhance their life. When you die, rigor mortis sets in and stiffens your body! You cannot be in motion if you are dead! Get them moving! When you are in motion you tire! God Blesses Motion!

I sometimes get asked, "Which of your children is your favorite A.W.?" Each one of my children is my favorite child. There is no one above the other. I think it is because I am part of a select breed of men who have four daughters that people ask me harmlessly do I have a favorite kid. How is it possible to love one more than the others? My mom never did any homework with me but would write 50-page papers for my brother and complete all of his homework assignments and school projects. She had a master's degree in elementary education, and yet I did not know what a thesis statement was in the ninth grade! My brother got everything I always wanted that my mom refused to buy me. I got a hooptie for my first car that cost $25 dollars, and he wrecked his first used Acura within months of my mom paying cash for it and then she turned around and bought him a brand new 40-thousand-dollar Ford Explorer. Within six months the Explorer looked like it had aged 20 years due to the maltreatment of my brother. My mom has spent tens of thousands of dollars on Air Jordans for my brother! She has spent thousands on summer trips for my brother and his children and his baby's mother and grandmother but has never taken or purchased one trip for my kids! I put down my down payment for my home when my mom put the down payment on my brother's!

Never pick favorites between your kids because you are undoubtedly and essentially showing one kid more love than the other and the other child how much you love them less. Your scales of love should balance between your children and will never equate to a healthy relationship between either kid if you pick favorites.

My father was not good enough for the parental role as my dad and so God Himself is the only Father I know. This was painful to know that I could never call some man dad or father. How can you be blessed and granted this wish and afforded this opportunity from God, and as a man, you let your children blow in the wind like a gnat's severed wing? I would run until I caught my child's wing. This is the pain you endure as a parent. When your muscles are screaming to stop because they are burning or are sore from the previous day's work out, think of it as the pain coming out and the love coming in. First comes the pain then comes the pleasure. Before you birth a baby or business, there tends to be plenty of blood, sweat, and tears of pain and eventually by grace they subside to transform into tears of joy! You have to have been put to the test to be able to stand up to testify and sing your testimony! TEST. I. MONY! First I get the "TEST." Then "I" get the "MONEY!" You go to college to learn a trade. You are trading time for money with the University to learn how to execute a certain profession. Studying for the test and committing to learn your craft is difficult. But once you get through it to the other side by way of graduating, now you can get the money, or if you are that excellent at what you do, the money will come and get you at an early age like Michael Jackson*, LeBron James, Gary Coleman*, and Moziah Bridges of Mo's Bows.

As a parent, no one should care more about your children than you. If you do not care about their safety, education, and well-being than give them to somebody who will care about them. To choose to party or someone over them does not make sense to me. God chose you to care for His priceless creation, and this is how you choose to take care of His product. The keyword is "choose!" They cannot feed themselves or pay bills. They cannot put a roof over their head or clothe or protect themselves. How do you feed yourself or change your diaper or administer the proper amount of medication when you are a child? Why don't you give them the keys to your car? The Lord will not give you more than you can handle and if it is more than you can manage, ask for help. I say all of this because as parents we sometimes believe that we are the only ones experiencing unique situations with our children and so we question our parenting skills thinking that we may not be or have not been the best parents based on how our children turn out. First of all, I want you to know that just about every human being I know both personally and professionally, regardless of economic status, wealthy, rich, moderate, poor, destitute, political affiliation, influential or not, demographics, degrees of education or not, religious preferences or sexual identities, we all come from some level of dysfunction. The difference is how we will cope with the dysfunction. Will we be proactive and get help to cure the generational curse in our DNA and bloodline or will we bury our senses in the sand and hear no, speak no, see no or smell no evil and allow this dysfunction to continue festering and attacking our loved ones like infectious disease, germ, or vermin until it finally comes for someone's life and now have no choice to confront the forces that are plaguing and torturing your soul?

I have a phenomenal friend who's ego is the same as mine and who had a mirrored experience with his daughter as I did. His oldest daughter had the audacity to move into their house with roaches and bed bugs. When he asked her "why she continued to lie to him about the issue" she informed him that "she was embarrassed, to tell the truth!" She had a legendary lengthy record of lying to him and his wife no matter what it cost. She lied at 15 about spending the night over a friend's house when in fact she was over her future 2-time baby's donor's house because she told his grandparents that she was a runaway from an abusive home. My friend called the cops one day because they thought someone had broken into their house and stole their laptop. Years later they found the laptop in the attic attached to her bedroom. She had taken it from his home office and was "too scared to tell him and his wife!" At 16, she got arrested for shoplifting at the mall with several other girlfriends who they never met because her donor had put merchandise in their bags. That gave her a misdemeanor on her record. They did not find out about the arrest until five years later when his wife handed him a letter from Amazon stating that "because of your failure to disclose your criminal background, your application has been formally withdrawn." He had never applied for a job at Amazon and then it hit him that it was his daughter's letter because his wife had taken her on a job interview a few weeks prior and because she was named after him and her name was so similar to his that his wife thought it was a bill from Amazon.

Solutions To Permanently Eradicate Domestic Violence, Child Abuse, and Bullying

She stole clothes, shoes, and jewelry from her mother. She stole their car when their youngest child was in the hospital overnight for several weeks. She stole her mother's cell phone for weeks only for one of her sisters to spot her using it at a family member's home. She pawned the tablet they got her for college, and instead of enrolling in college with the money they gave her for clothes, books, school supplies, and tuition, she took the down payment for college and bought drugs and clothes.

All these constant lies from her that his daughter always found herself in reverse. He always told his daughter that she was hustling backwards in life. He worked hard for his wife and kids to live in a certain zip code so they could go to the best schools and live in the best and safest homes and neighborhoods. She wanted to be in the worst and most dangerous neighborhood in all of Maryland. Do you think the people who live in those dangerous and impoverished neighborhoods there would stay there if they hit the lottery for a million dollars? Only an idiot who is not on a charitable mission would want that type of living for themselves or their children.

He and his wife worked beyond hard, so his wife could stay with the babies during their most formative years, and they could sleep at night knowing their children were not being molested, abused, or neglected in a daycare. Being an at-home mom is the hardest, sleepless, most underappreciated, thankless job in the world, but the reward comes when your children get off to a phenomenal start in life without any pain and harm that will stay and haunt them forever. They then put them in the best private Christian school at a yearly payment for four that was most people's annual salary. He always thanked God and his employer for giving him the opportunity to earn so his kids could get the best education!

His daughter's donor to this day does not even have a driver's license. He has never kept a job for more than a year and is famous for being in and out of jail for domestic violence or destruction of property centered around his daughter other family or drugs. She would not stand up to him or tell her dad about the abuse, but she would talk major shizzle to her dad, her mother, and her little sisters. He too was locked up when baby number 2 came into the world, and like me, my friend paid for both babies to come into this world. He told his daughter to change their last name to his since he paid for them and their car seats, cribs, diapers, wipes, clothes, food, miscellaneous, birthday and Christmas toys. He was the Grandfather, not the father.

She never appreciated him or her mom! Her donor never appreciated her dad taking him to DMV at least six times to try and get his license. When her dad found out her donor never studied for the driver's permit test that was a wrap for him. Again, if a father does not care about having a driver's license so he can get to and from work for his children, then society is working with a person who does not want to do what is best for his children. His daughter continued lying to her father about him and the abuse that her father eventually whipped his ass twice for putting his hands on his daughter and it was not his daughter who told him, but rather it was his then 2 and 4-year-old grandson who told him that "My daddy made my mommy cry, Grandpa!"

My friend swore that after the second time at spanking his daughter's donor's a**, he would never lay hands on him again, because seeing how he was a coward and she was not strong enough to tell her dad anything about the abuse and was still habitually lying to him and his wife, he had to get away from both of them before he ended up in jail or the penitentiary behind two irresponsible, lying, and uncaring parents!

As it would be, his daughter and the baby's daddy fought to the point where his daughter had to leave the house she had been in since she had the first baby. He brought her and his two grandsons into his house to try and get them off to a more productive start in life. When they initially came to his house, he went and bought them bunk beds and a new bathroom set. They had their room to share with their mother. She got promoted to manager at her job by a great friend of his. She was no longer giving her check to her drug-using and dealing babies donor. She got a bank account and began to save money, and she even paid him back just about all the debt she owed him since the boys were born. She went and got a cell phone and financed her first car. He refused to buy another car because the first one he bought her he told her that he had her on his insurance and to not let anyone drive the car and all the neighbors said that the donor was driving the car. Without a license? She or he wrecked the car within three days of him handing her the keys. He still does not know the truth to this day, and he doubts he ever will because she is probably "too embarrassed to tell him!" The blessing behind that car is he got it repaired by an awesome businessman who had always been transparent with him for a great cash price. He let the car sit there for four months even though it was repaired because he did not want to even think about returning the car to his daughter.

Solutions To Permanently Eradicate Domestic Violence, Child Abuse, and Bullying

He got the car back, and that week he headed to Cleveland and got a frantic text from his wife that she had been in an accident and that she was okay but that the car had been totaled. He did not know his wife had taken his daughter's car that morning because her battery was dead, and she had to get his other kids to school. The car was totaled, his wife was not injured, and the insurance company paid him $4000 more than what he had paid for the car. The very next year his daughter asked him to help her get a car when she got her tax returns back. As much as he wanted his money back that she owed him from financing his grandson's births and beyond, he told her he would. Seeing how he was an insurance adjuster, he just called a few people and headed to the auction with his wife, daughter, and newest grandson. He got inside the auction and began to get an overwhelming feeling of nausea. He fought through it, so he could get her a car and leave. Well, it began to rain. He told me that anyone who knows how to appraise a used car professionally knows you never buy a car in the rain because you cannot feel or visually spot paintwork and damage. He told his daughter it was time to go and to get her deposit back because they were not buying a car in the rain and because he was about to puke. He hurried back to the car and told his wife to go make sure his daughter gets her money back because they weren't getting a car that day because of the rain. Within 20 minutes his wife was back at the car shaking her head saying that their daughter had purchased a car even though they told her not to on that rainy day. He said he started his car and pulled off with his wife and the baby.

She arrived about two hours later and picked up the baby. He never saw her because he was in bed with chills. 2 days later his daughter called his wife to say she had been in an accident on the highway with both children in the back of the car and that the car had been totaled, and the insurance company was not going to pay because she did not have full comprehensive coverage, as he had instructed her to always get, on the car and only had liability which meant she just lost all of her money. He never saw the vehicle, but he knew it was a piece of crap car because no airbags deployed, and it was a frontal collision, and she was speeding more than 60 miles per hour. She could have been killed in that car, but since she bought an "As Is" car at the auction, there was no recourse or legal position for him to take against the auction. In two years she was involved in 2 accidents where her cars had been in an accident. He told her he would no longer enable her, and she would have to do buy a car on her own because she did not appreciate him.

Fast forward to where she has moved back in with him with her 2 young sons in January and before the months end both were enrolled in daycare where the oldest graduated in May with the ability to now write his name, read and do math, and socialize with his peers rather than around drug-using or dealing adults with their other unarticulated relatives. Her kids were not being left at just anyone's house where they were exposed to criminals and criminal behavior and were subject to violence, molestation, and child abuse. They ate three meals daily at routine times with regular baths and reading times. She had a full-time job that she did not have to worry about her donor coming to the job with foolishness or dropping the kids off because "He was tired of babysitting his kids!" He did not have a job to go after dropping them off at her job forcing her to lose her job and possibly credibility from the employer. She now had her own cell phone and did not have to worry about him smashing it against the wall or throwing it at her or putting it and her wallet down the street sewer. She did not have to worry about him cutting up her clothes when she went to work so she could not go out with her friends. Her kids no longer had to be exposed to this violent and immature behavior from their donor as well as her two cents on the matter.

What does she do when things are going great for her and her children? She decides to fight her mother on Superbowl Sunday and gets her a** beat by her mother who had been refusing to put her hands on her baby her entire older teen, young adult life. His wife could no longer treat his daughter as her child, but because of the serious disrespect, she was forced to chin check her and let her know that you will always respect your mother and yourself, regardless of how damn old you are. His other daughters looked on as if in amazement because they were not expecting ever to see that side of craziness from their mother. He told me he could have stopped it, but his daughter had been forewarned by him on multiple occasions throughout the years regarding her slick talk and sly mouthpiece and that her mother loved them so much that outside of the normal ways to correct and discipline your children she never saw herself ever fighting to harm one of her babies as a remedy for appropriate discipline.

And even then, his wife still held back on their daughter, despite his daughter throwing the first punch. His wife did not call the police because that would have made matters worse in his mind with no resolution for his daughter. They forgave her, and for the sake of the grandkids they allowed her to stay, but she definitely had to pay them rent so she could appreciate what they were doing for her. He thought that if she put some skin in the game, an equitable position, that she would be less likely to bug out and would think twice before she rolled the dice on being thrown out. She paid respectfully for four months, and so when June rolled up, she said she was going to be late paying them because she was going to need the money to put down on an apartment where she had to pay a deposit and first month's rent. No problem he thought. She was moving forward to get her own. That is good! But then five days passed, and she said she did not get approved for the place. Ok, he thought, where is the rent money so she could stay there for the next month.

She went off and refused to pay and called him and his wife every name in the book and that "He was not shizzle and that he was robbing her and that none of her friends had to pay their parents rent!" He said A.W., "We are talking apples to footballs when it comes to comparing her life to her friend's life. She had a kid in high school at 17 and another one two years later. She had two friends who have had no children to date, and they both graduated from college and are back home paying off their student loans and making car payments. One of them also has a brother still in college, and the other has two grown brothers still at home and two retired parents. She has a friend who has a son who is independent, has an apartment with her boyfriend and she works at the bank." He went on to say that "The bottom line is that he did not particularly give a rat's a** about what Tracey, Diana, or Hillary was doing in their household because they were not contributing a damn thing to him as he was to his daughter. His daughter showed them what not to do!"

He wondered if "Her parent's friends were dealing with the same horrendous attitude and unbelievable level of disrespect that he and his wife were experiencing? Have they spent thousands of dollars ensuring their grandchildren are fed and protected? Oh, that's right, they do not have any grandchildren or a derelict baby daddy donor to deal with and an ungrateful daughter." He went on to say, "Man, A.W., I do not have to explain my damn self to this 23-year-old who absolutely is clueless on my level of love. In an instant, my tolerance level was filled to enough! That is it. She has got to go. Maybe a homeless shelter will make her appreciate her parents, sisters, this home, and all the millions of things we have deposited into her life and that of her children. Get the hell out of my house right now while you are still able to get to your car on your own two feet. Get out NOW!"

Now here comes the tears and the "I'm sorry please!" At this point, I asked my friend, "Did his daughter think about the consequences of her actions before she just impulsively popped off? Did she think about her children as she fought her mother months ago? Was she thinking about her children when she allowed her donor to bully and terrorize her in front of her children giving them the blueprint on how to treat their mother and their future girlfriends and wives? Did she think about her children and how her actions will now impact where they must go to school? Was she ever thinking about her children when now they do not have their own bed to sleep in and a bathroom to go in private and no one trying to bring any harm to them when she was away at work? Did she think about her brothers and sister who deserved a great night's rest and peaceful weekends but had to put up listening to her arguments and rants with her parents or cries from her babies? Did she think about everything she had lied to them about and the things she hid from them that are now impacting her career possibilities and ultimately her children? Did she think about the vermin of bugs that were biting and walking over her children as they slept on the brand-new bunk beds that her parents bought for them and the lower bunk that she slept on too? Did she think her menial funky little "rent" impacted or positively contributed to their household budget when she and her children cost them more in monthly expenses?" He said that "Within six months the room looked like a college fraternity house. Filthy, disheveled and funky best describes the room. The bunk bed looked like it had been age-progressed. Mildew and sour-smelling unlaundered clothes draped the floor and were piled high to the ceiling. The roaches and bed bugs were beginning to fester and were getting in position to attack."

He was questioning had he done the right thing by putting her and his grandchildren out. The only thing I could tell my friend was that "He should not feel guilty for doing what he believed was the right thing to do at the time. I asked if he had rented that room out to a stranger would he have tolerated the same negative behavior from a stranger that his daughter had and brought into his home that impacted every family member." He emphatically replied, "Hell Nah, A.W.!" My point to him is that "If you and your family continue to tolerate the abuse, violence, and mistreatment from your daughter you are an enabler who is telling your child and your grandchildren that there are no consequences for such behavior and that she can continue to run as a pack leader of untamed wild, rabid and crazy dogs, showing her boys how to go on a rampage traumatizing, torturing, terrorizing, and infecting those who are close to them with her rabid tongue and giving even less of a damn to non-pack and family members. This type of behavior only ends in the death of someone, whether it be a homicide or suicide, or a trip to the hospital, penitentiary, or worse, the psychiatric ward." I suggested he get his daughter help!

Horrific parents do not hear their babies' cries, nor do they see their babies' tears. These parents give you toxic stress, tainted bloodlines, and generational curses. They cannot console you or hug you because they are numb, unconscious and unconcerned. They do not love you or themselves but love the trauma.

There was no money for college for me because my mom gave the money to a deadbeat sperm donor to start a bus transportation company — the same man who was a serial cheater with a billion or so kids by multiples of different women. He was greedy, noncommittal, self-serving, cruel and truly undeserving of receiving someone else's college fund when he was not even a positive contributor in anyone's life, especially his own children.

I despise any man or woman who abandons their children, their children's other parent, and their parental responsibilities and requirements. My dad copped out of his parental duties when he chose to be violent towards my mother and her family as well as when he decided to shoot at innocent boys, the police, and they justifiably killed him. This event put in place in the atmosphere and my bloodline the dysfunction and abuse from my mother who was violently abused and assaulted in every possible fashion by my sperm donor father. She consequently hated me for being the seed from the degenerate, derelict, devil who changed her life pattern as a strong independent woman by bringing shame and embarrassment during her senior year of college, to her and her family.

Back then, to be an unmarried, pregnant single parent was sacrilegious and one of the main reasons back-alley abortions happened at an alarming rate. I think she tried to kill me in the womb, and this was the reason why I was born so small and so sick that they thought I was premature and the very reason why I stayed in the hospital for so long after birth to where she went home before me.

As a result of this tragedy, I wanted to be a dad who provided, protected, and prayed for my children! Educate them both in and out of the classroom! I raise my kids to be an alpha wolf and before they could be an alpha anything they had to first serve in other roles in the pack! How can you be the head of the pack if you have never served as a great number two, three, or ten?

I had my daughter say to my wife and me, "I can't wait until I am 18 so I can leave!" Amen to that! Hell, I cannot wait until you turn 18 so you can leave too! Real talk! Truth be told! I wish you could go now! No rules, no respect, no boundaries, no consequences! Hit the bricks sister! You will come to appreciate us!

The reason we do not kick them out now is that we know they are not quite prepared for the wilderness and jungle that is out there filled with predators and snares that are unforgiving! When my daughter finally got out there on her own, she called me crying saying she wanted to come back home and that she now understands why I am the way I am regarding be a wolf.

Now you got what you wanted what are you going to do daughter? You are in the jungle with no protection from the Alpha daddy or mommy! Now you are free and so are we! Free from your torture and abuse against your family who has done nothing but helps and support you! The blessing is you have the tools to succeed and your daddy can still hear your howls for help in the event you still need help!

I am tired of responsible people having to pay for irresponsible people's mishaps! I will never call or ever imply babies are mistakes because babies come from God in heaven. They are His will, pride and joy, and His deliberate creation.

Like my life, sometimes He uses the most heinous individuals to get the most significant people to earth! The will of God is powerful and purposefully clever! I heard Pastor Dr. Gregory Moss give this incredible example with Doug and Eric Edwards one night in South Carolina. Pastor Moss said, *"Take for instance in the Bible with the example of Judas who sold out Jesus to Pontius Pilate. First and foremost, Judas was one of the 12 disciples picked by Jesus and who rolled with Jesus! My heart tells me that this is why Judas threw the petty amount of fool's gold in the form of 30 silver coins because it was then at that very moment in his life, and forevermore, when he realized Jesus Christ was innocent and was truly the Savior, and he was ultimately responsible for the execution of the King of Love!* [64] *How else would Jesus have been crucified for our unworthy sins only to return as our Savior! This was all in God's plan."* [65] It was the will of God to use Judas for our benefit.

The crucifixion was the ultimate example of a child trusting a parent enough by doing what their parent had instructed them to do, putting their life on the line, and in this case, His life on the cross, knowing the pain He was facing for a crime He never committed, yet trusting God the Father enough despite His own fear and sacrifice of His life! For all we know Judas was just a cleverly designed and strategic plan by God because He so loved the world, and as a result, Judas is with the other disciples in heaven who, despite turning their backs on Jesus and denying Him and His miracles, even though they witnessed or heard of the many other miracles performed by Jesus, and yet they did not come to His rescue on the cross and did not believe in Him until after He was resurrected and then ascended into heaven! The disciples all became martyrs to show their love for God because it was after Jesus was ascended into heaven that they became believers in Jesus Christ, our Father God from heaven, on earth in the flesh! There is pleasure after pain!

My dad/donor was a human piece of shizzle that tortured my mother's life to where God ordained him to be justifiably killed by the Baltimore police, before I was ever born, because he was not mature or man enough to be my father, dad, friend, provider, prayer warrior or protector and only God Himself could fill the position! Also where my mother tried to kill me, never defended me, chose serving men over me, or going into the military at the latest possible age, away from me again, never supported my athletic career or academics, and had to drink until she was figuratively blind and wasted as a way for her to cope in raising me or to publicly humiliate and embarrass me! All I could ever rely on was God my Father!

It is amazing how brazen and audacious your kids can be to the point where they treat you like they are your parents and you are their kid! They have gotten things twisted, and ultimately they must be chin checked and reminded who the parent is and who is the child. I am not speaking of violence against the child to prove your parental status! I am speaking about sometimes they have to experience stepping on their own we-we or falling on their butts to honestly know you had their best intentions because you love them. Most of us did not understand what any of our parents were saying until we had our own children and went through similar instances. Hey, that is not just tough love, it is life! They will never know or grow!

I am tired of suburban or wanna be a hood thug and gangster children trying to pretend to be hard or claiming their life was or is so tough. This is foolish thinking and behavior. Just because you went to jail for some reason do you think you have earned street credibility and a badge of honor? Real gangsters know that fools get caught and go to jail. Going to jail puts your money on pause. Survive prison and tell us that you were a thug in there running it and maybe with evidence supporting your statements we will believe it. The crazy part is the children who have to actually live in such violent, hostile and deplorable conditions of a neighborhood would leave that dangerous environment in a second. If you hit the lottery for $500 million, would you stay in the same zip code? Not! Warren Buffett never moved? Why not?

I have given my eldest daughter a "mercy pass and virtual killing!" If I did not get my child out of my house, I would probably have harmed her 23-year-old butt. The dam was about to break, and I was about to flood her with the most spectacular a** whooping you could bestow upon a grown-up child! If she had been my son, by now he would have been missing all of his teeth, but I chilled! I know that physically harming anyone does not work. This was a test for me to "pass" her on to her destiny! A destiny ordained by the will of God. If she is bold enough to stand toe to toe with her mother and me, then she can face the other societal animals in the jungle! Putting your children out to the world is a faith test that you just have to trust and believe that you have given them enough over the years that they will survive in the wilderness. Do not forget that they have your resilience in their blood!

On a few occasions, I have had to temporarily exterminate my child from my life. I have done this with other negative and hidden agenda family members and associates because at that time her spirit and energy was so negative, filthy, unsatisfied, ungrateful, and disgruntled. She added stress and no value to my life and was taking away the harmony that is due to my life as a parent and human being!

A positive and a negative energy will always equal a negative until the negative becomes a positive! They can set themselves free to be in or out of control of their own lives! As parents, we must speak life, not death, into the lives of our children and the people around us! There is life and death in our tongues! The confidence we give to our children will pay off in their lives and ours too.

When we encourage them, those brilliant words of confidence get planted as permanent seeds of esteem, and the more you nurture those seeds with water, which is a required nutrient for life, we will eventually see the incredibly beautiful disposition blossoms of the fruits of our labor! Moreover, these ingrained seeds will now get implanted into their children's esteem, and as a result, will perpetually get planted and continually germinate into their children's, children's, children's esteem!

I will never be labeled as an enabler who is just as guilty as the individual who is perpetuating the problem. If my child was on crack cocaine or heroin or opioids would I be her banker the one buying the drugs for her or giving her the legal permission as her doctor prescribing them or giving them to her as a pharmacist by distributing them to her or a cohort using the drugs and getting high or low with her and using every excuse in the world to justify using them and stealing from hard-working innocent people to pay for the habit. Being an enabler kills them faster!

Do not be a victim leading your own search party! There are people out here in the world right now who want you to sympathize and empathize for them when they are excuse-filled, lazy, and pitiless people. They have an incredibly high level of entitlement when they have been spoiled and cuddled by loved ones trying to make their lives less of a struggle than the pains and strife's that their loved ones had to overcome and endure while they have not been earning respect or rights to being entitled. Let your kids taste the sweat it takes to put a dollar in their pocket.

Parents have been bombarded by the lying and disrespectful behavior and are quite frankly fed up and frustrated because all of us have a boiling point and certain tolerance level. But when is enough, enough? When do you go from forgiveness to forgetting when someone keeps jabbing you in the same bruised area of your body, and the pain keeps getting worse, and there is no relief in sight or pain remedy you can administer? **I HAD TO GET RID OF THE CONSTANT PAIN BEFORE IT KILLED ME OR MY RELATIONSHIPS WITH OTHER LOVED ONES! I STAY AWAY FROM THE PAIN BEFORE I GET HURT & THE PAIN SPREADS!**

Just remember that you never put your children out of your life and out of your house! Your child put themselves out of your life and out of your home as a result of their horrific behavior, torturous actions, and disrespectful attitude towards you. If they were not your child would you accept this type of behavior from a stranger, neighbor, or co-worker? Of course, you would not and should not have to take this abuse and offensive behavior from your child if you know you have raised them right and done everything that you possibly could have done to provide, protect, & care for them properly! I am not talking abandonment.***#preserveyourlife***

Do not lose sleep over an individual who is selfish, and inconsiderate of your feelings and moreover, the love you have given them their entire life. Children such as these typically never appreciate their parents until their parents have cut them off or out of their lives. These abusive kids who have treated their parents like crap and stole their parent's joy and jewelry are the ones you see crying uncontrollably to the point where they are inconsolable and eventually passed out unconsciously on the church floor or at the burial site, because they know they tortured, terrorized and traumatized the very special and sometimes only person on the planet, who truly loved them and cared about their welfare. Children know too!

Kids do not always understand the unbelievable love commitment it takes to deliver the daily sacrifices it takes to provide safe shelter, food, clothes, education, entertainment, and any other luxuries! These types of kids do not care about your tears and your stress! I will never let anyone be an "emotional terrorist" blackmailing and holding me and my family hostage until we meet their ransom demands.

My wife and I were dealing with my critically ill child and youngest daughter's continuous battle of refractory epileptic seizures. When she had her first seizure, I was living the American dream! I was coming off two consecutive years of having been named the manager for the #1 Certified Pre-Owned automotive dealership in America and was making a serious six-figure annual income.

However, going through the trials and tests that come with having a chronically ill family member is one thing, but also having another child steal your car and laptop while this is all playing out is an entirely different set of fish to fry. We enrolled her in college with new clothes, books, a laptop, and supplies, only to find out she took the money for college, sold the clothes, exchanged the school supplies for cash and pawned the laptop. I should have gotten her professional help!

Despite it all, we never gave up on her, and she is doing exceptionally well today. I am proud of her and my other three daughters who are doing phenomenal as well in their space of life. They benefitted from learning from their sister's tests in life and their own set of failures. They listened to their dad and mom's testimonies!

Is it not ironic how we always say we would never be like our parents or we would never do the negative things that our parents did to us, but sometimes we subliminally or innately find ourselves doing the exact same negative things our parents did to us to someone who has significance to us? In my case, I inherited from my father and innately became physically, psychologically violent and abusive to my girlfriend and closest relatives. I have learned to talk with and not at my kids!

From my mother and aunt, I retained the attributes of just being verbally cruel and dangerously abusive! I wanted to push people away before they left me forever by choice or force as recourse to my abusive behavior. I was a hypocrite in my mind until Dr. Ryans told me that children often live and do what they learn and see at home from family or other influences. Some kids are polar opposites though!

I nearly repeated my father's heinous behavior which ultimately cost him his life by being shot and killed by the Baltimore police! The only difference was I was in his home state of Virginia, and I did not have a shootout with the police, but the similarities of how I put myself in the penitentiary was a near carbon copy of what he had done to my mother 21 years earlier. This cannot possibly be my legacy and a repeat of a tragedy! My children and their children will be better than me.

I am pointing out such men who have beat their haters and the forces of oppression to achieve the seemingly impossible dreams that come true for just a few in certain communities and scenarios. Terrell Owens and Deion Sanders are "Prime" examples of individuals who kept a singular focus on doing whatever it takes by using every possible form of inspiration to fight for their dreams while making other people's dreams come true too! You have to love you some you to make it through!

Both had biological fathers who lived near them, not in their house with them or their mothers, but influenced them in unconventional methods, so with laser focus, big heart, best intentions, and hard work, the good Lord gave them fame and fortune because He knew He would be "Owen" T.O. for the rest of his life and because Deion did not always have a "Buck" to his name as a child!

Deion's two dads were two of the biggest influences in his life, both positive and negative. He said he never drank or smoked because his dads taught him what not to do, and he focused on his goal of making a better life for his mom. Sanders, however, had nothing but love for his dads, even though they weren't always the typical father-son relationships.

Mims Sanders, who died at age 50, gave his son the flashy side of his personality. A standout baseball player and high-stepping drum major in high school, Sanders' dad was known as Daddy Buck. "He was that dude," Sanders said. "He was the entertainment side of me. He was Prime Time. But that's why I'm always careful of what I show my kids. My dad didn't have bouts with drugs; he was Mike Tyson with drugs. There were no bouts. I remember walking in on him one time. I worked at Bojangles in high school. Me and a friend of mine, Gerald Lephart, used to look out for our daddies. His daddy was in the same boat. We used to take food from Bojangles to our fathers after work. I actually walked in on him in shooting up.

I was like, 'Come on, man? You got to clean yourself up.' I was like the father, and he was like the son." Connie Knight married Willie Knight in 1975, and they moved out of the projects into a single-family home next to a graveyard on Henderson Street, about five blocks away. Willie Knight was a foreman at a lumber yard who also left an indelible impression on Sanders. "He drank a lot, but one thing my stepfather did was he went to work," Sanders said. "No matter what, he went to work. He would drink. He was a good home drinker. He didn't go out and drink in the clubs. He would drink right in his car or in his room. He was a good, hard worker. He wasn't abusive or nasty. He taught me work ethic, along with my mother, just to see him put on that uniform and go to work every morning." [66] Both wanted to be providers, so their mom, grandmother, and family would no longer have to be in the struggle.

T.O. had to *"Love me some me!"*™ [67] *and Deion had to be all about "Prime Time" "Neon Deion"* [68] because their biological fathers were not there to build them as men and so outside of a maternal and a grandmother's love, the best example they had as men were coaches or taking the best attributes of their dads and stepdads and making it work for themselves. My man T.O. and I were in the dark, under the covers of secrecy and "Don't tell him!" about our dads for a significant part of our lives and so all we had was loneliness, confusion and a simple plea to just being told the truth about who our dad was because not that it would ease the pain of never knowing a dad's love, I just wanted to know who he was and why he abandoned me and mom.

I just wanted to know why I was not a part of my dad's family. We needed acknowledgment from a man and the teachings of a man on how to love a woman and your children properly and appropriately! T.O.'s dad was across the street from his house the entire time living as a married man with kids. The only reason they told T.O. who his dad was, was because T.O. began showing an interest in the girl across the street in that house, which he quickly found out was his sister! I cried for T.O.! I could not imagine what was going through his head when he found out.

Why didn't someone come for me? My man Deion learned what to do and what not to do as a man from the men who were significantly involved in his life and found the best attributes of his dad to be a part of who he was! That is "Prime Time" love in my book and my heart! That taught me that you can always find a positive in the negative. This is why I have such unconditional love for Allen Iverson, Ray Allen, Kevin Garnett, Shaquille O'Neal, Kevin Durant, Dwyane Wade, Demaryius Thomas, and LeBron James. They never gave up or gave in to excuses despite their circumstances! They persevered with their mom, friends, and or family despite the dark clouds and death of relationships both personal and corporate.

Every morning when my feet hit the floor I always think about my wife and kids and how much they mean to me. Trena, Antoneya, Ava, Andira, and Anisa are the sole reason for me to get up every morning to go to work to provide, protect, and pray. I also think on different occasions about certain men, God rest their souls, like my Grandpa Burgess* and Alfred Glover's dad, Rogers Glover Sr.*, who would rise without fail and without excuses to feed their family and the many others they were accountable for! Mr. Glover, like what I was told about my Grandpa James Burgess, was a man's man who symbolized what it meant to love his wife and raise his children in a Godly home! ***These men's feet were the first to hit the floor daily!***

Both were God-fearing men who were as reliable and dependable as the air we breathe. What I saw with my own eyes and heard with my ears in Mr. Glover was an honorable display of showing his kids how to love and pray with a special side of wisdom! He, as is the case with all the family men I love and respect, will with most certainty, be drafted into heaven with all the other men and women soldiers in God's Military! I salute men and women who have served others sacrificially and without complaint. Mr. and Mrs. Glover*, you have a phenomenal son in Alfred, beautiful children and grandchildren, along with incredible sons and daughters-in-law to match, and you truly will always be in my thoughts and prayers!

Just know that you served your family well and proudly. What an example of a man you were to me, Mr. Glover! Alfred and his brothers and sisters are great people!

To my friends, family, and to all eyes and ears who read and listen to this book, always remember that your kids are always watching and listening to you and are innately taking mental notes! They will either repeat how you treat others, or they will use you as their motivation to do everything opposite of you, resenting you in their mind forever for the pain you bestowed upon them and others who they love or respect. To the abuser who violently assaults your mate in any manner, you cannot possibly love your kids or yourself if you hurt your kid's parent! When you harm your child's other parent, you harm your child and the relationship you have with them. If you love your child, regardless of the relationship with an ex, respect them.

At the end of your life, will you be proud of how you showed your kids how to love themselves and their kids? Will you pass on the love or hate gene in their DNA and your bloodline? Did you at least try to correct your errors before you died? It is never too late! What will be your lasting legacy? How you treat your children will often represent how they will treat others! They will either be duplicates of your behavior or absolute opposites of how you treated them. Always opt for love because love will never let you down or betray you and it will certainly never harm your children or legacy. Choose Love! Choose Life!

My Wife's Cousin's Baby Shower
A Loving Display of Family Support Welcoming The Baby

The Walden, Burgess, and Battiste Family

IN THE WORLD OF VIOLENCE and ABUSE, YOU EITHER BECOME WHAT YOU HATED AT SOME POINT IN YOUR LIFE and WHATEVER PROCESS or WHOEVER HARMED YOU TYPICALLY BECOMES YOUR PROCESS TO HARM OTHERS and YOURSELF! IF YOU ARE BLESSED or RECEIVED HELP, I PRAY THAT YOU BECOME A LOVING PERSON! YOU and YOUR FAMILY DESERVE TO LIVE A LIFE FREE OF DOMESTIC VIOLENCE!

ULTIMATELY, AS THE EVIL PERPETRATOR, YOU HAVE TO DECIDE TO PROACTIVELY GET THE LIFE-SKILLS and COPING TECHNIQUES TO PERMANENTLY CHANGE YOU and YOUR PROCESSES AS AN OFFENDER OR YOU WILL CONTINUE TO BE REACTIVE TO VIOLENCE AND ABUSE ONLY TO HIT THE REPEAT CYCLE BUTTON ON YOUR LIFE! THE QUESTION THEN BECOMES, IS THIS HOW YOU TRULY WISH TO LIVE YOUR LIFE and BE REMEMBERED BY OTHERS? DO YOU CHOOSE TO BE REMEMBERED AS A PERSON WHO PURPOSELY CHOSE TO BE A ZERO TO THE PEOPLE WHO LOVED and CARED ABOUT YOU? I CHOOSE TODAY and FOREVERMORE TO BE A HERO and NEVER AGAIN A ZERO TO MYSELF and THOSE WHO LOVE ME! I OWE THAT TO MY BLOODLINE!

LOOK AT THE FORMIDABLE FAMILY MEN IN THE PHOTO WHO ARE STANDING WITH THEIR WIFE and KID! LOOK AT THE SUPPORT FROM AUNTS and COUSINS! CHOOSE FAMILY LOVE! BE GRATEFUL FOR HAVING A LOVING FAMILY! SMILE and GIVE LOVE!

L.O.V.E- LOVE ONLY VISITED EVERYONE ELSE
You Are A Nobody Until Somebody Loves You!
Everyone Deserves To Be Loved Healthily!

As a kid, I did not believe in true love and the sanctity of it or the holy institution of marriage because all I ever saw and remembered was violence and hypocrisy! I saw a widowed grandmother who never had any man in her life after the death of my grandpa. My mother never married yet she dated a married man who she had a stillborn baby with when I was around 7. She graduated to a separate relationship with a devious, habitually cheating, noncommittal, selfish prick, who she stayed with for twenty plus years, despite him having about a billion children from a million baby mommas, who she considered her "boyfriend," who was twenty years older than her, and who, at the ripe age of 55+, had his alleged last child.

I witnessed countless front row episodes of my aunts and uncles adulterous and cheating abusive and violent affairs outside of their marriages and relationships. With sincere, loving respect, I had plenty of exposure to the sweetest gay uncle and most genuine gentleman aunt who I will forever love unconditionally and without any judgment, who never married because it was not legal in Baltimore then. I saw the worst in marriages and couples who shacked up for centuries. Love equated to deception. The Screen Actors Guild should have passed out SAG cards and awards to my family for the live performances I witnessed at the various stages of my life as it pertained to loving relationships. These relationships set the stage for my dealings with girls and women. My normalcy was abuse and cheating in a relationship with a woman prior to prison. I realized that I could not be happy if I was cheating but somehow the thrill of cheating made me happy! What is LOVE?

For the few marriages that I did see, whether it was family, friends, neighbors, or people at church, it turned out that many of their marriages were filled with dysfunction too such as alcohol or drug abuse, domestic violence, adultery, lies, betrayal, and deception. I witnessed the sagas, and the negative impact of divorce on my cousins from my aunts and uncles failed marriages. I saw the picture of pain in the faces of my aunts and uncles who found out they were cheated on by their spouses. I felt there and my cousins' pain and grieved in silence for them. Divorce is devastating for the entire family! I remember distinctly thinking, "How come certain family members and friends do not come around anymore? If he is not the birth father, who is? He had a baby outside of his marriage? What is a swinger?

What is free love? How come the ladies on Baltimore street said it cost money? What is Spanish Fly? I thought they were blood brothers? Why did he sleep with his best friend's girlfriend? Why did she sleep with his best friend? Is he the father?" In my way of loving a friend, there is absolutely nothing a woman could ever do for me if she once had any semblance of a relationship with any of my friends. Loyalty is everything to me. Today, I will walk away from any relationship that proves to not reciprocate the same healthy love and respect I have given.

I am amazed at the level of disloyalty that lies in many relationships today. There are just some lines in a relationship that should never be crossed. If any friend ever thought that it would be cool to step over the line to another friend's spouse or friend, I would challenge them on their level of love for themselves because you cannot possibly say you love me as your friend if you are willing to hurt yourself first knowing that you are getting into a forbidden relationship that started out deceptively. Your relationship is built on the foundation of lying and manipulation. Get out and terminate your current relationship formally before you start another serious relationship, especially a deceptive hookup. Sure there will be a bunch of tears for all people impacted by your decision to move on but trust me when I say all people should heal over time if you exited the relationship with respect and dignity. Being in love or lust with 2 or more different people will end tragically!

Domestic violence, bullying, and child abuse are complicated in that you are learning to hate what is trying to love you because what is trying to love you is what is showing you how to hate yourself and others. What is supposed to love you is harming you. Children indeed are a product of their environment in most cases because they learn what they live and how they are living will be how they live with others in their future. My mom, aunt, and uncle were trying to harm me vs. love me!

If you teach and show them violence and that is all they see, hear or feel it is with some certainty that they will become a character to play out in their own life's drama and reality show that contributes some form of violence and abuse or bullying to those people closest to them. They literally will be a "hit" to the people around them that will chip away at the love others have for them to the point where they bruise and sour a fruitful relationship. No child deserves to have those negative influences around them. That is an incredibly scary and traumatic experience for somebody's baby regardless of the child's age. This was why I had to and shamefully still do, stay away from my family because I cannot fully comprehend how I can associate with those individuals who tried to harm me and not help me. Could you imagine drowning at the hands of an individual who is keeping you from coming up for air and you know other people are watching this crime occur, and they are standing poolside with life preservers and a phone to call 911, and no one helps! Would you befriend them or associate with them if somehow God miraculously saved you? But because you are family with your abusers you have to stay cordial?

I forgave them for their actions to heal myself, but true forgiveness is forgetting, and that is indeed a miracle that only God can perform. So for me, my way of healing and coping is loving from a distance, because in my heart and mind I sincerely hope never to see another act of violence and abuse from the people who allegedly have a love for me. Also, because I have children, I cannot and will not expose them to my perpetrators or those who have harmed my wife over her life, because I do not trust those same volatile environments. Yes, I have love for them, but it is just a healthier way for me to cope and love them because I trust myself more because I am in control of my environment and what my family is exposed to versus taking the chance of someone, namely me, from harming them ever again.

Love hurts, and rejection is a weapon of mass destruction if you do not know how to put your arms around it and disengage the arms properly. We were not made to hate! We were made to love one another, but somehow someone else's pain overwhelmed our innocence. Never let your pain and hurt, hurt or pain others. I am used to making "painments," not "payments," with women in my life. I said earlier in the book that women to me are "Fee-Males" and not "Free-Males" meaning that they are more than worthy and deserving of a man who takes care of them and comforts them as God initially ordained, by providing for them, praying for and with them, and protecting them from harm! Women want love "Payments" and not "Painmeants"(ABUSE) directly deposited into their hands, hearts, and lives, to provide mental and physical comfort for them! There was a time in my life where all I ever seemed to get in return was a "Pain-Meant" to strike my hands and heart!

I am definitely from a different wolf pack because I am altruistic and benevolent by nature in that I am generally concerned about the welfare of others. If I have a pizza to eat, you have a pizza to eat! My love is like those friends who are there for you when you need help moving to a new residence and cleaning up after a party! I am the friend who will be there for you at the very lowest and worst times of your life and who you can trust to pick up your kids from school in an emergency and who you ultimately can leave your children to in your will and who will testify to the world on behalf of your character and who will right you when you are wrong and who will be there for your family when you have exited the earth, all with a pure heart and no agenda! I am the friend who makes sure that before I pull off in my car, I make sure your car starts or you get in the house safely.

When I say I will be your friend until the end of time and beyond, I am saying I will love you until I join you in heaven for eternity! Through my trials, tribulations, dark shadows, death walks, and lonely near-death moments, I have learned that when others are fleeing from you, hatefully cursing your name, untethering their anchors from you, running for their lives, and your foundation is rocked from its base with the towers shivering hot and are coming unraveled by the fiery crash and your life as you see it is over, I am the one who is holding your hand with the inferno to our backs as we take an angelic leap of faith together to our heavenly destiny.

I have spent enough time on people who know me but who do not truly know and love me. They already know how I feel about them, but to you I only have seconds, a moment, to show and prove my love to you! Do not leave me. Please stay with me! Can we go to heaven together! I love You! Do you not have love me? You are here for someone else and not me? Why not me? Foster kids, I LOVE YOU!

I am the extraordinary centurion running to you like the first responders running up the hundred-plus flights of stairs as the winds of many cool our overheating hearts as they passed us sprinting down the steps. All I can think of is saving you and not me or anything or anyone else. I've spent enough time for them to know and love me, so they already know how I feel about them, but to you I only have seconds, a moment, to show and prove to you how much I do love you! Don't leave me! Please stay with me! I will see you in heaven one day, my friend!

Solutions To Permanently Eradicate Domestic Violence, Child Abuse, and Bullying

<u>LOYALTY</u>

A FRIEND UNTIL WE GET TO HEAVEN TOGETHER!
I FORGIVE EVERYONE 7 X 7 X7 X 7 X 7 X 7 X7 X 7!
I LOVE YOU MORE THAN YOU COULD EVER POSSIBLY LOVE ME!
YOU WILL NEVER MEET ANYONE ELSE LIKE ME!
I CARE ABOUT YOUR HEART, NOT YOUR $$$!
I AM TOO DAMN LOYAL!

ON THE REAL! DO NOT ACCEPT MY MEEKNESS AS WEAKNESS!

Solutions To Permanently Eradicate Domestic Violence, Child Abuse, and Bullying

**ARE YOU DECEPTIVE? A WOLF IN SHEEPS CLOTHING?
I WAS A COWARD, NOT A MAN, IN MY OWN CLOTHING!
A.W. the MANIMAL! 50% Man + 50% Animal = 100% FAKE**

(FACE MERGER BY ANTONIO JENNINGS)

WHO ARE YOU WHEN NO ONE IS LOOKING and THE DEVICES SUCH AS A CELL PHONE OR CAMERA ARE NOT RECORDING? ARE YOU A SECURE and MATURE MAN OR WOMAN, OR ARE YOU AN INSECURE, IMMATURE, WILD, RECKLESS, UNAWARE, OUT OF CONTROL, UNACCOUNTABLE ANIMAL? YOU HAVE TO BE MADE WHOLE TO BE HAPPY! FIND THE SOLUTION NOW TO GET YOU CLOSER TO ETERNAL HAPPINESS and A PERMANENT ERADICATION OF DOMESTIC VIOLENCE, CHILD ABUSE, and BULLYING! A POSITIVE and A NEGATIVE WILL ALWAYS EQUAL A NEGATIVE! I AM 1000% CERTAIN YOU CAN NOT BE AN ABUSER and HERO IF YOU ARE BOTH IN THE DARK! THE LIGHT WILL APPEAR, and IT WILL EXPOSE YOUR REAR! GET IN GEAR BEFORE "IT" COST YOU EVERYTHING DEAR! CAN YOU HEAR?

Solutions To Permanently Eradicate Domestic Violence, Child Abuse, and Bullying

THE DICHOTOMY OF A MANIMAL! HERO and HYPOCRITE! VICTIM and VICTIMIZER...A.W. BURGESS

Who Or What Does The World Get On Any Given Day? A Respectful Shero/Hero Man or Woman or a Diabolical Sociopath Zero Terrorizing Innocent People?

It was just another night for me as an 8-year-old. I climbed into bed as I always had and was shortly joined in the same bed by my mom who I slept next to since I could remember! I cannot recall the time of the night, but I do remember it was late, and all I remember is my left arm and leg hitting the wall because the bed was pressed up on the wall. I remember thinking that I could not breathe! Why was a pillow covering my face? Why can't I remove it? Why can't I get up? Why can't I move? Am I dreaming? The reality was I was pinned down, being smothered by my mother with a pillow, and my arms and legs were doing their best to escape. I was not dreaming. I was nightmaring! As I was fading, I remember hearing my aunt banging on the locked door exclaiming, "What's going on in there? Open the door Loisey!" And before I knew it, I was being pulled to freedom and rushed to another room! The door closed rapidly to the door and locked instantly. I remember my mom trying to knock the door down and screaming give me back my baby! When she could not get in, she went outside and knocked on the window shouting the same, "Give me back my baby!" I hurt for my mom because I think she had buyer's remorse! I want to believe her intent was not malicious intent, but I still cannot resolve why? Was I still on the postpartum list? I blame cowardly Jimmy Thompson for doing this to my mom and me! ***MAN DAMN!***

I do not remember seeing my mother for a time after "the incident!" I was confused about "the incident" and why **"IT"** happened. I remember when my new bedding arrangements occurred! I remember thinking "Why can't I be with my mom? Why did she leave me and where did she go?" Then the world went silent and eventually retreated to the faraway fairytale town of deadly family secrets. No one ever spoke of **"IT"** or about **"IT"** ever again! Little did I know how **"IT"** would harm me. The next time I remember being around my mom she had gifts for me! I was happy to see her, and she looked happy to see me! I was glad she was around me. I remember not long after that, she sat me down and said, "What have I always wanted to do in my entire life?" I had not a clue as to what that answer would ever be! Was she getting her own house and we were leaving my grandmother's home?

And then she blurted out, "I am going into the Army! I am going to be gone for several weeks of boot camp training in Fort Dix New Jersey!" I remember thinking "She is going to be gone forever to Atlantic City." And then poof, "Voila," she was gone to Fort Dix! Why did she have to leave again? I did not want her to leave again! I remember being mad at her for leaving! I cursed her out in my mind and when I was by myself on many days for leaving me behind again by myself! What a long. lonely summer to wait for her return. I do not even remember being that excited about her return. What was the purpose of going into the military? $$$

One of the most landmark days in my life was when at 13 years old, one Friday evening, my mother wanted me to go to dinner with her and her loud, arrogant, boisterous "boyfriend" Mr. Dorsey. She was going to surprise Mr. Dorsey with me joining them for dinner because, during that period, I imagine I was like most teens who thought it would be corny, whack, or embarrassing to be seen with a parent in public. I usually would be somewhere riding a bike or playing a sport with friends or in the city with my cousin Teeny, but on this particular evening, I opted to be with them for a meal.

We arrived at Mr. Dorsey's apartment, and my mom opens the door with her key, and we entered in and quickly stood in the kitchen. My mom assumed Mr. Dorsey was not home because it was eerily quiet in the apartment. She told me to go to his bedroom to see if he was sleeping. I went to the back, opened his door, and to his and my surprise, he was in the middle of a sex act with another woman. Before I could shut the door, my mother was right behind me and had just witnessed what I did. He and the woman had to have known someone had just witnessed them having sex because my mother slammed the door. Before my mother and I could get back to the kitchen, my mom was exclaiming, "You didn't see anything!" I knew what I had just seen and proceeded to shout back louder to her that "I saw what I saw, regardless of whether you saw it or not, and I know you saw it exactly how I saw it too Ma! Give me the keys to the car! I will be in the car waiting!" If I had been carrying my gun, I would have emptied the bullets in him for dissing my mom!

I slammed the door as I exited his apartment and kept thinking this man Mr. Dorsey is a piece of shizzle and my mother is a fool for dealing with the man who has like 15 kids with a billion different women and who does not and has never taken care of any of his kids. Just the fact that he has 15+ kids with countless different women tells you he is not committed to any women, children or parental responsibilities. This being was an animal, not a man, who was committed to being a deadbeat dad, and a serial cheater who will have sex with anyone who would have sex with him, not excluding animals! This dude was a chump and a bum to me.

Shortly after that, out of the apartment comes the other woman, with her walk of shame. She hurried up and sped off in her car. Minutes later, with him in a robe and draped all over my mom like they were walking down the aisle after just being married, out comes Mr. Dorsey and my mom! This was the moment where I thought my mother was the dumbest b**** on the planet who plays the fool on the regular with an equally b**** a** dude who does not give a free f*** about my mother, definitely not me, and his 15 kids. He abandoned all those kids and their mothers, and this is who my mom is all clutched up with hubby dubby style? His abandonment reflects that he is heartless and does not care about himself or anyone for that matter! They were both suckers who needed one another to satisfy each other's weaknesses as humans. If I would have had my gun on me I would have shot both of them for being so diggity damn sorry as parents. ***MAN DAMN! Go to hell!***

From that point forward, I never looked him in the eyes or respected him. I do not believe I said 15 words to that sperm donor ever again respectfully until my mother brought them to my wedding 10 years later, which only included her him, my brother Tony, and my mother-in-law. When he died, I do not even remember being notified or asked to the funeral let alone attending the funeral and don't even remember my mom telling me he had died for months after the funeral. Why should I have cared for a person like him who never cared about me? He was my little brother's dad, not mine. I saw him as a selfish and greedy goblin who was a liar and cheater who refused to take care of his kids. I do not understand how he was a catch!

Quite frankly, not telling me about relatives and close family friend's deaths was normal for me. Outside of my favorite aunts Marty and Mary, I never attended anyone else's funeral, burial, or memorials. What does that say about the condition or state of your relationship with your mother and family when you are not even told about a significant family member or individual's death for months or even years after they have died? I understood not attending these funerals when I was in the penitentiary, but I never understood why I was not told or even invited to close family members and friend's funerals. I was only 3 hours away in college.#smh

Nonetheless, my mother and grandmother were "Silence Keepers" and "Sideliners" who sat on the sidelines in that they never said or did anything to my mother, aunt or uncle to permanently protect me from the abuse and violent offenses. They never even thought of getting me preventive help or counseling when it was obvious as a kid, and then eventually a teenage young adult, I was violently dealing with some real issues and was terrorizing, bullying, fighting, punishing and torturing other family members, friends and others alike such as Toby*, my dog. They did absolutely nothing. Maybe they did not know how to get me help and were just ignorant about getting me the necessary help. Maybe they thought I would grow out of it and eventually I or the problem would go away. Maybe they thought that by kicking me out that would solve my issues. Maybe they were like a lot of people who just sat on the sidelines scratching their heads silently and baffled about what to do with this child to correct these character deficiencies and propensity for hostility and violence. Maybe they were embarrassed and did not want anyone to know what was going on inside our house or that they would be viewed as parental failures. Maybe they thought they would lose their jobs in the school system if school administrators and authorities learned of the despicable acts of violence and child abuse committed against me as a child! Maybe they thought the department of child protective services and welfare would have been notified and after the investigation, the other children in the house and I would have been removed and placed into the prejudicial foster "uncare" system.

I do not exactly know what they were thinking or why they were thinking about what they were thinking. The only thing I do know is they did not do anything to prevent themselves and others from violently harming and abusing me and simply put in motion the blueprints for me on how to domestically bully, abuse and victimize women, children, other people, and animals. That blueprint, along with failing to properly protect me from perpetrators of violence and abuse coupled with their silence to my violence and avoidance to get me the necessary help led me fatefully to the penitentiary and psychiatric hospital. The amazing or ridiculous part about me ending up in prison and the psychiatric hospital is the very treatment I received there could have been obtained well before I even got arrested and I could have gotten it for free. ***MAN DAMN!*** How could, would, or should I have known I could have gotten help from school resources? I imagine I had the "Silence to Violence" gene in my DNA just like my mother and grandmother.

When I got out of the penitentiary, it did not take me long enough to realize that I owe my life and legacy to the victims and victimizers of violence, bullying, and abuse against women, children, and animals! People have asked me why do you care about helping domestic violence offenders, child abusers, bullies and animal cruelest? My reply has always been, who will speak for the individuals who cannot or will not speak for themselves? Who will fight the seemingly winless fight for the insignificant and invisible people who society deems as its most vulnerable, as well as, its disposables? I put my nonjudgmental arms around these throwaways. The ones society has given up on, the shamed, judged, outcasts, the unwanted, abandoned, blackballed, blacklisted, pieces of crap, black mold undesirables, unhireables, uninvited, the black and imperfect sheep!

Who wants misfits? Who will put stock in the lives of individuals whose lives have no value? Who will speak for the unwanted, detestable, undesirable black mold deplorables? Who will stand up for those murdered from domestic violence and child abuse? Who will speak for the children and young adults who commit suicide because of bullying? Who will appear on behalf of the invisible and articulately speak for the muzzled and muted? Who will defend the abandoned and neglected? Who will encourage the downtrodden and hopeless? Who will help employ the deplorable, despicable and easily disposable? I will! I will create a loving den for this pack to get fed the knowledge that someone obviously did not do right!

I am a former domestic violence abuser, offender, and bully. As an abuser who knows how to get inside the mind of an abuser better than me, an apex abuser, bully, and domestic violence offender? I am the predator and the prey! There was a time in my life where I was physically, mentally, emotionally, and psychologically abusing my girlfriend, family, and friends. I was a depraved, tortured soul as a child who grew to become a violent menace and terrorist to anyone who was close to me! The hypocrisy of my life was that I was a hero at work and in sports, but I was a zero at home and school to those people who truly loved me. Because of this abusive and violent behavior, I ended up in the penitentiary and a psychiatric hospital and came depressingly close to committing suicide. I can candidly say that the greatest mistake of my life was taking too long to get help for my violent and dysfunctional behavior. I got the help that ultimately saved my life and the lives of others too.

Today, I have the required coping techniques and life skills that afford me the opportunity to lead a mentally healthy, fully functional and productive life. I am pleading and howling to all domestic violence offenders, child abusers, bullies, and victimizers to commit to permanently eradicating domestic violence, child abuse, and bullying! It would be my pleasure to serve, help and partner with anyone to save their life and legacy! So commit to never hit! You only get one life to live, how will people remember you and how will your tombstone read? I would rather love and hug you than rub and shove you. I respect and value all women! Sexual assault and sexual harassment truth matters to me and not just because I have four daughters.

I know firsthand what it feels like to be abused, neglected and abandoned! I am my brother and sister's keeper! I will keep innocent individuals from being harmed by reaching the predator who is unequipped to mentally and healthily love anyone because they do not know how to first love themselves! If I can eradicate the violence and abuse in their psyche they will learn not to harm others and themselves permanently.

When a woman or young female dresses in all black, baggy clothes, and hoodies to cover their hair and faces because they do not want to draw attention to themselves they are in trauma! I blame the lame fathers and parents who abandoned their children and the family members who did not believe them when they said they were abused by a family member, friend, or a trusted authority! We have to believe our babies because to not believe them traumatizes them even further, Put simply, if I saw an individual beating a woman, child, or animal, I would do everything humanly possible to stop the individual from continuing the abuse. If I stop the individual abuser, I stop the abuse, and thus both the victim and the abuser are no longer being harmed or harming another. If I just put my body around the victim as a shield, then now I am being abused too, and the abuser continues to be a violent offender just to another person and the person I am shielding is still in a position to be harmed and mentally unsettled and tortured. The abuser or problem in this case never goes away, and the victim continues to be victimized. It is a circle of destruction going nowhere except to the blackhole grave or the living cemetery or "cement-ery" called the penitentiary. No more black clothes for victims. Pure white!

To answer the people asking me why do you care about helping domestic violence offenders, child abusers, bullies and animal cruelest, I hope they now see that I am one of the best solutions for permanently eradicating domestic violence, child abuse, bullying, and animal cruelty? What would have my life been had someone helped my dad? It may have turned out entirely different than him being dead and my mom scared to live a life as a single mom trying to raise a boy in Baltimore! Who will shield the innocent victim and the abuser? I will! A.W. Burgess will! My life will be defined as my will to serve others to eradicate domestic violence and abuse against women, children, and animals, to preserve the lives and legacies of these individuals who are victims of violence and the violent offenders and abusers who are victimizers or are on their way to becoming one!

Solutions To Permanently Eradicate Domestic Violence, Child Abuse, and Bullying

I made my name in the business world by "making chicken salad out of chicken shizzle!" I see the potential and positive in the negative. When the worst offender of domestic violence and abuse transforms and transitions to the greatest advocate and defender against violence and abuse against women and children, all things become possible only if one is accountable and aware of yourself! Like the Baltimore athletic apparel company DTLR, who made their brand famous by taking the hardest athletic apparel to sell and selling out the inventory, I will make a way out of the seemingly impossible by taking society's pariah and throwaways and the hardest to change and convince, polish them up with new techniques towards coping and life skills as it pertains to ending domestic violence and child abuse against women and children and by the will of God, I will let destiny do the rest!

Domestic violence and abuse are dangerous if left untreated. If domestic violence and child abuse is not permanently eradicated, meaning you are totally healed and not simply treated, it is not a matter of **"IF"** the violence and abuse will happen again, but a matter of **"WHEN"** the violence and abuse will occur again and rear its horrendous head over and over and over until someone dies, gets incarcerated or until Jesus intervenes! The impact you have on others lasts a lifetime. Parents were not given children by God for them to destroy His creation. Spouses and couples were never made to offend or abuse each other violently. A pet would never want to be abused or neglected purposely when the sole purpose for having a pet is meant to bring joy and companionship to its owner! Even a pet deserves to be free!

As a child, what do you do when your mother tries to kill you, and then your family does absolutely nothing to protect you from future harm? No one talked to me about "it" or even asked me how I felt about the entire situation. I was kept in the same environment as if nothing ever happened. The betrayal came when the very aunt who saved me became the bully and torturer I hated most in life. Her immature mind games and torturous treatment at night was just an amusing form of intimidation for her. She would punch me in the face, slap me, choke me or even hit me in the head with a rotary telephone. I always thought as a kid that one day I will get her and my sorry uncle who was mean for no reason and who would steal from us or wear our clothes at his leisure, often time stretching them to the point where we could no longer fit our clothes. I am so glad I did not murder my family!

Where were you to protect me, Mommy? Teacher of the Year at work but a mother who could not teach me how to love properly at home. What were you teaching me? For my aunt to put us in the basement with the lights completely out just made me madder and more upset because I did not like the way my cousins were scared, screaming, and crying. I never possessed fear, and because I never cried or showed an impenetrable spirit, it became my aunt's mission to break my will. It became my uncle's quest to keep thumping me in my sternum. All I could ever think about was getting bigger and stronger so that one day I would make her, him and you mommy, feel the way she made my cousins feel and their and your level of disrespect by not protecting me! This is why I was ashamed of being born into this world and this family because I was taking the brutal and harsh punishment for someone else's crime and pain. I was paying the price for someone else's crime? Jimmy Thompson's crime! Your crime! Thus, I would learn to do the same to other people. I would learn to harm other innocent people like Teeny, Michelle, & Toby*!

I am a tremendously flawed man! A filthy rag who is trying to bleach away the bloodstains on my life that will never fade or go away. I am a dysfunctional human being trying to function in a dysfunctional and hypocritical society. I am a spiritual being and believer and not a religious person. I am incredibly tainted yet incredibly blessed and am simply trying to deliver a message of truth and love to prevent individuals from harming others, themselves, and their legacies. It is not possible for me to accomplish this by myself and so I humbly and respectfully ask for your support in any capacity to help those of us who truly need to be protected from violence and abuse and to help the many overcome being an abuser and violent offender, while also preventing others from becoming victims or victimizers!

What mark will I leave on the world? How will I always be remembered? Will I be remembered as the domestic violence and child abuse predator whisperer or will I permanently be remembered as a failure, felon, batterer, woman beater, domestic violence offender, an abuser of someone else's child, a closet animal cruelty individual, or a pure waste of talent by people who have the right to judge me or defined by loved ones, friends and business associates as a legendary husband, father, friend, and business consultant who cared about impacting and serving the lives of others even after he was no longer on the earth. I refuse to have those claims as my legacy and would rather be known as a humanitarian who changed his mindset, evil ways and behavior to change the world to a better place. At one time, I was a fighter of women. But I decided to take on the fight against domestic violence and child abuse by embracing the violent offenders and child abusers to convince them to choose to fight, batter, abuse and defeat their personal pains and demons and not their children, wives, girlfriends, boyfriends, co-workers, fellow citizens, animals, personal and corporate legacies and most of all....................themselves.

These are my confessions as a domestic violence offender and child abuse-"her!" You have got to own the abuse to be able to throw away the abuse. If you buy anything, you have a basic fundamental right to discard it at your leisure. If you never buy into the idea of owning your abuse, then it will eventually own and discard you at its convenience. I was a definitive abuser of multiple types such as mental(psychological), physical, emotional and verbal. Whether it was mind games or the silent treatment or harmful personal verbal assaults, disappearing for days with no communication or pissing on her dreams by telling her she was stupid for wanting to be a teacher because they did not make any money or killing her esteem and self-beauty by telling her she was fat and out of shape because she possessed the "fat gene" and she did not work out or just simply calling her a dumb b**** or fat b**** pig or hog or accusing her of sleeping around because she was a whore a** cheating b**** who was not loyal and could never be trusted! Or simply telling her, she was "weak" and that I made her significant and she was a nobody without me! Everything I told her she was, is what I truly was as a person on the inside. I was the nobody when she was somebody. I was the insignificant b**** and bully who was internally and mentally weak and who carried the "abuse and hate genes" respectfully. I was the one who was the cheating a** b**** whore. Never her!

I am sincerely sorry & apologize to God for abusing His priceless creation, Michelle! I am sincerely sorry and apologize to her parents for being a hypocrite and abusing their baby that God trusted so much that of all the people on the earth at that time, He chose them to raise His baby! I am sincerely sorry and apologize to her sister for abusing the big sister who was worthy of looking up to but also a big sister who always took pride in her baby sister. I am sincerely sorry and apologize to her husband for abusing his bride and best friend that God had put together for no man to put asunder! I am sincerely sorry and apologize to her children for harming their Mommy! I am sincerely sorry and apologize to her family and friends for harming their precious loved one and friend! I am sincerely sorry and apologize to Dr. William Harvey and Hampton University for being a threat on their campus and bringing unnecessary attention to their great institution for higher learning! I pray that my actions and the negative attention that was received in the media, as a result, did not translate to prospective students choosing not to attend out of fear! My violence impacted so many people. One never knows the ripple effect of violence!

Solutions To Permanently Eradicate Domestic Violence, Child Abuse, and Bullying

If you ever want to know where you stand with any relationship, take the money out of the relationship. Go and tell your spouse or significant other that you need to file bankruptcy because you lost your job six months ago and you have zero dollars, the credit cards are maxed out, the house is in foreclosure, the car is being repossessed, the kid's college fund is gone, along with an empty 401k, and your credit is so bad you cannot finance a pack of bubblegum! Tell them you are waiting for several pawn shops and homeless shelters to call you back. Ask them what are they thinking? Will they stay, or will they go? If they stay, they are there for you for better or worse and not for the party freebies! If you did not have money or influence would people want to interact with you? Would they want you to marry their child? Would they laugh as hard and loud at your jokes? Would they put up with your bullcrap? Would you accept me into your club, fraternity, sorority, or college and give me an honorary degree? Would you invite me to your home, church, or neighborhood and introduce me to your family and friends? Now find out I am a domestic violence offender or a child abuser? Will you still love and accept me the same? Will you allow your stock and brand to suffer and plummet because of your association with me? Am I now an asset or a** to you and the organization?

I once angrily said to my family, F*** Family! F*** Y'All MuthaF******, after learning that my uncle had lied to my mother and grandmother about him not stealing my money and they believed him. Some families have family members and friends who screw over their family and friends a million different ways to get what they want. Some church and school leaders are screwing over their parishioners and students financially, figuratively, and literally. Show me what you are giving back and not just taking from people. I love Jesus, and He is the King of All Kings, and He would wash your feet and ask you what you need and how can He meet your needs! Man is the polar opposite who wants you to wash his feet and meet all of his needs along with the needs of his wife, children, bank account and sexual fantasies!

Let us talk about real economics, and more specifically a lack thereof or an abundance thereof, contributing to perpetuating and glorifying abuse and violence against women and children because the world financially benefits and greedily loves and displays violence and abuse without playing an impactful part in the eradication or solutions to domestic violence and child abuse against women and children. Sex, crime, and violence sells! Why are we still watching these forms of entertainment and yet America's Most Wanted was taken off the air by Fox, replaced by "Animation Domination" and then eventually from CNN with John Walsh's second attempt at capturing dangerous fugitives! Thank You God for the Justice Network and John Walsh! How many fugitives are caught now with AMW gone?

Hollywood and corporate America does not want to be responsible for showcasing the solutions but would rather put on display and glorify the most heinous murderers, serial rapists, pedophiles, gangsters, horror stories or movies! If you do not trust what I am saying take a look at the shows that have been and are currently available to view for your pleasure whether it is on network, cable, satellite, streaming television networks and services. CBS, NBC, CNN, HLN, OWN, Reelz, E, Amazon Prime, Netflix, Hulu, Bravo, MTV, VH1, Paramount Network(It Was Him), USA, Syfy, Investigation Discovery(ID), BET, BetHer, TVone, IFC, ION, WGN, CNBC, MSNBC, 48 Hours, Dateline, TNT, TruTV, Lifetime, LMN, AMC, We, A&E, National Geographic, etc. I am tired of hearing about Ted Bundy*, John Gotti*, Al Capone*, Pablo Escobar*, Bill Cosby and Harvey Weinstein! How does it benefit my life watching the stories of serial killers, rapists, pedophiles, stalkers and the most heinous people to have lived? Society does not promote the good news stories until the last 2 minutes of a program going off the air. We are teaching some of our kids how cool it is to be notoriously infamous!

I am creating a good news movement, meaning a loving movement that showcases, encourages uplift, and empowerment towards human beings who are breaking their silence and coming out of the doldrums of death to live and love prosperous, meaningful lives where they stop harming themselves first and then others. I have seen enough faces of death in life that I do not need to see this on television and in the movies. Do not confuse pain with entertainment where people are benefiting from other people's misfortunes in life. I want a festival that signifies the victory of good over evil, the arrival of LIFE and the end of DEATH, and for many, a festive day to meet others, play and laugh, forget and forgive, live and learn from each other's experiences while repairing broken hearts and relationships. I pray that when I walk into any room, my aura and presence embodies and overwhelms individuals to be engaged in being a significant difference in eradicating domestic violence, child abuse, and bullying. ***Faces of Death*** the movie was a hoax and lie!

Your life should never become relevant after somebody kills you! Now you are a somebody if someone kills you? That is ridiculous in that society wants to know as much about the killer than the victim! Why do you only become relevant after you are dead? Why do you only become relevant after you have committed a heinous crime? Why can't your life be significant now? You only get one life, and this is how it ends or is this where it begins? What kills you is what builds you. The journey is full of black holes, landmines, and quicksand, along with a grim forecast of torrential downpours, mudslides, tornadoes, hurricanes, and brush fires being muddy, murky, foggy, dusty, and cloudy paths. And yet, we still seem to track through the mud, see through the fog, dust, and clouds find a way to make it to our destination. The twisters will rapidly move on and disappear as fast as they appeared, as they always do! Know that it does not rain torrentially every day, and eventually, the floods will subside, the dam and levies won't be breached, the black clouds will dissipate like the black hole and the quicksand and mud will dry up alongside your tears, and the sun will shine and breakthrough and provide relief. Your prayers were heard by God and answered! You are alive! But more than anything, you have just proven your will is unbreakable and cannot be shaken from your foundation because you are built to survive. I have a heart for showcasing the victim's stories because I know they will never get a Wikipedia page like most of the heinous murderers and other criminals. Is it not crazy that we remember the crimes and the criminals more than the legacy of the victims? If we want to celebrate the criminals, let us celebrate the criminals who have performed a 180-degree turnaround to contribute positively back to the community it robbed. Let us showcase these changes to inspire other victimizers to change their lives to victorious citizens who went from torturers to carrying the torch of love.

Because I suffered from Stockholm Syndrome, the more I was abused by my abusers, the more I wanted to be with my abusers. I empathized with them until they ultimately pushed me away. Sad but true, as was the case for me, you oftentimes become the abuser you said you would never be. I was so used to this emotional detachment, abandonment, neglect, and lack of genuine support and parental protection from my mom and the constant fighting, bullying, fear tactics and intimidation from my aunt and uncle that violence always made me believe it was not possible for others to love me because they would realize they had made a mistake in loving me and would eventually leave.

As a result, I would rather push away any person showing me love before they ultimately pushed me away because of my predictable propensity to be unsupportive, neglectful, and an absentee friend who was constantly abusive and violent by fighting, bullying, and intimidating. I was so used to being pushed away, unsupported and abandoned, being left alone was always my norm that I became accustomed to my entire life! I was used to being a lone wolf! No one cheering in the stands for me because I was not worthy of their time? Who or what took more precedence over being there for me and supporting what was important to me? Getting attention from a person who never had any marriage intentions or long-term love interests versus going and watching "your" star athlete child. What was more important than your child's happiness and esteem? What lesson were you trying to enforce? Did you get what you wanted from the individual you chose over your child? Did they fulfill or kill your dreams? Did you become whole as a person?

My life will never be an individual who sat on the sidelines watching television, playing on the internet, going to work and raising my family without being engaged, involved, and impacting the community. I just will not be satisfied with mediocrity knowing that there are people who are living their lives either perpetuating violence or absorbing the pain of the perpetrator of violence. I have to help the victim and the victimizer because if I do not, other people will die or continue to perpetuate violence. No human being or animal deserves to be a victim or deserves to continue their acts of violence without any intervention to show them a better way to live or cope. We have interventions for drug and alcohol addiction, but we have not provided a permanent solution to managing domestic violence and child abuse. I wish to be incredibly intentional in helping prevent deaths and providing the coping and life skills to any receptive, accountable individual, whether they are violent or nonviolent. I need the help of many individuals and corporations to accomplish this vision. So who am I and what am I trying to accomplish?

I am the face of domestic violence, bullying, and child abuse solutions! I protect abused women, men, and children! I keep them from death and from stalkers! We have violence against our women, children, LGBTQ, animals, and law enforcement! Violence is in our homes, churches, schools, workplace, synagogues, hotels, elevators, entertainment venues of art, music concerts, movie theatres, yoga spas, bars, clubs, jobs, military bases, sporting events, casinos, parks, hospitals, bloodlines, and DNA. Is there any safe place? Waiting for a loved one to be found dead or alive must be one of the very worst experiences a human being could ever endure! Time must feel like it is either stopped or it is moving a million miles a second! The air must be heavy like a thousand pounds of weight on your chest. How do you process your loved one has been discovered dead? How do you resurrect your child from the dead?

What is going through the mind of the victim as their life is being taken from them? What is going through the head of the individual taking the life of someone else's baby and family member or friend? Who gave them the Godly permission and authority to pull the lever, switch, or trigger or push the button or needle to release the chemicals? What is comparable to the death or molestation of a baby?

Everyone is someone's baby! I am someone's baby. I want my legacy to be as a benevolent, humanitarian, author, speaker, family man, and the face of the American solution to domestic violence, bullying and child abuse! I am a certified Manimal- A Man and An Alpha Male Wolf! I am the leader of my family, the company FAMILY MANKIND™, and am an advocate for women, children, animals, and abusers. It is not where I am from, but it is where I am and moreover, where I am going and where I want to be! From Baltimore Boy to Maryland Man! From felon to freedom! From victim to victimizer to victor! From being America's Most Wanted to America's Most Wanted man! You cannot be on the run forever!

Stop! Turn around! Face what is trying to kill you and your legacy! Submit! Admit! Commit! Forgive! Conquer it! Serve others! I am the one providing solutions to end domestic violence and abuse against women and children! I speak for the invisible, irrelevant and muzzled human beings who are being abused, violently offended, bullied, stalked, threatened, manipulated or silenced by others or institutions. I am a man who does not have his father's last name. I am a man who does not even have a father's name listed on his birth certificate. A child denied death benefits because his mother could not prove his father's paternity! My name is not Antoine William Burgess because Burgess is my mother's birth name not the last name from marriage. My legal birth last name, according to the people who say a man named James, who was my mother's abusive and violent sperm donor, should be Thompson. Imagine looking at your birth certificate, and there is no one listed as your father. Was my father an alien or ghost or was his name blank?

I am in the business of saving lives and legacies. The essence of what I am is I care more about an individual's life than I do about their economics, political, religious, sexuality, demographics, or social affiliations. When you are in the midst of being abused or violently offended, do you care about the associations of the individual trying to save your life? I possess an altruistic soul in that I am genuinely concerned about the welfare of others. I am an uniter of all people, not a divider! FAMILY MANKIND™ literally translates to "For All Mankind I Love You! Managing Anger and Abuse Now, Kindly!" All I know is love! Evil only wins when Good does absolutely nothing! I am the "Good Guy" looking to partner with other

"Good People!" There are no hidden agendas, but rather complete accountability and transparency! Domestic violence and child abuse does *NOT* care about anything or anyone and is *NOT* looking for a permanent solution! *NOT* has me in **KNOTS**!

I also suffer from chronic victim's guilt and remorse! A pain of guilt and remorse placed in the core of my heart, soul, and mind! Why could I *not* save them or prevented my friend, Shaniya Davis*, Zahra Baker*, or Tahjir Smith* from being killed and violently abused by their parents and caretakers? These were their caretakers, *not* undertakers? Why did someone *not* say or do anything to help them? Why could I have **NOT** saved Cherica Adams*, Nicole Brown Simpson* or myself? Why did someone **NOT** show James Ernest Thompson* a better way to treat women so that the Baltimore Police would *not* have justifiably killed him? I am fatherless!

Why is it that husbands, boyfriends, estranged former husbands, and ex-boyfriends abuse and kill their wives, girlfriends, and children? Why do parents abuse and murder their children? I thought they made vows before God and to each other to love one another? Why did they throw away their relationship? Where did the love go? How can this possibly be? What happened to respect? How did these demons of death and destruction get in these individuals? Why do evil and hate think it has won? Where are you good and love? Someone or something put them and such pain in them? Who put it in them? What happened? Let us run it out to kill it!

Why did someone *NOT* say or do anything to prevent them from being harmed or killed! I have victim's remorse that fuels me, and as a result, I will always be proactive to protect and fight for any all individuals of abuse and violence! The remorse and guilt are real and has been in me since I was a child.

When I was in the 7th grade, a female classmate was scald to death in her bathtub at the hands of her mother. I remember the shock and confusion that overwhelmed me and all of us close to her immediately after we were told. I remember vividly how my little crew of friends went silent and naturally as pubescent boys we did not cry or show any public emotion about her death. We were numb and mum to the point that I do not even recall being afforded the opportunity to attend her funeral. Now I truly understand why after a school tragedy, grief counselors are dispatched to offer counseling services to students. As I had always done after a traumatic event, I simply held it in and took it as another test of my manhood to not cry because boys never cry as my uncles and male cousins instilled in me! I just remember thinking why her mother did that to her and in an instant the remembrance and confusion set in on me that my mother also had tried to smother me to death in years prior and had it not been for my investigative aunt hearing my arm bang against her wall, I would have been dead just like many other children.

What could, or should I have done as a 12-year-old 7th grader prior to and after her death? How come I did not know she was being abused! How would I have known? My remembrance of her was a pistol of fire who could hang with any boy or girl when it came to joking on one another in a dozens joke competition! She was witty as hell despite the fact that she was thought of or known as the most unattractive girl in our school! Her beauty to me was her fierce, take no prisoners attitude and relentless funny perspective on boys in our crew or class. How could her mom take her spirit? Was her mom abused by a man like my mom or was she abused as a child and either way, she took it out on my friend? God needed her beautiful soul back in heaven. He needed a jester in heaven to keep the angels in healthy stitches of laughter! God needed her more than I could have ever imagined!

A few years later, here comes the death of my McDonogh tutor Ceres Horn*. Then, almost a year to the day, my close friend Brandon Wilson* dies on the New Jersey Turnpike in a one-car accident! And as if death was supposed to come regularly to my life, my childhood friend Darell Dixon* is murdered in Baltimore a few years later. Death, dark, gray, black, tears, puddles, and piss! Am I next Lord?

Then I end up in jail as a result of abduction, which is kidnapping, and the illegal possession of a firearm during the commission of a crime, all stemming from domestic violence and abuse against my former girlfriend and am eventually housed in the same cell with Thomas Beavers*, who eventually would claim a bed on Virginia's Death Row! What could I have done to have prevented Tommy from raping, robbing, and ultimately murdering his elderly neighbor, Margaret Lowery* and raping others? I would have kept him off of death row and receiving a lethal injection, but more than anything, Ms. Lowery would have lived out her glorious destiny and not die at the hands of violence and abuse! **_MAN DAMN!_**

Fast Forward to 1996 and one of my childhood heroes, O.J. Simpson is on trial for killing his ex-wife Nicole Brown Simpson* and Ronald Goldman*. I could not believe he was on trial for a double murder, but equally, I was as hurt to learn he had been abusing Nicole violently for years! What I was also most disgusted with was the reality that I was no better than O.J. when it came to abusing the woman and friend who loved me despite my many character flaws. The abuse of Michelle, many years before Nicole and Ron's murder made me cry. I single-handedly killed my friend's esteem and all she ever did was love me. What kind of friend was I to hurt and abuse? How can I be called a friend to anybody? Women will fear me!

Of course, the world now knows O.J. was not convicted of their murders, but what the world also knows, and subsequently convicted in the court of public opinion, is that he violently abused his wife and many still allege he murdered them! I wish I could have done something to prevent Nicole, Ron, and O.J.'s demise! Would Aaron Hernandez* and Odin Lloyd*, still be here had I been there for Aaron? I hurt for Aaron's daughter, fiancé, Odin Lloyd's family, and the NFL! I'm sorry Joe Mixon! I hurt deeply for not helping my man Chris Brown! I did not run fast enough and arrived too late to help save the special life of Lawrence Phillips*, who was always running for his life, and who had abused women running for theirs! Would my tireless and inspirational great friend Saundra Adams be living a life forced on her rather than by her choice and would her beautifully ambitious first-round pick of a daughter Cherica Adams* still be here and Rae Carruth, an NFL first-round draft pick by the Carolina Panthers, be a convicted felon and conspirator to convict murder, but rather a free man providing and caring for his incredibly God's strength and heavenly sent son Chancellor Lee? None would have a * next to their name.

I will forever believe that it was my fault that I was not in a position to protect or prevent the abuse and violence to save the lives of Tahjir Smith*, Zahra Baker*, Shaniya Davis*, Fred Lane*, Phylicia Barnes*, and Cherica Adams*! I could not howl or growl for them and sat morbidly silent on the sidelines with a chained muzzle covering my mouth! I contributed absolutely nothing to their or my own well-being! I did not "Howl for Help" for them and was not accountable to them or myself! I want any mature individual to join me and help other offenders, abusers, and bullies not go down the same streets of violence that have devastated the lives and legacies of people they know personally and those whom they will never know personally or professionally!

By no means am I now or will I ever try to diminish or make light of or justify the torturous acts of violence and abuse against any women or children committed by the famous, infamous or not famous individuals mentioned in this book! What I am simply trying to convey is that based on my own life and personal tragedies and experiences, the fact is the way I see a successful, permanent, solution to saving the lives and legacies of women and children, and thus preserving their legacies, is to ensure that the victimizers are truly getting genuine support by way of proactive, accountable protocols and coping techniques that lead to these abusers being permanently healed and not temporarily treated and thus the cycle of abuse and violence continues to perpetuate until someone gets tragically injured and abused or violently murdered!

Think about it this way! An individual beats, slaps, or chokes a loved one albeit a wife, girlfriend, or baby, toddler, or child. What happens to the women or children? Most times they flee to a family member or friend's home or shelter or are placed in the custody of the state's version of child protective services and welfare or department of social services! Where does the offender go? Jail? And if so, for how long and where does he go when he is released and what is protecting the victims from this offender? Why did the victim have to run and hide when they did nothing? Are we penalizing the victims when they did absolutely nothing wrong, but yet they and their families, friends, and co-workers are running and hiding for their lives, and chances are they are going to be forced or by circumstantial choice, to be right back in the same residence with their abuser and violent offender! When a pit bull or wild animal mauls a human being, animal control comes out and secures the animal and then takes it to be trained, euthanized, or released back in the wild! What do we do when domestic violence occurrences? We return them to the victim!

In most cases, the abusers are returning to their residence where the abuse has occurred with little to no consequences and with even less impactful solutions to curve their behavior, and thus the cycle of abuse and violence continues! What is even worse is often times the abuse is never reported! These perpetrators know there are no consequences and until they know real consequences or solutions to actually heal them, they will only know the repetition of abuse and violence with no consequences and no permanent solutions! Bottom line: If I can get through to the abusers and violent offenders, I will prevent abuse and violence against women and children, while preserving the lives and legacies of each! I will change the direction of the normal expectations of victimizers. I know it is a daunting task to believe or bet on individuals that society deems as pieces of a missing puzzle, but the real sacrifice is painful! Pain comes before pleasure like the birth of a baby! The pain is coming out and leaving because the love is coming in! Pain is replaced by pleasure which is love! We have to give love a try. I put my life on the line for this cause which is our cause. Boys will not be boys when they are taught to be men, and that life is not for horseplay! Real men do not cry wolf! Real men Stay Hungry! I am simply here to help people who cannot help themselves. I hope to be a part of the permanent solution and the perfect partner and follow up to the Metoomovement.

The world will quickly know that for my one lifetime, I am a 1000% Genuine, Authentic, Certified Man! I am an ALPHA Man and Wolf who is intense, hostile, and vigilant for a cause, but who is an accountable, conscious, respectful, benevolent, altruistic, and philanthropic FAMILY MAN!™

I always wanted to help save the people society deemed as living waste, who are irrelevant and invisible pariahs, hopeless, and just those who are stuck between a rock and hell! This is why my passion and affinity for those impacted by domestic violence and child abuse is what churns my heart! This is absolutely why I care about the foster kids and those that time out of the foster care system without ever being adopted! I was not relevant as a child to my mother. I could be viewed as the hero kid to other parents, teachers, and kids because of my exceptional athletic talents, smarts in and out of the classroom, and respectful manners to adults, but I was a zero in my own home! This was further displayed in my mother's actions when she tried to kill me or allowed my aunt and uncle to abuse me whenever she chose a man or personal project over my needs and supports. No one ever came to my defense when my aunt and uncle were fighting me! I always felt like my life had zero meaning and purpose whenever my mother said she wished she had aborted me by flushing me down the toilet when she had the chance or that I was mean just like my dad!

I always felt like a discarded piece of trash and an unwanted throw away like many of our foster kids and abused children who never got adopted or adopted by horrible parents! This unknowingly became my motivation for striving to be the very best at whatever I put my hands to, so I could get out of a place where I never felt I belonged! All things are possible to me, and I will vigilantly and ferociously work until I eventually see the invisible become invincible!

I felt like the famous horse Sunday Silence. *When Sunday Silence was born, he had crooked back legs and was deemed an unlikeable horse by all who laid eyes on him. All the experts said he was a skinny zero horse who would never amount to a doggone thing. His owner tried to sell him twice, but no one wanted to buy him! He had no foreseeable future value in their eyes. The horse no one wanted! No one wanted him like a foster child who never got adopted! He went to auction and was purchased for $17,000 dollars which was the 4th lowest purchase amount out of 160 horses sold at auction that day. On top of that, as he was traveling home from the auction, the van transporting him wrecked in a trailer accident killing six thoroughbreds on a foggy northwest Arkansas highway!* [75]

All the experts said he was damaged goods who would soon die of the injuries from the accident. His owner told them to just put him out in the pasture for the remainder of his life. And just as miracles happen, to the amazement of all, about a week later when they went to check on him, he was out in the pasture "jumping around, frolicking, and running like he was as a foal. There was nothing wrong with him, and he had totally recovered from the accident!" Thank God that his owner Arthur Hancock didn't take him out to pasture to "take him out!" He saw Sunday Silence just as himself. He once said, "I had a heartfelt affinity for Sunday Silence because he was a horse that no one wanted! I wasn't wanted! So, we both were in the same boat!" [69]

If Sunday Silence could have spoken to his owner Arthur Hancock, I know he would have said, "Do not put me out! Put me out to pasture! I am the miracle you prayed for to God to help save your life!" He proved to his owner that if you have the faith of a mustard seed by believing in me, do not give up on me, invest in me, then you can bet the farm on me, and I will be a benefit to your life forever! He showed the world that he was a diamond in the rough so please do not just throw away anything based on its outside appearance but judge them for their heart and will to win! Bet the farm on me! Miracles do come in different packages if you believe! Sunday Silence reminds me of the people that society judges on appearances and emphatically counts them out before they even enter the race due to their physical stature inefficiencies, economic deficiencies, and zip codes! What they fail to realize is when you are scrawny, disabled, weak, and deficient God overcompensates the size of your heart, your unmatchable work ethic, and your supernatural will to win in the game of life! Sunday Silence has it! I have it and have seen it firsthand with my wife and kids and the many sheroes and heroes I have listed such as Anne and Allen Iverson, Saundra and Lee Adams, along with Muggsy and Brittney Bogues, Julius Peppers, Leon and Barbara Levine, and Steve Smith Sr!

The baddest man is an individual who can provide solutions like a blind man who can see through the other senses of hearing, touching, tasting, and smelling the things we cannot with intimate details. I see things differently than most people! I see words and meanings different than most people. For instance, the word Cancer! Most see the word as Can-Cer! Speak life(VIVE) into it! I see it as Can-Cer-Vive! Can Survive! It's all in how you look at it! Look now! He'll- HE Will- HE'LL=HEAL= HE(God) Will Heal You! Atheist- AT(HE IS)T or HE IS sits right in the middle of the word, but someone or something has blinded your perception! God is right in the middle! Look at it this way, at-he-is-t Who beat the HE out of your life? Atheist to me means HE IS THE TRUTH! Do not be insecure but rather be secure in Jesus and you will have all the security in knowing you are going to be alright! You have to trust and have FAITH! No Jesus Know Harm! Know Jesus No Harm! My friend and one of my God consultants and spiritual experts Martuan Woodley once told me about the word WORLD- "When the world took the LORD and His WORD out of the word WORLD, look at how the world and the WORD of God has changed our world. The WORD and our LORD is the only thing we can truly trust and rely on forever." This is how I operate in the world…on Faith and Love.

After prison, all that was on my brain was the thought of who was going to love or hire an undesirable like me? I did not think or believe I was ever capable of being loved or hired by a respected, great paying corporation again once I went to the penitentiary and psychiatric hospital. I truly did not ever believe anyone, or anything would ever want to love or hire me especially now that I was a freshly minted convicted felon and a former "psychiatric " inpatient! Who would want to be my friend or hire me or want to marry me or have children by me or share their life with someone as heinous and dangerous as me, let alone hire me with those nefarious credentials? This feeling was intensified upon my release from prison. I was uncertain whether I was capable of healthily loving another woman because I did not trust that I was healed from abusing another externally and internally beautiful and altruistic woman and friend like Michelle. I imagine you could say I had post penitentiary trepidation towards seriously dating someone or looking for work at a reputable company because I sincerely did not want to hurt anyone else literally and figuratively, including myself! I was shell shocked and quite apprehensive about approaching companies and women romantically for fear of rejection after I disclosed the reasons for my recent penitentiary vacation! I simply needed a job to please my parole obligations and a friend to be a friend because, throughout my entire incarceration, I had little to no meaningful companionship with anyone who was looking forward to my release!

I was alone in prison literally and metaphorically mentally and could already see I was going to be alone upon my release and imprisoned in my apartment and mind literally and metaphorically. This was a feeling I knew all too well as a child and during my years at McDonogh and Oklahoma State University. Besides, I had not graduated from college, and my INROADS internship at Ingram Industries and Ingram Book Company was in perilous jeopardy! I had systematically destroyed my personal and corporate lives! From 0 to #1 back to 0! Started from the bottom and now I am back here? I was hustling backwards! ***MAN DAMN!***

I recall the greatest reluctance and embarrassment, yet a burning desire of respect, to speak with my mentor E. Bronson Ingram who was in Nashville! When I finally got him on the phone, after getting past his gatekeepers, I remember the embarrassment and shame I felt because I had let him and the many others responsible for my direct success at Ingram down! They had invested their time and money in training me and the financial commitment and investments Mr. Ingram had made in my future at his company! I remember telling him that I would repay him for the money he had previously compensated me, now that I could no longer become a corporate attorney or trusted corporate managing executive seeing how I was now a paroled, disenfranchised felon versus a graduate from Hampton University with a Bachelor's of Science(B.S.) Degree in Finance and a first-year law school student at Vanderbilt University where he suggested I attend because he was going to pay for me to go to law school while still working as a corporate attorney or executive management trainee at Ingram Industries. After allowing me to vent about what I had just been through since I spoke with him last in person, the very first words out of his mouth were, "Are you okay and do you need any money or anything? What can I help you with to get your life back on the successful track it was on before this ordeal?" I could not believe what I was hearing, yet I could, because he was who he had always been and who I knew him to be, but like everyone else, I thought he would have abandoned me because I had let him down!

In my mind and heart, I was restored professionally because of him, but the reality was that because I had such a lengthy parole that restricted me from leaving the state of Virginia, it was impossible for me to go back to Ingram Industries! He did everything to help me, but it was an unsalvageable venture that could never be realized. I will never forget the overwhelming sense of shame and the incredible level of disgust for blowing the opportunity E. Bronson Ingram had bestowed upon me and my future with not just his company, but also his family! I will always remember how he did not judge me, but rather, how he met me where I was and merely wanted to know how he could help me grow from there! That is a trait that is innately resident in my soul and has carried me in developing business for companies and growing their employees. If I could see him today I would probably cry in his arms, not for the alterations I had for my career with him, but because I never had the personal opportunity to tell him how sorry I was for not being a return on his investment and to thank him for not judging me and for wanting to help me! ***MAN DAMN!***

I am trying to uniquely domesticate and tame the abusers and violent offenders who some may compare to out of control wild animals. We cannot always tranquilize or euthanize these individuals because that is not always applicable or the best solution, so we must find alternative ways to eradicate and prevent domestic violence and child abuse. Do you know what it is like to see a dead living person? Abuse victims and their victimizers who have spent more time in jail or prison than on the streets because they cannot break their addiction to drugs, alcohol, pornography, sex, gambling, and abuse! I ask society this question? What do you think would happen if zookeepers released all their apex predators such as lions, tigers, bears, or hyenas into society? What would society do? How would society react? Would there be mass hysteria where people are running for their lives and are locking every door or window? Is everyone arming up with a gun or bow and arrow to shoot these wild animals? Does the media have helicopters in the sky tracking their whereabouts? How would the animals respond? Would they do what comes naturally to them? Jail and prison are our zoos being secured by our wardens the zookeepers.

What happens when a child abuser or domestic violence offender is released from jail or prison or a bully is set to return to school following a suspension? If we as a society do not have a proactive solution for these apex predators, then we will only be reactive soon after they do what comes naturally to them! If you got abused or are a victim of domestic violence, how would you feel knowing this predator of an individual will be released? Why not release Jerry Sandusky or Larry Nassar to test the theory? How about releasing convicted murderers Scott or Drew Peterson or Jesse Matthew Jr or George Huguely V? What do you think of the idea? Bill Cosby has gone from America's Dad to America's Had. If you do not learn from his behavior, you are destined for disaster. Kareem Hunt and Tyreek Hill be careful, or exit left with Ray Rice and Chad Ochocinco. It is a long, hard-fought journey paid with many sacrifices to get to the professional and expert level of any industry. Then if you are blessed or fortunate in becoming a famous celebrity or corporate executive, in just seconds, with the capture of a digital camera or someone coming forward to make a nefarious claim against you, everything that you worked for is gone and never the same as you remembered it! Your legacy is systematically destroyed or tainted! Bill Cosby, Harvey Weinstein, Darren Sharper, O.J.Simpson, Aaron Hernandez*, Chad "Ochocinco" Johnson, Matt Lauer, Russell Simmons, Asia Argento, Tyreek Hill, Kareem Hunt, Ray Rice,

Kevin Spacey, Charlie Rose, Joe Mixon, Mario Batali, Marshall Faulk, Heath Evans, Donovan McNabb, Ike Taylor, Warren Sapp. Who's next? I pray not you!

Although I fear nothing, if I had one it would be along the lines of leaving no life insurance for my family and no legacy of impact in the lives of people I came into contact with during my life! Just know that when I tell a person, I will pray for them I don't wait I pray right then and there for them, and with them, so they know I meant what I said, and they genuinely know I care about them. If it is the Lord's Will, I want my legacy to continue through my children and grandchildren and their children's children's children along with the many others who partnered with me to eradicate domestic violence and child abuse against women, children, LGBTQ, and animals while fighting recidivism.

I do not want my legacy to die when I die! I do not mind being labeled a felon or an abuser or domestic violence offender if and only if it means I prevent others from being abused and assaulted or being the abuser or violent offender. I was and still am aggressive, hostile, and relentless. It is just that now my aggression, hostility, and relentless spirit is controlled and focused on formidable and purposeful activities and solutions.

I pray that God intervenes with anyone who is trying to beat the domestic violence and child abuse curse. I pray that my actions restore me to a credible status in our society so that America knows I am the closest living example of a person who is corporate and street certified, qualified, official, original, genuine and authentic when it comes to saving lives and legacies by helping abusers to no longer be domestic violence offenders, child abusers, bullies, or cruel to animals.

I know God has meaning and a significant purpose for my life to be used to help those individuals who can not necessarily always help themselves! I gladly accept and embrace the challenge and commitment. I am an authentic brand that many people can relate to and associate themselves! I have been battle-tested and have stood the many tests of time!

My situation of going to prison for domestic violence and abuse is not so unique, but me leading a movement by confessing to the world as an abuser that the solution to domestic violence, child abuse, and bullying is when the abuser admits they have an issue and takes the necessary steps to mentally get help to permanently eradicate domestic violence is something very few people have actually initiated. How I am going about changing the final destiny, meaning the lives and legacies of victimizers and victims, most definitely is one of a kind!

Solutions To Permanently Eradicate Domestic Violence, Child Abuse, and Bullying

There are millions of people like me who were traumatized and victimized as children and subsequently ended up being victimizers. There are millions of people who have been impacted by predators of domestic violence, child abuse, sexual assault, and bullying! We are not glorifying the violence, abuse or bullying, but rather the accountability and awareness of providing hope to victims and their victimizers that real change is in fact possible.

To go from the pits of traumatizing people to a drama-free palace of reality is only possible if you believe in real change as it pertains to mental wellness! How else would you explain my reality and miraculous destination in life?

I want everyone to see a therapist whether they believe they need to see one or not. Why do you think most therapists see a therapist on a consistent basis?

Just like you go to a gym consistently for physical wellness it is that important to go to a psychiatrist, psychologist or counselor on a consistent basis for your mental health!

To All Humankind, Stay Accountable! Stay Aware and Conscious! Stay Uncomfortable! Stay Hungry Like A Wolf! Stay Relentless! Stay Prepared! Stay Focused and Driven! But under no circumstances, after you get healed and delivered from abusing others do you Stay Still and Settle? If you do you are dead! God blesses motion! Get in motion and make an impact on your family, friends, job, community, and the world by displaying love, respect, and peace.

One Final Thought: If Your Spouse, Parents, Boss, Pastor, Doctor, or Local Chief of Police Were To Browse Your Search History On Your Computer, What Would They See, Find, or Learn About You? If You Would Be Ashamed or Embarrassed About What They Would Find, You Should Change What You Are Googling and Get To Cleansing Your Mind! Get Off The Internet!!

Do Not Be A HYPOCRITE! Choose To Be A HERO or SHERO For God's Sake!

YOUR MENTAL HEALTH IS AS EQUALLY OR MORE IMPORTANT THAN YOUR PHYSICAL HEALTH!

YOU ONLY GET ONE LIFETIME TO MAKE AN IMPACT! WHAT ARE YOU DOING WITH THE ONLY ONE YOU GET ON THIS EARTH?

SPEAKING FOR THE INNOCENT* IMPACTED BY VIOLENCE!

Zahra Baker*, Shaniya Davis*, Erica Parsons*, Tahjir Smith*, Cherica Adams*, Sharra Ferger*, Elissa Self*, Caylee Anthony*, Jim Vansickle, Ortralla Mosley*, JonBenet Ramsey*, Alisha and Ava Bromfield*, Yeardley Love*, Dawnia Dacosta*, Tashonda Bethea*, Sharon Nance*, Audrey Spain*, Valencia Jumper*, Michelle Stinson*, Vanessa Little Mack*, Betty Jean Baucom*, Brandi June Henderson*, Caroline Love*, Shawna Hawk*, Beverly Carter*, Valencia Blair,* Ka'Loni Flynn* and her unborn baby,* Molly Tibbetts*, Chrissy Long*, Stephanie Rabsatt, Sharra Ferger*, Jamel Myles*, Wynetta* and Jaylin Wright*, Connie Jones, Shania Gray*, Michelle Thorton*, Kristopher Miller*, A.J. Freund*, Kelly Stansfield,* #MeToo, #TimesUp, Jessica Sacco*, Heather Heyer*, Laci Peterson*, Hannah Elizabeth Graham*, Tyler Clementi*, Stacy Peterson*, Chiquita Tate*, Shania Gray*, Denita Monique Smith*, Kristopher Miller*, Shanann*, Celeste*, and Bella Watts*, Ahkenya Johnson*, Tamika Huston*, Steve McNair*, Gladys Ricart*, Fred Lane*, Stephanie Rabsatt* and her unborn baby boy Jaden*, Ida and Jana Randolph*, Arrijana Hill* and her unborn twin babies*, Ericka Bradley*, Jonathan Harris*, Riley Howell*, Candice Parchment*, Kim Thomas*, Ashley Pegram*, Liza Steen*, Susan Still, Beverly Hope Roscoe Melton*, Crystal Parker*, Corinne Gustavson*, Faith Moody, Cara Knott*, Kim Medlin*, Freda Edwards, Hae Min Lee, Jessica Rovell, Tyshika Askins*, Michelle Thornton*, Jessica Padgett*, Yvette Cade, Kim Medlin*, Alesa Richardson, Ida* and Jana Randolph*, Maleah Davis*, Nancy Schwartzman, Michelle Robinson, Christy Simms, my Mom, Aunt, Cousins, and In-Laws!

I will never forget what happened to you! I will never forget what I did to others! I am working to make sure it does not happen to anyone else! I will not be silenced by violence! I will do everything I can to ensure you, your life was not in vain! You showed me the way! You showed me the light! I can see now!

Solutions To Permanently Eradicate Domestic Violence, Child Abuse, and Bullying

CASES: DOMESTIC VIOLENCE, CHILD ABUSE, and BULLYING
When Domestic Violence, Abuse, And Bullying Are Not Permanently Eradicated,
It Is Not A Matter Of "IF" Tragedy Will Happen, It Is A Matter Of "WHEN!"

America has such an obsession with showcasing violence and abuse against women and children that they have corporations committed to profiting from it and patrons who do not mind supporting them. America has no problem glorifying the crime but has no solutions to support eradicating the human issue that caused the initial problem. This is a perpetuation of the cycle of violence and abuse against women and children because we are telling our youth and individuals who have no coping skills that to become relevant or famous, go out and harm someone. Look at the mass shootings in our schools, churches and other public places and look at the lives of the shooters leading up to the horrendous tragedy. Gun violence is one thing, but the core of the issue was the shooter's mental capacity. If they did not have a gun, they would have found another weapon to kill! The most lethal weapon that is available to all people and not regulated by the government is the mind! I pray that the victim's families are profiting from the loss of their loved ones when their loved one's story is being told to the world, and they are always having to relive and visit the pain and horror emotionally. I have seen enough faces of death in real life that I do not ever need to see any more negative images for as long as I breathe.

We are obsessed with the bad guy's story and not the good guys. Why or how did they become a monster? Do we study this phenomenon for intriguing behavior purposes? Do we study these criminals to be able to profile and identify the next heinous criminal who may fit the pattern? We do not showcase the good guy's story because there is no money or attraction to it! One of my very lowest and baffling days was when the show "America's Most Wanted" was canceled. In 25 seasons the show successfully captured more than 1200 fugitives. How many heinous criminals would have potentially evaded justice had it not been for the viewers who were also seeking justice on behalf of the victims? Were they "snitching" or hungry for justice? I have always been obsessed with watching these crime shows as the next individual who is drawn to hearing and seeing how certain violent offenses unfolded, but what intrigues me most is not how these individuals died but why they were killed by the murderer, how the killer was captured, and the justice that the family received by way of the price that the perpetrator had to pay. These stories have to be told so we can celebrate the lives of the victims and the individuals who brought their abusers and violent offenders to justice. If we want to put a dent in crime, we have to teach our children and abusers how to cope, so they have no desire or reason to kill or harm anyone or anything. I am tired of other people's painmeants™! Pain meant for victims! No names of the victimizers! No glorifying here!

Zahra Clare Baker (November 16, 1999 – September 24, 2010) was born in Wagga Wagga, Australia, and was reported missing on October 9, 2010. Only 10 years old at the time of her death, her dismembered remains were found in November 2010. Because of the crime's gruesome nature and the series of events leading up to her death, Zahra's murder received worldwide media coverage. In September 2011, the victim's stepmother pleaded guilty to murdering Zahra, and was sentenced to eighteen years in prison. [70]

The North Carolina Supreme Court on Friday upheld the death sentence and conviction for the September 2009 murder of 5-year-old Shaniya Davis of Fayetteville. Shaniya's murder was one of Fayetteville's most notorious instances of human trafficking. Her mother told the police she gave Shaniya to him to satisfy a $200 debt. There was evidence that Shaniya was sexually assaulted before she was asphyxiated, and her body was dumped in the woods out in the country. [71]

19-year-old mother and her 26-year-old boyfriend who beat 4-year-old Tahjir Smith* to death and a forensic pathologist ruled the manner of death homicide after finding that the four-year-old died of multiple blunt and thermal injuries and shock, as a result of what a district attorney called "a violent, sustained beating." All for spilling cereal. [72]

Susan Still is an American women's rights activist and keynote speaker on domestic violence. After suffering years of extreme abuse from her husband, Still was awarded custody of her sons, and her husband was jailed for 36 years, the longest sentence ever imposed for non-lethal violence. Her abuse was captured on video being filmed by her children at the direction of her husband. [73]

Jessica Sacco- She and ex-boyfriend got into an argument and he stabbed her in the abdomen. Hours later, he would suffocate her with a plastic bag. She fought him off at first, ripping the first bag and scratching him, but succumbed after he wrapped her face in a second bag. With the help of 4 friends he dismembered and disposed of her body. He was sentenced to life in prison with the possibility of parole in 42 years! [74]

Yvette Cade, of Maryland, was nearly burned to death by her ex-husband. She tells women trapped in violent domestic relationships to get out as quick as they can. She didn't, and it nearly cost Cade her life. Cade was attacked in 2005 by her ex-

husband, who doused her with gasoline and set her on fire in her office in front of customers and co-workers. She suffered third-degree burns over 60 percent of her body and spent three months in a hospital. She's had numerous surgeries and is extensively scarred. "I felt the intense flame hit my back. The flames were 1,500 degrees," Cade told about 320 people at the luncheon in the DoubleTree Hotel. "I saw my flesh dripping to my feet." Her ex-husband was sentenced to life in prison. Three weeks before the attack, a judge ignored Cade's pleas to extend a protective order barring the ex-husband from visiting her. [75]

Freda Edwards, 39, is being treated in the Washington Hospital Center's burn unit for second- and third-degree burns to her face, neck and upper body. According to police investigators, her husband, 40, a self-employed landscaper, took the fuel tank off of a gasoline-powered weed trimmer and doused Edwards with the fuel before setting her ablaze around 3 a.m. Saturday. Police said the two had argued before the attack. Edwards earlier obtained a restraining order against him but visited him late Friday night at his home in Hyattsville. Edwards ran to her family's Hyattsville home after the attack, where a relative placed a 911 emergency call. He later surrendered to police at a friend's home. He was charged with first- and second-degree attempted murder and first- and second-degree assault, Copeland said. He was being held without bond at Prince George's County Detention Center. The attack is the second such case in Prince George's County in less than a year. On Oct. 10, Yvette Cade, 32, was attacked by her estranged husband at the cellular telephone store where she worked. Her ex doused her with gasoline and chased her into the parking lot. When she fell, he ignited the liquid. [76]

McDaniel Smith lll*- Shot multiple times and killed by Damien Pipkins* who interceded as Smith was abusing the mother of his children. He had 6 kids by 4 different women. Smith was a great father and friend, but he was an abuser who paid with his life in exchange for his domestic violence and abuse against his baby's mother. Damien Pipkins was never charged for McDaniel Smith's murder and this was the second time he had killed a man who he thought was violently abusing a woman. [77]

Chrissy Long- An online predator confessed to strangling Christina Long in his car during sex in a Danbury, Connecticut parking lot. He further stated that he dumped her body in a brook in Greenwich, CT, 35 miles away, and threw the girl's purse in a gas station dumpster. The FBI placed him under arrest for "using the Internet to entice a minor into sexual activity," a federal crime, after he admitted to meeting Christina Long online and having sex with her on two different occasions. The following day he led investigators to her body, court documents say.

In the ensuing days and months, he would be charged by the state of Connecticut with one count of first-degree manslaughter and three counts of sexual assault and one count of risk of injury to a minor. His wife would file for divorce. And the Federal Government charged him with two counts of using the Internet to entice a minor and two counts of interstate travel to engage in sexual activity with a minor, plus one count for using the Internet to entice another minor in the summer of 1998. He was sentenced to 25 years without parole. Chrissy Long was the first person ever killed by an online predator. [78]

A former friend who was obsessed with Priyanka Kumari. Both attended Green Hope High School in Cary, NC but Priyanka moved to Holly Springs High School in late 2015 because he was stalking her. The attack happened after she got off a school bus near her Apex home on January 12, She suffered deep cuts to her face, head, and neck from the blows of his machete. [79]

Hae Min Lee (October 15, 1980 – c. January 13, 1999) was a Korean American high school senior at Woodlawn High School in Baltimore County, Maryland, United States, who disappeared on January 13, 1999. Her body was found four weeks later in Leakin Park, the victim of murder by manual strangulation. Her ex-boyfriend was convicted in February 2000 of first-degree murder and given a life sentence plus 30 years. [80]

A Mecklenburg County Sheriff's Deputy shot her husband with her service weapon in January after he threw things at her and threatened her with a knife, according to an autopsy report. James Hawkins, who was 35 and also a Mecklenburg County Sheriff's Deputy, was pronounced dead at the couple's northeast Charlotte home on Jan. 15. His wife is on paid administrative leave until the investigation into her husband's death is finished, the sheriff's office said. No one has been charged in James Hawkins' death. The autopsy found that James Hawkins' cause of death was a gunshot wound to the neck. He was also shot in the hand, and that bullet may have then entered his abdomen, the autopsy said. Autopsy reports include a summary section that discusses the circumstances surrounding a death. In this case, the report said, there was an argument. [81]

(CNN)A 9-year-old boy in Colorado took his life days after starting the fourth-grade last week. He had recently come out as gay to his mother, who believes that bullying was a factor in his death, she told HLN's Mike Galanos on Tuesday. "The same kids who picked on him last year were even meaner to him once he came out and said he was gay," said Leia Pierce, Jamel Myles' mother. "They hurt my baby." Denver Police said that Jamel's death appears to be a suicide. [82]

By 2009, Connie Jones's 21-year marriage was cascading into violent chaos. She and her husband been fighting a lot, court records say, and at one point, he fractured her rib cage. On May 6, 2009, he threatened to kill his wife in front of their 12-year-old *son, screaming expletives and telling the boy his mother didn't care about him. "I will take you out to the ... pool and drown you," he told his wife, according to court records. Connie Jones called police that day. Less than a week later, she filed for divorce. Her husband was arrested and taken to two psychiatric hospitals, where he stayed for several days. He was discharged, even though doctors found that his mental state was deteriorating. He "will continue to unravel...he will become increasingly paranoid, likely psychotic, and pose an even greater risk of perpetrating violence," according to an assessment by Steven Pitt, a prominent forensic psychiatrist who had consulted in several high-profile criminal cases. And unravel him did. He spent the past several years living in hotel rooms, embittered by his divorce and consumed with long-held grudges, police say. In hours-long, rambling videos posted in a YouTube channel called "exposing lowlifes," he railed against his perceived enemies — judges, psychiatrists, lawyers, counselors, and his ex-wife — whom he accused of conspiring to paint him as an abusive and troubled man, to deprive him of his son. He claimed that his former spouse was the abuser, and she had concocted a dubious tale of a battered wife. His anger boiled over last week, in a violent rampage that sent police on a days-long manhunt and rattled Scottsdale, Ariz., a Phoenix suburb known for its golf courses, resorts, and nightlife. Police say ***** swiftly targeted people who had been involved in his divorce proceedings, including the forensic psychiatrist who had examined him. The killing spree would end in *****'s death, police say, after the 56-year-old wanted for killing six people shot himself inside a hotel room. Connie Jones, 52, described her ex-husband as a "very emotionally disturbed person." "As a medical professional and a citizen, I am deeply saddened by the tragedy caused by my ex-husband ... Personally, I have feared for my safety for the past nine years," Jones, who is a doctor, said in a brief statement. "I cannot express the emotions I feel for the innocent families touched by this senseless violence."*

    His rampage began Thursday when police say he shot and killed Pitt. The 59-year-old psychiatrist was killed in broad daylight outside his office on the outskirts of Scottsdale. Less than 24 hours later, he went to the law firm his wife had retained during the divorce. There, police say, he shot Valeria Sharp, 48, and Laura Anderson, 49, two paralegals who worked for the firm in downtown Scottsdale. With a gunshot wound to her head, Sharp made her way out of the office and flagged a bus driver for help before she died. Police followed her blood trail back to the office and found Anderson. The next victim was psychologist Marshall Levine, 72, who was not tied to Jones's divorce case but happened to share an office space with someone who was: another psychologist Jones's son was required to see as part of the divorce proceedings. Levine's girlfriend found his body just after midnight Saturday, police said. By midnight Monday, police *found two more bodies. Mary Simmons, 70, and Bryon Thomas, 72, were shot to death in their home in Fountain Hills, a town outside Phoenix. Investigators believe he went to that home Sunday afternoon and killed the two, though they have not said why. He killed himself inside an Extended Stay hotel room, where he had been living, as tactical team members closed in Monday morning. Police have not said what kind of weapon ***** used in the killings, or how he got it. For days, the attacks placed many in the legal and mental-health communities on edge and raised speculations that Pitt, the most well-known of the victims, may have been killed because of his profession, which required him to study the minds of criminals. Some feared that the attacker was indiscriminately killing people involved in the criminal justice and court system. Police said they received more than a hundred tips about the attacks. One came from Connie Jones and her husband, a retired detective who recognized some of the victims' connections to the divorce case, Connie Jones said in her statement. Little is known about him. He had a GED but no college degree. He and his ex-wife were married in 1988 in Fayetteville, N.C. Their son was born nine years later, in 1997. For much of their marriage, he stayed at home and took care of their son, while Connie Jones worked. Her substantial salary as a radiologist afforded them a house in Scottsdale, two Mercedes-Benz cars and a Toyota. By 2009, he had descended into troubling behavior. In January of that year, his son's school in Scottsdale sought harassment orders against him after he assaulted administrators, the Arizona Republic reported. The boy was transferred to another school.*

In April of that year, he attacked his wife in front of their son because she asked the boy to turn down the TV. He pinned his wife down on the couch, with his knee pressed against her chest. If she disrespected him, he said, "she would be found at the bottom of the pool," according to court records cited by the Republic. The abuse led to a police standoff on May 6, 2009, when Connie Jones secretly called 911. After police arrived, he refused to come out of the house, and the boy was inside with him, court records say. He told his son that his mother was a whore. "She's got these cops out there ready to kill me ... your mom wants me to die ... she wants you to die," he told his son, according to court records. He was charged and later pleaded guilty to disorderly conduct, a misdemeanor, public records show. Pitt, the psychiatrist, testified during the divorce proceedings that he had anxiety and mood disorders, that he was antisocial, narcissistic and paranoid. He lacked remorse and frequently suspected his ex-wife of infidelity, even without justification. He had no friends or confidants but had a "grandiose sense of self-importance" and required "excessive admiration," court records say. He had made egregious claims that Connie Jones sexually abused their son. He also was often armed. According to a psychologist's report, he "always had a weapon because of a disagreement he had with the landscape company." he, though, loved his son "very deeply," court records say. And at one point after his parents separated, the boy was missing his father. The divorce left the child traumatized, staring into space or falling asleep during sessions with counselors. The marriage was dissolved in 2010, and Connie Jones was given sole custody of the son. A judge allowed supervised visits every week, despite his abusive behavior and experts' assessments that he was mentally unstable.

Before the attacks, he is believed to have created several "narrated" YouTube videos, said Sgt. Ben Hoster, spokesman for the Scottsdale Police Department. Some were posted as recently as a week ago. None of the videos showed his face; some just showed a white mask as a man's voice can be heard talking about a corrupt court system he claimed had been rigged against him, according to the Arizona Republic's description of the videos. [83]

Shanann Watts (born January 10, 1984), who was pregnant and her two young daughters, Bella, 4, Celeste, 3, was murdered by her husband in their home in Frederick, Colorado. Shanann's husband and the father of the two children and her unborn child, pled guilty on November 6, 2018, to multiple counts of first-degree murder. He was sentenced to five consecutive life sentences. The body of 34-year-old Shanann Watts was found in a shallow grave Thursday near the oil tank where the bodies of 3-year-old Celeste and 4-year-old Bella were found submerged. This was a love triangle that went horrifically wrong. [84]

Chiquita Harris*, a successful attorney was murdered by her habitual abuser and controlling personality husband. [85]

A 37-year-old Plainfield man will spend the rest of his life in jail for the first-degree intentional murder of Alisha Bromfield * and her unborn baby Ava Lucille*. Man sentenced to 2 life terms for killing pregnant woman. He was found guilty of first-degree intentional homicide in May for the August 2012 slaying of 21-year-old Alisha Bromfield, who had traveled with Cooper to Wisconsin's Door County to attend his sister's wedding, according to county court records. Cooper also was found guilty of third-degree sexual assault for having sex with Bromfield's body after he strangled her to death in their resort bedroom after the wedding. [86]

Hannah Elizabeth Graham (February 25, 1996 – c. September 13, 2014) was an 18-year-old second-year British American student at the University of Virginia who went missing on September 13, 2014. She was last seen early in the morning that day, at the Downtown Mall in Charlottesville, Virginia. Five weeks later, her remains were discovered on an abandoned property in nearby Albemarle County. Her killer pled guilty to murdering Graham and was given a lifetime prison sentence. He was also found guilty and sentenced to three additional lifetimes for other, previous crimes. [87]

Solutions To Permanently Eradicate Domestic Violence, Child Abuse, and Bullying

The murder of Yeardley Love took place in May 2010 in Charlottesville, Virginia. Love, a University of Virginia (UVA) women's lacrosse student-athlete, was found unresponsive in her Charlottesville apartment on May 3. Later that day, a UVA men's lacrosse player, originally of Chevy Chase, Maryland, was arrested by Charlottesville Police. He was tried and found guilty of Love's murder. On August 30, 2012, he was formally sentenced to 23 years in prison by Judge Edward Hogshire, with sentences of 23 years for the second-degree murder conviction and one year for the grand larceny conviction to run concurrently. He is scheduled to be released in late 2035. [88]

A 28-year-old man sentenced to death for the heinous murder and several rapes of Shania Gray, 16. "A cowardly individual with an extensive history of abusing women. He is the epitome of an evil, soulless, manipulative, conniving monster." His attorneys tried to convince the jury by saying "He grew up in a violent, drug-ridden area of St. Louis, "an urban American nightmare." They said he had been molested by his siblings and grandfather and neglected by his mother, who was raped and murdered in 1997. "It would have been better if those children had been raised by wolves," defense attorney Brady Wyatt said during the trial. "Wolves protect their pups." [89]

A 25-year-old man was sentenced to life in prison after a jury found him guilty in the gruesome rape and stabbing death of a 9-year-old Pasco County girl in 1997. Jurors deliberated just over an hour before finding the killer guilty in the slaying of Sharra Ferger, whose body was found in October 1997 in a field near her Blanton home, north of Dade City. She was sexually assaulted, bitten and stabbed 46 times. The killer, who was 17 at that time of the killing, could not be sentenced to death because of a U.S. Supreme Court ruling barring the execution of juveniles. He was a friend of the girl's uncle, Her uncle, 39, who also is charged and could get the death penalty if convicted at trial later this year. Prosecutors said the girl's head had been stabbed nine times, her chest 33 times and her neck four times. Six of the head wounds went through her skull. Five of the chest wounds pierced her lungs and heart. [90]

A Seattle man was found guilty of murdering a Belltown woman and stuffing her body in a closet, was sentenced to 254 months — about 21 years. According to Seattle police detectives, He was found half-naked in the closet of her apartment. Detectives said her apartment showed signs of a struggle. The detectives said that evidence at the scene suggested that she had been sexually assaulted, and the King County Medical Examiner said she was strangled to death. Detectives started putting pieces together after eyewitness testimony pointed the finger to him. Detectives said Thornton and him, knew each other through a number of drugs. Apartment surveillance video shows him going in and out of Thornton's apartment various times throughout the months leading up to the murder. Detectives took DNA samples and fingerprints found at Thornton's apartment and said the tests were a positive match to him. The fingerprints at the crime scene were taken from various surfaces of the apartment and his fingerprints were found in the living room where it appeared the struggle took place. The DNA was matched to him through a national database. He has a felony criminal history in Utah. He was found guilty of second-degree murder Sept. 21. He received the maximum sentence for the charge. "Michele Thornton was murdered in her own apartment by a killer who tried very hard to cover his tracks," King County Prosecutor Dan Satterberg said. "Thanks to diligent police work by Seattle Police detectives and skillful prosecution, we were able to identify her killer and hold him accountable." [91]

A D.C. police officer was convicted Thursday of killing his mistress outside a Hillcrest Heights community center, then driving their daughter to a nearby apartment complex and leaving her in a hot SUV to die. Prosecutors had accused the married, undercover vice officer of fatally shooting 20-year-old Wynetta Wright in May 2011 because he did not want to acknowledge his child or pay her child support. The slaying occurred hours before he was to submit a DNA sample that would ultimately prove he was the father of Wright's 11-month-old daughter, Jaylin Wright. After killing Wynetta Wright, prosecutors said, he drove the woman's SUV to a nearby apartment complex, leaving Jaylin in the vehicle to die in the heat. (By Matt Zapotosky, Washington Post, January 17, 2013), According to Criminally Intrigued, December 29, 2017, on the evening of February 12, 1988, was shot by her husband. The injuries she sustained as a result of the shooting rendered her a paraplegic. He also shot and killed Janice Morris and her boyfriend, Ralph Swain. He received the death penalty! [92]

Tyler Clementi became the victim of a horrible act of cyber-harassment, a type of bullying or cruelty that takes place using the internet. One night, Tyler asked his dorm mate, ****** ****, for some privacy because he had a date. Ravi agreed but what Tyler didn't know was that **** was planning a horrible act of humiliation; he secretly pointed his computer's webcam at Tyler's bed, and then left. The camera captured Tyler in an intimate act, as **** invited other students to view it online. Many students at the university contributed to this invasion of privacy by not reporting or stopping what was happening to Tyler. Tyler discovered what his abuser had done when he viewed his roommate's Twitter feed. He learned he had widely become a topic of ridicule in his new social environment. He also found out that his roommate was planning a second attempt to broadcast from the webcam. Several days later, Tyler Clementi ended his life by jumping off the George Washington Bridge. He was 18. [93]

Kristopher Miller*- A community service police officer murdered by his girlfriend Kim Griffin's stalker, at the time, soon to be ex-husband and Pastor. He was sentenced to life in prison. [94]

Steve McNair*- On July 4, 2009, McNair was found dead from multiple gunshot wounds, murdered by 20-year-old mistress. McNair had been shot twice in the body and twice in the head. He was believed to have been asleep on the couch when he was murdered. She had a worsening financial situation and also suspected that he was in another extramarital relationship. [95]

Fred Lane*, my neighbor- Former NFL player murdered by his wife. On July 6, 2000, Fred's wife, shot and killed Lane. His keys were still in the lock and he had been shot twice with a 12-gauge shotgun - once in the chest and a second time in the back of the head, apparently at point-blank range. ******** pleaded guilty to voluntary manslaughter in 2003. Prosecutors at her sentencing described ****** as an abusive woman who killed her husband for insurance money. Defense attorneys called her a battered wife who killed in self-defense. A judge sentenced her to seven years and 11 months, ruling her actions were premeditated and deliberate, that she acted with malice and shot him a second time after he'd already been rendered helpless. She received credit for jail time served waiting on a federal charge of conspiracy to commit bank larceny. She pleaded guilty and served four months for that charge. She was released on March 3, 2009. [96]

Stephanie Rabsatt* and her unborn baby boy Jaden*- A 17-year-old, 30 weeks pregnant, murdered by being shot in the head and abdomen by her boyfriend and baby's daddy, 17-year-old ****** "********" ****. He didn't want to be a father. He was sentenced to 50 years in prison. [97]

Ida and Jana Randolph*- Murdered by Jana's ex-boyfriend, for revenge over being thrown out of their apartment and for their credit and debit cards for money. He had two coconspirators. One was sentenced to 50 years to life. The other sentenced 17 years to life. One coconspirator received just 14 years as a plea for her testimony against the boyfriend and other coconspirator. [98]

Arrijana Hill* and her unborn twin babies*- A 16-year-old, pregnant with twin boys was murdered by being stabbed to death by her boyfriend and babies' daddy, 16-year-old **** ********. He wanted her to get an abortion so as to not mess up his future. He didn't want to be a father. He was convicted of capital murder and sentenced to life in prison. [99]

Ericka Bradley*- A 17-year-old, murdered by her high school sweetheart and father of her 5-month-old baby, 18-year-old **********. He ran her over with his car after an abusive argument over his infidelity. It is alleged that he had been physically and emotionally abusing Ericka throughout their relationship. He received a sentence of natural life with no chance of parole. [100]

Jonathan Harris*- A two-time survivor of kidney failure murdered and robbed by his drug-addicted and uncontrollable and revengeful girlfriend and her co-conspirators after he threw her out of his apartment. But before the proceedings could begin for her murder trial she died of brain cancer. One co-conspirator received 5 years in exchange for her testimony against the other two while the other co-conspirator received 40 years to life. [101]

Candice Parchment*- A 15-year-old murdered by 19-year-old ***** who had previously attempted to rape her with 16-year-old *****. It is alleged he killed her to cover up the attempted rape. He received life without parole plus 50 years. She documented the attempted rape in her diary which when discovered by her mom after her death, led detectives straight to ********and******. ****** was sentenced to 20 years with 15 suspended and because he was a minor he has the opportunity to have this removed from his records due to the first offender probation program. Had it not been the stigma of sexual assault, if she had come forth with the attempted rape it may have saved her life. [102]

Crystal Parker*- East Point Georgia Police Officer murdered by former female lover after the two had split up she learned Crystal had moved on. The woman accused of killing an East Point police officer pleaded guilty Wednesday and was sentenced to life in prison, plus five years. [103]

Cara Knott* was murdered by a former California Highway Interstate Patrolman after he pulled her over, he strangled her and dumped her body in a remote area. He didn't want a DNA test. Sentenced him to 25 years to life. [104]

Kim Medlin*- Murdered by a former Monroe, NC police officer after he pulled her over. He's serving a life sentence. [105]

Jessica Padgett*- She was murdered by her stepfather for the specific purpose of having sex with her corpse. He was actually caught on tape sexually abusing her corpse. He was sentenced to life in prison without parole. [106]

Ex-Boyfriend Kills Bride-to-Be on Wedding Day in Front of Family

Gladys Ricart*, 39, a bride to be, was shot dead in front of her family yesterday by a former boyfriend who walked uninvited into her New Jersey home as the family was about to leave for the wedding, the authorities said.

The former boyfriend, dressed as if for a wedding, walked in about 4 P.M. as the woman was posing for a final round of photographs, pulled a gun out of a briefcase and shot her repeatedly, prosecutors said. He was immediately restrained by the bride's *brother, who held him until the police arrived, the authorities said.* [107] *He was sentenced to life!*

Liza Steen, Victim In Murder-Suicide, Feared '******', The woman gunned down Thursday had taken out multiple stalking orders against ***** "******" ******. By John Ferak, Patch Staff | Nov 9, 2018 5:44 pm ET | Updated Nov 10, 2018 1:44 am ET [108]

JOLIET, IL - The 37-year-old woman who was slain in a murder-suicide in Bolingbrook had visited the Will County Courthouse on multiple occasions since July in hopes of getting a stalking no-contact order against ***** ****** "******" ******, court records reflect. On Thursday morning, ******, 44, fatally shot his ex-girlfriend, Millizza "Liza" Steen, at her house in the 200 block of Douglass Way, police said.

He was later found dead in the yard from a self-inflicted gunshot wound, Bolingbrook Police said. He and Steen had a rocky and turbulent relationship over the past several years, and Steen decided that she wanted him out of her life over the summer.

He, however, was not willing to move on, court records show.

"***** and I have been together for 13 years and there's a history of abuse. He has pushed me before and tried to hold me down. I am afraid because he has a history of domestic battery and he told me he stalked his ex-girlfriend and that he paid someone to come to her job to jump on her," Steen wrote Will County's judicial system in July, when she obtained her first order of protection against the man who would kill her four months later, according to police.

In fact, his friends warned Steen that he can't tolerate rejection from a woman who wants to break off a romantic relationship with him, court documents from July show.

"His friends told me that he becomes very crazy when a female is trying to leave him. He showed up at my mother's home last night (July 7) and she allowed him to make a phone call. My mom doesn't feel safe because of his violent temper and I don't want him near my mother's home," Steen wrote the court in July.

Court documents on file at the Will County Courthouse show that Steen filed for a second stalking no-contact order against him in October. The one she got in July was later dismissed, court documents show.

One of the court records reviewed by the Joliet Patch on Friday shows that a Plenary Stalking No Contact Order was issued on Oct. 30 at 9:43 a.m. and would remain "in effect until Oct. 30, 2020, at 5 p.m. The court paper indicates that Steen, the petitioner, was given a copy of the Order in open court last week, on Oct. 30.

Since July, Associate Will County Judge Fred Harvey has handled the domestic complaints filed by Steen against the man who would ultimately kill her, court documents indicate.

On Oct. 8, court records show, he showed up at his ex-girlfriend's place of employment in Willowbrook "after repeatedly being told not to. He entered my workplace and came to my desk and waited for me," Steen wrote Will County's judicial system in October.

"I was hiding in the bathroom and texting him to please leave or I would call the police. My coworker also asked him to leave, but he wouldn't."

October's protection order petition also states that Steen's ex-boyfriend on Oct. 7 "sent a text to my phone stating, 'Liza you may as well as move out of town if you think you're leaving me because if I ever see you with somebody and I know it is likely, I'm acting a fool and they gonna respect it (sic).'"

That same day, Oct. 7, he showed up at her house in Bolingbrook "uninvited and unannounced. He can be seen on the front doorbell camera ringing and knocking on the door. Can also be seen on the backyard camera jumping the fence to peek through the blinds/curtains to see if I were home," court documents show.

Steen's October protection order petition indicated "he could see me inside sitting on the couch. He also tried to yank the back door open but was unsuccessful."

The previous day, Oct. 6, he had called Steen "over 20 times and left over 10 voicemails because I refused to pick up his calls. His general message was, 'Where are you? I am going to be without you. Why are you doing this? You know we should be together; you know I love you. He went from being angry to being nice throughout these texts and calls. "Steen and he had been boyfriend-girlfriend and had shared a common dwelling together, until July, when she wanted him out of her life, court records show.

"He and I were having an argument in the car and he struck me in my face. He pulled over and parked and continued to hit me in the face. He pulled me out of the car, and I was trying to fight back, but he kept pounding on my face and all over my body," Steen wrote the court in July.

The Bolingbrook woman stated, "someone pulled him off of me and I ran to get my purse from the car, and he chased me and tugged on my purse and the strap on my purse broke and he fell back, so I ran and called the police."

The Will County Courthouse documents indicate that "The police came immediately and arrested him," Steen wrote in her July protection order.

Court records filed in Will County, however, aren't clear what community and what law enforcement jurisdiction handled the July 7 domestic violence episode occurred.

Solutions To Permanently Eradicate Domestic Violence, Child Abuse, and Bullying

Thursday's domestic violence murder victim was survived by a 17-year-old daughter, court records show. He and Steen did not have any children together, court records indicate.

Court records listed his address as Berwyn. Bolingbrook Police said he lived on Twin Falls Drive in Plainfield. The Will County Coroner's Office, on Friday night, classified him as being a Bolingbrook resident. [108]

I learned of this incredible story from Liza Steen's endearing friend Asafonie Obed-Horton as I was about to board a plane to Chicago. Asafonie was so wonderful and brave like her friend Liza, to share such a gut-wrenching story of loss to me that I promised her I would share Liza's story so it could help any person who is a victim or violent offender of domestic violence to prevent another murder-suicide stemming from intimate partner violence. Liza did everything to protect her life by getting the system involved and letting her family and friends know what was violently happening to her. I let her down and so did the judicial system who failed to protect her as a civic duty and responsibility! I wish I could have reached him before all this tragedy unfolded to change the lives and legacies of all people who knew Liza Steen! I know we could have reached her ex to prevent this outcome!

One of the most defining times in my life is when my youngest daughter was sick, and we ended up in a prestigious university research hospital. There was a little boy in the intensive care unit with us! He was in a coma and we could see them as they could see us because the rooms all had glass walls! The entire ICU was quarantined due to a breakout of MRSA, and so no one could leave the ICU, and no one could visit the ICU unless you were hospital personnel!

Everyone, including parents, had on what seemed like hazmat yellow suits covering our mouths and noses! One of the little boy's family members walked up to me and asked me to pray for her! When I asked what I was to pray for she simply replied, "Peace!"

I later found out that her grandson was actually on life support and that they were keeping him alive until his dad and other family members could see him for the last time. It turns out he was beaten to death by the teenage babysitter who was having an illicit affair with the baby's adult mother. The teenage boy assumed the baby was his because the baby's actual father was serving time across seas in the military.

When the father was set to come home, the teenage boy wanted the mother to tell her husband that she was divorcing him(the husband) to be in a permanent relationship with the teenage boy since he was the father of the baby. The mother of the baby told the teenager that she had lied to him about him being the baby's father, and when he realized the mother, who had been essentially molesting him, had lied to him and that he was the baby's actual father, he snapped and beat the baby to death when he was alone with the child.

This is why the boy's paternal grandmother wanted me to pray for peace because everyone on both sides of the family wanted to kill her daughter-in-law for being the root cause for the baby's death and the eternal pain her son and family will always have to live with for the rest of their lives. How or why does this tragedy happen to our babies because of irresponsible parents? That baby paid for a crime he did not commit!

Then, there was an inconsolable little girl probably no more than 3 years old trolling the hallway just crying and crying as if she didn't have a friend in the entire world! The nurses pulled me to the side to tell me that "she had been removed by social services and that she did not have any family there for her until the courts assigned a family member or foster home."

I could go on and on with case after case of violence. Victimizers of violence are violators of trust and breakers of love contracts despite being parents, spouses, friends, gamers, classmates, sworn law enforcement, pastors, priests, bishops, teachers, doctors or coaches who solemnly swear to God and make vows to God and repeat oaths to God on bibles with their left hands in the air and before God. So Help Me God!

What is about to happen is zero tolerance from victims. The fight has begun! ENOUGH! The Howlers™ and Grounders™ are here for the insecure. No more silence to the violence, abuse, and bullying! No more running, hiding, crying, or living in fear. Hear the howl offenders! Time's up for the insecure because no one sets out to say, "Yes! Me too mom! I am a victim!" If you are struggling with bullying, violence, and abuse, be honest and get Help Now! I am serious my friend! It will save lives & legacies of innocent people & U!

Solutions To Permanently Eradicate Domestic Violence, Child Abuse, and Bullying

<u>To ALL Abusers</u>: THE ABUSER'S ACCOUNTABILITY and TRANSPARENCY MOVEMENT HAS BEGUN! YOUR TIMES UP! NO MORE SECRETS! NO MORE SILENCE! NO MORE HIDING! NO MORE VIOLENCE! NO MORE RUNNING! NO MORE CRYING! NO MORE CURSING! NO MORE LYING! NO MORE TORTURE & HATE IN OUR BLOODLINES! NO MORE GENERATIONAL CURSES! NO MORE BIBLE VERSES! NO MORE ME TOO! BUT MORE OF, "THE COPS ARE HERE FOR YOU!" Join A.W. <u>Now</u>

Solutions To Permanently Eradicate Domestic Violence, Child Abuse, and Bullying

STATISTICS

Know Your Numbers! It Is What You Do Not Know That Can Hurt You!
Numbers Tell A Story! If You Can't Measure "It" You Can't Manage "It"!

WHAT IS DOMESTIC VIOLENCE?

According to the National Coalition Against Domestic Violence, *"Domestic violence is the willful intimidation, physical assault, battery, sexual assault and/or other abusive behavior as part of a systematic pattern of power and control perpetrated by one intimate partner against another. It includes physical violence, sexual violence, threats, and emotional/psychological abuse. The frequency and severity of domestic violence varies dramatically."*

NATIONAL STATISTICS FOR YOU TO KNOW?

- **3 women are murdered every day** by a current or former male partner in the U.S.[109]
- In the United States, an average of 20 people experience intimate partner physical violence every minute. This equates to more than 10 million abuse victims annually.[110]
- 1 in 4 women and 1 in 7 men have been victims of severe physical violence (e.g. beating, burning, strangling) by an intimate partner in their lifetime 1 in 4 women and 1 in 9 men experience severe intimate partner physical violence, intimate partner contact sexual violence, and/or intimate partner stalking with impacts such as injury, fearfulness, posttraumatic stress disorder, use of victim services, contraction of sexually transmitted diseases, etc. [111]

  This is commonly considered "domestic violence".
- 1 in 3 women and 1 in 4 men have experienced some form of physical violence by an intimate partner. This includes a range of behaviors and in some cases might not be considered "domestic violence". [112]
- 1 in 7 women and 1 in 25 men have been injured by an intimate partner. [113]
- 1 in 10 women have been raped by an intimate partner. No data on male victims.[114]
- 1 in 7 women and 1 in 18 men have been stalked. Stalking causes the target to fear she/he/they or someone close to her/him/them will be harmed or killed. [115]
- On a typical day, domestic violence hotlines nationwide receive over 20,000 calls.[116]
- An abuser's access to a firearm increases the risk of intimate partner femicide by 400%.[117]
- Intimate partner violence accounts for 15% of all violent crime.[118]
- Intimate partner violence is most common against women between the ages of 18-24.[119]
- 19% of intimate partner violence involves a weapon.[120]

WHY IT MATTERS

The National Coalition Against Domestic Violence *also says "Domestic violence is prevalent in every community, and affects all people regardless of age, socio-economic status, sexual orientation, gender, race, religion, or nationality. Physical violence is often accompanied by emotionally abusive and controlling behavior as part of a much larger, systematic pattern of dominance and control. Domestic violence can result in physical injury, psychological trauma, and even death. The devastating consequences of domestic violence can cross generations and last a lifetime."*

RAPE-SEXUAL ASSAULT

- 1 in 5 women and 1 in 59 men in the United States is raped during his/her lifetime. [121]

- 9.4% of women in the United States experience intimate partner sexual assault in their lifetimes. Almost half of female (46.7%) and male (44.9%) victims of rape in the United States were raped by an acquaintance. Of these, 45.4% of female rape victims and 29% of male rape victims were raped by an intimate partner. [122]

STALKING

- 19.3 million women and 5.1 million men in the United States have been stalked in their lifetime. [123]

- 66.2% of female stalking victims and 43.5% men reported stalking by a current or former intimate partner.[124]

HOMICIDE

- 1 in 3 female murder victims and 1 in 20 male murder victims are killed by intimate partners.[125]

- A study of intimate partner homicides found 20% of victims were family members or friends of the abused partner, neighbors, persons who intervened, law enforcement responders, or bystanders.[126]

- 72% of all murder-suicides are perpetrated by intimate partners.[127]

- 94% of murder-suicide victims are female. A study of intimate partner homicides found that 20% of victims were not the intimate partners themselves, but family members, friends, neighbors, persons who intervened, law enforcement responders, or bystanders.[128]

PHYSICAL/MENTAL EFFECTS

- Victims of intimate partner violence are at increased risk of contracting HIV or other STI's due to forced intercourse and/or prolonged exposure to stress.[129]

- Studies suggest that there is a relationship between Intimate partner victimization is correlated with a higher rate of depression and suicidal behavior. [130]

- Only 34% of people who are injured by intimate partners receive medical care for their injuries. Physical, mental, and sexual and reproductive health effects have been linked with intimate partner violence including adolescent pregnancy, unintended pregnancy in general, miscarriage, stillbirth, intrauterine hemorrhage, nutritional deficiency, abdominal pain and other gastrointestinal problems, neurological disorders, chronic pain, disability, anxiety and post-traumatic stress disorder (PTSD), as well as noncommunicable diseases such as hypertension, cancer and cardiovascular diseases. Victims of domestic violence are also at higher risk for developing addictions to alcohol, tobacco, or drugs.[131]

ECONOMIC EFFECTS

- Victims of intimate partner violence lose a total of 8,000,000 million days of paid work each year, the equivalent of 32,000 full-time jobs.[132]

- Intimate partner violence is estimated to cost the US economy between $5.8 billion and $12.6 billion annually, up to 0.125% of the national gross domestic product.[133]

- Between 21-60% of victims of intimate partner violence lose their jobs due to reasons stemming from the abuse.[134]

- Between 2003 and 2008, 142 women were murdered in their workplace by former or current intimate partners. This amounts to 22% of workplace homicides among women.[135]

CHILDREN AND DOMESTIC VIOLENCE

- 1 in 15 children are exposed to intimate partner violence each year, and 90% of these children are eyewitnesses to this violence.[136]

- The Department of Justice estimates that 10 million children in America see their mothers get physically abused every year.[137]

- Studies have also shown that almost **70 percent** of children under age **16** who are arrested for a crime were either abused themselves or witnessed abuse[138], says Lisa Bloch Rodwin, the prosecutor who helped put Ulner Still behind bars.

- According to the Bureau of Justice statistics, African American women are **35%** more likely to be the victims of domestic violence than white women.[139]

- It's estimated that more than **20 women** are killed by a romantic partner in the U.S. each week. Of those, half of them are African American.[140]

- According to the CDC, over **3,500** women and girls were murdered in the United States in 2015.[141] More than **500** were pregnant at the time of their murder.[142]

- Also, **24%** of violent offenders reported being under the influence of drugs at the time they committed their crime. In cases where victims and perpetrators are in a relationship, more than half of the offenders admitted to drinking or using drugs at the time the crime was committed.[143]

Solutions To Permanently Eradicate Domestic Violence, Child Abuse, and Bullying

- **1 in 3** women who are murdered in the U.S. each day are murdered by their husbands, boyfriends, or former ex-husbands or boyfriends.[144] When spouses or partners cheat on one another in a relationship in domestic type murders infidelity is often part of the motive of someone's death.

- In 15 states, **more than 40%** of all homicides of women in each state involved intimate partner violence.[145]

- 85% of domestic violence victims are female, and 15% are male.[146]

- Approximately **63%** of homeless women have experienced domestic violence in their adult lives.[147]

- Nearly half of all women and men in the US will experience psychological aggression by an intimate partner in their lifetime.[148]

- Approximately **5 million children** are exposed to domestic violence every year. Children exposed are more likely to attempt suicide, abuse drugs and alcohol, run away from home, engage in teenage prostitution, and commit sexual assault crimes.[149]

- **40 million** adult Americans grew up living with domestic violence. [150]

- Children from homes with violence are much more likely to experience significant psychological problems short- and long-term. [151]

- Children who've experienced domestic violence often meet the diagnostic criteria for Post-Traumatic Stress Disorder(PTSD) and the effects on their brain are similar to those experienced by combat veterans. [152]

- Domestic violence in childhood is directly correlated with difficulties learning, lower IQ scores, deficiencies in visual-motor skills and problems with attention and memory.[153]

- Living with domestic violence significantly alters a child's DNA, aging them prematurely **7-10** years.[154]

- Children in homes with violence are physically abused or seriously neglected at a rate of **1500%** higher than the national average.[155]

- Those who grow up with domestic violence are **6 times** more likely to commit suicide and **50%** more likely to abuse drugs and alcohol.[156]

- If you grow up with domestic violence, you're **74%** more likely to commit a violent crime against someone else.[157]

- Children of domestic violence are **3 times** more likely to repeat the cycle in adulthood, as growing up with domestic violence is the most significant predictor of whether or not someone will be engaged in domestic violence later in life.[158]

- **40%** of domestic violence cases have children under **18** in the home.[159]

- **50%** of batterers who abuse their intimate partners also abuse their children.[160]

Solutions To Permanently Eradicate Domestic Violence, Child Abuse, and Bullying

- **81%** of women and **35%** of men who experienced rape, stalking, or physical violence by an intimate partner reported significant short- or long-term impact such as post-traumatic stress disorder symptoms and injury.[161]
- **4%** of high school students report being hit, slapped, or physically hurt on purpose by their boyfriend or girlfriend in the last **12 months**.[162]
- Only **1 out of 3** people who are injured during a domestic violence incident will ever receive medical care for their injuries.[163]
- **Most cases of domestic violence are never reported to police.**[164]
- Men who are victimized are substantially less likely than women to report their situation to police.[165]

In December of 2017, the Huffington Posts wrote an article titled, ***30 Shocking Domestic Violence Statistics That Remind Us It's An Epidemic.*** *The number of American troops killed in Afghanistan and Iraq between 2001 and 2012 was* ***6,488.*** *The number of American women who were murdered by current or ex male partners during that time was* ***11,766.*** *That's nearly double the amount of casualties lost during war.*[166]

Women are much more likely to be victims of intimate partner violence with 85 percent of domestic abuse victims being women and 15 percent men. Too many women have been held captive by domestic violence — whether through physical abuse, financial abuse, emotional abuse or a combination of all three.[167] *We are inundated with news stories about domestic violence, from athletes beating their significant others in public elevators or in their own homes to celebrities publicly abusing their girlfriends. This problem is not one that will go away quickly or quietly.*[168] *Domestic violence is not a singular incident, it's an insidious problem deeply rooted in our culture — and these numbers prove that.*[169]

3-   ***The number of women murdered every day by a current or former male partner in the U.S.***[170]

38,028,000- *The number of women who have experienced physical intimate partner violence in their lifetimes.*[171]

40%- *Women with disabilities are 40% more likely to experience intimate partner violence- especially severe violence-than women without disabilities according to the American Psychological Association.*[172]

4,774,000- *The number of women in the U.S. who experience physical violence by an intimate partner every year.*[173]

1,509- *The number of women murdered by men they knew in 2011. Of the 1,509 women,* ***926*** *were killed by an intimate partner and* ***264*** *of those were killed by an intimate partner during an argument. CDC and Prevention.*[174]

18,000- *The number of women who have been killed by men in domestic violence disputes since 2003.*[175]

Solutions To Permanently Eradicate Domestic Violence, Child Abuse, and Bullying

3 to 4-   *According to the World Health Organization, Worldwide, men who were exposed to domestic violence as children are 3 to 4 times more likely to perpetrate intimate partner violence as adults than men who did not experience domestic abuse as children.[176]*

9 seconds-   *A woman is beaten every 9 seconds in the U.S. according to Domestic Violence Statistics.[177]*

18,500,000-   *The number of mental health care visits due to intimate partner violence.[178]*

$948-   *The average cost of emergency care for intimate partner violence-related incidents for women. The average cost for men is $387.[179]*

IPV-   *Intimate Partner Violence is the leading cause of female homicide (femicide) and injury-related deaths during pregnancy according to the American Psychological Association. [180]*

2 in 5-   *The number of gay or bisexual men who will experience intimate partner violence in their lifetimes. [181]*

50%-   *The % of lesbian women who will experience domestic violence (not necessarily intimate partner violence) in their lifetimes. [182]*

81-   *The percentage of women who are stalked by a current or former male partner who are also physically abused by that partner. [183]*

98%-   *The % of financial abuse that occurs in all domestic violence cases. The number one reason domestic violence survivors stay or return to the abusive relationship is that the abuser controls their money supply, leaving them with no financial resources to break free. [184]*

21-   *The # of LGBT people murdered by their intimate partners in 2013. 50% of them were people of color. The highest documented level of domestic violence homicide in the LGBT community in history. [185]*

2.6x-   *The # of times more likely a transgender person of color will become a victim of intimate partner violence than a non-LGBT person. [186]*

3rd-   *Domestic violence is the 3rd leading cause of homelessness according to the National Coalition for the Homelessness. [187]*

70x-   *The # of times more likely a woman is to be murdered in the few weeks after leaving her abusive partner than at any other time in the relationship. [188]*

25%-   *The percentage of physical assaults perpetrated against women that are reported to the police annually. [189]*

Solutions To Permanently Eradicate Domestic Violence, Child Abuse, and Bullying

CHILD ABUSE

❖ Approximately, **5 children die every day because of child abuse**. [190] In the U.S. between four and seven children on average die daily to child abuse and neglect.[190,191]

❖ **A report of child abuse is made every ten seconds.** [190] Yearly, referrals to state child protective services involve **6.6 million children,** and around 3.2 million of those children are subject to an investigated report.[191] These agencies found in 2014, an estimated **702,000 victims** of child maltreatment. [191]

❖ In 2014, state agencies identified an estimated **1,580 children who died** as a result of abuse and neglect — between **four and five children a day.** [192] However, studies also indicate significant undercounting of child maltreatment fatalities by state agencies — by **50% or more**. [192]

❖ More than **70%** of the children who died as a result of child abuse or neglect were two years of age or younger. More than 80% were not yet old enough for kindergarten. [193]

❖ Around **80%** of child maltreatment fatalities involve at least one parent as perpetrator.[193]

❖ **1 in 3 girls and 1 out of 5 boys will be sexually abused before they reach age 18.** [194]

❖ **90%** of child sexual abuse victims know the perpetrator in some way. **68%** are abused by a family member. [195]

❖ In 2012, **82.2%** of child abuse perpetrators were found to be between the ages of **18-44**, of which **39.6%** were recorded to be between the ages of **25-34**. [196]

❖ Boys (48.5%) Girls (51.2%) become victims at nearly the same rate. [197]

❖ 2.9 million cases of child abuse are reported every year in the U.S. [198]

❖ Children who experience child abuse and neglect are 59% more likely to be arrested as a juvenile, 28% more likely to be arrested as an adult, and 30% more likely to commit violent crime. [199]

❖ About 80% of 21-year-olds who were abused as children met criteria for at least one psychological disorder. [200]

❖ A study of 513 children exposed to drugs in-utero, **rates of abuse were 2 to 3 times that of other children in the same geographical area**. [201]

❖ As many as two-thirds of the people in treatment for drug abuse reported being abused or neglected as children.[202]

❖ 14% of all men and **36%** of women in prison in the USA were abused as children, about twice the frequency seen in the general population.[203]

❖ For new cases in 2008 alone, lifetime estimates of lost worker productivity, health care costs, special education costs, child welfare expenditures, and criminal justice expenditures added up to $124 billion.[204]

❖ Children who experience child abuse and neglect are about 9 times more likely to become involved in criminal activity.[205]

❖ The U.S. Centers for Disease Control and Prevention links adverse childhood experiences(which include other household dysfunctions along with abuse and neglect)with a range of long-term health impacts.[206]

❖ Individuals who reported six or more adverse childhood experiences had an average life expectancy two decades shorter than those who reported none.[206]

❖ Ischemic heart disease (IHD), Chronic obstructive pulmonary disease (COPD), liver disease and other health-related quality of life issues are tied to child abuse. [206]

❖ Abused children are less likely to practice safe sex, putting them at greater risk for STDs. They're also **25%** more likely to experience teen pregnancy. [207]

BULLYING

In 2014, the Centers for Disease Control and the Department of Education released the first federal uniform definition of bullying for research and surveillance.1 The core elements of the definition include: unwanted aggressive behavior; observed or perceived power imbalance; and repetition of behaviors or high likelihood of repetition. There are many different modes and types of bullying.

The current definition acknowledges two modes and four types by which youth can be bullied or can bully others. The two modes of bullying include direct (e.g., bullying that occurs in the presence of a targeted youth) and indirect (e.g., bullying not directly communicated to a targeted youth such as spreading rumors).

In addition to these two modes, the four types of bullying include broad categories of physical, verbal, relational (e.g., efforts to harm the reputation or relationships of the targeted youth), and damage to property.

Bullying can happen in any number of places, contexts, or locations. Sometimes that place is online or through a cellphone. Bullying that occurs using technology (including but not limited to phones, email, chat rooms, instant messaging, and online posts) is considered electronic bullying and is viewed as a context or location.

Electronic bullying or cyberbullying involves primarily verbal aggression (e.g., threatening or harassing electronic communications) and relational aggression (e.g., spreading rumors electronically). Electronic bullying or cyberbullying can also involve property damage resulting from electronic attacks that lead to the modification, dissemination, damage, or destruction of a youth's privately stored electronic information.

Some bullying actions can fall into criminal categories, such as harassment, hazing, or assault. Journalists and other content creators can use this definition to determine whether an incident they are covering is actually bullying. Media pieces often mistakenly use the word "bullying" to describe events such as one-time physical fights, online arguments, or incidents between adults.

According to the American Society for the Positive Care of Children, bullying is unwanted, aggressive behavior that involves a real or perceived power imbalance. The behavior is repeated or has the potential to be repeated over time. Both kids who are bullied and who bully others may have serious, lasting problems.

In order to be considered bullying, the behavior must be aggressive and include:

- An imbalance of power: Kids who bully use their power, physical strength, access to embarrassing information, or popularity, to control or harm others. Power imbalances can change over time and in different situations, even if they involve the same people.

- Repetition: Bullying behaviors happen more than once or have the potential to happen more than once.

Bullying includes actions such as making threats, spreading rumors, attacking someone physically or verbally, and excluding someone from a group on purpose. Bullying has become an epidemic that affects not only children but parents, teachers and the community.

According to the National Education Association, PACER Center, Stopbullying.gov, and The American Society for the Positive Care of Children:

60,000 kids per day skips school for fear of being bullied.[208]

When bystanders intervene, bullying stops within **10 seconds 57%** of the time.[209]

The American Society for the Positive Care of Children also states:

The 3 B's of Bullying

1. **Bullier – 30%** of youth admit to bullying
2. **Bullied – 1 in 3** students bullied at school
3. **Bystander – 70%** have witnessed bullying

BEEN BULLIED

28% of U.S. students in grades 6–12 experienced bullying.[210]

20% of U.S. students in grades 9–12 experienced bullying.[211]

BULLIED OTHERS

Approximately 30% of young people admit to bullying others in surveys.[212]

WITNESSED BULLYING

70.6% of young people say they have seen bullying in their schools.[213]

70.4% of school staff have seen bullying. 62% witnessed bullying two or more times in the last month and 41% witness bullying once a week or more.[214]

When bystanders intervene, bullying stops within 10 seconds 57% of the time.[209]

Solutions To Permanently Eradicate Domestic Violence, Child Abuse, and Bullying

BEEN CYBERBULLIED

6% of students in grades 6–12 experienced cyberbullying.[215]

16% of high school students (grades 9–12) were electronically bullied in the past year.[216]

However, 55.2% of LGBT students experienced cyberbullying.[217]

RISK FACTORS FOR BULLYING

No single factor puts a child at risk of being bullied or bullying others. Bullying can happen anywhere—cities, suburbs, or rural towns. Depending on the environment, some groups, such as lesbian, gay, bisexual, or transgendered (LGBT) youth,[218] youth with disabilities,[219] and socially isolated youth, may be at an increased risk of being bullied.

Generally, children who are bullied have one or more of the following risk factors: [220]

- *Are perceived as different from their peers, such as being overweight or underweight, wearing glasses or different clothing, being new to a school, or being unable to afford what kids consider "cool"*

- *Are perceived as weak or unable to defend themselves*

- *Are depressed, anxious, or have low self-esteem*

- *Are less popular than others and have few friends*

- *Do not get along well with others, seen as annoying or provoking, or antagonize others for attention*

StopBullying.gov statistics: [221]

➢ *1 in 7 students in grades K – 12 are either a bully or have been a victim of bullying.*

➢ *An estimated 160,000 U.S. children miss school every day due to fear of attack or intimidation by other students.*

➢ *83% of girls and 79% of boys report experiencing harassment.*

➢ *Six out of 10 teenagers say they witness bullying in school once a day.*

➢ *35% of kids have been threatened online.*

➢ *Nearly 9 out of 10 LGBTQ youth report being verbally harassed at school in the past year because of their sexual orientation.*

➢ *57% of boys and 43% of girls reported being bullied because of religious or cultural differences.*

➢ *Bullies often go on to perpetrate violence later in life: 40% of boys identified as bullies in grades 6 through 9 had three or more arrests by age 30.*

➢ *One out of every 10 students who drop out of school does so because of repeated incidents of bullying.*

➢ *75% of shooting incidents at schools have been linked to bullying and harassment.*

➢ *64% of children who were bullied did not report it.*

Solutions To Permanently Eradicate Domestic Violence, Child Abuse, and Bullying

➤ Nearly **70%** of students think schools respond poorly to bullying.

➤ When bystanders intervene, bullying stops within **10 seconds 57%** of the time.

Bullying has serious, adverse educational effects, and students who are targets often experience extreme stress that can lead to symptoms of physical illness and a diminished ability to learn, according to the National Education Association. This translates into increased absenteeism and impaired performance, as indicated by decreased test scores. [222]

NATIONAL STATISTICS

According to the stopbullyingnowfoundation.gov, the overall outlook of the long-term effects of bullying upon society is grim: [223]

➤ 60% of middle school students say that they have been bullied, while 16% of staff believes that students are bullied.

➤ 160,000 students stay home from school every day due to bullying. (National Education Association)

➤ 30% of students who reported they had been bullied said they had at times brought weapons to school.

➤ A bully is 6 times more likely to be incarcerated by the age of 24.

➤ A bully is 5 times more likely to have a serious criminal record when he grows up.

➤ 2/3 of students who are targets become bullies.

➤ 20% of all children say they have been bullied.

➤ 20% of high school students say they have seriously considered suicide within the last 12 months.

➤ 25% of students say that teachers intervened in bullying incidents while 71% of teachers say they intervened.

➤ The average child has watched 8,000 televised murders and 100,000 acts of violence before finishing elementary school.

➤ In schools where there are anti-bullying programs, bullying is reduced by 50%.

➤ Bullying was a factor in 2/3 of the 37 school shootings reviewed by the US Secret Service.

➤ The National Institute of Occupational Safety Health (NIOSH) (Sauter, et al.,1990), there is a loss of employment amounting to $19 billion and a drop-in productivity of $3 billion due to workplace bullying!

➤ Law enforcement costs related to bullying are enormous. Since 1999, the Office on Violence against Women (OVW) has spent $98 million in assistance to address campus sexual violence.

How Often Bullied [224]

➤ *Every 7 minutes a child is bullied!*

> In one large study, about 49% of children in grades 4–12 reported being bullied by other students at school at least once during the past month, whereas 30.8% reported bullying others during that time.

> Defining "frequent" involvement in bullying as occurring two or more times within the past month, 40.6% of students reported some type of frequent involvement in bullying, with 23.2% being the youth frequently bullied, 8.0% being the youth who frequently bullied others, and 9.4% playing both roles frequently.

Types of Bullying [225]

> The most common types of bullying are verbal and social. Physical bullying happens less often. Cyberbullying happens the least frequently.

> According to one large study, the following percentages of middle schools' students had experienced these various types of bullying: name-calling (44.2 %); teasing (43.3 %); spreading rumors or lies (36.3%); pushing or shoving (32.4%); hitting, slapping, or kicking (29.2%); leaving out (28.5%); threatening (27.4%); stealing belongings (27.3%); sexual comments or gestures (23.7%); e-mail or blogging (9.9%).

Where Bullying Occurs [226]

> Most bullying takes place in school, outside on school grounds, and on the school bus. Bullying also happens wherever kids gather in the community. And of course, cyberbullying occurs on cell phones and online.

> According to one large study, the following percentages of middle schools' students had experienced bullying in these various places at school: classroom (29.3%); hallway or lockers (29.0%); cafeteria (23.4%); gym or PE class (19.5%); bathroom (43.0%); playground or recess (6.2%).

How Often Adult Notified [227]

> Only about 20 to 30% of students who are bullied notify adults about the bullying.
> Adult Intervention 15%, Peer Intervention 4%, No Intervention 85%

BULLYING AND SUICIDE [228]

The relationship between bullying and suicide is complex. Many media reports oversimplify this relationship, insinuating or directly stating that bullying can cause suicide. The facts tell a different story. In particular, it is not accurate and potentially dangerous to present bullying as the "cause" or "reason" for a suicide, or to suggest that suicide is a natural response to bullying. We recommend the media not use the word "bully-cide."

Research indicates that persistent bullying can lead to or worsen feelings of isolation, rejection, exclusion, and despair, as well as depression and anxiety, which can contribute to suicidal behavior. The vast majority of young people who are bullied do not become suicidal. Most young people who die by suicide have multiple risk factors. Some youth, such as LGBTQ youth, are at increased risk for suicide attempts even when bullying is not a factor.

Solutions To Permanently Eradicate Domestic Violence, Child Abuse, and Bullying

TARGETED GROUPS [229]

Bullying can affect any young person, but there are characteristics and circumstances that put certain young people at higher risk. Read more about risk factors.

Special Note About LGBTQ Youth:18Research shows that LGBTQ youth are at a heightened risk for being the target of bullying, and this is an important story angle. However, media should balance coverage with information about the many facets of bullying and the wide range of youth involved.

Information and support is available for victims of abuse, their friends and family:

- *If you are in danger, call 911, a local hotline or a national hotline.*
- *U.S. National Domestic Violence Hotline provides confidential and anonymous support by phone 1-800-799-SAFE(7233) or TTY 1-800-787-3224*
- *Bullying Lifeline and Suicide Prevention Hotline 1-800-273-TALK(8255)*
- *U.S. National Teen Dating Abuse Hotline: Love Is Respect: provides teens and young adults confidential and anonymous support by phone 1-866-331-9474 or online real-time chat.*
- *WomensLaw has legal information and resources for victims.*
- *The National Resource Center on Domestic Violence has information for survivors on the Domestic Violence Awareness Project site.*
- *The Allstate Foundation has resources to end financial abuse at PurplePurse.com.*
- *Postpartum Support International Help Line 1-800-944-4773*
- *National Human trafficking Hotline 1-888-373-7888*
- *Substance Abuse and Mental Health Services Administration(SAMHSA) 1-800-662-HELP(4357)*

- ***National Domestic Violence Offenders, Child Abusers, and Bullies Howl for Help Talk, Text, and Chat HELP-LINE 1-833-3HOWLER 1-(833-346-9537) An Anonymous Abusers Hotline Set Up For Victimizers And Victims Of Domestic Violence, Child Abuse, and Bullying! Call Now! Don't Wait! Don't Hesitate! Call Now Before A Tragedy Occurs! Save Your Life!***

"IT" = "VIOLENCE": Political Men Hate Women

SHEROES and HEROES OFTEN PAY WITH THEIR LIVES! WHY? UNACCOUNTABILITY, WHICH IS AN AWARENESS TOWARDS THE SERIOUSNESS OF DOMESTIC VIOLENCE! LAWS and MEN WILL NOT CHANGE OR START CARING UNTIL "IT" HAPPENS TO THEM OR THEIR LOVED ONES OR AN INFLUENTIAL & WEALTHY CONSTITUENT!

LIKE THE SILENCE OF VIOLENCE, MOST OF OUR POLITICIANS ARE REACTIVE TO VIOLENCE and NOT PROACTIVE! LET US HOPE "IT" HAPPENS TO THEM FOR CHANGE TO COME ABOUT! WHAT WOULD HAPPEN IF A MALE POLITICIAN WERE A VICTIM OF DOMESTIC VIOLENCE, CHILD ABUSE, BULLYING, OR RAPE BY ANOTHER MAN? I AM TALKING ABOUT AN 8 FOOT, 800LB. MUSCLE BOUND DUDE WHO HAS BEEN ON DEATH ROW FOR 30 YEARS WITH AN INSATIABLE APPETITE FOR MEN WHO LOOK JUST LIKE THE ALOOF POLITICIAN! WOULD THE LAWS CHANGE THEN?

Solutions To Permanently Eradicate Domestic Violence, Child Abuse, and Bullying

SHEROES and HEROES

Due To Man Being So Despicable, God Needed Them More Back In Heaven!

The word hero would not exist without "her" being in the front of "o"! SHEROES sounds better to me like, "She Rolls" or "She Rose" above! Respectfully, one day I pray that I am worthy to be considered a HERO if I may be so lucky and blessed. How do I define SHERO and HERO? All SHEROES and HEROES who lost their lives as a result of domestic violence, bullying, neglect or child abuse and those fearless survivors who stood up to, fought the great fight, overcame their struggles and eradicated violence and abuse in their corner of the world! Any survivor of domestic violence, any individual that once was a victimizer who made the commitment to get help and are continuing the journey to end their legacy of abuse towards any human being or animal! No hate, physical, mental, verbal, or emotional abuse, discrimination, bullying, rape, stalking, sexual deviance, threats, terrorizing towards anyone or anything! Caretakers of the disabled and elderly. People who not just believe in second chances, but who provides hope to those receiving the second chance! Any individual who did not succumb to their abuser's torturous dungeon and mental prison! In the face of a horrific set of events, they conquered their oppressors to make fear flee. Those who kept their lives moving forward and in-flight despite having the wind halt and their wings severed! Those who gathered the rationale that they will not ever be bullied, silenced, intimidated, abused or violated and that they will die defending the only life they get. My SHEROES and HEROES are murdered kids*, Zahra Baker*, Shaniya Davis*, Tahjir Smith*, Cherica Adams*, her son Chancellor Lee, her mom Sandra Adams, my wife and kids, interveners, and Shaquille O'Neal. A heartfelt thanks to Shaquille O'Neal...You know why Shaq! I love you, Bruh! What a heart! My mom, aunt, and my wife's family members are sheroes who overcame domestic violence to live free of trauma and drama later in their lives! They are all resilient warrior Queens!

Many of these innocent women are victims of womanizing and adulterous men who have maliciously killed their unsuspecting wives, girlfriends, mistresses or children because they either panicked or willfully murdered them because she was pregnant, and they did not want to have the baby or babies, or they didn't want to pay child support or have their affair publicly broadcasted to break up their happy home with their wife or long-term girlfriend, or they just hated the child and were unfit to care for them! The angelic children are victims of parents who have chosen a dangerous lifestyle and culture that does not make the welfare of the child a safe priority. There is an ultimate price that all these SHEROES and HEROES have paid for others that can never be repaid or restored by anyone, only by God Himself!

My SHEROES and HEROES are those survivors who did not surrender or submit and who outlasted injustice with their ferocious, tireless and fearless fight for justice! Those who turned their muddy and messy dispositions into solid, impenetrable and unbreakable brick foundations! Lastly, the abuser and violent offenders who became accountable and aware of their violent action and sought help and continued a lifelong commitment to continuous treatment whereby they never abused another human being or animal again in their life. All the anonymous and known victims who come forward to press charges against their violent abusers are SHEROES and HEROES!

All the grandmothers in my and my wife's family who are the true beacons of strength—Henrietta Burgess, Rosetta Wilkerson, and Vernell Walden! The pain you endured was phenomenal and beyond comprehension! You are the family glue!

My SHEROES and HEROES. Zahra Baker*, Shaniya Davis*, Erica Parsons*, Tahjir Smith*, Sharra Ferger*, Elissa Self*, Caylee Anthony*, Jim Vansickle, Ortralla Mosley*, JonBenet Ramsey*, Alisha and Ava Bromfield*, Sherry Anicich, Yeardley*, Sherry and John Love, Riker Newhouse, A.J. Freund*, The Turpin children, Dawnia Dacosta*, Tashonda Bethea*, Sharon Nance*, Audrey Spain*, Valencia Jumper*, Michelle Stinson*, Vanessa Little Mack*, Betty Jean Baucom*, Brandi June Henderson*, Caroline Love*, Shawna Hawk*, Dee Sumpter and Judy Williams, Founders of Mothers of Murdered Offspring, Beverly Carter*, Valencia Blair,* Ka'Loni Flynn* and her unborn baby,* Asai Miller, Miller and Riddick Family, Molly Tibbetts*, Chester Bennington*, The victims in Aurora, Pittsburgh, Thousand Oaks, Santa Fe, Annapolis, Parkland, Las Vegas, Sutherland Springs, Charleston, Orlando, Rosenburg, Washington Navy Yard, Newtown, Ft. Hood, Geneva and Samson, Binghamton, Blacksburg, Red Lake, N.Y. City, Wichita, Atlanta, Columbine, Palatine, Killeen, Jacksonville, UNC Charlotte, Edmond, San Ysidro, Brooklyn, and Seattle, Dr. Gerald Grant, Dr. William Gallentine, Chris Cornell, Kelly Stansfield,* Office of Violence Against Women, #MeToo-Tarana Burke, #TimesUp-Lisa Borders, Rod Demery, Sheriff Garry McFadden, Kerr Putney, Chief Rodney Monroe, the FBI, David Quinn and Vincent Velasquez, Heather Heyer* and mother Susan Bro, Tereon Grant, Crisis Assistance Ministry, DNA, Crime Scene Investigators, Cold Case and Homicide Detectives,

Child Protective and Welfare Services' Employees, Police, Sheriffs, State Troopers, CSI, Forensic Files- Peter Thomas, High-Quality Surveillance Cameras, Drs. Watson and Crick, Laci Peterson*, Stacy Peterson*, Chiquita Tate*, Shania Gray*, Asha Degree, Miguel Sabillion- New Options for Violent Actions, Denita Monique Smith*, Kristopher Miller*, Shanann, Celeste, and Bella Watts, Ahkenya Johnson*, Tamika Huston*, Steve McNair*, Fred Lane*, Stephanie Rabsatt* and her unborn baby boy Jaden*, Ida and Jana Randolph*, Arrijana Hill* and her unborn twin babies*, Ericka Bradley*, Jonathan Harris*, Riley Howell*, Candice Parchment*, Jordan McNair and his parents Tonya Wilson and Martin "Marty" McNair, Tamron Hall, Kelis, Paul Williams lll, Jerry and Channel Timmons, Alesa Richardson, Alexa Dews, Ali Avalon, Brandon Dehoff, Alicia Boggs, Amanda Bray, Todd Rose, Kareem "Biggs" Burke, Chef Jeff Henderson*(FF), Amanda Carpenter, Girlsinc, Angela Rhys, Francis Augustus "Frank" Bender, Judy Smith, Adam Howland, Adam Stevenson, Adara Thomas, Ahmet Metveagaci, John and Tammy Martin, A.J. Jordan, Kim Thomas*, Al Glover, Ashley Pegram*, All ethical law enforcement officers and agents sworn to uphold the law and serve their citizens of the community by protecting them. Beverly Hope Roscoe Melton*, Crystal Parker*, Jay Emory, Darryl Thompson, Mr. and Mrs. William Christian, Billy Christian, Derrick and Frances Frost, Captain Jim Craft, Monique Oden, Tony Thorton, JD Day, Dr. Rinelda Horton, Jerome Davis, Derek McEwen, Al Silva, Janet Herrera, Marisela Gutierrez, Maribel Real, Vanessa Hart, Stephany Contreras, Kierra Ward, Kim Rossmo- Geographic Profiler, Corinne Gustavson*, Faith Moody, Children's Advocate, Rape Crisis Counselor at the Sexual Abuse Response Center, Cara Knott*, Kim Medlin*, Hae Min Lee, Jessica Rovell--who went to the police and brought charges against her attacker which lead to his demise and the freedom for others to come forward! She prevented others from being raped! She testified too! She gives others the courage to come forward and seek justice! Joann Buttaro- Rape survivor of a serial rapist who stated in court at his sentence hearing and her victim's impact statement that her rapist *"did something terrible to me. I couldn't defend myself. He violated me, and that can never be undone...Ever!" She also told the judge that "someone who affected someone's life so greatly and in such a negative way. It was important that his life be changed so greatly in a negative way!"* [231] Tyshika Askins*, Michelle Thornton*, Jessica Padgett*, John Cameron- A Detective's Detective and a living angel to families of slain individuals. He's the face of cold case solutions. Ellen Pence*, Amanda Coxe, Jeff and Renee Leake,

Amour Lopez, Johnathan Washington, George Fitzgerald, Gary Leibowitz, Slade Machamer, Joey Crowley, Candice Geouge Hellyar, Rodney Scott, Matt Smith, John Allen, Matthew Gelber, U2, Robert Henderson, Kingdom Covenant Church, Kevin Allen, Loren Townes, Gregg Bell, Michael Mackey, Shan "Shableek" Richardson, Asher Rubin, Mario Roberts, Adrienne Watson Carver, Tony Sutton, Tiffany Rogers, Claudine Rogers, Billy Rogers, Thomas Young, Jeff Hardy, Andre Battiste, Sr. and Jr., Bill Hamilton, Jonni Aidoo, Jose Ruiz, Shriners, Wounded Warriors, St. Jude's Hospital, Duncan L. Anderson Jr. and lll(Tre), Devyn and Mindy Anderson, Jermaine Venable, Keyshia Cole, Jeff Marcus, John Rush, Coretta Livingston, Emma Allen, David Mieldon, Warren, Laura, Lauren, and Lance Wallace, Richard Mason ll, Angela Neuhauser, Robert McMullin, The Sanborns, Darren & Heather Ford, Mariah Carey, E. Bronson Ingram, Rick Hendrick, Jeff Teague, Ken Hall, Jerry Adams, Jessica Perredes, Alvin Heggs, Jerome Pendergrass, Bill Bowditch, Jeremy and Jan Guenther, Art Casey, Bill Havican, Andre Blaylock, Jim Bethard, JJ Stokes, Bill Franklin, Andre, Juanita, Symone and Gregory Shanks, Brian Clift, Carl Riley, Louis Dorsey, Andrei Obilinsky, Andrew Gomez, Geneva Highlander, Joe Alvares, Andy Johnson, Bill Britt, James White, Angie Brown, George Russell, Ann Blaney, George Guilford, Annetria Lattimore, Jason Dunham, Anthony Elder, Scott Miller, Gerald Johnson, Fabrizzio Molinari, Anthony Lane, Kevin Giles, Jason Hackney, Anthony Lutz, Keri McClanahan, Nevest Coleman, Lori Anna Parker, Donna Gladden, John Haines, John, Cynthia and Jewel Ham, Gerard Matthews, Antwain Jordan, Gerardo "JT" Tuazon, Archie Brown, Gerry and Saranah Walden, Judge Faith Jenkins, Mariah Woods, Cherica*, Chancellor Lee and Sandra Adams, John Violet, K-Michelle, The American Cookie Company, Friends of the Homeless Shelter- Newport News, Virginia, Crystal Parker*, Shay Williams-Relationship Expert, Tina Turner, Herb Chambers, Tego Dorsett, Glenn Sutton, Fantasia Barrino, George Cuff, Chef Gordon Ramsey, Ike Nwaneri, Desmond Corcoran, Phillip Lemp, Lolita "Roxanne Shante" Gooden, Yvette Cade, Lily Rose Lee, Rachel Denhollander, Jack Gross- 1 Jeans Group, Ronan Farrow, Bobbi Hague, Mark Bowling, Shereece Patton, Jordan Taylor, Jalen Roddy, Darren Ray, Bobby Roussell, John Tapper, Wynetta and Jaylin Wright, J.J. Watt, Terry Brown, Wade Younger, George Laughrun, Alfred, Baxter, Olivia, and Josette Glover, Mr. and Mrs. Rogers Glover Sr, Billy, Ruth, and Franklin Graham, Owen Ray, William Henderson, Chip Harris, Greg Sher, Glenn Counts, Beverly Cooper, Sam Listenbee, Rob Long, Todd Katz, Thomas Chandler, Tony James, Jon

Justice, Camille Frances, Kraig Holt, Wayne Brady, George Crayton, Wiley Little, Demar Derozan, Kevin Roberts, Brian Hackney, Bryan VanHuystee, Bryant Wardlow, Candace Szeliga, Carlton Phillips, Kevin Love, Justify, Fisher Beasley, Thomas Guy, Dale Brown- Threat Management System, Terrell and Susan Murphy, Harry Vannie, David and Niki Stephens, Elon Musk, Linda Pfaff, Terrence, Pam, Miles, and Noland Martino, Kevin Smith, Nikki McPhatter, Pastor Mark Carson, Patrice Johnson, Ann and Allen Iverson, Betsy Patton, Lenny Gonzales, Greg Armstrong, Harold Cogdell Jr., Tyler Perry, Mike Tomlin, Kristin Cilingiroglu, Harry Collins, James Outten, Ted Venetoulis, Thomas Davis, Kyle Kinzer, Whoopi Goldberg, Hasaan Kirkland, Liza Rios, Serena Williams, Roderick Wright, Tamika Norton, Kevin Brown, Nancy Grace, Nate Holloway, Patrice Wood, Ashley Benfield, Koy Billings, George Dubose, Willie Robinson, Ann Parks, Jeni Howe, Rob Roth, Rachel Clemmons, Na'Shanda Jackson, Russ Redgate, Steven Inge, Majed Aliah, Jeff Weiner, Joe Kenda, Candice Delong, Kendra Moore, Henry Parks, Phaedra Parks, Paula Byrd, Sunday Silence, NeNe and Gregg Leakes, Karriem Ricks, Alan and Tara Robinson, Boyd Byrd, Kyle Penske, Carlton Weddington, Israel Perdomo, Kelly Shirley, Jackie Young, Kyle Thomas, Miko Baldwin, Shawn Blackiston, Carol Richardson, Kelvin Perry, Julieanne Eads, Laurie Gallagher, Kristi Walker, Justin Leverette, George Hurst, Adrian Branch, Alexander Behringer, Chris Holcombe, James Brown, Alan Keim, Michelle Weiner, Peggy Holtz Fancer, The Holtz's, Kash Bishop, Germain Kirkland, Thomas and Joyce Moorehead, Peter Boesen, Kim Pursely, Ken Holland, Ken Morrand, Hasaan Kirkland, Dana, Brian and Jason Hackney, Amy Heekin, Pastor Acquinetta Davis, Larry Cox, Isaac Dorbor, Luther and Ann Gooden, Patricia Owens, Alan Macloughlin, Shawn Richardson, Anthony Lane, Gabby Melendez, Toni Johnson, Randy Threatt, Julian Gooch, Gabrielle Abinion, Julie Brafmann-Dorkan, Kevin Durant, Patrick Cannon, The entire Curry Family Dell, Sonya, Stephon, Ayesha, Seth, Sydell, Dr Rochelle Brandon, Dr. Carl Foulks, Dr. Shawn and Joann Williams, Samuel Riddle lll, Ashanti Shackleford, Julia Crutchfield, Carlos Walton, Juanita Smith, Randy Harris, Victor Williams, Mark Duncan, Don Galloway, Dr. Robert and Sharay Seldon, Dr. Danielle Funny, Larry and Joy Foster, Randy Achenburg, Linda and Jerry "Jay" Woods, John Hubbard, Don Evans, Kimberly Chambers, Brad Chambers, Chris Beach, Dwain Campbell, Allan "Big Al" Jones, John Licka, Alonzo "Poochy" and Petey Davenport and their phenomenal mother Constance, Evelyn Lozada who stated, ***"You don't have to fight for your marriage if you're being fought by your***

Solutions To Permanently Eradicate Domestic Violence, Child Abuse, and Bullying

husband 2 seconds into the marriage because it's only going to get worse from this point forward." [230] Pastor Ivan T. Harris, Shivonne Evans Battle, Maria, Freddie and Lindsey Evans, Davis Holland, Chip Diggs, Nene Lashea, James Outten, Matthew Whiteside, Princess Wright-Johnston, Don Pendleton, Chris Cuomo, Archie and Olivia Manning, Amber Armand, Donald Armand Sr and Jr., Erica Bryant, Joe Crowley, Alisyn Camerota, Joe Folck, Dr. Jean Ronel Corbier, Isaac and Renee Powell, Vernell and Alison Walden, Anderson Cooper, Jake Randolph, James Burns, Don Lemon, Joe Munson, John Gast, Carol Costello, Doc Simeon Frazier, Michaela Pereira, Victor Blackwell, Jason Wollwert, Peggy Dillard, John Anderson, John Dear, Robin Meade, Christi Paul, Kenny Gullette, Erica Hill, Kevin Edwards, SE Cupp, Kevin Myers, Christine Romans, John Sutterfield, Erik Terkelsen, Fredricka Whitfield, John and Donna Sieverts, Evelyn Camilo, John Easton, Peter G, Donnie Hoover, Jay Holcomb, Libby McElduff, Jay Ishmael, Eric Norman, Van Jones, Eddie Owens, Tom Joyner, Kim Walker, Exoneration Projects, Kraig Holt, Kris Beacham, Roland "Lil Duvall" Powell, Les Boyd, Rickey Smiley, Cedric "The Entertainer", D.L. Hughley, Kristen Poole, Coach Tom Holiday of Oklahoma State, Kevin, Michelle, Zachary, Kailyn, and Julian Price, Mitch Clemens, George and LaKesha Kearney Hicks, Arthur Bootsy Townsend, Keith Gaines, Andre L. Palmer, Martha Henderson, LaQuinta Finnie, Elrod Hendricks, Police, Fire Department, EMT and All First Responders, Teachers, Bob Barker, Steve Smith Sr. and wife Angie, PETA, Amanda Thomashow, Callahan, Reve, Meghan, Hayden, and John Walsh, Michel'le, Cheryl "Pepsii" Riley, Jennie Willoughby, Fred Beans, Larry Aronson, Colbie Holderness, Jada Pinkett Smith, Josh Allison, JR Lane, Leon Thompson, Robin Givens, Leroy Hendricks, Baltimore Attorney Billy Murphy, Frank Endress, Brad Hackendahl, Brad and Maha Johnson, Lori Montero, Katie Crater, Tyrone "Muggsy" Bogues, Reggie Lewis, Randy Kaiser, Morgan Steenhoek, Thurgood Marshall, Morris Smith Sr. and Jr., Katey Yeats, Louis Giron, Barry Rollins, Kelly Alston, Ben Hannah, Tom Joyner, Gunmemorial.com, Anthony and Vernon Watts, Charlize Theron, Kelly Paul, Arly Pedroza, Floyd Perry, Kelly Randall, Armando Love, Frank Dehoff, Arneisha Gore, Niki Jones, Arthur Moore, Noah Snyder, Ashley Anderson, Larry, Torina*, Chad, Carlae, and Shawn Cook, Barrett Schrader, Raphael Ray, Rula Lenska, Barry Davis, Randy and Kourtney Fox, Isaiah Thomas, Ben and Kathy Heatly, Bev Watford, Fred Lockhart, Christina Aguilera, Bill Kuniej, Jamelia, Bill Marsh, Ray Robbins, Shawn Cochran, Juan Santos, Beverley Knight, Rihanna, Susan Still, Individuals who adopt! Blaine Decker, Bob Sanchez, The children who never got adopted! 9/11 and the OKC bombing survivors. The school shooting Victims: Columbine, Sandy Hook, Stoneman Douglas, Kentucky. Those with Survivors Guilt. The throwaways nobody wants! Steve Wilkos, Dr. Martin Luther King Jr and Coretta Scott King, Bernice King, Raymond Harris, Nockey Hunter, Adam Rippon. Individuals and Corporations that provide second chances to deserving individuals, so those disenfranchised people can live an ongoing productive life and serve others! Sybrina Fulton, Tracy, and Trayvon Martin*, Eddie Johnson-Chicago Superintendent, Ryan Young- CNN Correspondent, Gene Dennis, Tony Debastani, Hannibal Buress! All the women who came and are still coming forward as a member of the #METOO/#TimesUp movement! All of Larry Nassar and Jerry Sandusky survivors. The parents of the organization Mothers of Murdered Offspring (Momo), The brave individuals who came forward to expose Alvin Levy. All organizations dedicated to safe housing victims of domestic violence and child abuse! National Center of Violence Against Women, Center for Missing and Exploited Children. Individuals who adopt children and save them from perilous situations. The media who believes in no more public shame or character assassination to victims of violence, abuse, and bullying. Marsalee Nicholas-Marsy's Law, Gloria Allred, Bill Kurtis- Cold Case Files and American Justice, Erica Parsons victim, Richie Akers, Paige and Andre Armstrong, Mike Brabham, Judy Williams, Karinne Stephens, Scott Jones, Kevin Garay, Robin Thomas, Mike Davies, Dr. James Seward, Edwin Mason, Steve Hoyle, Roosevelt Fulmore, Danielle Wallace, Michelle Disoza, Silvanus Walden, Ted Creecy, Mike Beck, Dyan Trent, Mike Bowman, Ed Haggerty, Maria Walden, TC Jones, Reggie White, Steve Reed, Renee Barrineau, Jada Pinkett Smith and Adrienne Banfield-Jones, Marshall Morris, Robert Sherrill, Santiago Valentin, Monica Hessey, Celeste Hedley, and Katie Herzkall, Tommy Renshaw, Donnie, Tamika, Jasmine and Zion Pack, Steve Howell, Tracy Myers, Ernie Swords, Doug Alexander, Stan Anders, Edward Eppes Jr., Danielle Jennings, Rob Poliquin, Steven Stearns, Doug DeSloover, Symone Miller, Van Olp, Velma Burgess, Brian "Sincere" Smith, Tom Fulp, Edward Skeeter, Tony Bastfield, Steve Bansek, Gary Lawrence, Mike Bowman, Douglas Miranda, Douglas Moore, Stuart Harris, Dques Reid, Marvin Wilson, Dr. Gregory Moss, Ed Mazyck, Toni Hannah, Ron Frazier, Carroll Stewart, Yolanda Ford, Stuart Harris, Eric Dresing, Damian Mills, Todd Dewey, Shannon and Monique Tharp, Shawn Tyler, Tommy Hill, Mandeep Sidhu, Eugene Roberts, Tracie Wiggins-James, Michael Strahan, Caryn Brewer, Tim

Barnes, Rob Krasow, Tim Rodman, James Exum, Stacy and Monica Walker, Wade Rouse, Maj Aliah, Rob Vendetti, Malcolm Reid, Cesar Mancebo, Thomas Washington, Winford Galmon, Elaine Ruffolo, Wayne Wilkerson, Tim Ellerbee, Chad Cochran, Mike Davis, Tyrone Fields, William Buie, Tyrone Williams, Elsie Henderson, Richard Kay, Will and Danielle West, Chad Rudy, Tim Fleming, Tim and Heather Horning, Mike Smith, Titus Walden, Charles Everage, Tejon Robinson, Donnie Hoover, Ron Wyche, Dr. Michael and Heather Spicola, Dr. Candace Howell, Emile Williams, Charles, Jordan, and Justin Gooden, Ron and Pam Jacobs, Jeredith Shearin Green, Sean and Anita Matthews, Ross Blackstock, Dave Kendrick, Matt Donovan, Dave Umlor, Mark Samples, Dean Bishop, Mehdi Benzakhour, Robert Anstey, De'Andrea Jackson, Ronda Lawrence Scullen, Derek Rico, Albert "Rusty" Mills, Direk Mickey, Dave Waco, Rob Pearson, Rob Perite, Mitch Abernethy, Dave Washington, Emir and Pat Abinion, Davian Velez, Junious Theodore Lockett, Sikina Lockett, Sheunna Billingsley, David Caldwell, Erik Mihelich, Victor Jones, David Chan, David Ellis, Ed Keady, Charles Graustauk, Robert Fleming, David English, Charles Howard Parker, Charles Stewart, Martin Lewis, Charles Winton, Richard Warner, Cheis Garrus, RJ Harvey, Damon and Robert Young, Dan Downing, Mariann Taylor, Robert Gosten, Daniel Able, Chip Diggs, Chip Harris, Mike Martin, Scott Jaggers, Damian Kingsbury, Chiwahn Walden, Mark Baloun, Kendra Koski-Sachs, Indye Caplan Gersh, Taylor Hart, Chris Beach, Martaun and Adrienne Woodley, Marqaun Woodley, Chris Carter, Marvin and Tina White, Chris Conway, Damian and Jermaine Johnson of No Grease Barbers, Rob Solomon, Chris Henderson, Mark Mahoney, Chris Hobart, Robert and Jackie, Kourtney, and Kennedy Jones, Nick Nichols, Chris Jones, Victor Hussey, Michael Blakely, Rebecca Moore-Leach, Chris Monds, Mike Rainey, Chris Mullis, Chris Perry, Sylvester Sr., Simone, Sylvester Jr., Sarai, Sylas, Sophia, and Solomon, Chris Saunders, Terence Jones, David Livingston, Manny Zapata, David Manning, Sean Jordan, Marcus Pryor, Stephanie Petrone, David Niland, Nydia Pastoriza, Syrell Daniels, Tate Feinstrum, Marcus Wiggins, David Shrieve, David Strickland, David Sykes, Shivan Daniels, Michael Johnson, Theron Green, Spike Troy Whitehurst, David Tennant, Christine Liberto, Dana McCracken, Rodney Moore, Christopher and Cadillac Carrothers, Daniel Hackenmeyer, Daniel Williams, Richard Kay, Travis Adams, Onekki Smith, Daren Norman, Cindy Mynatt, Darron Mills, Zachary Edmonds, Shon Jennings, Darryl Autry, Tom Godfrey, Clarence Woods, Claudia Cuellar, Woody Haynes, Darryl Smith, Rodney and Betsy

Williams, Todd Ruley, Winston Pittman Jr, Simeon Frazier, Ryan Lallensack, Ohmar Land, Rory Griggs, Claudie White, Daryl Parham, Nancy Harver, Cody Favery, Sonny James, Reggie Major, Colin Harrison, Roger and Matt Gregg, Shelley Giles, Paola Vargas, Rick Reyes, Stephany Contreras, Con Errico, William Felix, Stacy Sanders, Corey Simmons, Country, Tom Gregg, Damon Lester, Sid Barron, Tom Priest, Ronnie Reddick, Courtney Stewart, Todd King, Steve Hurst, Tiana Montes, Cris Carter, Tim Vaughn, Dr. Curtis DeSena, Trey Harb, Sonny James, Tim Jones, Curtis Goliday, Tony Smith, Cyndi Jackson, Shirley Europa, Tonya Bass, D.R. Bacife, Rod Taylor, Torren Millbrooks, William Broughton, Margaret Walden, Rosetta Wilkerson, Sean Richardson, Tracey Taylor, Felix Bighem, Nicole and Netro McKay, Nathaniel "Pierre" Armstrong, Todd Brown, Tim and Mark Funderburk, Tony and Listeria Clawson, Michael Griggs, Eze Napant, Mark Hankins, Jim Mayfield, Richard and Joe Bosley III, Tamara Pope, Casey and Emily Clark, Andrew Levin, Anthony Evans, John Redmond, Cristina Love, Melissa Brooks, Damon Austin, Robert Fails, Deshane Granger, Sandra Neuhauser, Kisa Pangburn, Magi Berger, Mark Hankins, Lelita Walden, Jailynn Gaines, Telaya Bacote, Tracey Nathaniel, JT and Sangai Thompson, Ron, Karrol, Patricia, Amy, Shirley, Jack, Brian, David, Laurie and Kevin Kowitz, John and Carmen Dorsey, Corey Bradley, Eugene Soh, Damon Brown, Sr., Eddie Owens, Sean Cates, Nellie Damrauer, Marcus A. Costley, Rick Ferrer, Clarence Maurice and Louwana Ball, Robert Mason, Manual Zapata, Katherin Koorbanoff Hoegy, Nikki Austin, Star Spencer, Jeff Felton, David Robinson, John Rallo, Dusky Holman, Kevin Wilson, Neena Seymour, Claudia Orellana, Jeff Haze, Wynn Walden, Elaine Stevens Robinson, Rob Bark, Brian Bark, Brian Rosenblatt, Russ Dlin, Kraig Lattimore, Cortland D. Wylie, Doug and Eric Edwards, David Washington, Andrew Waskey, Richard Brown, Brad and Julie Childers, Roxanne Washington, DeMarco Crump, Cam Stewart, William Caldwell, Chester, (RIP), Joyce(RIP), Jonathan and Anthony Washington, Heather Weissberg Randall, Akenna Vaught Blackmon, Darien M. Norman Sr., Colleen Butler, Rob Lewis, Dericus Scott, Carlo Gilotte, Steven Michael Goldstein, Cheryl Wilson, David Pacy, Jerry Witowsky, Jason Tutman, Patrick Wilson, Corey Jenkins, Paul Pruitt, Lawrence Chang, Jeff Goldstein, Kenneth Thompson, Paul Faust, Frank Savage, Aaron Short, Beth Woods, Toni Wallace, Bienvenido Benedicto, Katey Yates, Sharon Lipa, Eskias and Crystal McDaniels, Andre L. Palmer, Heather Dozier Drayton, Amanda Wilkinson Orr, Derrick "Big Diesel" Jones, John Peacock, John

O'Neal, Todd Smith, Paul Smith*, Dawn Wilson- Jennings, Leslie Sauls Clark, Eric Mangrum, Annalyssia Marie, Allen Gatling Sr, Xavier Blackwell, Cecil Marrow, Ali Talebi, Claudie White Jr., Jarrod Schwartz, Asafonie Obed-Horton, Liza Steen, Brandon Lawyer, Toriallyn Brodie, Joe and Angela Badgett, Daniel Hagen, Libby McElduff, Mark Campbell, Randy Myers, Nancy Wilkinson, Michelle Hart Wheaton, Manual Floyd, Taylor Martino, Jed Carmona, Brittany Hunter, Christina Catanzaro, Monica Mroz, Lisa and Kevin(RIP) Reaves, Chris Conway, Sandi Ross Poole, Pastor Stacy and DeNae LeMay, Tracey Clarke, Stevie and Jeffrey Clark, Ervin and Andrew Locust, Mark Young, Julia Ana Diaz, Roberto Diaz, Logan Burris, Marcie Jones, Paul Williams lll, Lloyd "Tony" and Loretta Bastfield, David Ro, David Punzalan, Delano Santos, Steve Manness, Bonnie Van Metre, Marsha LeQueux, Jeff Thomas, John Dear, Lisa Levin Beck, Jen Machamer, Brian Robinson, Julian Gooch, Corey Parker, Zac Williams, Chris Monds, Guy Walden, Christopher Carter, Laura Stone Ellis, Kimberley Warden, Chris Midgette, Jeff Belsky, Gigi Bodwin, Vanessa Jackson, Herb Wilson, Alex Mansolino, Bill Franklin, David Fulton, Nina Jones, Bill Batten, Scott Harris, Corey and Tanya Simmons, Dr. Gregory Moss Sr., Renado Robinson, Shauntae Jordan, Mae Walden, Felicia Mack, Greg Hutchinson, Stan Dorsey, Alberto Diaz, Carla Sewell Bluitt, Darcia Parker, John Wilkey, Cedric White Sr., James Weaver, James Johnson, O'Dell McKinney, Antonio "Too Tuff Tony" Martinez, Nsenga Burton, Eric Thomas, Victoria Watlington, Juan Ramos, Paul Williams, Vic Grant, Jennifer Tyler, Ted and Stacie Peddy, Doug Miller, Sylvia Coates, Vicki Foster, Carlos Pauling, Louis Martinez, Dawn Watts, Chantel Scott, Orlando Shropshire, Marcus Shields, Amy Warner Benjamin, Greg Hayes, Richard McGough, Andy Klaff, Darren Ashley, Byron Brown, Fran Milbower, Beth Skinner Lavery, Stephanie Franklin, Missy Becke Lemke, Tehara Bryant, Rob Maupin, Daryl Hutton, Tiffany Lynette May-Byrd, D'Keonia Eddington, Brenda Peterson, Nikki Clifton, Les Allen Jr., Signe Whitson, Mackenzie Galbraith Dougherty, Hasaan Kirkland, Dana Morgan Fady, Robert Wilson, Ernest Johnson, Scott Frank, Colleen Anderson, David Rosenbaum, Libby Emma, Tammie Ventura, James Baack, Dawn McCain, Finesse McCain, Fred Collymore, Kimberly Joy Walker, Elizabeth Levy-Hembling, Trevor Ingle, Mina Wender, Michelle Zimlin Yospa, Joseph W. Parran, Gigi D'Antonio Liberati, Elizabeth Waller, Troy Germain, Dan Yochelson, Julian Wright, Jennifer Sponseller Webber, Janine Davis, No Limit Larry, Fly Ty, Tone X, Nate Quick(RIP), BJ Murphy, Victor Fakhoury, Tiffany England, Eva Griffith, Ally

Leonard, Simone Motton, Mark Vincent, Mark and Ari Blum, The Seals, Roderick Ware, Duane Goins, Rodney Goggins, Albert Black, Nina Massey-McReed, Christine Mendez, Jen Fields, Anita Boyd Harris, Alan Oliver, Robert Sherrill, Vanessa Hill, Brian Timian, Kelly Turner-Woolford, Haywood Carl Butler, Richard DeVayne, Amia Mimi Croom, Linwood Bolles, Barbara Peacock, Mike McCravy Sr.(RIP) and Jr., Kevin Smith, Frankie Day, Aaron Hall, Kim Morales, Sylvia Bass, Ronique Donaldson, Daniel S. Levine, Beth Miller vonBriesen, Christine, Mary, Tina, Penny, Tub, Raymond-Rainbow, Charles, Leonard, Bruce, Carl-Leo, Richard, Buddy, Lyle, Linwood, and Chris Smith, Eric Copeland, Steve Tuttle, Rebecca Ratliff, Bishop Walter Thomas, Kassie Street, Byron Thomas, Tom Kelly, Tina S. Miles, Deborah Stockwell, Kaitlyn Michelle Walsh, Jim Sabo, Laurie Sabo Burns, LaPronda Spann, Darren Sanders, Buzz Mayer, Larry Wedgewood, Jabarr E. Adams, Tawanna Rosenbaum, Andre Burnell, Stuart Watson, Jason Stoogenke, Delancey Daniels, Brett Ingerman, Jack Waters, Navid Lotfi, John Seal, Geoff Trussell, Cass O'Meara, Wanda Pulliam, Carl Gustafson Jr., Douglas Jones, Bobby Gibson, Doug Weaver, Seth Bondroff, Elsa Cornish, Christopher Evans, Michelle Mayer, Amanda Talbott, Derrick McDonald, Rick Williams, Robert Arce Jr., Zack Dillard, Ronald Fleshman, Steven Brodie, Troy Wilson, Dr. Kim Anderson, Dr. Tiky Swain, John Higgins lll, Derek Newton, Evers Burns, Ant Scott, Carla Williams, Chip Newton, Chris Moran, Lisa Davis, Dwayne Cooper, Lamont Cooper, Toby Rivers Sr., Jamie Camilo, David Manning, Ray West, Cyndi Jackson, Emily Isaacs Dugan, David Hands, David Porter, Padej Yakamna, Pam Smith, Jason Daniel Whitley, Jeff Bloom, Dena Marcia, Laura Sellars, Lavell Derwin Jones, Joe Gast, The Gast Family, Leroy Hendricks, Trini House, Chad Lockhart, Brent Lewis, Horatious Harris, Adrian Wilson, Todd Axelrod, Tameran Davenport, Michael Dorsey, James Day, Karen Bennett Yates, Tony and Ronald Isaacs, Brian Litofsy, Pervis Coleman, Todd Webber, Michael Rojo, Kelly and William McGlenn, Eric Douglas, Pat McCarthy, Michele Benyi, Paul M. Bonk, Aliceson King, Jeff Sindler, Will Scovill, Seth Dykes, Rebecca Mules, Ted Maher, George Kimbrow Jr., Bobby Newton, Martin McKibbin Jr, Harry Leo White Jr., Jeremy Shroeder, Lamar Smith, Reggie Newton, Leon Newsome, Stacie Ludwig Dowling, Terri and Jimmy Dowla, Eric Twiggs, Steve Rutherford, Jack Mitchell, Angela Duncan Minor, Shenique Mens Smith, Jaden, and James "Man" Smith, Diane Hemphill, Svenya Nimmons, Ethan Bost, Jason Dansicker, Erica Cook, Josh Hetzel, Joe Netta, Chuck Vanderburg, Shani Maria, Bob Mayberry Hyundai, Pam Harrell-Killette, Melissa

Willen Hyatt, Marty Smith, Chris Perry, Vaughn and Kim Hebron, Scott Athen, Grailen Archie, Bill Weitzenkorn, Rob Ferrer, Amy Mandell Gainsburg, Mike Brabham, Nomy Delgado, Ali Louise Avalon, Malik Shabazz, Cheryl, Damon and Bobby Royster, Kristian Moore, Franklin Fitzgerald, Rich Reamer, Tom Gregg, Eric and Leanna Jones, Ray Faust, David Ellis, Arnie Connor, Will Pridgen, Scott Weller, Lorie Lennon, Alberto Silva, Linwood Franklin, Andrew Wilen, Kenneth Thompson, Austin Jefferson, Marcus Wiggins, Jamie Ingerman Parks, Jody Prettyman Isaacs, Tyler Mosley, Jordan Forman, John Sutterfield, Tom Klaff, Jason Turnipseed, Scott Alan Sweren, Stacey Rosenblatt Battaglia, Dwayne Mitchell, David Ahn, Cheryl Patterson-Coad, Jill Cohn Shaw, Maya Mohamed KaiKai, Niki Cosby, George Hurst, Roderick Wayne Hart Sr., Tracey Gladden, Angel Walden, Melanie D. Fenwick Thompson, Marnie Fenwick, Sean "DJ Spen" Spencer, Wayne Mallory, Manny Gillis, Jack Green*, Mark Treece, Troy and Mark Hines, Derrick Asbell, Charles Ali Everage, William S. Parrish Sr., Kyle Potocki, Brian Clift, Bruce Pickus, Marvin Chambers, Brian Rice, Jeffrey Ervin, Ashley Graham and Justin Ervin, Adell Pickens, Terrence Price, Molly Clark Jefferds, Alexandria Davis, Todd Griffin, Jovie Bodie Bohan, Shane Purser, Kevin Leitch, Donald Cureton Jr., Josh Rice, Changa Bell, Jack Soliman, Katie Del Carmen Byram, Bobby Escalante, Jonathan Reamer, Jeff Teague, Susan Kirchhausen, Chris Carter, Michael Block, Geoff Streat, Tommy Koulianos, Jay Donald, Taylor Rock, Jim Caswell, Rachel French, Sandy Wetzel, Haley Whitley, Paul Girard, Andy Seagal, Jonathan Davis, Brian Wah, Howard Wiseman, Brian Castillo, Justin Kraus, Steve Papaminas, Gian Aleece, Kristin Greenwald Ruark, Tesah Spriggs, Chuckie and Kyra Waters, Antonio Hunter, Billy Bryant, Michael Pinckney, Sharon Strauss, Troi Gordon, Eric Aldrich, Portia Kee, Byron Cage, Giselle Graves, Pastor Jamal Bryant, Maggi Apollon, Ted Boyle, Hamani and Kendria Fisher, Sharon Satisky Lynn, Todd Inman, Michael Bennett, Tony Lawson, Brian Maier, Jenny Cline, Nate Holloway, Latonya Hines, Chip Hammonds, Joel Cunningham, Rachelle Ellie Westover, Rochelle Jones, Greg D'Alesandro, Tony Armstrong, Jermaine Walker, Shonelle Gibson, Stephen Illyefalvi, Michael Gormley, Greg Cooley, Nick Williams, Damian Kingsberry, Aubri T. Ames, Sharrard Alexander, Antujuan Marshall, Reverend Howard V. Booker, Joseph "Monkey" Butler, Reverend H. Blunt, William T. Baker, Jerry Bias, Karin Booker, Angela Bowles, Duane W. Cephas, Amanda Brown, Christin Bluford, Scott Miller, James Becton, Eric Dunmire, Iverson Davis, Shawna Daniels, Charles Booker, David Dewberry, Dr. William Coker, York Eggleston,

Sadi El-Amin, Fernando Davis, Moses Outlaw, James Nowell, Vernard McBeth, Sheila Hawkins, Nikki Webbe, Tamiko Fung, Gerald J. Freytes, Danielle France, Mark Ashe, William H. Graham, Alonzo Ellison, Maurice Gillis, Gwendolyn Jackson, Clara Brown, Cornelius Ivey, Clarence Jackson Jr., Darnell Haskins, Chiny Hinton, Angela Harvell, Robert Jones Jr., Stephen Hyman, Mike Jereb, James Noell, Tina Hankins, Eric Jones, Camica Harris, Carl Johnson, Veronica James, Pamela Leggette, Geno Harris, Joe and Pat Township, Pellum Murray, John E. Mann, David Maitland, Gary Phillpott, Yolanda Powell, Prescilla Roberts, Darnell Rogers, Derick "Skee" Robinson, Michael Ramsey, Sam Simkins, Tony Schultz, Jeff Simmons, Kiesha Townes, Chonda Whitaker, Calvin Veney, Weldon Terry, Donald Trott, Matthew Valentine, Gene Vaughan, Jesse Lee Williams, John Whiteside, Ron Ward, Brian Forbes, Ron Ward, Darryl Witron, Scott Taylor, Scott Hamilton, Angela Bowles, Chanelle Gray, Charlotte Rose, Ron Kelly, James Leary, James W. Devore, Michael R. Young, Don C. McFadden, Randy M. Estenson lll, Samuel Eloud, Joseph Doughtie, Marlon Burns, Jason Ellington, Alvin Darden, James S. Redmen, Robert Drouin, William H. Lewis, Chad Ross, Kendall Debrick, Jerome Spratley, Leroy Savage, Corey Smith, Steve Nesbitt, Frank Drigotus, Marl Boesen, Mitch Cuthbertson, Larry Picone, Cheryl Godwin, Bob Sanchez, Todd King, Bonita Dent, Russell Fleury, Bob Atwood, Rex Welton, Don Galloway, Bob Meade, Clem Ashford, Walter Thompson, Hensy Fenton, Emily Yang, Kari Carpenter, Deirdre Halverstade, Doug Winchester*, Mark Russell, Bryant K. Alexander, Dr. Brian Killian, Omar "Rasheed" Bailey, Franklin Butts, Otis Burnette, Larry Burris Sr. and Jr., Patrice Wood, Vic Black, Paul Bearden, Whitney Brackett, Laney Cole, Malcolm Graham, George Doggett, Andre Blaylock, Michelle Thomas, Charleon Maria Macon, Dan Deviller, Zeke Farrington lll, John Farrar, Brian Freeland, Terence Felder, Tyrone and Kelly Gorham, J.J. Grey, Mark Bryant Howie, Tony Harris, Angie Hughes, Derek Harris, Quentin Johnson, Ed Kitchen, Ed Knowles, Rob Love, Kevin Liggon, May May and Edith Liggons, Ed Keady, David Livingston, Bruce Little, Greg Metcalf, Eric McDonald, Gerard Matthews, Derek McSwain, Keith Mason, Wanda McConico, Nikki Nance, Donnie Moore, Antonio Jennings, Patrick Milner, Randy Richardson, Todd Rose, Adam Jones, George and Eva Raftelis, Steve Rownd, Andre Reynolds, Captain Robert Willis, Robert McMullins, Clyde Brian Smith, Norman Spencer, Keith and Rosalind Vinson, Chris Walker, Vince Jefferson, Wali Molina, Charlene Salyers, Martin Padgett, Mackenzie Dougherty, Tina Adams, Orlando Lee, Dave Blunt, Chris Fischesser,

Belinda Gribble, Will Jones, Richard Zamora, Leslie Clark, Andy Couture, Andrew VonBargen, Samantha Montgomery, Tony Nelson, Bruce Stewart, Phil Hautzenroed, Chuck Weisbrod, Robert Fails, Kenan Nelson, Amanda Labarbera, Terri Paola, Brandon Walsh, Eric Thomas, Steve Witham, Bradford White, Bill Atwood, Coach Summerville, Cheryl McCullough, Omari, Christopher, Christophia, Wayne Sr., and Jr Patterson, the Crowley's and Springhettis, Brett Walsh, Chip Jergens, Andreas Burket, Andy Hyman, Chris O'Donnell, Bill, Coach, Darryl, Zach Glutz, Anthony Destefano, Sean "Suede" Nelson, Derek Davis, James, Ina, and Sylvia Sutton, Patrice Jones, Greg Penn, Keith Hunter, Ellison Clary, Susan Malveaux, Donna Buie, Dave Farace, Mark Koski, and Orlando Spears, Cynthia Coates, Dr. Rani Singh, Robert Smoot, Robert Seigman, and Maleah Davis*.

Growing up in Baltimore, my heroes were Tony Dorsett who donned the jersey # 33, Reggie Williams 33, Eddie Murray 33, Magic Johnson 33 in college and 32 with the Lakers because the man Kareem Abdul Jabbar wore 33, Andrew Locust 33, Antoine Harris 23, Jim Brown 32, David Thompson 33, Herschel Walker 34, Michael Jordan 23, Scottie Pippen 33, Adrian Branch 24, Deion Sanders 21, Len Bias 34, David Wingate 40, Ricky Hendricks 24, Cal Ripken Jr 8, Earl Weaver 4, Elrod Hendricks 44, Reggie Jackson 44, Brian Jordan 40, Rodney Monroe 21, Sam Mills 51 and the incomparable Tyrone "Muggsy" Bogues 14!

The entire Burgess Family, James*(RIP), Henrietta Sands, William "Snookie"*, Roslyn, Marjorie, William "Boonie"*, Thomas* & Jason*, Delores, Marty*, Doris, Joyce Ann, Jason*, Jackie Earl, Morris "Chip"*, Royce "Chubby" Burgess, Teeny Turner, Antonio, Kamari, and Riley Dorsey, Rachel Griggs, Gregory Hutchinson, Aliyah Tucker, Richard Blackwell II, Brandy Blackwell and Kyli Savage, Richard Blackwell III and Kylia Blackwell, Maurice, Cody, and McKenzie Burgess, Kristin, and Avery Dennis, Jordan Burgess, Taylor, Zorie and Sydney Plotkin Burgess, Trisha Burgess, Darnell Dorsey, Michael Carter, Eboni Hatchet, Phoenix Elizabeth Mitchell, William and Elizabeth* Hatchet, Uncle Vince* and Aunt Cissy* Anderson, Anita and Neet Neet, Carlos, and Peaches, Mr. and Mrs. Ryan and Buddy, Kim, Keith, Beth Anne and Marcus Costley, Mr. Leonard and Mrs. Irene! The Hodges and Tuckers. My cousins Joe, Kenny, Danelle, and Nicole Wilkerson, Edwin Ebby, and Gina* White, Alice, Nathaniel, Shawn, Carla, and Brandon Phillips, Darrell, Christopher "Peanut" and Andrew* Sands, and Aunt Joan, Aunt Helen*, Bev, Angel, and Cindy! Gary Gardner, Barbara Ann, Little Gary*, Tyrone, Telly, and Tara Smith, Uncle Soul*, Momma Ruth*, Paul*, Aunt

Mary*, Uncle Pete*, Phyllis, Ruth, Vanessa, Kurt*, Tammy, & Shawn Dorsey, Deion and Breyonne Young, Stephanie and Steve Harris, Phyllis, and George Williams, Dennis and Sylvia, Clairenette, and Charlotte Johnson, Nicky Nell, Big and Little Herman, Jason* & Leslie Reynolds, Joe*, Mary Lou, Sherry, Brian, Little Joe, and Darryl* Butler, Karen, Hanky, Charlene, and Joan King, Mr. and Mrs. Fats Dorsey*, and Mickey Dorsey, Phillips, Rogers, Waters, Nicholson, Rich, the Sidnores, Ryan, Harris, Washington, White, Davis, Owens, Altamese Nealy, Joe Naylor, Griggs, Smith, King, Lyles, Joe and Carl Sands, #1 Drummer & Singer in the World, Dennis, D'Nisha & Renee Chambers, Betty, Joe, and Eddie Sharp! Juanita, Stewart, Genny, & Lillian Murray! Larry Rich and Jackie Waters. My wife Trena, Antoneya, Ava, Andira, and Anisa Burgess, Justin & Jaxon Henderson, the Walden, Wilkerson, Battiste, Gaines, Bacote, Smith, Mens, Samuel, Jones, Brown, Williams, Anderson, Hicks, David, Maria, Sydney, Lola, & Olivia Stephens family.

I will never forget the hero in my life who unscrambled the Rubik's Cube in my head, Dr. Miller M. Ryans(RIP)! Dr. Ryans gave me the solutions for me to cope healthily after prison. Margaret "Maggi" L. Curry-Williams has been my shero for restoring my belief that society would forgive me when she accepted me to Old Dominion University. E. Bronson Ingram for showing the ultimate display of love for still believing in me after I had thrown away my life and the investment he had made in my future. Rick Hendrick for giving me a living wage despite my background. My wife for loving me in spite of me. To the victims and families of domestic violence, child abuse, and bullying you truly are my heroes and sheroes. To the individuals who decided to get help to stop the violence, abuse, torture, and bullying, you are now on my list of heroes and sheroes. God Bless You All for choosing life over death! Kevin Brown of Charleston, SC, thank you for housing me at a desperately needed time in my life! You are truly are a brother's keeper!

Tahjir Smith*, Zahra Baker*, Shaniya Davis*, Erica Parsons*, Liza Steen*, Cherica Adams* and many others, I will never forget you. Your life will always serve a meaningful purpose! You are beyond a SHERO and HERO to me. You were an angel on earth to me and I am so sorry that I couldn't have gotten this book into the hands of the people who harmed you before they took your precious life! Your family, friends, and people like me will forever love you! Your name will forever live in my heart and mind. I can't wait to see you in heaven one day! Your Bro, Your Bruh, and Your Friend, A.W. BURGESS. I'm so so so so so sorry that I was not in a position to help God save your life! Your legacy will live in me!

PATRICK B. McDERMOTT P. C.
ATTORNEYS AT LAW

PATRICK B. McDERMOTT   532 SETTLERS LANDING ROAD   TELEPHONE (804) 722-0611
DEBORAH S. ROE   P. O. BOX 28   FAX   (804) 722-1312
STEPHEN K. SMITH   HAMPTON, VIRGINIA 23669   TOLL FREE (800) 882-3063

April 13, 1992

Milton Dorsey
3407 Auroro Lane, Apt. M
Baltimore, MD 21207

       Re: Antoine Burgess

Dear Mr. Dorsey:

    I went to visit Antoine on Friday morning, April 10, 1992, and he is looking very good. He has put on some weight and he is a trustee in the jail, which means he has special privileges that the other inmates do not. He says he has talked with his job counselor at Ingram Industries and the counselor told him to get his life straight and then get in touch with Ingram when he is ready to seek employment.

    I asked him if he had been in touch with you or his mom. He said no. I asked if his mother had written and at first he said he had not heard from his mother, then he admitted that he had sent his letters from her back. I asked why and he said he did not want her emotional or financial support anymore. I told him that part of his healing process would be making amends with her and he said no, he was going to go about his life and not be close to anyone. I am sure he's hurting inside and this is his defense mechanism, but it's a shame he won't write his mother.

    If either you or Ms. Burgess has any questions or concerns, please call.

                  Very truly yours,

                  Deborah S. Roe, Esq.

DSR/kp

---

[232] *WHY IS MY LAWYER TALKING TO HIM? HE DID NOT <u>WANT</u> HIS OWN KIDS! SENDING ME MY OWN MONEY IS FINANCIAL SUPPORT? MY MOM COULD NOT COME TO MY GAMES and THE 2 TIMES SHE DID SHE WAS DRUNK AS A SKUNK; SHE <u>WANTED</u> HIM SO MY COLLEGE SAVINGS WENT TO HIS BUS BUSINESS; SHE MADE ME A HOMELESS COLLEGE KID and NOW SHE <u>WANTS</u> TO COMMUNICATE WITH ME and VISIT ME IN JAIL? YOU <u>WANT</u> "HIM" AROUND ME? EVERYONE WAS CLUELESS TO <u>WANTING</u> ME and WHAT I <u>WANTED</u>! <u>ONLY GOD WANTED ME</u>!*

Solutions To Permanently Eradicate Domestic Violence, Child Abuse, and Bullying

THE WANTED* and UNWANTED*

Titles No Human Being Ever Wants! I Want You To Be Wanted, Not Wanted*!

I have my wayward walk in life because of violence that cost me more than just a short staycation in prison. I have lost significant friendships to domestic violence and abuse and am emphatic towards making people think twice about the only life they will ever have and how they are impacting others. You only get one life. What will you do with the only one you get? How will others remember you? How do you want others to remember you? When someone calls your name what is the first thing that jumps in their head? When you have a medical emergency such as a broken an arm or leg, you go to the hospital! When you get sick, you go to your primary caretaker like your local doctor! When you have cancer or are on dialysis, you go to a treatment center! When you have a mental break down or domestic violence or child abuse incident where you have abused a loved one, where do you go? Do you call 911 on yourself? Does someone call on your behalf? What are you prescribed or what do you take to stop your abuse of others? If you do not want to be unwanted, you have to want to be helped now! Your mental wellness is at stake.

I often think about a great middle school friend to this day still disturbed and upset that her mother could kill her, a 12-year-old seventh grader, by placing her in a scalding hot tub! That image will play in my mind until I see her in heaven. I always wished she could have told me she was being abused and needed my help so that I could have said something to someone! She too was on mute. The violence silenced her. The regret and remorse I have never lessens and will never go away!

When I think about Cherica Adams* or see her mom and son, I feel like it is unfair that I knew a woman who her son will never know! I know the feeling of having a parent die from violence before you are born and all the misfortune's and non-benefits that come with it! I always try to find the positive in a negative or tragedy and so I pray that others will possess the wisdom to see the after-effects of such violence & abuse that they decide not to harm anyone, anything, or themselves.

I have long forgiven Bonita's mom, Rae Carruth, Van Brett Watkins, Stanley Abraham, and Michael Kennedy, for permanently changing the lives and family of Cherica, Saundra, and Chancellor Lee Adams, as well as, permanently changing their families and their own lives! I do not harbor any hate towards them, nor do I judge them because that is reserved for God only. I would ask them though, as I said to myself so many times in and out of prison or when I lost significant opportunities in life as a result of my violence, **WAS IT ALL WORTH IT? IF YOU COULD TAKE IT BACK WOULD YOU? I KNOW YOU WOULD!**

As I had to deal with the harsh realities that come with post-prison, Rae is going to have to grasp the scope of his new life. As a former professional football player and college graduate, can you field these questions, Rae? What do you say to your son about his mom? What do you say to her mother about her daughter's life and death? How are you going to earn a formidable living for your son and his grandmother? How are you going to repay them and reimburse them for their permanent losses? Can you ever settle the debt? Can you ever get your good name and credibility back or is it gone forever? Can you raise the dead and breathe life back into their lifeless bodies or make a disabled person walk normally? Can you take away or erase the pain or the thoughts of what is lost? **WAS IT WORTH IT NOW?** I pray people look at our stories of violence and abuse and get the wisdom to learn from our transgressions that harmed the lives and legacies of incredible individuals! Welcome to the unwanted club and family Rae, Van Brett, Stanley, and Michael. I am a lifetime member of the club you joined. A club where when people learn of you they hesitate. A club that no sane person wishes to get a membership.

To all domestic violence offenders, child abusers, and bullies: **STOP** being so damn insecure! You are preventing yourself from executing your future! Either take a step forward towards a solution or your problems will be stuck where you are, or you will be taking a step backward leading to greater losses, pain and more overall traumatic experiences! I am not playing when I say **DO NOT PLAY WITH THIS!**

You have to be a FAMILY MAN™ about taking care of the responsibilities of your family. No one is ever going to care more about your children than you. The mothers and grandmothers who are raising the world of kids are proving every day that the game of life still goes on when the Queen is in check! The women are the royal forces holding the family together even when the so-called King has self checked out or even been replaced by a new squire in her court. When the King is in check, the game is over mate. I have raised my daughters to be the Queen supporting their King. The King should respectfully support her and her dreams too as she supports his dreams. Together you can have fun and get your dreams done!

When a man and woman support each other they can rule the world but when you do not support each other you have just killed the dynamics of a dynasty where no one rules, and eventually, you are both setting the kingdom up to be overthrown! Do not lose yourself in another person. Love yourself more than you love another person. When you love yourself less than you love another person, who or what do you become when that person leaves you? If you are always in love with you first, you will never have to worry about you running out on you and having your heart shattered into a trillion pieces. You have to love you more than anything!

If you, like me, have ever been wanted by law enforcement or are considered "unwanted" because you have been or currently are a domestic violence offender, child abuser or bully, what I truly want you to know is I sincerely love you and cannot judge you. There was a time not so long ago that I was sitting exactly where you are now, and then because I did not listen to the girlfriend I was abusing to get the help I so desperately needed, and I ended up in the penitentiary and psychiatric hospital. I will not have that for your life, and that is why I refuse to judge you and would rather talk to you or hug you if that is what is needed. Judgment is reserved for Your Maker. My position in life is to do everything I can to ensure another human being or animal will never be a traumatic or tragic victim of domestic violence, bullying or child abuse. I will stop the abuse by fixing the abuser!

What I know and believe is that most abused people go on to abuse people because all they know as their normal is abuse! When abuse and violence occurs, I feel that I let them down by not doing enough or saying anything to prevent and protect them from evil's harm. I let down the victims, abusers, violent offenders, and the positive and productive law-abiding members of our society. I failed them because I muzzled and froze in my tracks! God Blesses Motion! I gotta get moving! I want you to lay down your burdens and pain and submit yourself to finding the solutions to your pain! The Lord wants you to rest! Sit down, reveal to be healed, and let the Lord bring out the pain so that the love can come into your heart, mind, and soul. As my great friend from Baltimore Duncan Anderson Jr always says, "Meditate before you Medicate!" Before you put a pill, blunt, or raise an alcohol or stronger drink to your lips, is your mind healthy? Is your mind sober to receive love?

Think about this, if you are a victimizer, meaning a domestic violence offender, child abuser or bully, I want to help you permanently! If you are a victim of domestic violence, child abuse or are being bullied I want to help you. I will not judge you, but instead, I will love and hug you. Just know that I cannot help to fix your problems of domestic violence, child abuse or bullying, unless we fix the root cause of the violence, abuse and bullying which begins with the mentality of the victimizer, abuser, or bully. To permanently eradicate the violence, abuse, and bullying we have to permanently eradicate whatever is traumatically causing the violence and bullying in the victimizer! We have to sever the weights of pain, so we do not become weighed down by the pain. Put a 45lb weight on your back and walk!

Do not be an abuser!(ABUSE-HER) Do not abuse her, the child, or the pet! Abuse me! Domestic violate me! Try to control and manipulate me! A full-blooded alpha man! A wolf who can tolerate hearing about your violence, abuse, and pain because I care about getting your mind right so that you can live a healthy, productive and prosperous life. When the world throws you away, where do you go? I want to give you the love, coping and life skills, along with non-judgment, to focus and move forward with your life! I have unconditional love for you! No judgment!

I visit inmates not out of sympathy or empathy, but as a necessity to prevent perpetuating violence and abuse. I am a humanitarian first. Where will they go and what will they do once released? Are they equipped to cope or are they a U-turn away from returning to jail or prison as a result of abuse and violence? Are they institutionalized and destined for disaster? Like you, I was part of the problem, and now I am part of the solution. Take a definitive stand with me against violence and abuse against women and children. I do not want you to fall into recidivism as a result of violence. Recidivism is a losing game. When you think you are all alone or dealing with an unbearable situation remember God is carrying you and your burden! The poem, *"Footprints In The Sand"* is simply powerful and a message to anyone that you are never going through anything alone. The poem honestly had a profound effect on me to let me know that God does care about me. Here is the poem. I pray that you understand that you have people who understand and can help.

"One night I dreamed a dream. As I was walking along the beach with my Lord. Across the dark sky flashed scenes from my life. For each scene, I noticed two sets of footprints in the sand, One belonging to me and one to my Lord. After the last scene of my life flashed before me, I looked back at the footprints in the sand. I noticed that at many times along the path of my life, especially at the very lowest and saddest times, there was only one set of footprints. This really troubled me, so I asked the Lord about it. "Lord, you said once I decided to follow you, You'd walk with me all the way. But I noticed that during the saddest and most troublesome times of my life, there was only one set of footprints. I don't understand why, when I needed You the most, You would leave me." He whispered, "My precious child, I love you and will never leave you. Never, ever, during your trials and testings. When you saw only one set of footprints, It was then that I carried you." [233]

You are never going through anything by yourself! I have gone from hero to zero and back to hero only by the grace and mercy of God and other people who chose to willingly help me despite my criminal history and domestic violence past. I will always be thankful for their understanding and not forever holding my pass against me. Their mercy provided me with hope and belief that prayers do eventually get answered by God! I prayed to God that if I were given another chance to prove I was no monster I would do something in the earth to manifest His love for humankind! The commitment is dangerous to me, and it has to be as serious to those connected with me. To begin the journey to eradicate violence and abuse, offenders and predators must admit and commit to never again hit!

You only get one lifetime! What are you doing with the only one permitted to you? What will be your legacy to humanity? I want you to get an R.O. I. (Return On Investment) on you. Are you an investment? Are you worthy of investing in yourself? Are others willing and worthy of investing in you and showing you grace and mercy? I say this because time is money. We give all of our time to other people's dreams, but rarely to our own. Invest in your life and freedom. Expense you! Get an R.O.I. on you and your dreams.

I know firsthand how incredibly difficult it is to confess to anyone that you are an abuser! I know the fear of judgment and rejection, but you have to think big picture and long-term when it comes to your life as you know it and as you want to know it! Not everyone is going to support your journey as a confessed admitted abuser and violent offender. Some people will never forgive you for your crime or violent behavior against another human being or animal just because of the way it has impacted them or their own set of beliefs.

Violence and abuse are like trying to figure the Rubik's cube out, and you have never seen it before or read the solutions manual, and by the way, you are two years old! What are your odds at conquering the solution to the seemingly impossible to solve Rubik's Cube or will you take the stickers off and cheat or get so frustrated with it that you smash it into a trillion pieces? Do not gamble with your life! We all have a Blu-ray Ultra HD 3D DVD movie that will eventually come out!

Are you a cold-hearted, cold-blooded person? Do you epitomize evil? Do you have a conscious? Are you remorseful? Do you realize you cannot replace a life or innocence? The person who you are abusing accepts your apologies, but what they truly need is your actions to permanently change this violent behavior so that where it is possible, they will want to stay with you by and not by force.

Solutions To Permanently Eradicate Domestic Violence, Child Abuse, and Bullying

Your broken promises to never do **"IT"** again makes people numb, incoherent and despondent, and simply chips at any hope that you will become the person who they first fell in love with and could relate to as a friend. Just think about how your expression of "I am sorry!" If you say it over and over again, each time it gets worse! "I am sorry. I am sorry. I am sorry. I am sorry." Yes, you are right! You are a SORRY son of a gun and not a sincere and genuinely apologetic individual and friend who is not working to make your life better and free of pain, drama, trauma, and dysfunction! I would rather be a castaway on a deserted island than hurt anyone or anything in my life purposely without working towards a permanent and healthy solution in any of my relationships! ***END "IT"----- DO NOT MEND "IT"!***

You have been abusing people for some time, and this violence comes with irreparable and in some cases, irreversible consequences that are never negotiable or even up for discussion. The problem as an abuser is that you still believe that your actions do not matter to the people you are abusing when they significantly do! Right now, all that matters is not harming those individuals and yourself ever again by getting help! I am not here to save you, only God Saves, but to inform you that this is not a request to get help, but a requirement to get the help that leads to a permanent healing solution, not treatment! Do you want to be healed or treated?

Do not forfeit your right to live amongst us due to your actions. It is cool seeing the wild and dangerous animals at the zoo behind the glass or in their fenced-in enclosures. But who wants to snap pictures now that the wild animal is set free and there are no glass, steel, or cement enclosures? Do not lose your freedom and have the world fearing any personal or corporate relationship with you. You have your freedom to go anywhere in the world with the freedom to do just about anything you want to choose to do and be. Now you have to free yourself from what is causing your pain making you violent and abusive. Do you think if the animals at the zoo could free themselves they would? Do you think they would rather be back in the wild where God intended them to be? They do not have a choice regarding their destiny, but you do!

You have to see a world outside of your hate and violence. The trajectory of your life will change when you choose to change. No excuse for the abuse. There are no justifications that will be permissible. You cannot change the past, but you can change and write a new today and tomorrow. Your life is your script, and you are the writer and director of your book, play, musical and movie.

Whenever you are abused and hurt and are improperly loved by those closest to you or someone in a position of authority over you, like family, friends, neighbors, educators, various types of teachers, coaches or church administrators, I know that you are destined to harm yourself and others because abused and hurt people, abuse and hurt other people! You have to get your mental health right to get on the right path to total relationship wellness! The decision to change your mind and behavior is owned and controlled by you. You cannot worry about what you cannot control and how others will think about your choices for a better future. I cannot use a magic eraser to clean up or clear my felony background. I have to live with the asterisk and notification that is next to my name and often shared and whispered to others to diminish my character and respect levels with others.

Always know that *"No weapons formed against you shall prosper!"* [234] The key phrase is knowing that weapons will form against you! However, they will not prosper, win, or conquer you! **<u>HATERS ARE GOING TO HATE ALWAYS!</u>**

I once was stuck up on my way home walking with a friend, and before I knew it there was a gun pointed at my face and a guy dressed in all black with a burglar's black ski mask on shouting, "Run it down, son! You know what time it is!" The crazy part about this transaction was knowing that I was not even afraid for my life or scared to die. My life didn't flash in front of me! I didn't think about my family or future. All I remember next is hearing the rapid sound of cha cha cha cha cha like scurrying feet that sounded like the leaves blowing profusely with hurricane winds like Usain Bolt running down the track to set the Olympic and World records.

Before I knew it, the stick-up kid was looking me straight in the eye, and within a flash, he took off his mask and said, "Antoine! Boyyy, I almost served your a** N****! You didn't even flinch. You looked like you wanted me to shoot you or you didn't care if I did! You got heart little homie! Who the hell was that chicken who ran? Was that your cousin Teeny?" It wasn't Teeny! Teeny would have never left my side. Teeny would have stood there expecting me to do something heroic. He definitely would have stayed with me if it meant we both lost our lives.

I told him it was not my cousin and told him it was nobody I knew and that we were just walking home from the basketball courts. The truth was that if he knew who it was, the streets would have relentlessly joked, robbed, jacked, teed off, tenderized and pulverized that kid for the rest of his life. He would have had to turn in his man card because he would have been emasculated by the boys and girls in the neighborhood and at school for the rest of his days. The sad truth is my friend who ran, lost his life just a few years later. His death still bothers me because had I been around, he would still be here making money with me. Laughing at his jokes and hearing his raspy voice made my day! His murder is still unsolved after 30 years.

The bottom line is the reason I did not flinch was quite simple in that how do you kill something that is already dead or prepared to die? I was heartless and heartbroken at the same time from the abuse. My uncles and older cousins always said, "I would be a sissy if I cried or ran away from anything and that real men just take it on the chin and in the chest like a soldier ready to die!" The irony is none of them ever served in the military or even volunteered civilly for anything to my knowledge. My aunt Marty and mother, a couple of great uncles by marriage, cousins, distant relatives, and a few neighbors are the only ones that I know of who served, and they never challenged my manhood in that regard! Military men are ok!

You have to begin by trusting someone and that someone is God. If He made you and you were made in His image and likeness, then you have it in you to be royalty and respected regardless of whether people like you or not! If He is the Creator and we were made in His image, that makes us all Creators! You just have to change your mind and believe. ***"God created mankind in his own image."*** [235] ***Do not be conformed to this world, but be transformed by the renewal of your mind, that by testing you may discern what is the will of God, what is good and acceptable and perfect."*** [236]

You will certainly open up a universe that you probably would have thought never existed. Like the University of Maryland Baltimore County (UMBC) men's basketball team against number one seeded Virginia in the 2018 NCAA men's basketball tournament. A number sixteen seeded team had never beaten a number 1 ranked team in the history of the college tournament. What the world believed would be impossible becomes possible! Ask Heavyweight Boxing Champion and an even greater Champion of Fathers, George Foreman about restoration with the "Foreman Grill" and winning the title at that oldest age at the time by defeating youthful Michael Moore. As long as you have breath in your body and are of sound mind, you can change and be the person you want to be and must be to function in any environment properly.

What would you do if you spotted a poisonous snake or wild animals such as a wolf, grizzly bear, lion, or alligator just outside the window of your school classroom? Would you just sit there and not say something to your teacher or would you ignore it? What if you saw there were some other students about to unknowingly leave the school and were to go straight out the door into the path of the poisonous and wild animal? Would you say or do something? How would you react? How would you feel if you were one of the unknowing students just about to go out the door right into the path of a dangerous animal? Would you want someone to let you know? Would you sit silently, or would you sound the alarm? Bystanders and Sideliners are letting violence, child abuse, and bullying to exist because they are not saying or doing anything!

Please join me in a FAMILY MANKIND™ environment for a fireside chat with others just like you and others there to support and encourage you. We have a No Judgment Law and a FAMILY MANKIND™ private and privileged discussion! You do not have to be careful with whom you share your deepest thoughts unless you plan on putting them in a book or play script and they are copywritten because your thoughts will not be used against you with the persons you shared them. No one will be mad or upset with you nor have any hidden agendas.

Our environment is abuser-friendly whereby we understand some friends and family are too reckless when it comes to your feelings. Some are vindictive and very vengeful and don't mind profiting off of your pain. Here we like telling secrets because to be healed it must be revealed. The truth will truly set your mind and soul free! It does not rain every day. Eventually, the sun will shine again. Get with me and let us shine together. Our culture is 1000% ANONYMOUS in nature!

Embrace your asterisk and change the meaning behind the asterisk next to your name. Admit your weaknesses and ignorance's that are killing your relationships. Come out of the shadows and darkness that is clouding your judgment and preventing you from being what you want to be to others.

Stay out of court for any and everything negative. Have a clean driver's license record. Ask yourself, "Do you want someone to send police officers to your family's residence for a death notification? Do you want to steal someone else's sunshine? How will you live your only lifetime impacting people around you?" Just know that when your will and talent exceeds your deficiencies, adversities or disabilities, success and money will chase you down.

Your talents will overcome all hindrances, disabilities, and adversities! If you are at the bottom and have experienced incredible losses just know that the Lord will restore! I pray for you right now, "Lord, Let My Will Be Done!" Maybe your reward is only going to be for Heaven and not on this earth! So be anxious for nothing and do not fret what people think about you. What do you think about you?

What does God think about you? He forgives and forgets. Renew yourself and cleanse your spirit and soul with a new way of living right now! You are exactly why I created FAMILY MANKIND™! For All Mankind I Love You! Managing Anger and Abuse Now Kindly! I want to help people like you who were just like me...UNWANTED AND BROKEN HEARTED! We just have to be KIND and non-judgmental in our approach to help each other and people who are just like us!

I know what happens to an individual once society deems you a social pariah and has judged you as a worthless piece of crap? Do you want your epitaph to read deadbeat, woman or wife beater, batterer, man-eater, animal cruelest, federal hate offender, homophobic? How will you be remembered and how do you want to be remembered? Have you destroyed or tainted your legacy? Is there an asterisk next to your name? Where do you go to live and earn income to take care of yourself and those relying entirely on you to exist when you have been blackballed and blacklisted? Who forgives these heinous human beings and their despicable acts? How long will this black cloud rain down a fire of misery? Is there an ass for every seat when it comes to these individuals? How and why do you hurt the ones you love, including yourself, and who love you? How do they ease the pain when they know that you are coming back to them again? What is (this type of) love? Baby don't hurt me! Don't hurt me! Don't hurt me! No more! No more! No more!

What is amazing to me is that many of these victimizers are great philosophers and promise-makers and are masquerading as a FAMILY MAN™ or the Good Guy/Girl or a Man's Man or Woman's Woman. They are pleasant to talk to or write or even visit at the penitentiary or jail, but who are they in reality when the cameras aren't rolling, or figures of authority and those they respect aren't around to see or listen to the real monster or prevent violence and abuse from occurring! What happens when these individuals are set to be released? Have they conned the probation and parole authorities or the correctional administrators or the mental health caretaker? Are they prepared or scared to be involved in any relationship? Does excitement remain or is it replaced with fear and anxiety-like an escaped wild animal from the zoo? Society now has to deal with this released manimal or womanimal. In some cases, it is a loved one, colleague, child, animal, or an individual who is hated just because of their sexual identity who bears the brunt of this untamed inhumane offender.

Your negative actions impact others! Ask your children or your boss if you or your boss can potentially lose your or their job for keeping you employed! Is that not right Rob Porter and Tony Baker? How many people will stop supporting you, your cause, or business and unfollow or unlike you on social media platforms? Are you prepared to be the head of hypocrisy? No one will ever care about your fame, but rather your character and your legacy will forever be remembered impactfully for what you positively contributed to someone's life! Do you believe you can get away with domestic violence, child abuse, rape, murder, molestation, or stalking? Are you that arrogant that you actually believe you can beat and outwit ballistic science, well-seasoned veteran investigative detectives, DNA, CSI, Forensics, License Plate Readers, surveillance cameras everywhere, scientific, GPS, cell phone tracking technology, digital wanted signs, Live PD, Amber Alerts, Code Adam, and amazing grace prayers? Are you a coward who is willing to commit a crime because you are a jealous predator not willing to accept rejection or move on away from her? Instead of facing a judge, jury or God you thought it was best to murder?

How can you possibly win if every heinous criminal is always eventually caught? Was it worth it? Would you do it differently if you could take it back? What type of person can literally and figuratively watch the life; soul, and spirit of an individual leave their body? You cannot possibly be human to witness such an act upon an innocent individual! How do you cope? Do you attend Family Mankind™ meetings consistently? Why couldn't I have spoken to Rae Carruth or Van Brett Watkins and their co-conspirators long or seconds before they brought upon a tragedy of horrific proportions? I would have at least tried to be the voice of reason and consequence. Now my little guy Lee and his mighty right hand of God strength grandmother Saundra have to push past the pain every single day for the rest of their lives? Who will take care of Lee when Saundra is in heaven with Cherica? Cherica and Lee were somebody's baby's too! Did you think about the pain you would cause your family Ray or Van Brett? Aren't you someone's baby too? My videotape is not out there or gone viral for the world to see like Ray Rice, Kareem Hunt, or O.J. Simpson's and Chad "Ochocinco" Johnson's former wife's black-eyed photograph but I and many others in the dark and behind the walls are just as guilty, and many have done even worse! I do not want another professional athlete or any fan to experience the incredible pain, hardships, losses, and embarrassment that comes with the after effects of domestic violence! We cannot blame anyone but ourselves!

God has to take back some of His babies sooner than others because of the inhumane ways of man and He needs to add to His continuous growing army of angels. Let Him make those calls up to heaven! We should never think that we can harm God's property or play God to decide someone's ultimate fate on earth!

The crazy thing about being an abuser is I tried to control my girlfriend and wife in so many violent and abusive ways, that the only ironic aspect about "control" was that I wanted people to respect my "control," but I was the one who could not even "control" or respect myself. I was completely out of "control and my mind!"

The truth about *Violence and Abuse* is if left untreated, "**It**" is not a matter of "**If**" "**It**" will occur again, but rather it is "**When**" "**It**" will happen again and again. I am a testimony that "**It**" will happen again without professional help or without help from an organization like Family Mankind™! I made the common mistake of thinking I could beat "**It**" by myself! Domestic violence has beaten World Champs! If you think you can or cannot beat "**It**" (*Violence and Abuse*), you are already defeated and destined for destruction, doom, and death! If you want to fight or beat up someone or something, fight Violence and Abuse! I promise you that the *Violence and Abuse* is an undisputed champion against individuals who think they can beat "**It**" alone in the ring of life. If you doubt you can beat "**It**" *Violence and Abuse* has already won. You are an amateur to this and that is why you must seek a professional. "**It**" even once put retired boxing champion Floyd Mayweather Jr. on his back and in jail for a short period. He is the G.O.A.T, undisputed, undefeated champion. If "**It**" happened to the money man as hard-hitting as he is, who are you? Why Floyd Jr? *"It"* defeated Floyd Mayweather Sr.

This challenge should make you stronger, not weaker. If you are face down or your back is on the canvas rise to your challenger and take your destiny! Are you a coward afraid of facing rejection from others? There are consequences for your actions! Now you will not be invited back as the featured alumni speaking at the graduation commencement or fundraising event where they auction off a signed item of yours. You were clearly once the talk of the town and the big man on campus whose tweets, and YouTube videos went viral! Now you are just viral to social media, and you are unliked on Instagram, no longer followed by others on Twitter, and unfriended on Facebook. I want our heroes & sheroes to stay heroes & sheroes!

Someone will melt your Heisman to the ground, or you will be asked to return it with the key to the city and your honorary degrees! Your statue will permanently be removed or sold for scraps. Hall of Fame, absolutely not now or possibly never because of the possible political fallout and no one willing to vote for you, but definitely a vote for the Hall of Shame or Infamy! Think twice or more!

Solutions To Permanently Eradicate Domestic Violence, Child Abuse, and Bullying

Are you going to abandon your responsibilities? Is it that easy to run away from your mental health and meaningful relationships? What is the value of your freedom? Would you kill someone for any amount of money? If someone disrespected you would you kill them? Are you a contender or pretender? I get you & want you? What is your deal? ***You have to eradicate the pain in your brain Bro!***

Violence and abuse against women, children, or animals will dethrone you even if you are the king of boxing like Mike Tyson or knock you down like Riddick Bowe. It will sack your legacy and potentially sideline you like Ray Rice, Michael Vick, Tyreek Hill or Kareem Hunt. Your Heisman Trophy and chances to get into the Hall of Fame or the removal of your statue will be melted down, diminished and destroyed like the legacy of O.J. Simpson, Chad "Ochocinco" Johnson or Joe Paterno!

You may have to resign or retire from your post under suspicion or job allegedly like Urban Meyer and may never get elected to any office if you are like Eric Schneiderman or Tony Baker! CEO will no longer stand for Chief Executive or Entertaining Officer and will be replaced by Chief Exited Official like Russell Simmons or Harvey Weinstein! No one wants to see your movies or television shows Kevin Spacey! To hell with your music R. Kelly! Here comes the suits G!

Now you have to sell or leave your own company that you have headed since day one! Jerry Richardson, Mario Batali, and Russell Simmons can testify to this fact. Your parking spot that was painted or had a post with your name and title along with the placard on your door and your picture and name on the company's official website has been repainted, replaced, or removed immediately and permanently!

How can you be a mentor to young men and our youth if you are not living up to what you are preaching and coaching, or you are culpable by not saying anything or doing enough to protect victims of domestic violence and child abuse? Is winning a football game more important than protecting the innocent and helpless or was it about the money or defending your violent and abusive friend's secret more critical? Was it that important now?

Now your legacy is permanently tied to harboring and protecting a violent offender? Would you have protected them the way you have so loyally had it been your child or wife they were abusing or violently offending? No one who has been impacted by violence or who is a sympathizer and empathizer wants your autograph, interview, opinion, time, money, or anything to do with you and anything you are associated. Your stock is worth zero, and you have just been served a death sentence for something you could have changed if you had decided to be proactive about a solution to prevent violence and abuse against women or children! A child's age does matter and it ain't just a number R. Kelly! Great men like Urban Meyer and Joe Paterno were scorched because of someone else's criminal behavior as a result of being an alleged bystander and "Sideliner" to the crimes! Nobody is going to support the "Sideliner" for supporting the alleged abuser!

Now you know a millionth of a fraction of what your victims feel like to be silenced by violence, abused and violated! How does it feel? Do you like your new position in life? Do you like the black carpet and the press now? After being made famous for your reporting and interviews the interviewer and writer of headlines who is paid millions annually to do it five times a week, now the article and headlines are about you! Do you like the fact that no one laughs at you no matter how funny or corny they be! Is that not right Louie C.K., Bill Cosby, or Al Franken? We do not want to hear your perspective on politics and news commentary Matt Lauer, Tom Brokaw, and Charlie Rose! Welcome to the club of the wanted* and unwanted*!

The #MeToo and #TimesUp movement is justified and will never go away or lose momentum! I live for the day when politically positioned men start getting raped or violently beat and abused by their partners and strange men on the street, not just when they are incarcerated, and the world now becomes a foreign place they can't recognize, only then will they know how women and children feel! They will also see how the lenient a** laws and the violent and abusive politicians who legislate these biased, shameful, weak laws, that do not punish and rehabilitate abusers and violent offenders! When they as a victim now feels the life sentence of pain! Only then will the laws become fair and just to the victims too! When someone violently abuses an innocent, defenseless woman, child, member of the LGBTQ community, a disabled person, or an animal and is found guilty of it and receives a light sentence if any sentence at all, is another slap in the face to the abused! Let the violator feel a stiff punch in the face or gut by the strong arm of the law! Let them awake in a jail or prison cell or hospital bed or coffin confused, reluctant to tell, stuck, beat, bruised, bleeding or ashamed, filled with self-blame or survivor's remorse or embarrassed or helpless or dead!

Victims of violence and abuse receive a life sentence or worst, a death sentence! For their entire lives, they are reminded in subtle and blatant ways of your torture that keeps them locked up in their minds or confined and imprisoned to a lifetime of secrecy and shame! Does it matter when or why you abused, threatened, or harassed your victim? No excuses, exceptions, or passes.

If you want a chance for your spouse or children to stay with you, you must immediately admit that you are an abuser and then you must submit to getting help and continuous treatment and solutions for domestic violence or child abuse. You must get healed entirely and delivered from the pain in your mind, body, and soul and the only way to achieve a permanent solution is to learn proven techniques through a repetitive, proactive process! Prescription pain relievers are temporary tactics like putting a Band-Aid on a gunshot wound. Do not be ashamed and do not battle the pain by yourself in the dark because you and your situation are not unique to domestic violence, bullying, and child abuse. People are standing by who are ready to take the journey with you into the light, just as someone has done with them.

What title do you want to be crowned? A Permanently Labeled Abuser, Domestic Violence Offender, Batterer, Victimizer of Violence, Woman Beater, Predator, Silencer! Be still and hear me clearly Bro! Psalm 46:10. ***Come out of the shadows of death and never step into the darkness that prohibits people from shining their "little lights!"*** [237] Do not be publicly "marked for death" or feel the humiliation, shame, and embarrassment that comes with being labeled an abuser, bully, or domestic violence offender.

In all of my dreams or nightmares, I never saw myself as that kind of person who would be permanently labeled as a victimizer of violence or predator. If you are going to be labeled something be labeled a success or server of others or a genuine friend or a professional/expert of some profession or industry. Be labeled an author or teacher or encourager. The label and asterisk that will always stay next to my name and will follow me to the grave on my headstone will be B.A.P. The B stands for "Benevolent" which means disposed to doing good. The A is for "Altruistic!" which means I am generally concerned about the welfare of others! The P stands for "Philanthropic" which means I am working to give money to charitable organizations for humanitarian purposes.

Sure I will permanently be labeled a convicted felon, but that will never define my life but rather a moment in time that built me to become "The FAMILY MAN™!" The same would define you if you decided to become who you wanted to be in your one lifetime. So, what that you made a mistake or an unfortunate error in judgment that has other people judging you! Who's opinion really matters other than God Almighty? God forgives us and does not continue to judge after repenting!

What most of these abusers want and so desperately need are love and respect! This is why I am not calling them out, but instead, I am calling them in to receive the love and respect from an individual who is just like them but has the secret sauce to get them on a mentally healthy path, so they do not harm others via domestic violence, child abuse or bullying! They should not need to join a gang or a cult to be accepted. They do it to be acknowledged, respected and moreover to feel loved and a part of a semblance of a family! How would you feel if you were abandoned or abused by your parents or family?

What if you were never adopted and timed out of foster care? The human body, soul, and mind needs love as much as food and water! People are lonely and alone trying to satisfy society's rules of acceptance. Meanwhile, kids are timing out of the foster care system, not being adopted, are not dating, and not going to the prom because no one asked them. No one should be celebrating birthdays alone. No one is in the stands cheerleading for their children and loved ones. No one should be alone in the hospital because no one can come to visit. No one is bringing housewarming gifts to your new home. No one should be having a lonely baby or bridal shower! We should be celebrating life's best positive moments and experiences together that stand the tests of time.

Get up every morning to the book of Proverbs and go to bed to the book of Psalms. You will rest peacefully when you purposely are working to make a difference in your life that ultimately makes an impact in other people's lives. Meditate on this verse as I do daily and what gave me peace during and after my time in the penitentiary and psychiatric hospital. These were the instructions on how to deal with the many different scenarios that play out in your life and the ways to overcome certain scenarios and deal with people.

Psalm 23-A Psalm of David.

1-The Lord is my shepherd; I shall not want and lack nothing. 2- He makes me lie down in green pastures, He leads me beside quiet waters, 3- He refreshes and restores my soul. He guides me along the right paths of righteousness for His name's sake. 4- Even though I walk through the darkest valley of the shadows of death, I will fear no evil, for You are with me; Your rod and Your staff, they comfort me. 5- You prepare a table before me in the presence of my enemies. You anoint my head with oil; my cup overflows and runneth over!

6- Surely Your goodness and love will follow me all the days of my life, and I will dwell in the house of the Lord forever. [238]

Always remember, *"No weapons formed against you shall prosper!"* [234] Think about what that says. Weapons, or in this case, life will send some bad situations, things and people your way, but they will not prosper, meaning they will not break you, your will, or your spirit! They will never conquer you because God is with you. You are His greatest creation! Your life is priceless and never meant to be destroyed or diminished! You are worth more than anything of value! Know that He is fighting your battles, but you have to be a soldier in His Military and not Man's!

Where did the pain, trauma, or drama originate to cause you to become an abuser? What were the specific, detailed moments in your life that caused you to become an abuser? Who was the specific individual who influenced your character to become an abuser? Can you imagine someone abusing your child the way you abuse another individual's child? How do you want your epitaph to read? How do you wish to be remembered from a legacy standpoint? You do realize you are living your first, last, and only lifetime? What traits did you give to your future bloodline? It is never too late, unless you're dead, to rewrite your legacy or at least write the finale or final chapter or act correctly to make things Right! Who wants to be remembered as an abuser or have that inscribed on their tombstone or written in the obituary? If God created you, that act alone states that you were made perfectly and priceless! God did not make a mistake. Man screws up what God intended to be beautiful and loved respectfully. It is that we have not been shown or educated properly and appropriately on how to cope and love others as well as ourselves.

I always think about how I truly believed I could beat being an abuser by myself without professional guidance and support. Like I could just hit a switch or perform a magic trick and "poof be gone abuse!" Dealing with the issue of being an abuser is like trying to separate conjoined twins from the head and heart, and you've never performed or witnessed any surgery in your life or trying to figure out a Rubik's cube for the very first time. Generally speaking, only a handful of geniuses on this planet can accomplish such daunting feats and even then how many would take the chance. For any individual struggling to figure abuse out or worse, believing they can heal themselves of the disease without the appropriate solution, truly is destined for a self-prescribed repeat of pain, trauma, crying, destruction and final dose of death! If I handed you a Rubik's cube for the very first time and told you had 4 minutes to solve it or you are dead could you do it? What if I handed you a grenade with a combination on it that could stop it from exploding and then I pulled the pin without telling you the combination would you be able to figure it out? Not getting help for your issues is as lethal as any example I have provided!

You have never been trained or seen how to provide the solution to your abusive nature, and so naturally, it is going to explode in your face killing you and possibly those around you! The sad or ignorant part is that should you live long enough you will then probably get the help you need, not by choice but rather by force! Again, my greatest regret and mistake in life is waiting too long to get the help I so desperately needed and as a result, the violence ended up beating me to the doctors in the psychiatric ward of a prison hospital. Don't wait before it's too late.

I WANT YOU AROUND TO EXPERIENCE THE MOMENTS IN YOUR CHILDREN'S LIVES THAT WILL BE DEFINING MOMENTS TO BOTH YOU AND THEM THAT THEY WILL NEVER FORGET AS LONG AS THEY HAVE BREATH AND CHERISH FOREVER! YOU MUST BE THERE, TO BE THERE FOR THEM OR YOU RUN THE RISK OF THEM QUESTIONING WHY YOU WERE NOT THERE AT THOSE TIMES!

Dear Domestic Violence Offender, Batterer, Woman Beater, Child Abuser, and Bully, If you have just a moment to listen to me, I would just like to tell you that I love you and would never judge you! You are wanted by me and the many others who love you! You have to want to be the better person you want to be and the person everyone who loves you knows you are capable of being, which is a loving & phenomenal person…A Family Man!

I have the title and label no one wants: Permanently Disenfranchised Convicted Felon! I am an executive platinum, diamond, gold and key club member of the WANTED* and UNWANTED* ASS-OCIATION reserved exclusively for individuals who abuse their intimate partners, spouses, and mates! Trust me when I tell you that this behavior is dangerous for your life and legacy. If you love your partner or mate more than yourself, you really need to get with me now so we can discuss how we can eradicate the violence in your life!

They are not your property! You should never think "If I can't have 'em, no one else will!" They belong to God just like you do friend. Is it right to through acid in their face to disfigure them for life? How'd you like someone to do that to you or someone you actually care about like a parent or child? ***<u>You should not want what does not want you! Let them go on to their destination so you can too!</u>***

Solutions To Permanently Eradicate Domestic Violence, Child Abuse, and Bullying

My greatest failure in life was to not take the advice immediately from individuals who honestly had a genuine love for me and my welfare! I chose to not get help with my violent temper and propensity to violence towards humankind and my dog Toby, and it cost me a path in life that I wish upon no one. I plead to all violent offenders, child abusers, and bullies to please stand up, step forward, ***HOWL*** and ***GET HELP NOW! DO NOT WAIT!***

If you or someone you love is a domestic violence offender, child abuser, or bully, please call or text the National Batterers, Child Abusers, and Bullies Howl For Helpline at **833-3HOWLER (833-346-9537)** or go to our website to chat at www.familymankind.org.

If you are a victim of domestic violence call the National Domestic Violence Hotline at **1-800-799-7233 or TTY at 1-800-787-3224.**

If you are a rape victim, please call the National Sexual Assault Hotline at **1-800-656-4673**.

If you are a child abuse victim, please call or text ChildHelp National Child Abuse Hotline at **1-800-422-4453.**

If you are being bullied and are having feelings of suicide, please call the **LIFELINE at 1-800-273-(TALK)8255.**
DO NOT WAIT LIKE I DID! MAKE THE CALL or TEXT NOW!
SAVE YOUR LIFE or The LIFE of SOMEONE YOU LOVE!
YOUR CALLS WILL REMAIN COMPLETELY ANONYMOUS.
1-833-3HOWLER or 1-833-346-9537

Solutions To Permanently Eradicate Domestic Violence, Child Abuse, and Bullying

ARE YOU A WOLF OR CHICKEN?

The Speed Of The Pack Depends On The Speed Of The Leader!
The "Life" Of The Family Depends On The "Life" Of The Leader!

People ask me all the time what does A.W. stand for and I about always say "A Wolf" with an "Amazing Will" because I have an "Awesome Wife" and four daughters and thus I have "All Women" in my house! I have always been hungry like "A Wolf" when it comes to working for an income. I even have a picture of me going to first grade with a briefcase type satchel. (Go Back To Page 106)

I realized early in life I had to be a wolf, a leader, when my mother would, "Always Whine" and complain that she never had enough money to buy me name brand clothes or jewelry or Air Jordans because she was a teacher and "Teachers do not make a lot of money!" Right then my mission became crystal clear that if I could not get what I wanted in life from my mom, I would have to go get it myself because no one was going to give it to me for free or if they did there was a hidden agenda in exchange for what they had given me. Receiving something for free for me was a bad option or a slave's contract and dangerous proposition or bait for someone to extort or pimp me. I was never going to sign up for that "Baltimore Trap" deal.

I was a natural negotiator who always knew my worth corporately! The strange truth is when I was selling cars as a 25-year-old youngster, the older men, Greg Hayes, and Richard McGough use to affectionately say A.W. stood for "Always Working" or "At Work" because of my relentless and tireless work ethic. I truly appreciated the encouragement and was always flattered by their comments because I respected them from the fact that these two men truly were family men who fiercely committed their lives to take care of their responsibilities as husbands and fathers! Greg Hayes had successfully navigated his way up the ladder of success at the Hendrick Automotive Group, and I remember asking him what it took to make big money at Hendrick and in his fatherly direct manner of communicating he replied, "Results and Relationships!" He made it very clear to me that I had to be relentless and not ruthless when it came to making a name for myself at Hendrick.

It was obvious to me that all I needed to do was out-hustle any and every employee, regardless of their goals and dreams! I had to think like I was the owner and this business was my baby to care for because nobody was going to give me anything to take care of my family and my legacy. I worked seven days a week for

Hendrick Imports which is now called Hendrick BMW, Hendrick Porsche, and Land Rover of Charlotte located in Charlotte, North Carolina off of Independence Blvd.

The dealership was open six days and closed on Sundays. Mr. Hendrick was a phenomenal owner who treated and compensated us like royalty. I knew that for me to stand out in the Hendrick pack, my results and attitude would separate me from the others who shared the same corporate ambitions. There were no other options and excuses left for me other than to be phenomenal and passionate! I was there on Sunday's by choice, working the car lot to provide information such as brochures or to answer any customer questions without ever being pushy or sounding like a car salesperson. I was there strictly to build honest relationships because I was not from Charlotte and knew absolutely no one. How do you make a name for yourself when you know no one? I stayed focus and hungry to get to my dreams! I wanted not only to outwork my fellow colleagues, but I also wanted to outwork all BMW salespeople in the world, not just North or South Carolina.

In my mind, I always thought like the owner, and so this was "Burgess BMW" and I was taking care of my customers! The fact was I was treating Mr. Hendrick's dealership as if I was babysitting one of his children. If the boss trusted you enough to babysit and care for his child at his house, you would be incredibly diligent and make sure the baby never wanted or needed anything. You would ensure the baby was properly cared for by way of making sure they were fed on time and burping them so that they would not get colicky. You would keep their diapers fresh and dry! They would be bathed properly and oiled and powdered to look and smell like a brand-new car just bought and driven off the new car showroom floor. You would guard, protect and defend them with your life like the secret service guarding the President of the United States of America. You would pray for them and their safety, so they would never be harmed and for them to live a healthy and prosperous life. You would do this not because it was your job or duty, but to protect your good name so you would never be fired for doing a horrible job with the boss's baby! I carried these sentiments with me every day I went to work at Hendrick. I believed that if I took care of his babies, he would naturally take care of my babies.

I got permission to work the lot on Sundays from the executive general manager John Fornshell. We referred to him as "The Great White" because he had pearly white hair and because like the apex of all sharks in the ocean is called "The Great White Shark" he was the apex "Great White Manager" for 5 dealerships. He exuded respect and strength from all employees. He was direct and honest with you and never threw a punch that you did not see coming or deserved. He was incredibly passionate and possessed a relentless will to win and make as much money as humanly possible but within the laws of the land.

He, E. Bronson Ingram and Rick Hendrick singlehandedly became the best examples for me of how to manage a business and people. They were individuals who corporately gave two bits about my future and who displayed firsthand how a man is supposed to provide and protect his family. Rogers Glover Sr. would soon after that show me this same type of love on a personal level through his phenomenal son Alfred. These men were all "Men's Men!" These men were "Stand Up Guys!" I always wanted to be considered a "Man's Man" by anyone who came into contact with me. All these men inspired me to always know that within me lies an "Amazing Will" that will always motivate me to do right by my family, friends, and society!

These men in my eyes of the world are viewed as figurative Apex wolves to me. How and why you might ask? Wolves travel in packs, which means they are traveling and living with their family members. They balance and create a healthy and thriving ecosystem! Ask the park rangers at Yellowstone National Park about the significance of the reintroduction of the wolf and the benefits to the other animals and plant life along with that of humankind. The benefits outweigh the costs!

Wolves are accountable to their young and each other. The success of the pack depends on how each contributes to their role. If one gets out of line or tries to disrespect the pack, the alpha male or female usually jumps in and corrects them. If one wolf decides to get greedy or becomes selfish with their agenda they put the entire pack at risk of not being successful predators to eat and survive. This accountability increases the packs' chances for a formidable and prosperous future as hunters because the odds of prey escaping the pack once they are locked in on them are minimal. The speed and direction of the pack are directly dependent on the speed and direction of the leadership of the pack. These alphas are showing their offspring and other family members what you have to do to survive now and tomorrow in the wilderness. They are giving you the tools to get and stay out of the mud and quicksand and how to survive through the treacherous droughts and winters.

I am a felon who is considered the great wolf in the business world because of my professional aggression towards making deals and my positive hostile energy towards having an impact on people's lives and legacies. This positive and professional aggression is what sets me apart from others, but it indeed is who I am as a sincere person. America loves to see that criminal bad boy, aggressive and hostile role on television or in the movies, a play or juicy book, but what happens to those same sentiments when it moves next door to you or it is staring you in the0 face asking for a job, so they can feed themselves, their babies or their family?

A wolf is a pure killer if you do not know how to treat it properly. It is the purest and most aggressive form of a domesticated dog. A healthy portion of America loves dogs. It has become a part of the family and American culture. When I got older, all I heard was, "I just want to get married, have 2 kids and a dog...2.5." The difference today though is that America hates the aggressive breeds of dogs and are excluding them when and wherever they can. I see on housing and rental agreements "No aggressive breeds permitted! No Exceptions!" Think about animal cruelty and abuse.

You will hear all the experts say that the dogs who attack are direct reflections of how they were treated and trained by their owners or handlers. Most animals are out to please and pleasure their owners and are just trying to display their loyalty and respect. The animals are suffering for no sound reason other than they were just an animal and their owners are just lazy, ignorant, ruthless, and heartless savages. Then we kill them when they attack or do what is normal to them!

Like people, most animals who attack, such as dogs, lions, tigers, and elephants are trained under abusive conditions by mentally unhealthy individuals. These are wild animals that we are trying to domesticate, but we humans are the ones committing domestic violence and abuse against them as if we are animals too.

Growing up I have witnessed dogs killed by some pretty psychotic and evil individuals who were senseless and unable to have compassion. I know because I was once one of them. I saw my friend kill an "annoying" dog with a skateboard to show and prove his masculinity. This act of violence did not even phase me when it happened, and I was almost happy that this dog would no longer be "annoying" or bothering us on our way home from school! I was numb to the violence and unphased by the welfare or fate of the dog let alone the feelings of the dog's owners.

I could not imagine today being around any individual who would even think of committing such a vile and evil act towards any innocent and defenseless animal, let alone being a "Sideliner" who does not stop it. I know I would never be able to witness the sights or sounds from such a killing. How cruel and cowardice of such an evil and hateful individual. No one with love in their body would allow such an act today, but the sad reality is these types of acts or worst play out against humans and animals every single day in the world. Babies, women, great-hearted men, children, churchgoers, students, athletes, musicians, members of the LGBTQ community, neighbors, pets, zoo animals, and even wild animals are literally being hunted down, killed, unfairly abused and violently offended every single day!

This violence is just deplorable and has to stop because too many people are unjustly losing their lives and innocence to ignorant, violent and evil people who are heartless, spiritually dead and numb to the abuse and pain they are inflicting. These individuals are crying out for help and are desperate to know why this is happening to them. All I can say is that I did not have any sensitivity to feelings when it came to dealing with animals because humans were always the sources of my pain. But when I met a dog named Roscoe, who was the family dog of my former girlfriend's family, I felt unconditional and reciprocal love. This dog was a hilarious and intuitive friend who never judged me, and whenever I came around, he greeted me with respect, hugs & a ton of slobber. He was the animal friend I always needed!

When I think about my love for Roscoe and Toby, I am reminded by the rapper DMX. After reading his book *E.A.R.L,* and just following his career and life, I always knew why he turned out the way he did because I can relate! Like me, why couldn't his parents, not just his grandmother, love him the way his dogs loved him and the way he loved his dogs, so that he would have been able to healthily first love himself and then his wife and children? Why couldn't his parents be proud and excited to see him and his talents like his children once did as babies and dogs do all the time when they look at him when he gets home from work. He was just like them as a baby and child excited and extremely happy to see his parents too but where were they and where did they go when he needed them most as a child? All he could ever rely on and trust with no pain in return was his grandma and his dogs to give him love and receive his love in return. Earl Simmons will always be my brother because we share the same heart and love for dogs and serving others. I know his reasons for staying in and out of jail and prison too. That's his story to tell!

I cried out for God to answer me why I destroyed my life and how I arrived in the penitentiary and psychiatric hospital when I should have been graduating from college and getting married to my high school sweetheart and working for Ingram Industries while attending law school in pursuit of a J.D. and MBA. Why Lord? Why me? Why now? Why my life? The amazing answers did not come to me until I read in the Bible about Solomon and his son David. Solomon and money. The why and heart to encourage yourself by David. You have to read those stories on your own versus getting the synopsis from me. All I can tell you is it will give you inspiration regarding coming to your own rescue and that money will not solve your problems. All the solutions to your problems are already in you waiting for you!

My question to you is, "Are you a wolf or chicken?" The original breed of man! Authentic and genuine! A breed apart! A breed like no other. A true one of a kind. Are you a wolf in sheep's clothing who is deceptive with a hidden agenda or are you a vampire which is a bloodsucker who sucks the life out of people? I am still passionate and hungry for helping others but please do not take my meekness for weakness! When a wolf smiles you still see the wolf's teeth. It is just that now I am professionally aggressive and hostile about getting domestic violence offenders, child abusers, and bullies' permanent solutions to eradicate violence and abuse.

I want you to trust me when I say I have the best intentions and interests of the victimizers and the victims of violence. I say this because I have always seen things different from others! Remember, most people see the word CANCER or as you break it down CAN-CER. I see it this way...add **VIVE** to it, meaning *"long life"*... CAN-SUR... meaning CAN SURVIVE™! We have to push past the pain and see the possibility of a *long life* on the other side of violence and abuse. Give it life!

The difference though is to accomplish this seemingly impossible task you the victimizer must first ***"Know your numbers!"*** When you are trying to get healthy you go to the doctor so they can run a series of test to check your total health such as for high blood pressure, cholesterol levels, blood glucose levels, etc., to see where you are health-wise, so you can live longer! What you do not *"**know**"* can kill you!

That is what I need from everyone around me, so we can always ***know*** what we do well as a functioning human being and then where are our deficiencies and dysfunctions so that we can grow as individuals from there! Once we know where the deficiencies lie we can work towards the solutions. This is where the transformation begins from being a puppy to a full-fledged wolf. This is where we are leaving the dysfunctions of acting like a chicken, winging our daily problems with no solutions, to be an accountable, mentally healthy ***FAMILY INDIVIDUAL!***

The main reason I ask people are they a wolf or chicken is that I am trying to see what type of spirit and heart they possess towards others and themselves! Wolves travel in what? That is right. They travel in packs! In essence, they are traveling with their family. Each pack has an alpha male and female leader who is either successfully guiding the pack to survival, surrender submission, or death! The pack is relying on its leaders to make decisions about eating, warding off other predators and a safe habitat. The difference between a mediocre alpha male and an Apex alpha male is life or death. The pack only follows and fulfills their roles in the pack only if they respect the leadership meeting the needs of the family! The leaders of the pack only reciprocate their love for the pack if those individual wolves are respecting the leadership and are humbly fulfilling their roles in the pack without challenging the authority of the alpha male and female.

When everyone understands their role and fulfills their part, the group hunts successfully, and they collectively ward off other predators. Contrarily though, when a member of the pack decides not to fulfill their role, the pack suffers, and the individual wolf often pays a stiff penalty if not death from the alpha male or female or another predator if they stray away from the pack! The point is, there are alot of people who claim to be wolves, but they really are wolves in sheep's clothing or worse yet, they are really bloodsucking vampires or chickens using another person as a source for survival because they are either lazy or manipulative and would instead let that someone else do all the hard work and once that's done they will slide up to the table to eat more than their fair share.

Wolves do not wait for the food to come to them, they go to the menu. They are strategically fixated on always hunting, whereas chickens are always waiting for someone to come and feed them. That is why their food is literally called "feed"! Wolves do not wait long before they are in hunt mode again. Wolves have this aggressive survival spirit innately planted in their DNA. As leaders of families, if you do not have this in your DNA, it is because it has not been nurtured or you just are not meant to be a leader. I cannot and will not wait for my ship to come in to be successful in life, I have to swim out and find my ship like a pirate and take my ship before someone else claims it for themselves. Always remember that chickens do not eat wolves, but wolves certainly eat chickens. Wolves are strategic planners and hunters whereas chickens are "winging it" every second of their life just waiting to eat or die. Chickens are always running around in fear because they know their necks are easy to snap and that's why they are so nervous and jittery when anything or anyone other than another chicken comes around them.

As a decent and respectful human being, you naturally have it in you to be a successful person who lives a healthy and prosperous mental, physical, emotional and spiritual life. You are not a chicken because you were not built by God to be afraid of anything except Him. Sure, you are going to have your fair share of setbacks in life, but it is how you choose to manage and cope during life's greatest tests and obstacles that depends on how you will survive.

After decades of marriage many ask, "What is the secret to being married a long time A.W.?" Do the things you did to make her love you from the beginning! If you bought her roses and chocolates every day never stop doing so until she tells you to stop! All the promises you made to her keep your word and make good on them. Never go back on your word especially if you know it is going to hurt her feelings. Be early and at worst case be on time for everything. If you are going to be late, make sure you call or text and apologize sincerely and if possible, make it up in a special way by asking them how you can make it right! Do not make this a habit though because then you may become unreliable with your words and promises! Know how to apologize and say sorry for any and everything. Would you rather win the battle but end up losing the war? Win the wars, and you win the war of their heart and soul. Do not lose the war and become a prisoner in your own relationship!

Also, you must be absolutely transparent about your likes and dislikes as well as your finances and goals. Many individuals have domestic issues based on the lies they have said that cannot be substantiated throughout the relationship! For instance, if you meet someone for the first time and you lie about your how much money you have and make or the type of job you have or the type of person you are and how sweet and genuine you are as an individual then what happens when you do not respond accordingly based on your testimonies?

What happens is you are viewed as a fake, shady, hypocritical liar! You have become a traitor and spy in your relationship and this betrayal is tough to make right. Now you are tasked with trying to be something you are not naturally! In essence, you were once viewed as a wolf, a loyal and respectful leader, by the individual who first trusted you, but now you are just a rabid shady domesticated dog! You promised to be the king of the wild and the head of the pack leading the family by becoming a consistent provider, fearless protector, and displaying healthy examples of family love and unity!

You must be a fearless and strategic alpha wolf that has earned the right through sheer respect to provide and protect the pack! When an alpha wolf can no longer provide and protect as a leader, they are either run off, kicked out of the pack or worst, killed by another alpha wolf or pack! The future or preservation of the pack depends solely on the ability of the alpha wolf's abilities and aptitude to lead! It is a mutually reciprocated beneficial relationship based on respect and trust.

What separates a wolf from being a domesticated dog is 1% in the DNA! However, that 1% difference of DNA is incredibly significant in that it makes a wolf an instinctual predator, killer, self-providing strategic hunter and planner versus a domestic dog that relies on humans to provide food and shelter from predators like man and the elements in the world such as the weather and other predators in the wild that can kill it! That 1% is the difference between surviving life and death!

I am certainly not judging, but if at all possible, do not get caught up in the drug game or gang life! I absolutely understand wholeheartedly why people do both because I did both as a youth and as a young adult! I wanted money, power, and respect like most individuals who decide to participate in such activities and a way of life. The truth at the core of it all outside of the fact that if you sell drugs and are making some substantial cash, then the draw of hood fame and notoriety gives you the fancy name brand clothes, shoes, jewelry, cars, vacations, furniture, and electronic devices which ultimately draws the women! What no one tells you, especially the ones committing the crimes with you is that it also draws the police, special law enforcement, competitive drug dealers, rival gangs, street enforcers such as hitmen or as we say in the streets shooters, goons, thugs, stick up kids, or young comer-uppers trying to get a hardcore reputation! No one tells you that the very ones next to you telling you that they keep it real, g, and 100 or 1000% with you all day every day and that you are their brother from another mother will more than likely be the one who "sets" you up to be murdered or robbed or indicted on incredibly serious state and federal charges leading to an even worst seriously long prison stint or date with the devil in hell! Committing crimes with friends will kill friendships!

That is why we say we are at the "set" (at home with our friends/homeboys) because eventually, some of us will get "set" up by someone we know! How many seemingly successful gangsters, drug dealers, bank robbers, and murderers made it out alive or with all the money? The answer is not one! Not one! The trick is they pay with their life and freedom and do not even get to profit from their crimes and others do! Their lawyers become even greater millionaires. The prosecutors and judges make career cases and advances from them and some even profit from book deals and speaking engagements from the notoriety! ***Someone killed my friend!***

Ask Whitey Bulger*, John Gotti*, Pablo Escobar*, Bonnie* and Clyde*, Stanley "Tookie" Williams* who was Co-Founder of the Westside Crips and who consequently died by lethal injection on California's death row, Demetrius "Big Meech" Flenory, Larry Hoover, Howard "Pappy" Mason, Lorenzo "Fat Cat"

Nichols, Kenneth "Supreme" McGriff, Guy Fisher, Jeff Fort, Alpo Martinez, American Gangster Frank Lucas, Sammy "The Bull" Gravano, Rayful Edmond, Nicky Barnes, and Freeway Ricky Ross if crime pays and how fair of a deal they received by the government from the many friends and government officials who snitched on them to save their own life or who set them up for a planned failure.

I would be honored and pissed at the same time every time I heard my name in a song or my image in a television show or movie or on social or print media because of the fool's gold I was deceptively given! Cigarettes, Moonshine, and now weed in some states was once illegal and look at the companies that came up out of the illegal ashes, mountain crops, and backyard distilleries and the forever unimpeded financial fortunes of profit for these illegal individuals! Hell, I did not even realize one could get their hands on propofol or fentanyl until Michael Jackson and Prince were killed! Two icons conned by someone because of tremendous pain.

Fentanyl is stronger and more lethal than heroin or crack, but it is legal. My point is that our games are rigged for someone to win and for us to lose. We become temporary media exploited millionaires and infamous while others become famously silent billionaires. We sell drugs on the corners, right? Where do pharmacies sell their legally prescribed drugs? On the corners! Some drugs are even sold on the internet! We absorb all the risk for an illegal transaction, drug distribution, even though we did not manufacturer or ship the drug from its original country! Pharmacy distributors and pharmaceutical companies pay lobbyists to go to D.C. to make their distribution activities legal!

We either are forced to be snitches that the world now turns on and calls them b*****s which consequently can cause them or others to end up in one of two ditches...the grave or the living dead grave called a penitentiary cell on an extended year stay such as life without parole or federal years where you have got to do at least 85% of the time! That means that in most cases we go into the criminal injustice system as youth and very young men and women and come out as older, wiser soldiers whose best youthful years have passed, and many monumental moments have passed such as births, deaths, birthdays, graduations, and a plethora of significant events one can never get back including the freedom that lies inside you!

If you are going to snitch to save your life after you have committed a crime, you are destined to die as a cowardly hypocrite who receives no respect from anyone. When you snitch to save the life of someone else, you are destined to live and be viewed as a SHERO or HERO. Understand how the game is played so you do not lose precious time in the game of life! The time ticks so slow yet so fast in the penitentiary and before you know it you are *"**shoulding**"* all over yourself..."I **should** have done this...I **should** have done that...I **should** be..." ***MAN DAMN!***

Once time has passed, you can never get it back! Do not be deceived and caught up in the traps of money, power, sex, material things and committing crimes unless you are willing to trade your freedom for a muzzle over your mouth. No one will ever hear your howl from a penitentiary cell. Your pack(family) will suffer now that you are gone away for an extended period! Who is going to protect the pack?

When you are a wolf out there in the wilderness trying to eat, the Lord knows you have to eat to survive. He will provide if you believe and have faith. As a testimony, there was a time in my life when I was homeless literally and figuratively in my mind, and then I walked into the shelter for a bed and walked out as a volunteer and soon after that a board member. When you serve others for a greater good, you do not chance losing the opportunities to serve them because the reality is you will be losing the opportunity to benefit yourself which is the very reason why you stay fulfilled and full of love, peace, and happiness.

My brothers and friends, who probably did not realize then and even do not now, Tre Riddle, Venard Macbeth, Kenny, and Eric at Red Lobster and Mark Bryant Howie were vital and instrumental in my mental healthiness in that when I got out of the penitentiary they truly kept me in motion by getting me out of my apartment to socialize and help me rehabilitate from my trauma and drama. Like wolves, they would not leave another wolf behind, and when another wolf is injured, they helped by licking my wounds. They refused to abandon me and let me go starving in the wilderness. I wanted to be sedentary and stay in my apartment because I had given up on love and was apprehensive and reluctant to get involved with another woman after what I had just put myself and Michelle through, along with our family, friends and the citizens of Hampton University. If it was not for the beautiful, intelligent, young and mature women like Kisa Pangburn, Danielle Green, Nicole McKay and her fiery sister Netro McKay, Priscilla Roberts, Tammy P, Amanda Brown, Shawna Daniels, Chandra, Terri Dowla, and of course Trena Walden, I would have never believed I was even capable of giving or receiving love from any animal or human especially a woman.

I would have never been able to say yes to Trena when she asked me to marry her on a Monday and was married that same Friday. I would have never trusted another woman ever again had it not been for the love and time each gave me as a friend and nothing beyond just being a friend with no benefits!

People saw the best in me when I was at my very lowest times in life. Many inmates, jail and prison staff, law officials, wardens, correctional and parole officers, judges and medical professionals provided me with hope and inspiration, and I wish I could personally thank them for contributing to my mental wellness during my stay in the Virginia correctional system and Central State Mental Hospital, back in September of 1991 through January of 1993.

Like Ann Iverson speaking life into her son Bubba Chuck, whom the world knows as Allen Iverson, the penitentiary counselor, Mr. Parker, would always say, "Man, you honestly do not belong in here man! You belong in here as much as a fish needs to be out of the water! You just needed to get mentally healthy!"

The judge who handled my case and who consequently ordered the involuntary psychiatric treatment, kept shaking his head because as he stated over and over, "I cannot comprehend how with all the extraordinary positives ahead of you as a result of the extraordinary dedicated work you have put in as a college student, corporate intern, and community volunteer to get you these exceptional opportunities, why would you throw all of that away for some girl? There has got to be a sounder reason, and I will not stop wondering until I know for certain why and how you arrived here in front of me!"

My prison psychiatrist, Dr. Miller M. Ryans*(RIP) kept telling me after we had talked extensively for weeks and when he was finished with his diagnoses and assessments of me he said, "I am surprised that you did not severely, if not fatally, harm yourself or others earlier in your life after all that you have been through and endured! You could have received this treatment without ever having to come to prison to get it! I will do everything possible to get you healthy and out of the system as soon as heavenly possible so that you can get on with your life son! This place has served its purpose and so let us get you out of here so you can serve your purpose in the world!"

I want victimizers to admit that they are batterers, emotional, financial, psychological, and verbal abusers who try to control every aspect of their victim's lives. These are not easy things to talk about, admit to, or disclose publicly! Although it is hard to admit to this despicable behavior, it is worse admitting to the world that you did them intentionally to a loved one!

Solutions To Permanently Eradicate Domestic Violence, Child Abuse, and Bullying

<u>YOU ARE WHAT YOU DO WHEN NO ONE IS LOOKING!</u>

SERVING AT THE SPECIAL OLYMPICS IN 1987

LITTLE DID I KNOW THEN THAT THOSE MOMENTS OF SERVING CHILDREN WITH SPECIAL NEEDS-DISABILITIES WAS PREPARING ME FOR MY OWN CHILD WHO HAS SPECIAL NEEDS AND A LEARNING DISABILITY! I THANK YOU, GOD, FOR CHOOSING ME, MY WIFE AND OUR OTHER CHILDREN TO TAKE CARE OF HER!

Antoinne Burgess and his new friend enjoy a game of Bingo dur-

IF YOU EVER WANT TO MAKE AN IMPACT IN YOUR LIFE, MAKE AN IMPACT IN SOMEONE ELSE'S LIFE! SERVING OTHERS WILL ULTIMATELY SERVE A SIGNIFICANT PURPOSE TO YOUR LIFE!

Solutions To Permanently Eradicate Domestic Violence, Child Abuse, and Bullying

KNOW THE VALUE OF YOUR LIFE!

If God Made You, Your Life Is Priceless and Can Never Be Devalued!

Babies come from God. God does not make mistakes ever! The bottom line is your life is priceless and no person has a right or reason to abuse, neglect, destroy or kill God's creation and property. Every life has a purpose and meaning, despite the circumstances of how it arrives at earth. No one should ever feel ashamed of being born or be punished for a crime they never committed! The truth is simple in that some people just should not be allowed to have children! When you choose a reckless lifestyle, an insignificant other, any addiction, or partying all the time, over loving and taking care of your children and the responsibilities that automatically come with being a parent or friend, you should never be a parent or a friend in any relationship and should get a divorce or separation or surrender your parental rights to a loved one or have your children placed for adoption so someone can love them properly and provide a safe home where they can be treated as decent human beings. You do not deserve to be called mom or dad or husband or wife, or boyfriend or girlfriend because you are unfit and not qualified for the role. You have forfeited your right to fulfill your heavenly responsibility to take care of God's property unless you can find the love.

As a child who was abused and abandoned, when your life is not valued, and you are not loved appropriately by your parents you stop caring about love and you turn into an evil, angry, mean, confused, devious and uncaring individual incapable of properly giving or receiving love because your feelings are unbalanced. You do not possess a soul and your heart fills with hate. You are emotionless and are insensitive to other people's feelings. If you are not nurtured by your parents, especially your mother, from the very beginning of your life, you learn to not be nurtured and that becomes your normal which is not normal. If you do not hear her heartbeat as you are pressed up under her bosom, no one will ever hear yours and you will be considered heartless. How do you love another someone if no one ever appropriately loved you and you consider yourself a nobody? How do you love anyone or anything properly if no one or nothing ever loved you properly or showed you how to appropriately love another?

If all you have ever seen, known, and felt is hate, rejection, torture, pain, abuse, losses, abandonment or a roller coaster of emotions how do you possess love, a confident self-esteem self, or even care for others? If no one has ever made you feel secure there is no wonder why you are insecure. If you have never felt safe then no one will feel safe around you. If you are not in control of your emotions there is no wonder why your emotions are out of control. How do you even smile or possess the will to see each day? Who do you respect or trust when your own disrespectful parents or caretakers are the cause for your pain? How do you acclimate or fit in with those who are lovingly functioning people when you are an unloved dysfunctional diabolical human being? In math, a negative and a positive will always equal a negative. I am positive that I was a negative person.

Have you ever been punched, slapped, choked, strangled, kicked, neglected or abandoned? Do you know what it is like to not be picked on a team by your own parents and they select other people over you to be on their team? Do you know what it is like to be abused by a family member and your parent sits on the sidelines and does not stand up, come to your defense and fight for you? They are silenced to your violence. Have you ever wished that tomorrow would never come or for your parent to not be your parent or your family not be your family? Do you know what it is like to be invisible and your words falling on deaf ears to your parents? You are unwanted by the very people who should be wanting you!

On several occasions in my young child and adult life, I was so depressed that I battled thoughts of suicide. I felt that if I died I would no longer have to face the pain of each day. The very lowest time of my life came during my return to my senior year of college at Hampton University. I was homeless, living out of my car and spending my nights at Ingram in the bathroom. I was already estranged from my family in Baltimore I thought, well at the very least I had my girlfriend Michelle who loved me unconditionally with all of my flaws and bull crap and our young dog Toby.

I was returning to college after a stint of homelessness and a summer so filled with the traps of Baltimore that I was glad and amazed at the same time that I escaped with my freedom, sanity, and life. I survived being mistakenly identified and pulled over by a helicopter at gunpoint by a super-aggressive Baltimore police department looking for liquor store murderers and robbers. I survived two full-scale race riots. One at Polock Johnny's and the other at a pool party in Randallstown. I witnessed an innocent, unsuspecting homeless man get purposely pushed in the Baltimore Harbor and nearly killed by a crazed man, feet from me because he was tired of homeless people begging him for money. And despite the odds, I was going to finish college and walk into a phenomenal corporate career with Ingram Industries and an even better personal life being married to my high school sweetheart Michelle. All of this negativity means what?

I was not a spiritual man as I am today. I walk by faith today. At that time in my life, it was not meant to be in the cards of life that were dealt to me! Because of my history of domestic violence and abuse against my girlfriend of 6 years, she justifiably decided to end our relationship before the beginning of our senior year and move on to her proper place in life minus me the abuser. She was conscious!

What happened to my master plan of being married to her with children, a set of twins specifically, Toby, and me being a corporate attorney for Ingram? What happened? My family was gone out of my life and so I now no longer have my future family? I survived being abused and abandoned by family, and now she has chosen to get away from me too? I have got to be the reason why everyone is choosing to run from me. I am the reason why they are running for their life. I am pushing them away! Why should I live? Who would even care if I am dead & gone?

I fell into a depression that I could not find my way out of no matter how much I tried. Life scenarios like these are not easy to solve when you have no coping skills or any parental counseling. I had no one to run to for advice. I was in no position to manage so many unexplained why's. I could not figure out what was causing me to harm those closest to me. It had always been this way my entire life. As soon as I got close to someone, they went away by choice or force. This was a normal that I was tired of enduring. My tear ducts were dry. I was ready to descend to the other side where the grass was brown. The side that is the underbelly of the grass. The side that you have to shovel at least 6000 feet south to a blazing inferno.

My condo roommate William Buie, who was my homeboy from Baltimore and a sincere friend who just wanted me to realize that there were plenty of other "fish in the sea" given that I was at a learning institution that had a 20 to 1 female to male student population, and I was an attractive man about to receive a freshly minted Bachelor of Science Degree in Finance, headed to Vanderbilt, the Baltimore School of Law or Georgetown in pursuit of a Juris Doctorate MBA! He insisted that I had to see the many women who were interested since I was no longer in a committed relationship. He was right, but I could not get past the loss of Michelle, my family, and the whole confusion of loss! I was not going to go run into the arms of another beautiful woman and someone else's baby only to terrorize them and be left standing alone with the same feelings of guilt and shame knowing I was the reason for them leaving because "it" happened again. I could not do that again to anyone or myself! I was a monster. I was not a respectable man! I was not a friend! I was not capable of loving a woman without abusing them in some negative fashion physically, mentally, verbally, emotionally, financially, or psychologically!

I was the reason why these people ran for their lives! I had bullied many others like my cousins Teeny Turner & Ebby White, family friends Anthony Parker, John Washington, Wilbert White, Bryan Adams*(R.I.P), Darren Davis, Darrell Dixon*(R.I.P) and many others. I had violently abused my mother, aunt Annie, and uncle Chubby once I was big enough to make them pay for what they had done to me as a child. They truly do not realize how much I wanted to harm them. I wanted to beat their a**** into the dirt! No one tried to understand that my reality was death to me because I blamed myself for abusing them all including sending my homeboy and roommate William Buie to the hospital for calling me "weak for being whipped over one girl who doesn't love or want me anymore!" I stayed awake for several days because I assumed he had called the police on me. He kept the Baltimore "No Snitch Code" and never called the police, and I should have trusted he would never have because as he ran out of the condo bleeding and crying in pain physically, but more of a broken heart, he shouted, "I love you, man! I will always love you, man!" *MAN DAMN! William Buie, "I love you too man! You are a brother's keeper!"*

Here I was again pushing loving people away from me at the hands of violence. In my mind, I knew that I was not worthy of anyone's love or friendship, because I would either harm them or myself! I was not even worthy of being a pet parent to my young dog Toby the boxer. He was such a good boy and nonjudgmental pleaser of a dog, and I even managed to abuse him and treat him as bad as anyone else close to me. I neglected him because he was an afterthought and he reminded me of how much I loved Michelle, and so he was fallout from a failed relationship. I would leave him in the apartment or out on the balcony for days during the "dog days":(of my life. I fed him but gave no love! That was so wrong and cruel to take it out on something that was so innocent and could not possibly take care of itself.

When I saw how in less than 60 days my life had gone from depression to homelessness to escaping death to escaping jail, to an incredible corporate and personal future, to losing my family, to lonely, to homelessness, to losing my girlfriend, to losing weight, to losing my roommate William, to losing my mind, to losing hope and purpose, to losing my life, it was then that I realized I was the problem and I began to make plans to take my life! I thought out and believed suicide would be best! My plan was to go to Applebee's or Bennigan's for my last supper.

My last meal consisted of endless riblets, Buffalo Wings and fries with several pitchers of Miller High Life even though I was a low life!

I chose Applebee's. When I got back to the condo, I was tipsy but resolute in ending my life. I got in the dry tub and began to pour diesel fuel over my head in the shower with the goal of setting myself on fire. The problem was I was drunk, and I could not get my Bic to flick meaning my lighter was so drenched in the fuel and with my fingertips being so soft and smooth I could not ignite the lighter and I remember an overwhelming diesel smell and then lights out! It was either the diesel from the gas can or the "diesel" from the pitchers. I was high as a Georgia pine! I was "lit" from the pitchers of Miller High Life! I was out and feeling no pain.

I remember the feeling of someone carrying me as I was sleeping peacefully for what seemed like an eternity and dreaming about someone banging like the police trying to break down my door. And then I awakened! Holy Moly! Someone was banging on my door. I thought to myself how was I going to go to the door smelling profusely like diesel fuel? Was it Michelle? I had been calling her like a stalker. Was it Will Buie? Was it the police? Then I heard Toby crying out on the patio because it was raining, cold and dark. I decided to get him first, so he could put whoever was at the door at ease and would give me an excuse to hand him off, so I could go and clean off the diesel fuel. When I got to the door no one was there to my relief and dismay. I assumed later that because of Toby's 2 am piercing cries that one of my neighbors banged on the door to let me know to get him off the balcony.

I was hurt and happy at that same time that no one was at the door, but it was more reason to get to the other side as soon as I could possibly! I fed Toby and washed him and myself up. My dog looked at me as if to say "Aren't you lucky I saved you B****? Now feed me you selfish and insensitive jerk! What took you so long to save me? Where's my dinner?" Then I thought God had intervened! I remember thinking that the only friend I had in the entire world was Toby and I had almost neglectfully killed him!

I had to get rid of him because I was no longer fit to care for him, and so I put an ad in the paper listing his age, markings. AKC registry status, full health records of shots and most of all "Free to a loving and deserving homeowner with a family and kids!" That was a listing I should have advertised for myself and one I wish I could have placed for myself as a child. Toby deserved better than what I could do for him at that time. I knew what it was like to be shamed, ridiculed, neglected, abandoned and abused and so I had to send him away because I could not bear to look at him because a few weeks prior I spanked him until he pissed on his self in complete submission. I am so sorry Toby*. You did not deserve me as a dad!

How mean and cruel could I be to harm an innocent dog that never did anything to me except fight for my attention and love? He was so great and loyal to me, and I managed to turn an obedient dog into a stranger in my mind. It was not his fault! He was a baby at just seven months old! I had become and probably always was a scary monster taking my rage out on my helpless and innocent baby boxer Toby* who was solely relying on me to survive! I was the one who was ashamed just for being born, and now I am blaming and punishing my dog for a crime that was not his to pay for with his hind. Toby was a boxer for a reason…he was a fighter! He showed me how to ask for help when he was out on the porch sobbing for someone to come to his rescue. He was smart enough to ask for help when he could not save himself from the elements in the wild! If more people studied how and why people love their dogs they would understand how to love and engage with each other unconditionally and without judgment.

One of the saddest days of my life was when I gave Toby to a Virginia Beach FAMILY MAN™ who swore to me that Toby* would live the life of a King and that he and his wife and kids would never harm him. As they were pulling off, with Toby in the rear of the car, Toby looked out the back window at me as if to say, "I don't want to leave you! Don't give up on me. Just get better and come back to get me after you get healed! I will be waiting with this foster family until then!" I cried for days because again another loved one was gone at the hands of my violence.

My mother, aunt, and uncle made me feel ashamed for just being born! No one tried to understand that I was a child taking the blame, shame, ridicule, neglect, abandonment and punishment for my father's crime or perhaps their own dysfunction and pain influenced by someone else. My father was the domestic violence offender and abuser, not me? He was the bully and intimidator not me to my mother and her siblings. Why did my family speak death into my life by saying "You are mean and evil just like your father!" What was the issue of why people wanted to harm me as a child? Now I understand why they harmed me and forgive them and love them from a distance today! This is a healthy coping solution for me!

When I was first arrested, my attorney recommended I voluntarily commit to getting treatment to show the court and judge that this was a mistake in judgment and that I was changing for the better! I remember ending up in the hospital and the nurse carefully yet constantly inquiring about why I wanted to take my life. I told her I was not wanted, and I was inflicting pain on everyone and everything! I was without a family, homeless, the best thing ever in my life my former friend Michelle and her family, school, Will Buie my roommate, Toby, and my future! What purpose did I have to live? What was always confusing for me, and although I believed I was a genius in my mind, was I knew firsthand what it was to be unwanted, abused and abandoned by a loved one, but yet I could not figure out why I was doing to those closest to me what I hated others doing to me as a child and young adult.

What a Rubik's cube for me? The answer is simple in that tortured people, torture people until they discover or reveal the source of their pain, and then, and only then, can they find the solutions to get permanently healed. Until then, if you do not receive professional help, you will continue to be harvested and poached by the most dysfunctional worst behavior in yourself or by others, for your talents, like organic super greens, and once you are eaten and processed through the body for all of its nutrients to benefit the host's system, you will be processed like crap and quickly flushed down the toilet. Know the value of your life and never let someone exploit you or your talents and if by chance you are an abuser abusing others get help right now, so you do not let your talents turn into crap. Shout out to Mo'Nique from Baltimore for showing the world her value in that we are Baltimoreans and we never back down; we stand our ground and dig in! Never be pimped or prostituted ever by anyone! Never let someone blow your flame out or steal your wick!

I thank God for The American Cookie Company who allowed me the opportunity to deliver their cookies to the many homeless people in Newport News, Virginia! Kroger and Harris Teeter, you are a blessing for giving food to the second harvest food bank and many other charitable displays of love! I pray I will have many more examples of corporate generosity to share in my sequels to this book in the years to come. I will partner with phenomenal companies who care about others!

Can you imagine providing a solution to the world's problems or just for entertainment purposes by creating or inventing something only for someone else to steal, benefit, or plagiarize your creativity, idea, patent, copyright or intellectual property only for you to get no profits or recognition for your efforts? How would you feel? Can you imagine hearing your song on the radio or YouTube or Google Play or being offered for sale on iTunes or other music streaming services and you get no money or residuals, royalties, recognition or financial credits and considerations while someone else is literally enjoying the fruits of your labor and intellectual property? Your intellectual property is your collateral and future down payment for life's capacity of expenses. Some entertainers, musicians, and artists only got paid peanuts for a song or movie that they wrote, produced, composed, and sang, and the song became a hit, and they never received any residuals or royalties from their creativity and intellectual property.

The following individuals epitomize betting on themselves and not standing for injustice because they knew the value of their life. Jim Brown, Muhammad Ali, James Brown, Thurgood Marshall, Allison Walden, James Burgess, Barry Sanders, Le'veon Bell, Judges Greg Mathis and Faith Jenkins, Oprah Winfrey, Ray Charles, Deion Sanders, Ava Duvernay, Spike Lee, Samuel L. Jackson, Taraji P. Henson, Steve Harvey, Tom Joyner, Tyra Banks, Sean "Diddy" Combs, Kenan Ivory Wayans, Mo'Nique, Beyoncé, Master P, Ludacris, Tyler Perry, Tupac, Dave Chappelle, Jay Z, Ice Cube, Dr, Dre, 50 Cent, Bob Johnson, Eminem, Queen Latifah, Biggie, LL Cool James, Vivica A. Fox, Little Richard, Chance the Rapper, LeBron James, Stephon Curry, Kevin Durant, Lil Wayne, Nicki Minaj, Drake, Chris Paul, Carmelo Anthony, Bobby Brown, Bill Russell, Trina, Kevin Hart, Trick Daddy, Aaron Donald, Steve Smith Sr, DeAngelo Williams, Shonda Rhimes, Whoopi Goldberg, Roxanne Shante, Nas, Birdman, Sam Cook, Quincy Jones, Sidney Poitier, Redd Foxx, Tina Turner, Prince, Will Smith, Michelle Thompson, Delores Burgess, E40, Michael Jackson, and A.W. Burgess. YOU? U!

I want to thank a few people for keeping me sane! I enjoyed laughing at Redd Foxx*(R.I.P), Eddie Murphy, Richard Pryor*(R.I.P), Sinbad, Deon Cole, Earthquake, Capone, Talent, Mike Epps, Steve Harvey, Katt Williams, Lil Duval, Cedric The Entertainer, Charlie Murphy*(R.I.P), Eddie Griffin, Kevin Hart, Jeff Ross, and Charles Walden. Your talents inspired me. I thank God for your life because your talent kept me laughing or entertained when life was not always funny.

I am a man. I am a brand! My brand is accountability and awareness of one's own mental health! The brand for people who have made mistakes and terrible errors in judgment but who learned from those errors and never returned to harming others! I am from a group of people where there are no eyes on the prize called peace, but we end up noble with a prize called peace! I represent those who were counted out forever but bet on themselves when the chips were down and grabbed their obstacles and turned them into opportunities that paid off well!

Know the value of your life before someone else does and you do not benefit from your life and your God-given talents! Triumph over devastation, death, and tragedy! I stopped writing the script to my own death, drama, and tragedy! I will never let anyone blow out my flame where I get stuck in the wax! I will always stay focused on being a Family Man because distractions are killing us literally and figuratively!

Solutions To Permanently Eradicate Domestic Violence, Child Abuse, and Bullying

Remember:

EVIL

ONLY WINS

WHEN

GOOD DOES

NOTHING!™

Solutions To Permanently Eradicate Domestic Violence, Child Abuse, and Bullying

FAMILY MANKIND™

F.A.M.I.L.Y. M.A.N. KIND
For All Mankind I Love You! Managing Anger and Abuse Now, Kindly!

I created Family Mankind™ to prevent domestic violence offenders, child abusers, and bullies from harming innocent women, children, and animals as well as preventing these violent individuals from being arrested, being labeled a felon or simply having a criminal background as a result of domestic violence! I did not want any individual to end up in the penitentiary or psychiatric hospital as I did because they did not get the required psychiatric therapy to improve their mental health and quality of life. I do not want anyone to harm themselves or another human being or animal and destroy not just the victim's life and legacy, but their very own too! If I can inspire an individual to institute a permanent change mentally, as was done for me, then I can stop the abuse and permanently prevent someone from self-destructing and harming others! How can someone kill you if they no longer have the weapons to kill you or themselves, especially their mind! When I hear of a person who has committed suicide, or I see an individual addicted to drugs, alcohol, both, has overdosed or are consistently in and out of rehab or jail or are just mentally unstable, I always ask, "What caused, what was or what is their pain? What can I do to help them now!" How did their mom or dad love and protect them? Children learn what they live and how life treats them! What should I or any adult think of a parent who tells their child when it comes to you "I should have had an abortion! I should have flushed you down the toilet! You ruined my life!"

The ultimate objective for the Family Mankind™ organization is to be the solution for those struggling with domestic violence, child abuse, and bullying as comparable to what Alcoholics Anonymous® is to individuals struggling with alcohol addiction. We wish to establish services and a culture where victimizers are proactively coming forward out of the darkness for a high-quality mental health and behavioral solution to permanently eradicate violence, bullying, and abuse. *I am not challenging or calling bullies, abusers and domestic violence offenders out, but rather I am calling them in to receive their permanent healing!* Like a call from the wild, this is one wolf's howl to another wolf to help them! It is time to proactively change the culture. Trying to publicly call out, challenge and shame a child or sexual abuser, bully, or domestic violence offender to change their criminal behavior does not work, and in fact, it angers them further or forces them to go further into isolation or worsen their actions towards their current or new victims. I want to inspire them to change for the better. What I want them to know is your physical well-being must match your mental well-being! Abusing someone physically and then also torturing them mentally is the ultimate sign you urgently need help! Bruises may heal, but the psychological effects may linger for a lifetime for an individual. Do not be a toxic agent. Toxic agents are dangerous to all bodies!

There is always a first to try and then eventually accomplish the impossible dream! That first in my world is me. The first to come out of the shadows of domestic violence secrecy and abuse! I am no longer running and hiding from the truth of my past and the horrific chapters of abuse and violence and so I have chosen transparency and accountability to help me help others acquire the coping skills and life techniques to live a mentally healthy life as I have been afforded. This behavior does not permanently stop until you permanently stop the perpetrator of the violence, bullying, and abuse. I am requiring, not requesting, all men, women, children, and young adult abusers, bullies and violent offenders of all types to come out of the shadows of their souls to get with me, my corporate partners and associates so they can get themselves the required and necessary continued treatment that will lead to a permanent healing and change that will impact their and their loved ones' lives and legacies and prevent a dangerous cycle and pattern of violence and abuse against all mankind, animals and moreover, themselves.

Our authorities in schools, sports, youth activities, and churches, have a completely legal and moral responsibility to keep all children safe from predators and bullies and with most certainty should never be the violators of the trust that parents and society bestowed upon them. Thousands of children have been sexually abused and tortured by priests throughout the world! Just having one child molested is too many for me. Few are going to prison for these crimes and if they do it is generally for the minimal time before they are free to roam society again. The audacity about their crimes is that they mentally sentence the victims to life without parole or a death sentence because the victim can no longer live with the pain stemming from the crime. Who's going to pay for these deaths? Their families will pay the price for the rest of their lives. Who will settle their hearts, spirits, and mind? I do not care how much financially victims of violence are compensated via restitution for their tragic losses, those funds or settlement checks will never exceed their pain or put the fun back into their lives or settle them completely. Tell me how does one permanently remove the thought of the death of their child or innocence?

Solutions To Permanently Eradicate Domestic Violence, Child Abuse, and Bullying

What is worst is when they die at the hands of a caretaker that the parent entrusted such as a former boy or girlfriend, spouse, their new spouse, boyfriend, girlfriend, relative, friend or friend of a friend, adopted or foster parent, teacher, coach or anyone in a position of authority in church. There are some things in life that only God Almighty can remove because man simply cannot! Again, please inform me how does any loving parent ever recover from the death of a child?

When the world throws you away, where do you go? Family Mankind™ gives you love, coping and life skills, along with, non-judgment to focus and move forward with your life! We visit inmates not out of sympathy or empathy, but as a necessity to prevent perpetuating violence and abuse. We are humanitarians first. Where will they go and what will they do once released back into society? Are they equipped to cope or are they a U-turn away from returning to jail or prison as a result of abuse and violence? Are they institutionalized and destined for disaster?

Why is it that absolutely nothing changes until someone is killed or a tragedy occurs to a significant somebody? Are certain lives worth more than others? Yes, it depends on who was killed or how much money it is going to cost someone literally or figuratively before a permanent change comes about to the rescue. Why are women and children globally, regardless of race, religion or culture still being raped and molested in our churches and schools and no one is going to prison? How come our children are not safe in their own homes surrounded by internal and external predators, molesters, and bullies. Should it matter what neighborhood you live in to keep your children safe from the worst predators in your state? We all pay taxes in some form or another, so it should not matter where you live or what school your children attend for them to be safe from predators! No person's life is more important than any other person's life! Period!

There should never be a statute of limitations on sexual abuse because we are talking about the violent murder of an individual's innocence that is sentenced to the death penalty and if you are lucky you receive life without parole and painfully subjected to the ridiculous and insultingly act of a government that just slaps the violent offenders and perpetrators with fines, timeout incarceration periods, or no punishment at all and simply lets them continue their systemic cycle of abuse and violence because there are no honest consequences and better solutions for them to permanently stop harming others. These violators of trust need to go get their healing and stop stealing from others and themselves, their opportunity for a loving, prosperous life and legacy! I am not asking them to get help, but rather, it is a requirement, to learn the appropriate coping and life skills and techniques before they are afforded a position of trust or job. What good is it to have a trillion dollars in your pocket or bank from your corporate talents and yet you abuse others? What good is it to have a Ph.D. from the highest learning institution or be a Rhodes Scholar from Oxford University and you have the worst attitude on the planet and people despise being around you? I would rather have a Ph.D. in common sense and a phenomenal character than any Ph.D. or high paying job! What good is it to have everything you want materialistically, but then you have nothing to fulfill your purpose in life and no one at all to share the materialistic things with you. You will end up spiritually, emotionally, and quite possibly, physically dead! You will be a prisoner serving time in the dungeons of your mind and soul.

At Family Mankind™, we never judge victimizers or victims of violence, but we do love and hug! We are huggers who embrace hope and change! We choose to "love our enemies as ourselves!" It is a place where victims of violence and violent offenders come together to share their stories to heal and support each other with the help of volunteers to eventually become victors of violence! We want recovering individuals to know they will no longer be defined by their crimes as victims or victimizers but vindicated conquerors! We are servant leaders because the greatest honor and blessing is when you serve others you are actually serving yourself. Imagine when there is only one seat left on the plane to heaven, and you tell the person behind you, you can go in front of me in my place! What one does not realize is there is a reserved seat in the cockpit next to the captain.

Our client and customer is the abuser and violent offender of innocent, abused, bullied and children, women, and animals. The women and children are boldly stepping forward to rightfully take claim to no longer being a victim! What I, society, and victims of violence and abuse need is for the victimizers and abusers of women and children to come out of the shadows of darkness and death of their self-mutilating, shameful, vile, reprehensible and despicable behavior and boldly commit to getting a permanent solution to their problems to permanently preserve their lives and legacies. I require these violent offenders and abusers, to stand up and step forward to take accountability for their life! Society will never impact domestic violence and child abuse until we impact the domestic violence offender and child abusers!

To stop the violence and abuse behavior, we have to stop the behavior of the violent offender and abuser. Women, children, students or pet animals should never feel worried that their days are numbered on earth and that they are just buying time before they are seriously harmed or killed by a current spouse, friend, classmate, significant other, former spouse, friend, parent, foster or adopted parent, caretaker or even a pet parent. No man, woman, child or pet should be endangered or mistreated in any fashion because it is simply inhumane and fundamentally wrong to intimidate, bully, harass or torture anyone or anything. No surviving victims of violence should ever be silenced. Silence the victimizers and abusers with real proactive coping and life solutions or with stiffer penalties and sentences that will lead to the appropriate rehabilitative mental health solutions and support, so they do not become a habitual abuser and violent offender, recidivist or murderer.

Our corporate vision is to assist individuals in breaking generational curses of abusers in their family bloodlines. Abusers are not born they are created. We are born to love and manufactured to hate! Monsters get created through certain life scenarios or someone is pushing their pain, sickness, abuse, and illness onto another innocent person, by way of force or choice, who is undoubtedly unaware and incapable of stopping that individual's agenda. Whether it is seeing or hearing, one is learning the behavior from some traumatic experience or an individual(s), television, movies, books, magazines, radio or any other forms of mass communication.

If a child was molested by their parent and witnessed them commit crimes or be a prostitute, how would you think that child is going to turn out as a human being? Can you ever imagine a child knowingly having sex with their parent? What an unimaginable image! Many serial killers, rapists, and psychopaths got their violent behavior from their parents who abused, killed, and dissected animals as a child! It is not natural to be born a hater, violent physical or mental abuser, pediphiler, rapist, arsonist, or murderer! It is like a baby or child that has never laughed or smiled! ***What caused that baby or child to stop laughing, smiling, or loving?*** If you are laughing or smiling uncontrollably and then suddenly someone comes up to you and suddenly severely pinches you or punches you in the face or gut your smile suddenly retreats to a frown or a look of bewilderment, and your body sends out negative signals because now you are focused on pain! Imagine this behavior happens consistently enough to become the norm or enough to impact you for the rest of your life and all you ever know or remember is the pain. It could also lie dormant and not resurface until triggered! Because of the exposure to hate or violence this individual knows how to inflict pain on others and is immune to love, hate, or violence! They have zero feelings because they simply lack emotions and the ability to care. If all you have ever known is hate and have never been loved or shown how to properly love another human being, how is it possible to normally love another human being, animal, plant, or valuables! Violence and destructive behavior will surface if there is never any coping skills learned to diminish or forever suppress this learned behavior!

Whatever happens to you is eventually, and quite possibly, what you learn to do to others! Whatever you are exposed to is what you possibly will expose to others! If your parent(s), guardian(s), never love you or love you adequately how do you learn to love others adequately or sufficiently if no adequate or sufficient love is in you? If you are exposed to porn or alcoholism or pyrotechnics or violence or horror movies, why is it a surprise when children and adults become what they've been exposed to at impressionable times in their lives! How can you go never adopted and be in foster care until you age out of the system! No one wants to love me or has ever loved me? What is wrong with me? How do we function in a dysfunctional world? How can you properly love anyone or anything if you have never been properly loved? When you hurt someone or damage something, you are really damaging yourself! If you abuse her or your child you are really abusing yourself! If you bully them, you are bullying yourself! If you hate them, you hate yourself! Who would do that to their self? Your physical well-being must match your mental well-being! Abusing someone physically and then also torturing them mentally is the ultimate sign you urgently need an intervention! Bruises may heal, but the psychological effects may linger for a lifetime for an individual. Domestic violence leads to silence and is destined for the death of a living entity and legacy! Domestic violence leads to loneliness, death and a cursed bloodline that continues to perpetuate the same cycle of violence and destruction!

Women and children suffer in silence until they are killed by violence. They have an incredibly high lethality rate. There is only so much that the criminal justice and healthcare system can do to prevent violence and abuse! Our mission is to convince the seemingly inconvincible to change their violent and abusive behavior before they destroy lives and legacies. We are not talking prevention or awareness to domestic violence and child abuse or bullying in our homes, schools, and workplaces, but rather we are speaking of eradication of domestic violence, child abuse and bullying against our women and children. Batterer's groups traditionally have incredibly low success rates. The definition of insanity is doing the same thing over and over again expecting better results. The statistical success rates of batterers groups are 5%-8%. Batterers groups do not work because they do not show you how to properly manage your anger and abuse because they are too busy telling you what to do from an educational viewpoint rather than from a theoretical, mechanical and applicable standpoint! Who is leading the meetings? What is their skin in the game? What agenda and goal do they possibly possess? How can they respectfully reach and touch the batterers and abusers to make a permanent impact when so many are resistant to change? We are not teaching a way to prevent domestic violence and child abuse. We are telling our children, women, and all victims of domestic violence and child abuse to go suffer in silence and just be prepared to properly continue receiving the violence and abuse because the only "Justice" you have as a victim is "Just Us" or "Just Ice" which are cold shoulders to helping protect your life and legacy! In many states, because we have many male politicians, who may just be ignorant of the issue of domestic violence and child abuse against women and children or this may not be a priority on their political agenda or whom themselves may be domestic violence and child abuse sympathizers, we do not even have stern laws to protect the victims from their victimizers once they get out of prison.

The message we are sending to the abusers of these children and women is I can continue to abuse, and there are no significant consequences? Who were the politicians who changed the laws whereby when a person assaults another there no longer is an immediate warrant for their arrest, thus putting the victim and children in greater harm's way? Most violent offenders and abusers will tell you that they never received any real or significant rehabilitation during and post-incarceration and so they are destined and are highly likely to re-offend and so recidivism occurs. Meanwhile, the entire time the offender is locked up, the victims and their families are worried about the day their abuser, or domestic terrorist is released, and so they too are genuinely sentenced with them just that they are imprisoned in their minds. A few domestic violence batterers group meetings or anger management classes are not the solutions to eradicating or even preventing violence and abuse against children and women. We are not talking about quitting smoking or any other addiction. We are talking about violence and abuse that will kill you or someone you love!

As "The FAMILY MAN™," I have successfully transitioned from a convicted felon to convicting and convincing other domestic violence offenders and abusers to find the solutions that will permanently free them and their families of violence and abuse, so they are not destroying their relationships or legacies! I embrace being The World's #1 Felon & Abuser if it means that the price I paid for my dysfunction does not cause another domestic violence offender or child abuser to harm another human or animal and as a result destroy their lives and legacies and those of the people who love them! Domestic violence and abuse against women and children absolutely destroys any semblance of a loving, healthy relationship and often is a gateway that leads straight into bullying and animal cruelty!

Violence and abuse prevention and awareness is not enough for me and was not what prevented me from abusing my mother, girlfriend, dog, family members, and friends or even complete strangers. It did not prevent me from going to prison or a psychiatric hospital or from nearly committing suicide. I was aware I was violent and abusive, but I did not know how to permanently change my behavior because I did not have the appropriate coping or life skills and techniques! If it was not for a concerned judge, prison officials, and an exceptional psychiatric doctor who properly assessed and diagnosed me and got me the appropriate treatment and rehabilitation, I would have been a habitual domestic violence offender and abuser whose crimes and behavior would have most likely escalated to far worse situations and crimes such as suicide or murder! At best I would have been a positive contributor to society as a recidivist and a burden to taxpayers. Talking is not enough. It takes several anchors to hold down an aircraft carrier. I am required to be a change agent and champion for a permanent and healthy change, not a toxic agent!

Trying to figure out domestic violence and child abuse is like a 4-month-old baby trying to figure out a freshly scrambled Rubik's cube or the sensitive method of defusing a live bomb after the first time they have seen it. The solutions are beyond complex and complicated. The difference is there is no room for error!

We begin the relationship with abusers and violent offenders by first being a sincere non-judgmental, non-denominational, non-discriminatory, and non-partisan affiliated organization. We serve as humanitarians with an altruistic spirit whereas we are generally concerned about the welfare of children, women and their abusers.

At Family Mankind™ we do not care about your race, religious belief, political affiliation, demographics, disability, socioeconomic or education status! We do care about your level of love, care, heart, and health as it pertains to helping to permanently eradicate domestic violence and child abuse! We will never give up on people, to show people to never give up on their life, family and their legacy!

We need individual and corporate partnerships that help us reach our ultimate goal of saving the lives and legacies of women, children, animals, and their abusers. We also partner with domestic violence support groups to give empathy, encouragement, education, support and hope not just to the victims but to their violent offenders so that the offenders can be impacted by seeing and feeling the harm and devastation they have caused through the eyes of victims.

Imagine when I can get abusers, violent offenders and bullies to commit to never hit! Imagine when they realize there is never an excuse for abuse! Imagine when there is no silence to violence from victims and their victimizers, and they choose to get help to end their abuse! I want anyone who knows me and the mission I serve to always know that I will stand up and fight violence ferociously with my voice and servitude. Ending the silence to domestic violence! No excuse for child abuse! Violence and abuse emit toxic stress and generational curses of violence and abuse against women and children. Now you see why I want the domestic violence offenders, child abusers, and bullies! We are the hazmat team for people to permanently eradicate violence like removing black mold, Ebola, flesh-eating diseases, viruses, and infestations.

When you first hear the term "FAMILY MAN™" what comes to your mind? Because of where my life took me and the pain I have caused others, I owe my life to the families of the victims of violence, child abuse, and bullying by trying to make the impossible possible by relentlessly trying to end domestic violence and child abuse against women and children. If I at least try, then just maybe I and my associates, corporate partners, MenTours™, WomenTours™ and volunteers will prevent one person from tragically harming or scarring someone else's loved one for life, and we will also be helping to eradicate recidivism while benefiting the individual from becoming an abuser to someone else, themselves, their family, and society!

Family Mankind™ will be the global leader in the humanitarian efforts of eradicating domestic violence, bullying, and abuse against women and children! We absolutely have a lifelong commitment to giving society a broader portfolio on leading abusers and violent offenders to coping skills and alternative techniques that work!

When the world throws certain individuals away, where do they go? We give them the love, coping and life skills, along with, non-judgment to focus and move forward with their life! We visit inmates not out of sympathy or empathy, but as a necessity to prevent perpetuating violence and abuse. We are humanitarians first. Where will they go and what will they do once released? Are they equipped to cope or are they a U-turn away from returning to jail or prison as a result of abuse and violence? Are they institutionalized and destined for disaster?

How can anyone hurt anyone or anything that they are charged with protecting, providing, and caring for, and simply loving? Children, the disabled, elderly, and animals are beyond vulnerable and cannot care or protect and provide for themselves! They are helpless, vulnerable and innocent as a newborn baby!

Domestic violence, child abuse, and bullying does not exclude anyone and can happen anywhere regardless of their family's name, fortune, race, religion, demographics, education level, degree, G.E.D or nothing, socioeconomics, or job title. We have seen or heard of domestic violence and child abuse rearing its ugly head in our homes, churches, hospitals, schools and colleges, the workplace, the Olympics, Hollywood, Congress, the Senate, and even the White House! This is not a black or white or religious or economic situation, it is about love and the solutions that come about using love tactics and techniques to combat violence, We strive to prevent deaths and individual legacies.

If violence and abuse can come from parents, friends, neighbors, law enforcement, coaches, educators, doctors, members of the clergy, politicians or pure strangers how do we defend against it? The Solution is the Family Mankind™ organization. God Blesses Motion and *"Evil only wins when Good does nothing!"*™ To be a change agent to do something good for others, we must be actively engaged with phenomenal energy. Think about it. A car does not move until you put it in the drive position. But like anything else, it takes a lot of energy and resources to put the car in motion. Before you can operate a car legally, you must first possess a driver's license. Then you must purchase a vehicle, register it at the DMV, put insurance on it and then you must buy gas and keep it well maintained regularly. If you do not have any money to buy the gas, your vehicle stays parked. No gas equates to no motion. Like any form of transportation to get us to our destination, we must have resources and energy to fuel our mode of transportation.

What separates Family Mankind™ is we are proactive in our accountability and eradication solutions approach to domestic violence, child abuse, and bullying versus just making people aware of the issue or prevention where there is no effective impact on an individual's life, legacy or community. To God, All Victims of Violence, the abusers, bullies, and violent offenders, I owe you the sincerest apology from my heart and soul!

Just like you, and I could quite possibly be wrong, and if I am, please forgive me when I say that I was not properly loved and shown how to love another properly, and as a result, I became a domestic violence offender, bully, and abuser of someone else's child. I contributed majorly in attempting to destroy God's property and their physical, mental, and emotional well-being! I had no right or authority to do such a vile, cowardly, and heinous act towards another human being! My significance and our company mission are to provide permanent solutions to violence against women and children!

Have you ever seen a dead living person? ***How can you love anyone or anything properly if you have never been appropriately loved or shown how to love another human or animal properly?*** What if you have never seen a healthy functioning relationship? What if you were never adopted and were passed over by 5, 10, 20 or more foster families? How about being passed over by just one family? How about never knowing one or both parents?

Have you ever wished you were not born? ***Have you ever been blamed or punished by a loved one or stranger for a crime you did not commit?*** This is why I want to bring hope to abusers and those they abuse! Have you ever asked the question "What is wrong with me?" Domestic violence and child abuse are like an infestation of rats, bed bugs, and roaches, just breeding and breeding until they overrun your dwelling and then they or their diseases will kill you. You just cannot sweep them under the carpet before the infestation eats or carries the floor away. If you do not get them under attack, they will grow to attack you continuously.

Silence promotes and perpetuates violence! It is not a matter of if but when violence will occur again unless you get help mentally! Domestic violence leads to silence and is destined for the death of a living entity and legacy! Domestic violence leads to loneliness, death, and a cursed bloodline that continues to perpetuate the same cycle of violence and destruction! Do not keep giving your love to someone who does not return the same or greater healthier love and respect! I never want to be with anyone that does not want to indeed be with me and love me how I love them! Love is a constant compromise and reciprocated internal belief that my fellow mankind would ***Never Ever*** intentionally harm me in any fashion! In

Solutions To Permanently Eradicate Domestic Violence, Child Abuse, and Bullying

short, *love me or move on so I can give love and be loved by the person God has intended me to spend a glorious lifetime without contention, drama or trauma!*

At Family Mankind™ we recognize we have a serious humanitarian challenge. We must first get violent offenders, child abusers, and bullies to come out of the shadows of death and darkness to permanently commit to non-violence against women, children, and animals. Then commit to 1.) getting lifelong therapy. 2.) ending the cycle of violence in their family bloodline. 3.) serving by joining the other family men committed to loving themselves, others, and family values!

I pray I become a reason for abusers and those they abuse to believe in hope! Hope that there is a solution to end violence against all humanity such as men, women, children, lesbians, bisexuals, gays, transgenders, queers, the disabled and animals! To provide hope that they will not be killed or disfigured and there will be a return to normalcy. The very worst thing any human can do is display violence towards another human and systematically, consequently, destroy their legacy and potentially the legacy of their children!

Can you ever imagine being responsible for killing another individual's dreams or legacy? How about knowing you can create or do something better than anyone on the planet and your past will not allow you to do so? How about a debt that will never be repaid and being judged for it for the rest of your life! I am a significant part of a global community issue that must be reckoned with because unless we get educated or motivated to deliver a permanent solution, where do we go and what do we do productively with society's throwaways and degenerates? Stop allowing your insecurities to defeat your life's destination!

What most of these abusers want and need is RESPECT! Therefore, I must show them LOVE. They should not have a need to join a gang or a cult to be accepted. They do it to be acknowledged, respected and moreover to feel loved and a part of a semblance of a family! How would you feel if you were abandoned or abused by your parents or family? What if you were never adopted and timed out of foster care? The human body, soul, and mind needs love as much as food and water! People are lonely and alone trying to satisfy society's rules of acceptance meanwhile kids are timing out of the foster care system, not being adopted, are being assaulted, children are being abused and bullied, celebrating birthdays alone, no one is in the stands cheerleading for them, they are alone in the hospital because no one can come to visit, and they are homeless or are in jail where there are no visitors! What would make someone love you for a lifetime? What is the source of their pain? We will get to the root cause! You do not have to be lonely at Family Mankind™. You do not!

What will happen if Family Mankind™ and I do not try to help the future helpless, hopeless, and innocent individuals and their abusers or bullies? The bottom-line is Family Mankind™ is a human services organization that addresses the impact of intimate partner, interpersonal violence and toxic stress of domestic violence, bullying, and child abuse by getting to the root cause of chronic violent behavior and mental illness; and the unhealthy environment children are exposed to that consequentially harm innocent individuals, perpetuate cycles of violence and abuse, the destruction of lives, legacies and the communities where they reside. To help adults and children proactively move forward to receive the mental health solutions and love that will lead to permanent eradication of violence, abuse, and bullying.

Family Mankind™ Is An Abuser Focused Organization! No One Deserves To Constantly Live Under The Threat Of Death! Life Under Constant Threat Is Not Living But Is The Closest Proximity To Death Without Being In A Grave. Nothing Changes Until The Abuser's Mind Changes!

Solutions To Permanently Eradicate Domestic Violence, Child Abuse, and Bullying

Adult children thrive to survive

SURVIVOR'S GUIDE

Frederick Levy

NOTE TO READERS: *This column is for adult children of alcoholics. It will appear the third Thursday of each month.*

There is often a look about them. Adult children of alcoholics (ACoA) may seem successful and well put together, yet have an haunted expression, an underlying sadness that betrays the quietest confidence. Just as riches cannot buy happiness, all manner of striving can't seem to produce a sense of belonging and connectedness. They yearn for intimacy. It is their greatest longing, and greatest fear.

This fear is the step-child of years of emotional, and sometimes physical, violence in the home. Normally, a child learns about relationships by interactions with his or her parents, and successful parental modeling. In an alcoholic home, all relating occurs through "the bottle." The alcoholic is addicted to the alcohol; the spouse addicted to the alcoholic. The marriage becomes a vortex, drawing all available love and energy cataclysmically to its center, until ultimately all are swept away.

Survival, therefore, becomes the keynote of existence. Children of alcoholics (CoA) find a variety of means to stay afloat. The lucky ones may have another adult nearby; a neighbor, relative, teacher or member of the clergy from whom they draw support. These are the "supercopers;" they may emerge with fewer difficulties.

The majority, however, have to "make do." Some spend many lonely hours in their rooms, trying to read, listening to music; pretending to be invisible. Numbness and a dreamless sleep is their reward, if they can make it through the night.

Others take a more activist approach; these are the rescuers. Seeing the non-alcoholic parent in distress, they physically intervene, often at great risk, to prevent the violence. This is effective training for a great warrior or protector, but hardly teaches the kind of vulnerability that is essential in forming mutually nurturing relationships.

There are many approaches CoAs take to handle the stress. Some, sensing the family's need for relief, provide humor, distraction; anything to attract attention. Surrounded by chaos, little they do is taken seriously. Ironically, the more attention the child receives, the less of the person anyone sees. The clown is rendered invisible.

The angry child, the family sacrifice, absorbs the pain. His words going unnoticed, he lashes out, hoping someone will see what is happening, and help. Instead, he is carted away, to the principal's office, to detention, to the drug dealers. The family shakes its head in dismay; the alcoholism goes unrecognized. Powerless, he sinks into despair and isolation, sometimes finding solace in the streets.

Without effective parental models, the ACoA finds that he has few tools with which to build healthy romantic relationships. The rush of excitement springing from mutual attraction and discovery can be thrilling, and may promise a sense of renewal to the lonely and depressed adult child.

But ultimately, issues need to be raised, and problems worked out. Repetition of the same self-defeating patterns of connecting and communicating are the hallmark of ACoA relationships.

Yet, ACoAs can change how they live.

Adult children are people with vast emotional resources; having struggled to survive, they can learn to thrive. And thriving begins on the note of recognition.

Levy, a licensed clinical social worker specializing in the concerns of adult children of alcoholics, is associated with Bennett Garner M.D. and Associates in Newport News. Send questions to Survivors Guide, c/o Daily Press, MP 1203, 7505 Warwick Blvd., Newport News, VA 23607.

Solutions To Permanently Eradicate Domestic Violence, Child Abuse, and Bullying

ACCOUNTABILITY and AWARENESS: VIOLENCE SURVEY
*If You Want To Be Healed, "**IT**" Must Be Revealed!*

This survey was designed to help you heal! Do you want to be temporarily treated or permanently healed? I am here to help you, not judge you. If you want to be healed, **IT** must be revealed! Do not let your hurt, hurt others... especially you! No more secrets or excuses! The time has come to release the trauma-drama to refreshingly receive your freedom and peace. God Blesses motion! Taking this initial step-up means you are rising above your abuse and making the commitment to impact your life and the lives of the people impacted by your behavior! What is done in the dark will always come to light eventually, because **IT** is not a matter of "*if* **IT** will" resurface but "*when* **IT** will" resurface if you do not get **IT** permanently healed and not temporarily treated. I love you! Do not let **IT** fool you! **IT** is cunning.

This survey will establish if you are a domestic violence offender, child abuser, or bully in need of mental wellness or group therapy sessions. Again, if you want to be healed, **IT** must be revealed. You must throw **IT** up and get **IT** out of your system so we can identify the root cause of the violence and abuse and throw **IT** out to get to a solution, so you can properly move forward in your one lifetime!

This is not domestic violence, bullying, and child abuse awareness and prevention. This is domestic violence, bullying, and child abuse eradication. Your physical well-being must match your mental well-being! If the mind is not healthy the body will soon follow suit. How will you heal if you do nothing? **IT** is EVIL!

Abusing someone physically and then also torturing them mentally is the ultimate sign you urgently need an intervention! Bruises may heal, but the psychological effects may linger for a lifetime for an individual. I am here to help you. What good is **IT** for me to tell you that you have a flat tire and not at least help you fix the problem! I am here to show the abusers how to permanently fix or replace the flat tire! How fast can you go on a flat tire? Eventually, you are going to damage the metal frame of the wheel. How long before you flip the car over because you are experiencing the remnants of a blowout? What you are experiencing is the progression of violence, abuse, and bullying. **IT** goes from bad to worse to a tragedy. You are in motion and then before you know **IT** you have come to a screeching and grinding halt not by choice but by force. What will **IT** be? **You** choose? **IT** chooses? I told my girlfriend, "Honey, I promise you **IT** will not happen again!" I was wrong! **IT** happened over and over and over again until she left, and I ended up in prison!

Please answer the survey honestly so you can be on an honest path towards a permanent mentally healthy solution. The more detailed you are will help to speed up your permanent diagnostic and recovery.

LET US GET TO THE ROOT CAUSE OF "IT" -------YOUR PROBLEM! TELL ME WHAT HAPPENED... EVERYTHING! TAKE MY HAND...LET US GO GET YOUR HEALING! "IT" WILL NOT WIN!

Solutions To Permanently Eradicate Domestic Violence, Child Abuse, and Bullying

(MOST ANSWERS ONLY REQUIRE A YES-Y OR NO-N RESPONSE)

- ☐ Have you ever been arrested for domestic violence, child abuse or bullying?_____
- ☐ If so, when and what was your sentence and length of incarceration?_____
  _____
  _____

- ☐ Did you go to jail or prison, or receive probation, parole, community service, a fine, or alternative corrective action?_____
- ☐ Ever been arrested for child abuse or negligence or reckless endangerment?_____
- ☐ Ever been arrested for witness retaliation, false Imprisonment, abduction, kidnapping, aggravated assault, aggravated stalking, witness intimidation or extortion?_____
- ☐ If yes, when and what was your crime, sentence and length of incarceration?_____
  _____

- ☐ Ever been to jail, prison, probation, parole, community service, fine, alternative corrective action? _____
- ☐ Has the Department of Social Services or Child Welfare Protective Services ever been called on you? If yes, when and what was the outcome?_____
  _____

- ☐ If you lost custody of your kids, did you ever get them back?_____
  If not, why?_____
- ☐ Were you ever abused as a child?_____
- ☐ If yes, was the abuse physical, mental, verbal, emotional, or sexual?_____
- ☐ Who abused you?_____
- ☐ Did you ever witness a traumatic event?_____
- ☐ Did you ever participate or take part in a traumatic event?_____
- ☐ Did you have both parents growing up?_____
- ☐ Were they ever divorced?_____
- ☐ Did you ever witness them committing violence and abuse towards one another?__
- ☐ Was any parent an absentee parent?_____ If yes, why did they leave?_____
  _____

- ☐ How did you feel about it?_____
- ☐ What, if any, kind of relationship do you have with them today?_____
- ☐ Were you adopted as a child?_____
- ☐ If yes, how was your family experience?_____
  _____

- ☐ Were you ever in the foster care system?_____
- ☐ Were you ever adopted?___If yes, how did you feel about the experience?_____
  _____
  _____

☐ If no, how did you feel about the experience?_____

_____

_____

☐ Did you time out of the foster care system?_____

☐ If yes, how do you feel about never being adopted?_____

_____

_____

☐ Were you ever abused during your time as an adopted or foster child?_____

☐ If so, who abused you and how did they abuse you?_____

_____

_____

☐ Did you ever want to run away?_____ Why did you want to run away?_____

_____

_____

☐ Did you ever run away?_____ If yes, Why?_____

☐ Were you ever bullied?_____ If yes, by whom and when?_____

_____

☐ Have you ever bullied anyone or any living thing?_____

☐ Are you a controlling person?_____ If yes, Why?_____

☐ Do you prefer to be controlled?_____

☐ Do you control where a woman/man goes?_____

☐ Who she/he can see or not see or talk to?_____

☐ What she/he wears clothes wise?_____

☐ What type of makeup she can put on her face?_____

☐ How she/he styles her hair?_____

☐ Where she/he can work?_____

☐ Her/His personal and work schedule?_____

☐ Her/His passwords?_____

☐ Do you monitor her/his cell phone, text, email, voicemail, or computer usage?_____

☐ Can she freely go out with family or friends without your permission?_____

☐ Do you isolate them from their family and friends?_____

☐ Do you hate any of her family, friends, animals, activities or hobbies?_____

☐ If so, which ones specifically do you hate the most and why?_____

_____

_____

☐ Do you constantly wonder what they are doing, where they are and who they are with?_____ Why?_____

☐ Can she/he have a friend of the opposite sex?_____

☐ Do you have an obsessive personality?_____

- ☐ Are you obsessed with your mates?_____ Why?_____
- ☐ Ever called/text your mate or someone you were mad at by phone/text more than 5 successive times?_____ Why?_____
- ☐ Have you ever left more than 5 successive voicemails at one time?_____
- ☐ Did you grow more upset each time they did not pick up the phone?_____
- ☐ Ever recorded your mate in hopes of catching them lying or cheating on you?_____
- ☐ Did you move her/him or your child far away from her/his/their family and or friends?_____Why?_____
- ☐ Have you ever cut, burned, bleached or destroyed your significant other's clothes?__
- ☐ Have you ever stolen clothes or shoes from an ex?_____
- ☐ Have you ever destroyed anything of value of a significant other or ex?_____
- ☐ Have you ever vandalized a significant other or ex's home or vehicle?_____
- ☐ Ever taken back or stolen items you once gave to a significant other or ex?_____
- ☐ Have you ever broken into an ex's residence?_____
- ☐ Have you ever broken into their vehicle?_____
- ☐ Do you consider her/him or your child a slave?_____
- ☐ Have you ever called her/him or your child a slave?_____
- ☐ Ever made any of the following statements: See what you made me do! Look what you made me do to you! It is your fault for making me act this way towards you! Watch your mouth! You better check yourself before you wreck yourself! Do not say another word if I were you! Say one more word and see what I am going to do to you!_____ What did you say?_____
- ☐ Ever physically, mentally, verbally, or emotionally abused her/him/ or your child in front of others?_____If so, where were you?_____
- ☐ How did you feel afterwards?_____
- ☐ Have you ever allowed others to abuse her/him or your child?_____
- ☐ Have you ever strangled or choked her/him or your child?_____Both?_____
- ☐ Ever slapped, smacked, or punched her/him or a child in the face?_____
- ☐ Ever shook a baby or child profusely?____ If yes, What was the reason?_____
  _____
- ☐ Ever bruised a body part? Broke any of their bones? Knocked out any of their teeth?_____ If yes, Why?_____
- ☐ Ever take them to urgent care or the hospital as a result of your violence and abuse?_____ Did you lie to the hospital personnel about what happened?_____
- ☐ Ever been arrested as a result of your violence and abuse on her/him or child?_____
- ☐ If yes, when and what was your sentence or punishment as a result?_____
  _____
- ☐ Used an object to beat up, whoop, or spank?____ What did you use?_____
- ☐ Have you ever spit at or on her/him/or a child?_____

- ☐ Ever beat, slap, choke, threaten, sexually assaulted, or raped a pregnant woman?____
- ☐ What caused you to want to commit the act?_____
  _____

- ☐ Do you take your anger out on your children?_____
- ☐ Do you blame your children for your problems?_____
- ☐ Do you wish you never had children?_____
  If yes, what makes you feel this way?_____
  _____

- ☐ Do you wish your kids were out of your life?_____
  If yes, what makes you feel this way?_____
  _____

- ☐ Have you ever punished a child by withholding a meal or starving them?_____
  If yes, what did they do to make you withhold their meal?_____
  _____
  How did you feel afterwards?_____
- ☐ Do you feel held back in life as a result of your children?_____
  If yes, why do you feel held back?_____
  _____

- ☐ Do you feel held back in life as a result of your mate?_____
  If so, why?_____
- ☐ Do you blame your spouse for the pregnancy?_____
- ☐ Do you wish you never met your mate?_____
- ☐ Do you wish your mate/child/fellow student was dead?_____
- ☐ Do you blame all of your problems on your mate/child/fellow student?_____
- ☐ Do you have any issues with your sexuality or gender identification?_____
- ☐ When you are sad, angry, or depressed, what ways do you find to cope?_____
  _____

- ☐ Did you ever wish you were never born?_____ Why? _____
  _____

- ☐ Ever feel you were blamed or punished for things or crimes you never committed?__
  Why do you feel this way?_____
- ☐ Ever harmed an animal?___ If yes, explain in great detail why you did?_____
  _____
  _____
  _____

- ☐ Did you feel remorseful for harming the animal?_____
- ☐ Did you harm any other animals thereafter?____If yes, explain in great detail?_____
  _____
  _____

_____

_____

☐ Do you feel compelled to harm more animals?_____

☐ Have you ever sought mental health counseling?_____
   If so, when and for what ailment?_____
   How long were you in treatment?_____ Was it effective?_____

☐ Do you enjoy torturing others?_____If so, why?_____

☐ Do you enjoy being tortured?____ If so, why?_____

☐ Have you ever held anyone hostage or against their will?_____If yes, when,
   why, and what was the outcome?_____

☐ Were you ever convicted of abduction or kidnapping?_____

☐ What was the extent of the offense?_____

☐ Do you thrive off of controlling or intimidating others?_____

☐ Have you ever wondered why you were born?_____

☐ Do you have or suffer from separation anxiety?_____

☐ Have you ever been abandoned?_____
   By whom and when?_____
   How did it make you feel?_____

☐ Do you have a Dr. Jekyll and Mr. Hyde personality?_____

☐ Are you a hero at work but a zero at home?_____

☐ Have you ever been called weird or bizarre?_____

☐ Have you ever been called a loose cannon?_____

☐ If you ever broke up with a mate or spouse did you allow them to move on?_____

☐ How did you feel about them dating a new person?_____

☐ Do you come from a dysfunctional family?_____

☐ What was the dysfunction?_____

☐ Have you ever received counseling for this dysfunction?_____

☐ How do you cope with this dysfunction?_____

☐ Do you or have you ever perpetuated this dysfunction?_____

☐ Are you the product of a divorce?_____

☐ Was the divorce amicable or was it war of the roses between your parents?_____

☐ If you had to pick one parent or both, who is the root cause of all your problems?____

☐ What addictions do you currently have?_____

☐ Addictions in Your Past?_____

☐ If yes, what were they?_____

☐ If someone were to ask your children have they ever seen or heard violence or physical, verbal, or emotional abuse in your house by one or both of their parents/caretakers, what would they say?_____

☐ How often are you angry?_____

☐ Do you ever have feelings of losing control?_____

☐ Have you ever displayed psychopathic behavior?_____

☐ Have you ever had or thought of having sex with a child?_____

☐ Have you ever had or thought about having sex with an animal?_____

☐ Ever had sex with an inanimate object like a sex toy or blow up doll?_____

☐ Have you ever molested anyone?_____

☐ Have you ever been molested?_____

☐ If yes, were you molested by a family member, friend, close acquaintance such as a teacher, coach, pastor or stranger?_____

☐ Have you ever thought of having sex with a corpse?_____ Ever had?_____

☐ Have you ever raped or dreamed of raping anyone?____ If so which act?_____

☐ Have you ever used a date rape drug to have sex?___ If yes, when?_____

☐ Ever lied or impersonated a professional position to attract a mate/child?_____

☐ Do you treat women/men/children properly or like property?_____

☐ Did you ever hit any parent/guardian/teacher as a child?_____

☐ Ever hit or beat up a sibling or family member or friend?___ If yes, who?_____

☐ Were your mom/dad/guardians strict disciplinarians?_____

☐ Have you ever been told you were insecure?_____ By whom?_____

☐ Do you think you are an insecure person?_____

☐ Have people warned others of you and your temper?_____

☐ Do you punch walls or throw things when you are mad?_____

☐ How well do you handle rejection?_____

☐ Have you ever attended anger management classes either by choice or government court ordered?_____

☐ Have you ever had "Road Rage" while driving?_____

☐ Did the "Road Rage" escalate to an act of violence?_____

☐ If yes, did anyone get harmed as a result?_____

☐ Were you ever charged as a result of "Road Rage?"_____

☐ Do you take prescribed medicine for your anger and temperament?_____

☐ If yes, which medications have you been prescribed?_____

☐ Currently take or have taken in the past, illegal or black-market drugs for pain?_____

☐ If yes, which ones?_____

☐ Have you ever been diagnosed with Schizophrenia or PTSD or ADHD?_____

Solutions To Permanently Eradicate Domestic Violence, Child Abuse, and Bullying

- Which one?_____ If not, what other diagnosis?_____
- ☐ Besides legal hunting, have you ever harmed or killed any animals?_____
- ☐ If yes, which ones?_____
- ☐ When was the first and last time this occurred?_____
- ☐ What made you harm or kill the animal?_____
- ☐ Did you take enjoyment out of harming or killing the animal?_____
- ☐ Do you enjoy fire? If yes, what fascinates you the most about fires?_____
- ☐ Ever been arrested for arson or any charges related to damaging a property?_____
- ☐ Do you find yourself argumentative?_____
- ☐ How do you feel about losing an argument?_____
- ☐ Are you a confrontational type person?_____If yes, what makes you confrontational?
  _____

- ☐ Do you think women/men/children/animals are weak?_____
- ☐ Did you have a child/children as a teenager?_____
- ☐ How did having children as a teenager impact your childhood and way of living?____
  _____

- ☐ Do you wish you never had your child/children?___ If yes, why?_____
  _____

- ☐ Are you still in a relationship with the individual you had the child/children with when you were a teenager?_____ If not why?_____
- ☐ How would you describe your relationship with them?_____
- ☐ Are they a good parent?_____ Please explain why?_____
  _____

- ☐ Do you have a son, daughter, both, or none?_____
- ☐ Do you regret having children?_____
- ☐ Do you hate children?_____ If yes, why?_____
- ☐ Are you currently employed?____ If yes, what do you do for a living?_____
- ☐ If no, how long have you been unemployed?_____
- ☐ Why have you not been hired?_____
- ☐ What is your dream job?_____ What would you do for free if money was not an issue?_____
- ☐ What do you do for fun and relaxation when you are not at work or during your spare time?_____
- ☐ What are your hobbies?_____
- ☐ Do you belong to any professional organizations?_____ Which ones?_____
- ☐ Who or what was/is your greatest inspiration in your life?_____
- ☐ Why do/did they inspire you?_____
- ☐ Who is your favorite entertainer?_____

Solutions To Permanently Eradicate Domestic Violence, Child Abuse, and Bullying

- [ ] Why are they your favorite?_____
- [ ] What type/genres of music do you listen to?_____
- [ ] What category of movies do you prefer?_____
- [ ] Why do you prefer them?_____
- [ ] What is your favorite television show(s)?_____
- [ ] What makes them your favorite?_____
- [ ] What is your favorite television network? Why?_____
- [ ] What famous living/dead female celebrity do you like and respect?_____
  Why?_____
- [ ] What famous living/dead male celebrity do you like and respect?_____
  Why?_____
- [ ] What celebrity living/dead do you hate with a passion?_____
  Why?_____
- [ ] What does accountability mean to you?_____
- [ ] Do you consider yourself a responsible person?_____
- [ ] Do you consider yourself a respectful person?_____
- [ ] Do you respect most people in your family or life?_____
- [ ] Who do you respect the most and why?_____
- [ ] Who do you respect the least and why?_____
- [ ] Are you respected at work?_____ If yes/no why?_____
- [ ] Do you respect management at your job?_____
- [ ] Do you pay court ordered child support?_____
- [ ] Are you paid up to date and current on your child support?_____
- [ ] Have you ever been incarcerated for failure to pay your child support?_____
- [ ] What is your favorite color?_____
- [ ] What is your favorite number?_____
- [ ] What is your favorite food?_____
- [ ] What is your favorite beverage?_____
- [ ] Are you a hoarder?_____ If yes, why?_____
- [ ] How would you describe your level of hoarding?_____
- [ ] What would you be most ashamed of if people found out certain things about you?_____
  _____

- [ ] When no one is looking, what would you want most people to know about you?_____
  _____

- [ ] If there was a secret or secrets you would like to tell because it is killing you from within, what would it be?_____
  _____

Solutions To Permanently Eradicate Domestic Violence, Child Abuse, and Bullying

- ❏ Are you easily provoked by men/women/children?_____
- ❏ What sets you off the most about men/women/children when you are in a relationship with them?_____
- ❏ What calms/settles you down from getting agitated or angry?_____
- ❏ On a scale of 1-10 (10 is the highest level of love), how much do you love yourself and why?_____
- ❏ On a scale of 1-10 (10 is the highest level of love), how much do others love you and why?_____
- ❏ On a scale of 1-10 (10 is the highest level of love), how much do you want others to love you and why?_____
- ❏ Do you consider yourself a relevant, valuable asset to society or an invisible pariah who society holds in its butt crack?_____
- ❏ On a scale of 1-10 (10 is the highest level of hate), how much do others hate you and why?_____
- ❏ What do you hate about yourself?_____
- ❏ What redeeming qualities do you possess that would make someone love you?_____
  _____
- ❏ What negative qualities do you possess that causes people to hate you?_____
  _____
- ❏ Do you go from 0 to 100 as far as your temperament?_____
- ❏ Are you a leader or follower?_____
- ❏ Are you a closet physical, sexual, mental, verbal, emotional abuser of a loved one, friend, colleague, student, neighbor associate, or stranger?_____
- ❏ What is your religion/faith/belief/or none at all?_____
- ❏ Are you a highly religious or spiritual person?_____
- ❏ When was the last time you partook in religious or spiritual activities?_____
- ❏ What causes you to continue participating in the activities?_____
- ❏ What caused you to stop participating in the activities?_____
- ❏ Do you like sports?_____ If yes, which ones?_____
- ❏ Where, when, why, and who first abused you?_____
- ❏ Are they still abusing you?_____
- ❏ Where, when, why, and who did you first abuse?_____
- ❏ What was the nature of the abuse?_____
- ❏ Do you have a long or short fuse/temper?_____
- ❏ Do you drink/do drugs?_____
- ❏ Are you an alcoholic/addict?_____ What is your drink/drug?_____
- ❏ Recovering alcoholic/addict?_____ What was your drink/drug?_____
- ❏ Are you addicted to porn?_____ What type(s)?_____

Solutions To Permanently Eradicate Domestic Violence, Child Abuse, and Bullying

- ☐ How addicted are you to porn?_____
- ☐ Do you act on your sexual impulses?_____
- ☐ If yes, how do you respond to your urges?_____
- ☐ Have you ever paid for sex?_____ If yes, was it an escort or street prostitute?_____
- ☐ How often do you participate in such activities?_____ When was the last time?_____
- ☐ Do you have any sexually transmitted diseases (STDs)?_____
- ☐ Is your disease communicable, transferable, or contagious?_____
- ☐ Are you currently receiving treatment for your STD?_____
- ☐ Do you smoke?_____ If yes, what do you smoke?_____
- ☐ Ever been on a high-speed chase from police or other law enforcement authorities? _____ If yes, why did you run?_____
- ☐ Have you ever been a fugitive or wanted by the law?_____
- ☐ Ever been on probation or parole or court ordered to do community service hours? _____If yes, what were you on or ordered?_____
- ☐ Currently on probation, parole, or fulfilling court ordered community service hours?___ If yes, what are you on or ordered?_____
- ☐ If yes, what is the remaining time of your probation, parole, community service hours?_____
- ☐ Who is your probation or parole officer?_____
- ☐ Ever violated the terms/conditions of your probation, parole, or required community service hours?_____ If yes, when and what was the violation?____ _____
- ☐ Are you a registered sex offender?_____
- ☐ If yes, how long have you been on the registry?_____
- ☐ Have you ever reoffended?_____ If yes, when?_____
- ☐ Do you have a valid driver's license?_____ What state?_____
- ☐ Do you have a state identification card in lieu of a driver's license?_____
- ☐ What is your greatest strength?_____
- ☐ What is your greatest weakness?_____
- ☐ What is your greatest accomplishment to date in your life?_____
- ☐ What is your greatest failure?_____
- ☐ Are you legally disabled?_____ What's your disability?_____
- ☐ Are you in pain as a result of your disability?_____
- ☐ Do you have a caretaker to assist you?_____
- ☐ Have you always been disabled?_____
- ☐ If not, when did you become disabled?_____
- ☐ Are you angry about your disability?_____

Solutions To Permanently Eradicate Domestic Violence, Child Abuse, and Bullying

☐ If you could love anyone or anything in the world right now, who or what would it be and why?_____

☐ If you could kill anyone or anything in the world right now, who or what would it be and why?_____

_____

☐ If you had a dying wish right now, what would it be?_____

☐ Why are you passionate about that specific wish?_____

☐ If you could be a superhero the world has never seen, who would you be?_____

☐ What would your superpower(s) be?_____

☐ Do you cuss? Are you a profanity laced cursor/cusser?_____

☐ What curse/cuss words do you use regularly?_____

☐ Were you ever cursed at as a child?_____

☐ Were you ever put down as a child?_____

☐ Ever body shame a woman or child?_____ Call them fat, pigs, or ugly?_____

☐ Ever call women or girls b*****s, whores, sluts, hoes, prostitutes, "THOTs"?_____

☐ Call women/girls/kids b*****s, whores, sluts, hoes, prostitutes, or "THOTS" now?__

☐ Do you hate men/women/kids/classmates?_____ If yes, why?_____

☐ Do you hate children?_____ If yes, why?_____

☐ Do you hate animals?____ If yes, which ones and why?_____

☐ Do you hate anyone in the lesbian, gay, bisexual, transgender, or queer (LGBTQ) community?____ If yes, why?_____

☐ Ever harmed, abused, assaulted, damaged or offended anyone or anything in the LGBTQ community?_____ If yes, what was the extent of the violence, abuse or damage?_____

☐ Ever arrested as a result?_____ If yes, what was your sentence or conditions of release?_____

☐ Are you receiving any services, treatment or medication for your PTSD or ADHD?

_____

☐ Have you ever stalked or criminally harassed anyone or anything?_____

☐ Ever exhibited the behavior of a stalker or harasser such as calling compulsively and leaving mean or terrorizing threats?_____

☐ Ever stalked them or harassed them at their job or school or anywhere they were?_____Why?_____

☐ Ever shown up uninvited to where they were and acted violently or with intimidation? _____Why?_____

☐ Ever waited for them no matter the wait just to see and talk with them?_____ Why?_____

☐ If yes, who and when?_____

Solutions To Permanently Eradicate Domestic Violence, Child Abuse, and Bullying

- ☐ Followed them and watched them as if you were running government surveillance and intelligence on them?_____ Why?_____
- ☐ Did you buy them gifts or send them items hoping to rekindle the relationship?_____
- ☐ Did they accept the gift?_____ How did you react if they refused the gift?____
  _____

- ☐ Have you ever returned to a job you have been fired from?_____
- ☐ Do you have an impulsive explosive disorder?_____
- ☐ Ever commit a crime after a fight with a wife, girlfriend, or parent?_____
- ☐ Ever commit a crime after a breakup, separation, or divorce from a spouse, or mate?____ If yes, what?_____
- ☐ Have you ever been thrown out of a residence or place of business?_____
  Why?_____
- ☐ Were you ever arrested as a result of such behavior?_____
- ☐ If yes, what was the outcome?_____
- ☐ Have you ever vandalized a car, home, business or church?_____ If yes, why?_____
- ☐ Were you prosecuted, or court ordered to pay restitution to the victims?_____
- ☐ If yes, what was the extent of the sentence or amount ordered to repay the victim?
  _____

- ☐ What do you most fear or are most afraid of or have a phobia that petrifies you?_____
  _____

- ☐ How long have you been this way?_____
- ☐ Were you ever able to overcome this fear or phobia?_____
- ☐ What did you do to conquer your fear or phobia?_____
- ☐ Do you suffer from "Psychological Syndrome" where the more you were abused by your abuser, the more you wanted to be with your abuser?_____
- ☐ Do you have an obsessive, impulsive, compulsive, dominant or controlling personality?_____
- ☐ Have you ever had a food addiction?_____ What foods?_____
- ☐ Have you ever been anorexic, bulimic, or morbidly obese?_____
- ☐ Have you ever cheated sexually on your spouse or significant other?_____
- ☐ Has someone ever cheated sexually on you with another person?_____
- ☐ Are you a sexual predator?_____
- ☐ Have you ever attempted suicide?_____ If so, when and why?_____
  _____

- ☐ Are you fully recovered from suicidal thoughts?_____
- ☐ When was the last time you attempted suicide?_____
- ☐ Have you ever suffered from depression?_____

Solutions To Permanently Eradicate Domestic Violence, Child Abuse, and Bullying

- ☐ If yes, what was the trigger of the depression?_____
- ☐ Are you fully recovered from depression?_____
- ☐ Are you currently taking any medication for depression?_____
- ☐ Ever served others by being a volunteer and contributor to your community?_____
- ☐ If yes, what or where did you serve?_____
- ☐ How did you feel about serving others?_____
- ☐ Have you ever lied to bring attention or sympathy to yourself?_____
- ☐ Do you lie even when you know the truth?_____
- ☐ Have you ever been a peeping Tom?_____
- ☐ Have you ever been arrested for being a peeping Tom?_____
- ☐ If yes, when and what causes you to want to peep?_____
- ☐ When was the last time you peeped?_____
- ☐ Do you seem to always find yourself in toxic or abusive Relationships?_____
- ☐ Do you argue with just about anyone close to you?_____
- ☐ Are you addicted to drama and trauma?_____
- ☐ Do you hate yourself?_____ If yes, why?_____
  _____
- ☐ Do you hate your mom, dad, or both parents?_____ If yes, why?_____
  _____
- ☐ Do you hate women, men, or both?_____ If yes, why?_____
  _____
- ☐ Do you hate children?_____ If yes, why!_____
  _____
- ☐ Do you hate animals?_____ If yes, why and which ones?_____
  _____
- ☐ Do you hate any member of the LGBTQ community?_____If yes, who and
  why?_____
- ☐ Do you easily bond with people or does it take a while for you to warm up and trust
  any person?_____
- ☐ Ever abandoned at any point in your life?_____ If yes, who abandoned you and
  why?_____
- ☐ Have you ever served in the military?_____ If yes, what branch?_____
- ☐ Were you full time or in the reserves?_____
- ☐ Did you retire from the military?_____ If yes, your final rank and total length
  of time served?_____
- ☐ If you did not retire, how long did you serve and why did you leave the military?__
  _____
- ☐ Were you honorably or dishonorably discharged?_____
  If dishonorably charged, what was the reason(s)?_____

Solutions To Permanently Eradicate Domestic Violence, Child Abuse, and Bullying

☐ Do you have any regrets about what caused your discharge?_____

☐ Have you ever been in any war or potential kill zone?_____

☐ Have you ever killed anyone?_____

☐ Have you ever witnessed a murder while serving in the military or as a civilian?_____

☐ Ever seen a dead body other than one at a funeral while serving or as a civilian?_____

☐ Have you ever witnessed a rape while serving in the military or as a civilian?_____

☐ Ever fantasize about killing, raping, or torturing anyone?_____ If yes, which ones and why?_____

☐ Are you a jealous person?_____ What makes you jealous?_____

☐ Are you an insecure person?_____ What do you believe is the root cause for you being or feeling insecure?_____

☐ Are you afraid of people leaving you permanently?_____

☐ Are you an introvert, hermit, or isolationist?_____

☐ Ever had sex from an individual off a dating, social, or pornographic website?____ Which site?_____ Why do you like this site?_____
_____

☐ Are you a sex addict?_____ Why do you think you are a sex addict?_____
_____

☐ Are you capable of healthily loving others?_____

☐ Are you capable of receiving healthy love from others?_____

☐ Did you witness healthy or unhealthy relationships growing up as a child?_____

☐ Do you think as a child you were shown how to properly love another person?_____

☐ Do you just want to be loved?_____

☐ Do you give hugs?_____ Do you like or dislike hugs?_____

☐ Are you comfortable receiving hugs?_____

☐ Has anyone ever hugged you?_____

☐ Have you ever been missing?_____

☐ Have you ever run away?_____

☐ If there was one person or thing that is the root of cause for all your pain and suffering who or what would you say is the cause?_____

☐ Has anyone ever suggested you get counseling or professional help, or you should see a psychiatrist or psychologist or receive psychotherapy?_____

☐ If so, who recommended the services and when?_____

☐ How well can you give advice, negative critiquing or criticism?_____

☐ How well can you take advice, negative critiquing or criticism from others?_____

☐ Did you take their advice?_____ If yes, what were the results and your opinion?
_____

☐ If no, why did you feel you didn't require the services?_____

☐ Have you ever been homeless?_____ If yes, when?_____

☐ What was the reason you became homeless?_____

☐ How did you overcome your homelessness?_____

☐ Were you raised in the suburbs, the city streets, a house, military housing, section 8 government housing, from home to home with no permanent dwelling because you were never adopted, "the hood," in a trailer park, or in the projects?_____

☐ Do you punch or kick walls, slam doors or destroy property?_____

☐ Ever thrown, broken, or destroyed a cell phone or any electronic device?_____

☐ Ever cheated on your spouse or girl/boyfriend?_____

☐ Ever accused your partner of cheating?_____

☐ Ever been accused of cheating?_____

☐ Ever denied any of your children?_____ If yes, why?_____

☐ Ever fought or beat up your Mom or Dad?_____

☐ Ever set a person or animal on fire?_____

☐ Ever put a baby, child, or adult person in a trashcan/dumpster after killing them?____

☐ Ever dismember an animal or human being?_____

☐ Ever been questioned by the police or any law enforcement?_____

☐ Ever voluntarily or involuntarily been committed to a treatment center or hospital?__

☐ Ever put a tracking device on a car, phone or electronic device of mate?_____

☐ Why did you feel you had to monitor them?_____

☐ Have you ever had warrants?_____ If yes, what were they?_____

☐ Do you believe in retaliation, getting even with or getting some "get back" on someone who you believe stabbed you in the back, wronged or crossed you?_____

☐ Ever had your children removed from your custody and why?_____
_____
_____

☐ Have you ever received or attended anger management classes?_____
When and For what reason?_____

☐ Do you have anger issues?_____ Why are you so angry or what does your anger stem from? _____
_____

☐ Did you witness violence as a child?_____ What did you see?_____
_____

☐ How do you feel towards the individuals committing the violence against you or a loved one? _____
_____
_____

☐ Do you make great choices and decisions for your life?_____

☐ How about for your children?_____

☐ Do you think before you react?_____

☐ Do you think before you speak?_____

☐ Are you remorseful or regret abusing someone after you have violently assaulted or abused them?_____

☐ Have you ever had a Domestic Violence Protective Order (also called a "50B," "DVPO," "protective order, or "restraining order"), served on you?_____

☐ How did you feel about the order being served on you?_____

☐ How did you want to respond to the person placing the order on you?_____
   _____

☐ How did you respond to the order placed on you?_____

☐ Did you comply or violate the order?_____

☐ Did you lose custody of your children as a result of the order?_____

☐ Do you run from confrontations or face confrontations with violence?_____

☐ Do you minimize your violence, deny it, or blame others for it?_____

☐ Are you a difficult or petty person?_____

☐ How many foster homes have you been in during your life?_____

☐ How many times were you passed over for adoption?_____ Ever adopted?_____

☐ Were you ever abused in foster care?____ If yes, by whom?_____

☐ Why do you think they abused you?_____

☐ Ever put or throw a person or animal out of a car?_____ Why?_____

☐ Have you ever promised an individual that you violently physically assaulted or abused that "you would never do it again?"_____ Did you keep your promise?_____

☐ When you are in a relationship, do you control every aspect of your mate's life?____ Does your mate become your property?_____ Do you think you own them?

☐ Are you a leader or follower?_____Why?_____

☐ Do you know if you are capable of being loved?_____

☐ Do you realize there are people in the world who actually care about your life?_____

☐ Are you willing to do everything humanly possible to get well mentally so that you may be totally healed from domestic violence, child abuse or bullying?_____

☐ How many times have you been married?_____

☐ What's the longest you have been married?_____

☐ How many divorces have you experienced?_____

☐ What has been the main reason you have gotten a divorce?_____

☐ Do you believe you can be what you want to be?_____

☐ When was the last time you remember being happy and actually loving your life?___
   _____

☐ Are you a lovable person?_____

Solutions To Permanently Eradicate Domestic Violence, Child Abuse, and Bullying

☐   What makes you a loveable person?_____

☐   If you are not loveable, what are you?_____

☐   Why do you say that about yourself?_____
    _____
    _____

☐   Do you want to be permanently healed or treated?_____

☐   Who harmed you?_____

☐   What happened?_____
    _____
    _____
    _____
    _____
    _____
    _____
    _____
    _____
    _____
    _____
    _____
    _____
    _____

☐   What specifically caused you to become violent, abusive, or violent to others?
    _____
    _____
    _____
    _____
    _____
    _____
    _____
    _____
    _____
    _____
    _____
    _____
    _____
    _____

☐   Would you be willing to take a lie detector test to prove your truthfulness to the
    answers you gave to this survey?_____

Solutions To Permanently Eradicate Domestic Violence, Child Abuse, and Bullying

If no, why?_____

❏ What questions would you add to this survey?_____

_____

_____

_____

_____

_____

_____

_____

❏ What questions would you delete from the survey?_____

_____

_____

_____

_____

_____

Why? _____

_____

Thank You For Beginning The Process of Getting Healed! This Accountability and Awareness Violence Survey is completely 1000% Anonymous. You Have The Right To Take Back Your Survey At Any Time Up To 30 Days! After 30 Days The Survey Is Destroyed Via Shredder. Family Mankind™ Uses The Survey Strictly For Consultation With The Volunteer Domestic Violence Offender, Child Abuser, Or Bully. The Employees and Volunteers of Family Mankind™ Are Not Licensed Physicians, Psychologists, Psychiatrists, Psychotherapists or Counselors! As Such, We Are Only Offering Suggestions And Opinions To Help Domestic Violence Offenders, Child Abusers, and Bullies To Try To Overcome and Permanently Eradicate Domestic Violence, Child Abuse, and Bullying! Our Methods, Techniques, and Coping Skills Are Merely Recommendations, Opinions, and Suggestions From Individuals Who Have Overcome Domestic Violence, Child Abuse, and Bullying! We Are Not Offering Licensed Clinical Psychologist or Psychiatrists Expert Opinions or Advice! Thank You and God Bless You For Your Participation and Willingness To Get Healthy!

Solutions To Permanently Eradicate Domestic Violence, Child Abuse, and Bullying

SOLUTIONS

Evil Only Wins, When Good Does Nothing! The Definition of Insanity Is Doing The Same Thing Over and Over Again, Expecting Different Results! God Blesses Motion! Get In Motion and Do Something Positive! Do Something Now! Are You Part Of The Solution or Problem?

You are probably wondering why I did not put these solutions to permanently eradicating domestic violence, child abuse, bullying, and all of the aftereffects and nasty vines of violence, abuse and bullying such as rape, sexual assault, sexual harassment, human trafficking, workplace, church and school massacres, animal cruelty, along with LGBTQ discrimination and hate, at the beginning or middle of the book! I am not deliberately saving the best for last, I simply wanted you to see the making and history of a monster and then present the solutions. To present the solutions first is like giving you the answers to the test first without knowing the dynamics of the problem. The formula and example to solve the equation is why we go to school so that we can learn the theory of why we have a problem, then learn and practice the mechanics to understand how to overcome the issues, and then finally we are able to use these winning solutions to these complex and sensitive life situations, so we can now apply them to our daily lives. Everyone loves the climactic finale of an exceptional novel or movie, only if we are witnessing someone else's pain, but moreover, the solution to end the pain. I pray I provide that for you with my journey through domestic violence, child abuse, and bullying.

Before anything can permanently change and truly be eradicated, your mind has to be fully receptive to the required changes you will have to make. The body will always follow what the brain says to do. Mental health is equally as important if not as more significant than your physical health. Get help now by way of psychiatric therapy or counseling. "Honey, I promise I will not do it again!" does not work and has never worked. Victims don't want you to tell them you won't do it again they want you to show them you will never do "it" again! Making a promise that you are not 1000% sure you will keep is a solemn commitment, and when you break that commitment in the future, it pushes your victim further away from believing you are capable of a permanent change and more likely to harm them more often and worse than before. You genuinely are pulling away from them and pulling closer to the mental or actual cemetery and or penitentiary. I promise you that you cannot keep a promise such as never assaulting them again unless you truly get professional mental health and psychological services and into a proactive healthy lifestyle that includes an aggressive continuum of post-treatment services.

Like any solution to addiction, please know that if you are doing it to appease a judge's court order or the one you have been abusing and violently offending to get back into their good graces, STOP Right Now! It will not work! Is your attitude magnetic and drawing people to you or is it repulsively repelling? The saying used to be, "Treat people the way you would want to be treated!" Surprisingly enough though, you can not apply that initially to a violent offender, child abuser, bully, or even a college student hazing another classmate. Here is why. Violence, abuse, bullying, intimidation, stalking, torture, hazing or anything to describe intentionally harming anyone is their normal and regardless of the degree of it, to the person being violated and offended, no matter what you call it, to them it is violence. But to the violent offenders, this abuse is the way they are used to being treated and is their normalcy for treatment to others. The term should be, "Treat people the way nonviolent and non-abusive people treat others!" Treat people the way they want to be treated is what I have learned in my personal and business life. Not everyone wants the red-carpet treatment, but they do wish to be treated with respect! Some people would prefer a white or purple carpet versus that of a red carpet! Make a commitment and resolution you can keep and take to the grave. Each day commit to getting your mental health and personal relationships into shape!

It took me 21 years from birth to be broken so for me to expect to be healed entirely tomorrow is truly unrealistic! Sure there are a few who went cold turkey and did it instantly, but they are the exception and not the rule. Rome was not built in a day and neither was your life. Freedom from pain will be made well when you develop the right coping skills, life techniques and support services into the very concrete foundation of your life. I certainly was not the exception as others were to be rapidly delivered from being a domestic violence offender and abuser, but I can for certain tell you that your permanent healing, like my healing, will come if you are doing everything to eliminate the abuse triggers by getting to the root cause of your pain. If it happened to me, it will definitely happen for you and much sooner than me because I am giving you my secret sauces to achieve your permanent pain solution. My solutions are practical in the simplest application form versus clinical.

FAMILY MANKIND™ provides a range of flexible domestic violence and child abuse solutions, powerful life skill techniques and extensive demographic and global reach for curing and curbing violence, child abuse, and bullying. This call, howl, and shout out, is for all men and women, and in some cases youthful abusers, bullies, and violent offenders to stand up and move forward to a permanent coping solution. This is not a pledge or request to stop violence and abuse against women and children by me, but rather, it is a requirement and lifelong commitment to love and respect yourself, others, and your legacy!

1. Submit, Admit, Commit! Submit to the Pain! Admit You Have A Pain! What's The Root Cause Of The Pain? Then Commit To Finding The Solution To The Pain In Your Brain! Go See A Licensed Professional!

You must commit first to submit, admit and commit to the continuous process and techniques to prevent violence, bullying, and abuse against women and children that will get you healed not treated. Do you want to be treated or cured? You have to get on your knees, sit still, or bow down and submit to tapping out to a force that will kill your life and legacy! You have to surrender to yourself and resolve in your mind that you alone can never defeat the internal battle between you and what is causing you to be a violent offender, abuser, and bully. Then you must respectfully admit that you are what you are at this time and it is what it is at this time but your declaration to permanently eradicate and seek mental wellness solutions and acknowledgment of being an offender, abuser, and bully will positively change your future forever. Commit to the consistent and continued mental wellness journey so as to retain the proper life and coping skills and techniques to strengthen the healing of your mind, body, soul and relationships with others so how you eradicated and overcame your deficiencies will be your legacy and testimony and ultimately show you and the world how much you loved and respected yourself and them! Must truly fall in love with yourself? How can you love others if you do not have a love for yourself?

2. Learn Coping Skills & Techniques To Set You Up Effectively In Life!

You have to build your fuse box called coping skills. What happens to a house where there is no fuse box and breakers? The house burns down! Your fuses will save your life and others. You have to find the root cause of your pain to get to the solution! Stand up to violence and no longer stand for being an abuser, bully, or violent offender. You have to be in your right mind so that you are not out of your mind! You must find what keeps you of sound mind, so you do not lose yourself! This may sound a bit insane and I am not advocating the use or selling of illegal drugs but if smoking marijuana keeps certain people from committing heinous crimes and abuse against women, children and animals then light up and smoke to your heart's content. If that act alone keeps them from harming others then beam them up! I had to learn to be a respectful loser! I hated losing more than winning! I could not stand to lose to anyone at anything. I was quite provocative in that I would push buttons and hit below the belt if it meant the difference of me proving my point or winning versus losing. There was nothing off limits or established boundaries of fairness. My behavior and treatment to those people closest to me were incredibly disrespectful, cruel, repugnant and despicable! Just to share a few examples of my bullying as a child, I remember pushing an unhinged, weighted screen door on top of my cousin Teeny; throwing a boulder on top of the head of family friend Johnathan Washington, bullying Darell Dixon* and Bryan Adams* (R.I.P my friends) and many others for their lunch or other things I desired; beating up cousin Ebby and family friend Anthony; and forcing grass into the mouth of my friend Wilbert White all before I hit junior high school. I did not know how to manage myself properly because I was an out of control bully with zero coping skills.

The bottom line is I was wild and totally out of control for as long as I can remember. For the sake of others, there was never any glamour or humor for me when it came to bullying others. It was always all about my attitude to give respect and be respected by all people. When I show up on the scene, I wanted everyone to know I was there like a lion, without me having to announce I was there. When you were as wild as I was and subject to go off on someone at any time for no particular reason, people always know where you are. I know this type of attitude today is dangerous if you are not respectfully respected by others. What does society do when a wild animal mauls or kills a human? We hunt down the animal, and if we can find it, we often kill it. However, what if there is no report of the mauling or killing or worst we put the animal back in society, not being domesticated, or worst we allow the animal to continue roaming with zero consequences! Absolute chaos!

This is what it was like for me growing up as a bully, and especially when I became well known for my athleticism too. This is what the government and society does with violent and abusive offenders. Would you want to get in a cage with the tiger that mauled Roy of Siegfried and Roy or in a pool with the serial killer whale Tilikum after he has just attacked or killed one of his trainers? We put our women and children back in the homes of their parents, caretakers, or boyfriends and husbands with these abusers and violent offenders who have not received any consequences or appropriate training and solutions for their behavior or they come home from being incarcerated because of their violent actions only to abuse again or take their abuse and violence to a greater extent because they are being returned to the same environment with the same people and no new coping skills and techniques. We have to trust and believe that people can change and only change with effective techniques and a permanent support system. This is one of the valid reasons why I never returned as a permanent citizen to Baltimore. I was going right back to the environment that built and nurtured me as a violent offender, abuser, and bully. That would be insanity. I had choices that allowed me to stay away. What if I did not have options to stay away? I would be worse off.

3. The Rubik's Cube- Can A 4-Month-Old Baby Figure It Out?

Solving the Rubik's cube is like solving domestic violence. Buy a Rubik's cube! A Rubik's cube is a puzzle with multicolored squares, where you attempt to twist and turn so that all the squares on each face are of the same color. You scramble the cube to where there are no back to back, side to side same colors. The mission of the game is to try to figure the cube, so all sides have the same color. How long did it take you to figure **IT** out? Now, scramble **IT** again as you did previously. Once **IT** is all scrambled again, hand the cube to a 4-month-old baby. Set the stopwatch to 4 minutes! Go! Did the baby figure it out? Trying to figure out domestic violence and child abuse is like a 4-month-old baby trying to figure out a freshly scrambled Rubik's cube or the sensitive method of defusing a live bomb after the first time they have ever seen **IT**. The solutions are beyond complex and complicated. The difference is there is no room for error! Trying to figure out how to stop domestic violence, bullying, and child abuse on your own is like trying to solve the Rubik's cube with a ticking time bomb implanted in **IT**. However, this is the very first time you have ever seen one and you only have seconds to unscramble & defuse **IT**. You must get help in the form of professional mental treatment before the bomb goes off killing us all. Get help now! Domestic violence is not a game to play with because **IT** can blow up in your face at any time or place. If you are no longer a domestic violence offender, child abuser, or bully, I proudly salute you and tell you to put your solved Rubik's Cube on your mantle for the world to see. Boom!

4. Apologize-Understand The Power Of Telling Someone You Wronged Them! There Is Incredible Healing For All With A Sincere Apology!

Apologize sincerely to your victims and all individuals impacted by your abuse. Victims should not be the first person to reach out to their victimizer for their healing. The victimizer should be more accountable and aware that the healing process begins with their victimizers proactively apologizing to them when their victims are ready to receive their apology. If your victim beats you to an apology, they are genuinely trying to free themselves from your anchor of pain, and it should be you to cut the cord to free them, not them cutting the anchor you put around their neck and on their brain and back.

5.　The Commitment Oath

No Excuses Policy! "Excuses are tools of the incompetent which builds monuments of nothingness and those who specialize in using them seldom accomplish anything!" There is never an excuse for abuse! It does not matter why or when you abuse your victim! What matters is your proactive approach to apologizing to your victims by having your actions line up with your apology if you are sincere about permanently stopping your abuse and helping others just like you to overcome their inadequacies! I will never hit or be hit! I will never abuse or be abused! I will never bully anyone or be bullied by anyone! I will never silence anyone because of violence, and I will never be silenced by violence by anyone! I will yell, tell, scream, holler, and snitch before I end up with a stitch or in a permanent ditch! I will never abuse or violently offend anyone or anything, including myself, whether it be physically, mentally, verbally, or emotionally, and I will not be a victim of abuse by anyone or anything! I will never remain silent when I see, hear, or learn of any child abuse or domestic violence! I will howl and growl until I am heard! I will preserve the lives and legacies of abused women, children, and abusers through proactive prevention! I will forever be accountable and aware of my life and behavior and will never use any excuse to justify my abuse!

6.　No More Secrets or Sitting idle in solid silence! "I will never sit in silence to violence! I will be a HOWLER™ and GROUNDER™!"

I will Howl For Help! Child Abuse, Bullying and Domestic Violence Helpline! Text, Telephone, Email, Chat! I will stand up to violence! We must howl and growl for our lives and the lives of others being abused!" A wolf's howl can be heard over 6 miles by other wolves in a forest and ten miles on the tundra! When you hear a wolf's howl what do you think? Silence is just as bad as the abuse and only leads to regret and second-guessing once your loved one is gone forever. We have to mark our territory and leave a scent to attract other wolves to help other wolves! Do you want to be treated or healed? If you want to be healed, it must be revealed! Whether you are a victim of violence and abuse or the one who is or has victimized others, I need you! Do you want to be wanted for helping others or WANTED by law enforcement? If you want to be healed, it must be revealed! My secret was I was abused, and consequently I became an abuser who never got help and as a result, became a convicted felon because of domestic violence and abuse against my former girlfriend! "I systematically destroyed my life! What is your benefit or gain for you to abuse or kill anyone? Throw Up your pain by talking and walking it out! Have you ever thrown up and felt better afterward?

7. Stay Away From and Get Out of Toxic Relationships Strategically

Some relationships breed toxic fumes that are bad for your overall health, which will smother you and eventually kill your entire existence. Do not ever be around or stay with someone that does not want to be with you! Why would you stay in a relationship with someone who does not want to be with you? That is what I did not want to accept when my former girlfriend told me "it was over!" If I had been more mature or better yet, more prepared, I would have gathered my things, thanked her for the great memories, apologized for the bad ones, and moved on to see another day. Sure I would be upset and be stunned by that person's decision to no longer want to be with me, but the reality of their choice is when someone says you are not the one for them, you should be thanking them for being honest with their feelings and their position in the relationship. I have replayed that scenario in my mind a trillion times over the years after my stint in the penitentiary. The bottom line is you never want to continue any relationship if one party makes it clear you are no longer a welcomed guest in their life or party. Run, do not walk, from the relationship and find someone who wants to be with you. What you will do is keep the possibilities of a successful relationship open with someone else rather than doing something violent that will cause you and the person you once loved and who once loved you, a set of negative circumstances that may be irrevocable, as was the case for me. That same sentiment includes any company that does not appreciate what you bring to the table by way of your results at work. If you are bringing it at work and they do not see the value in you as an employee, then upgrade yourself by finding a better job solution and move on to your destiny. My girlfriend rightfully ran for her life from me because I was dangerous! She got out! I was a toxic agent.

8. No Insecurities! Secure Your Life! Who & What Made You Insecure?

Tons of relationships suffer at the hands of insecure people! Many people become insecure because someone, generally a parent, has not made them secure as an individual and as a result they cannot trust that the next person is going to make them feel secure enough because they have been abused and neglected by the very individuals who should have been securing safety, a healthy and stable environment and love in their life. When any human being is abused, bullied and neglected by a loved one how does it become possible for them to feel secure in any relationship or environment when they have been deviously betrayed by the individuals who should have been loving them and not harming them? They and their environment often become carbon copies of their abusers because that is their normal and that insecurity is what has been placed in their heart, soul, and mind.

If your parent is beating the life out of you or your other parent and no one comes to rescue you how much hope do you have that the next "loving" person in your life will not traumatize the same way? If a school official or other classmates sit on the sidelines and watch you get bullied or beat down and no one comes to the rescue how secure or hopeful is that child that tomorrow will be a better school day? Eventually, enough is enough because either an individual's tolerance level is tired of bullying or being bullied and something will give in the process. "I am not a bully, child abuser, or domestic violence offender!" should be what we are teaching in health education or citizenship class at school and in the church to all individuals of all ages. We should be seeing those banners and not state champions banners or retired jersey numbers hanging in the school cafeterias or raptors in the gymnasium! We should be wearing wrist bands, T-shirts, or chains that declares any message that we are against violence, abuse, and bullying and are about love and respect for one another! When an abuser or bully knows that you have an entire family, school, or community that does not tolerate that behavior, they are less likely to be offenders. When a bully or abuser knows that they do not have to try to make a team that they are already on and that they are loved and will not be harmed, they will be less likely to harm another and more likely to love another and themselves. We have to continually plant these seeds of love and encouragement in our children to give them the coping skills and techniques to live a mentally healthy, balanced and secure life. What will it take to make you feel safe and secure? You must find your security!

9. **Consequential Critical Thinking? Think Twice Before You Roll The Life Dice! Absolutely No Regrets For The Only Lifetime You Get! Healing Is In Your Mentality!**

You can learn a lot from an individual who has lost in life! Sure we are all going to make our fair share of mistakes and errors in life that ultimately strengthens and builds solid character in some of us. But what about those mistakes in judgment that can never be made right like getting a felony criminal record or taking an innocent individual's life or peace of mind. You cannot get that person's life back once they are gone forever. How do you personally restore a victim's peace of mind? How do you win back the communities trust once you are labeled a convicted felon? What will it cost you or the ones you love when you do not get help? The definition of insanity is doing the same things over and over again while expecting different results. Before you react or overreact, you best think things through critically because the consequences could be irreversible or irreparable or irreplaceable! When it comes to any violence, it will always let you down! You lose all hope of reconciliation when you cross a line that can never be made right with the victim of your abuse. Where your apology may never be accepted and the way you remember life can never be restored to its original condition. Now I will always hold onto hope, and the belief that all things are possible through the Lord but even then miracles only come about like winning the Powerball. Then there is the disbelief that sets in that you can have zero contact with them. The dreams you have in your sleep are real but then you wake to your reality, and the real-life nightmare now becomes your reality! What did you gain by winning the battle and losing the war? Do you now wish you could take it back and that it would have never happened? What about your relationship with your kids, family, job, colleagues, community, church? Now you have an arrest record and criminal background history! Do you love yourself? If so, why did you do this to yourself?

10. **Volunteer Your Time With Purposeful Activities! Serving Others Will Help You To Focus On Helping Others Which Will In Turn Help You!**

It is not about how you lived, but how you served others! Serve others. Less about you and more about meeting the needs of others! Serving others will fulfill you with a purpose! ***Do not be mad at the solution if you are part of the problem and not working towards a solution.*** Occupy your time with fruitful relationships such as any cause that you can personally relate to and help individuals who can benefit from your talents, resources, influence, and skillsets. You have to believe in the cause you are serving. If you are a former domestic violence offender, child abuser, or bully I need and want you with me. For years when I first got out of the penitentiary, I volunteered at a homeless shelter. The volunteering gave me a purpose and a commitment to help others. It had me focus on helping and serving others when the truth was it was serving and fulfilling me. There are great charities and causes like Susan G Komen, Shriners Hospital, local food banks, Habitat for Humanity, St. Jude's Children's Research Hospital, and FAMILY MANKIND™!

11. You Are What You Devote Your Time To Daily! Find Your Sanctuary! Your Peace! Positive Activities Breeds A Positive Spirit!

Be involved in positive activities such as volunteering, joining a gym and working out, hobbies, learning a trade or language, traveling, being involved in the church, the arts of music, theatre, writing music or plays or a movie, filming, making beats, painting, drawing, dancing, singing, deejaying, playing Xbox, PlayStation, supporting a political candidate, reading to children, coaching, cheerleading, online gaming, playing fantasy sports, start a blog, podcast, or a book or dining club, wine or beer tasting club or cigar review club, or play chess, checkers, or card games such as spades, bid whist or bid wiz, tonk, poker or pitch horse shoes, corn hole, or ride a horse, building a business, running for political office, read to children, coach, or jet ski or learn to swim or hike, fish, hunt, canoe, or box or karate, taekwondo, or learn to cook or bake or bead or crochet or yard sell or restore old things like cars or collect baseball cards or stamps or coins or exotic vehicles, animals or women, be a comedian, write jokes funny skits, church activities, volunteer at a hospital or meals for wheels. Teaching other sports such as Lacrosse, Crew(Rowing), Boxing, Bowling, Cycling, Rugby, Track and Field, Fencing, Weightlifting/Bodybuilding, Reading/Writing Clubs, Equestrian, Dog Breeding, Chess, Gaming, Journalism, Police Law Enforcement, Pilots, Broadcasting, Real Estate, Music Production, Promotions, Engineering! Do something that is fulfilling to you and benefits others. Idle time is a waste of energy that leads to death... occupy and fill your time with something that fulfills you inside until you become extraordinary and not ordinary! Work with what God gave you as a talent or skill set like my boy Lee Adams who has a smile Ministry! We are all good at something. Just find what makes you smile.

Let your little light shine for the world to see and know! Bring value to the world! Do not take away from it and never replenish or upgrade it! Be the first! Be #1 or a loyal and dedicated number 2! Occupy your time loving one another not shoving or shoveling one another! Let your life be remembered for your triumph and not your tragedy! Do not be Comfortable, Do not settle, Stay Hungry! Time kills Dreams! Get Busy Living Your One and Only Lifetime! Idle hands belong to the devil! God blesses motion. Evil only wins when good does nothing! Positive activities breed positive results. You are what you constantly do! Own it better than anyone in the world!

12. Mirrors- Whatever They See Is What They Will Probably Be!

You are giving your children the roadmap on how to treat other people and how to destroy themselves! As a parent, would you walk up to a baby and hand them a live grenade? Eventually, they will somehow manage to pull the pin on themselves or society will pull the pin for them based on their behavior. If you abuse them, eventually they will abuse themselves or their babies or family members and friends. Maybe they do not physically harm others, but they have to resort to drugs, alcohol, sex or other forms of addiction such as becoming a workaholic. Do not get stuck in the mirror whereas your children who come to visit you in jail think you are stuck in the mirror because they can see you through the visitor's glass, but they are unable to touch you! All we want to do as parents is protect our children from pain. Are you protecting your children from pain or are you the root cause of their pain?

13. MenTours™ and WomenTours™ At Family Mankind! Partnerships!

Most men and women need *"Tour Guides"* in life. Serve others to serve you! Be a servant leader volunteer in your community. Less about you and more about helping others will eventually show you that serving others helps to heal your mind and spirit! We can use you at Family Mankind! Share your testimony!

14. No Bullying School Platform

Snitching Saves Lives Howl and Growl Helpline! Society has made it acceptable and uncool not to snitch or tell the authorities on someone. We have to create a new culture and make it acceptable and comfortable for our children in our communities by instilling life whistles in our children that it is okay to tell someone that another person is harming you or about to hurt you! Many children do not feel safe and are committing suicide or homicide as a result of feeling threatened or insecure in the belief that they can be helped by other children, adults, parents, the police, school officials and counselors.

15. Parents, School Staff, and Other Caring Adults Have A Role To Play In Preventing Bullying. Adults Must Intervene Immediately!

According to Stopbullying.gov, to help kids, You MUST: Help kids understand bullying. Talk about what bullying is and how to stand up to it safely. Tell kids bullying is unacceptable. Make sure kids know how to get help. Keep the lines of communication open. Check-in with kids often. Listen to them. Know their friends, ask about school, and understand their concerns. Encourage kids to do what they love. Special activities, interests, and hobbies can boost confidence, help kids make friends, and protect them from bullying behavior. Model how to treat others with kindness and respect. ***The sooner adults are involved, the sooner bullying STOPS!***

Solutions To Permanently Eradicate Domestic Violence, Child Abuse, and Bullying

Twelve Ways You Can Prevent Bullying [240]

i. **Understand the nature and extent of the bullying.** *Bullying is prevalent among students, with nearly one in five students reporting that they have been bullied on school property, and one in nine students reporting that they have been cyberbullied in the previous year.* [241,242,243,244]

ii. **Understand the risk factors that contribute to bullying**, *such as a dysfunctional or abusive home life, behavioral difficulties, mental health issues, and socially disorganized communities.* [245]

iii. **Establish an open dialogue with your child.** *Simply listening to what children have to say can be quite revealing. It's better to have an acute ear to see what is really going on in a child's life than to lecture the child. Engaging a child in a discussion about school, friends, and after-school activities can be a constructive way to find out what your child is involved in, and with whom.*

iv. **Set boundaries with consequences for your child's actions.** *Waiting until children have committed acts of violence may be too late. Children benefit from discipline and boundaries that keep them safe and teach them about acceptable behaviors. Your child should know that stepping outside those boundaries is not only inappropriate but results in consequences.*

v. **Set an example for your child.** *From an early age, children are influenced by their parents. Whether consciously or subconsciously, children begin to mimic their parents, including how their parents handle stress and display prejudice.* [246] *When children observe physical or psychological abuse at home, they may use similar techniques to solve problems at school.*

vi. **Be aware of warning signs.** *Parents should be aware of behavioral changes in their children. The following is a list of symptoms that may appear:*
   - *Physical signs of injury*
   - *Sudden or persistent darkness, sadness, or withdrawal from family and friends*
   - *Missing or damaged personal property*
   - *Torn or disheveled clothing*
   - *Complaints of illness when there are no visible symptoms*
   - *Skipping one or more classes*
   - *Not wanting to ride the school bus*

- o   *Running away from home for short periods of time*
- o   *Carrying a weapon, whether a nail file, a screwdriver or a knife*
- o   *References to suicide, or statements about not wanting to be around anymore*
- o   *Angry threats about getting even with another student*

- **Be proactive in your child's schooling.** *Know which classes a child is taking, the names of teachers and school counselors, assignments due, and grades achieved. Being in touch with your child's school can help you spot problematic behavior and deal with it promptly.*

- **Teach your child to recognize and avoid violence.** *Teach your child to be aware of precipitating factors which may lead to violence. Help him or her become aware of possible perpetrators and teach your child to avoid them at all costs, even if that means not being part of a clique at school.*

- **Identify a safe haven at school.** *Be aware of the physical layout of your child's school. Go on a Saturday or Sunday when school is out and locate the safest place your child can go in the event he or she senses violence. This could be a classroom, the nurse's office, the principal's office, or the hall outside it. Explain to your child that they are not running away, but instead are preventing themselves from becoming involved in a physical altercation which may lead to their own discipline.*

- **Teach the difference between tattling and whistleblowing.** *No one likes a bully. Your child should know that reporting a bully to a teacher or school staff member is not weak or cowardly, but a commendable act that helps all students.*

- **Help your child develop a buddy system.** *It's important for your child to be among friends at school. The more the better. There is safety in numbers. It is less likely a bully will attack your child when he or she is among friends. Know who your child's friends are. If your child doesn't seem to have many, speak with the parents of other children who may have things in common with your child. This is especially helpful if your child is shy.*

- **Enroll your child in a self-defense class.** *Self-defense classes teach your child how to defend themselves and instill self-confidence and self-esteem.*

Violence Prevention Strategies for Schools [247]

a. **Fulfill the legal duty of care.** *Schools have a legal and moral duty to make their property safe so students are not unduly harmed. This begins with teachers. Teachers must identify to the school administration students who may potentially be problematic. Administrators have a duty to intervene and avoid becoming negligent.*

b. **Stay informed about daily events and incidents.** *Teachers and school administrators must be aware of what is going in the halls, locker rooms, on the field, and at after-school activities. Keeping involved by speaking with students and listening to their concerns can be crucial, especially when there's a sense of impending violence.*

c. **Host guest speakers to discuss bullying.** *Guest speakers, such as police officers, lawyers, and social workers, can have a positive impact on students.*

d. **Encourage students to report concerns and incidents.** *Identifying the catalysts to possible confrontations can help reduce the incidents of violence. Let students know that they can remain anonymous when reporting concerns.*

e. **Engage parents about inappropriate behavior.** *Opening the eyes of parents can help to stem or eliminate acts of student violence.* [247]

16. Write Your Own Sermon, Obituary, & Epitaph Before Someone Else!

What will your epitaph read on your tombstone? How will your legacy impact your bloodline? Are you passing a DNA generational curse and legacy of abuse and violence? How do you want to be remembered by others? It is better you write and tell your story the way you want to be remembered rather than someone else tell the world who they believed you were to the world! You want to be remembered as a wolf on your tombstone, but someone writes that you were a chicken because you did not write your will! That is the impression they had of you!

17. Turn Around And Look At Your Crap! What Are You Doo-Doing To Others? In The Toilet What Does "IT" Say About Your Attitude?

You are what you consistently do! Either you are the S***, or You Are A Piece of S***! **Do not be a broken full toilet where people cannot do s*** with you!** You have to be respectful and moldable. Nobody wants to work with a David Downer or Negative Nancy. You have to be magnetic, so people want to be drawn and attracted to you to want to help you win and watch you succeed in life!

18. Hate The Hate, Not The Person! There Is No Greater Love Than To Love Yourself! If You Don't Love Yourself, How Do You Love Others?

You cannot hate what God created. Hate what you have done to others but fall back in love with yourself! You cannot stop loving yourself because there is no way to love others if you fall out of love with yourself. Once you see how valuable of an asset you are to yourself, you will not have to live a life worried about what others think of you because what will matter is how you feel about yourself. Live to please yourself, and that will spill over into other people's happiness. If your family, friends, and colleagues see your happiness, many people want a piece of that sunshine because they are in the dark! *Let Your Little Light Shine and Shine Bright!*

19. Let Me Get A Copy Of Your DVD! Will You Make A Copy Of Your Life To Pass Out? Should Your Life's Movie Be On Netflix Or Hulu?

If every moment in your life was filmed unedited, would you pass out copies, destroy the master copy, try and edit or delete the negative parts, or would you pass out from what's being passed out? Everyone has a DVD of their life. What if your darkest secrets were recorded on a DVD when you were actually committing the offenses? Would you want to make copies and pass them out or sell them for the world to see? Would you want your life on Netflix, Hulu, YouTube, or Amazon?

20. Legacy Lynchpin-Bloodline Of Violence And Abuse In Our DNA.

In the womb, while my dad was committing acts of violence and abuse against my mother, and eventually him being killed in a shootout with the Baltimore Police! I apologize to the cop for my father putting him and his colleagues in that position that day! A crime that I nearly perpetuated subliminally! This is your last day on earth. How will you be remembered? How do you want to be remembered? Do you control yours?

21. Can Not Let Her Go? Why Would You Ever Want To Be With Anyone Who Does Not Want To Be With You? How Would You Feel If Someone Tried To Control You? Are You A Game Hunter? Let Go!

Would you upgrade your car, house, diamond, or winning lottery number winnings if you could? Of course? So why can you not let her go? Two-year-old in the "mine" phase? You do not own anyone, and no one owns you! Do not be foolish? Are you a power and control freak? Let her return where she was before you. When you get fired from a job do you continue to show up for work? What would happen to you if you did that? Move on to the next one! But are you the reason they leave? How would you feel if someone refused to accept your severance and stalked you?

22. There Is Never An Excuse for Abuse! They Are Somebody's Baby!

It is not about you and what you lost. It is about the pain you inflicted upon another. You have violated that person's human rights! No more promises that "IT won't happen again, baby!" Do not fight a battle you cannot beat by yourself! Get the help that will save your life and your loved ones too! You are somebody's baby! They are somebody's baby! How do you treat a baby? We are all somebody's baby! Harming the harmless! How do you justify beating the mother of your child? Did you separate her from your child? Do you see her as a human and someone worthy of respect? How do you justify abusing a baby or child of any age? How do you justify bullying a classmate? What did they ever do to you to cause you to maltreat them? And if they did mistreat you, why did you choose to stay and tolerate the continuous maltreatment? If you saw a baby get punched in the face **WWYD**?

23. Listen To What Loved Ones Are Saying About Your Mental Health

Sometimes we need to be saved from ourselves. When someone who has your best interest tells you that you need help or there is a formal family intervention to tell you directly about your behavior that is negatively impacting your and their lives, LISTEN and RESPOND YESTERDAY! There is no tomorrow! Get help now while you can and with the full support of loved ones. Do not overthink things or over-analyze this situation because your life is about to significantly change for the better or worse depending on what you decide to do for your mental wellness. My greatest regret is that I did not listen to the loved ones in my corner and it changed the direction of my future. If I had listened to them I would not be a felon today!

23. RECIDIVISM: Definition of Insanity? Doing The Same Things Over and Over Expecting Different Results-Do Not Be A Zero In The Zoo!

I have had friends who stayed in and out of jail as if they were high wage-earning road warriors working a job that kept them on the road for significant stints or a military person on a long-term deployment or a wealthy individual who spends part of the year out of the country in some remote wealthier country like beautiful Monaco or a retiree bluebird who flies to Florida for the frigid winter months of their home state and returning in the livelier spring months! When jail or prison becomes a better option and place to live than your actual home with your family, America has a serious problem! If the only place you could go to receive proper nutrition or medical treatment would you go there? How about a safe environment free from child molesters, muggers, stick up kids, drug dealers, and addicts, or violent home invasion burglars? How about a place where you can get your own bed and get a quality education? How about a place where you are relevant and not invisible? How about a place where you can receive love? A place where you can be yourself and be a part of a family you call your gang! A place where you can work out and get healthy? A place where you can make money and have worldly possessions? A place where you can get all of your reading and television programming and other forms of entertainment such as gambling or sports or even taking the time to write rap lyrics or even a book? A place where you are the man or woman. A place where you find peace of mind! If prison and jail is more attractive and sexier, compared to what you deal with at home, how many convincing arguments do you have to make to an individual that is choosing how to survive and self-preserve with the basic choices to being a human being such as food, water, shelter, clothing, sanitation, education, and healthcare. The solution is rooted in what is causing the pain and suffering and getting the appropriate coping skills and techniques to extinguish the problems and pain permanently! Then comes economic and education solutions to provide purpose and fulfillment and reasons for someone to live! Serving others in need with opportunities and activities to keep them focused on others and not just on their pain! Sometimes you can be healed by healing others needing a bigger bandage and carrying heavier baggage than you! Activities breeds activities! New environments because the definition of insanity is doing the same things over and over again expecting different results! I saw a better life when I got out of the dungeon! It is hard to dream in those dark places when the light is off in your head. Your mind is on the pain and not the pleasure! Surround yourself with a positive environment and positive people who support your wellness and wellbeing.

24. This Is Your Loved One's Last Day On Earth! What Will You Say? How Will You Act? You Have 24 Hours Before The Great Send-Off!

This is the very last time that you will ever see them. Have you told them that you loved them and appreciated their impact on your life? I know I will not live forever, but I pray my legacy as a humanitarian serves as a never-ending perpetual lifelong gift to inspire humanity always to let one another know how much we loved each other! I love you! Let them know before you or they permanently leave!

25. Be Proactive & Not Reactive! Self Report By Choice & Not By Force!

A dedicated Domestic Violence, Child Abuse, and Bullying Hotline via Text, Telephone, Email, or Chat Mail, exclusively for children, women, men and any individuals for self-admitted domestic violence offenders, bullies, child abusers, molesters, pedophiles, and animal abusers who are seeking help as well as anyone who is being abused or witnessing child abuse and domestic violence! Violence occurs in all zip codes and demographics! It does not care where you went to school and from where you graduated and the degree you received. It does not care about your party affiliation or political influences. It does not care about your executive job title and how much money and power you possess! Your house, car, and other possessions will not defeat violence alone. The Solution is ***Love You First***! When you honestly love anything you would never purposely harm it in any way! Love does not keep score or try to get its way! This is an Accountability Call for Victims, Victimizers, and Volunteers impacted by abuse and those wanting to make an impact towards eradicating domestic violence and child abuse! You Only Get One Life Here on Earth! So Stand Up, Step Forward and Move Towards a continuous, Healthy Resolution of Love for Your Life, Your Family and Those Around You! I need you even if you have never abused or have been abused! I need your expertise, support, and labor of love! We all become victims of violence if better solutions and awareness is not provided to the select individuals who currently are receiving abuse or who are abusers that are showing our children and women that you will eventually become a victim or abuser! I am trying to prevent the next abusive fatality, tragedy or act of violence or domestic terrorism that occurs every day on this earth! So how can you partner with us? First, make the commitment! Second, decide how you wish to be involved in supporting the FAMILY MAN! Lastly, Get in Motion by contacting your nearest FAMILY MAN™ office! ***Call, Text, Chat 833.3HOWLER Help Line! 1-833-346-9537. Be A Howler™ & Grounder™!***

26. Do Not Be A "PLUNGER" In A Relationship! FOREVER! EVER!

Sean Matthews' fiery and loving wife Anita Matthews is a truth talker. She says, ***"In a relationship, you cannot be a plunger!"*** In a relationship, when you have disagreements or problems that you have argued to the end and then everyone forgives everyone and all becomes well, ***"You Can't Keep Bringing Up The Old S*** that is causing the arguments!"*** It is over, so let it be over! True forgiving is forgetting and not a game of keeping score or record of what someone did to harm you, especially if it was not a crime! I am not naïve though because pain is pain. However, if you cannot get beyond the pain, MOVE ON! Put your left foot forward. Put your right foot facing backward! Now walk! You cannot move! You are stuck in the same place. I am not advocating leaving your mate. I am advocating taking the impasse that you and your intimate partner get professional help to get past and through the impasse that is seemingly plunging your relationship into the toilet!

27. What Type Of Grad Are You On The Totem Pole Of Violence And Abuse? WHAT TYPE OF DEGREE WILL YOU GET? 1ST OR 2ND?

Violence and abuse graduates from a harsh verbal offensive or emotional mind game of statements to a grab or shake to a choke or strangle to a slap or backhand to a punch to a beating to a killing! Where are you on the totem pole of violence and abuse? As an abuser, we are violators of trust, contract breakers, career killers, generational cursors, and affiliation and association assassins! Ask all the people who were fired on your watch and who were accountable for you! How many resigned or forced to retire earlier then they had planned, as a result of your illicit, immoral, inappropriate or unethical actions? How many people now have a tainted legacy and asterisk next to their name and on their headstone? How many serve a life sentence while free on the street and imprisoned to the confines of their trauma while you live each day free, regardless if you have served your time and are free or have life without parole as if you never had anything to do with traumatizing this individual! Is that fair or rightful to do harm to another human and think they will exist normally after an abnormal subhuman act was committed against them?

28. STOP, DROP, And ROLL! JAY Z And SOLANGE IN THE ELEVATOR! WE CAN LEARN FROM JAY Z STAYING *COOL!*

If you have ever seen the "elevator incident" between Jay Z and Beyoncé's sister Solange, what you witness is a man who has incredible self-control and respect for his family and business! Jay Z is an iconic brand married to an iconic brand. Had he assaulted his sister-in-law in any fashion, he could have damaged his solid corporate image, plummeted his assets, and jeopardized his relationship with his wife, kids, and in-laws. Instead, he displayed incredible control and respect. We need to study that elevator tape more than any taped song or movie he has ever made! Unfortunately, many individuals have been captured in elevators committing domestic violence assaults and it has cost people their careers and good names. A few seconds out of control can change your life for the absolute, unrecoverable worst such as a Ray Rice or a few seconds being in control which can save lives... Jay Z!

If you are on fire, we were taught to Stop, Drop and Roll! What if you were never taught those basic fundamentals? What would happen? Would you die? What do you do when you get your buttons pushed too hot, and your anger gauge goes from 0 to 1000? What should you do? You certainly can STOP and think about what the potential long-term consequences for a violent reaction are about to occur! You can also DROP down to the ground and curl up in the fetal position to submit to your potential victim and scream aloud that you love them, yourself, your children, and your life and that you sincerely do not wish to harm them, and you just need them to give you your space, so you can continue to love them right! ROLL out of there like you are on fire running for your life! Cooler heads prevail! You are really running to freedom.

29. STAY- Follow These Commands Like A Great Wolf, Not A Dog!

a) Stay away from strip clubs if you are married or are in a committed relationship. Never take your wife or girlfriend to one even if it is their idea! No men taking men to see men too! Strip clubs make their insecurities go crazy because they begin comparing themselves to other people. How do you feel when a brand-new Lamborghini or Lexus pulls up next to you and you are driving an old hooptie? What if she asked you to go watch naked men and that was not your cup of tea, would you go watch then?

b) Never cheat or have threesomes with your spouse or intimate partner! This is a deadly transaction that typically ends in the death of your relationship or the death of you, your spouse, or the other person. If the person you love is not enough sexually, you have to find a healthy solution or get out before you get an STD that will kill you or your self-esteem. Tell your next potential partner you have a communicable disease and see their response.

c) Stay away from pornography or using social media to try to engage with people from the past for the purpose of hooking up for sex! In fact, stay off the internet looking for any individual who is willing to have sex whether casually or via an escort service. I do not want to see you escorted to the morgue or grave!

30. LAW ENFORCEMENT- DO NOT LET US OUT IMMEDIATELY!

If a domestic violence offender has been charged with domestic violence I am ordering you to not let them out on any type of bond or electronic monitoring system or a laughable restraining order. This may seem harsh or unusual, but what is stirring in the mind of that offender is, "I am going to kill that B**** ASAP! I am going to F*** them or their S*** up as soon as I get the chance!" This person cannot be "restrained" because their mind and life are totally out of "order" right now! What this person needs is help immediately. I committed 2 acts of violence and abuse against my former girlfriend within weeks of the first violent offense! I needed focused and intense therapy, but all I received was a get out of jail free card, restraining order, and a disturbingly hostile battle inside my brain on whether to kill myself or my former girlfriend! Both were not healthy options for my girlfriend, me, our families, law enforcement, the community, and our futures. I was in a fragile mental state needing mental help, not freedom! Stop aiding, enabling, & abetting us.

31. SOMEBODY'S BABY! SOMEBODY'S BODY! *GOD'S PROPERTY!*

What would you do if you saw a person punch a baby in the face or stomach with all of their human strength? ***IS THAT PERSON YOU?*** If you were the baby, what would you think? Would you want someone to come to your rescue? What if a gang of 8 foot, 800lb. savages surrounded you to violently assault you for what you did to the innocent baby? What would you want them to do to you? Would you want mercy? How would you feel if that were someone you loved or a favorite pet?

32. WHERE IS YOUR DADDY? WAS YOUR MOM A GREAT MOM?

Many of us suffer in our personal lives as children and adults because of the pain inflicted on us from the abandonment of our father or mother. When you are a child you need both parents to raise you along with aunts, uncles, cousins, siblings, and grandparents. Both parents give you the balance you need mentally and emotionally. Both give you security that all children desire. When you do not receive this security, most people become insecure, and as a result they become relationship dividers and immature. They suffer in personal relationships because they are not whole. When you are the parent who abandons your children or shows them violence and abuse, you are setting the stage for them to live a very difficult, insecure, complicated, and drama filled life because they are often perpetuating the cycle that you created. A child with two mentally healthy parents will often turn out a secure, balanced adult!

33. PRAY! TALK TO YOUR GOD! PRAYER & MEDITATION HELPS

God would never do anything to harm you in any way. Do not be deceived and wonder, "Why did God allow this abuse to happen to me? Why did God make me a monster of an abuser?" If we believe God is love, why would we ever believe He would purposely harm us! Man has caused our pain. Not God! He made us! It is the wicked ways of man who has inflicted this torture and pain on us. To overcome violence and abuse we have to find a higher being and a love bigger than us who gives us an eternal peace, divine understanding, and a supernatural strength to overcome our deficiencies, pains, and fears to live prosperously through each day. Our mind becomes free when we know God is the source of our healing…not man.

I WAS *COMMITTED* TO A PSYCHIATRIC FACILITY FOR HELP!

JOHN RANDOLPH HOSPITAL

Hopewell, Virginia

RADIOLOGY CONSULT

NAME: BURGESS, ANTOIN	X-RAY NO.: 112228
AGE: 21	REFERRING PHYSICIAN: RYANS, M.
ROOM OR ADDRESS CSH	DATE: 12/3/91

REPORT

CT HEAD SCAN WITH AND WITHOUT CONTRAST ENHANCEMENT:

Serial transaxial cuts of the bony calvarium reveals the attenuation over the hemispheres to be uniform with and without contrast enhancement. The lateral ventricles are normal. Third ventricle and basilar cisterns unremarkable. There is no mass effect. No acute intracerebral or extra axial hemorrhage noted.

OPINION: Normal CT head scan with and without contrast enhancement.

T.R. Howell, M.D.
Radiologist
TRH/MRS
12/3/91dt10

I Ended Up In Central State Hospital In The Care Of Dr. Miller Ryans*! He Got Me Right!

Solutions To Permanently Eradicate Domestic Violence, Child Abuse, and Bullying

THE COMMITMENT

If You Are Not Committed, You Are Destined To Be Committed!

My name is A.W. Burgess, and I am a former domestic violence abuser, offender, and bully. There was a time in my life when I was physically, verbally, mentally, emotionally, financially, and psychologically abusing and torturing my girlfriend, family, friends, and even my dog. I was a tortured soul who became a violent menace and terrorist to anyone who was close to me! The hypocrisy of my life was that I was a hero at work and in sports, but I was a zero at home and school to those people who truly loved me. As a result of this abusive and violent behavior, I ended up in the penitentiary and a psychiatric hospital and came depressingly close to committing suicide and **QUITE POSSIBLY FEMICIDE!** I was dysfunctional!

Candidly, the greatest mistake of my life was taking too long to get help for my violent and dysfunctional behavior. I got the help that ultimately saved my life and the lives of others too. Today, I have the required coping techniques and life skills that afford me the opportunity to lead a mentally healthy, fully functional and productive life. I am pleading and howling to all domestic violence offenders, child abusers, bullies, and any type of violent victimizers to commit to permanently eradicating domestic violence, child abuse, and bullying! It would be my pleasure to serve, help and partner with any individual or entity to preserve someone's life and legacy! We must all commit to end domestic violence! We only get one life to live. How will people remember us individually and how will our tombstone read?

Whenever there is a new year, many people make and take solemn swears, oaths, vows, promises, commitments, and resolutions to get their physical bodies in shape. Some even join weight reduction organizations and gyms for zero dollars down, ten dollars a month with no long-term commitments or contracts! How many decide to get their mental health in shape? How many people have joined an organization to get their minds in shape? What's the investment in your mental wellness? How many have pledged to stop beating up, bullying and abusing their children, spouses, and classmates? "I promise I won't hit you ever again! I promise I won't do **IT** again! I promise I will break my promise to you! I promise I will!"

How many abusers have seen the sad commercials where there is a desperate cry from a charitable company to save sick or disabled children, wounded veterans, or abused animals and they choose to financially support that organization's cause but that same individual will not hear the desperate cries and pleas of their victims and choose not to invest in themselves? What sense does it make to go into another year making pledges to others and to yourself that you will never honor or support? You will help a stranger's cause but not loved ones' or classmates'? You will send strangers the change in your pockets, but you will not dig down in the pockets of your life to make a permanent change that rewards your life and that of your victim's permanently!

You do not have to wait for another year, next month, week, or today because you can begin the change right now. You and your victims can not afford to wait. Stop making commitments or promises you will not keep. What is the cost or down payment for a healthy mind and relationship that only has a binding contract to love one another? How would you feel to know that you were the root cause of someone committing suicide? Commit or be committed!

THE COMMITMENT

1. I love myself. Therefore, I will never hurt anyone or anything I love, beginning with myself! How can I love others if I do not first love me! I love me! I love myself! I will commit to never hit with my hands, feet, mouth, or mind! I will commit to getting my mind healthy, so my body will follow the same energy! I will run away from or sit in the fetal position submitting that you have won the battle before I fight a losing cause and destroy what I love so very much! I will submit before I hit. I will always get help to never hit anyone! I will never harm myself! To love others I must love me!

2. I am a life beater! I am not an intimate partner, child, student, animal or any type of abuser, baterrer or bully. I am a winner!

3. I am fully aware that this dysfunctional disease of violence and abuse will always be in and or near me and can only resurface if I permit it or am relaxed or too comfortable with my treatment.

4. My life and legacy will not be as a victim or victimizer but as a humbled and flawed champion who became a sincere and apologetic vindicator, restorer, empathizer, and victor who once fell down but arose to help, not harm, humanity or the animal kingdom! My legacy will be that I was more than a conquerer.

Solutions To Permanently Eradicate Domestic Violence, Child Abuse, and Bullying

5. I will never jeopardize, compromise, or take for granted my life, freedom, community, family, future or legacy ever. Breaking the law or being incarcerated is never an option! I am not a recidivist!

6. I will never abandon my responsibilities as a citizen, student, friend, spouse, parent, employee, or humanitarian! I love others!

7. I am my brother and sister's, keeper! I will keep you from being harmed! I will ground violence and not stand for it!

8. I will be proactive to negative scenarios and think infinitely about the costs and painmeants!™ I will not lose my freedom for shizzle!

9. I am an encourager. I will always speak life, and not death, into the lives of all around me! My life matters and so do the lives of the people I impact. I will always look and find the positive in others.

10. I will sit down, breathe, meditate or pray to reflect as often as I am able! I will kneel to find the sanctuary within my heart and mind.

11. I sincerely apologize with all my heart to my victims for being the cause of their pain & suffering! I will show them & the world how sincere my apology means with my loving actions & behavior.

12. I will stay out of ALL courts such as traffic, criminal, and family. I will focus on my health, family, education, or employment! I will stay out of and away from toxic, negative people, situations, scenarios and relationships to avoid ever being prosecuted.

13. My mental and physical health will always be a top priority in my life! My mental health must always be equal to or exceed my physical health. If the mind is weak, the body is weaker. If the mind is strong, the body is as strong! I will be mentally stronger.

14. I will never commit any act of violence against women, children, the LGBTQ, animals, any other individual, especially, including myself! Victims are innocent individuals who deserve only love!

15. I will never break the law or get myself arrested unless it is a peaceful protest, or I am defending my life or that of a loving individual! My freedom is priceless and comes at a high cost!

16. If I find myself tempted to break my commitment, I will get help immediately! I will sprint from temptation and never look back.

17. I will always commit my life to faithfully protecting my good name, legacy, and bloodline! I am a generational curse breaker!

18. I will encourage others to join me in being a transparent, altruistic humanitarian who can truly call themselves a Family Man™!

19. I will never provoke another or be provoked into the traps of violence and abuse. There is a difference between arguing, fussing, cussing, sparring verbally and debating respectfully.

20. I will find positive activities and hobbies that keep my focus on staying mentally, physically, verbally, and emotionally healthy. Occupy your time with positive activities and people when you are severely lonely and depressed but moreover, get professional help to help you get over your trauma.

21. I will enthusiastically serve others and fulfill my life's purpose.

22. I will always choose love over hate. Life over death!

23. For my one lifetime, I realize I was an abuser or violent offender, or bully. I will never be reactive to violence. I have the opportunity to never be a bully, abuser, or violent offender again and so I choose a proactive approach and commitment to preventing others from harming others, including myself! I will be a shining example of positive change. I will never resort to violence as a solution.

24. I will not use or sell any drugs or alcohol that will alter my mind. Horrific crimes of abuse and violent offenses occur when people have substances altering their minds and behavior.

25. Secrets kill and silence the strong. If the strong are silenced, evil wins. To take back my strength and defeat the evil that is killing me, I have to talk it out. I have to extract the pain that is torturing and traumatizing the love in me. I am taking back the love for myself and others while freeing my mind and soul! I have control over what is controlling me! I will never choose silence to violence because I know silence to violence will ultimately kill someone.

Solutions To Permanently Eradicate Domestic Violence, Child Abuse, and Bullying

26. I will move away from any provocative people or circumstances. Sometimes a change in scenery, people, or career will keep me from scenarios that will bring out the worst in my natural behavior.

27. I can and will let go of any failed love! I never want to be in a relationship with any individual or entity that does not love me any longer and does not want to be with me! I will free them & myself!

28. I will not be an insecure individual but rather I will be comforted in the knowledge that I will do everything to control my love for myself first and trust that I cannot control others but rather I can control myself! I will be a mentally secure and mature person.

29. I will always be a positive person who surrounds myself with people and organizations as positive or greater than I am. I will always exude positivity! I am beyond certain of this! I am positive!

30. I will never quit on my life, family, children, friends, or dreams!

31. I will never forget to stay focused on impacting my life and legacy!

32. I will always be R.E.A.L.- Really Effective At Loving not Lying!

33. I will never do anything to permanently destroy my life or legacy.

This is my commitment never to abuse! I will commit to never abuse, bully, or violently offend any human being or animal, including myself. Below, I will sign the requirement and not a request commitment to my one precious life of love, respect, nonviolence, and peace!

I sign this commitment on the shield I call my heart. My word and signature is my bond! I will never renege on this commitment because my life and my legacy depend on my truth to this contract. I am not a liar or hypocrite! I WILL NOT BREAK MY CONTRACT TO MYSELF OR COMMUNITY!

Help me God to overcome the obstacles that together we will forever overcome! You made me God! Help me help myself become whole! My commitment is sincere, I am on bending knees, and I will not void my contract!

I AM FREE FROM THIS CYCLE OF VIOLENCE and ABUSE! BEFORE I HIT, I WILL SUBMIT and COMMIT NEVER TO HIT! I REFUSE TO ABUSE BECAUSE I CHOOSE TO LOVE MYSELF ABOVE ALL! WITH HONOR and RESPECT TO MYSELF and THE OTHERS WHO LOVE ME and CALL ME FRIEND, AS AN OATH TO GOD, I SIGN MY NAME BELOW TO SHOW MY COMMITMENT TO MY PERSONAL and CORPORATE FAMILY, FRIENDS, COMMUNITY and TO THE ONLY GOD I SERVE!

PRINTED NAME   **SIGNATURE**   **DATE**

FAMILYMAN

Eradicating Domestic Violence | Child Abuse | Bullying

Solutions To Permanently Eradicate Domestic Violence, Child Abuse, and Bullying

IF YOU KNEW THIS WAS YOUR LAST DAY ON EARTH, HOW WOULD YOU SPEND YOUR LAST 24 HOURS?

IN LIFE, EVERY MAN & WOMAN NEEDS A MEN-TOUR™ WHO WILL GUIDE YOU WITH WISE COUNSEL AND HUMOR?

(Above) George Hurst Sharing A Laugh And Life's Best Lessons With Me

I Have Met Phenomenal "MenTours™" & "WomenTours™" in Business. Many of These Men and Women Taught Me More Through Their Painful Losses In Life, Along With Their "Secret Sauces" To Winning! I Learned From Peter Boesen, Carroll Stewart & The Man Above…Allison Walden*!

Solutions To Permanently Eradicate Domestic Violence, Child Abuse, and Bullying

MENTOURS – WOMENTOURS – PARTNERSHIPS
WILL YOU GUIDE ME THROUGH THE DARK?
TWO HEADS ARE BETTER THAN ONE

They say, "Time is money!" and that you never have enough of both! What are you doing with the one lifetime you get on this earth? Your time is vital, but your wisdom and sacrifice are worth more than money! Your life examples that display exemplary resilience and success are priceless. Your willingness to help with the fight is beyond comprehension. You are more than a volunteer, you are a guiding light, and that is why you are called a Womentour™ and Mentour™! You guide girls, boys, women, and men into shining examples of what a mature, secure adult and parent looks, sounds, and acts like at home, work, school and in personal and corporate relationships. You show them how to shine their little light.

There are many crossroads in a person's life where critical decisions are made without the wise counsel or ear of a loving individual who has your best interest, best intentions and solutions for your life that impact your existence now, in the future and your legacy. I think about the many times of depression and my anger, girls, sex, fighting, politics, coaches, death, and the many struggles as a child, young adult, and adult. The decision to go to McDonogh versus going to a public school or another school where I would have been more appreciated and exposed as a result of my sports talents. What college should I attend to better my chances at reaching a Major League Baseball or NFL contract versus which school will provide me with a quality free education and degree that will sustain me in the future?

I was so used to not having anyone in the stands personally cheering and caring about me that I wanted to get as far away as possible from my family and Baltimore without realizing I did not have a clear support system around me in Stillwater, Oklahoma at Oklahoma State University. Then in a flash, I impulsively left a full scholarship from Oklahoma State! Giving away my dog Toby* when he brought nothing but joy and unconditional love to my life. All the times before and after I violently offended, abused or bullied my former girlfriend, friends, and family. How about the decision I made to take my own life or to feloniously force my way to speak to my former girlfriend with and without a gun, twice? Why I did not complete college. Why I chose to be in the car business and sales?

Why I was told I was so special in sports but yet I did not have a dad, mom, or family cheerleading for me in life and at my games? When I was asked to "marry

Solutions To Permanently Eradicate Domestic Violence, Child Abuse, and Bullying

her" by my wife, and I did not hesitate to say yes, and I never respectfully asked her father for her hand in marriage. Selling my wife's wedding ring and not having money for my kids for college or life insurance because I had to drain the college fund, 401k, investment accounts, home equity and savings accounts to pay for critical medical bills only to still end up with a seriously ill child, no money, no home, a repossessed car and bad credit when the entire time we qualified for Medicaid and I did not know it! What is a beacon score? What is a mentor? No dad?

I think about how I left great relationships such as E. Bronson Ingram and Mr. Hendrick and never communicated properly back to either of them when they reached out to me. I think about the countless times my former girlfriend told me humbly and respectfully to get help and I ignored her pleas as only an ignorant and foolish person would have done. How I sat in elementary, junior and senior high school as well as college, bottled up with secrets, rage, shame, and guilt. I think about the hypocrisy of being a hero in public and a zero in private to my family and friends. How I could not understand why I could not save myself from repeating the violence, abuse, and bullying. I think about how I was wanted for all the wrong reasons. I am paying for a lifelong debt that can never be settled and wish I had a Mentour™ or Womentour™ guiding me in life well before I committed the acts of bullying, violence, and abuse that cost me this permanent life and death sentence? Can you imagine a wolf or a lion with no teeth or a black mamba with no fangs? You will die in the wild or jungle if you are not equipped with how to lovingly use your God-given talents appropriately. Mentours™ and Womentours™ keep you accountable and aware of the evil and monstrous snares that are lurking in the valleys of the shadows of death and darkness. How do you have sex or make love?

To honestly win in life you have to serve others and make their lives better which will, in turn, make your life better! Positive opportunities will chase you down if you are doing the right things for people by serving them as a sincerely loyal and humble servant. If there is no honest passion to go with the spirit of servitude in helping others to achieve their dreams and happiness, then you will never prosper, and those opportunities you are hoping to receive will flee to more deserving causes for people to be served. The bottom line is, _whatever you would do for free, with no hidden agendas and a sincere heart, is what you should be!_ You must be definitive in serving others so that others will want to humbly help you. How can I serve you?

I want you! I need you! I cannot get it done without you! Partner with me to end violence, bullying, and abuse against innocent and undeserving people! Start a FAMILY MANKIND™ Branch or Group today! I need your guiding light to bring those individuals out of the depths of darkness and the valleys of the shadows of death. I am looking for Mentours™ and Womentours™ and corporate entities to be change agents to guide men and women in the right direction of life by showing those who are in need how to live a violent and abuse-free life while helping provide resources to keep the vision continuously moving forward! As leaders, we will deter those who are a razor blade fence from committing violence and abuse by giving hope to violent offenders and abusers that they can be healed from their disease if they believe that it is not a matter of if they will be cured but rather when they will be healed! Will you join me in saving and preserving lives and legacies? ***Whoever claims to love God yet hates a brother or sister is a liar. For anyone who does not love his brother whom he has seen, cannot love God, whom he has not seen!*** [248]

Two Heads Are Better Than One

Somebody has to be the first to take the first step into battle. However, the war is not won alone until others follow you into battle to combat and conquer what's trying to kill you and others! When I think about some of the most significant corporations in this world, they all started with a vital mission and vision. However, what made them a presence in the marketplace and world was the love, talent, passion and respect leadership had for one another. There was trust, respect, and a laser beam focus to serve others with a great product or service. As a result, they always attracted the best talents that the world offered and was able to survive the toughest of times due to the unbreakable will of its leaders! I need those types of rare individuals around me twenty-four seven, three sixty-six! I have taken the first step, "Will you take the next step with me? Join me and let us combat and conquer domestic violence, bullying, and child abuse!" I am prayerfully and humbly asking a few people and entities to be bold and partner with me to no longer stand for domestic violence, child abuse, and bullying by becoming a FAMILY MAN™ for humanity's sake! Everybody needs LOVE and PROTECTION from harm! There is nothing more important than an individual's life! If I can provide hope to the hopeless and convince the inconvincible that the impossible is possible if they just do the right things, then my life will have served a meaningful purpose. Without appropriate and effective solutions, techniques and strategies, it is not a matter of if, but when the next act of violence will choose its next victim!

Domestic violence, child abuse, and bullying can be prevented and permanently eradicated in violent offenders, abusers, and bullies, especially when the mighty righteous authority of a pack community is brought together as an alliance and family. Community-wide strategies can help identify and support adults and children who are victims and victimizers, redirect the evil behavior of those who violently offend, abuse and bully children, and change the attitudes of adults and youth who tolerate despicable behaviors in homes, schools, and communities.

STRATEGICALLY FUNCTIONING AS 1 PACK OF HOWLERS™ and GROUNDERS™

Domestic Violence, Child Abuse, and Bullying does not just happen at home or at school. Volunteers and Community leaders can strategically use their intellectual capacities, resources, influences, affiliations, community relationships and skillsets to prevent and eradicate domestic violence, child abuse, and bullying wherever it occurs. Together as one pack, we will send an undeniable HOWL that we will never tolerate domestic violence, child abuse, or bullying.

Do not Stand For Domestic Violence, Child Abuse, or Bullying! No More Silence to Domestic Violence, Child Abuse or Bullying Sideliners! Do Not Stand For "IT" Ever!

Anyone who suspects or witnesses domestic violence, child abuse or bullying, either in person, as a neighbor, friend, family member, co-worker, classmate or online, is considered a sideliner. Friends, students, peers, teachers, school staff, parents, coaches, and other youth who are serving children and adults can be sideliners. Using social media platforms, where anyone can comment, chat, or blog with cyberbullying, even strangers can be considered sideliners.

Mature adults, young adults, and school-aged children willfully or unwilfully engaged in domestic violence, child abuse, and bullying serve in significant capacities. Witnessing violence, abuse and bullying is upsetting and affects the Grounder™ too. Sideliners can make an impact on domestic violence, child abuse, and bullying situations by becoming a Grounder™. A Grounder™ is someone who does not stand for violence, abuse or bullying and proactively sees what happens and strategically intervenes, interrupts, or speaks up to permanently eradicate the violence, abuse, bullying.

Strategic Grounders™- Neighbors, friends, family, members of the media, co-workers, classmates or social media cohorts online, must become Strategic Grounders™ and not sideliners. Friends, students, peers, teachers, school staff, parents, coaches, and other youth who are victims often feel even more alone because there are witnesses who do nothing. When no one intervenes the person being targeted may feel that grounders do not care, or they agree with what is happening. There are many reasons why a sideliner may not interject, even if they believe that domestic violence, child abuse or bullying is wrong. They may fear retaliation or becoming the target of violence, abuse, or bullying themselves. They may also think getting involved could have negative social consequences.

I repeat, a Grounder™ is someone who does not stand for violence, abuse or bullying and proactively sees what happens and strategically intervenes, interrupts, or speaks up to permanently eradicate the violence, abuse, bullying. A Grounder™ is someone who takes action when they witness domestic violence, child abuse, and bullying. Grounders™ realize their support can make an impact in the life for someone who is being assaulted, harassed, beaten or bullied. When victims and victimizers know they have allies and are defended and supported by others, they are less anxious and depressed than those who are not.

Imagine when mental health professionals, law enforcement, government agencies, corporations, faith-based and non-profit organizations, local associations, and education institutions proactively come together to heal the victims and victimizers of violence, abuse, and bullying before any evil occurs.

These are impactful actions that sideliners to domestic violence, child abuse, and bullying can do to become Grounders™: Do Not Sit On The Sidelines. Get In The Game!

- ☐ Society must use different approaches to eradicate nefarious behavior permanently.
- ☐ Change the victimizer's behavior so that we can shift the focus to mental wellness.
- ☐ Two heads are better than one. There is strength in a pack! Grounders™ can intercede as a family to show some people want to help change the behavior.
- ☐ We will not continue to allow victims to suffer in silence.
- ☐ We will strategically howl with the person who is the target of violence to help diffuse potential abusive interactions.
- ☐ Communicate strategically with the person who is the victim and the victimizer to let them know we do not agree with the behavior and that we care. We will make an impact!
- ☐ We will display winning examples of how to be SHEROES, HEROES, and Grounders™.

Everyone can help adults and children learn how to cope with life's obstacles. Strategies to focus on an individual's mental wellness to prevent violence, abuse, and bullying. Especially tactics that use a pack system nurtures relationships and helps them develop empathy. When Sideliners™ become Grounders™ it helps the victims and victimizers but shows other Sideliners™ how to proactively prevent or approach domestic violence, child abuse, and bullying. If you are on the sidelines you are not in the game and you are watching the game doing nothing! You are standing by viewing the game of life where one player is getting punished by another person who is on the same team! What sense does that make to anyone?

Each day, everyday folks sit on the sidelines eating popcorn and view violence as if they are watching an award-winning play! This abuse is not a play to the victim who is being bullied, abused or violently assaulted. The individual committing this assault needs to be grounded permanently! How can you witness someone get pummeled and do nothing? You just watched a horrific car accident and the car just caught on fire and you are going to stand there and not try to get the trapped people out? Whether you hear the screams for help or not you know someone is in the car and is in imminent need of help because their lives hang in the balance. Call or text 911 if you are too scared or frozen to respond. When you see someone in need do something! Kids and any victims of violence need to always be safe and know that someone will protect them and keep them safe! What would you want someone to do for you? You are a great wolf who will always be the Grounder™ who will take down any predator of any size for the sake of the family and preservation of life! Who can silence the howl of a wolf? No one can ever silence a wolf's howl! When one wolf is howling for help we must help because precious seconds hang in the balance between life and death for an innocent person. If you have been a victim, your pain will not go in vain! God will use you to help others and prevent others from harm. If you are like me and have been a victimizer then you can impact others by showing the world you are remorseful, and your actions of change are showing the world you are a Grounder™ who believes in taking down the insecurities in others so that they no longer hurt others!

Bye standers!

I need you! Two heads are better than one! Together we can change destinies and legacies forever! We will eradicate bullying, abuse and domestic violence towards women and children while showing their abusers an appropriate way to live and love! We never want our children to be labeled as an abuser or victim of violence! As corporate leaders, we do not want to be labeled either as a place that condoned such conduct and reacted only in the response of a negligent backlash politically but instead, proactively encouraged all employees and customers alike to take the appropriate approach to thwart domestic violence, child abuse, and bullying! As Grounders™, we will not sit silently towards domestic violence, child abuse, and bullying will always encourage everyone to "Howl for Help!"

Thank God for those incredibly brave individuals who came forward to "Ground" violent offenders, child abusers, and bullies! Partner with me, please! *IF YOU EVER WONDER WHY I NEED YOUR HELP TO HELP PEOPLE THIS IS WHY I DO WHAT I DO AND WHY I DREAM AND PRAY!*

3- *WOMEN MURDERED EVERY DAY FROM*

DOMESTIC VIOLENCE [170]

5- *CHILDREN DIE EVERY DAY FROM*

CHILD ABUSE [190]

7- *EVERY 7 MINUTES A CHILD IS BULLIED* [224]

Solutions To Permanently Eradicate Domestic Violence, Child Abuse, and Bullying

GOD! ALL I WANT FOR CHRISTMAS IS FOR MY DREAMS AND PRAYERS TO COME TRUE SO THAT NO ONE COMMITS DOMESTIC VIOLENCE, CHILD ABUSE, AND BULLYING! USE ME SO NO ONE EVER HAS TO DIE OR BE HARMED BY ANY FORM OF VIOLENCE!

Solutions To Permanently Eradicate Domestic Violence, Child Abuse, and Bullying

DREAMS
If You Are Not Dreaming, You Are Already Dead!

The very last thing we do at the end of every day is going to sleep. Whether we remember them or not we literally have many dreams at night consciously or subconsciously. My dreams are not so unique in that like many accountable adults, my dreams are about leaving a legacy where my children's children's children benefit from the sweat of my labor and figuratively speaking, they forever enjoy not just the fruits from my labor, but also bread, meats, nuts, vegetables and everything else that a successful life can offer! What good is living a life where you never impacted others?

In my dreams, I climb above the clouds beyond extreme altitudes! All things become possible in my mind. Sure, I dream like most people for financial security for my family after I have died, but my dreams are different and more substantial to benefit them and others forever, especially when I am no longer on this earth! I have always said that when it comes to choosing what you want to do as a career in life, "***You Should Be Whatever You Would Do For Free!***"™ and that way you will not become a slave to a job, but rather, you will enjoy a career where the money will track you down, and if it is not about the money, then it is about your freedom, passion, and legacy! I want to make my impact and contribution to the world now and many years after I die! I owe the victims my life!

I do not think there are too many things more exciting for me than to be a servant leader and successful part of helping someone else's dreams come true! Would I love to have a street, school, bridge, tunnel, athletic field or court, library, airport, trophy or an award named in my honor for my humanitarian efforts or perhaps have a highway, school, mountain, stadium, arena, museum, center, hospital, or airport named in my honor as a legacy to my family and all whom have helped and supported me, so they never stop trying to eradicate death from violence? A legacy that will never die!

I would love to have a specialty drink, sandwich, dish, or any meal with my name if it reminds people of the cause I fight for each day? I would even take an appliance or cooking device with my name on it if every time someone used it, it reminded them to not stand for bullying, child abuse, and domestic violence! Yes! I would love to have a commemorative stamp or named holiday or a life-size wax replica or statue of myself out in front of a historical landmark, building or monument named after me if it was meant as a reminder to the people that were to live after me to remember the historical humanitarian significance of my life's work! I would be honored to be recognized as the hero of the year by CNN or winner of the prestigious "Diana Award" if it brought more domestic violence offenders, child abusers, and bullies out of the shadows to get the required help to improve their mental health so as to permanently prevent humans and animals from becoming victims of violence and abuse. My dreams are for no innocent individual to be subjected to the threat of any violence!

How about my own clothing, cologne or jewelry line for my millions of fans, followers, and supporters on social media so they are reminded of my life and legacy saving humanitarian efforts every time they wear my clothes, cologne, or jewelry! I dream of children of all ages buying my action figure doll, video game, or Halloween costume and mask of me as a justice fighter, bully and abuse preventer! I would love for people to Google me and read on Wikipedia how my dysfunctional life story confessing that I was a product of child abuse, bullying, and violence and as a result I went on to be an abuser, bully and domestic violence offender who went from tragedy to triumph by impacting other people's lives and preventing domestic violence and child abuse! I can be a premium brand too!

I dream of people quoting me in their speeches or everyday talks! I would love to have my own theme song, or a song called A.W. Burgess, or some actor or recording artist shout out my name in one of their movies or hit songs to bring awareness to what FAMILY MANKIND™ is doing for victims, abusers, legacies and society in general! I dream of being a superhero with the power to permanently erase the pain and trauma of victims as well as abolishing the minds of and change hardened child abusers, bullies, violent domestic violence offenders, and sexual deviants into loving individuals who will never know how to ever harm or bully a human, animal, or themselves!

How about my bobblehead or a toy created in my image that combats bullying, domestic violence, and child abuse! I would love to sign autographs and take selfies with others if it was my way of thanking them sincerely for believing in the care of others and for changing their violent and abusive ways forever! I would love to have my self-named tv show or a reality intervention show helping abused victims and their abusers! Let us show abusers who changed! I want to see their stories, not their killers!

I dream of a book and movie written about my life, oh snap, you are reading my book and the significant impact I contributed to the lives and legacies of others that ultimately leads to me receiving a Hollywood Star on the walk of fame. I would love to be named Time Magazine's "Person of the Year" and People Magazine's "Sexiest Man Alive" if it draws attention to the platform of ending violence and abuse against women and children. How about an A.W. roast? Or how about me being a breeder of wolves or Boxer dogs that people are demanding because it is the most protective breed of dog on the planet and it is an A.W. Burgess bred dog whose pedigree is flawless and protects people from any form of violence, abuse, and bullying! The breed will attack and hold until they submit!

Since I am still dreaming, let us get turned up by dreaming about someday winning the Nobel Peace Prize for my humanitarian efforts like so many incredible humanitarians before me and thus spawning and inspiring a new generation of humanitarians! I pray one day Dr. Lewis Gates reveals my family's genealogy, so I can see who the originator of violence in my lineage was! I would love to know what sparked the violence gene that I eventually put out! I would love to have the question posed by Alex Trebek to contestants on Jeopardy that says, "This world-renown humanitarian, Bestseller Author and Human Rights Activist fought to eradicate violence and abuse against women and children along with bullying, animal cruelty and recidivism?" and a contestant rings in and says, "Who is A.W. Burgess?" Or my name is the answer to the category Historical People puzzle on Wheel of Fortune. *__I Am The Superhero With The Superpower To Permanently Eradicate Domestic Violence, Child Abuse, & Bullying! Saving Lives & Legacies!__*

I dream of someone giving me the deed to thousands of acres of land that could never be sold for the purpose of building a private school for the throwaway children in our society such as foster children and runaways alongside the very brightest and wealthiest children so that both can see their commonalities and build on their differences while supporting one another! I dream about the day I have buildings to house the stalkers, child abusers and violent offenders to teach them how to cope and properly love those they should be loving and not harming! A Hall of Fame or memorial to never forget the children and victims of domestic violence, child abuse and bullying who died as a result to positively commemorate the children and individuals who paid with their lives as victims of domestic violence and child abuse as well as celebrating the individuals and corporations who have supported the eradication of domestic violence and child abuse! Their life was not disposable like a non-degradable piece of trash. We will recycle their story so it will always serve a meaningful purpose for others to live well and treat others with respect and love. I and society should never forget them!

What if murdered victims of domestic violence and child abuse were buried with an A.W. Burgess FAMILY MAN™ Jersey on or some FAMILY MAN™ paraphernalia was placed in their casket as a reminder to the world that this is the end result of what happens to an innocent and vulnerable individual who suffered at the hands of another individual who chose not to get help, and someone had to pay with their life. What if we created a FAMILY MAN™ media and entertainment corporation that distributed movies, music, television shows and digital magazines dedicated to ridding the world of violence, child abuse, and bullying and we had programming that got the hardest children adopted! (What would you think if no one wanted to adopt you ever? Why doesn't anyone love or want me? Am I that ugly and undesirable or am I not worthy to be loved? I am a throwaway?) I wish I could adopt all the kids who were either never adopted or were adopted a seemingly trillion times or never felt they were truly loved. I pray I inspire people whereas they name their baby A.W.! What if a state put out the A.W. personalized license plate.

It would be a dream if someone requested to meet me as a Make A Wish foundation request. I dream that I could heal them or any other person of their pain regardless of what their pain may be! Please, auction off my possessions for charity! To all the abuse I wish I could block the abuser's strike and convince them they are truly abusing themselves and the ones who really love them unconditionally! I wish I could bring my dad back to prevent him from harming my Mom, those who loved him, those impacted by his abusive actions and me! I wish I could bring back all the victims of any form of terrorism and the school shootings! I wish I could take away survivor's guilt. Take away the guilt I have believing I could have or should have said or done something that could have helped or prevented this disgusting tragedy! I wish it were me that could have died instead of your baby!

I dream of 3 bills named after victims of domestic violence, child abuse, and bullying because of the countless hours of humanitarian efforts, nonpartisan laws, that requires all licensed drivers of motor vehicles regardless of class, military personnel, law enforcement, politicians, educators, college students, healthcare officials, etc., to submit a DNA test with fingerprints, that goes into the Federal CODIS (Combined DNA Index System) and NDIS (National DNA Index System) database systems to prevent individuals from committing illegal or immoral crimes while also fighting to mandate stiffer penalties to any and all individuals who abuse, commit violent acts, threaten, or stalk women and children regardless of the criminal's previous criminal history! Remember it is typically who we do not know that kills and rapes! Criminals and potential criminals will think twice when they know their DNA is on file.

The second law is where, by law, all gun manufacturers and sellers are required to have the actual fired marked bullets and its digital photo of the bullet and record of the gun sold placed in a federal registry like fingerprints and DNA records of the names of these gun sellers and registered gun owners since no two guns are the same and we do not have to worry about finding the owner or identifying the exact gun and in some cases the body of the victims! Now we know who's gun fired the bullet! This is the end of non-traceable guns! Legislation Holding every gun manufacturer and gun seller accountable and responsible to keeping the fired bullet and spent casing on federal files to always know who actually owns the gun and before you sell it to the next owner the change of ownership must be recorded or it's a felony!

Lastly, a law that severely punishes any individual who has malice and criminal intent and deceptively portrays or devises a schematic ruse or impersonates a professional career position on any website or app for the purpose of attracting an individual for nefarious behavior! Let us be proactive and stop them before they commit murder, rape, robbery or assault.

As a convicted felon I dream of a Presidential Pardon and Kennedy Medal of Honor for my life's efforts in preventing abuse, violence, and bullying against adults, children, and animals! I am definitely dreaming because for me to believe I can figuratively go from a criminal man on America's Most Wanted to America's Most Wanted Man has to be a dream. But you know what? The beautiful thing about dreams is that they are just hopeful thoughts until you get into motion and act towards accomplishing them. Dreams with no meaningful and justifiable action just become fatiguing like running a race with no finish line and a nightmare and not your reality! I am a leader...a man...a movement...a brand!!!

I have had many visions that I did nothing with, and they slowly evaporated into division which for me really stands for the death of my vision and dreams called "dievision!" As I have always believed, this is a classic case where "time kills deals!" How can you ever get your dream job if you never apply or go to the interview? The longer you take getting to your dreams you keep moving the finish line further away!

My ultimate dreams are for violence and abuse victims, along with abusers and violent offenders to have their loving dreams become a reality! No human ever deserves to be harmed and unloved! They deserve to live in a loving and healthy environment surrounded by mentally healthy individuals who know how to cope with life skills and without dysfunction or addiction. I too dream of a website that forever remembers the lives of children and women who have been murdered by the hands of child abuse and domestic violence or as a consequence of bullying so that they will never be forgotten and the world will know their life and legacy served a purpose and has a definitive meaning so any other human seeing their story never becomes an individual who causes this horrific demise of another human and will never opt to cause this pain and torture to anyone or anything including themselves but would become proactive in getting a solution that forever prevents them from ever harming another and themselves!

I dream of having a voluntary or court-ordered inpatient or outpatient, Domestic Violence Recovery Center for child abusers and domestic violence offenders! The grounds will be paved with bricks or concrete with the inscribed names of victims of domestic violence and child abuse who paid with their lives so that child abusers and domestic violence offenders know the end result to not getting continuous help for their violent behavior! I would love for these abusers to work in a zoo or veterinarian hospital or raise puppies and horses from birth on our corporate grounds, so they can appreciate life and somebody totally relying on them to exist in life and know the importance of why anyone would want to do harm to this vulnerable baby at any point of their life! This is God's creation, somebody's baby and a member of someone's family. Their life is priceless and invaluable, and it truly is never for sale to anyone other than its Creator. Better yet, let them work in a hospital or funeral home to see the trauma and death of domestic violence and child abuse.

When you do the kind of work I do, the dangers I face, the sacrifices and compromises I face personally and professionally, along with the horrific and tragic things I see and hear firsthand from victims of abuse, bullying violence, you don't dream of being famous and the price that comes with it, you dream of a world where we no longer do harm and commit sinister acts against another human being, and we opt for loving one another! I dream that if Caesar Milan is the dog whisperer, I imagine one day someone would say I'm the domestic violence, bully, and abuser whisperer or chin checker and violent silencer assassin! The truth is, your internal motor called your brain, never shuts off because as long as evil exists, it only wins when good does nothing! That alone keeps you up at night, not being famous. I always feel like I am running out of time to serve others and prevent someone from being harmed or thwarting someone from harming others or their self, while not forgetting family, friends, and myself in the mix! You only get one lifetime and so I imagine I will sleep peacefully when we get to heaven with our loved ones!

We can only howl and growl for help at the abuser and violent offenders who choose not to get help to heal themselves from what ails their mind, body, and soul! However, I warn against shunning or overly judging the abusers or victimizers, if we do not offer a realistic, tangible approach and solution to get them healed, not treated.

My ultimate dream is for random people to come up to me, associated individuals and corporate partners to say "A.W., you and X corporation or you and Joe Doe saved my life and my husband's too! He no longer beats me up physically, verbally, mentally, sexually or emotionally! Or "because of the FAMILY MANKIND™'s Howl for Help Communication Center, my Call, Email or Text to the helpline, my child was able to tell us they were being bullied and as a result, they and their bully are now great friends because their bully got help!" Or a child that walks up to me and says "A.W. I no longer live in fear that I or my parent or my pet am going to be killed by my parent because my parent got the required help they needed, and they now consistently attend the FAMILY MANKIND™ meetings and certified training sessions!

Since life is a game filled with many gambles, when it deals you a bad hand in life, in essence, wrongs people have influenced upon you, I want to try and help make it right by bettering the odds that they win in life! I dream of a Broadway play about my life as a humanitarian and advocate! Starts with the death of my dad and the impact it had on my mother and my life. "Who is going to show him how to be a FAMILY MAN™? The first 10 minutes we stand to commemorate the "X" women, "X" children and "X" animals who lost their lives to violence and abuse. Your life had significant meaning and relevance and you will forever live in our hearts and minds and will always serve as an inspiration to eradicate domestic violence, child abuse, bullying, and animal cruelty. Your life is the reason why we work to permanently change the mindsets and behavior of violent offenders and abusers, so they will never harm anyone or anything including themselves. We do this for you and your family but most of all for your legacy. You will never be forgotten!

I stand naked in front of you to humbly bare my heart and soul, without a hair of untruth and absolute unworthiness, but to also say transparently and respectfully that I possess no secrets, hidden agendas or anything to hide! I am free and delivered from the tortuous trauma that was at the root of my cantankerous drama! I want my only lifetime to be a legacy that helped to save lives and legacies of both the victims and victimizers of domestic violence, child abuse, and bullying! My dad lost his life because of domestic violence and consequently, my mother who was once the victim became my victimizer along with her younger sister and brother. If she did not value my life, why would anyone, including me, value my life?

My passion, mission, vision, and gift is simple in that I am trying to help God save other people's lives and legacies by doing all I can to help and prevent anyone from being a victim or victimizer and keep innocent people out of harm's way. I never want to see anyone impulsively and intentionally enter into depression, divorce proceedings or the penitentiary as I did only to come out with a permanent criminal history, or worse, end up in a morgue, coffin, grave, on death row, on life support, in a psychiatric hospital or watching their dreams never become a reality and thus their legacy is forever impacted. We are ending recidivism and generation curses in bloodlines. All of these scenarios lead to the death and destruction in the lives of families and legacies. I will accomplish protecting the lives and legacies of innocent people by showing domestic violence offenders, child abusers, and bullies how to permanently eradicate their evil behavior by getting them the mental health they so desperately require! That is what I owe to the human race! I pray I can inspire humanity! I do not want any human being or animal harmed or harming themselves. I never want them to end up as I once did when it could have been prevented.

I dream of bullies, child abusers, and domestic violence offenders getting the required help to become permanently healed from what has caused them to be violent. I want to see their conversions transform them to my side of life and way of thinking to where they become benevolent and altruistic partners with me and fellow humanitarians, philanthropist, and nonpartisan lobbyists and victim's advocates. I do not and will not ever claim to be a know it all to any and everything, but what I do know by living on this earth this long is that many people doubt that what I am trying to accomplish a daunting task with individuals who may not be worthy of putting forth such an effort, but all I can say to the haters, doubters, naysayers, critics, and cynics is that my motives are to purely help contribute to saving lives, legacies, relationships, family bloodlines, and friendships to end generational curses and destructive cyclical behavior that leads to death! Even though **America has a gun control problem and an equally if not greater mental health issue,** I know, trust, and believe that *"WITH MEN THIS IS IMPOSSIBLE, BUT WITH GOD ALL THINGS ARE POSSIBLE!"*[249] **YOU JUST HAVE TO BELIEVE IN THE CHANGE YOU SEEK! I CAN SEE THE ENDLESS POSITIVE POSSIBILITIES FOR THOSE WISHING TO CHANGE!** *YOU CAN TOO!*

IMPOSSIBLE

I M POSSIBLE

I AM POSSIBLE

With that being said, the possibilities are endless if you simply believe you can permanently change and get in motion so that the impossible becomes possible! If no one has told you lately I will tell you I Love You! Thank You so very much for your time in allowing me to vent and share my story with you. I pray you will receive something of significant value after reading my life's motion picture. Please get help if you need it. There is no shame or embarrassment in getting your mental health to its optimal, healthiest level! I need your help! Will you please help me! I cannot do it alone!

Love You! The Wolf!

Your Brother…A.W. Burgess!

See You In Heaven!

THE FINAL THOUGHT

Domestic violence is no joke to me and should not be to anyone with a sound mind! I am in a business where violence does not care about your religion, politics, money, zip code, affiliations, demographics, job title, or college degree! I pray that this book will bring an awareness to any individuals struggling to resolve domestic violence so they can be permanently healed from a preventable issue. I truly desire to help God preserve lives and legacies of victims and their victimizers!

I pray that any individual living in a constant threat of death is permanently relieved of the pain so that they can live a phenomenal life free of domestic violence, child abuse, and bullying! I am so sorry for the pain I have caused innocent individuals and the people who invested their time in me as a young kid in Baltimore, only for me to throw a phenomenal set of opportunities away because of my stubbornness and ignorance to getting help for my violent behavior.

Solutions To Permanently Eradicate Domestic Violence, Child Abuse, and Bullying

I KNOW THE SOLUTION TO DOMESTIC VIOLENCE, CHILD ABUSE, and BULLYING! I HAVE THE ANTIDOTE...THE CURE!

"We must tackle domestic violence at the source which is focusing on the mental wellness of the abuser. To bring about a permanent change and healing we have to bring abusers and bullies in anonymously and respectfully, to bring out the out the root cause of the violence, without ever judging and shaming them! We must take the mental gun from them! Or in my case, help to heal them while in legal custody!"

I CAN NOT DO THIS BY MYSELF! I NEED YOUR HELP! THANK YOU FOR YOUR SUPPORT and THANK YOU MORE FOR YOUR PRAYERS! YOUR FRIEND.... YOUR BROTHER....THE WOLF....
A.W. BURGESS.... THE FAMILY MAN

REFERENCES

1. Captain Francesco Schettino https://www.reuters.com/article/us-italy-ship/top-italian-court-upholds-conviction-of-costa-concordia-captain-idUSKBN1882MF/., 2. https://listverse.com/2016/08/30/10-tragic-stories-from-the-childhood-of-charles-manson/., 3. Children learn discipline from their first teachers, Deborah W. Higgenbotham, The Progress Index, Monday, January 6, 1992., 4. https://www.pressreade r.com/., 5. https://en.wikipedia.org/wiki/Stop_Snitchin%27, 6. Carmelo Anthony, https://en.wikipedia.org/wiki/Stop_Snitchin%27/., 7. Corrupt 8 Baltimore Cops https://www.bbc.com/news/world-us-canada-43035628;In Baltimore, Brazen Officers Took Every Chance to Rob and Cheat https://www.nytimes.com/2018/02/06/us/baltimore-police-corruption.html/., 8. Page Attorney: Leader Of Corrupt BPD Task Force and Sean Suiter Investigated Phylicia Barnes Murder Case https://baltimore.cbslocal.com/2018/03/27/sean-suiter-phylicia-barnes-murder-case/;Baltimore judge acquits man accused of killing Phylicia Barnes https://www.baltimoresun.com/news/maryland/crime/bs-md-ci-phylicia-barnes-motion-acquittal-20180330-story.html/., 9. https://en.wikipedia.org/wiki/Murder_of_Phylicia_Barnes/., 10. Sheila Dixon- https://en.wikipedia.org/wiki/Sheila_Dixon https://www.baltimoresun.com/news/bal-dixonphoto2-0106-photo.html/., 11. Reggie Lewis Friend http://articles.latimes.com/1995-03-21/sports/sp-45134_1_reggie-lewis/., 12. Derrick Lewis Friend recants nhttps://www.nytimes.com/1995/03/22/sports/friend-of-lewis-s-recants.html/., 13. https://www.baltimoresun.com/news/maryland/freddie-gray/bs-md-ci-boe-20150908-story.html, The Baltimore Sun, Freddie Gray Case, September 8, 2015, Baltimore to pay Freddie Gray's Family $6.4 million to settle civic claim. By Yvonne Wenger., 14. Jameson C (2010). "The Short Step From Love to Hypnosis: A Reconsideration of the Stockholm Syndrome". Journal for Cultural Research. 14.4: 337–355. https://en.wikipedia.org/wiki/Stockholm_syndrome., 15. Breslau N, Davis GC, Andreski P, Peterson E. Traumatic Events and Posttraumatic Stress Disorder in an Urban Population of Young Adults. Arch Gen Psychiatry. 1991;48(3):216–222. doi:10.1001/archpsyc.1991.01810270028003, https://en.wikipedia.org/wiki/Stockholm_syndrome., 16. Exposure to violence and post-traumatic stress disorder in urban adolescents, Berton, Margaret Wright; Stabb, Sally D. Adolescence; Roslyn Heights Vol. 31, Iss. 122, (Summer 1996): 489-98., https://search.proquest.com/openview/56cb52d71c60b28ab6dca07c278d1fc0/1?pq-origsite=gscholarandcbl=41539, 17. By Quint Forgery https://www.politico.com/story/2018/08/26/jacksonville-florida-mass-shooting-reported-797271/., 18. https://www.usatoday.com/story/news/2018/09/25/baltimore-homicide-murder-rate-fbi-statistics-death-crime-killings/1426739002/., 19. https://www.washingtonpost.com/investigations/as-police-struggle-to-solve-homicides-baltimore-residents-see-an-open-season-for-killing/2018/12/26/7ee561e4-fb24-11e8-8c9a-860ce2a8148f_story.html?utm_term=.9a751c893b84/., 20. https://baltimore.cbslocal.com/2018/02/19/baltimore-named-nations-most-dangerous-city-by-usa-today/., 21. The Baltimore Sun, January 1987., 22. The Baltimore Sun, January 1987., 23. https://www.findagrave.com/memorial/94985863/ceres-millicent-horn/., 24. https://www.findagrave.com/memorial/94985863/ceres-millicent-horn/., 25. https://www.apnews.com/68db0a53599a248e56e486aea665c45e., 26. The Baltimore Sun, January 1988., 27. The Baltimore Sun, January 1988., 28. USA TODAY, March 1988., 29. USA TODAY, March 1988., 30. Randallstown Times, June 1988., 31. "To much is given, much is required and expected!" (reads Luke 12:48 in the King James Version.)., 32. History of Omega Psi Phi- https://www.oppf.org/about_omega.aspan/., 33.The Jumpman logo- https://en.wikipedia.org/wiki/Jumpman_(logo)/., 34. http://mentalfloss.com/article/63386/enduring-legacy-pied-piper-hamelin/., 35. https://time.com/4821911/king-james-bible-history/., 36. https://en.wikipedia.org/wiki/Central_State_Hospital_(Virginia)/., 37. Ingram Industries News, July 1989, Page 7, Three Students Added To INROADS Program., 38. OYMA 1992 Outstanding Young Men of America., 39. Warrants for Arrest issued by Hampton City Police Department 10/28/1991 and 11/15/1991/., 40. https://www.dailypress.com/news/dp-xpm-19911101-1991-11-01-9111010122-story.html Hu Student Abducted By Former Boyfriend, November 1, 1991 Cheryl L. Reed Daily Press., 41. https://www.dailypress.com/news/dp-xpm-19911116-1991-11-16-9111160060-story.htmlBaltimore Man Jailed In Second Abduction, November 16, 1991 David Chernicky Daily Press., 42. https://www.gotquestions.org/dominion-over-animals.html God has sovereign power over His creation and has delegated the authority to mankind to have dominion over the animals (Genesis 1:26)., 43. https://www.biblegateway.com/passage/?search=Isaiah+54%3A17andversion=NKJV Isaiah 54:17 New King James Version (NKJV)No weapon formed against you shall prosper, 44. https://www.dictionary.com/browse/recidivism Definition of recidivism., 45. https://www.cga.ct.gov/2003/olrdata/jud/rpt/2003-r-0333.htm Consequences of a Felony Conviction By: Christopher Reinhart, Associate Attorney., 46. http://www.washingtonpost.com/wp-srv/national/daily/feb99/felons22.htm Voting Rights for Felons Win Support By Michael A. Fletcher, Washington Post Staff Writer Monday, February 22, 1999; Page A1Jerome A. Gray., 47. http://www.washingtonpost.com/wp-srv/national/daily/feb99/felons22.htm Voting Rights for Felons Win Support By Michael A. Fletcher, Washington Post Staff Writer Monday, February 22, 1999 Hilary Shelton., 48. https://www.politifact.com/truth-o-meter/article/2018/apr/25/understanding-felon-voting-rights-restoration/., 49.Thomas Beavers Daily Press, Ken Armstrong June 11,1992, Murder Jury Acts Quickly, Rapist Guilty. https://www.dailypress.com/news/dp-xpm-19920611-1992-06-11-9206110033-story.html,50. https://www.dailypress.com/news/dp-xpm-19920610-1992-06-10-9206100192-story.html, 50.Thomas Beavers Daily Press, Ken Armstrong 1992, "Deep Voice of the Devil" June 10, 1992., 51. https://www.dailypress.com/news/dp-xpm-19920708-1992-07-08-9207080148-story.html? Ken Armstrong, Daily Press, July 8,1992 Terrified Young Man., 52. https://kids.nationalgeographic.com/animals/emperor-penguin/#emperor-penguin-group-snow.jpg., 53. https://www.biblegateway.com/passage/?search=Proverbs+18%3A22andversion=NKJV, Proverbs 18:22 New King James Version (NKJV) 22 He who finds a wife finds a good thing. And obtains favor from the Lord., 54. https://biblehub.com/genesis/2-24.htm King James Version, Therefore shall a man leave his father and his mother and shall cleave unto his wife: and they shall be one flesh.., 55. https://me.me/i/the-female-wolf-appears-to-hide-under-the-male-shes-5361542., 56. BMW Master's Academy Photo and Formal Letter 10/98., 57. BMW Diversity and Marketing Conference Photo 11/97 and Letter 10/97., 58. NAACP Conference Representative Photo and Formal Letter, July 1998., 59. Charlotte Business Journal, August 1, 1997.and, March 16,1998, 60. The Acura Certified Experience Magazine, 61. https://archive.org/details/MSNBCW_20180826_113000_Your_Business Jack Gross of the 1 Jeans Group., 62. https://biblehub.com/matthew/6-10.htm "Lord Let Your Will Be Done!"., 63. https://www.biblegateway.com/passage/?search=Proverbs+16%3A27-29andversion=TLB "Idle hands are the devil's workshop"., 64. https://www.biblegateway.com/passage/?search=Matthew+27andversion=NIV Matthew 27 New International Version (NIV) Judas Hangs Himself., 27 Early in the morning, all the chief priests and the elders of the people made their plans how to have Jesus executed. 2 So they bound him, led him away and handed him over to Pilate the governor. 3 When Judas, who had betrayed him, saw that Jesus was condemned, he was seized with remorse and returned the thirty pieces of silver to the chief priests and the elders. 4 "I have sinned," he said, "for I have betrayed innocent blood."., 65. https://www.biblegateway.com/passage/?search=Matthew+26andversion=NIV 54 But how then would the Scriptures be fulfilled that say it must happen in this way?"., 66. https://www.star-telegram.com/sports/article3828485.html Deion Sanders, Deion went from rough streets to Prime spot in Canton By Clarence E. Hill Jr – Chill@star-telegram.com 8/05/11 11:51 PM, Updated 1/12/12 8:31am., 67. https://www.forbes.com/pictures/ffje45eem/terrell-owens-i-love-me-some-me/#60e70_a2b2905 Terrell Owens "I Love Me Some Me"™., 68. "Prime Time" "Neon Deion", Deion Luwynn Sanders Sr. (/ˈdiːɒn/; born August 9, 1967), nicknamed "Prime Time" and "Neon Deion"., 69. https://www.nbcsports.com/video/event/dark-horses "I had a heartfelt affinity for Sunday Silence because he was a horse that no one

wanted! I wasn't wanted! So, we both were in the same boat!"., 70. https://en.wikipedia.org/wiki/Death_of_Zahra_Baker, 71. Shaniya Davis (Fayetteville Observer-06/08/ 2018), 72. https://www.cbsnews.com/news/penn-couple-beat-4-year-old-boy-to-death-for-spilling- cereal-police/, 73. https://en.wikipedia.org/wiki/Susan_Still_(women's_rights_activist, 74. https://www.oxygen.com/blogs/21-year-old-dismembered-by-man-she-met-online-and-his-juggalo- friends., 75. http://www.washingtonpost.com/wp-dyn/content/article/2010/06/18/AR2010061804508 .html., 76. https://www.foxnews.com/story/maryland-man-charged-with-setting-ex-wife-on-fire., 77. https://www.ksla.com/story/17083134/arrest-made-in-allendale-homicide/., 78. https://www.westchestermagazine.com/Westchester-Magazine/March-2003/The-Short-Sad-Life- of- Christina-Long/., 79. https://www.wral.com/cary-man-pleads-guilty-in-machete-attack-on-ex-girlfriend/17664260/, 80. https://en.wikipedia.org/wiki/Murder_of_Hae_Min_Lee., 81. https://www.charlotteobserver.com/news/local/article206767109.html., 82. https://www.cnn.com/2018/08/28/health/preteen-suicide-jamel-myles/index.html., 83. https://www.washingtonpost.com/news/post-nation/wp/2018/06/05/ he-was-deemed-paranoid-and-psychotic-years-later-he-killed-six-in-arizona-police-say/?utm_term=.706962c70b20., 84. Https://en.wikipedia.org/wiki/Watts_family_homicides)., 85. http://www.cnn.com/2009/CRIME/03/28/louisiana.lawyer.slain/., 86. https://www.chicagotribune.com/suburbs/bolingbrook-plainfield/ct-brian-cooper-murder-sentencing-plainfield-tl-07-20140728-story.html., 87. https://en.wikipedia.org/wiki/Murder_of_Hannah_Graham., 88.https://en.wikipedia.org/wiki/Murder_of_Yeardley_Love., 89. https://www.dallasnews.com/news/crime/2013/11/16/franklin-davis-sentenced-to-death-for-killing-teen- rape-accuser., 90. https://www.gainesville.com/news/20050921/man-guilty-in-girls-rape-slaying/., 91. https://q13fox.com/2012/10/26/convicted-felon-sentenced-to-21-years-for-2011-murder-of-belltown- woman/ POSTED 11:37 AM, OCTOBER 26, 2012, BY BRETT CIHON, 92. https://law.justia.com/cases/alabama/court-of-appeals-criminal/1996/cr-94-387-0.html., 93. https://tylerclementi.org/tylers-story/., 94. https://www.startribune.com/ex-pastor-convicted-in-north-high-staffer-s-slaying/138235249/., 95. https://en.wikipedia.org/wiki/Steve_McNair., 96. https://en.wikipedia.org/wiki/Fred_Lane_(American_football)., 97. https://www.sun-sentinel.com/news/fl-xpm-2012-04-12-fl-babbs-murder-sentencing-20120412-story.html/., 98. https://pix11.com/2015/03/17/man-found-guilty-of-murdering-bronx-mother-and-daughter/., 99. https://www.chron.com/news/houston-texas/houston/article/Closing-arguments-begin-in-pearland-teens-murder-6219184.php., 100. (https://www.wrdw.com/home/headlines/39581372.html)., 101. (https://www.wusa9.com/article/news/local/killer-of-kidney-transplant-survivor-found-guilty/74167270)., 102. (https://www.ajc.com/news/local/authorities-diary-leads-alleged-killer-missing-teen/89SDIRLWDRuZnqkKVD1kRO/)., 103. https://www.ajc.com/news/girlfriend-gets-life-prison-for-police-officer-death/ql0nwPpvQrHL2bJuzviCzH/., 104. (https://en.wikipedia.org/wiki/Murder_of_Cara_Knott)., 105. (https://caselaw.findlaw.com/nc-court-of-appeals/1428041.html)., 106. https://www.monstersandcritics.com/smallscreen/gregory-graf-murdered-stepdaughter-jessica-padgett-and-then-filmed-himself-sexually-abusing-her-corpse/., 107. https://www.nytimes.com/1999/09/27/nyregion/ex-boyfriend-kills-bride-to-be-on-wedding-day-in-front-of-family.html., 108. https://patch.com/illinois/joliet/woman-killed-murder-suicide-feared-shorty-would-harm-her., 109. National Network To End Domestic Violence, http://ajph.aphapublications.org/doi/abs/10.2105/AJPH.2013.301582., 110. Black, M.C., Basile, K.C., Breiding, M.J., Smith, S.G., Walters, M.L., Merrick, M.T., Chen, J. and Stevens, M. (2011). The national intimate partner and sexual violence, survey: 2010 summary report. Retrieved from http://www.cdc.gov/violenceprevention/pdf/nisvs_report2010-a.pdf., 111. National Center for Injury Prevention and Control, Center for Disease Control and Prevention (n.d.). Infographic based on data from the intimate partner and sexual violence survey (nisvs): 2010-2012 state report. https://www.cdc.gov/violenceprevention/pdf/NISVS-infographic-2016.pdf., 112. Black, M.C., Basile, K.C., Breiding, M.J., Smith, S.G., Walters, M.L., Merrick, M.T., Chen, J. and Stevens, M. (2011). The national intimate partner and sexual violence, survey: 2010 summary report. Retrieved from http://www.cdc.gov/violenceprevention/pdf/nisvs_report2010-a.pdf., 113. Ibid., 114. Ibid., 115. 112 Ibid., 116. National Network to End Domestic Violence (2017). Domestic violence counts national summary. Retrieved from https://nnedv.org/mdocsposts/census_2016_handout_national-summary/., 117. Campbell, J.C., Webster, D., Koziol-McLain, J., Block, C., Campbell, D., Curry, M. A., Gary, F., Glass, N., McFarlane, J., Sachs, C., Sharps, P., Ulrich, Y., Wilt, S., Manganello, J., Xu, X, Schollenberger, J., Frye, V. and Lauphon, K. (2003). Risk factors for femicide in abusive relationships: Results from a multisite case control study. American Journal of Public Health, 93(7), 1089-1097., 118. Truman, J. L. and Morgan, R. E. (2014). Nonfatal domestic violence, 2003-2012. Retrieved from http://www.bjs.gov/content/pub/pdf/ndv0312.pdf., 119. Ibid., 120. Ibid., 121. Black, M.C., Basile, K.C., Breiding, M.J., Smith, S.G., Walters, M.L., Merrick, M.T., Chen, J. and Stevens, M. (2011). The national intimate partner and sexual violence survey: 2010 summary report. Retrieved from http://www.cdc.gov/violenceprevention/pdf/nisvs_report2010-a.pdf., 122. Ibid., 123. Ibid., 124. Ibid., 125. Bridges, F.S., Tatum, K. M., and Kunselman, J.C. (2008). Domestic violence statutes and rates of intimate partner and family homicide: A research note. Criminal Justice Policy Review, 19(1), 117-130., 126. Smith, S., Fowler, K. and Nileon, P. (2014). Intimate partner homicide and corollary victims in 16 states: National violent death reporting system, 2003-2009. American Journal of Public Health, 104(3), 461-466. doi: 10.2105/AJPH.2013.301582., 127. Violence Policy Center. (2012). American roulette: Murder-suicide in the United States. Retrieved from www.vpc.org/studies/amroul2012.pdf., 128. Ibid., 129. World Health Organization (2013). Global and regional estimates of violence against women: Prevalence and health effects of intimate partner violence and nonpartner sexual violence. http://apps.who.int/iris/bitstream/10665/85239/1/9789241564625_eng.pdf?ua=1., 130. Ibid., 131. Truman, J. L. and Morgan, R. E. (2014). Nonfatal domestic violence, 2003-2012. Retrieved from http://www.bjs.gov/content/pub/pdf/ndv0312.pdf., 132. Rothman, E., Hathaway, J., Stidsen, A. and de Vries, H. (2007). How employment helps female victims of intimate partner abuse: A qualitative study. Journal of Occupational Health Psychology, 12(2), 136-143. doi: 10.1037/1076-8998.12.2.136., 133. University of Minnesota's Institute on Domestic Violence in the African American Community World Health Organization (2004). The economic dimensions of intimate partner violence. Retrieved from http://apps.who.int/iris/bitstream/10665/42944/1/9241591609.pdf., 134. Ibid., 102. Finkelhor, D., Turner, H., Ormrod, R. and Hamby, S. (2011). Children's exposure to intimate partner violence and other family violence. Retrieved from https://www.ncjrs.gov/pdffiles1/ojjdp/232272.pdf., 135. Workplace Homicides Among U.S. Women: The Role of Intimate Partner Violence Hope M. Tiesman, PhD, Kelly K. Gurka, PhD, Srinivas Konda, MPH, Jeffrey M. Coben, MD, and Harlan E. Amandus, PhD, taken from https://www.ncbi.nlm.nih.gov/pmc/articles/PMC4687019/ .,136. U.S. Department of Justice Office of Justice Programs Office of Juvenile Justice and Delinquency Prevention, Children's Exposure to Intimate Partner Violence and Other Family Violence Sherry Hamby, David Finkelhor, Heather Turner, and Richard Ormrod., 137.-138. Bureau of Justice statistics., 139.-143. Center for Disease Control Statistics., 144. Center for American Progress article, Women Under The Gun., 145. HuffPost, article, At Least A Third Of All Women Murdered In The U.S. Are Killed By Male Partners ., 146. National Coalition for the Homeless., 147. Department of Justice Office of Justice Programs, article, Nearly One in Four Intimate Partner Violence Cases Involved A Child Witness., 148.-158. Childhood Domestic Violence Association, article, 10 Startling Statistics About Children of Domestic Violence, (51), Social Solutions., 159.-164. National Intimate Partner and Sexual Violence Survey, 2010 Summary Report National Center for Injury Prevention and Control, Division of Violence Prevention, Atlanta, GA, and Control of the Centers for Disease Control and Prevention., 165.-168. HuffPost, Dec 06, 2017, 30 Shocking Domestic Violence Statistics That Remind Us It's An Epidemic, 169.-170. National Network To End Domestic Violence., 171. American Psychological Association, Intimate Partner Violence Facts and Resources, 172. Prevalence and Characteristics of Sexual Violence, Stalking, and Intimate Partner Violence Victimization — National Intimate Partner and Sexual Violence Survey, United States, 2011, Surveillance Summaries, September 5, 2014 / 63(SS08);1-18, Matthew J. Breiding, PhD, Sharon G. Smith, PhD, Kathleen C. Basile, PhD, Mikel L. Walters, PhD, Jieru Chen, MS, Melissa T. Merrick, PhD, Division of Violence Prevention, National Center

Solutions To Permanently Eradicate Domestic Violence, Child Abuse, and Bullying

for Injury Prevention and Control, CDC, Corresponding author: Matthew J. Breiding, Division of Violence Prevention, National Center for Injury Prevention and Control, CDC., 173. Violence Policy Center, When Men Murder Women: An Analysis of 2011 Homicide Data Females Murdered by Males in Single Victim/Single Offender Incidents, 174. HuffPost, December 6, 2017, At Least A Third Of All Women Murdered In The U.S. Are Killed By Male Partners, By Alissa Scheller, 175. World Health Organization, 176. Domesticviolencestatistics.org, 177. Costs of Intimate Partner Violence Against Women in the United States Department of Health and Human Services Centers for Disease Control and Prevention National Center for Injury Prevention and Control March 2003, 178. Domesticviolencestatistics.org, (72)American Psychological Association, 179.-181 National Coalition Against Domestic Violence, article, Domestic Violence and Lesbian, Gay, Bisexual and Transgender Relationships, 182. American Bar Association, 183. U.S. News and World Report, How to Stop Domestic Financial Abuse, How to prevent, and recover, from this type of dangerous behavior., By Tim Chen, April 26, 2011, 184.-185. University of Minnesota's Institute on Domestic Violence in the African American Community, 186. National Coalition for the Homelessness., 187. Domestic Violence Intervention Program, 188. U.S. Department of Justice Office of Justice Programs National Institute of Justice research report Extent, Nature, and Consequences of Intimate Partner Violence, 189. CDC, Adverse Childhood Experiences (ACE) Study, 190. Child Maltreatment, 2014, 191. GAO-U.S. Governments Accountability Office, 192. Kids Count, 193. The Advocacy Center. "The Facts About Youth Sexual Abuse." Accessed February 21, 2014, http://www.theadvocacycenter.org/adv_abuse.html., 194. U.S. Department of Justice. "Sexual Assault of Young Children as Reported to Law Enforcement: Victim, Incident, and Offender Characteristics." Bureau of Justice Statics. Accessed February 21, 2014, Retrieved From http://www.bjs.gov/content/pub/pdf/saycrle.pdf., 195.-198. Safe Horizon. "Child Abuse Facts." Accessed March 3, 2015., 199. Amy B. Silverman, Helen Z. Reinherz, Rose M. Giaconia, The long-term sequelae of child and adolescent abuse: A longitudinal community study, Child Abuse and Neglect, Volume 20, Issue 8, August 1996, Pages 709-723., 200. Jaudes, P. K., Ekwo, E., and Van Voorhis, J. (1995). Association of drug abuse and child abuse. Child Abuse and Neglect, 19(9), 1065-1075, 201. Swan, N. (1998). Exploring the role of child abuse on later drug abuse: Researchers face broad gaps in information. NIDA Notes, 13(2)., 202. Harlow, CW. Prior Abuse Reported by Inmates and Probationers. Washington, DC: US Dept. of Justice, Office of Justice Programs, Bureau of Justice Statistics, 1999, 203. Fang, X., et al. The economic burden of child maltreatment in the United States and implications for prevention. Child Abuse and Neglect (2012), doi:10.1016/j.chiabu.2011.10.006, 204. CDC, Adverse Childhood Experiences (ACE) Study, 205. Brown, D. et al. Adverse Childhood Experiences and the Risk of Premature Mortality; Am. J. of Preventative Medicine (2009) Vol. 37, Iss. 5, 206. ChildHelp. "Child Abuse Statistics and Facts." ChildHelp. Accessed March 3, 2015., 207. U.S. Dept. of Justice, 208. Hawkins, D. L., Pepler, D., and Craig, W. M. (2001). Peer interventions in playground bullying. Social Development, 10, 512-527., 209. National Center for Education Statistics and Bureau of Justice Statistics, School Crime Supplement, 2008–2009, 210. Centers for Disease Control and Prevention, Youth Risk Behavior Surveillance System, 2011, 211.-213. Bradshaw, C.P., Sawyer, A.L., and O'Brennan, L.M. (2007). Bullying and peer victimization at school: Perceptual differences between students and school staff. School Psychology Review, 36 (3), 361-382., 214. National Center for Education Statistics and Bureau of Justice Statistics, School Crime Supplement, 2008–2009, 215-216. Centers for Disease Control and Prevention, Youth Risk Behavior Surveillance System, 2011., Kosciw, J. G., Greytak, E. A., Bartkiewicz, M. J., Boesen, M. J., and Palmer, N. A. (2012). The 2, 179. 011 National School Climate Survey: The experiences of lesbian, gay, bisexual and transgender youth in our nation's schools. New York: GLSEN., 217-218. At risk groups, 219. Youth with disabilities, Federally Collected Data Reports, 2011 Youth Risk Behavior Surveillance System (Centers for Disease Control and Prevention).The 2008–2009 School Crime Supplement (National Center for Education Statistics and Bureau of Justice Statistics). 220.-222. Stopbullying.gov, 223.-229. Stopbullyingnowfoundation.gov, 230. Evelyn Lozada, 231. Joann Buttaro- https://www.investigationdiscovery.com/tv-shows/web-of-lies/full-episodes/playing-doctor ... #speakout, 232. Deborah Roe, Attorney, Letter to Milton Dorsey, This is why we have privacy laws, 233. Footprints In The Sand, The authorship of the poem is disputed, with a number of people claiming to have written it. In 2008, Rachel Aviv in a Poetry Foundation article[1] discusses the claims of Burrell Webb, Mary Stevenson, Margaret Fishback Powers, and Carolyn Joyce Carty. Later that year, The Washington Post, covering a lawsuit between the claims of Stevenson, Powers and Carty, said that "At least a dozen people" had claimed credit for the poem.[2]The three authors who have most strenuously promoted their authorship are Margaret Powers (née Fishback), Carolyn Carty, and Mary Stevenson. Powers says she wrote the poem on Canadian Thanksgiving weekend, in mid-October 1964.[3] Powers is among the contenders who have resorted to litigation in hopes of establishing a claim. She is occasionally confused with American writer Margaret Fishback. Powers published an autobiography in 1993.[3] Carolyn Carty also claims to have written the poem in 1963 when she was six years old based on an earlier work by her great-great aunt, a Sunday school teacher. She is known to be a hostile contender of the "Footprints" poem and declines to be interviewed about it, although she writes letters to those who write about the poem online.[1]A collection of poetry by Carty with a claim to authorship of "Footprints" was published in 2004.[4] Mary Stevenson is also a purported author of the poem circa 1936.[5][6] A Stevenson biography was published in 1995.[7] Aviv, Rachel (March 19, 2008). "Enter Sandman: Who wrote footprints?". Poetry Foundation. Retrieved 2008-08-05. Stuever, Hank (June 1, 2008). "Search to Divine Authorship Leads 'Footprints' to Court". The Washington Post. Retrieved 2017-11-05. Powers, Margaret Fishback (2012). Footprints: The True Story Behind the Poem That Inspired Millions. HarperCollins. p. 252. ISBN 978-1-44341-233-9. Carty, Carolyn Joyce; Scharring-Hausen, Robert Louis; Scharring-Hausen, Ella H. (2004). Footprints in the Sand: One Night a Man Had a Dream. Authorhouse. p. 77. ISBN 1418448532. Colombo, Carmen. "Footprints in the Sand". Wowzone. Retrieved 2016-09-19 Colombo, Carmen. "Footprints in the Sand - The Full Story". Wowzone. Retrieved 2016-09-19. Giorgio, Gail (1995). Footprints in the Sand: The Life Story of Mary Stevenson, Author of the Immortal Poem. Gold Leaf Press. p. 133. ISBN 1-882723-24-4.234. https://www.biblegateway.com/passage/?search=Isaiah+54%3A17andversion=KJV Isaiah 54:17 King James Version (KJV) No weapon that is formed against thee shall prosper; "No weapons formed against you shall prosper!", 235. Genesis 1:27 New International Version (NIV), 27 So God created mankind in his own image, in the image of God he created them; male and female he created them., 236. https://www.biblegateway.com/passage/?search=Romans +12%3A1-2andversion=ESV Do not be conformed to this world,[c] but be transformed by the renewal of your mind, that by testing you may discern what is the will of God, what is good and acceptable and perfect.", 237. https://biblehub.com/psalms/46-10.htm "Come out of the shadows of death and never step into the darkness that prohibits people from shining their "little lights!" 238. https://biblehub.com/psalms/23-4 .htm "Yea, though I walk through the shadows of death, I fear no evil! Your rod and staff they comfort me! Psalm 23-A Psalm of David. 4- Even though I walk through the darkest valley of the shadows of death, I will fear no evil, for You are with me; Your rod and Your staff, they comfort me., 239. Survivors Guide, Frederick Levy, Daily Press, 240. 12 Ways to Prevent Bullying, https://www.injuryclaimcoach.com/protect-your-child .html, 241. Centers for Disease Control (CDC) School Violence: Data and Statistics, http://www.cdc.gov/violenceprevention/youthviolence/schoolviolence/data_stats.html., 242. Center For Disease Control and Prevention (CDC) "Fact Sheet", http://www.cdc.gov/violenceprevention/pdf/school_violence_fact_sheet-a.pdf., 243. Center for Disease Control and Prevention (CDC) Understanding School Violence, http://www.cdc.gov/violenceprevention/pdf/school_violence_fact_sheet-a.pdf., 244. Center for Disease Control and Prevention:Youth Violence: Risk and Protective Factors, http://www.cdc.gov/violenceprevention/youthviolence/riskprotectivefactors.html#RiskFactors., 245. Center for Disease Control and Prevention: "Understanding School Violence Fact Sheet", http://www.cdc.gov/violenceprevention/pdf/school_violence_fact_sheet-a.pdf., 246. (*Referrence no longer available.*), 247. About Education http://712educators.about.com/od/schoolviolence/tp/prevent_school_violence.htm, 248. Love Comes Frm God https://biblehub.com/1_john/4-20.htm 249. Bible Gateway Matthew:19:26, New King James Version, "With God All Things Are Possible."

Solutions To Permanently Eradicate Domestic Violence, Child Abuse, and Bullying

CPSIA information can be obtained
at www.ICGtesting.com
Printed in the USA
LVHW081452181219
640936LV00002B/37/P